# WOMEN'S LEGAL LANDMARKS

*Women's Legal Landmarks* commemorates the centenary of women's admission in 1919 to the legal profession in the UK and Ireland by identifying key legal landmarks in women's legal history. Over 80 authors write about landmarks that represent a significant achievement or turning point in women's engagement with law and law reform. The landmarks cover a wide range of topics, including matrimonial property, the right to vote, prostitution, surrogacy and assisted reproduction, rape, domestic violence, FGM, equal pay, abortion, image-based sexual abuse, and the ordination of women bishops, as well as the life stories of women who were the first to undertake key legal roles and positions. Together the landmarks offer a scholarly intervention in the recovery of women's lost history and in the development of methodology of feminist legal history as well as a demonstration of women's agency and activism in the achievement of law reform and justice.

# Women's Legal Landmarks

*Celebrating the History of Women and Law in the UK and Ireland*

Edited by
Erika Rackley
and
Rosemary Auchmuty

•HART•
OXFORD • LONDON • NEW YORK • NEW DELHI • SYDNEY

HART PUBLISHING
Bloomsbury Publishing Plc
Kemp House, Chawley Park, Cumnor Hill, Oxford, OX2 9PH, UK

HART PUBLISHING, the Hart/Stag logo, BLOOMSBURY and the Diana logo are trademarks of Bloomsbury Publishing Plc

First published in hardback, 2019
Paperback edition, 2019



A catalogue record for this book is available from the British Library.

Library of Congress Cataloging-in-Publication data

Names: Rackley, Erika, editor. | Auchmuty, Rosemary, editor.

Title: Women's legal landmarks : celebrating the history of women and law in the UK and Ireland / edited by Erika Rackley and Rosemary Auchmuty.

Description: Oxford, UK ; Portland, Oregon : Hart Publishing, 2019.

Identifiers: LCCN 2018034445 (print) | LCCN 2018035208 (ebook) |

ISBN 9781782259787 (Epub) | ISBN 9781782259770 (hardback : alk. paper)

Subjects: LCSH: Women—Legal status, laws, etc.—Great Britain—History. | Women—Legal status, laws, etc.—Ireland—History.

Classification: LCC KD734 (ebook) | LCC KD734 .W664 2018 (print) | DDC 342.4108/78—dc23

LC record available at https://lccn.loc.gov/2018034445

ISBN: HB: 978-1-78225-977-0
PB: 978-1-50993-566-6
ePDF: 978-1-78225-979-4
ePub: 978-1-78225-978-7

Typeset by Compuscript Ltd, Shannon

To find out more about our authors and books visit www.hartpublishing.co.uk. Here you will find extracts, author information, details of forthcoming events and the option to sign up for our newsletters.

# FOREWORD

This fascinating book tells the story of the law and the legal profession from the perspective of women. That in itself is a landmark. Until comparatively recently, the law was made by men, either in the highest courts of our land or in Parliament, and there was barely a woman to be seen. Legal academic commentators in the universities were also men. When notable cases were documented, they were certainly not reflecting women's priorities or the reality of women's lives. Like most history, historical scholarship of the law has too often ignored women. Unless a heroine, villain or victim, women went unmentioned.

This project, however, subverts that old order as it celebrates 100 years since women were admitted to the legal profession in the UK and Ireland. It documents major events and cases which marked women's progress towards equality and justice. In a suitably collaborative endeavour, a huge team, from diverse backgrounds and of differing ages, volunteered to choose and then research a significant happening in our history of the last thousand years. The selection of stories inspires and at times shocks. They set out what took place at the time but also describe what followed. Progress is never linear and sometimes events led to a dragging of feet or even a backlash.

When I was called to the Bar in 1972, only seven per cent of barristers were women. Many chambers were forthright in saying they did not take women. The law was for men. In fact, it was largely for men of a certain class and race. The solicitors' profession was not very different. Then the Sex Discrimination Act was passed in 1975 and for a while, when challenged, Heads of Chambers would say: 'Women? We've got one.' And that sole creature would often be pushed into the family law niche.

When feminists of my generation started shining a spotlight on law's failures, we were met with outrage and dogged denial that there was any discrimination whatsoever. The law is neutral, we were told. Justice is blind. If gender played any part at all, they insisted, it was displayed in chivalrous leniency towards women. The fact that there were myths about female deceit and stereotypes about what constituted appropriate womanhood was unrecognised. That there were double sexual standards in the courts allowing for conduct in men that brought ignominy on the head of a woman was endemic but unacknowledged. To suggest that judges might disguise their misogyny with intellectual dishonesty was dismissed as absolute calumny. The notion that women should be on the Bench in equal numbers was a source of great amusement.

The exclusively male clerks who distributed work in chambers also had a very poor view of women because they assumed we would go off and have babies and would not bring a decent return on the investment of their energy. They earned 10 per cent of our earnings so what money we barristers might generate was all important. The clerks-rooms were papered with Pirelli calendars showing naked women draped across cars and Page 3 pinups. Female applicants for pupillages would be asked by older male barristers if they had a fiancé and were planning marriage. Breaking down the male exclusivity of the profession was a long and hard struggle, and to younger generations many of these accounts now sound prehistoric. However, we demanded change because, if the institutions of law were riddled with such attitudes and such a culture pervaded the law, how could confidence in the system be secured? *How could there be justice?*

Today more than half of law graduates are women and they are entering the legal profession in large numbers. The judiciary too has many brilliant women – though not enough at the highest levels. This book shows just how much progress has been made for women across society and how law has played an essential role in creating that change. Many of the accounts are of legal 'firsts' – the first barrister and solicitor, our first senior judges. Indeed, many of the writers were involved in the legal landmarks themselves, like Lady Hale, the President of the UK Supreme Court. The cases and events engage with issues like marital rights, divorce, suffrage, property rights, abortion, equal pay, domestic violence and rape and all the struggles against the miserable indignities and unfairness which blight women's lives.

*Women's Legal Landmarks* reveals the important role played by feminists in bringing about legal change. The landmarks rarely happened without the determination of committed women who knew that law mattered and who wanted reform; too often legal history is told as though laws were enthusiastically passed through willing Parliaments or cases resolved by generous men in long wigs. In fact, much of the change was grudging. Reform was often met with resistance and opposition. Of course, there have also been male allies who have championed women's rights and there are now many men in the law who are proud to call themselves feminists too and who join women in pushing for change. But the gains were never made without struggle.

The collection is a model of feminist legal history. It should make us both proud and angry. It should open our eyes wider to the ways in which law still fails women and the need for more women of all kinds to take their place in senior roles in the legal profession, Parliament, in the academy and in the judiciary. Only then will we secure justice and equality for us all.

Helena Kennedy
*June 2018*

# ACKNOWLEDGEMENTS

Coordinating the Women's Legal Landmarks Project, which took five years and had over 100 participants, was a huge challenge. We are grateful for the collegiality, commitment and patience of everyone involved.

In particular, we would like to thank those who presented at our training workshops, including Elizabeth Dawson (Institute of Advanced Legal Studies), David Foster (The National Archives), Guy Holborn (Lincoln's Inn), Alison Lindsay (National Records of Scotland), Gillian Murphy (Women's Library at the LSE), Rebecca Probert (then at the University of Warwick), June Purvis (editor of the *Women's History Review* and convenor of the Women's History Network), Polly Russell and Jonathan Sims (the British Library) and Mari Takayanagi (UK Parliamentary Archives).

It would not have been possible to organise a project on this scale without considerable financial support. We are therefore extremely grateful to the Society of Legal Scholars, the journal *Social and Legal Studies*, the Leverhulme Trust and the British Academy as well as the law schools at the University of Birmingham and the University of Reading. In particular, we want to thank Laura-Anne Goulding and Jonathan Laidlow, based at the University of Birmingham, for their sterling work on our website.

We also wish to put on record our appreciation of the financial and practical support given by Bristol Law School, Durham Law School and the Law Department at the LSE, and especially by Jules Winterton and Belinda Crothers at the Institute of Advanced Legal Studies. In addition, many contributors owe a debt to their own institutions for helping to fund their participation. In these times of economic stringency, targets, and competition, it is heartening that the academic community is still prepared to support collaborative projects like this one, and we hope it will long continue.

Erika Rackley and Rosemary Auchmuty

# CONTENTS

# LIST OF CONTRIBUTORS

**Rosemary Auchmuty** is Professor of Law at the University of Reading.

**Susan Atkins** is a retired public servant and former Director of the Women and Equality Unit in the Cabinet Office.

**Ivana Bacik** is Reid Professor of Criminal Law, Criminology and Penology at Trinity College, Dublin, Leader of the Labour Party in the Seanad and Senator for the University of Dublin.

**Kim Barker** is a Lecturer in Law at the University of Stirling.

**Joanne Beswick** is a Senior Lecturer at Staffordshire University.

**Lois Bibbings** is a Professor of Law, Gender and History in the Law School at the University of Bristol.

**Hazel Biggs** is Professor of Healthcare Law and Bioethics at the University of Southampton.

**Laura Binger** is a Postgraduate Research Student in the Law School at the University of Kent.

**Judith Bourne** is a Senior Lecturer on the Law Programme at St Mary's University, Twickenham, London.

**Frances Burton** is a Senior Lecturer in Law at the University of Buckingham.

**Laura Cahillane** is a Lecturer in the School of Law, University of Limerick.

**Catriona Cairns** is a Solicitor at the Treasury Solicitor's Department.

**Meghan Campbell** is a Lecturer in Law at the University of Birmingham.

**Helen Carr** is a Professor in the Law School at the University of Kent.

**Katharine Cockin** is Professor of English Literature at the University of Essex.

**Joanne Conaghan** is a Professor in the Law School at the University of Bristol.

**Fiona Cownie** is a Professor of Law at Keele University.

**Elizabeth Cruickshank** is a historian and non-practising solicitor.

**Dana Denis-Smith** is founder of the First 100 Years and a non-practising solicitor.

**Fiona de Londras** is Professor of Global Legal Studies at the University of Birmingham.

**Caroline Derry** is a Lecturer in Law at The Open University.

**Alison Diduck** is a Professor in the Faculty of Laws at University College London.

**Julia Downes** is a Lecturer in Criminology and Social Policy at The Open University.

**Susan Edwards** is Professor and Dean of Law at the University of Buckingham.

**Máiréad Enright** is a Senior Lecturer in the Law School at the University of Birmingham.

**Marie Fox** is Queen Victoria Chair of Law at the School of Law and Social Justice, University of Liverpool.

**Nikki Godden-Rasul** is a Lecturer at Newcastle Law School, University of Newcastle.

**Liz Goldthorpe** is a legal biographer and retired judge.

**Sarah Greer** is Professor and Deputy Vice Chancellor at the University of Worcester.

**Brenda Hale** is President of the UK Supreme Court.

**Rosie Harding** is Professor of Law and Society at Birmingham Law School, University of Birmingham.

**Andy Hayward** is an Assistant Professor at Durham Law School, Durham University.

**Jonathan Herring** is a Professor of Law at the University of Oxford.

**Nora Honkala** is a Lecturer in Law at The City Law School of City, University of London.

**Kirsty Horsey** is a Reader in the Law School at the University of Kent.

**Carol Howells** is a Senior Lecturer in Law at The Open University.

**Rosemary Hunter** is Professor of Law and Socio-Legal Studies at the University of Kent.

**Emma Hutchinson** is a barrister at the Bar of Northern Ireland.

**Catrin Fflûr Huws** is a Senior Lecturer in the Department of Law and Criminology at Aberstwyth University.

**Harini Iyengar** is a barrister at 11 King's Bench Walk.

**Anna Jobe** is a Teaching Fellow and Postgraduate Research Student in the Law School at Durham University.

**Natalie L Jones** is a Research Fellow in the History Department at the University of Warwick.

**Olga Jurasz** is a Senior Lecturer in Law at The Open University.

**Felicity Kaganas** is a Professor of Law at Brunel University, London.

**Sonia Kalsi** is a Teaching Fellow in Criminal law at University College London and a non-practising barrister.

**Helen Kay** is an activist and historian.

**Kay Lalor** is a Senior Lecturer in Manchester Law School, Manchester Metropolitan University.

**Laura Lammasniemi** is Assistant Professor in the Law School at the University of Warwick

**Ruth Lamont** is a Senior Lecturer in Family and Child Law at the University of Manchester.

**Jacqueline Lane** is a Senior Lecturer in the Law School at the University of Huddersfield.

**Susan Leahy** is a Lecturer in Law at the University of Limerick.

**Alison Lindsay** is Head of the Historical and Legal Search Rooms at the National Records of Scotland.

**Phyllis Livaha** is a Senior Lecturer at Erasmus University College, Erasmus University Rotterdam.

**Anne Logan** is a Reader in Social History at the University of Kent's School of Social Policy, Sociology and Social Research's Medway campus.

**Clare McGlynn** is Professor of Law at Durham University.

**Sheelagh McGuinness** is a Reader in the Law School at the University of Bristol.

**Sarah Mercer** is a retired Lecturer from Northumbria University.

**Colin Moore** is a Lecturer in Law at the University of Essex.

**Anne Morris** is an Honorary Senior Research Fellow in the School of Law and Social Justice, University of Liverpool.

**Debra Morris** is Professor of Law and Dean of the School of Law and Social Justice, University of Liverpool.

**Linda Mulcahy** is Professor of Law at the London School of Economics.

**Ann Mumford** is Professor of Law at Dickson Poon Law School, Kings College London.

**Emma Nottingham** is a Senior Lecturer in the Department of Law at the University of Winchester

**Aoife O'Donoghue** is Professor of Law at Durham University.

**Maeve O'Rourke** is a barrister at 33 Bedford Row, London.

**Leonora Onaran** is a Senior Lecturer at Southampton Law School, University of Southampton.

**Marie Parker** is a Lecturer in Family and Welfare Law at Bangor University.

**Pragna Patel** is a founding member and Director of Southall Black Sisters.

**Supuni Perera** is a Postgraduate Research Student in the Law School, University of Southampton.

**Nicky Priaulx** is Professor of Law in the School of Law and Politics at Cardiff University.

**Rose Pipes** is an independent researcher.

**Erika Rackley** is a Professor in the Law School at the University of Kent.

**Penelope Russell** is a Lecturer in the Law School at the University of Sheffield.

**Harriet Samuels** is a Reader in the Law Department at the University of Westminster.

**Janet Smith** is an independent historian and a member of the National Coalition of Independent Scholars.

**Teresa Sutton** is a Lecturer in Law at the University of Sussex.

**Mari Takayanagi** is Senior Archivist at the Parliamentary Archives.

**Sharon Thompson** is a Senior Lecturer in Law in the School of Law and Politics at Cardiff University.

**Miranda Threlfall-Holmes** is Team Rector of the St Luke in the City Team Parish, Liverpool, and member of General Synod 2007–12 and 2015–17.

**Leah Treanor** is a barrister and Postgraduate Research Student at Queen's University Belfast.

**Steven Vaughan** is a Senior Lecturer in Environmental Law at University College London.

**F Vera-Gray** is an Assistant Professor in Sociology at Durham University.

**Lucy Vickers** is Professor of Law at Oxford Brookes University.

**Dawn Watkins** is a Professor at Leicester Law School, University of Leicester.

**Annapurna Waughray** is a Reader in Manchester Law School, Manchester Metropolitan University.

**Siobhan Weare** is a Lecturer in Law at Lancaster University.

**Elizabeth Woodcraft** is a former barrister and author.

# 1

# Women's Legal Landmarks: An Introduction

ERIKA RACKLEY AND ROSEMARY AUCHMUTY

Landmark [land-mahrk]

Noun:

1. a significant event, juncture or achievement marking an important stage or turning point in something;
2. a prominent or distinguishing object or feature that is easily seen, especially at a distance, which serves as a guide and/or that marks a site or location.

Verb (used with object):

1. to declare (a building, occasion) a landmark.

2019 marks the centenary of women's formal entry into the legal profession. This was, of course, a key legal landmark for women. But it was not the first: feminists have long had recourse to law as a key means of achieving equality. Nor was it the last: there have been, and continue to be, important legal advances for women. Women's legal history is full of landmarks, turning points in law's response to women's lives and experiences. The Women's Legal Landmarks Project was a multidisciplinary collaboration involving feminist scholars engaging in the process of 'landmarking' key legal events, cases and statutes for women in the UK and Ireland. Our aim was to offer a scholarly intervention into the recovery of women's lost history by combining legal and historical expertise to create the first scholarly anthology of legal landmarks for women. Together we worked to produce a collection of landmarks that demonstrated women's agency and activism in the achievement of law reform and justice. This book is the result.

## I. The Women's Legal Landmarks Project

As with many good ideas, the impetus for the project arose out of an afternoon of procrastination. A chance happening upon the blurb of a promised but yet-to-be-written book led to a conversation about the possibility of a large, collaborative project – along the lines of the UK Feminist Judgments Project[1] – bringing together lawyers and historians

[1] The UK Feminist Judgments Project (FJP) ran from 2008 to 2010. Building on and developing the methodology of the Women's Court of Canada, participants sought to put feminist theory into practice by writing 'missing' feminist judgments to key cases in England and Wales (see further Rosemary Hunter, Clare McGlynn

to identify and write about legal landmarks for women. The forthcoming anniversary of women's entry into the legal profession – then just over five years away – seemed a good 'hook' to hang it on, as well as a target to aim for. The Women's Legal Landmarks Project was underway.

We realised early on that the project's scope would require a large number of participants with a range of expertise. A call for expressions of interest followed. We asked only that the landmark – case, statute, event or monument – be from the UK (England, Wales, Scotland and Northern Ireland) or Ireland and 'be significant for feminists'. The response was exceptionally positive. After an initial sift we selected around 75 potential landmarks, narrowing our focus down to those that had had a *positive* impact – however small or fleeting – on the lives of women. This is, of course, often a matter of judgement. We allowed the case for inclusion to be made, and sometimes we were persuaded. We also introduced a further category of 'first women', to include those who were the first women to undertake key legal roles and positions.

One consequence of this approach is that, notwithstanding our efforts to commission 'missing' landmarks, the collection may seem eclectic – eccentric even. It is evident that some fairly obvious landmarks for women are not present, though they will probably be referred to somewhere in the text (for example, though there is no landmark chapter on the Equal Pay Act 1970, it is discussed in the Dagenham Car Plant Strike, 1968 and *Birmingham City Council v Abdulla* (2012) landmarks). Others may seem arcane and of limited scope (for example, the Married Women (Restraint Upon Anticipation) Act 1949). Still others do not immediately suggest themselves as particularly concerned with women (for example, the Mental Capacity Act 2005) or indeed law (*A Pageant of Great Women*, Cicely Hamilton, 1909–12). However, the final list is not as random as it might, at first, seem. In particular, the preponderance of landmarks on property and/or money and women's bodily integrity is not a coincidence. There are more landmarks on these issues because, throughout history, men's control of women's property, money and body has been the most powerful means of keeping women in subjection. And because as feminist scholars we work and write on issues that matter most to women, the most basic denials.

The collection, while comprehensive, is not therefore definitive. It was never our aim to produce an encyclopedia. Rather it was to bring together a collection that reflected women's involvement in and experience of law and law reform. Although we hoped to reach a round number – first 20, then 50 and later 100 – our list of landmarks was not closed: indeed, we accepted (and lost) a new entry just six weeks before we submitted the manuscript, and accepted another – on the Irish abortion law Referendum in May 2018 – during the publication process. In total there are 92 landmarks.[2] We hope that in future, other people will identify – and fill – the gaps. There is certainly space for a second or third volume of equal interest and relevance.

and Erika Rackley (eds), *Feminist Judgments: From Theory to Practice* (Hart Publishing, 2010)). To date there have been FJPs in Australia, New Zealand, Northern/Ireland, the US, India and Scotland as well as related projects on international law, medical law and ethics, 'wild law' and children's rights.

[2] With the exception of this introduction, text that appears in bold indicates another landmark entry. This allows for connections across and among landmarks. We have also done our best to ensure that the index is as comprehensive as possible, including references to all individuals, organisations, statutes and cases mentioned by name in the text.

The landmarks were developed through a series of workshops supported by the Society of Legal Scholars, the journal *Social and Legal Studies*, the Institute of Advanced Legal Studies and several universities,[3] at which contributors discussed drafts and shared knowledge and insights into both the legal area and the historical context. Contributions followed the same basic structure: summary of landmark; context; detail of the landmark; what happened next; and significance for women.[4] At the workshops we grouped the landmarks within themes – property; crime; first women; public law and professions; equality, employment and discrimination; family and medical law – which enabled participants to locate their landmark within a common substantive but broad historical context. The 'crime' workshop, for example, discussed landmarks spanning almost 200 years.[5] A number of participants attended multiple workshops which allowed connections to be made across the themes. Workshops were also attended by other academics and scholars as well as postgraduates with an interest in the field.

With the support of the Institute of Advanced Legal Studies, we also held two methodology and training events, one on working with archival sources (at which experts introduced participants to relevant collections and sources and led them through the processes of finding and interrogating primary sources) and the other on the production of secondary sources in women's legal history.[6] For a number of participants this was their first time engaging in historical (as opposed to legal or even historically legal) research and so these events were important not only to ensure the academic rigour of the individual landmarks and the project as a whole, but also in relation to our broader aim of developing the discipline of feminist legal history. In addition to the feedback participants received at and after the workshops, the landmarks were subjected to an intensive editorial process involving detailed comments and suggestions on successive drafts.

In total, over 100 people have been involved in the project in some form. The 87 landmark authors are drawn from wide-ranging academic disciplines and backgrounds, including law, history, English literature, theology and criminology, and also include independent historians, parliamentary archivists, parliamentarians, civil servants, activists, lawyers and judges from across the four jurisdictions. We are proud that our authors range from established scholars to postgraduate and early career researchers as well as those who have retired from their professional employment. Another pertinent characteristic of a number

[3] Durham, London School of Economics (twice), Reading, Bristol, and Birmingham.

[4] The 'first women' landmarks followed more or less the same structure, with a discussion of the woman's life coming before a discussion of the context, what happened next and her landmark's significance for women.

[5] For the book, however, after some deliberation, we decided to present the landmarks chronologically rather than in related subject groups. We do so mindful of the danger of presenting what might appear to be a Whiggish tale of women's steady progress from injustice to equality, though we hope that the inclusion of sections on 'What happened next' and 'Significance' might go some way to avoiding that impression. We adopted a chronological approach because we wanted to demonstrate the full sweep of the historical development, to show how a number of issues might be being debated at any one period and how the same people might be involved in different landmarks (we know that feminist campaigners have always been active in a range of causes) and to give a sense of what was going on at any one time. We were also keen to encourage our readers, especially the academic ones, not to confine themselves to their specialist area of law and to read outside of their area, as they might not have done if we had arranged the landmarks in subject groups. This arrangement had the additional practical benefit of enabling us as editors to avoid having to allocate each landmark to a single category when, in reality, its effects might spread across several areas of law.

[6] Women's Legal Landmarks Archival Training Day, Institute of Advanced Legal Studies, London, 25 June 2015; Doing Women's Legal History, Institute of Advanced Legal Studies, London, 26 October 2016.

of our authors is that they were involved in some way in one or more of the landmarks.[7] Where authors wrote about landmarks in which they had played a role, we did not ask them to adopt the guise of academic distance or objectivity, but simply to note the fact of their involvement.

We are also aware that there are divergent feminist views on a number of the issues raised by the landmarks – and indeed in relation to some of the landmarks themselves. However, while we know that not all will agree, we think that in all cases the argument that the landmark had some positive impact on women (however limited, fleeting or vexed) can be – and has been – made.

## II. Doing Feminist Legal History

Despite a fairly well-established tradition of feminist legal history in North America and elsewhere,[8] legal history scholarship in the UK and Ireland largely ignores women. With some notable exceptions,[9] at best it plays down women's perspectives and agency[10] and at worst, reduces mentions of women to the occasional paragraph.[11] In contrast to the well-established and vigorously theorised sub-discipline of feminist *history*, feminist *legal* history is under-utilised as a resource or method within feminist legal scholarship in the UK and Ireland.[12] This is true notwithstanding the proliferation of projects, exhibitions and events marking the centenary of women lawyers. There is an important (though often unremarked) difference between doing feminist legal history and collating accounts of the lives of women lawyers and/or women in law. A feminist legal historian does not simply collect

[7] eg Susan Atkins, Ivana Bacik, Frances Burton, Elizabeth Cruickshank, Mairead Enright, Fiona de Londras, Brenda Hale, Rosemary Hunter, Clare McGlynn, Maeve O'Rourke, Pragna Patel, Erika Rackley, Miranda Threlfall-Holmes, Elizabeth Woodcraft.

[8] eg Mary-Jane Mossman, *The First Women Lawyers: A Comparative Study of Gender, Law and the Legal Professions* (Hart Publishing, 2016); Diane Kirkby (ed), *Past law, Present Histories* (ANU E Press, 2012); Tracy Thomas and Tracey Boisseau (eds), *Feminist Legal History: Essays on Women and Law* (New York University Press, 2011); Felice Batlan (ed), 'Women's Legal History: A Global Perspective' (2012) 87(2) *Chicago-Kent Law Review* 331–704; Eileen Spring, *Land, Law and Family: Aristocratic Inheritance in England, 1300 to 1800* (University of North Carolina Press, 1993); Susan Staves, *Married Women's Separate Property in England, 1660–1833* (Harvard University Press, 1990); Dorothy M Stetson, *A Woman's Issue: The Politics of Family Law Reform in England* (Greenwood Press, 1982).

[9] eg Rosemary Auchmuty, 'Whatever happened to Miss Bebb? *Bebb v The Law Society* and women's legal history' (2012) 31 *Legal Studies* 199–230; Rosemary Auchmuty, 'Recovering lost lives: researching women in legal history' (2015) 42 *Journal of Law and Society* 34; Patrick Polden, 'The Lady of Tower Bridge: Sybil Campbell, England's first woman judge' (1993) 8 *Women's History Review* 505; Patrick Polden, 'Portia's Progress: Women and the Bar, 1919–1939' (2005) 12 *International Journal of the Legal Profession* 293; Ivana Bacik, Cathryn Costello and Eileen Drew, *Gender inJustice: feminising the legal professions* (Trinity College Dublin Law School, 2003).

[10] eg Michael Birks, *Gentlemen of the Law* (Stevens, 1960).

[11] eg AH Manchester, *Modern Legal History* 1750–1950 (Butterworths, 1980).

[12] Again with notable exceptions, eg, Albie Sachs and Joan Hoff Wilson, *Sexism and the Law: A Study of Male Beliefs and Judicial Bias in Britain and America* (Wiley-Blackwell, 1978); Sally Sheldon, '"Who is the Mother to Make the Judgement": Constructions of Woman in UK Abortion Law' (1993) 1 *Feminist Legal Studies* 3; Rosemary Auchmuty, 'Law and the Power of Feminism: How marriage lost its power to oppress women' (2012) 20 *Feminist Legal Studies* 71; Máiréad Enright and Emilie Cloatre, '"On the Perimeter of the Lawful": Enduring Illegality in the Irish Family Planning Movement, 1972–1985' (2017) 44(4) *Journal of Law and Society* 471.

and assemble the 'facts' of an event or person's life. Rather feminist legal history seeks to produce a new, accurate, inclusive account by:

1. asking the 'woman question' (where are the women in this account?);[13]
2. foregrounding *gender* as an organising principle in society and the *dynamic* between the sexes;
3. including *women's* stories, experiences and voices (often hidden, ignored and silenced in dominant narratives) and locating *men's* position – their opposition or support – within these;
4. establishing women as *agents* rather than simply subjects of law;
5. focusing on law (broadly conceived), with a nuanced view of how it operates;
6. placing events in their historical context and rejecting the assumption that change occurs merely through shifts in social attitudes and institutional reform;
7. challenging assumptions of unabated progress and liberal incrementalism by showing that legal reform is often messy, disjointed and episodic, that there is very often a backlash and regrouping by opponents, and that hard-won gains are easily lost as momentum and focus shift elsewhere.

Feminist legal history is, then, at root a political project. Its purpose is transformative, not descriptive. It requires its authors to commit not only to uncovering the silences and the silenced and to locating the specific in the general, but also to take a further step and use these histories to challenge and change the dominant narrative not only of the past, but also the future. In other words, while its substance may require the author to look back, the motivation of feminist legal history is forward-looking.

With this in mind, the Women's Legal Landmarks Project had both academic and political ambitions.

Academically, it sought to blur disciplinary boundaries by applying a feminist lens to an under explored research methodology in the UK and Ireland, where legal history – let alone *feminist* legal history – remains a relatively niche subject. It sought to carve out a space for feminist legal history, so that it might push at the boundaries of knowledge and critical engagement in legal history and feminist legal studies generally. It also aimed to foster a broader study of law reform and legal change across academic disciplines by harnessing a range of multi-disciplinary expertise and creating a space in which the insights of scholars and professionals from many backgrounds could be brought to bear on a specific case, statute and/or event. Our hope was that the landmarks could be located – and stand up to scrutiny – within any relevant discipline.

In particular, we wanted the subject-specific expertise of legally-trained scholars to ensure the accurate interpretation of complex legal provisions, sometimes missing in historical research. And we wanted the subject-expertise of historians to ensure that the contributions were permeated by an understanding of historiography – the idea that history is not simply a collection of established facts assembled in an unchallengeable narrative, but has been, and should be, a dialogue between past and present, acknowledged to come from a range of perspectives and viewpoints. This approach had the effect of forcing legal scholars to widen their focus beyond the *legal* sources which all too often

[13] See Katharine T Bartlett, 'Feminist Legal Methods' (1990) 103 *Harvard Law Review* 829.

constitute the compass of legal research and which therefore frequently overlook or exclude women simply because women were not present in public office or practically involved in law before the twentieth century, and continue to be in a substantial minority in the law-making process.

Taken together, the landmarks challenge the 'top-down' gender-neutral and ahistorical understanding of law which dominates much of UK legal education.[14] Many law students graduate knowing little about legal history and even less about *women's* legal history. The revised 'statement of standards for university law library provision in the United Kingdom', prepared by the Libraries Sub-Committee of the Society of Legal Scholars in 2009 to 'assist law libraries to meet the needs of the research and teaching objectives of … university law schools', makes just one mention of gender and feminism (in the titles of the *Harvard Journal of Law and Gender* and *Feminist Legal Studies*[15] respectively).[16] Gender is not included as a separate 'subject source' in a list that runs to 43 entries and includes computer law, construction law and tax/revenue law. While legal history does make the Sub-Committee's list, the main thrust of legal education is one that encourages little sense of historical perspective beyond the development of certain precedents. In lectures and textbooks, current principles are often stripped of context and critique, while the emphasis on the *legal* actors (mainly judges, but also politicians), rather than the politics and/or activism that influenced the court or Parliament, ensures (so long as women continue to be in the minority in such positions) the continued dominance of the perspectives and agency of *men*. The process of law reform is presented as a tale in which enlightened institutions gradually reform themselves. And if women's legal history is mentioned at all, it appears as one of steady progress from injustice and inequality toward justice and equality, in which women are subjects rather than agents of change. For the authors of this collection, however, the landmarks are a reflection of the determination and commitment of women and groups of women in the ongoing struggle to achieve justice and equality for women.

Of course, this view of women's legal history is not only found in law schools. It is found across academic disciplines and beyond. Thus, the challenge to debunk the myth of 'women's linear progress from oppression under the law to equal opportunity in modern times'[17] is *political* as well as academic. With this in mind, the Women's Legal Landmarks Project had two further aims: first, through the recognition of hitherto overlooked or suppressed histories, to expose the continued marginalisation of women in law, public policy and social justice, and, second, by providing a deeper understanding of the impact of law on the lived experience of women and the impact of women on law, to inform strategies adopted by those *currently* seeking social justice. The history of women's admission to the legal profession is a case in point.

[14] Though see Susan Atkins and Brenda Hoggett, *Women and the Law* (Wiley-Blackwell, 1984); Rosemary Auchmuty (ed), *Great Debates in Gender and Law* (Palgrave, 2018).

[15] See *Feminist Legal Studies* Journal, 1993.

[16] Libraries Sub-Committee of the Society of Legal Scholars, 'A library for the modern law school: a statement of standards for university law library provision in the United Kingdom' (Society of Legal Scholars, 2009 revision): http://www.legalscholars.ac.uk/wp-content/uploads/2016/05/SLS-Library-for-a-Modern-Law-School-Statement-2009.pdf.

[17] Thomas and Boisseau (eds), n 9 above, 2.

## III. The Reason for the Project: Celebrating the Centenary of Women's Admission to the Legal Profession

This Project celebrates the admission of women to the legal profession in the UK and Ireland following the enactment of the Sex Disqualification (Removal) Act 1919. This admission was not gained easily, though existing accounts might lead one to imagine it was, perhaps as a reward for women's service during the First World War or as part of the natural progress of women's rights.[18] In fact, women's admission had been resisted for decades by a profession that clung to its male monopoly on law-making and the power that accompanied the status and income of lawyers. Law was among the last professions in the UK to admit women; and it was able to keep them out for so long because lawyers, judges and MPs, all of them men, controlled the very means by which their entrance was to be achieved.

Even after women had demonstrated their mastery of the legal technicalities involved in their many campaigns to reform the law relating to domestic violence, married women's property, prostitution and other legal issues;[19] even after they had shown they could compete intellectually with male students in the university law schools;[20] even after they could be observed carrying out professional legal functions, as did Eliza Orme in the law office she ran with women friends in Chancery Lane between 1875 and 1904,[21] or Gwyneth Bebb in prosecuting employers who fell foul of labour laws before the First World War and black marketeers during the war,[22] still the professions held out. Women were unsuited to legal work, they argued; they were too emotional, and unable to reason: the Earl of Halsbury (of *Halsbury's Laws*) objected that 'a woman had no recognition of any side but her own'.[23] Many men feared the competition of women, and claimed that there was not enough work to go around. They were sure that clients would not want to be represented by women. Barristers especially resisted women's invasion of their masculine spaces where they could freely indulge their masculine customs.[24] All these objections were aired in debates at the Law Society (for solicitors) and the Bar (for barristers) and motions to admit women were repeatedly lost.[25]

There was evidence that women had occupied legal offices and performed legal functions in the distant past. In a book published in 1894, Charlotte Carmichael Stopes gave examples of titled women who had appeared as advocates in mediaeval times and Tudor women who had been judges in County courts.[26] But, like the vote, women had

[18] Birks, n 11 above; Manchester, n 12 above.

[19] See, eg, Gaols Act 1823; Married Women's Property Act 1882; Section 5(1) of the Criminal Law Amendment Act 1885.

[20] Rosemary Auchmuty, 'Early Women Law Students at Cambridge and Oxford' (2008) 29 *Journal of Legal History* 63.

[21] Leslie Howsam, 'Eliza Orme (1848–1937), social activist and lawyer' in *Oxford Dictionary of National Biography* (2004).

[22] Rosemary Auchmuty, 'Whatever happened to Miss Bebb? *Bebb v The Law Society* and women's legal history' (2012) 31 *Legal Studies* 199–230.

[23] Nellie Alden Granz, *English Women Enter the Professions* (privately printed, 1965) 275.

[24] Elsie Lang, *British Women in the Twentieth Century* (T Werner Laurie, 1929) chapter 6.

[25] See further First Woman Solicitor in England and Wales, Carrie Morrison, 1922.

[26] Charlotte Carmichael Stopes, *British Freewomen. Their Historical Privilege* (Swan Sonnenschein & Co, 1894) 47, 64. See also Lang, n 24 above, 145.

ceased to participate in law and politics by the time industrialisation took hold in the eighteenth century and the doctrine of separate spheres (men for public life, women for the home) became the ideal and the enforced reality. Middle-class women's frustration with this arrangement, combined with an expanding economy (and a plummeting marriage rate) in the nineteenth century, led to the first wave of feminism and campaigns that included finding opportunities for women to support themselves and pursue careers. Better education for girls was the first target. Then, following a successful campaign to open higher education to women, Cambridge and then London and Oxford permitted women to attend lectures and take the university examinations from the 1870s onwards.[27] A very few women chose to study law, cognisant of its usefulness to the women's movement quite as much as its career potential.[28] In 1878 a 'Small Group for the Promotion of Legal Education' was founded, and in 1888 Eliza Orme became the first woman law graduate when she successfully completed the external LLB at London University.[29] (Oxford and Cambridge did not grant degrees to women until 1920 and 1948 respectively.)

But the possession of a law degree was not sufficient – was not, indeed, required – to become a practising lawyer.[30] For that, one needed to pass the professional examinations authorised by each of the two branches of the legal profession; and to these, women were not admitted. In 1871 Maria Grey was refused permission to attend the lectures at Lincoln's Inn (for the Bar). In 1878 Eliza Orme was refused permission to take the Law Society's examinations (to become a solicitor). We emphasise these dates to reinforce the point that women had been campaigning for *almost 50 years* before finally winning admission to the legal profession in 1919.

If the traditional legal histories record one event in this long, sustained, highly organised feminist campaign, it is the case of *Bebb v Law Society*.[31] Gywneth Bebb held the equivalent of a first-class honours degree in law from Oxford University. Along with three companions, she applied to the Law Society to be permitted to sit the examinations to become a solicitor. The women were refused on account of their sex. Miss Bebb thereupon challenged the Law Society in the High Court and then in the Court of Appeal. Her supporters and legal advisers, who included the distinguished male barristers who represented her in court and the sympathetic male solicitors who briefed them, relied primarily on section 48 of the Solicitors Act 1843, which stated that

> every Word importing the Masculine Gender only shall extend and be applied to a Female as well as a Male … unless it be otherwise specially provided or there be something in the Subject or Context repugnant to such construction.

In spite of this textbook case of statutory interpretation – the very statute regulating solicitors stated that women were encompassed in 'men' – Miss Bebb lost. All four judges

[27] Auchmuty, n 20 above. Although not to take degrees.

[28] Christabel Pankhurst, for example, graduated from Manchester University with a first in law in 1906, having applied unsuccessfully to the Bar in 1903. See further Rosemary Auchmuty, 'Feminists as stakeholders in the law school' in Fiona Cownie (ed), *Stakeholders in the Law School* (Hart Publishing, 2010) 35.

[29] Mossman, n 8 above, 121–37; Howsam, n 21 above.

[30] This is still the case.

[31] *Bebb v Law Society* [1914] 1 Ch 286. See further Rosemary Auchmuty, 'Whatever happened to Miss Bebb? *Bebb v The Law Society* and women's legal history' (2011) 31 *Legal Studies* 199.

(one in the High Court and three in the Court of Appeal) contended that they were bound by 'long uniform and uninterrupted usage, which we ought … to be very loth to depart from'.[32] Since only men had ever been solicitors, they said, women could not become solicitors until Parliament passed explicit legislation admitting them.

Miss Bebb's case was important for attracting huge publicity (and general press approval) for the women's cause. But it was only one of a range of strategies the feminists adopted in pursuit of their goal. Campaigning was stepped up, with the formation of the Committee to Open the Legal Profession to Women in 1914, whose members included distinguished establishment figures from the Conservative, Liberal, and Labour parties as well as representatives of all the feminist groups (and even some opponents of votes for women, like Mary Ward). There were meetings, debates, heated discussions in the solicitors' and barristers' professional associations and a succession of private member's Bills in Parliament.

The First World War proved to be the catalyst for a change of heart among solicitors, not just because women 'proved their worth' in keeping services going while the men were at the front but because so many young men were lost that women were needed to fill the gap. After the war, therefore, the Law Society voted to admit women. The Bar remained obdurate to the end. Only with the enactment of the Sex Disqualification (Removal) Act 1919 were they forced to admit women, and they did so with poor grace. Women who went down the barrister's route found themselves excluded, unsupported, criticised and harassed, and struggled to succeed at the Bar for decades thereafter.[33]

Women's admission to the legal profession in the UK and Ireland is, then, not just the historical peg upon which the Women's Legal Landmarks Project hangs, but is itself a landmark in women's legal history itself, paradigmatic of the landmarks in this book, for the following reasons.

First, the whole story of women's admission to the legal profession is not well-known and, where told, tends to take forms that this project hopes to correct. Second, the *Bebb* case dominates discussions for the simple reason that it is a *legal* source, and legal scholars are infamous for relying on legal sources and ignoring or dismissing extra-legal ones. This explains why their accounts so often display ignorance of or indifference to the background and context of the *Bebb* litigation and the wider campaign of which it was a part. Moreover, focusing on *Bebb* allows traditional historians to isolate Miss Bebb as the first and only complainant, instead of revealing her to be one of a large and longstanding group of campaigners on this issue. Worse, it encourages us to elevate Miss Bebb to the status of heroine. However attractive such presentations may appear at first sight for those in pursuit of suitable role models for young people and inspirations for today's equality campaigns, this is something we must guard against. To embrace an individual as a heroine risks falling into the trap that men's history has set for us, where she becomes one lone voice instead of representative of a mass movement, and personally courageous rather than carried along by a host of supporters. It takes attention away from the *real* story, which is

[32] This despite the fact that Counsel for Miss Bebb listed the names of women who had held legal functions in days gone by.

[33] See further First Woman to be Admitted to an Inn of Court, Helena Normanton, 1919; Helena Kennedy, 'Women at the Bar' in Robert Hazell (ed), *The Bar on Trial* (Quartet Books Ltd, 1978) 148.

the decades-long resistance of the male lawyers, MPs and judges to the idea of allowing women to be lawyers, and the need for feminist campaigners to strategise on all fronts to shift attitudes, since they had no say in changing the law. While feminists today have a far greater say in the processes and outcomes of law reform, the need to make visible the extent to which feminist campaigns stand on the shoulders of those who came before them is as important as ever.

What makes women's admission to the legal profession particularly *significant* for a project on women's legal landmarks is that, as with votes for women, feminists had high hopes for what it would achieve. Both changes, coming so close together, seemed to signify the advent of a new legal era for women in which women would be *directly* involved in the law-making process instead of having to rely on men to take up their causes. And so it has been. Even if not all women lawyers or MPs have been feminists, it is clear from the landmarks in this collection how often the feminists among them have indeed been involved in women's causes and how often it has been the participation of feminist lawyers, MPs and, eventually, judges that has pushed women's issues and perspectives onto the legal agenda, sometimes with marked success.[34]

But progress has been astonishingly slow. The 1919 Act gave women the right to sit on juries[35] and to be appointed as magistrates (judges in the lower courts), and it was a long-term feminist goal to have women on the senior judiciary, as these judges were appointed from the ranks of barristers at the time. Although magistrate appointments were made immediately,[36] the arrival of women in the higher courts proved to take much longer than any of the campaigners of 1919 would have envisaged, as men's grip on the top levels of the judiciary held firm through their ability to decide who was chosen, and later through their ability to interpret 'merit'.[37] Few of those entering the profession in 1919 would have imagined that it would take another 85 years for the first woman – Brenda Hale – to be appointed to the Appellate Committee of the House of Lords, then the most UK's most senior court.[38] Even fewer would think that it would take (on current predictions) somewhere *between 150 and 200 years* for there to be parity across the judiciary between women and men judges.[39]

The trajectory of women's representation in the legal profession and the judiciary thus shows how landmarks for women are always partial and circumscribed, and almost always followed by a tightening of control by those whose power has been breached. The achievement of a landmark is rarely, if ever, the end of the story. Too often it signifies the start of

[34] eg Education Act 1944; Family Allowances Act 1945; Dagenham Car Plant Strike, 1968; *R v Ahulwalia* (1992); First Woman President of the UK Supreme Court, Lady Hale, 2017.

[35] See Sex Disqualification (Removal) Act 1919 and Section 25 of the Criminal Justice Act 1972.

[36] First Women Justices of the Peace, 1919.

[37] Although the ability of the judiciary to be 'self-selecting' formally ended when the Judicial Appointments Commission (JAC) was established in 2006, it has been suggested that during its first decade the JAC been 'hemmed in' to varying degrees by its judicial stakeholders (Graham Gee and Erika Rackley, 'Introduction: Diversity and the JAC's First Ten Years' in Graham Gee and Erika Rackley (eds), *Debating Judicial Appointments in an Age of Diversity* (Routledge, 2017)).

[38] Susan Denham was appointed to the Supreme Court of Ireland in 1992, becoming Chief Justice in 2011, a position she held until her retirement in 2017.

[39] Lord Sumption, 'Home Truths about Judicial Diversity', Bar Council Law Reform Lecture, 15 November 2012; Alan Paterson and Chris Paterson, *Guarding the guardians? Towards an independent, accountable and diverse senior judiciary* (CentreForum, 2012) 37.

another struggle; an even more bitter one since the impediments to justice and equality for women are no longer explicit but may be hidden, informal, and bolstered by practices not yet forbidden or even recognised, and always able to be denied by opponents protesting that 'women are equal now'.

# IV. The Landmarks

Together, the landmarks in this collection span eleven centuries. The earliest – The Laws of Hywel Dda, which detail the legal status of women in mediaeval Wales[40] – comes from the tenth century. Most of the rest date from the latter half of the twentieth century, thanks no doubt to women's greater participation in law-making as well as successive tides of feminist activism. In between, some of the landmarks are familiar steps in the history of women's emancipation, such as the Married Women's Property Act 1882, which gave married women the ability to own and manage property independently of their husbands, and the Representation of the People Act 1918, which gave women over 30 who met a property requirement the vote. Others are important milestones in women's social or political history: the Abortion Act 1967, which provided for legal abortion in England and Wales in certain defined circumstances; the Health (Family Planning) Act 1979, which regulated the importation and provision of contraception in Ireland; the Housing (Homeless Persons) Act 1977, which increased legislative protection for women escaping from domestic violence; and the ordination of women bishops.[41] Still others feature regularly on undergraduate law degrees, such as *Williams & Glyn's Bank v Boland* (1980), which accepted that wives might have an overriding interest in the family home instead of merely a personal right by virtue of being married to the legal owner; *R v Ahluwalia* (1992), which recognised Battered Woman Syndrome as evidence to support the defences of diminished responsibility and provocation in homicide; and Section 41 of the Youth Justice and Criminal Evidence Act 1999, which sought to limit the use of sexual history evidence in criminal trials.

Other landmarks will be less familiar as feminist landmarks or to non-lawyers: for example, the Criminal Law Amendment Act 1885,[42] best known for criminalising homosexual acts between men but which also raised the age of consent for girls; the Maternity and Child Welfare Act 1918, which obliged local authorities to set up maternal and child welfare clinics; Article 7 of the Covenant of the League of Nations 1919, which gave space for women's participation in public international law; and *Gill and Coote v El Vino Co Ltd* (1982), which overturned a rule that women would not be served at a London bar.

## A. Jurisdiction

Not all the landmarks in this collection apply equally to the whole of the UK and Ireland. The description 'UK and Ireland' encompasses the jurisdictions of England and Wales,

[40] Cyfraith Hywel (The Laws of Hywel Dda), c. 940.

[41] Bishops and Priests (Consecration and Ordination of Women) Measure 2014 and Canon C2, 'Of the Consecration of Bishops', 2014.

[42] See Section 5(1) of the Criminal Law Amendment Act 1885.

Scotland and Northern Ireland – which make up the United Kingdom of Great Britain and Northern Ireland – and the Republic of Ireland, as well as the UK itself in international matters. Some of the landmarks apply across all these jurisdictions, others to only to some or one of them. During the time period of the collection, these jurisdictions have come together, separated, been created, and co-existed to varying degrees.

At the time of our first landmark – circa 950 – what we now know as Wales, Ireland, Scotland and England looked very different indeed. The borders between England and Wales, and England and Scotland were yet to be settled, and the geographic areas were largely ruled by a system of small kingdoms, each with their own laws and customs. Fast-forward almost 800 years to our next landmark and England and Wales have become distinct countries, but a single jurisdiction by virtue of the Laws in Wales Act 1535–42. Scotland is also part of a political union with England and Wales – known as the United Kingdom of Great Britain – following the Treaty of Union in 1707. There is just one Parliament sitting in Westminster. But Scotland retains its own legal system, and still does today.[43]

100 years later, the Union expands further. On 1 January 1801, Ireland becomes part of 'the United Kingdom of Great Britain and Ireland'.[44] A group of protestant MPs take up their seats at Westminster and the Irish Government votes to abolish itself. This remained the political and legal status quo until the partition of Ireland and the creation of Northern Ireland in 1921 under the Government of Ireland Act and the establishment of the Irish Free State in 1922.[45] From this point on, Ireland (once again) had a separate and distinct legal system. Just over a quarter of the landmarks discussed in this collection fall within the period prior to 1922, so will apply to the whole of the UK unless expressly excluded. The Married Women's Property Act 1882, for instance, applied to England and Wales and the unified Ireland but not to Scotland, which has always had its own property law.

Fast-forward another 50 years and a new site of law-making joined the mix: the (then) European Economic Community (EEC), now the European Union (EU). This introduced to both the UK, by virtue of the European Communities Act 1972, and to Ireland, following a referendum the same year, a new – and expansive – site of law-making via the EU institutions and the Court of Justice of the European Union. 30 years later, in 1998, the institutional landscape of law-making across the UK altered again. There are now devolved legislatures in Scotland (the Scottish Parliament), Northern Ireland (the Northern Ireland Assembly) and Wales (the National Assembly of Wales). The latter provides us with two landmarks: the National Assembly of Wales Election, 2003, following which the Assembly became the first legislative chamber to elect equal numbers of men and women, and the Violence Against Women, Domestic Abuse and Sexual Violence (Wales) Act 2015.

[43] See further William Gordon, 'Scotland as a Mixed Jurisdiction' in William Gordon, *Roman Law, Scots Law and Legal History: Selected Essays* (Edinburgh University Press, 2007).

[44] By virtue of the Acts of Union 1800. In fact, English law was first imported into Ireland, and had 'held sway', since the Anglo-Norman invasion of 1170 (Bacik et al, n 9 above, 40).

[45] Basil Chubb, *The Politics of the Irish Constitution* (Institute of Public Administration, 1991).

## B. Types of Landmarks

It is often imagined that the only significant legal landmarks are those enshrined in legislation or, occasionally, case law in the higher courts. This collection shows that a range of influences, including pressure from outside the legal and political establishment, can bring about shifts in legal thinking and practice. That said, many of the landmarks are indeed statutes, beginning with the Gaols Act 1823, which identified women prisoners as a special group and created standards of health and inspection, and ending with Section 2 of the Abusive Behaviour and Sexual Harm (Scotland) Act 2016, the first legislation in the UK and Ireland to address varied forms of image-based sexual abuse.

A further group of landmarks is legal cases. The first, *The Slave, Grace* (1827), though substantively about the position of (women) slaves in England, establishes the importance of feminist organisation in pursuance of law reform from the early nineteenth century onwards. As Rosemary Auchmuty notes:

> The anti-slavery movement gave women experience in organising around political issues, dealing with male opposition, identifying the ways that privilege worked, and making links between the oppression of other women and their own, which was to stand them in good stead when, the emancipation of slaves achieved, they turned their attention to the emancipation of women.[46]

Other cases include *R v Jackson* (1891), which held that no one had the right to imprison another person, even his wife, *St George's Healthcare NHS Trust v S* (1998), which confirmed that a competent pregnant woman can refuse medical treatment even if that may result in harm to her or the foetus, *White v White* (2000), which established the equal-sharing principle on divorce, and our final case, *In the Matter of an Application for Judicial Review by the Northern Ireland Human Rights Commission* (2015), which ruled that, in denying terminations to women who were carrying a foetus with a fatal abnormality or who had become pregnant as a result of rape or incest, Northern Irish abortion law was not human rights compliant (under article 8 of the European Convention on Human Rights).

Another group of landmarks coalesces around key events in which women were the primary participants and which either led to legislation – such as the strikes by match-workers at the Bryant and May factory in 1888[47] and, 80 years later, by Ford workers at the Dagenham car plant[48] – or, as is the case with the Women's Peace Camp at Greenham Common 1981–2000, had a significant impact on the development of the common law.

The collection also includes discussion of two parliamentary reports – the Committee on the Employment of Women on Police Duties, 1920 and the Warnock Report, 1984 – and of international obligations that follow from the UK Ratification of the Optional Protocol to the Convention on the Elimination of all Forms of Discrimination Against Women (OP-CEDAW), 2005 and the United Nation's recognition in 2011 of the Irish State's failure to protect the girls and women who were involuntarily confined in the Magdalene Laundries.[49]

[46] *The Slave, Grace* (1827), 53.

[47] See Match Women's Strike 1888.

[48] See Dagenham Car Plant Strike, 1968.

[49] Concluding Observations of the UN Committee against Torture, Recommendation to Ireland regarding the Magdalene Laundries 2011.

A final subset of landmarks encompasses books, journals and plays. These include popular works such as Mary Wollstonecraft's call for equality and for the extension of civil and political rights in *A Vindication of the Rights of Woman* (1792),[50] Barbara Leigh Smith Bodichon's *A Brief Summary of the Most Important Laws Concerning Women*, 1854, which set out the law that shaped and underpinned campaigns for women's rights, Cicely Hamilton's *A Pageant of Great Women*, which presented arguments for women's enfranchisement, and Radclyffe Hall's *Well of Loneliness*,[51] whose banning in 1928 brought the issue of lesbian freedom into the public domain. In addition, we include the first text to comprehensively examine the gendered nature of law and the legal inter-relationships between women's private and public lives and between men and women, the agenda-shaping *Women and the Law* by Susan Atkins and Brenda Hoggett (now Lady Hale), and the first feminist law journal in the UK, *Feminist Legal Studies*.

Interwoven among the substantive landmarks are short biographies of women lawyers, judges, politicians and academics who were the first to fill a particular role or position, beginning with Helen Taylor (the first woman to run an election campaign for Parliament in 1885) and ending with Brenda Hale's ground-breaking appointment as President of the UK Supreme Court in 2017. These personal histories allow for exploration of the role played by these women in the substantive landmarks considered (for example, Helena Normanton and the Married Women's Property Act 1964, and Mary Robinson[52] and the Health (Family Planning) Act 1979 and the Fifteenth Amendment of the Constitution Act 1995), as well as for direct consideration of the differences in viewpoint, ambition and feminism among women. We include their stories, mindful of the invidiousness of singling out individual women from what are often collective endeavours and aware that the designation of 'the first' is often – as many women 'firsts' (though not, we note, men) acknowledge – a matter of 'being in the right place at the right time'.

We are also aware that there are many other 'firsts' who are not included in the collection, such as Agnes Twiston Hughes who, in 1923, became the first woman solicitor in Wales, or Linda Dobbs, the first black woman appointed to the High Court in 2004. We could also have included Elish Angiolini, the first woman to be appointed Lord Advocate in Scotland in 2006, Denise McBride and Siobhan Keegan who, in October 2015, became the first women to sit on the High Court in Northern Ireland or, perhaps more controversially, Margaret Thatcher, the first woman UK Prime Minister. There are many others.[53] Some we wanted to include, but lost along the way. Other notable women in law were excluded because, while they had undoubtedly made outstanding contributions to women's legal progress, there was not a significant UK or Irish 'first' peg on which to hang their inclusion. Cornelia Sorabji, the first woman to study law at Oxford – but not the first woman to study law – was excluded for this reason, as was Chrystal Macmillan, the first woman to plead a case before the House of Lords. As with the collection as a whole, the purpose of our list of 'first women' is not to be exhaustive, but representative. However, their stories are important not only in order to celebrate the significant personal achievements of these landmark women but as a lens through which to acknowledge the contribution of other women, known and unknown,

[50] *A Vindication of the Rights of Woman*, Mary Wollstonecraft, 1792.
[51] *DPP v Jonathan Cape and Leopold Hill* (1928).
[52] First Woman President of Ireland, Mary Robinson, 1990.
[53] See further, First 100 years: https://first100years.org.uk/.

who appear in these and other entries in the collection (and who are listed in the index). The collective history of women lawyers is also considered in the chapters on the appointment of the first women Justices of the Peace, and the foundation of the Association of Women Solicitors, 1919, and the Association of Women Barristers, 1991.

## C. Topics

Just as every area of law affects women (though this is far from obvious in the undergraduate law curriculum today), so the landmarks in this volume come from a wide range of legal fields, public and private, national and international: from tort law to family law, property law to employment law, medical law to human rights law, criminal law to tax law. Many deal with subject-matter that might be considered paradigmatically feminist: issues of immediate concern to women's lives such as domestic and sexual violence,[54] marriage and divorce,[55] reproduction and childcare,[56] workplace discrimination,[57] as well as access to professions and political institutions.[58] Indeed, some were causes célèbres for feminist activism in law, such as the Women's Peace Camp at Greenham Common 1981–2000, Section 41 of the Youth Justice and Criminal Evidence Act 1999 and the Irish referendum on the 8th Amendment in May 2018. However, others – such as the British Nationality Act 1948 (which conferred on women the same right as men to retain or change their nationality, irrespective of their marital status) and Section 32 of the Finance Act 1988 (which introduced separate taxation for married women) – wear their (no less significant) feminist credentials more lightly. Several of the landmarks consider intersectional issues of class,[59] race and ethnicity,[60] disability,[61] age,[62] sexuality[63] and religion.[64]

[54] eg *R v Jackson* (1891); First Women's Refuge, 1971; First Rape Crisis Centre, 1976; Section 4 of the Sexual Offences (Amendment) Act 1976; Housing (Homeless Persons) Act 1977; *Davis v Johnson* (1978); Section 5 of the Criminal Law (Rape) (Amendment) Act 1990; *R v Ahluwalia* (1992); Section 1 of the Sexual Offences Act 2003, Section 14 of the Policing and Crime Act 2009; Section 2 of the Abusive Behaviour and Sexual Harm (Scotland) Act 2016.

[55] eg Divorce and Matrimonial Causes Act 1857; Married Women's Property Act 1882; Matrimonial Causes Act 1923; Married Women (Restraint Upon Anticipation) Act 1949; Married Women's Property Act 1964; *White v White* (2000); Forced Marriage (Civil Protection) Act 2007; *Radmacher v Grantino* (2010).

[56] eg Maternity and Child Welfare Act 1918; Family Allowances Act 1945; Abortion Act 1967; National Health Service (Family Planning) Act 1967; Health (Family Planning) Act 1979; Warnock Report, 1984; Protection of Life During Pregnancy Act 2013; *In the Matter of an Application for Judicial Review by the Northern Ireland Human Rights Commission* (2015); Thirty-sixth Amendment to the Irish Constitution, 2018.

[57] eg Education Act 1944; Dagenham Car Plant Strike, 1968; Sex Discrimination Act 1975; *Webb v EMO Air Cargo (UK) Ltd (No 2)* (1994); *Birmingham City Council v Abdulla* (2012); Bishops and Priests (Consecration and Ordination of Women) Measure 2014 and Canon C2, 'Of the Consecration of Bishops', 2014.

[58] eg Sex Disqualification (Removal) Act 1919; Article 7 of the Covenant of the League of Nations, 1919; Committee on the Employment of Women on Police Duties, 1920; Life Peerages Act 1958; Bishops and Priests (Consecration and Ordination of Women) Measure 2014 and Canon C2, 'Of the Consecration of Bishops', 2014.

[59] eg Match Women's Strike, 1888.

[60] eg *The Slave, Grace* (1827); British Nationality Act 1948; Prohibition of Female Circumcision Act 1985; *Islam v Secretary of State for the Home Department, R v Immigration Appeal Tribunal and Another, ex parte Shah* (1999); Forced Marriage (Civil Protection) Act 2007.

[61] eg Mental Capacity Act 2005.

[62] eg *Gillick v West Norfolk and Wisbech Area Health Authority* (1985).

[63] eg *DPP v Jonathan Cape and Leopold Hill* (1928).

[64] eg Bishops and Priests (Consecration and Ordination of Women) Measure 2014 and Canon C2, 'Of the Consecration of Bishops', 2014.

## D. Themes

There are a number of themes that emerge from the landmarks and which cut across different areas of law and different times and places. These include issues relating to justice, power and equality, representation and agency, feminist networks and organisations, as well as the use and abuse of law.

### *(i) Equality, Justice and (Gendered) Power*

Conventional legal histories of women portray a gradual trajectory towards the equality we are supposed to enjoy today. As these landmarks demonstrate, however, this description is far from accurate. Though there has undoubtedly been progress, the trajectory is not always and unremittingly upwards, but rather proceeds in fits and starts, and sometimes goes backwards. Moreover, as many of the landmarks make clear, in spite of equality legislation and policies, women still do not enjoy full equality today,[65] and some women continue to be more equal than others.

Throughout most of the nineteenth century, equality was not the only – or indeed the primary – issue at stake. The main target of the Victorian feminist campaigns was the removal of the worst examples of men's privileges and women's oppression. Indeed, the very notion of equality is problematic when it means equality with masculine institutions and practices that we deplore. Thus, while the pursuit of equality features across many landmarks, it is not the most important theme that links them. If there is any feminist goal that characterises them all, it is probably the search for *justice* – for fair legal treatment for women, for freedom from gender-based oppression, as well as freedom to act as full citizens.

Central to the achievement of justice for women is an analysis of gendered power. 'Gender' is an expression that is used to distinguish men from women but it is also a relationship, one in which, throughout most of history, men have held power *over* women through their control of both the public and the private spheres. Women's legal landmarks are therefore linked by the theme of *resistance to male power and control*, whether it be in politics (Representation of the People Act 1918, Life Peerages Act 1958), in the workplace (for example, Match Women's Strike 1888, Dagenham Car Plant Strike, 1968), in informal masculine institutions (*Gill and Coote v El Vino Co Ltd* (1982)) or in the home (First Women's Refuge, 1971; *Davis v Johnson* (1978)). Many other landmarks are about *men's brutality and women's basic need for protection*, before they could even think about justice and equality (for example, Section 5(1) of the Criminal Law Amendment Act 1885; First Rape Crisis Centre, 1976; Section 5 of the Criminal Law (Rape) (Amendment) Act 1990; Violence Against Women, Domestic Abuse and Sexual Violence (Wales) Act 2015). The same is true of women at the heart of landmarks involving the *use (and abuse) of state power* (for example, *Islam v Secretary of State for the Home Department, R v Immigration*

[65] This is starkly demonstrated by the inclusion of both the Dagenham Car Plant Strike (1968), which led to equal pay for women, and the UK Supreme Court case of *Birmingham City Council v Abdulla* (2012), a test case brought by 170 women and four men in relation to 11,000 equal pay claims against Birmingham City Council 40 years later.

*Appeal Tribunal and Another, ex parte Shah* (1999); Housing (Homeless Persons) Act 1977; Concluding Observations of the UN Committee against Torture, Recommendation to Ireland regarding the Magdalene Laundries, 2011; *In the Matter of an Application for Judicial Review by the Northern Ireland Human Rights Commission* (2015)).

## *(ii) Representation, Access and Agency*

In a book about *legal* landmarks it is unsurprising that women's *representation in law-making* at every level is a recurring theme: from their admission to the legal profession itself and as JPs and jurors[66] to their gradual inroads into the higher judiciary (many examples in this book) and the legal academy (First Woman Professor of Law in Ireland, Frances Moran, 1925; First Woman Professor of Law in the United Kingdom, Claire Palley, 1970); and from securing the vote to being able to sit in Parliament, whether as MPs,[67] members of the House of Lords (Life Peerages Act 1958) or bishops of the Church of England (Bishops and Priests (Consecration and Ordination of Women) Measure 2014 and Canon C2, 'Of the Consecration of Bishops', 2014).

Of course, legal and political representation is just one form of access. Other landmarks demonstrate women's struggle for *access*, not just to rights and opportunities enjoyed by men (for example, in the workplace[68] or the public sphere)[69] but to *sex-specific rights and services* related to pregnancy and abortion,[70] whose denial has limited or prevented women's participation in civil society. Access to *good health* is equally important and several landmarks focus on the removal of restrictions on the medical care necessary to ensure this.[71]

Access to *money and to property* are particularly important feminist goals for women since women's independence depends on being able to support themselves free of men's control. A number of the landmarks address this, including the Family Allowances Act 1945, which by paying the newly-established family allowance to *mothers* provided them with a level of control over the family finances, the Married Women's Property Act 1964, which established that housekeeping money belongs jointly to husband and wife, and *White v White* (2000), which laid down the equal-sharing principle on divorce. Other landmarks focus on *preventing* others from accessing (and appropriating) women's property – whether by virtue of marriage (Married Women's Property Act 1882; *Barclays Bank v O'Brien* (1993); *Radmacher v Grantino* (2010)) or cohabitation (*Grant v Edwards* (1986), which facilitated women's acquisition of property rights through informal means). Closely allied to access

[66] First Women Justices of the Peace, 1919; Section 25 of the Criminal Justice Act 1972.

[67] Sex Discrimination (Election Candidates) Act 2002; National Assembly for Wales election, 2003 Electoral (Amendment) Act 2012.

[68] eg Sex Disqualification (Removal) Act 1919; Article 7 of the Covenant of the League of Nations, 1919; Bishops and Priests (Consecration and Ordination of Women) Measure 2014 and Canon C2, 'Of the Consecration of Bishops', 2014.

[69] eg *Gill and Coote v El Vino Co Ltd* (1982); *R v Nimmo and Sorley* (2014).

[70] eg Abortion Act 1967; National Health Service (Family Planning) Act 1967; Health (Family Planning) Act 1979; Warnock Report, 1984; *Gillick v West Norfolk and Wisbech Area Health Authority* 1985); *Webb v EMO Air Cargo (UK) Ltd (No 2)* (1994); Protection of Life During Pregnancy Act 2013; *In the Matter of an Application for Judicial Review by the Northern Ireland Human Rights Commission* (2015).

[71] eg Maternity and Child Welfare Act 1918; Health (Family Planning) Act 1979.

is the acceptance and recognition of women's agency, whether through the systematic dismantling of coverture (whereby married women's legal personality was subsumed in their husband's, for example, the Married Women's Property Act 1882, the Married Women (Restraint Upon Anticipation Act) 1949, and *Williams & Glyn's Bank v Boland* (1980)), or by being treated as competent to agree to or refuse medical treatment (*Gillick v West Norfolk and Wisbech Area Health Authority* (1985); *St George's Healthcare NHS Trust v S* (1998); Mental Capacity Act 2005).

## *(iii) Feminist Organisations, Networks and Campaigns*

The importance of feminist networks, organisations and campaigns is another strong theme across the landmarks. Across the centuries, feminists have used a range of strategies to publicise, educate and influence, some of which have been noted here as landmarks in their own right (*A Vindication of the Rights of Woman*, 1792 (Mary Wollstonecraft), *A Brief Summary of the Most Important Laws Concerning Women*, 1854 (Barbara Bodichon), *A Pageant of Great Women*, 1909–12 (Cicely Hamilton), *Women and the Law*, 1984 (Susan Atkins and Brenda Hoggett), and the *Feminist Legal Studies* journal, 1993). Other common features of feminist tactics have been networking among women and alliances with those with power, whether these be professional associations (Association of Women Solicitors, 1921; Association of Women Barristers, 1991) or interest groups focused on a single issue (for example, votes for women), or links with legal men and male MPs before 1919 and with feminist lawyers and politicians thereafter. Sometimes leaders emerge, and their names are noted, but second-wave feminism resisted the idea of individual spokeswomen who could be isolated by opponents or made to speak for a range of different views. The Women's Peace Camp at Greenham Common 1981–2000 represents the high point of collective action.

Many of the landmarks have come as a direct result of feminist campaigning, even though when the official story is told some other cause is generally found, as we found with women's entry into the legal profession. Some are well known: votes for women is an obvious example. Others are overlooked or not known at all, such as the lobbying of women-led NGOs at the Paris Peace Conference in 1919, which ensured that women were at the heart of the emerging mechanisms of global governance through their membership of the League of Nations Secretariat,[72] and the Married Women's Property Act 1964, which allowed wives to keep half the housekeeping allowance. Across the centuries these sometimes lengthy and often hard-fought campaigns have made, and continue to make, a significant difference to women's lives. The match women's and the Dagenham car worker's strikes advanced women's claims to a fair wage and better conditions of work and the Justice for Magdalene campaign revealed the oppression of Irish women by the state and fought for compensation for survivors.[73] Feminist campaigns have led to statutory reforms relating to prostitution,[74]

[72] Article 7 of the Covenant of the League of Nations, 1919.

[73] Concluding Observations of the UN Committee against Torture, Recommendation to Ireland regarding the Magdalene Laundries, 2011.

[74] Section 14 of the Policing and Crime Act 2009.

rape and sexual history evidence,[75] domestic violence,[76] forced marriage,[77] the provision of contraception,[78] the appointment of women bishops,[79] and so-called 'revenge porn'.[80] *R v Nimmo and Sorely* (2014), the first prosecution for online threats of rape and sexual violence, may also fit within this category – though in this case the feminist campaign (to ensure women's representation on UK bank notes) provided the 'trigger' for the defendants' actions. Some of these landmarks do not at first sight appear to benefit women specifically, yet were fought for with women in mind: for example, the Housing (Homeless Persons) Act 1977 and *Birmingham City Council v Abdulla* (2012), fought on behalf of predominantly female workers. The inclusion of the UK's ratification of the Optional Protocol to CEDAW provides an opportunity to consider future avenues for feminist campaigns and a 'call to arms' to utilise its provisions to hold governments to account for systemic gender inequality.

## *(iv) The Use and Abuse of Law*

Finally, the landmarks demonstrate how law has been used to control and discipline women. Though for most of the time period covered by the collection, women were formally excluded from the mechanisms of law, this did not mean it did not touch their lives; rather the reverse. Throughout the nineteenth and into the twentieth century, women were subject to sex-specific laws designed to restrict their access to many of the rights of men. As Barbara Leigh Smith Bodichon noted in her *Brief Summary*, 'women, more than any other members of the community, suffer from over-legislation'.[81] As in 1854, so too in 2017.

The landmarks also reveal law as a tool that can be used by women to advance their cause, whether simply for their protection[82] or for wider goals like equality. They recognised the power of law to lead public opinion and to disrupt the 'normal' gender relations in which women were subject to men. In some cases, they hoped that the legal intervention would be short-lived, that it would lead to a world where protective legislation was not needed.[83] They looked forward to a new era in which women's voices would be heard, women's concerns addressed, and women's injustices and inequalities righted; when gender would cease to be a justification for differential treatment in law.

But this is not to say that feminists, then and now, were unaware of the limits of legal reform. Each generation of feminists dismisses earlier movements as naïve and over-optimistic because they failed to achieve perfect equality and justice for women, but even nineteenth-century feminists quickly learned to be wary of expecting too much from

[75] eg Section 4 of the Sexual Offences (Amendment) Act 1976; Section 5 of the Criminal Law (Rape) (Amendment) Act 1990; Section 41 of the Youth Justice and Criminal Evidence Act 1999; Section 1 of the Sexual Offences Act 2003.

[76] *R v Ahluwalia* (1992).

[77] Forced Marriage (Civil Protection) Act 2007.

[78] Health (Family Planning) Act 1979.

[79] Bishops and Priests (Consecration and Ordination of Women) Measure 2014 and Canon C2, 'Of the Consecration of Bishops', 2014.

[80] Section 2 of the Abusive Behaviour and Sexual Harm (Scotland) Act 2016.

[81] Barbara Leigh Smith Bodichon, *A Brief Summary of the Most Important Laws Concerning Women*, 1854, 13.

[82] eg *R v Jackson* (1891).

[83] eg Section 4 of the Sexual Offences (Amendment) Act 1976; Sex Discrimination (Election Candidates) Act 2002; National Assembly for Wales election, 2003; Electoral (Amendment) Act 2012.

institutions so firmly controlled by men in the interests of men. This has not stopped others from seeking to lower women's expectations. Consider, for example, the warning in the White Paper that preceded the Sex Discrimination Act 1975: 'it is important to recognise the inevitable restraints on what can be achieved by legislation, so that it is seen in proper perspective, without arousing false expectations or encouraging a sense of complacency'.[84] In truth such warnings are unnecessary. History has taught women the limits of law.

Law reform is messy. It is unpredictable, usually time- and personality-dependent and often flawed. The legislation or decision that results is – more often than not – the product of compromise: a (hopefully temporary) foothold from which to secure further reform. It was, for example, another decade after the enactment of the Representation of the People Act 1918 before many of the women who campaigned for the vote were actually able to do so. It took over half a century for the double standard, put on a statutory footing in the Matrimonial Causes Act 1857 – allowing a husband to divorce his wife for adultery while requiring that a husband's adultery be compounded by another matrimonial offence – to be removed.[85] Meanwhile, women in Northern Ireland still are waiting to be able to access abortion, even on the limited terms provided for under the Abortion Act 1967.[86]

Nor does law reform *alone* secure real change in women's lives. It cannot stop male violence, pregnancy discrimination, pay inequality, exploitation and abuse. In fact, as many of the landmarks in this volume demonstrate, whenever there is a legal advance for women, there follows a backlash, as men attempt to re-assert the patriarchal control they formerly enjoyed. Successful campaigns for legislative reform are typically followed by decades of case law as both 'sides' turn to the courts to enforce or subvert Parliament's wishes. Sometimes, of course, the wrong side wins: it took less than six months for the House of Lords to 'read down' the provisions of section 41 of the Youth Justice and Criminal Evidence Act 1999.[87] But not always: it may have taken a couple of years, but in the end the judiciary was finally convinced that Parliament really had intended the Domestic Violence and Matrimonial Proceedings Act 1976 to enable a wife or cohabiting partner to exclude a husband or male partner from the family home in cases where her life was in serious or grave danger.[88] It took slightly longer for judges to widen the matrimonial offence of cruelty contained in the Matrimonial Causes Act 1857, to include non-violent mental cruelty, but they were well ahead of their time in doing so.[89] And, while we might have hoped that 40 years after the Equal Pay Act 1970, the long-promised reality of equal pay for equal work would have materialised, at least the UK Supreme Court in *Birmingham City Council v Abdulla* (2012) did what it could to facilitate the novel litigation strategy and claims of 11,000, predominately female, council workers.

[84] Home Office, *Equality for Women* (HMSO, Cmnd 5724, 1974) [21].

[85] By virtue of the Matrimonial Causes Act 1923.

[86] *In the Matter of an Application for Judicial Review by the Northern Ireland Human Rights Commission* (2015)).

[87] In *R v A (No 2)* [2001] UKHL 25. See further Clare McGlynn's feminist judgment – '*R v A (No 2)*' – in Hunter, McGlynn and Rackley (eds), n 1 above, 211.

[88] *Davis v Johnson* (1978).

[89] Matrimonial Causes Act 1857.

Without doubt, then, law is a blunt tool with which to try to secure, protect and enhance women's lives, experiences, and opportunities. It can be (and has been) used against us; it never quite achieves its goals; and it must be resorted to again and again to secure every little advance. But as Anne Morris points out in her discussion of *Gill and Coote v El Vino Co Ltd*, in the hands of determined women law can prove a powerful mechanism for change. This collection is evidence of that.

# The Landmarks

# 2

# Cyfraith Hywel (The Laws of Hywel Dda), c. 940

CAROL HOWELLS

Over 1000 years ago, and long before the admission of women into the legal profession in England and Wales, a Welsh prince, Hywel ap Cadwell (known as Hywel Dda), advanced and recognised the rights of women through the codification of existing laws. The legal framework he created (the *Cyfraith Hywel*) became widely known for its wisdom and justice, its respect for freedom and its humanity. In 2015 the *Law Society Gazette* described him as 'Britain's most enlightened lawmaker'.[1] Knowledge about his role in creating laws recognising the rights of women and children, and the system developed to administer them, stems from a number of manuscripts and books dating from the second quarter of the thirteenth century.[2] Whilst not treating men and women as equals in every respect, the laws provided some rights and protections and, in particular, recognised women not as chattels but as individuals with freedoms and responsibilities in their own right.

## I. Context

National boundaries and kingdoms within what we now know as the UK were once very different. Hywel Dda controlled much of what we would recognise as Wales. The settlements of the Anglo-Saxons had gradually separated the territory of Wales from the northern and southwestern territories within the UK. The successful Norman invasion of England in 1066, and failed conquest of Wales, led to the establishment of earldoms along the Welsh border. Wales was eventually conquered by Edward I some 200 years later in 1284. Although it retained its independence, much of the territory became an endowment for the heir to the English throne. Independence was finally lost with the Union with England in 1535–42.

Hywel Dda (Hywel) inherited a small kingdom in west Wales in the early tenth century. He was a state-builder, considerably extending his territories and recognising the

[1] 'Summit: Magna Carta? Hywel Dda was there first, says Wales', *Law Society Gazette*, 23 February 2015.

[2] A copy of the laws of Hywel Dda in Welsh, Manuscript NLW 20143A, has been digitised by Llyfrgell Genedlaethol Cymru (The National Library of Wales): https://www.llgc.org.uk/en/discover/digital-gallery/manuscripts/the-middle-ages/a-welsh-text-of-the-laws-of-hywel-dda/.

importance of law to successful government and peace. During his lifetime he successfully joined together the kingdoms of Wales. Hywel Dda translates as 'Hywel the Good' and it is widely believed that the description of 'good' was a recognition of his work in codifying Welsh laws.

It is not clear why Hywel decided to codify existing laws or use them to recognise the rights of both men and women. No evidence of his rationale exists but the practicality of providing cohesion and clarity and the uncertainty of invasion could have informed his decision. He would have been aware of the customary legal system in operation at the time of Roman occupation and of Roman law. He made a pilgrimage to Rome in 928 and was on good terms with the King of Wessex. On Hywel's death in 942, a chronicler described him as 'head and glory of all the British'.[3]

Although no original documents or records exist, a number of early manuscripts containing excerpts from the original Codes do survive. Prologues to these thirteenth-century manuscripts and books mention Hywel's name and relate a range of tales as to how Hywel brought together six experts, both legal and religious, from each area (*cantref / cymwd*) of his kingdom at Tŷ Gwyn (the White House) near Whitland. Those gathered – one prologue refers to about 1,000 men – revised and codified existing laws, retaining and refining those that were relevant. A number of the prologues make reference to the sanctioning authority of the King and mention that Papal ratification was also sought. Although these records were written down 300 years after his death, historians believe that at their core are the laws codified by Hywel in the 940s.

The laws were not universally welcomed. Christianity had been well established in Wales before moving to England, and the church was critical of a number of the laws including those on inheritance and marriage. Despite such criticisms, the system established by Hywel continued (with some alterations) and became a symbol of the struggles with England during the twelfth and thirteenth centuries.[4]

## II. The Landmark

The laws are divided into two categories, those relating to the King and officers of the Court and those relating to the 'country', that is society, kindred and status, animals, crimes and tort, property, contract, and the laws of women. Whilst they did not provide equality, the laws are noted and recognised for their enlightened attitude towards women. The laws placed a value upon the honour, life and limbs of both men and women, their property and belongings, and the people of Wales had freedom based on a right to move at will.

The laws also mention the position of the Queen.[5] This is unique, as Thomas Ellis commented in 1926 'in the early English laws, the Irish Laws, and the various Germanic Codes, there is a complete absence of any mention of the Queen at all'.[6] The mention of the

[3] Thomas Jones (ed & tr), *The Chronicle of the Princes, Brut y Tywysogyon* [AD 682–1282], Red Book of Hergest version (BCS History & Law series xvi, Cardiff, 1955) and DB Walters, 'Roman and Romano-canonical law and procedure in Wales', Recueil de mémoires et travaux publiés par la Société d'Histoire du Droit et des Institutions des anciens Pays de Droit écrit, fasc. 15 (Montpellier 1991) 80–91, 70.

[4] Introduction to law in Wales (Open University materials, 2016).

[5] The Queen was one of the three most important people at Court and had her own poet.

[6] Thomas P Ellis, *Welsh Tribal Law and Custom in the Middle Ages* (Clarendon Press, 1926) 31.

Queen and outlining of the Queen's position is therefore innovative and helps illustrate the degree of freedom possessed by women. The Queen was absolutely entitled to one-third of the King's income (from his personal land). A sum was intended for her own personal use. All officers of the household were also ranked below the Queen in terms of social status and the Queen was responsible for providing a gold ring to the Judge of Court (who had supreme judicial power) on investiture.

The society reflected in the laws is hierarchical, with community playing a central role and recognition being given to the role and rights of women. Each person within the society was recognised as having rights and responsibilities with a life value (*galanas*) and an injury value (*sarhaed*). The laws on the position of women also provided a level of freedom and protection. Daughters remained under the tutelage of their father until they reached the age of majority. They were recognised as having liability in tort from the age of seven (the same age as their brothers) and attained majority on puberty. If, on attaining majority, they had not married they had a choice as to whether to stay or leave[7] their father's 'platter'. On attaining majority they were also able to hold property and were free to live wherever they chose.[8] They could also enter contracts and inherit land in certain circumstances (although their land ownership could only be by clan '*tir gwelyauc*' or by a group, and not individual).[9]

All forms of marriage had their basis in contract. *Rodd o cenedl* (gift of kindred) involved the agreement and bestowal by relatives and was regarded as an honourable form of marriage; *lladrut* (stolen or clandestine) involved a choice by the women herself. There was also a form of personal bestowal, which did not involve consulting the woman's relatives, although the woman needed to have attained majority. In either form, the marriage would be legal and binding and children legitimate. Unlike the position in England where the laws of Edmund (940–46) required the blessing of the marriage by a priest, there was no legal requirement for there to be a religious marriage ceremony. Indeed, in the many tales of the *Mabinogion* (a text written in medieval Welsh which forms the earliest prose stories in Britain and is based on oral traditions)[10] only one mention is made of a religious marriage ceremony.

Moreover, unlike in Anglo-Saxon law, which did not recognise the right of a woman to dispose of herself in marriage, Welsh women were not regarded as chattels and had freedom and a choice in marriage. That said, when they married there was still money to be paid. In Anglo-Saxon law marriage involved the sale of the custody and protection of the woman by her male relatives and the payment of a '*weotuma*' to her male relations on the occasion of every marriage. In the Welsh laws a fee or '*amobr*' was payable to the King on the loss of the woman's virginity (whether on marriage or otherwise) and on marriage. The amount payable for *amobr* was fixed according to status (in the case of the King's daughter the amount was payable to the Queen). If it was not paid, it was recoverable through the courts. Responsibility for payment depended on the type of marriage and could either be that of the woman's relatives, (future) husband or indeed of the woman herself – if, for example, she entered a causal connection (a type of marriage). However, the King was not the only person who benefited financially from marriage – a payment of a '*cowyll*' was made

[7] 'Every woman is to go the way she willeth, freely': Law of Gwynedd see Ellis, ibid, 395.
[8] Ellis, n 6 above, 386.
[9] See the Dimetian Code ('Book of Blaegwyrd') and Ellis, n 6 above, 386 and 388.
[10] See n 22 below.

to the woman from her husband on the morning after the marriage, marking her transition from virgin to married woman.

The laws also detail the laws during marriage. A husband found to be unfaithful was required to pay his wife a fine, at least on the first two occasions – on the third the wife was entitled to a separation;[11] although, if she failed to take the opportunity to separate, she lost her rights to compensation for infidelity. The laws also indicated how possessions were to be divided upon separation. These ranged from household linen, cups, plates, tools, trinkets, flour, crops, furniture, debts and livestock. Children were entitled to any yarn, the husband to the plaid cloth and settle,[12] and the wife to use of a cart to remove her share of the possessions and to stay in the house for nine days. The laws also provided that the eldest and youngest child stayed with their father, while the middle child (or children) stayed with their mother. If the woman was pregnant at the time the couple separated she was entitled to financial support for the child for the first six months and, if after 12 months she decided to keep the child, the father was required to pay toward its upkeep (two-thirds of the cost until the child reached the age of 14).

A separation could also be granted on the ground of the wife's adultery, or by mutual agreement, or on the demand of one party, for example, if the other contracted leprosy or failed to produce an heir or otherwise failed to observe the terms of the marriage contract.[13] If a husband brought another woman to live in the household, to the dishonour of his wife, then the wife was entitled to kill that woman without any legal penalty (but only if she killed her with her own hands). The first seven years of marriage were regarded as trial period. If separation occurred prior to this, the wife as due an '*agweddi*'; that is, a proportion of the common pool of property owned by the couple. The exact amount of the *agweddi* depended on the woman's status by birth. If the marriage broke up after the end of seven years, the woman was entitled to half the common pool.

## III. What Happened Next

In many aspects – most notably in their recognition and respect of women's right to freedom of person, marriage and separation – Hywel Dda's laws were ahead of their time.[14] Certainly they compare favourably with comparable laws in England at the time, where the Norman Conquest had resulted in a rapid decline in women's status with the imposition of a military society and feudal law.[15] As Domesday historian John Moore has observed, the

[11] The laws use the word 'separation' or 'ysgar'.

[12] The plaid cloth was cloth woven on a loom – the modern equivalent would be checked tartan-style cloth. A settle is a wooden bench.

[13] In the Venedotian Code it states if a wife departed from her husband on one of three grounds, leprosy, impotency, or 'foetid breath' then she was entitled to her property. In other codes it says she 'is entitled to her agweddi'. See *Ancient Laws and Institutes of Wales; comprising laws supposed to be enacted by Howel the Good* (Commissioners of the Public Records, 1841).

[14] This is not to suggest they were perfect. Were a bride discovered not to be a virgin, for example, she would be taken outside, stripped naked from the waist down and given a young horse with a greased tail: 'If she can hold the horse by his tail she gets to keep it. If not, she gets nothing, as her family would not want her back': Rhodri Owen (BBC Wales), 'The Story of Wales: Dr Sara Elin Roberts on Hywel Dda's laws', *BBC News online*, 1 March 2012.

[15] The same is true in Ireland where women – although considered legally incompetent – had obtained rights within the marital relationship, including divorce, which were lost following the Norman Conquest. See, further,

Normans may have freed the remaining slaves 'but this must be set against their debasement of women in general'.[16] Little wonder then, that the precedent Hywel Dda's laws set was not welcomed in Norman England. As the former Lord Chancellor, Jack Straw, noted in 2009 in a lecture on the administration of Welsh law:

> the remarkably enlightened tenth century laws of Hywel Dda were abolished by King Edward I … on the tendentious but convenient claim by Edward's Archbishop of Canterbury Archbishop Peckham, that Hywel Dda's system 'emanated directly from the Devil'.[17]

Following the conquest by Edward I, Wales was largely governed by the laws of England. The 1284 Statute of Rhuddlan/Statute of Wales (passed by Edward I) replaced Welsh criminal law with English law. Most laws relating to the rights of women were repealed (as they failed to reflect those in existence in England) and English Common Law was introduced:

> The Divine Providence, which is unerring in its own government, among the gifts of its dispensation, wherewith it hath vouchsafed to distinguish us and our realm of England, hath now of its favour, wholly and entirely transferred under our proper dominion, the land of Wales, with its inhabitants, heretofore subject unto us, in feudal right, all obstacles whatsoever ceasing; and hath annexed and united the same unto the crown of the aforesaid realm, as a member of the same body.[18]

Welsh law continued to be used for civil cases (such as those involving contracts and sureties), though these laws too were changed – for example, to prevent illegitimate sons (the position of daughters is unknown) from claiming inheritance (as required in Canon law). This continued until the Laws in Wales Acts 1535 and 1542 (often referred to as the Acts of Union). Passed by Henry VIII,[19] these made Wales subject to English laws in both criminal and civil matters and, controversially, established English as the official language of government and law in Wales.[20] The Act declared its intention 'utterly to extirpate all and singular the sinister usages and customs differing [in Wales]',[21] including the 'sinister' recognition of women's rights:

> the dominion, principality, and country of Wales justly and righteously is and ever hath been incorporated, annexed, united, and subject to and under the imperial crown of this realm as a very member and joint of the same.

Ivana Bacik, Cathryn Costello and Eileen Drew, *Gender InJustice: Feminising the Legal Professions?* (Trinity College Dublin Law School, 2003) 41 and **Fifteenth Amendment of the Constitution Act 1995**.

[16] John S Moore, 'Domesday Slavery' in R Allen Brown (ed), *Anglo-Norman Studies: XI. Proceedings of the Battle Conference 1988* (Boydell & Brewer Ltd, 1989) 191, 220. See also Pauline Stafford, 'Women and the Norman Conquest' (1994) 4 *Transactions of the Royal Historical Society* 221–49.

[17] Jack Straw, 'Administration of Justice in Wales', Law Society Annual Lecture, 3 December 2009.

[18] Statute of Rhuddlan 1284. Also known as the Statute of Wales 1284 (12 Edward I). The statute was in fact a royal ordinance, not issued by Parliament. It was intended to settle the government of Wales after the execution of Dafydd ap Gruffydd in 1283. English criminal law was to be introduced, but Welsh custom and law were to operate in civil proceedings. Six sheriffdoms were established in Anglesey, Caernarfon, Merioneth, Flint, Carmarthen, and Cardiganshire.

[19] The Tudors (Tudur) had, of course, based some of their claims of succession though a bloodline linking them to Hywel Dda. Though, evidently, they did not feel the same level of connection to his laws.

[20] This was not repealed until 1993 (Welsh Language Act 1993).

[21] *An Acte for Laws & Justice to be ministred in Wales in like fourme as it is in this Realme* (27 Henry VIII c 26) repealed with effect from 21 December 1993. *An Acte for certaine Ordinaunces in the Kinges Majesties Domynion and Principalitie of Wales* (34 and 35 Henry VIII c 26) repealed with effect from 3 January 1995.

Despite this, the history of women's rights in Wales was not forgotten. It lived on through tales and traditions.[22] And, by the mid-nineteenth century, some of the legal rights medieval Welsh women had enjoyed and lost had begun to re-emerge. The **Matrimonial Causes Act 1857**, for example, allowed Victorian women to divorce in the civil courts, the **Married Women's Property Acts** 1870 and **1882**[23] gave married women the ability to own and manage property independently of their husbands, and the Guardianship of Infants Act 1886 allowed separated mothers custody of children under seven and access to older children. Others, such as the freedom of women and the right to choose, followed and can be seen as underpinning legislation such as the **Representation of the People Act 1918** (giving the right to vote) and the **Sex Disqualification (Removal) Act 1919**, which enabled women to enter the professions. Inevitably perhaps, many of the rights Hywel Dda gave to women, such as the seven-year trial marriage period or the precedence given to women's evidence of violation, would still be innovative today.[24]

## IV. Significance

The Laws of Hywel Dda provide an insight into both Welsh life and laws at the time. The laws covered all aspects of life and, in doing so, provided an insight into the society within which they were developed. They also provided the foundation for a Welsh legal system which functioned for the next 600 years until Union with England. They remained of cultural importance to people in Wales throughout their struggles in successive centuries. In 1926, Ellis dedicated his work on Welsh tribal law and custom 'to the memory of Hywel Dda who ruled in Wales a thousand years ago and who to this day personifies to his people law and justice'.[25]

The laws of women created a higher status for women than that found in other medieval societies, for example, within English Norman or Anglo-Saxon society. They provided a wide range of economic rights, inheritance rights and rights in relation to union with men. At a time when other systems regarded women as chattels, marriage was a form of contractual agreement and divorce permitted by common consent; if a wife found her husband committing adultery she was entitled to payment as compensation; if a divorce occurred after seven years of marriage the wife was entitled to half the husband's property and any children would be divided equitably as set out in the laws.

Today in Wales, the importance and influence of Hywel Dda are still recognised; the original home of the Welsh Assembly was Tŷ Hywel and the original Assembly chamber was known as Siambr Hywel. The Welsh Assembly and Welsh Government continue to look to the laws of Hywel Dda, and their innovative nature, as they pursue recognition for the role of women, women's rights and an equality agenda with vigour. At the 2015 Global

[22] See eg *The Mabinogion, Trioedd Ynys Prydein*. These tales and sagas also give insight into the implementation of the laws.

[23] **Married Women's Property Act 1882**.

[24] If a woman gave an oath that she has been violated (or not violated) then this was treated as conclusive proof she had been violated (or not violated): Ellis, n 6 above, 398.

[25] Ellis, n 6 above, dedication page.

Law Summit held to mark 800 years of the Magna Carta, the then Wales Economy Minister, Edwina Hart, stated:

> Hywel Dda was centuries ahead of his time, he was a great innovator and his laws predate Magna Carta by nearly 300 years which is a considerable achievement and something we are proud of. The Global Summit provides us with a great opportunity to highlight the fact that Wales has a very long history of innovation when it comes to the development and delivery of Law.[26]

Women's rights are seen as core to the work of both the Assembly and Welsh Government, evident in projects such as 'Diversity in Democracy' and 'Spark a conversation', equal representation on public sector boards and elected bodies, the living wage, single status pay arrangements, tackling gender stereotyping, the right to be safe, addressing occupational segregation and equal pay and providing support to enable women to access the careers of their choice (for example, the campaign to support women into public life). Recognising that many women experience poverty due to their position in the workplace and at home, they are also committed to tackling poverty as a gender-specific issue which affects men and women in different ways. In terms of legislation, the landmark **Violence against Women, Domestic Abuse and Sexual Violence (Wales) Act 2015**, is the first gender-specific law on domestic violence in the UK.

A less obvious legacy is the Hywel Dda memorial garden in Whitland, where the gathering which codified the laws is believed to have taken place. This memorial garden is designed as a contemplative environment in which to explore early medieval Welsh society and the laws of Hywel Dda. A series of six gardens represent the various categories of Hywel's laws. The 'Women's Garden' representing the 'Women' division of the laws is the largest of those gardens. It is designed to represent the enlightened attitude of the laws towards women, with slate plaques providing examples of the laws and rights of women.

## Further Reading


- Thomas Charles-Edwards, *The Welsh Laws* (Writers of Wales, 1989).
- Dafydd Jenkins and Morfydd E Owen (eds), *The Welsh Law of Women* (University of Wales Press, 1980).
- Arthur W Wade-Evans, *Welsh Medieval Law: Being a text of the Laws of Howel the Good* (Clarendon Press, 1909).


[26] Reported in *Law Society Gazette*, n 1 above.

# 3

# *A Vindication of the Rights of Woman*, Mary Wollstonecraft, 1792

ANNA JOBE

Mary Wollstonecraft's *A Vindication of the Rights of Woman*[1] is a call for equality and for the extension of civil and political rights to women. It links women's oppression directly to their lack of education, arguing that women could reason as well as men *if* they were educated, in which case there would be no justification for their exclusion. It was also critical of a number of other women's issues, including the lack of job opportunities, representation in government, and an independent civil existence outside of marriage. Wollstonecraft continues to be 'celebrated as the mother of English-language feminism'[2] and *Vindication*, as 'the intellectual manifesto of western feminism'.[3]

## I. Context

*Vindication* was published against the backdrop of social upheaval, intense political and ideological debate and transformation across a broad geographical scope. The American Revolution, which resulted in the overthrow of British rule and the foundation of the independent United States of America, had ended just four years previously. The French Revolution, during which power shifted from an absolutist monarchy, feudalist system and muscular Catholic Church to an emergent democratic French Republic, was still in full swing. Out of these revolutions emerged a discourse focusing on the rights of *men*, reflected in the American Declaration of Independence (1776) and the French *Declaration of the Rights of Man and of the Citizen* (1789).

However, the so-called 'Age of Enlightenment' had its blind spots. As pointedly noted by French playwright and activist, Olympe de Gouges, these rights did not extend to women. Her *Declaration of the Rights of Woman and the Female Citizen*, published a year before

[1] Mary Wollstonecraft, *A Vindication of the Rights of Woman: with Strictures on Political and Moral Subjects*. Hereinafter cited as '*Vindication*'. All references are to the Penguin Classics publication (2004, with Introduction and notes by Miriam Brody).

[2] Thomas Ford, 'Mary Wollstonecraft and the Motherhood of Feminism' (2009) 37 *Women's Studies Quarterly* 189.

[3] Barbara Taylor, 'Mary Wollstonecraft and the Wild Wish of Early Feminism' (1992) 33 *History Workshop* 197, 199.

*Vindication*, opened with the (somewhat optimistic) statement that 'Woman is born free and remains equal to man in rights'.

Reverberations from the French Revolution were felt in England, where political opinion was divided. Edmund Burke's controversial pamphlet 'Reflections on the Revolution in France' (1790), which was highly critical of the Revolution and its consequences for French society, provoked a number of responses, including Thomas Paine's *Rights of Man* (1791). However, in fact, the first response to Burke was written by Wollstonecraft. Her *Vindication of the Rights of Men, in a Letter to the Right Honourable Edmund Burke* (1790),[4] as Harriet Jump explained, used Burke's *Reflections*

> as a starting point from which to air her general disagreement with Burke and everything he had come to stand for: conservatism as opposed to democracy, tradition as opposed to innovation, society as opposed to the individual, patriarchy as opposed to feminism.[5]

Wollstonecraft was part of a radical intellectual circle that included Paine, Henry Fusili and William Blake. Born in London in 1759 to middle-class parents, she experienced the vulnerability of women's position at the time. Her family moved to Essex when her grandfather died so that her father could use his inheritance to become a 'gentleman farmer'. Abusive toward his wife – a 'despot … subject to alternate fits of kindness and cruelty'[6] – her father was also financially imprudent, and the family's financial situation deteriorated. With both parents favouring Wollstonecraft's older brother, it became necessary for Wollstonecraft to earn her own living.

Employment opportunities open to women at the time were limited. As Moira Ferguson notes, women were 'cast out of large sectors of the labor market' and 'many women sought marriage as one of the remaining viable legal options'.[7] However, marriage was not without considerable sacrifice. Under the doctrine of coverture, it entailed an immense transfer of power – and often money and property – to the husband. Married women could not own or control their own property, enter into contracts, or make a will:[8]

> By marriage, the husband and wife are one person in law, that is, the very being or legal existence of the woman is suspended during the marriage, or at least is incorporated and consolidated into that of the husband: under whose wing, protection and *cover* she performs everything.[9]

Wollstonecraft worked as a lady's companion, schoolteacher and governess. During her time as a governess she wrote a so-called 'conduct book' – common at the time and in keeping with what was deemed appropriate material to be written by a woman – entitled *Thoughts on the Education of Daughters, with Reflections on Female Conduct in the more important Duties of Life* (1787). Having sold this to renowned publisher Joseph Johnson, she began to take seriously the idea of writing to earn a living. She moved to London to

[4] Hereinafter cited as '*Rights of Men*'.

[5] Harriet Devine Jump, *Mary Wollstonecraft: Writer* (Harvester Wheatsheaf, 1994) 57.

[6] William Godwin, *Memoirs of the Author of a Vindication of the Rights of Woman* (first published 1798, Joseph Johnson) 7.

[7] Moira Ferguson, 'Introduction' in Moira Ferguson (ed), *First Feminists: British Women Writers 1578–1799* (Indiana University Press, 1985) 1.

[8] Tim Stretton and Krista Kesselring, 'Introduction' in Stretton and Kesselring (eds), *Married Women and the Law: Coverture in England and the Common Law World* (McGill-Queen's University Press, 2013) 8; See also **Married Women's Property Act 1882**; **Married Women (Restraint Upon Anticipation) Act 1949**.

[9] William Blackstone, *Commentaries on the Laws of England: Book the First* (1st edn, 1765–69, Oxford) 430.

live with Johnson in 1787. Print culture was booming. Between 1775 and 1800, the number of printed material titles increased from 3000 to 8000.[10] Crucially, this created space and employment opportunities for women: 'a radical historical shift that inevitably affected the conditions of women's existence to some extent, even if it did not lead to legal reform'.[11]

Wollstonecraft was well positioned to take advantage of this expansion. She took up translating, editing and publishing, as well as writing reviews for Johnson's new radical journal, the *Analytical Review*.[12] She reviewed Catharine Macaulay's *Letters on Education with Observations on Religious and Metaphysical Subjects* (1790), which argued that boys and girls should be educated together. In 1790, Wollstonecraft sent Macaulay a copy of the *Rights of Men*, writing in the accompanying note:[13]

> You are the only female writer who I coincide in opinion with respecting the rank our sex ought to endeavour to attain in the world. I respect Mrs Macaulay Graham because she contends for laurels whilst most of her sex only seek for flowers.[14]

Macaulay's response was equally warm; she wrote that she was 'highly pleased that this publication which I have so greatly admired … should have been written by a woman and thus to see my opinions of the powers and talents of the sex in your person so easily verified'.[15]

## II. The Landmark

Published by Johnson in 1792, *A Vindication of the Rights of Woman* was the product of Wollstonecraft's experience as a governess and school-teacher, her growing confidence in writing and publishing, and her increasing frustration with the subjugation of women. The origins of her arguments can be seen in her earlier publications – most notably, *Daughters* and the *Rights of Men*. She also 'drew upon the arguments of her immediate female predecessors',[16] including Macaulay. Indeed, as Miriam Brody notes, not only does *Vindication* 'not emerge out of the eighteenth century without antecedents … [it] is read far more profitably against this background of English feminism'.[17]

At its core, *Vindication* is a call for equality. It criticises contemporary conditions for women and argues for their civil and political rights to be recognised: 'Let women share the rights and she will emulate the virtues of man …'[18] For Wollstonecraft, the means of ensuring this is education. If, Wollstonecraft suggests, women were educated, they would be

[10] Michelle Levy, 'Women and Print Culture, 1750–1830' in Jacqueline Labbe (ed), *The History of British Women's Writing, 1750–1830* (Palgrave Macmillan, 2010) 31.

[11] Elizabeth Eger, *Bluestockings: Women of Reason from Enlightenment to Romanticism* (Palgrave Macmillan, 2010) 22.

[12] As Mitzi Myers notes, it can be difficult to ascertain the exact author of these reviews due to the tradition of using the authors' initials (Mitzi Myers, 'Mary Wollstonecraft's Literary Reviews' in Claudia L Johnson, *The Cambridge Companion to Mary Wollstonecraft* (Cambridge University Press, 2002) 82–83).

[13] Bridget Hill, 'The Links Between Mary Wollstonecraft and Catherine Macaulay: New Evidence' (1995) 4(2) *Women's History Review* 177.

[14] Letter from MW to Catharine Macaulay (December 1790).

[15] Letter from Catharine Macaulay to MW (December 1790).

[16] Eger, n 11 above, 22.

[17] Brody, 'Introduction', *Vindication*, xxx.

[18] *Vindication*, 242.

able to reason as effectively as men. And if this were the case, then there would be no need for the distinctions in treatment; that 'the sexual distinction which men have so warmly insisted upon, is arbitrary'.[19] 'Would men but generously snap our chains, and be content with rational fellowship instead of slavish obedience, they would find us more observant daughters, more affectionate sisters, more faithful wives, more reasonable mothers – in a word, better citizens.'[20]

With respect to women's 'follies and caprices', she continues, who can blame them?: 'Behold … the natural effect of ignorance! The mind will ever be unstable that has only prejudices to rest on, and the current will run with destructive fury when there are no barriers to break its force.'[21] Significantly, *Vindication* directly connected women's oppression with the realities of their everyday life:

> From the tyranny of man, I firmly believe, the greater number of female follies proceed; and the cunning … is produced by oppression … Asserting the rights which women in common with men ought to contend for, I have not attempted to extenuate their faults; but to prove them to be the natural consequence of their education and station in society.[22]

Wollstonecraft uses *Vindication* to set out her vision for national education,[23] where the sexes should be educated together 'to perfect both':[24]

> Strengthen the female mind by enlarging it, and there will be an end to blind obedience; but, as blind obedience is ever sought for by power, tyrants and sensualists are in the right when they endeavour to keep women in the dark, because the former only want slaves, and the latter a play-thing.[25]

She engages with, and criticises, several contemporary writers – all of whom were men – on the education of women:

> [A]ll the writers who have written on the subject of female education and manners … have contributed to render women more artificial, weak characters, than they would otherwise have been; and, consequently, more useless members of society … my objection extends to the whole purport of those books, which tend … to degrade one half of the human species, and render women pleasing at the expense of every solid virtue.[26]

Rousseau incurs Wollstonecraft's particular displeasure:

> Rousseau declares that a woman should never, for a moment, feel herself independent, that she should be … made a coquetish slave in order to render her a more alluring object of desire, a *sweeter* companion to man … obedience is the grand lesson which ought to be impressed with unrelenting rigour. What nonsense![27]

While for Wollstonecraft, knowledge and understanding were necessary to acquire true virtue, and – vitally – to allow women to be *free*, for Rousseau and 'most of the male writers

[19] ibid 241.
[20] ibid 186.
[21] ibid 28.
[22] ibid 241–42.
[23] See further **Education Act 1944**.
[24] *Vindication*, 216.
[25] ibid 34–35.
[26] ibid 31–32.
[27] ibid 36.

who have followed his steps … the whole tendency of female education ought to be directed to one point: – to render them pleasing'.[28] Men were content to maintain the status quo for their own purposes: 'She [woman] was created to be the toy of man, his rattle, and it must jingle in his ears whenever, dismissing reason, he chooses to be amused':[29]

> 'Educate women like men,' says Rousseau, 'and the more they resemble our sex the less power will they have over us.' This is the very point I aim at. I do not wish them to have power over men; but over themselves.[30]

And, of course, once women are properly educated there is no reason why they should not have increased opportunities. Women, Wollstonecraft argues, might be 'physicians', 'study politics', or pursue '[b]usiness of various kinds': 'How many women thus waste life away … who might have practised as physicians, regulated a farm, managed a shop, and stood erect, supported by their own industry …'[31]

Wollstonecraft also comments on women's legal and political position. She is critical of coverture: '[t]he laws respecting woman … make an absurd unit of a man and his wife; and then, by the easy transition of only considering him as responsible, she is reduced to a mere cypher'.[32] She refers to marriage as 'legal prostitution',[33] and argues that women should have financial independence from male relatives and spouses:

> [T]o render her really virtuous and useful, she must not … want, individually, the protection of civil laws; she must not be dependent on her husband's bounty for her subsistence during his life, or support after his death – for how can a being be generous who has nothing of its own? or, virtuous who is not free?[34]

Almost 130 years before Nancy Astor became the first woman MP to take her seat, Wollstonecraft also took on the lack of representation of women in government: 'I really think that women ought to have representatives, instead of being arbitrarily governed without having any direct share allowed them in the deliberations of government'.[35] However, Wollstonecraft's concern with the arbitrary exercise of power (where founded on anything other than reason) was not limited to the political sphere. In *Vindication* she challenged what she termed 'unconditional obedience', which she argued was the 'catch-word of tyrants'.[36] Other examples included 'the absurd duty, too often inculcated, of obeying a parent only on account of his being a parent, shackles the mind, and prepares it for a slavish submission to any power but reason'.[37] And, crucially, the disproportionate impact of this obedience on girls:

> It is the irregular exercise of parental authority that first injures the mind, and to those irregularities girls are more subject than boys … [Girls] are kept more down by their parents … and thus taught slavishly to submit to their parents, they are prepared for the slavery of marriage.[38]

[28] ibid 38.
[29] ibid 45.
[30] ibid 81.
[31] ibid 183–85.
[32] ibid 180.
[33] ibid 184.
[34] ibid 181–82.
[35] ibid 182.
[36] ibid 187.
[37] ibid 191.
[38] ibid 194, 193.

## III. What Happened Next

*Vindication* brought Wollstonecraft 'instant literary celebrity'.[39] It was initially applauded,[40] particularly in connection with its central message of female education, which was viewed as fairly uncontroversial. But it is clear that Wollstonecraft also recognised the complicity of the law in the oppression of women and identified it as an important site for contestation and reform. She indicated that she wished to write a second volume to *Vindication* that specifically addressed the laws associated with women: 'Many subjects, however, which I have cursorily alluded to, call for particular investigation, especially the laws relative to women.'[41] Sadly, this second volume did not emerge. However, some of these themes were explored in a novel, *The Wrongs of Woman, Or Maria*, which was published posthumously by her husband, William Godwin in 1798. While the novel's narrative concerns a woman – Maria – imprisoned by her husband in an asylum, as Thomas Ford notes, the 'wrongs' are 'in large part … inflicted through the physical and legal force exercised by men'.[42]

Wollstonecraft died in 1797 as a result of complications after the birth of her second daughter, Mary Godwin (later Mary Shelley, author of *Frankenstein*). After her death, William Godwin wrote a frank memoir of her life, against the wishes of her sisters and Johnson.[43] He described how Wollstonecraft had travelled to Paris to witness the effects of Revolutionary France, had fallen in love with Gilbert Imlay, an American businessman, and given birth to her first daughter outside of marriage – Fanny Imlay – in 1794.[44] He explained that Imlay had abandoned her, leading Wollstonecraft to attempt suicide twice. These aspects of her life shocked and outraged the audience of the time. Fame quickly turned to notoriety, and Wollstonecraft was vilified as 'sexually deviant, impious, and politically dangerous'.[45]

While Victorian moral outrage meant that it would be another century until *Vindication*'s influence was openly acknowledged, the influence of the ideas within *Vindication*, can be seen in *The Victim of Prejudice* (1799) by Mary Hays (who also probably wrote the anonymous *A Letter to the Men of Great Britain in Behalf of Woman* (1798))[46] and in Mary Robinson's *A Letter to the Women of England on the Injustice of Mental Subordination* (1799). In the latter, Robinson specifically notes that, 'it requires a legion of Wollstonecrafts to undermine the poison of prejudice and malevolence'.[47] In 1891, the suffragist Millicent Garrett Fawcett wrote in her introduction to a new edition of *Vindication* that Wollstonecraft was the women's rights movement's 'earliest confessor',[48]

[39] Jump (n 5 above), 89.

[40] See further RM Janes, 'On the Reception of Mary Wollstonecraft's: A Vindication of the Rights of Woman' (1978) 39(2) *Journal of the History of Ideas* 293–302.

[41] *Vindication*, 'Advertisement'.

[42] Ford (n 2 above), 192.

[43] Godwin (n 6 above).

[44] Raised by Godwin after Mary's death, Fanny committed suicide at the age of 22.

[45] Andrew McInnes, 'Wollstonecraft's Legion: Feminism in Crisis, 1799' (2013) 20(4) *Women's Writing* 479.

[46] ibid.

[47] Mary Robinson, *A Letter to the Women of England on the Injustice of Mental Subordination* (TN Longman and Others, 1799) 12.

[48] *A Vindication of the Rights of Woman: New Edition with an Introduction by Mrs Henry Fawcett* (T Fisher Unwin, 1891) 3.

and 'ahead of her time'.[49] Her *Women's Suffrage: A Short History of a Great Movement* published in 1912 began with the clear statement: 'WE suffragists have no cause to be ashamed of the founders of our movement … Mary Wollstonecraft started the demand of women for political liberty in England',[50] a sentiment echoed by Virginia Woolf, who in 1932 wrote that Wollstonecraft was 'alive and active … she argues and experiments, we hear her voice and trace her influence even now amongst the living'.[51]

## IV. Significance

While it may be anachronistic to describe Wollstonecraft as a 'revolutionary feminist',[52] without doubt *Vindication* remains 'a cornerstone of feminist thought'.[53] It is significant for women's legal history in two important respects. First, the ideas contained within the book constitute an eloquent and passionate articulation of women's equality and their need for civil and political rights. Second, those ideas have remained relevant over the course of the next two centuries and more, not just for feminist thought, but more broadly, with the result that, two centuries after its first publication, the issues that Wollstonecraft tackles – and the arguments and solutions she offers – continue to be central to women's social, economic, legal and political emancipation.[54]

## Further Reading

- Amaryta Sen, 'Mary, Mary, Quite Contrary!' (2005) 11(1) *Feminist Economics* 1.
- Barbara Taylor, *Mary Wollstonecraft and the Feminist Imagination* (Cambridge University Press, 2003).
- Mary Wollstonecraft, *A Vindication of the Rights of Woman* (1792).
- Mary Wollstonecraft, *The Wrongs of Woman; or Maria* (1798).

[49] ibid 26.
[50] Millicent Garrett Fawcett, 'Women's Suffrage: A Short History of a Great Movement' (TC and EC Jack, 1912) 5.
[51] Virginia Woolf, *The Common Reader: Volume 2* (Vintage, 2003 [1932]).
[52] Gary Kelly, *Revolutionary Feminism: The Mind and Career of Mary Wollstonecraft* (Macmillan, 1992) 1.
[53] Jump (n 5 above) 66.
[54] See eg Amaryta Sen, 'Mary, Mary, Quite Contrary!' (2005) 11(1) *Feminist Economics* 1, 2.

# 4

# Gaols Act 1823

RUTH LAMONT

The Gaols Act 1823[1] regulated the management of gaols (prisons) across England and Wales, providing regulations applying specifically to the circumstances of women prisoners. The regulations for women prisoners contained within the Act were drawn from the rules developed by Elizabeth Fry as part of her work from 1813 onwards with the women held in Newgate Gaol in London.[2] Fry sought to ensure better and separate treatment for women prisoners, reflecting a religious and reformatory aim of attempting to rehabilitate women, preventing further 'corruption' through association, and providing women prisoners with useful employment. The Act is a landmark in identifying women as having specific needs within the criminal justice system, providing new opportunities of employment for women, and in representing legislative change in response to a social campaign by a woman.

## I. Context

In the early nineteenth century, the role of the prison was undergoing significant change and development. The gaol system was administered by counties under the supervision of local magistrates and had been largely self-financing, with gaolers seeking payment from the persons incarcerated.[3] These arrangements led to significant differences between counties, depending on local willingness to finance expensive gaols, and variable treatment between prisoners. Men and women prisoners would not necessarily be separated from one another. The philanthropist and prison reformer John Howard, writing in 1777 in *The State of the Prisons in England and Wales*, had exposed the dreadful conditions and disorder prevailing in gaols across the country and provoked a national debate over the role and conditions of imprisonment.

[1] An Act for consolidating and amending the laws relating to the building, repairing and regulating of certain gaols and houses of correction in England and Wales, (1823) 4 Geo IV c 64.

[2] Elizabeth Fry was a Quaker prison reformer, who actively engaged with the education of women prisoners and their children in Newgate Gaol from 1813. In 1821, she helped found the 'British Ladies' Society for Promoting the Reformation of Female Prisoners', with the aim of rehabilitating women prisoners. She toured prisons across England and Scotland to examine the prevailing conditions, and published her findings, and campaigned for the reform of prisons across the UK. See further Anna Isba, *The Excellent Mrs Fry: The Unlikely Heroine* (Continuum International Publishing, 2010).

[3] Randall McGowen, 'The Well-Ordered Prison: England, 1780–1865' in Noval Morris and David J Rothman, *The Oxford History of the Prison: The Practice of Punishment in Western Society* (OUP, 1995) 72, 74.

Most prisoners in the eighteenth century were debtors or persons awaiting trial rather than being under sentence. By the nineteenth century, imprisonment as a form of punishment after trial became a more common sentence for a felon, but the gaol system at this point was clearly incapable of holding long-term prisoners. These difficulties and Howard's campaign had provoked calls for reform of the gaol system. In 1779, the Penitentiary Act aimed to create a men's prison and a separate women's prison, based on a regime of hard labour, religious instruction and solitary confinement. Although this reform failed, there was significant prison-building activity at county level in the 1780s and 1820s. Moreover, the role and purpose of imprisonment as a form of punishment was still being debated. Imprisonment as a punishment co-existed with transportation to Australia until 1853. Notably, in 1824, just one year after the Gaols Act, an Act to consolidate the rules on transportation[4] was passed, demonstrating that in the 1820s national policy was not solely focused on developing imprisonment as the primary form of punishment for felons.

Elizabeth Fry first visited Newgate gaol in 1813 and returned in 1816 to set up a school for children accompanying their mother in the prison. Newgate was different to many prisons in separating women prisoners from men but permitted open converse with the public through the gratings, enabling women to receive money and have access to alcohol, encouraging what Fry regarded as immoral behaviour. During Fry's initial visits to Newgate she witnessed the disorderly state of the prison and the women held there: 'begging, swearing, gaming, fighting, singing, dancing, dressing up in men's clothes – scenes too bad to be described'.[5] She began to read the Bible to the women prisoners and several women sought admission to her school. She was granted permission from the Sheriffs (who ran the prison) to appoint a matron to oversee the women prisoners, and to meet with the women and propose regulations, instruction and employment to them. To the surprise of the Sheriffs, the prisoners agreed to all these suggestions.

Fry's work at Newgate prison was a high-profile and central aspect of the Quaker prison reform campaign. In 1816, the 'Society for the Improvement of Prison Discipline' was established in part by Fry's brother, Joseph John Gurney, and her brothers-in-law, Thomas Fowell Buxton and Samuel Hoare. In 1817, Fry formed the 'Ladies' Association for the Improvement of the Female Prisoners at Newgate' to provide for the clothing, instruction and employment of the women. Its mission was to form habits of order, sobriety and industry to render women peaceable whilst in prison and respectable on leaving. Fry identified four 'essential elements' for reformation of women in prison: religious instruction, classification of prisoners, employment, and that women prisoners should be taken care of entirely by women, excepting a medical attendant or religious minister.[6] These four elements are clearly evident in the 1823 Act.

## II. The Landmark

The Gaols Act 1823 was passed at a time when the role and purpose of imprisonment as a form of punishment was still being debated in the context of a highly localised system.

[4] (1824) 5 Geo IV c 84.

[5] Evidence of Mrs Elizabeth Fry to House of Commons Select Committee on the Prisons within the City of London and Borough of Southwark, 27 February 1818.

[6] ibid.

It reflected the contested nature of these penal reforms and experienced a difficult passage through Parliament. Two earlier Bills failed before Robert Peel, the then Home Secretary, was able to pilot it through Parliament.

It followed a Select Committee report on the state of London's prisons,[7] to which a range of witnesses, including Fry, gave evidence, and marked a shift in developing national penal policy for the punishment of criminals. The Act covers a broad range of measures aimed at providing for the discipline of the prison and reformation of offenders generally. Section 5 created general regulations designed to apply in every prison, and specifically provided standards for the treatment of women prisoners. Regulations 2, 3 and 7 required a matron to be appointed in prisons where women prisoners were confined and that women prisoners be attended by women officers. Regulation 6 stated:

> The male and female prisoners shall be confined in separate buildings or parts of the prison so as to prevent them from seeing, conversing or holding any intercourse with each other; and the prisoners of each sex shall be divided into distinct classes.

Both men and women prisoners were to receive instruction in reading and writing. Although gaols remained under the control of, and funded by, the local counties, the 1823 Act represented an attempt to impose a nationwide standard on the conduct of prisons. The obligation to report on the conduct of the prison was designed to provide accountability, from the local to the national level, and reporting on the conditions for women prisoners and compliance with the standards outlined in the Act formed part of this process.

Contemporary reports from the Chester Gaol indicate that the passage of the Act provoked a response from local magistrates over the management of the prison. The County Lieutenant, Harry Potts, wrote in 1824:

> I advise you will take the earliest opportunity of calling the sessions attention of the Magistrates of this County, and impress upon them in the strongest Terms the absolute necessity of a strict compliance in future with the Provisions of the Acts in question.[8]

In fact, apart from the suggestion that women prisoners should have only women attendants, Fry's 'essential elements' were not new. What *was* new was that she had provided evidence of their potential impact. She had put them into practice at Newgate and had successfully reformed the behaviour of the prisoners. Her public campaign and the formation of the British Ladies' Society for Promoting the Reformation of Female Prisoners in 1821 also rendered her activities and their effects in Newgate visible to the public and part of a developing awareness of what might now be called 'social problems'. Fry's approach to reform of women prisoners focused on morality, religion and a desire to rescue women from further corruption. She was explicit in stating that access to religious education had a very satisfactory effect on the minds of the women, encouraging good conduct. The criminal woman was regarded as the opposite of the Victorian feminine ideal, endangering morality.

[7] Report from the Select Committee on the Prisons within the City of London and Borough of Southwark (19th Century HC Sessional Papers, 1818, 275).

[8] Letter from Stamford & Warrington Lieutenant to Dunham Massey, 1 July 1824, Chester Archives Miscellaneous records relating to Chester Gaol, QAB 6/5.

As a result, whereas men prisoners were regarded as requiring prison work to reform them into a productive member of the labour force on leaving prison, women prisoners were regarded as requiring moral regeneration, and Fry's work contributed to this perception.

## III. What Happened Next

The Act contributed towards improved conditions for women prisoners in England and Wales. However, Fry's reforms also had a wider impact. In 1823, she wrote to the Under-Secretary of State for the Colonies recommending the establishment of a 'female factory' in Hobart, Van Diemen's Land (now Tasmania). This would be supervised by a matron and would facilitate the reformation of transported convicts through education and work.[9] The factory was subsequently built and used for women convicts who were awaiting assignment as a servant to a private master or had been returned to the factory as punishment for infractions.

The reforms of the 1823 Act also provided new opportunities for employment for women, where there had previously existed few opportunities. As a consequence of the Act, it became necessary to appoint prison matrons. Mrs Todd, deputy governess of the Liverpool House of Industry, applied for the role of matron at Chester Gaol. She was the daughter of Edward Grayson, a shipbuilder in Liverpool, and a widow with three children to support.[10] The testimonial from the Liverpool governor described Mrs Todd as being

> of a most kind and humane disposition – a female of great modesty, unassuming, yet pleasing in manner and address, fair yet dignified, a most correct accountant – capable of keeping any books and writes with great facility.[11]

The nature of the governor's reference is as to her respectability and social position, referencing her friends and relatives, and on her feminine qualities of modesty and pleasing manner. Her competence as a supervisor of women prisoners is associated with her moral and social capacities, presumably providing a positive example to the prisoners. Mrs Todd also had to work to provide for her children and prison matron was a form of respectable employment for women.

Nor were these opportunities limited to working-women. Fry's activities, for example in forming 'Ladies' Committees', also encouraged non-working women to venture outside the private sphere of the family and motherhood. In emulation of her activities, a number of local committees were formed in places such as Bristol, Chester, Liverpool and Durham for the improvement of prison conditions for women through visiting and philanthropic activity.

[9] Kay Daniels, *Convict Women* (Allen & Unwin, 1998) 110–11.

[10] Letter from Mrs Todd to Mr Potts, Stamford & Warrington Lieutenant, 23 October 1823, Chester Archives, Miscellaneous records relating to Chester Gaol, QAB 6/5.

[11] Letter from William J Harding, Governor of Liverpool House of Industry, to the sitting Magistrates of the county gaol of Chester, 16 October 1823, Chester Archives Miscellaneous records relating to Chester Gaol, QAB 6/5.

More broadly, however, the Act did little to resolve the debates surrounding penal reform in Britain, particularly the role and purpose of prison.[12] In the short-term, many local gaols ignored at least some of the prescribed regulations and the requirement for an annual report.[13] Government policy developed an increasingly interventionist stance and the 1823 Act was repealed and replaced by the Prison Act in 1835, which established a central prison inspectorate to regularly report on the state of the county gaols, aimed at ensuring uniform administration.

The regulations for the classification and instruction of prisoners under the 1823 Act came under increasing criticism, with calls for systems of discipline based on labour and prevention of communication between prisoners. Fry was once again called to give evidence to a Parliamentary Select Committee in 1835. In her evidence she disapproved of the use for women of the treadmill, a form of non-productive labour, favouring instead the development of domestic skills.[14] However, in the years following the 1823 Act the influence of Fry's reformatory ideas had declined. In 1834, William Crawford of the 'Society for the Improvement of Prison Discipline' had completed his report into the American 'silent' or 'separate system' aimed at deterrence of crime, in which inmates were hooded and numbered to prevent identification, and communication between prisoners, and between prisoners and guards, was strictly prohibited.[15] While the Prison Act 1835 recommended no specific system of discipline, there was a distinct shift in the 1840s away from reforming prisoners and towards deterrence from crime through a prison regime of hard labour, and the 'silent' system was adopted for men in Pentonville prison in 1842. By contrast, while the approach to women prisoners continued to focus on reform, it did so by tending to identify women criminals as mentally ill and unstable, as evidenced by their departure from normalised patterns of female behaviour. Indeed, over the nineteenth century, there was an increasing focus on scientific and medical explanations for women's criminal deviance,[16] the impacts of which are still evident in understanding of women prisoners and criminals today.

## IV. Significance

The Gaols Act of 1823 is a small, yet fascinating, element of the sweeping nineteenth-century reforms affecting all aspects of the criminal justice system. The police force, definitions of crime and criminal behaviour, the conduct of criminal trials, and the management and punishment of offenders all saw fundamental change during this period.[17]

[12] Indeed, many still continue today. The differences in sentencing of men and women and their treatment within the prison reflect those originating in the 1823 Act.

[13] Clive Emsley, *Crime and Society in England, 1750–1900* (4th edn, Longman Pearson, 2010) 282. A Select Committee of the House of Lords appointed in 1835 to inquire into the present state of the several gaols and houses of correction in England and Wales identified that in some gaols, matrons and chaplains had not been appointed (19th Century HC Sessional Papers, 1835, 438–41).

[14] Evidence of Mrs Elizabeth Fry, Select Committee of the House of Lords appointed to inquire into the present state of the several gaols and houses of correction in England and Wales (19th Century HC Sessional Papers, ibid).

[15] Report of William Crawford on the Penitentiaries in the United States, addressed to the Home Department (19th Century HC Sessional Papers, 1834, 31).

[16] Lucia Zender, 'Women, Crime and Penal Responses: A historical approach' (1991) 14 *Crime and Justice* 307, 315.

[17] Barry Godfrey and Paul Lawrence, *Crime and Justice since 1750* (Routledge, 2014).

The 1823 Act is significant for women in two ways: first as an explicit identification of the needs of women within the criminal justice system, and secondly as an early example of women's campaigning and support of other women.

Women as criminals and prisoners were identified and managed differently as a result of the Act. Women prisoners had previously been treated differently in some aspects of punishment,[18] but the 1823 Act was the first to provide specifically for women prisoners' needs, including through the provision of women officers. This is largely a result of its direct link with the prison campaign work of the Quakers, most particularly the reforms proposed by Fry. The separation of women prisoners and supervision by women were important developments in a context where women could be highly vulnerable. Women were also treated – at least formally – equally, in having access to education and religious instruction. Interestingly, however, although Fry's original activities in Newgate prison had focused on the *children* of women inmates, neither she nor the Act acknowledged the position of women who were mothers.

Moreover, the reformatory and moral aims underpinning the 1823 Act influenced the debates surrounding women's criminality throughout the nineteenth century. The effect of these concepts on the treatment of women on conviction and in prison is only just beginning to be examined in detail by historians.[19] Thus, while Fry was an important social campaigner and activist, she perhaps unintentionally contributed to the ongoing, and at times unhelpful, perception of women as victims in need of moral reform. An appreciation of the social and economic environment of criminality in nineteenth-century London is notably absent from her understanding of criminal behaviour. However, despite these limitations, Fry's willingness to work with the outcasts of nineteenth-century society effected significant social change. And, without doubt, her humane reforms, and the legislation she informed, provided material and practical comfort to a large number of women, both within and without the penal system.

## Further Reading


- Elizabeth Fry, *Observations on the Visiting, Superintendence and Government of Female Prisoners* (J and A Arch, 1827).
- Anna Isba, *The Excellent Mrs Fry: The Unlikely Heroine* (Continuum International Publishing, 2010).
- Norval Morris and David J Rothman, *The Oxford History of the Prison: The Practice of Punishment in Western Society* (OUP, 1995).


[18] See eg An Act to abolish the punishment of public whipping of female offenders (1817) 57 Geo III c 75.
[19] See eg Lucy Williams, *Wayward Women: Female Offending in Victorian England* (Pen and Sword, 2016).

# 5

# *The Slave, Grace* (1827)

ROSEMARY AUCHMUTY

In *The Slave, Grace*, the High Court of Admiralty ruled that, although slavery did not exist in England, the English courts had no power to overrule the law of other countries where it did. Thus Grace James, who became free on a visit with her 'mistress' to England, was held to have become a slave again on her return to Antigua. The remedy awarded to her 'owner', however, was damages rather than restitution, so she obtained her freedom in fact if not in law.[1] Five years later slavery was abolished by Act of Parliament throughout the colonies, with slave-owners being awarded compensation for financial loss on this model.

## I. Context

Britain's industrial dominance in the eighteenth century owed much to its imperial slave labour. Africans were seized and shipped to America and the West Indies and sold as slaves to work on the sugar, cotton and tobacco plantations. Though Britain was not the only country engaged in this human trafficking, its industrial leadership along with its mastery of the seas enabled it to exploit its cheap labour most efficiently to become the richest manufacturing and trading nation in the world. Whole cities such as Bristol, Cardiff and Liverpool were built on profits from the slave trade. The country's leading banks and insurers derived their profits from it. Many people owed their comfortable standard of living to income from investments in the West Indies while, lower down the social scale, ordinary British workers obtained jobs in the manufacturing industries that flourished thanks to the exploitation of black slaves in the colonies.[2]

Under colonial law, slaves were the property of their owners. Legally, they were chattels, without any of the rights attaching to human beings. When the captain of a slave-ship threw a cargo of ailing slaves overboard in order to claim the insurance, the Solicitor-General argued in an English court that murder was an inappropriate description of what had occurred: 'This is a case of chattels or goods', he insisted.[3] As a domestic slave, Grace James

[1] *The Slave, Grace; R v Allan* (1827) 2 Haggard 94; 166 ER 179 (High Court of Admiralty).

[2] On the history of slavery in the British empire, see eg Peter Fryer, *Staying Power: The History of Black People in Britain* (Pluto, 1984); Trevor Phillips, *Britain's Slave Trade* (Channel 4 History, 2000); James Walvin, *Black Ivory: Slavery in the British Empire* (2nd edn, Wiley Blackwell, 2001).

[3] The *Zong* case, quoted in Fryer, n 2 above, 126.

occupied a position which was in some respects more privileged, but in some respects more dangerous, than that of other slaves. Domestic slaves were at their owner's beck and call any time of day or night. They could be punished for simple mistakes such as burning the dinner, and the punishments were severe, ranging from whipping to execution. They could be separated from their families and sold to other masters. They were made to work very hard, and from an early age. Sleep was rationed to four or five hours a night and food might also be restricted. As long as there was a steady supply of cheap labour coming into the colonies in the slave-ships, plantation owners might find it easier to work a slave to death and replace him or her than to provide the basic needs for survival. Women proved to be a better investment as they were hardier than men.

Women were useful in other ways. The reproduction of the workforce was assisted by intensive 'breeding'. Enslaved women were also sexual prey for the men of the house. Abolitionists agreed that life was worse for women slaves than for men. Yet they were also more troublesome than men. Women led slave uprisings in Jamaica in the eighteenth century, and the colony's records for 1824–26 showed that women incurred twice the number of punishments as men.[4] Women slaves earned a reputation for insubordination, evidenced by acts of resistance such as poisoning the family's food and extending the period of breast-feeding to avoid forced childbearing. Their position within the master's house gave domestic slaves access to books and newspapers, and many enslaved women (though not Grace James, who signed her petition with a cross) taught themselves to read and write. Not only did this challenge the plantation owners' desire to keep slaves ignorant and docile, it gave women a significant role in the acquisition and dissemination of knowledge and news to other slaves.

Legally, there was no slavery in England, Wales, Scotland or Ireland. The law was unclear, however, about whether a slave became free as soon as she or he landed in Britain. In 1749 Lord Chancellor Hardwicke rejected the idea – a 'Negro slave … is as much property as any other thing', he stated – but a later Lord Chancellor, Lord Henley, declared in a case of 1762 that 'as soon as a man sets foot on English ground he is free. … A Negro may maintain an action against his master for ill usage, and may have a *Habeas Corpus* if restrained of his liberty'.[5] The chronicler of the common law, William Blackstone, stated in the 1765 edition of his *Commentaries* that a slave who landed in England immediately became free, but a year later conceded that he [women are not mentioned] became free but 'the master's right to his service may probably still continue'.[6] In practice many courts ignored the precedents and routinely freed black petitioners.[7]

The case of *Somerset v Stewart*[8] is regarded as bringing slavery to an end in Britain. An African-born Virginia plantation slave who, having lived in Britain for some years, refused to return to America with his master, was seized and handed over to a slave-trader to be conveyed in chains to Jamaica to be sold. Lord Chief Justice Mansfield held that the seizure was unlawful on the ground that slavery was 'so odious, that nothing can be suffered

[4] On women slaves, see Beverley Bryan, Stella Dadzie and Suzanne Scafe, *The Heart of the Race: Black Women's Lives in Britain* (Virago, 1985).

[5] *Shanley v Harvey* (1762) 2 Eden 126; 28 ER 844.

[6] Fryer, n 2 above, 121.

[7] ibid 205.

[8] *Somerset v Stewart* (1772) 1 Lofft 1; 98 ER 499.

to support it but positive law', and, since English law did not support it, the man must be freed.

Yet plantation owners often visited and sometimes settled in Britain with their slaves in attendance. Black men and women were openly traded at auction in public market places, and slave-ships were a frequent sight in the ports. Even after *Somerset*, slave sales continued to take place in British cities and runaway slaves were still hunted down, like the woman seen by Hannah More in Bristol in 1790: the town crier had offered a guinea (£1.05) to anyone who would hand her over, and 'the poor trembling wretch was dragged out from a hole in the top of a house, where she had hid herself, and forced on board ship'.[9] Clearly, though Britons never could be slaves (as the patriotic song *Rule Britannia* claims), there was certainly slavery in Britain.

The British slave trade was abolished by Act of Parliament in 1807,[10] but slavery as an institution continued in America and the West Indies. Thus the status of slaves who, having been freed in Britain, returned to jurisdictions which still recognised the institution was unclear: did they remain free, or could they be re-enslaved?

The fact that Grace James's case came to court and was widely publicised was due to the efforts of the strong anti-slavery movement in Britain and the colonies. In this movement women played an important role. The Society for the Abolition of the Slave Trade was formed in 1787. At first women remained in the background, conscious that campaigners like William Wilberforce thought activism 'unsuited to the female character as delineated in Scripture'[11] and fearful that open participation would deter supporters who agreed that women should stay out of public life. But little by little they began to attend meetings, then to speak at them; to canvass at elections on the issue of abolition; to collect financial contributions, and then to make contributions themselves; to distribute pamphlets, and then to write them – published anonymously, in order to be taken seriously.[12] They gathered signatures for petitions, which became the most effective means of exerting pressure on a reluctant legislature. By the 1820s women's names began to dominate these petitions, as women capitalised on their social role as guardians of morality to point out the injustice of slavery and its appalling effects on women and children. In 1823, the first women's anti-slavery association was founded,[13] and by 1833, the year of emancipation, women's associations were responsible for one-third of the signatures on petitions.[14] A further, modern tactic was a boycott of slave-produced sugar. People were encouraged to enjoy their tea sugarless or with honey. Holding bazaars to raise money for the cause was also seen as an appropriate feminine activity, as was the wearing of bracelets and hairpins with the image of a black slave in chains upon them.[15]

[9] Letter from Hannah More to Horace Walpole, quoted in Fryer, n 2 above, 126.

[10] The (Abolition of the) Slave Trade Act 1807.

[11] Quoted in Elizabeth J Clapp, 'Introduction' in Elizabeth J Clapp and Julie Roy Jeffrey (eds), *Women, Dissent, and Anti-Slavery in Britain and America, 1790–1865* (OUP, 2011) 1.

[12] Timothy Whelan, 'Martha Gurney and the Anti-Slave Trade Movement, 1788–94' in Clapp and Jeffrey, n 11 above, chapter 2.

[13] Clare Midgley, *Women Against Slavery: The British Campaigns, 1780–1870* (Routledge, 1992) chapter 3.

[14] Christine Bolt, *The Women's Movements in the United States and Britain from the 1790s to the 1920s* (Harvester Wheatsheaf, 1993) 65; see also Bonnie Anderson, *The First International Women's Movement 1830–1860* (OUP, 2000) 115–27.

[15] Fryer, n 2 above, 210; Pam Hirsch, *Barbara Leigh Smith Bodichon* (Pimlico, 1999) 2–3, 28.

The London home of sisters Mary Sturch and Elizabeth Reid (who later founded Bedford College for women) served as headquarters for the activities of the women involved in the anti-slavery movement. Many supporters of abolition were active later in the feminist movement, including Barbara Leigh Smith Bodichon,[16] Josephine Butler,[17] Harriet Martineau and Bessie Rayner Parkes.[18]

## II. The Landmark

In 1822 Mrs Allan of Antigua came to England with her slave, Grace James, who, once she set foot on British soil, became a free woman. In 1823 Grace James returned voluntarily with her mistress to Antigua and lived as a free woman. After a 'trifling' incident in which she offended Mrs Allan, she was publicly flogged 'and told she was still a slave'. Her case attracted sympathy, and in 1825 she was seized by a customs officer 'as forfeited to the King, on suggestion of having been illegally imported in 1823' – it being illegal to detain a free person in slavery. Mr Allan claimed for her return, contending that Grace James was his property (his rather than his wife's because married women's property in common law belonged to their husband). The judge of the Vice-Admiralty Court of Antigua agreed, and ordered that she should be returned to the claimant. Grace James petitioned for her freedom, and the Crown appealed to the High Court of Admiralty in London to answer the point of principle of whether a slave, once freed in England, would revert to slavery on return to the colonies or would remain free.

*The Slave, Grace* was perceived as a test case by abolitionists and slave-owners alike. What looked at first sight like a dispute over forfeiture of property was in fact a claim for a freed slave to remain free, and the abolitionists – who included the customs officers who had engineered the slave's seizure and the colonial officials themselves – expected a sympathetic hearing in London, for the presiding judge, Lord Stowell, was known to be opposed to slavery. But Stowell ruled that England had no power to alter the laws of other jurisdictions, and thus that Grace James had indeed reverted to slavery on her return to Antigua.

The reason for this surprising and disappointing decision lies partly in the political context and partly in the character of the man. Although against slavery, Stowell was a conservative man who as an MP had opposed most reforms, including Catholic emancipation. In the turbulent period leading up to the 1833 Act, he was conscious of the grievances of the big slave-owners and industrial interests whose financial losses would be huge if and when slavery was abolished in the colonies. In a letter to an American colleague he wrote that English politics are 'in a very uncomfortable state, our revenue deficient, our people discontented, and a strong spirit of insubordination prevailing in the country'.[19] In the face

[16] See ***A Brief Summary of the Most Important Laws Concerning Women*, Barbara Leigh Smith Bodichon, 1854.**

[17] See **Section 5(1) Criminal Law Amendment Act 1885.**

[18] David Turley, 'Complicating the story: Religion and gender in historical writing on British and American anti-slavery' in Clapp and Jeffrey, n 11 above, 41; Alison Twells, '"We ought to obey God rather than Man": Women, anti-slavery and non-conformist religious cultures' in Clapp and Jeffrey, n 11 above, 67.

[19] Quoted in Justin Buckley Dyer, 'After the revolution: *Somerset* and the Anti-Slavery Tradition in Anglo-American Constitutional Development' (2009) 71(4) *Journal of Politics* 1422, 1433.

of conflicting pressures, he found it safer to distinguish *Somerset* which, he said, only established that 'the owners of slaves had no authority over them in England, nor any power of sending them back to the colonies',[20] and to draw on both 'floodgates' and 'security' arguments (the 'public inconvenience' of slaves who made their way to England to be freed and then returned as free men and women could be 'not only extremely burdensome to the colony, but … highly dangerous to its peace and security)'.[21] Thus, Justin Dyer suggests, cases like *The Slave, Grace* 'emerge not as manifestations of illiberal constitutional theories – valuing slavery for its own sake – but as conservative judicial attempts to preserve increasingly weakened constitutional orders'.[22]

By the time the case returned to court for remedy, however, Stowell had retired and the presiding judge was his successor, Sir Christopher Robinson, who, as King's Advocate, had argued Grace James's case in the hearing before Stowell and was sympathetic to her position. He refused to grant restitution and instead awarded damages to Mrs Allan. Thus Grace James achieved her freedom, in fact if not in law.

## III. What Happened Next

In 1833 Parliament passed An Act for the Abolition of Slavery throughout the British Colonies. Traditionally this has been presented as a high point of humanitarian reform 'within a narrative of empire that presented anti-slavery issues as having been resolved within the British imperial political and parliamentary system'.[23] In fact, the legislation was passed mainly because of the difficulties the plantation owners were experiencing in controlling their slave workforce and the increasing unprofitability of slave labour. The Industrial Revolution had ushered in a new system of wage labour which, in permitting employees to be hired and fired according to need, proved a cheaper option than one which required lifelong maintenance of one's workforce. By declining to advance the law judicially, Stowell opened the way for Parliament to negotiate a compromise settlement with the slave-owners in which they would be compensated for their losses on the model established by Robinson.

The 1833 Act contained 66 carefully-worked out sections dealing with the transfer of slaves into apprenticeship to their former owners and the compensation of slave-owners for the loss of their 'property'. Though 'emancipated', the slaves remained in subjection, forced to work for their former masters and deprived of access to land of their own: as Bryan, Dadzie and Scafe put it, 'Colonialism took over where slavery left off, ensuring that our labour would continue to bolster and maintain the British economy for years to come'.[24]

Women continued to campaign against the apprenticeship system as slavery under a different name, and a petition of 662,000 names hastened its demise in 1839.[25] Many joined the British and Foreign Anti-Slavery Society to work for the abolition of slavery throughout

[20] *The Slave, Grace* (n 1 above) 166 ER 179, 183.
[21] ibid, 186.
[22] Dyer, n 19 above, ibid.
[23] Turley, n 18 above, 25.
[24] Bryan, Dadzie and Scafe, n 4 above, 10.
[25] Midgley, n 13 above, 110.

the world. They raised money for the education of women and children in Africa and the West Indies and lent financial and moral support to the American anti-slavery movement – indeed, its leader, William Lloyd Garrison, called on American women to emulate the splendid record of their British sisters.[26]

But when Garrison brought an American delegation to the world Anti-Slavery Convention in London in 1840, the women were forbidden to speak and banished to the gallery. The experience of that public rebuff was never forgotten.[27] If the rejection of women's equal status within the anti-slavery movement was not the sole catalyst for the first wave of feminism, it was certainly a moment of awakening. Radical women could not help but see the similarities between the position of women – especially married women – and that of slaves, and indeed the language of slavery is present throughout the writings on women's rights. John Stuart Mill wrote in 1869 that 'Marriage is the only actual bondage known to our law. There remain no legal slaves, except the mistress of every house'.[28] Philippa Levine contends that when the Women's Emancipation Union spoke of 'the slavery of sex', they intentionally evoked the anti-slavery campaigns of the 1830s as 'a deliberate challenge to parliamentary reformers who had been active in the agitation but who seemed reluctant in this context closer to home'.[29]

## IV. Significance

The judgment in *The Slave, Grace* is remembered for representing a retreat from Lord Mansfield's declaration in *Somerset* that slavery was contrary to natural law, and a step backwards in the struggle for emancipation. Nevertheless, although she lost, *The Slave, Grace* was positive for women for several reasons. First, it drew attention to the fact that slavery existed on British soil, highlighted the country's hypocritical attitude to both slavery and women, and paved the way for slavery to be abolished throughout the colonies six years later. Many British women today are descended from enslaved women like Grace James. Her case is directly a part of their heritage, and the abolition of slavery that followed is perhaps the most significant legal landmark in their history.

Secondly, for Grace James personally, the case ended well when the Allans were awarded a financial remedy rather than restitution. Waddams suggests that there may have been judicial concern for her fate at the hands of owners against whom Grace James had already alleged cruelty, as well as sympathy for the fact that a return to slavery after three years of freedom would have been an undue hardship.[30] If so, this would be indicative of changed social attitudes towards slavery and concern for the subject – a black woman – as a person.

[26] Bolt, n 14 above, 65.

[27] Hirsch, n 15 above, 29. In an ironic illustration of the truism that history repeats itself, in 1963 black women activists were excluded from addressing the landmark civil rights march in Washington, USA; the women's movement that followed owed some of its impetus to this experience of political marginalisation. Louise Tickle, 'Freedom of Speech', *The Guardian*, 9 April 2018.

[28] John Stuart Mill, 'The Subjection of Women' (1869) in Alice S Rossi (ed), *Essays in Sex Equality* (University of Chicago Press, 1970) 217.

[29] Philippa Levine, *Victorian Feminism 1850–1900* (Hutchinson, 1987) 62.

[30] Stephen Waddams, 'The case of Grace James (1827)' (2006–07) 13 *Texas Wesleyan Law Review* 793.

Thirdly, the case is important because it gave women anti-slavery campaigners the example of a woman to demonstrate the cruelty and injustice of slavery. The anti-slavery movement was an important vehicle for women's political activism, leading inexorably into the first wave of feminism. As Clare Midgley points out, the anti-slavery campaigners' experience of questioning male authority represented 'an assertion of independence, and a recognition that their views were not adequately represented by men'.[31] The anti-slavery movement gave women experience in organising around political issues, dealing with male opposition, identifying the ways that privilege worked, and making links between the oppression of other women and their own, which was to stand them in good stead when, the emancipation of slaves achieved, they turned their attention to the emancipation of women.

## Further Reading

- Peter Fryer, *Staying Power: The History of Black People in Britain* (Pluto, 1984).
- Clare Midgley, *Women Against Slavery: The British Campaigns, 1780–1870* (Routledge, 1992).
- Stephen Waddams, 'The case of Grace James (1827)' (2006–07) 13 *Texas Wesleyan Law Review* 783–93.

[31] Midgley, n 13 above, 116.

# 6

# *A Brief Summary of the Most Important Laws Concerning Women*, Barbara Leigh Smith Bodichon, 1854

JOANNE CONAGHAN

*A Brief Summary in Plain Language of the Most Important Laws Concerning Women Together with a Few Observations Thereon* is an 18-page pamphlet published by John Chapman's publishing house in October 1854.[1] Although published anonymously, the booklet was written by Barbara Leigh Smith [later Bodichon] (1827–91), daughter of Benjamin Leigh Smith (1783–1860), a wealthy Unitarian and Whig social reformer. At the time of publication, Bodichon was relatively young (27) and had no legal training or profile as an author/commentator. Yet her pamphlet, which offered a concise, unadulterated account of the main provisions governing the legal status of women, proved both popular and provocative, running to a second edition in 1856 and a third, expanded edition in 1869.

After publication, Bodichon, encouraged by the Law Amendment Society (LAS), drew together a group of interested women, forming a committee to campaign for legislative reform of marriage laws. The committee, which first met in late 1855, collected evidence to support claims that as a result of the law, women were enduring real and substantial hardship, particularly in relation to property and access to earnings. Led by Bodichon, the committee drafted a petition which, in a few short months, collected over 26,000 signatures. The petition was presented in Parliament in March 1856 and in February 1857, Lord Brougham, on behalf of the LAS, introduced the first Married Women's Property Bill. Although failing to proceed beyond the first reading, the bill constituted the first shot across the bows in the long political battle culminating in the **Married Women's Property Act 1882**. Reflecting on Bodichon's achievements shortly after her death in 1891, her lifelong friend, Bessie Raynor Parkes, remarked that Bodichon's pamphlet was 'the small end of the wedge which was to change the whole fabric of the law'.[2]

[1] Hereinafter cited as '*Summary*'. All references are to the first edition (1854), unless otherwise stated.
[2] (July 1891) 210 *Englishwomen's Review* 147.

# I. Context

Barbara Leigh Smith was the oldest of five illegitimate children, the product of an 'irregular' union between her father, Benjamin, and her mother, Annie Longden, a milliner's apprentice who died when Barbara was seven. Barbara and her siblings were reared in a happy if highly unconventional household; blessed with wealth and charisma, Barbara was fortunate to make her own way in a world of education and privilege, moving from a young age in circles in which social, educational and legal reform were a frequent focus of conversation. When she reached 21, Bodichon's father settled upon her an annual income, allowing her the financial independence to pursue her many interests, including art, educational reform and women's employment. She was abreast of the intellectual issues of the day and acquainted with many writers and social commentators, including Elizabeth Gaskell and George Eliot. Her circle of friends also comprised women who were to make a significant mark on nineteenth-century feminist politics.[3] These included Emily Davies, with whom Bodichon co-founded Girton College in 1869, Bessie Raynor Parkes, with whom she started the *Englishwoman's Journal* in 1858, and Jessie Boucherett, with whom, in 1859, Bodichon helped to establish the Society for Promoting the Employment of Women.

A number of factors conspired to place Bodichon at the centre of early attempts to change the married women's property regime. Chief among these was her social proximity to members of the LAS. Founded in 1844, the Society for Promoting the Amendment of the Law was influenced by the ideas of Jeremy Bentham, attracting the support of Lord Brougham and other leading reformists.[4] Matthew Davenport Hill, the lawyer who advised Bodichon on writing the *Summary*, was among the Society's founding members, while his daughters – Florence and Rosamund Davenport Hill – were her friends and contemporaries. The LAS aimed to eliminate 'antiquated laws' and reduce the level of 'meddlesome legislation' inhibiting the free flourishing of trade and commerce.[5] They considered married women's property laws to be an example of the confusion and complexity occasioned by the parallel and often contradictory operations of law and equity[6] and indeed, in 1851, advocated the fusion of the two jurisdictions. Certain members of the LAS were aware of Bodichon's interest in law reform and encouraged it. Moreover, Bodichon was quick to express her attraction to the laissez-faire ideas the Society propagated.[7]

An additional factor likely to have fuelled Bodichon's zeal for reform was the very public plight of the writer and prominent social figure, Caroline Norton. Norton's story spans decades of marital misery and abuse, including prolonged separation from her children. In 1854, during the course of a financial disagreement with her long-estranged husband, Norton invoked public sympathy by writing for private circulation a pamphlet lamenting

[3] 'The families that dominated the reform movements of the 1860s and 1870s made up an intellectual aristocracy. The wives, daughters and maiden aunts of this intellectual elite became the leaders of the women's movement': Sheila Herstein, *A Mid-Victorian Feminist, Barbara Leigh Smith Bodichon* (Yale University Press, 1985) xii.

[4] OR McGregor, *Social History and Law Reform, The Hamlyn Lectures: Thirty-First Series* (Stevens & Sons, 1979) 18–22.

[5] Caroline Cornwallis, 'The Property of Married Women: Report of the Personal Laws Committee on the Laws relating to the Property of Married Women' (1856) 66 *Westminster Review* 331, 335 and 358.

[6] The contradictions between the two systems are highlighted, ibid 346–47.

[7] See eg *Summary*, 13.

the disadvantageous position accorded to women by existing marriage laws.[8] Bodichon was no doubt familiar with Norton's troubles; she would also have known Anna Jameson, a good friend of Bodichon's aunt, and another female author unfortunate enough to contract an unhappy marriage, periodically placing her in a perilous financial position notwithstanding the healthy income her writing generated but which in law was not her property.[9] These concerns also generated a debate about divorce law reform. In 1850 the government established a Royal Commission on Divorce, chaired by Lord Campbell. At that time, divorce was primarily governed by ecclesiastical law, with access to civil divorce available only through a Private Act of Parliament. Reporting in 1853, the Commission recommended the secularisation of divorce law via significant restructuring of the courts[10] and over the course of the next four years, divorce law reform featured frequently in Parliamentary debate, resulting in the enactment of the **Matrimonial Causes Act 1857**.

## II. The Landmark

During 1853 and 1854, Bodichon conducted extensive legal research under the advice and guidance of Matthew Davenport Hill, then Commissioner in Bankruptcy for Bristol. Her *Summary* was not the first 'modern' attempt systematically to expound women's status under law. In 1632, an anonymous author, 'T.E.', published a treatise which plotted women's legal position using categories reflecting their life progression from maiden through to wife and widow.[11] In 1777, another unknown author (commonly identified as Lady Elizabeth Chudleigh) penned a text listing the 'interests and duties' of women as 'daughters, wives, wards, widows, heiresses, spinsters, legatees, sisters, executrixes'.[12] Writing in the 1760s, Blackstone proffered no separate treatment of women. However, he devoted an entire chapter of the first volume of the *Commentaries* to the law governing the relation of husband (*baron*) and wife (*feme*), famously praising the common law for its benign treatment of the female sex.[13] Then in 1853, a year before Bodichon's intervention, John Wharton wrote a lengthy treatise entitled *Exposition of the Laws Relating to the Women of England*, of which some view the *Summary* as a concise condensation.[14] Certainly at 18 pages, and costing only a few pence, Bodichon's pamphlet was infinitely more accessible than 557 pages of dry legal text.

In October 1854, the *Summary* was published anonymously, appearing in the same year as Norton's *English Laws for Women*. The style and tone of the two texts, however, was markedly different. Norton's tract took the form of an emotional, highly personalised attack

[8] Caroline Norton, *English Laws for Women in the Nineteenth Century* (1854).

[9] Clara Thomas, *Love and Work Enough. The Life of Anna Jameson* (University of Toronto Press, 1967).

[10] Lawrence Stone, *Road to Divorce: England 1530–1987* (OUP, 1990) ch XII.

[11] TE, *The Lawes Resolution of Women's Rights or The Lawes Provision for Women* (1632).

[12] Anon, *The Laws Respecting Women, as they Regard Their Natural Rights or Their Connections and Conduct: in which their interests and duties as daughters, wards, heiresses, spinsters, sisters, wives, widows, mothers, legatees, executrixes, &c. are ascertained and enumerated: also, the obligations of parent and child, and the condition of minors* (1777).

[13] William Blackstone, *Commentaries on the Laws of England*, vol 1 ch XV, 434.

[14] Pam Hirsch, *Barbara Leigh Smith Bodichon, Feminist, Artist and Rebel* (Chatto & Windus, 1998) 86–87.

on the law; by contrast, the *Summary* was characterised by terse prose and a complete absence of personal or emotional embellishment. Following the convention of the time, Bodichon adopted a legal classificatory scheme in which rights and duties were assigned to the various statuses women acquired through their relationships with others. Like Blackstone, Bodichon distinguished the position of married women from that of 'unmarried women or spinsters', sketching a legal picture in which the latter were in broadly the same position as men, subject to 'special' laws prohibiting them from voting, holding public or clerical office, and so on.[15] Bodichon devoted separate attention to widows,[16] to 'women in other relationships' (for example, as agents, trustees, or executrixes),[17] and to 'the laws concerning illegitimate children and their mothers'.[18] However, the main focus of her attention was the legal situation of married women, which she spelled out in blunt and unambiguous terms:

> A man and wife are one person in law; the wife loses all her rights as a single woman and her existence is, as it were, entirely absorbed in that of her husband. He is civilly responsible for her wrongful acts … and she lives under his protection and cover.[19]

In contrast to Blackstone, Bodichon's exposition was not accompanied by any attempt to present the wife as a 'favourite' of English law. She emphasised that women 'lost' their rights and legal personality on marriage, that a husband might assign or dispose of a wife's personal property 'at his pleasure', and that a husband was under no formal obligation under common law to support her (although Bodichon acknowledged the possibility of equitable intervention in such contexts).[20] She also asserted (with, one suspects, deliberate provocation) that 'a woman's body belongs to her husband: she is in his custody, and he can enforce his right by a writ of *habeas corpus*'.[21] Rosemary Auchmuty argues that it was the very starkness of this prose, the itemised quality and lack of rhetorical embellishment, which made it such a powerful indictment of the law.[22]

Bodichon offered no generic conception of women's status under law; nor did she explicitly advocate women's legal equality.[23] Her objections to existing legal arrangements were framed largely in terms of their regressiveness, equating legal progress with the absence of regulation and the corresponding promotion of individual freedom:

> Philosophical thinkers have generally come to the conclusion that the tendency of progress is gradually to dispense with law – that is to say, as each individual man becomes unto himself a law,

[15] Bodichon commented that 'the professions of law and medicine, whether or not closed by law, are closed in fact' (*Summary*, 3). Later efforts to test this position confirmed Bodichon's bleak surmise as to the legality of women's access to the professions.

[16] ibid 10.

[17] ibid 11.

[18] ibid 11–13. Some biographers suggest that Bodichon's illegitimacy engendered in her a keen interest in the legal regulation of people's status and family relations (see eg Hirsch, n 14 above, 87–88).

[19] *Summary*, 6.

[20] ibid.

[21] ibid. In a later edition, Bodichon qualifies this by commenting that 'in practice this is greatly modified' (1869, 3rd edn).

[22] Rosemary Auchmuty, 'The Married Women's Property Acts: Equality was not the Issue' in Rosemary Hunter (ed), *Rethinking Equality Projects in Law* (Hart Publishing, 2008) 13, 34–35.

[23] ibid.

> less external restraint is necessary. And certainly the most urgently needed reforms are simple erasures from the statute book. Women, more than any other members of the community, suffer from over-legislation …[24]

She supported her argument by drawing from other jurisdictions, citing examples of laws more favourable to married women in France, Turkey, Hungary and the more liberal American States such as Ohio.[25] Her analysis, which evidenced an impressive grasp of law from someone with neither formal legal training nor practice experience, concluded in an exasperated cry for immediate reform: 'Why should not these legal devices be done away with, by the simple abolition of a law which we have outgrown?'.[26]

## III. What Happened Next

Bodichon's pamphlet was widely read and disseminated, causing something of a sensation among the Victorian intelligentsia. Marriage law reform became the subject of heated debate in leading journals, the *Westminster Review* commenting that the issue 'has obtained far more notice than is usually bestowed on the repeal of an old law'.[27] While some commentary was positive,[28] the issue also provoked significant criticism from those who considered either that such ideas were at war with nature and/or that concerns about husbands ill-treating their wives were greatly exaggerated.[29] To counter the latter suggestion, Bodichon and her newly formed committee of like-minded women sought out instances of marital injustice from up and down the country, many of which were gathered and published in a Report formally undertaken by the LAS in the *Westminster Review*.[30] At the same time she drafted a petition supporting the reform of marriage laws which in the space of a few months, and with the help of a nationwide army of activists, attracted tens of thousands of signatures.[31] The petition was eventually presented to Parliament, though, strikingly, Bodichon was not among the presenting delegation which was led by Anna Jameson and Mary Howitt, both well known writers. Presented by Lord Brougham in the House of Lords, and by Sir Erskine Perry in the Commons, the petition attracted favourable comment from the *Daily News*: 'The language of the petition is eminently temperate and judicious and it is numerously signed … it is the deliberate remonstrance of a whole sex against the perpetuation of gross injustice'.[32] Building on the momentum generated by the petition, the LAS

[24] *Summary*, 13.

[25] ibid 16–17. Hirsch suggests that Bodichon's Unitarian links proved particularly useful in gathering this comparative material (n 14 above, 91).

[26] *Summary*, 18.

[27] Cornwallis, n 5 above, 337.

[28] See eg JW Kaye, 'The Non-Existence of Women' (August 1855) 23 *North British Review* 536 (though mainly focuses on Norton's pamphlet) and Cornwallis, *Westminster Review* (n 5 above).

[29] See eg Margaret Oliphant, 'Laws Concerning Women' (April 1856) LXXIX *Blackwood's Edinburgh Magazine* 379–87; and 'Law for Ladies' (*Saturday Review*, 24 May 1856) ridiculing the LAS for 'join[ing] the ranks of feminine insurrection'.

[30] Cornwallis, n 5 above.

[31] 'When Sir Erskine Perry unrolled the petition in the Commons it reached the whole length of the House': Margaret Howitt (ed), *Mary Howitt: An Autobiography* (William Isbister Ltd, 1889) 116–17.

[32] *Daily News*, 14 March 1856.

drafted a Bill which was put before Parliament in 1857 but sadly did not get beyond first reading. The time was not yet right and, notwithstanding some support among the liberal intelligentsia,[33] there was still strong establishment and popular opposition to the very idea of unpicking the 'natural' gender hierarchy of which marriage was a core expression. Moreover, at just the same time as Bodichon's campaign for reform of married women's property laws was losing ground, the push to reform divorce law was taking firm hold and indeed some consider the success of the latter campaign to have contributed to the demise of the former.[34] In any event, Bodichon turned her attention to other social and political concerns and there is some evidence that she was in low spirits for a while.[35] It was to restore Bodichon's spirits as well as her sister's declining health that the Leigh Smith family sojourned in Algeria in 1856, where Barbara met and, eventually married, Doctor Eugene Bodichon.

## IV. Significance

The *Summary* was undoubtedly instrumental in bringing the issue of women's legal status to the fore in mid-nineteenth-century England. Bodichon's biographers are at one in asserting that it had a significant impact on contemporary public debate, Hester Burton describing the pamphlet's publication as 'like raising a standard or lighting a beacon'.[36] Yet, what followed is of equal importance, the campaign for married women's property reform which Bodichon led serving as the first organised campaign of the nascent women's movement. According to Shelia Herstein: 'the committee was the beginning of a communication network that linked women throughout the country and laid the foundation for organised feminist efforts of the future'.[37] In contrast to the individual crusades of feminist pioneers such as Mary Wollstonecraft or Caroline Norton, Bodichon ignited feminist activism, her committee evolving into the 'Langham Place Circle',[38] a hugely active and influential assemblage of nineteenth-century feminists. Of significance too was the way Bodichon went about formulating and supporting her core arguments, drawing on the experience of other jurisdictions as well as collecting empirical data, in the form of concrete instances of disadvantage occasioned by existing marriage laws. In methodological terms, her approach was an exemplar for modern law reform and the eventually successful outcome (albeit slow in coming), a prototype for the positive impact of social scientific study.

One question which is sometimes asked about Bodichon is why, given her individual achievements and wider involvement in a host of nineteenth-century social initiatives, she is not more widely known. Caroline Norton, for example, has garnered far greater fame

[33] See eg 'Liabilities of Husband and Wife' (January 1857) *Edinburgh Review* 181.

[34] Mary Lyndon Shanley, *Feminism, Marriage and the Law in Victorian England* (Princeton University Press, 1989) 35–49.

[35] Writing about Bodichon in her journal in 1856, George Eliot records 'we enjoyed her society very much but were deeply touched to see that three years had made her so much older and sadder' (Gordon S Haight, *George Eliot: A Biography* (OUP, 1968) 205).

[36] Hester Burton, *Barbara Bodichon* (Constable, 1949) 59.

[37] Herstein, n 3 above 78.

[38] Candida Ann Lacey (ed), *Barbara Leigh Smith Bodichon and the Langham Place Group* (Routledge, 1987).

and historical attention. Clearly, Bodichon did not seek the limelight. Notwithstanding that the 1856 petition was her 'grand scheme',[39] she asked Mrs Howitt and Jameson ('the literary ladies'[40]) to present it to Parliament, believing they would lend an appropriate cloak of respectability to the cause. Bodichon's biographers suggest that her strength lay in her inspiration and creativity, allowing her to serve as 'the source of seed',[41] 'to embrace a project briefly, albeit intensely'[42] but perhaps not necessarily enabling her to see things through to a satisfactory conclusion. However, looking at her life as a whole, and the many and diverse projects she initiated, what strikes me is how effective she was at engendering *collective* feminist engagement in the social and political affairs of the day. Candida Ann Lacey comments that 'her pioneering schemes to improve the status of women would make the following twenty years [from 1849+] some of the richest in debate and reform [in Victorian England]'.[43] In simple terms, Barbara Bodichon launched the modern women's movement.

## Further Reading

- Pam Hirsch, *Barbara Leigh Smith Bodichon: Feminist, Artist and Rebel* (Chatto & Windus, 1998).
- Candida Ann Lacey (ed), *Barbara Leigh Smith Bodichon and the Langham Place Group* (Routledge & Kegan Paul, 1987).
- Mary Lyndon Shanley, *Feminism, Marriage and the Law in Victorian England 1850–1895* (Princeton University Press, 1989).

[39] Letter of Mary Howitt, dated 3 December 1855, in *Mary Howitt: An Autobiography*, n 31 above.
[40] *Saturday Review*, n 29 above.
[41] Burton, n 36 above, 113.
[42] Herstein, n 3 above, 21.
[43] Lacey, n 38 above, 1.

# 7

# Matrimonial Causes Act 1857

PENELOPE RUSSELL

The Matrimonial Causes Act 1857 gave women in England and Wales legal standing to use the civil courts to seek a decree of divorce or nullity, enabling them to leave unhappy unions and remarry.[1] The statute has been described as a watershed, effectively legalising divorce.[2] It was the first Matrimonial Causes Act, culminating in our current statutory framework for divorce over a century later.[3] The constitutional law scholar Albert Venn Dicey wrote in 1905:

> The Divorce Act of 1857 on the face of it did no more than increase the facilities for obtaining divorce. It in reality gave national sanction to the contractual view of marriage … [and has] given strength to the belief that women ought, in the eye of the law, to stand substantially on an equality with men.[4]

## I. Context

Before the statute, seeking a divorce was a lengthy and complicated process which comprised three stages: obtaining first an order from the ecclesiastical court ('divorce *a mensa et thoro*', which permitted separation but not remarriage), second an order from the civil court for damages against the adulterous partner ('criminal conversation') and third dissolution of the marriage by private Act of Parliament ('divorce *a vincula matrimonii*'). The need for divorce reform was procedural: to rationalise the court system and to free up parliamentary time. In 1840 a Select Committee on Divorce Bills had been set up to consider the evidence in divorce cases but a vote by both Houses was still required and it remained a time-consuming process.

The grounds for divorce were limited and discriminatory: men were able to divorce on the basis of their wife's adultery alone, whereas women had to prove adultery aggravated by the marital offence of incest or bigamy. The different grounds were a reflection

[1] Divorcees had the option of remarriage, since the Marriage Act 1836 had introduced civil marriage and ended the church's exclusive right to solemnise marriages.

[2] Sybil Wolfram, 'Divorce in England 1700–1857' (1985) 5 *Oxford Journal of Legal Studies* 155, 158.

[3] The current statutory framework for divorce is set out in the Matrimonial Causes Act 1973.

[4] AV Dicey, *Lectures on the Relation between Law and Public Opinion in England During the Nineteenth Century* (London, 1905) 43.

of the widespread belief in the double standard of sexual morality: that a wife committing adultery could be less easily forgiven than the equivalent act of a husband.[5] Over a period of 187 years from 1670 to 1857 there were only eight women petitioners in total, of whom four were successful.[6] This can be contrasted with 321 divorces obtained by men over the same period.[7] Two of the successful women petitioners relied on their husband's affair with their sister; the other two were able to rely on adultery aggravated by bigamy.[8] Unsuccessful divorce Bills included those of Mrs Teush, Mrs Moffatt and Mrs Dawson who, although able to prove adultery, lacked the necessary element of bigamy or incest.[9]

Women suffered at least two impediments to accessing divorce: as well as the discriminatory grounds, there was also the practical cost of proceedings. A divorce under the old system was expensive, all three stages totalling between £200 and £5000.[10] This meant that divorce was only available to the upper echelons of society. The vast majority of women had not been able to petition for divorce because, even if they were married to a wealthy man, they lacked the independent means to do so. Married women were not able to make contracts or hold property in their own right, except under a trust, until the passage of the Married Women's Property Acts of 1870 and 1882.[11] A Royal Commission established in 1850 to enquire into the Law of Divorce concluded that the system should be simplified: 'The great expense and the long delay of these proceedings is a grievous hardship and oppression to individuals, and they amount in many cases to a denial of justice'.[12]

Members of the judiciary were of the same view. Mr Justice Maule's description of the divorce process in an 1845 bigamy case was scathing. He addressed the bigamist, a labourer called Thomas Hall:

> You ought first to have brought an action against your wife's seducer if you could have discovered him: that might have cost you money, and you say you are a poor working man, but that is not the fault of the law. You would then be obliged to prove by evidence your wife's criminality in a Court of Justice, and thus obtain a verdict with damages against the defendant, who was not unlikely to turn out a pauper. But so jealous is the law (which you ought to be aware is the perfection of reason) of the sanctity of the marriage tie, that in accomplishing all this you would only have fulfilled the lighter portion of your duty. You must then have gone, with your verdict in your hand, and petitioned the House of Lords for a divorce. It would cost you perhaps five or six hundred pounds and you do not seem to be worth as many pence.[13]

Mr Justice Maule only sentenced the bigamist to one day in prison. The speech was reported in *The Times*[14] and increased pressure for reform.

[5] Henry Kha and Warren Swain, 'The enactment of the Matrimonial Causes Act 1857: The Campbell Commission and the Parliamentary Debates' (2016) 37(3) *Journal of Legal History* 303, 318.
[6] Colin Gibson, *Dissolving Wedlock* (Routledge, 1994) 41.
[7] Roderick Phillips, *Untying the Knot* (Cambridge University Press, 1991) 66.
[8] ibid 68.
[9] Wolfram, n 2 above, 175.
[10] Gail Savage, 'The Operation of the 1857 Divorce Act, 1860–1910' (1982) 16 *Journal of Social History* 103, 103. However, see Wolfram, n 2 above, 166: the costs figure quoted by the Royal Commission on Divorce in 1853 was £700 but Wolfram calculates (based on the costs figures of published cases) that this is an over-estimate.
[11] **Married Women's Property Act 1882**.
[12] *The First Report of the commissioners … into the law of divorce*, BPP, 1852–53, vol 40, 269–70.
[13] *R v Hall* (1845) 1 Cox 231.
[14] *R v Hall* (1845) *The Times*, 3 April 1845, 7.

When compared to the vocal and well-organised campaigns for married women's property rights, arguments for reform of the double standard within divorce were scattered and muted.[15] Calls for reform of the law in the mid-Victorian era tended to focus on access to the court rather than the double standard. For example, in 1856 Barbara Leigh Smith Bodichon published a pamphlet critical of the inaccessibility of divorce saying 'a wife cannot be plaintiff, defendant, or witness in an important part of the proceedings for a divorce [the criminal conversation stage],[16] which evidently must lead to much injustice'.[17] In 1854 high-profile campaigner Caroline Norton published the first of two pamphlets on the issue, in which she referred to 'the jealous and exclusive guarding of masculine rights [which] is often the foundation of the most preposterous wrong'.[18]

The motivation for reform amongst parliamentarians was efficiency and enabling easier access to divorce for their male constituents, not ideals of equality. Reform was driven by powerful figures within the judiciary and legislature (all men),[19] challenging ecclesiastical control at a time of industrialisation and weakening church power.[20] The draft Bill for reform was presented as procedural only. When introducing the Bill to its second reading in the House of Lords, Lord Cranworth said that his aim was to establish 'on a rational footing what should be done when, unhappily, circumstances arose which naturally and justly led to the dissolution of the marriage tie'.[21] Many hours were engaged in heated debate about such issues as the scriptural authority for divorce, and the Opposition tried to delay the passage of the Bill by filibustering but Lord Palmerston promised that 'we shall return and sit here day by day and night by night until this Bill be concluded'.[22]

## II. The Landmark

The Matrimonial Causes Act 1857 came into effect on 1 January 1858. The statute greatly simplified and rationalised divorce procedure: the former three-stage process was reduced to one stage. Instead of using the ecclesiastical court, civil court and then Parliament, petitioners could now obtain a divorce from a civil court. All matrimonial litigation was transferred from the Church of England to a new secular Court for Divorce and Matrimonial Causes – the so-called 'Divorce Court'.[23]

The Act did not change the grounds for divorce; rather it simply codified past ecclesiastical and parliamentary practice. However, although the grounds for divorce remained

[15] Rebecca Probert, 'The double standard of morality in the Divorce and Matrimonial Causes Act 1857' (1999) 28 *Anglo-American Law Review* 73.

[16] JF Macqueen, *A practical treatise on the appellate jurisdiction of the House of Lords & Privy Council: together with the practice on parliamentary divorce* (London, 1842) 492.

[17] **Barbara Leigh Smith Bodichon, *A Brief Summary of the Most Important Laws Concerning Women*, 1854**, p 6.

[18] Caroline Norton, *English Laws for Women in the Nineteenth Century* (1854) 158.

[19] See Ray Strachey, *The Cause: A Short History of the Women's Movement in Great Britain* (Endeavour Press Ltd, 2016) 66. She asserts that the statute 'was no part of the regular Women's Movement'.

[20] For example, the 'high-water mark of industrial culture', the Great Exhibition took place in 1851: Edward Royle, *Modern Britain: A Social History 1750–1997* (Hodder Arnold, 1997) 396.

[21] HL Deb, 19 May 1857, vol 145 col 494.

[22] HC Deb, 13 August 1857, vol 147 col 1602.

[23] Section 6 of the Matrimonial Causes Act 1857.

the same (men could still use adultery on its own and women still had to prove adultery aggravated by a marital offence), the marital *offences* were expanded by the statute to include cruelty and desertion for two years, in addition to the prior offences of incest and bigamy.[24] These additional marital offences, when combined with the ground of adultery, made it easier for women to seek a divorce. Desertion was commonplace (many men had emigrated to North America and Australia)[25] and, within 10 years, cruelty had been widened judicially to include non-violent mental cruelty.[26]

The statute improved the position of women in other respects: under the statute a deserted wife could seek a court order protecting her earnings and property from her husband and his creditors.[27] In addition, the new Divorce Court had the power to make provision for the custody, maintenance and education of children as deemed by the court to be just and proper,[28] although Gail Savage has noted from an analysis of case histories reported in *The Times* that custody of children was not routinely allocated to the mother but to the party judged to be innocent in the divorce, which may have discouraged some petitioners.[29]

## III. What Happened Next

Before the enactment of the Act, there were on average two or three divorces a year.[30] Within the first year of the enactment, 253 divorce petitions were filed.[31] Successful divorces increased from 141 in 1861 to 580 in 1911.[32] The volume of divorce cases was greater than expected and in 1859 an editorial in *The Times* commented:

> We do not believe that any one either of the most eager supporters or violent opponents of the Divorce Bill of 1857 had the least idea of the quantity of matrimonial misery which was silent only for want of the opportunity to express itself until certified of the fact by the crowded state of the Court of Divorce, and the enormous pressure of the suitors.[33]

However, the numbers using the new divorce process were insignificant when compared to the size of the population. Lawrence Stone has pointed out that England was essentially a non-divorcing society.[34] England's divorce rate, even after the new statute, remained one of the lowest in the western world.[35]

[24] Section 27 of the Matrimonial Causes Act 1857.

[25] Wilbur Stanley Shepperson states that almost 17 million people emigrated from Britain in the nineteenth century in 'Industrial Emigration in Early Victorian Britain' (1953) *Journal of Economic History* 179–92.

[26] *Swatman v Swatman* (1864) 4 Sw & Tr 135, 164 ER 767; *Kelly v Kelly* (1870) LR 2 P & D 31.

[27] Section 21 of the Matrimonial Causes Act 1857.

[28] Section 35 of the Matrimonial Causes Act 1857.

[29] Savage, n 10 above, 106.

[30] Wolfram, n 2 above, 157.

[31] Allen Horstman, *Victorian Divorce* (St Martin's Press, 1985) 85.

[32] Lawrence Stone, *Road to Divorce* (OUP, 1990) 385.

[33] *The Times*, 12 January 1859, 8.

[34] Stone, n 32 above, 387.

[35] Being two per 100,000 population (compared to Germany 13, France 17, Switzerland 30 and the United States 55) Savage, n 10 above, 104 based on tables appended to *The Report of the Royal Commission on Divorce and Matrimonial Causes* (HMSO, 1912).

As well as the stigma of divorce, other reasons for the low numbers were the potentially dire consequences for women of marriage breakdown: the lack of state support and employment opportunities could result in severe financial hardship on marital separation. Although historical sources (including the census) are too unreliable to make generalisations about the level of married women's employment, studies of women working in London in Victorian times identify the work as casual and low paid, being most commonly domestic service, domestic cleaning, laundry, nursing and needlework.[36] This was exacerbated by the fact that the Divorce Court did not have power to order a lump sum or property settlement as part of the matrimonial proceedings, as the Matrimonial Causes Act 1857 did not contain provision for transfer of capital or property between parties.[37] The Court did have the power to order a husband to pay spousal maintenance but only if it could be secured (section 32), so the Court could not award maintenance to a wife if her husband did not own property, regardless of the level of the husband's income and his ability to pay.[38]

Another constraint on the number of petitioners was the fact that there was only one court, namely the Court for Divorce and Matrimonial Causes, which sat in London. The lack of jurisdiction of local lay courts was a deliberate tactic by the legislators to avoid jeopardising the institution of marriage.[39] John Macqueen, a barrister representing parties in the Divorce Court, wrote: 'There are two ways of withholding divorce from the poor. One is to say so in words; another is to erect an unapproachable tribunal'.[40] A divorce trial could last days, so a party's expenses would include not only legal representation and travel to London, but also overnight accommodation for them and their witnesses. A contemporary newspaper report writing about 'The Cost of a Divorce' in 1861 said:

> Some people think that a divorce is obtained cheaply now a-days, and that £50 or £60 will serve for that purpose, whereas the fact is that £200 – viz £100 for the wife's cost and £100 for the husband's is the smallest sum that can be calculated on.[41]

A sum of £50 or £60 would have been about a fifth of the cost under the old parliamentary procedure,[42] but was out of the reach of most people. In theory the statute gave legal standing to all women to petition for divorce; in reality divorce was only available to those who were able to make the financial sacrifice necessary to fund proceedings, effectively the middle and upper classes.

The hundreds using the centralised Divorce Court each year can be compared with the thousands using their local Magistrates Court to obtain an order for on-going maintenance: each year 11,000 such applications were made.[43] The Matrimonial Causes Act 1878, another landmark statute, gave women the right to apply to their local Magistrates Court for an order

[36] Pat Hudson, 'Women and industrialisation' in June Purvis (ed), *Women's History Britain 1850–1945* (UCL Press, 1995) 29.

[37] This did not come until 1970 by virtue of the Matrimonial Proceedings and Property Act.

[38] This did not change for 50 years until the implementation of the Matrimonial Causes Act 1907.

[39] Margaret K Woodhouse, 'The Marriage and Divorce Bill of 1857' (1959) 3 *American Journal of Legal History* 273–74.

[40] John F Macqueen, *A Practical Treatise on Divorce and Matrimonial Jurisdiction under the Act of 1857 and new orders* (W Maxwell, 1858) 129.

[41] *Galway Vindicator & Connaught Advertiser*, 21 December 1861, 4.

[42] Phillips, n 7 above, 129.

[43] Colin Gibson, *Dissolving Wedlock* (Routledge, 1994) 83.

in the following terms: that they no longer be bound to cohabit with their husband, that the husband pay to them a weekly sum of maintenance and that they have the custody of any children under the age of 10 (section 4). Following a successful campaign to help abused wives, led by activists such as Frances Power Cobbe, initially these remedies were available where the husband had been convicted of aggravated assault but were later extended to cases of desertion[44] and cruelty.[45] The Matrimonial Causes Act 1878 established cheaper, more accessible justice for working-class wives: a deliberate tactic by legislators to create a parallel system of the centralised Divorce Court for those who could afford it and local Magistrates Courts for those who could not.[46]

The magistrates' powers did not extend to granting a decree of divorce, and Stephen Cretney has pointed out that the lack of access to a divorce court condemned people to the 'living death of separation'.[47] It is noteworthy that, from an analysis of petitioners filing a divorce or nullity petition at the Divorce Court in 1858, 1868 and 1869, more than half went on to remarry.[48] By way of example, one of the first women to use the Divorce Court was Sarah Isabella Atkinson. She filed a petition for divorce in April 1858 at the age of 31, on the grounds of her husband's adultery and desertion. She had married Thomas Oliver (a barber and itinerant musician) on 22 January 1850 at St Mary's Parish Church in Lambeth but after only five weeks of marriage she discovered that her husband was having an affair with another woman (called Jane Carman) who had a child by him. The husband returned to live with his mistress but Sarah was forced to wait eight years until the Matrimonial Causes Act 1857 enabled her to petition for divorce. In his Answer to the Petition, the husband alleged that the breakdown of the marriage was caused by Sarah refusing to do housework ('The clothes when they got in such a beastly and dirty state I asked her to wash them, she told me she did not marry me to work or do washing') but he also asked for leniency so he could afford the upkeep of the four children he now had with Jane. Once Decree Absolute was pronounced, Sarah was able to remarry, which she did on 2 January 1860. Her second husband was Alfred Coates, a printer and compositor (the same occupation as her father). Sarah and Alfred went on to have seven children and their marriage lasted 45 years.[49]

## IV. Significance

Although procedural in nature, the Matrimonial Causes Act 1857 was a landmark step in women's emancipation.[50] When establishing a secular matrimonial jurisdiction, Parliament recognised that women should have legal standing to petition the civil court for divorce

[44] Married Women (Maintenance in Cases of Desertion) Act 1886.

[45] Summary Jurisdiction (Married Women) Act 1895.

[46] Stephen Cretney, *Family Law in the Twentieth Century* (OUP, 2005) 446.

[47] ibid 201.

[48] Using court documentation filed at the Court of Divorce and Matrimonial Causes and census data available in the National Archives. Results were corroborated by newspaper reports of the hearing of each case wherever available.

[49] London Metropolitan Archives, Saint Mary, Islington, Register of marriages, P83/MRY1, Item 1225; *England & Wales, Civil Registration Death Index, 1837–1915* [database online]. Provo, UT, USA: Ancestry.com Operations Inc, 2006.

[50] Wolfram, n 2 above, 179.

and, henceforth, despite the cost and inaccessibility of the court, 40 per cent of petitioners were women, compared to one per cent under the old parliamentary procedure.[51] Women went on to file the majority of petitions after equalisation of the divorce grounds, following the **Matrimonial Causes Act 1923**, over 60 years later.

## Further Reading

- Henry Kha and Warren Swain, 'The enactment of the Matrimonial Causes Act 1857: The Campbell Commission and the Parliamentary Debates' (2016) 37(3) *Journal of Legal History* 303–30.
- Griselda Rowntree and Norman Carrier, 'The Resort to Divorce in England and Wales, 1858–1957' (1958) 11(3) *Population Studies* 188.
- Sybil Wolfram, 'Divorce in England 1700–1857' (1985) 5 *Oxford Journal of Legal Studies* 155.

[51] Phillips, n 7 above, 130.

# 8

# Married Women's Property Act 1882

ANDY HAYWARD

The Married Women's Property Act 1882 was an Act of Parliament originally covering England and Wales and Ireland. Commencing on 1 January 1883, the Act provided for a married woman to hold all the property brought by her to the marriage or subsequently acquired thereafter as her 'separate property'. A married woman possessed for the first time the ability to acquire and dispose of all kinds of property 'as if she were a *feme sole* [single woman] without the intervention of any trustee' (section 1). It deserves its landmark status by virtue of the Act removing many, albeit not all, of the legal disadvantages flowing from coverture and for instigating a critical reappraisal of property holding within marriage.

## I. Context

Marriage generated multiple legal impediments for women in light of the unity of person doctrine. This common law doctrine conceptualised husband and wife as one person; that person, unsurprisingly, being the husband. Following marriage, the wife changed from '*feme-sole*' to a '*feme-covert*'; in essence, she became 'covered' by her 'baron' [husband]. In spite of these restrictions, the wife's impediments were often expressed as being favourable to women, as typified by Blackstone's remark that they were 'intended for her protection and benefit'[1] or by the views of Pollock and Maitland that they merely involved 'profitable guardianship' over the wife and her property.[2] Glanville Williams even described the unity of person doctrine as an instance of 'humanitarianism'.[3]

The doctrine had effects that were particularly extensive in relation to the wife's personal property, as upon coverture pre-marital property became the husband's in the same way as post-marital property and her earnings also became his. The effect on a wife's real property [land] was less extensive, as the husband was entitled to rents and profits during their joint life together. However, he could not sell the property without her consent and it would revert to her, along with her paraphernalia such as jewellery and dresses, if the husband

[1] William Blackstone, *Commentaries on the Laws of England* (21st edn, Sweet, Maxwell, Stevens and Norton, 1844) book 1, ch 1, 444.

[2] Frederick Pollock and FW Maitland, *The History of English Law Before the Time of Edward I* (2nd edn, Cambridge University Press, 1898) vol 1, 485.

[3] Glanville Williams, 'The Legal Unity of Husband and Wife' (1947) 10 *Modern Law Review* 16, 31.

were to predecease her. Nevertheless, the control of real property was largely vested in the husband. Paternalism suffused this doctrine, even though it should be noted that the position of wives before the Norman Conquest was far more favourable.

As divorce by an Act of Parliament was only open to the wealthy, the virtual inability of most people to get divorced prior to the **Divorce and Matrimonial Causes Act 1857** meant that the effects of coverture were for life. Even after that date and up until the **Matrimonial Causes Act 1923**, a wife, unlike a husband, had to prove aggravating factors to her husband's adultery to secure a divorce. Coverture also permeated other areas of the lives of married women; an inability to hold property separately, for example, meant that wives were also unable to enter contracts.

Despite these impediments, there was some mitigation of the effects of coverture at common law through the recognition of dower (a life interest in one-third of a husband's real property) coupled with the wife's right to be supported or maintained by her husband according to the husband's 'estate or condition'. Problematically, claims to dower could be thwarted by the husband placing his land in the names of third parties and a wife's right to be maintained was heavily restricted and difficult to enforce.[4]

In addition, the Court of Chancery provided that married women could have some of their property protected through trusts settling property for their separate use or through marriage settlements. Thus, for the rich, some of the effects of coverture could be alleviated through transferring property to trustees who would remain the owners at law but hold the property for the benefit of the wife. However, these inventions were less concerned with giving wives some financial independence than enabling fathers to protect their daughter's inheritance. The development of the restraint upon anticipation also further restricted these marriage settlements by preventing wives from alienating or charging their capital during marriage.[5]

## II. The Landmark

The campaign for reforming married women's property began in the 1850s but it is clear that many women felt the far-reaching effects of coverture before that period, as evidenced by several petitions made by wives to the Court of Requests in the late Tudor period.[6] The primary impetus for reform was the lack of protection of a wife's earnings, which under common law belonged absolutely to the husband. Although some cooperative savings banks might only allow the wife to withdraw payments, there was nothing preventing the husband suing the bank to seize these earnings, whether for his own use or to assign to his creditors. It was largely the combination of stories of high-profile women such as Sarah Siddons, a well-known actress, having their earnings seized, coupled with the stories of grave injustice in routine cases, that generated the momentum for change. The publication of Barbara Leigh Smith Bodichon's ***A Brief Summary, in Plain Language, of the Most Important Laws Concerning Women: Together With A Few Observations Thereon*** was

[4] See SN Grant-Bailey, *Lush on the Law of Husband and Wife* (4th edn, Stevens & Sons Ltd, 1933) ch 12.
[5] **Married Women (Restraint upon Anticipation) Act 1949**.
[6] See Tim Stretton, *Women Waging Law in Elizabethan England* (Cambridge University Press, 1998).

influential in explaining in an objective manner the impediments imposed upon married women by the common law.[7] Subsequently, a letter published in 1855 by Caroline Norton, a fashionable society hostess, sought the equalisation of legal treatment between married women who possessed a marriage settlement with those who did not.[8] Leigh Smith's publication was later given to the Law Amendment Society by Richard Monckton Milnes, a Liberal MP, and this assisted them in forming their 1856 Report calling for married women to have *feme sole* status over their property and contracts.

Early legislative time was spent on the issue after an attempt at introducing a Bill by Lord Henry Brougham, which was followed by another by Sir Erskine Perry that, unlike the former, passed to a second reading. Perry's Bill was quite radical in advocating not just legal recognition of separate property but rather the wife's ability to act as if she were a *feme sole*. The parliamentary debates reveal vivid examples of drunken husbands deserting wives and returning to seize their earnings. These accounts were challenged at the time by Sir John Buller who feared that foolish women, without the wise counsel of their husbands, would invest and squander property in 'worthless railway shares or in some unsound speculation'.[9] Although passing a second reading with a majority of 55 votes, the fact that the Matrimonial Causes Act 1857 had just been enacted with provisions offering some minimal protection for deserted wives meant that Perry's Bill was unlikely to proceed further. Divorce and judicial separation, which the 1857 Act provided for, were perceived as offering an *alternative* escape for women from the effects of coverture: if she were happily married, she had no need of protection; if unhappy, she could divorce.

The precursor to the 1882 Act was the Married Women's Property Act 1870 that enabled a woman to hold property for her separate use; yet a further Act was clearly required as it only related to a limited range of assets, namely, inter alia her earnings, savings bank deposits or real and personal property inherited by her through intestacy. The 1870 Act occurred around the time of two influential contributions: Frances Power Cobbe's essay 'Criminals, Idiots, Women and Minors',[10] published in 1868, and John Stuart Mill's *The Subjection of Women* published in 1869.[11] The former did not seek equality with men but systematically challenged the arguments in favour of retaining the common law position, whereas the latter called for equality between the sexes. Bringing these issues to a wider audience precipitated a series of Bills introduced in 1878, 1880 and 1881.

It was the Bill introduced into the House of Lords by Lord Selbourne that became the Married Women's Property Act 1882. As a government-backed measure, the Bill received support and its passage, according to Shanley, 'lacked drama and suspense'.[12] Nevertheless, and perhaps indicating the importance of feminist agency, Sir George Campbell lamented that 'the "women righters" had been exceedingly energetic' so much so that 'the case for

[7] In Candida Ann Lacey, *Barbara Leigh Smith Bodichon and the Langham Place Group* (Routledge and Kegan Paul, 1987) 23.

[8] Caroline Norton, 'A Letter to the Queen on Lord Chancellor Cranworth's Marriage and Divorce Bill' in Patricia Hollis, *Women in Public: The Women's Movement 1850–1900* (George Allen and Unwin, 1979) 183.

[9] HC Deb, 15 July 1857, vol 146 col 1515.

[10] Frances Power Cobbe, 'Criminals, Idiots, Women and Minors' [1868] in Susan Hamilton, *Criminals, Idiots, Women and Minors: Victorian Writing by Women on Women* (Broadview Press, 1995) 108.

[11] John Stuart Mill, *The Subjection of Women* (1st edn, Longmans, Green, Reader & Dyer, 1869).

[12] Mary Lyndon Shanley, *Feminism, Marriage, and the Law in Victorian England 1850–1895* (Princeton University Press, 1989) 124.

the poor married man was hopeless'.[13] In addition to this agency, the fact that the Liberals, many of whom were strong supporters of married women's property rights, gained control of Parliament in 1880 certainly assisted the passage of the Bill. Crucially, this Act provided that a married woman could acquire and dispose of all kinds of property 'as if she were a *feme sole* without the intervention of any trustee'.

## III. What Happened Next

It would be exaggeration to say that the Act ushered in an immediate change or brought to fruition the social revolution that many of the opponents of the Act feared. Very few women had any property to retain. In many ways, the Act was also drafted in a manner that perpetuated the status quo, yet was couched in the language of change or progression. For example, express marriage settlements where trustees held separate property for the wife were unaffected. Similarly, section 19 continued to permit the inclusion of restraints upon anticipation, thereby restricting the wife's ability to use her newly obtained property. Section 17, which enabled a judge to decide 'as he thinks fit' any question between husband and wife as to the title to or possession of property, also led to litigation enabling judges to restrictively interpret or even deny entitlements to married women in a manner fully justified by the esoteric scheme and wording of the Act.[14]

Most importantly, by insisting on 'separate property' the Act did not allow married women to hold property exactly like a man or single woman. It would have been simpler to say that marriage gave married women no entitlements or created no further impediments than what a woman would have if unmarried. Instead, by using the 'separate property' term-of-art, the level of understanding required of women regarding their own property rights was the same as that required previously in relation to the obscure and impenetrable marriage settlements.

The Act was subsequently amended in 1893, 1907, 1935, 1962 and 1969, mostly to remove lingering aspects of coverture or, alternatively, to resolve quite serious inconsistencies within the 1882 Act. For example, even after the Act's introduction, a husband remained liable for torts committed by his wife until the Law Reform (Married Women and Tortfeasors) Act 1935, and – even though married women could now enter into contracts in respect of their separate property – the general rule remained (again until the 1935 Act) that married women would not be liable under a contract.

## IV. Significance

The Married Women's Property Act 1882 is often lauded as a victory for *all* women. Referencing the early intervention of equity, Kenny evocatively noted that the Act gave 'the mangle, the teapot, and the sewing machine the same protection which diamonds and

[13] HC Deb, 11 August 1882, vol 273 col 1604.
[14] See *Gottliffe v Edelston* [1930] 2 KB 378.

consols had always purchased for themselves in the teeth of the law'.[15] To an extent, the Act can be conceptualised in this way because, as a matter of accepted fact, it did enable *all* married women to have a degree of control over their own separate property that was hitherto denied to them. This applause and optimism was inextricably bound up with hope of women's suffrage that in 1882 was now thought of as a real possibility, particularly as many women had been campaigning for both causes.

However, in many ways the actual reach of the Act, and the reform process preceding it, have been unduly romanticised by (generally male) legal historians, thereby making it appear like a triumph of equality bestowed upon women through the benevolent kindness of men. Staves has identified this narrative in the literature on the reform of married women's property, noting that 'legal history has most often been celebratory, explaining how the law was more and more beautifully adapted to the needs of society, more and more perfectly reflective of absolute justice'.[16]

A closer examination of the Act reveals that in many ways it was a watered-down concession that, despite having the appearance of radical change, indirectly enabled men to continue to control the property of women (much in the same way they had done directly through the imposition of trusts for separate use and marriage settlements). Therefore, it was neither 'a great victory of the principle of human equality over the unjust privilege of Sex'[17] nor 'the Magna Carta of women's liberties'.[18]

Viewed in isolation, the Act was not as far-reaching as it has been held to be by legal historians because, rather than recognising that marriage can often generate economic disadvantage, as vividly demonstrated by the cases highlighted in the process of reform, it adopted the more palatable and already existing language of 'separate property'. Indeed, it was far less progressive than the much earlier Perry Bill introduced in 1857. By perpetuating the language of separate property, it opted for a quick-fix and, more importantly, one where men remained the continuing arbiters controlling and determining whether property could, in fact, be deemed 'separate'. Choosing this legal construct reveals the fear of some Members of Parliament that since possession of property confers power and territory, wives with property could challenge the power-dynamics of marriage. The fact that the Act was subsequently amended on numerous occasions to chip away at the remaining vestiges of coverture is suggestive that real, as opposed to symbolic 'separate property', was begrudgingly conferred but only a long time after the Act's commencement in 1883.

Expecting more from the Act at that point in history is perhaps naïve. Women campaigning for reform primarily wanted the removal of legal impediments associated with coverture and clearly knew of the issues involved in going further by arguing that marriage could generate entitlement. As Caroline Norton revealed, women were not arguing for that 'wild and ridiculous doctrine of equality' and did not view themselves as equal.[19] Marriage was not at the time widely conceptualised as a partnership of equals. To reflect that sentiment in the Act would not only have constituted a dangerous flirtation with continental community of

[15] CS Kenny, *History of the Law of England as to the effects of Marriage on Property* (Reeves & Turner, 1879) 16. ('Consols' being 'consolidated annuities', which were irredeemable British Government securities).

[16] Susan Staves, *Married Women's Separate Property in England 1660–1833* (Harvard University Press 1990) 9.

[17] *Married Women's Property Committee Final Report* (1881) 34.

[18] Shanley, n 12 above, 124.

[19] Norton, n 8 above, 183.

property regimes, but would have severely hampered the Bill's chances of a passage through Parliament. Nevertheless, those ideas did emerge later in the twentieth century, particularly through the work of Otto Kahn-Freund who supported the introduction of a community of property.[20] Thus, it could be argued that the greatest triumph was not the actual provisions of the Act but the strategising of women lobbying for reform stretching back to the Langham Place Group. In the *English Woman's Review* article 'Property Rights of Women', published in 1859, the heresy contained within the Church of England's Marriage Service of a husband endowing a wife with all his worldly goods was forcibly challenged. The wife, as it noted, would not receive a farthing. Nevertheless, on the prospect of removing his entitlement to her property, it was said to be 'too much to expect such sweeping reform'.[21] Instead, a demand was made simply for retention of earnings acquired through the wife's labour or genius, which illustrates the incremental yet tactical and astute strategies adopted by women campaigning for separate property.

Alongside representing an achievement of feminist activism, the Act precipitated important debates in the 1940s onwards that questioned whether it should be accepted that marriage frequently generated economic disadvantage. Recognising separate property in 1882 was a crude solution and it side-stepped the bigger issue that most women had little or no property to hold. Quite ironically, this is perhaps why one provision of the Act, section 17, inserted to enable courts to determine whether property should be regarded as 'separate', was subsequently deployed as a means for women to *obtain* a share in property. Whilst that redistributive interpretation of section 17 was scotched by the House of Lords in *Pettitt v Pettitt* [1970] AC 777, the earlier litigation reveals that the 1882 Act gave this jurisdiction an important forum for a fundamental reappraisal of property holding within marriage.[22]

## Further Reading


- Rosemary Auchmuty, 'The Married Women's Property Acts: Equality was not the issue' in Rosemary Hunter (ed), *Rethinking Equality Projects in Law: Feminist Challenges* (Hart Publishing, 2008).
- Ben Griffin, 'Class, Gender, and Liberalism in Parliament, 1868–1882: The Case of the Married Women's Property Acts' (2003) 46 *The Historical Journal* 59.
- Mary Lyndon Shanley, *Feminism, Marriage, and the Law in Victorian England 1850–1895* (Princeton University Press, 1989).


[20] See Otto Kahn-Freund, 'Injustices and Inconsistencies in the Law of Husband and Wife' (1952) 15 *Modern Law Review* 135.

[21] Anon, 'Property Rights of Women' (1859) *English Woman's Journal*.

[22] See *Rimmer v Rimmer* [1952] 2 All ER 863 and *Fribance v Fribance* [1957] 1 All ER 357.

# 9

# First Woman Prospective Parliamentary Candidate, Helen Taylor, 1885

JANET SMITH

In 1885 Helen Taylor (1831–1907) became the first woman to be selected as a prospective parliamentary candidate. She was selected by Camberwell Radical Club as the Independent Radical Democrat candidate for the South London constituency of Camberwell North.[1] Taylor's candidature came 33 years before the Parliamentary (Qualification of Women) Act 1918 removed the bar on women sitting or voting in the House of Commons and the House of Lords.

## I. Life

Helen Taylor was born in 1831. Her mother, the suffragist Harriet Taylor, separated from Taylor's father in 1833 after meeting the philosopher John Stuart Mill. Taylor was educated at home in an enclosed but highly intellectual environment, amongst radicals who were determined to improve opportunities for women. In 1851 Harriet Taylor married Mill after the death of her husband. After her mother's death in 1858 Helen Taylor worked with Mill to promote women's suffrage. Mill and Taylor were among suffragists who set up the London National Society for Women's Suffrage in 1867. Following Mill's death in 1873, Taylor became an influential figure in land reform groups. She was an elected member of the London School Board (1876–85), a founder member of the Social Democratic Federation, and a supporter of Irish Home Rule. She was so well-known by the 1880s that the local press hailed her as 'the foremost women of her time'[2] on her arrival to speak in Preston on land nationalisation.

Taylor's manifesto was essentially that of the Social Democratic Federation. It demanded a six-hour working day, nationalisation of the land, graduated income tax, free elementary education, Home Rule for Ireland, universal suffrage, annual parliaments and payment of MPs. She campaigned vigorously, often facing violent hostility and fights at the hustings.[3]

[1] Letter from Camberwell Radical Club to Helen Taylor, 22 May 1885, Mill Taylor Collection (hereafter MTC), London School of Economics, file 18, no 5.

[2] *The Lancashire Evening Post*, 19 October 1886.

[3] *Lloyds Weekly Paper*, 1 November 1885.

She was branded by one opponent as 'an unsexed woman agitator'.[4] But the press acknowledged that she was likely to get a good number of votes from the working men of Camberwell, as she was popular in the borough for her work on the London School Board.[5] On the day of the submission of nomination papers, however, the Presiding Officer refused to accept hers as valid. The official maintained that under Section 4 of the Ballot Act 1872 candidates were referred to as 'his' and 'him', which excluded women. *The Standard* declared that Taylor had shown a lack of knowledge of 'the elementary rule of grammar in the differentiation between masculine and feminine genders'.[6] The *Law Journal*, however, concluded that if Taylor had taken legal advice she might well have secured her nomination. The Returning Officer might not have legally been able to reject her papers if they had been submitted by someone else, 'but she preferred boldly to avow her sex'.[7]

During the last decade of the nineteenth century Taylor withdrew from public life and, suffering from ill-health, lived mostly in Avignon, France. She died in Torquay, Devon, in 1907.

## II. Context

The Representation of the People Act 1832 excluded women from citizenship (and therefore the vote) through statute rather than, as before, by custom, by inserting the words 'male' and 'men' into the wording of the legislation.[8] Masculine pronouns were also adopted by the Representation of the People Act 1867 in spite of efforts by John Stuart Mill to persuade Parliament to amend the Bill using the word 'persons'. The Representation of the People Act 1884 extended the vote to a further tranch of men but, again, attempts by reformers to have women enfranchised on the same terms were defeated.[9]

The women's movement was active throughout this period in campaigns for votes for women. They achieved some minor successes: women were granted the right to vote in local elections under the Municipal Franchise Act 1869 and for school boards under the Education Act 1870. More importantly for Taylor's campaign, women were permitted to stand as Poor Law Guardians and School Board governors under those two statutes.

Taylor would have been aware that a woman had stood as a candidate for the US presidential election of 1872. Victoria Woodhall, the Equal Rights Party candidate, was in prison on the day of the election, for libel and for publishing an obscene article in which she claimed that a stockbroker called Challis had seduced young women. No ballot papers were issued in her name due to her imprisonment, as political parties were responsible for printing their own. Woodhall was found not guilty and took no further part in politics.[10]

[4] *Yorkshire Gazette*, 29 October 1885 and *Manchester Evening News*, 11 November 1885.

[5] *Pall Mall Gazette*, 21 November 1885.

[6] *The Standard*, 1 December 1885.

[7] *The Times*, 27 November 1885.

[8] **Representation of the People Act 1918.**

[9] Robert Blackburn, 'Laying the Foundation of the Modern Voting System: The Representation of the People Act 1918' (2011) 30(1) *Parliamentary History* 33–52, 36.

[10] Jad Adams, *Women and the Vote* (OUP, 2014) 160–69.

The basis of Taylor's claim for the right to stand for Parliament was section 4 of the Interpretation Act 1850, known as Lord Brougham's Act, which stated that 'unless expressly provided to the contrary', words importing the masculine gender would be 'deemed and taken to include female'. In claiming the right to stand for Parliament, Taylor and her supporters relied on a literal reading of this section. In 1867, however, thousands of feminists had registered to vote by arguing that this provision applied to the Representation of People Act, only to have their hopes dashed in *Chorlton v Lings*,[11] the first of a series of cases in which courts held that women were *not* persons for the purposes of the Act.[12] What these cases made clear was that the courts would look to other justifications, such as 'inveterate usage' (that is, there had only ever been male voters), for excluding women.

Nevertheless, feminists continued to make the point. Jessie Craigen, who set up the 'Miss Taylor Election Independent Aid Committee', issued an election handbill,[13] which noted that in pre-Reformation times, both Henry III and Edward III had summoned abbesses to Parliament. No statute existed, Craigen argued, to ban women from Parliament; neither was there anything in common law to forbid it.[14] The main feminist journal, the *English Women's Review*, supported Taylor's challenge but doubted it would further the women's suffrage cause. Rather, they felt it showed that '*men* shall be allowed to appoint what candidate they choose whoever that candidate might be'.[15] They also noted that the House of Lords, in *Gosling v Veley*,[16] had warned that if a woman were to be nominated as a candidate, the votes given for her would be invalid.[17]

The suffragist Alice Westlake wrote to Taylor that her candidature would be detrimental to the Women's Suffrage Bill 1885, which was due its second reading in the House of Commons. Westlake believed that Taylor should have waited until after the Bill before presenting herself as a candidate for 'we feel anxious about any step that will endanger it'.[18] Taylor, however, emphasised the importance of her campaign for women's suffrage, maintaining it would be 'a great impetus to the general advancement of women'. She believed her candidature was the only way to get the question of equal rights for women into the public domain: 'I feel I am acting as a pioneer and I expect at the next election there will be many women candidates for Parliament'.[19]

Taylor's main support from men came from the Camberwell Radical Club, whose secretary, Charles Ammon, declared that there was no statutory law against her candidature and that the 1832 Reform Act did not preclude women from standing as candidates or indeed voting.[20] As regards election candidates, he took the feminist line that the 1867 Reform Act referred to them as 'persons', which validated Taylor's candidature in the eyes of her supporters as it did not explicitly state that women were excluded. Portsmouth Radical Club sent their congratulations on her candidature, declaring 'that it will be a great step in the future

[11] *Chorlton v Lings* (1868–69) LR 4 CP 374.
[12] ***Edwards v Attorney General of Canada* (1929)**.
[13] MTC, box 7.
[14] ibid.
[15] ibid.
[16] *Gosling v Veley* (1850) 12 QB 328, 364.
[17] *English Women's Review*, 15 December 1885.
[18] Letter from Alice Westlake to Helen Taylor, 14 June 1885, MTC, file 13, no 361.
[19] ibid.
[20] *English Women's Review*, June 1885.

struggle for the equal rights of women'.[21] Taylor received the support of Social Democratic Federation colleagues and the American economist Henry George. She was also supported by many ordinary working people in Camberwell through her work on the London School Board.

Leading Irish nationalists also gave their support. Anna Parnell shared an election platform with Taylor. Parnell appealed to the Irish amongst the electorate to vote for Taylor, reminding them that Taylor had made a significant contribution to the Irish cause during the Land Wars, when tenant farmers had sought to assert their rights and to abolish the landlord system of land ownership. She had even physically erected Land League huts herself to house the evicted peasants. Michael Davitt, the founder of the Land League, also appealed to the Irish to vote for Taylor in a letter which Taylor made into a handbill.[22]

But Taylor had long been a thorn in the side of the Liberal party (as well as many in the suffrage movement) precisely because of her involvement with the Irish Land League. She had also opposed official Liberal policies on the London School Board when she had defended women teachers' employment rights and equal opportunities for girls. Many Liberals feared Taylor would split the progressive vote and allow a victory for the Conservative candidate.[23]

## III. What Happened Next

Reformers continued to argue that 'persons' legally included women in law. In 1891 the Court of Appeal heard the case of *De Souza v Cobden*[24] following the election of a woman London County Councillor who used this same argument. Miss Cobden lost; however, women gained the right to stand in local elections in 1894 under the Local Government Act.

The Parliamentary (Qualification of Women) Act 1918 finally gave women over 21 the right to sit in the House of Commons and House of Lords. In 1918 Constance Markievicz became the first woman to be elected as an MP but she did not take her seat. As a member of Sinn Fein, she sat in the rebel Irish Parliament in Dublin and resisted British rule in Ireland. Nancy Astor thus became the first woman to take her seat in the House of Commons in 1919.

Women's parliamentary representation remained woefully low throughout the twentieth century. Only 15 women were elected in 1931, 24 in 1945, 60 in 1993, 120 in 1997 and 191 in 2015.[25] The recent increase in the number of women MPs is largely a result of the **Sex Discrimination (Election Candidates) Act 2002**, which has allowed political parties to select candidates based on gender. Women have, however, exerted an influence at the heart of Government. In 1929 Margaret Bondfield became the first woman Cabinet member as Minister for Labour, and Ellen Wilkinson followed her as Minister of Education in 1945. Barbara Castle, as a Minister, improved the financial position of women through the Equal

[21] Letter from R Hale to Helen Taylor, 29 May 1885, MTC, file 18, no 60.
[22] MTC, box 7.
[23] *Sheffield Independent*, 24 October 1885.
[24] *De Souza v Cobden* [1891] 1 QB 687.
[25] This paragraph is indebted to Oonagh Gay and Richard Cracknell (eds), *Women in Parliament: Making a difference since 1918* (House of Commons Library Briefing Paper RP13-65, 2013).

Pay Act 1970, the Social Security Pensions Act 1975 and the Child Benefit Act 1975. Other influential women cabinet members have included Mo Mowlam, Harriet Harman and Margaret Beckett. Margaret Thatcher, then leader of the Conservative Party, became the first woman Prime Minister in 1979 but did not use her position to advance gender equality and proved a contentious politician. It remains to be seen what the legacy of Theresa May, who became the second woman Prime Minister in 2016, will be.

## IV. Significance

Taylor's campaign stands as a forgotten first for women. Though ultimately unsuccessful, her candidacy demonstrated that a woman (albeit one privileged by birth, social standing, connections and wealth) could secure the radical nomination as a prospective parliamentary candidate. Taylor ran a professional campaign and secured the support of men from the world of politics and economics and of working-class voters. It would be another 35 years until a woman entered the House of Commons as an MP. Taylor was a pioneer. She rightly regarded herself as a trailblazer in the fight for women's full citizenship, a view shared by the labour activist FW Soutter. Her (largely forgotten) story stands as a testimony to the fickleness of (women's) history.

## Further Reading


- Jad Adams, *Women and the Vote: A World History* (Oxford University Press, 2014).
- Joanne Conaghan, *Law and Gender* (Oxford University Press, 2013).
- June Purvis, *Women's History: Britain, 1850–1945. An Introduction* (Routledge, 1997).

# 10

# Section 5(1) of the Criminal Law Amendment Act 1885

LOIS BIBBINGS

According to the long title of the Criminal Law Amendment Act, its object was 'to make further provision for the Protection of Women and Girls, the suppression of brothels, and other purposes'.[1] Section 5(1) aimed at protecting girls from male sexual exploitation, an area of law, policy and practice which was a matter of particular concern in the last half of the nineteenth century, as it is in the early twenty-first century. It did so by raising the legal age of consent to 16 in the then United Kingdom of Great Britain and Ireland – at least in respect of unmarried girls, where the activity in question was penile-vaginal penetration ('carnal knowledge'[2] in the legal language of the time).[3]

## I. Context

Prior to the passing of the 1885 Act a number of individuals and groups had been concerned about the need to protect girls; there were fears about girls being led into prostitution and about 'white slavery',[4] worries about innocents robbed of their virginity and anxiety about seduction and sexually motivated abduction.[5]

A key figure in terms of those who wrote and spoke about the treatment of girls in matters sexual was Christian social reformer and women's rights campaigner Josephine Butler.

[1] The Act is perhaps best known for its 'criminalisation' of male homosexual acts. It created the offence of gross indecency which covered sexual acts between men that did not constitute buggery or where the latter offence could not be proved. Decriminalisation began in 1967.

[2] For a definition of 'carnal knowledge' see eg section 18 Offences Against the Person Act 1828, which provided that it required 'Proof of Penetration only.'

[3] The non-consensual offence of rape (which originally only covered penile-vaginal penetration) is not considered here.

[4] In the nineteenth century the 'white slave trade' was at first used to describe fears about the abduction of unworldly working-class country girls who, having been lured to London with promises of employment in domestic service, were then drugged and kept in brothels. Subsequently it also referred to a supposed European traffic in girls lured to the Continent.

[5] See eg Deborah Gorham, 'The "Maiden Tribute of Modern Babylon" Re-Examined: Child Prostitution and the Idea of Childhood in Late-Victorian England' (1978) 21(3) *Victorian Studies* 353.

In the 1860s–80s she focused her attention on prostitution and campaigned against the Contagious Diseases Acts of 1864, 1866 and 1869, which created an oppressive regime for many women and girls suspected of selling sex in specified locations connected to the Navy or Army; the statutes applied to England, Wales and Ireland.[6] In 1883 the Acts were suspended[7] and Butler's attention, along with that of some of her fellow campaigners, shifted to the need to protect girls from prostitution and white slavery – and to raise the age of consent for girls.

In terms of the legislative background to the 1885 Act, there had been various efforts to raise the age of consent for girls prior to 1885. For example, in 1861 Samuel Wilberforce, then Bishop of Oxford, attempted to raise the age of consent for penile-vaginal intercourse for girls, which was at this stage 12 (according to statutes in England and Wales and Ireland and under common law in Scotland).[8] These efforts received some support but were unsuccessful. Consequently, when the Offences Against the Person Act 1861, which applied to England, Wales and Ireland,[9] was passed, section 51 included the offence of 'unlawfully and carnally knowing any girl being above the age of 10 years and under the age of 12 years', leaving the age of consent unchanged – with arguments as to a girl's 'consent' to penetration being irrelevant (see, for example, *R v Ryland*[10] where a man was convicted for attempt in relation to section 51 despite a girl's supposed consent). Section 50 included the more serious equivalent offence in relation to under-10s – consent was irrelevant here too. As to mistake regarding age, the Court for Crown Cases Reserved[11] in *R v Prince*[12] was of the view that sections 50 and 51 of the 1861 Act should be read in a manner consistent with section 55, which dealt with the abduction of girls, making such a mistake irrelevant. One of the powerful statements made in the case is worth quoting, not least as the law was, unfortunately, not to remain in this protective stance towards girls for long. Here Blackburn J in the leading judgment (with which 9 out of 16 of his fellow judges concurred) said:

> It seems impossible to suppose that the intention of the legislature in those two sections [sections 50 and 51] could have been to make the crime depend upon the knowledge of the prisoner of the girl's actual age. It would produce the monstrous result that a man who had carnal

[6] In Scotland local and national measures had tended to become increasingly repressive both in relation to women identified as prostitutes and towards brothels at that time, but treatment in hospitals remained voluntary. See further, David G Barrie and Susan Broomhall, *Police Courts in Nineteenth-Century Scotland, Volume 2: Boundaries, Behaviours and Bodies* (Ashgate, 2014) 248–63.

[7] They were repealed, in large part as a result of the efforts of women's rights campaigners, by the Contagious Diseases Acts Repeal Act 1886. On opposition to them see Margaret Hamilton, 'Opposition to the Contagious Diseases Acts, 1864–1886' (1978) 10(1) *Albion: A Quarterly Journal Concerned with British Studies* 14.

[8] See the English Offences Against the Person Act 1828 section 17, the Offences Against the Person (Ireland) Act 1829 section 19 and in Scotland the offence of 'lewd, indecent and libidinous practices' which criminalised sexual conduct with pre-pubescent children – the legal age of puberty was 12 for girls and 14 for boys. See James Chalmers, 'Regulating Adolescent Sexuality: English and Scottish Approaches' (2011) 23(4) *Child and Family Law Quarterly* 450, 454.

[9] The common law in Scotland remained unchanged at this time.

[10] *R v Ryland* (1868) 11 Cox CC 101, 16 WR 941, 18 LT 538.

[11] The Court for Crown Cases Reserved heard references from trial judges on points of law post-conviction. It consisted of all the common law judges who went on circuit, presiding over the assizes around the country. Generally, cases were heard by a panel of five judges, however, in some controversial or important cases or where the judges were very much divided, the matter could be considered by the full court. *Prince* was considered to be just such an important case but only 16 of the then pool of 18 male judges were available to consider it. See Lois S Bibbings, *Binding Men: Stories about Violence and Law in Late Victorian England* (Routledge, 2014) 15–16.

[12] *R v Prince* (1875) LR 2 CCR 154; 39 JP 676.

> connection with a girl, in reality not quite ten years old, but whom he on reasonable grounds believed to be a little more than ten, was to escape altogether. He could not, in that view of the statute, be convicted of the felony, for he did not know her to be under ten. He could not be convicted of the misdemeanour, because she was in fact not above the age of ten. It seems to us that the intention of the legislature was to punish those who had connection with young girls, though with their consent, unless the girl was in fact old enough to give a valid consent. The man who has connection with a child, relying on her consent, does it at his peril, if she is below the statutable age.[13]

In 1871, alongside expressing concerns about girls tricked into prostitution, Josephine Butler had backed calls by a judge, Justice Willes, for the age of consent to penile-vaginal intercourse to be raised from 12 to 14 for girls.[14] A Private Member's Bill in 1873, entitled the Seduction Laws Amendment Bill, included a number of changes to improve the protection for girls. Amongst them was a provision which aimed to raise the age of consent. But it, too, failed to pass.[15] Shortly following this the Offences Against the Person Act 1875, which again applied to England, Wales and Ireland, repealed sections 50 and 51 of the 1861 Act and raised the age of consent for girls from 12 to 13. Section 4 made it a misdemeanour to carnally know and abuse a girl of 12 years of age 'whether with or without her consent'. The new more serious offence was included in section 3 and applied to girls under the age of 12. It seems probable that the view expressed by the majority in *Prince* continued to have authority for these provisions – as nothing to the contrary was either included in the 1875 Act or stated in the reported cases.

## II. The Landmark

In 1881 a House of Lords Select Committee Report into the issues of child prostitution and what we would now refer to as the 'trafficking' of girls for the purposes of prostitution laid the basis for the 1885 Act. The Report found that vice was widespread, especially in London, and included proposals for law reform.[16] Although much discussed, these were not destined to make a speedy passage into the statute books and kept foundering. Towards the end of March 1885 a third attempt to pass a bill based on the Report was made,[17] with the age of consent set at 16, despite previous efforts to raise it still further to 17[18] and with some arguing that it should be set at 18 or 21[19] – but its progress again seemed uncertain.[20] The fact that section 5(1), along with other provisions in the 1885 Act which aimed at protecting women and girls, came to be law was probably, as others have argued, helped by a child-prostitution-related scandal that same year.

[13] ibid, 171–72.

[14] See Josephine Butler, *The Constitution Violated. An Essay [Advocating the Repeal of the Contagious Diseases Acts 1866, 1868 and 1869]* (Edmonston and Douglas, 1871) 68, 137, 139–41.

[15] For discussions of the Bill see HC Deb, 2 April 1873, vol 215, cols 468–488.

[16] Report of the House of Lords Select Committee on the Law Relating to the Protection of Young Girls from Artifices to Induce them to Lead a Corrupt Life (1881).

[17] HL Deb, 26 March 1885, vol 296 col 621.

[18] See eg *The Times*, 27 June 1883, 11.

[19] See eg Gorham, n 5 above, 364, 365.

[20] See eg the view expressed in *The Times*, 14 April 1885, 9.

The so-called 'Maiden Tribute' revelations arose from the machinations depicted in a series of articles written by the editor of the *Pall Mall Gazette*.[21] William Thomas Stead, like Butler, had been a prominent campaigner against the Contagious Diseases Acts and was similarly concerned about the sexual exploitation of girls in the context of prostitution. Stead was determined to stage an undercover 'investigation' in order to expose the full extent of the problem already publicised by the Select Committee Report and bring about reform – but he opted for an alarming and immoral strategy to attempt this.

Headed 'The Maiden Tribute of Modern Babylon', Stead's newspaper reports purported to evidence the fact that young girls were being sold to wealthy men – and it did so in sensationalist terms. The articles had been researched by Stead, along with a number of his fellow campaigners including Butler, although the latter was not implicated in the most disturbing of his researches. Investigations included, for example, women posing as prostitutes and infiltrating brothels in order to gather information, as well as attempts to purchase children for the purposes of prostitution. However, it was felt by Stead that something more concrete and more dramatic was needed. He decided to buy a girl from her parents and create the impression that he had had sexual relations with her. The girl in question, Eliza Armstrong, was 13 when she was purchased from her mother at Stead's behest. Although she was told that Eliza would be going into service as a maid, it was assumed that the mother was aware that prostitution was the real purpose. Stead had the girl's virginity confirmed by a midwife and then she was then taken to a brothel, where she was drugged and placed in a bedroom. There, Stead created the impression that the girl had been acquired for him and that sexual activity had occurred. This story was then published as part of the 'Maiden Tribute' articles, with the details changed so that Armstrong was given a pseudonym and Stead's identity as the man for whom she was apparently bought was hidden. Reaction to the articles was considerable in terms of the general public, but it also had the effect of uniting the diverse groups who were already campaigning around the linked issues of child prostitution, the protection of girls from male sexual exploitation and, in particular, the age of consent for girls.

The story was published in early July 1885 as the age of consent measure progressed through Parliament. In early July campaigners, including Butler, made good use of the 'Maiden Tribute', keeping up the pressure for, amongst other things, the age of consent to be raised.[22] Discussion in the Houses included mention of the *Gazette* revelations and concern as to whether the Bill when enacted would be adequate to deal with the problems the reports highlighted.[23] On 14 August 1885 the Bill passed and the age of consent in relation to girls for penetrative sex was raised to 16 in England, Wales, Scotland and the then united Ireland.

Section 5(1) provided that 'any person' who '[u]nlawfully knows or attempts to have unlawful carnal knowledge of any girl being of or above the age of 13 years and under the age of sixteen years' was guilty of a misdemeanour and could be sentenced to up to two years imprisonment, with or without hard labour. The measure only applied to activity occurring

[21] 6 July 1885, 1–6; 7 July 1885, 1–6; 8 July 1885, 1–5; 10 July 1885, 1–6.
[22] See eg '"Modern Babylon" – Meeting in Exeter Hall', *Pall Mall Gazette*, 17 July 1885, 11.
[23] See eg report of an exchange in the House of Commons in *The Times*, 11 July 1885, 8.

outside lawful wedlock.[24] The question of the girl's apparent consent was irrelevant because of her age. The 'Maiden Tribute' revelations were not enough, however, to prevent the inclusion of provision for mistake as to age. The defendant could be acquitted if he was able to satisfy the court that, despite the fact that the girl was in fact younger, he had 'reasonable cause to believe that the girl was above the age of sixteen years.' Consequently, *Prince* held no sway in relation to section 5(1). Section 4 created the equivalent offence where the girl was aged 12 or under, and here the offence was more serious and both consent and mistake as to age were irrelevant.

The impact of the Stead articles continued, however, most notably with a huge demonstration in Hyde Park on 22 August 1885 demanding enforcement of the new legislation, calling for the 'Protection of Young Girls' and expressing concerns about the abuse of girls by the wealthy.[25]

## III. What Happened Next

In the period from 1885 to the time of writing in early 2018 there have been a number of key developments in relation to the age of consent in the different and shifting jurisdictions of the United Kingdom. For example, in England and Wales the Criminal Law Amendment Act 1922 repealed the provision as to mistakes of age and replaced it with a so-called 'young man's defence', making a mistaken belief that a girl was over 16 a defence to the section 5(1) offence where a man of 23 or younger had 'reasonable cause to believe the girl was over the age of sixteen years' but only on 'the first occasion on which he is charged'.[26] Today in England and Wales the age of consent remains fixed at 16 (for penile-vaginal intercourse along with other forms of sexual activity – and this age now applies to all children), with the distinction between children aged under 13 and 13, 14 and 15-year-olds maintained. The Sexual Offences Act 2003 contains a long list of sexual offences against children and young people, encompassing far more than was envisioned as being criminal at the time of the 1885 Act. Section 9 criminalises sexual activity with a child under 16 – this is the closest equivalent to section 5(1) of the 1885 Act. A person aged 18 or over is guilty of the offence if they intentionally sexually touch (with sexual touching including but not limited to various forms of penetration) a person under the age of 16. Here the prosecution must prove that accused did not reasonably believe that the victim was 16 or over. However, where the offence is committed against a victim under the age of 13 reasonable belief about their age is not relevant. 'Consent' is, of course, irrelevant in both instances. Child sexual offences committed by under 18s (including conduct that would constitute 'sexual activity with a child' under section 9 if committed by an adult) are criminalised by section 13 which provides for lower penalties for such offenders.

[24] The marriageable age was taken to be the legal age of puberty (12 for girls and 14 for boys) until the Age of Marriage Act 1929 in England, Wales and Scotland and until the Age of Marriage Act (Northern Ireland) 1951 in Northern Ireland.

[25] See further, Gorham, n 5 above, 361; Judith R Walkowitz, *City of Dreadful Delight: Narratives of Sexual Danger in Late-Victorian* (University of Chicago Press, 1992) 104–05.

[26] Section 2 of the Criminal Law Amendment Act 1922.

In Scotland, developments in English law have not been generally applied (although the young man's defence was) and for a time there was an, in places, confusing mix of common law and statute. The law was then consolidated in the Criminal Law (Consolidation) (Scotland) Act 1995.[27] Today this area is governed by the Sexual Offences (Scotland) Act 2009. As in England and Wales, the Act includes a long list of sexual offences against children and continues to make a distinction between offences committed against under 13s and those aged 13–15, with the age of consent maintained at 16 in relation to penile penetrative and orogenital contact, although it has been argued that an age of consent of 13 essentially applies in some circumstances for other forms of sexual contact.[28] Section 28, which criminalises intentional or reckless intercourse (penetration of the vagina, anus or mouth with the defendant's penis) with an 'older child', is the descendant of section 5(1). There is no need to establish an absence of consent as the offence is committed regardless of whether or not the child 'consents'. However, a defendant can claim reasonable belief that the victim was 16 as a possible defence (section 39) – but the offence can only be committed by someone aged 16 or above. Such conduct involving 'older children' is provided for in sections 37 and 38. Section 37 creates the offences of intentionally or recklessly 'engaging while an older child in sexual conduct with or towards another older child' and 'engaging while an older child in consensual sexual conduct with another older child', meaning that two teenagers who engage in intercourse involving penetration of the vagina, anus or mouth could, in some circumstances, both be liable to be convicted of an offence.[29] Consent in this context is defined in section 38.

In (what was to become) Northern Ireland, the 1885 Act continued to apply, albeit with amendments. There were some changes in relation to the sections 5 and 4 offences, most notably in 1923 when the reasonable belief as to age provision in section 5(1) was removed[30] and in 1950 when the age of consent in relation to section 5(1) was raised to 17,[31] and this remained the law until the twenty-first century.[32] Now the Sexual Offences (Northern Ireland) Order 2008 harmonises sexual offences law in the North with that in England and Wales. In particular, it lowered the age of consent from 17 to 16 – with this applying to all sexual activity. The relevant section numbers differ, however. Articles 16 and 20 mirror sections 9 and 13 of the 2003 English and Welsh measure.

## IV. Significance

Section 5(1) of the 1885 Act marked a major legal advance in efforts to protect girls – at least when it came to the letter of the law. And, despite a period of difference in Northern Ireland, 16 is still the age of consent for penile-vaginal intercourse within the UK. The notion of 'mistake' or 'reasonable belief' in relation to age has also endured in cases involving 'older child' victims, despite both the beginnings of efforts to responsibilise sexual behaviour in

[27] See further Chalmers, n 8 above.
[28] ibid.
[29] ibid.
[30] Section 2 of the Criminal Law Amendment Act (Northern Ireland) 1923.
[31] Section 13 of the Children and Young Persons Act (Northern Ireland) 1950.
[32] On the evolution of the law see further Lord Kerr in *R v Brown (Northern Ireland)* [2013] UKSC 43, [3]–[13].

other contexts[33] and an acceptance that '[w]hen the child is under 13 … [the accused] takes the risk that she may be younger than he thinks she is. The object is to make him take responsibility for what he chooses to do'.[34] Reasonable belief, it seems, is also a legacy of the 1885 Act.

But some things have changed. Conceptions of the child and thinking around sex, sexuality and equality have shifted – and the figure of the teenager has emerged. Now, sexual offences legislation attempts to encompass a wider range of sexual activity than was envisaged in the latter years of the nineteenth century, it applies to and seeks to protect both girls and boys and is now attempting to grapple with consensual teenage sexual experimentation.

However, there are also similarities which might be drawn between the background to and context of the raising of the age of consent in section 5(1) and the present day. Indeed, debates around section 5(1) and, more broadly, the issue of male exploitation of girls, take on a different significance and a horrifyingly familiar hue in the light of revelations such as those relating to the sexual abuse of large numbers of girls in Rochdale.[35] Although some of the terminology might have shifted, the issues are all too similar: predatory males, white slavery, grooming, sexually motivated abduction, girls being lured into prostitution, the exploitation of the vulnerable. And there were other disturbing ideas then that seem to persist now, including notions of a knowing or even predatory sort of young female sexuality, sexually 'precocious' girls, girls taking advantage of men, and girl prostitutes.

In this context, it seems facile but is nevertheless important to say that, whilst criminal law reforms which attempt to address these issues are important, changes to law alone do not alter attitudes and behaviours. Moreover, it is social attitudes which lead to these kinds of offences being committed (then and now), that result in girls (and boys) continuing to be preyed upon by men (and sometimes women) and that lead to the letter of the law being under- or unenforced.

## Further Reading


- Lois S Bibbings, *Binding Men: Stories about Violence and Law in Late Victorian England* (Routledge, 2014) chapter 1.
- James Chalmers, 'Regulating Adolescent Sexuality: English and Scottish Approaches' (2011) 23(4) *Child and Family Law Quarterly* 450.
- Deborah Gorham, 'The "Maiden Tribute of Modern Babylon" Re-Examined: Child Prostitution and the Idea of Childhood in Late-Victorian England' (1978) 21(3) *Victorian Studies* 353.
- House of Commons Home Affairs Select Committee, *Child Sexual Exploitation and the Response to Localised Grooming* (HC 68-I [Incorporating HC 182, 2012–13], 10 June 2013).
- Louise A Jackson, *Child Sexual Abuse in Victorian England* (Routledge, 2000).


[33] See eg Jane Scoular and Maggie O'Neill, 'Legal Incursions into Supply/Demand: Criminalising and Responsibilising the Buyers and Sellers of Sex in the UK' in Vanessa Munro and Marina Della Giusta, (eds), *Demanding Sex: Critical Reflections on the Regulation of Prostitution* (Ashgate, 2008) 13–34.

[34] Lady Hale in *R v G (Secretary of State for the Home Department intervening)* [2008] UKHL 37, [46].

[35] See eg House of Commons Home Affairs Select Committee, *Child Sexual Exploitation and the Response to Localised Grooming* (HC 68-I [Incorporating HC 182, 2012–13], 10 June 2013).

# 11

# Match Women's Strike, 1888

JACQUELINE LANE

The strike by match-workers, who were predominantly women, at the Bryant and May factory in Bow, East London, was an unprecedented, mass reaction to the appalling working conditions, low wages and illnesses caused by the use of the cheaper white phosphorus in the match-making process. It has been widely chronicled. Much of its notoriety can be attributed to its largely female participants and their suffering, but it was also a landmark in that legislative improvements to protect women in the workplace soon followed. Furthermore, the strike demonstrated that women could play a key role in gaining important rights through collective workplace bargaining.

## I. Context

In 1888, Bryant & May was the largest British employer of match-workers and of female casual labour in the East End of London. It had taken over rival factories, allowing it to reduce wages to lower than they had been 12 years previously. It claimed to be paying 10 to 12 shillings a week to 'steady' workers in 1876, but in 1888 the strike register showed women earning just four shillings a week.[1]

Late-nineteenth-century life in the East End of London was generally one of extreme poverty, deprivation and overpopulation. Wages were low, and workers were expected to work long hours in dire conditions in order to fuel the obsessive power of the Victorian capitalist classes. John Charlton notes that a number of conditions came together at this time which helped to explain the rise in strikes among unskilled workers. 'There were the basic facts of exploitation and oppression, both longer term and immediate shifts in the economy, and the birth and activity of the new socialist movement.' He also considered that the presence of a large Irish community in London, many of them refugees from the Great Famine, acted as a 'special ingredient'.[2] Society was still fundamentally patriarchal. Those who had the power – husbands and fathers – held sway over the women in their familial

[1] Louise Raw, *Striking a Light: The Bryant and May Matchwomen and their Place in History* (Continuum, 2011) 97.

[2] John Charlton, *It Just Went Like Tinder: The Mass Movement and New Unionism in Britain* (Redwords, 1999) 58.

circle, while employers and politicians were almost exclusively men. Similarly, the emerging craft unions were predominately a male preserve. In contrast, the match-workers' strike involved a predominantly young (largely teenage), non-unionised – and crucially – female workforce. The so-called 'match girls' at the centre of the strike were described by Charles Booth, reflecting the Victorian middle-class view of the working class as either feckless or victims, as 'a rough set of girls' in terms of both their class and their behaviour.[3] The persuasive language of 'girls' in discussions of the Bow match-worker's strike – as in so many other contexts – is revealing of representations of women in history.

As Lyn Brown MP put it on the 125th anniversary of the strike,

> Much of the telling of events at Bryant & May's factory has referred to match 'girls' and has presented a sentimentalised vision of young, helpless souls, dependent on the protection of others – who are, of course, older, wiser and 'better' men, as, in the main, are the historians who tell their stories. So today let us tell it as it was. Those workers were women with a fight on their hands to determine their own fate. Yes, some were young; all were working-class; many were … of Irish extraction; but they were women, not girls.[4]

In fact, Alice Francis, Kate Slater, Mary Driscoll, Jane Wakeling and Eliza Martin, the five women on the list of 'troublemakers' identified by Bryant and May, were 'capable, popular and charismatic [leaders] … earn[ing] the respect of colleagues, and sufficiently indomitable to have stood up to their employers in the cause of what they believed was right'.[5]

There had been previous political action by match-workers. In 1871, they protested outside Parliament, following the introduction of a match tax which threatened jobs. In 1882, the workers had attacked a statute of Liberal Prime Minister, William Gladstone, on Bow Road.

## II. The Landmark

In the early afternoon on or around 2 July 1888, around 1,400 Bryant and May factory workers came out on strike. The strike was sparked by the dismissal of (at least) one match-worker who was alleged to have fed information to the Fabian Society socialist, Annie Besant, about their working conditions. Other accounts suggest that there were three workers. Louise Raw cites from Besant's journal in which she wrote of three girls.[6] Besant was 'a phenomenon: a pioneer of pioneers', whose 'commitment to social betterment was certainly a cornerstone of her character', and whose 'energy and courage were of an extraordinary order'.[7] Though the Fabian Society, founded in 1884 by leading socialist thinkers Beatrice and Sidney Webb and George Bernard Shaw, had 'little interest in trade unions as vehicles for class struggle',[8] it used tactics such as boycotts or exposés of working conditions to embarrass unscrupulous employers. These become the hallmark of Besant's actions. However, in fact, though

[3] Raw, n 1 above, 47.
[4] 'Bow Match Women's Strike', HC Deb, 8 October 2013, 22WH.
[5] Raw, n 1 above, 223.
[6] ibid 130.
[7] Rosemary Dinnage, *Annie Besant* (Penguin, 1986) 12.
[8] Raw, n 1 above, 7.

Besant is inexorably linked to the 1888 strike, she was not in favour of direct action.[9] As Lyn Brown MP noted, drawing on the work of Louise Raw in a House of Common debate on the strike in October 2013:

> It is true that [Besant's] journalism and political activity played a pivotal role in the tale of the match women and the events that they precipitated. However, to present her role as one of leadership of the strike is to fall into the trap of seeing history solely from the perspective of the middle-class storyteller, and it frankly does not reflect the reality of the events as they unfolded. The women went against the advice of Annie Besant, who felt that they should not strike.[10]

At a meeting of the Society on 15 June 1888, Besant had listened to a talk about the situation of the workers at the Bryant and May factory. The owners of the factory and shareholders were enjoying large profits while paying their employees as little as four shillings a week – a fact that had come to light thanks to the evidence given to the enquiry of a House of Lords' Select Committee on sweated labour by Reverend Mr Adamson, the vicar of the parish of Old Ford where a number of the match-workers lived.[11] A resolution was moved and carried unanimously that the members would not purchase or use any matches manufactured by Bryant and May.

Besant went to the factory to speak to the workers. She discovered that the workers were subjected to long hours, while their poor wages were further reduced by a complex system of fines. Other workers suffered life-changing physical injuries or from the debilitating condition, necrosis of the jaw – so-called 'phossy jaw' – caused by the white phosphorus used in the match-making process and the lack of hand-washing and separate eating facilities. The phosphorus was absorbed through skin contact, inhalation or contaminated food. Besant subsequently published an exposé of the working conditions in the factory in *The Link* titled, 'White Slavery in London',[12] observing that 'chattel slaves' could not have been fed, clothed and housed for just four shillings a week.

> But who cares for the fate of these white wage slaves? Born in slums, driven to work while still children, undersized because underfed, oppressed because helpless, flung aside as soon as worked out, who cares if they die or go on the streets, provided only that the Bryant and May shareholders get their 23 per cent, and Mr Theodore Bryant can erect statues and buy parks? Oh if we had but a people's Dante, to make a special circle in the Inferno for those who live on this misery, and suck wealth out of the starvation of helpless girls.[13]

Shortly afterwards, three match-workers who had supplied information to Besant were dismissed as an act of revenge 'for the exposure of their iniquities'.[14]

Although the women were not formally unionised at this time, the workers came out on strike in support of their sacked colleague(s), first walking out on or around 2 July.

[9] ibid 136.

[10] 'Bow Match Women's Strike', n 4 above, 22WH–23WH.

[11] Louise Raw, 'Striking a Light: Bryant and May revisited' in Mary David (ed), *Class and Gender in British Labour History: Renewing the Debate of Starting it?* (Merlin Press, 1981) 155.

[12] Annie Besant, 'White Slavery in London', *The Link: A Journal for the Servants of Man*, 23 June 1888. *The Link*, co-founded by newspaper editor and campaigner WT Stead and Besant, regularly 'attacked sweated labour, extortionate landlords, unhealthy workshops, child labour and prostitution' (Dinnage, n 7 above, 63). The newspaper was described by Besant herself as 'a real light in the darkness' where 'petty injustices inflicted on the poor found voice': Annie Besant, *Annie Besant: An Autobiography* (Dossier Press, 1933), chapter XIV.

[13] *The Link*, ibid.

[14] Annie Besant, 'How Messrs. Bryant and May fight', *The Link*, 7 July 1888, 2.

An offer to reinstate the dismissed woman was not enough, for 'the spirit of revolt against cruel oppression had been aroused'.[15] The women demanded proper washrooms, regular lunch breaks and separate eating facilities in order to protect themselves from the effects of the white phosphorus. Besant was undeterred. As publicity grew, she openly confronted the factory owners, criticising them as 'cowards' for bullying their employees and suggesting that they sue her for libel. At the same time the Fabian Society set up a hardship fund to help any workers who were similarly dismissed.

As the strike continued, it caught the public imagination, no doubt in part because Bryant and May was a household name. It became the subject of questions in Parliament.[16] Charles Bradlaugh MP asked the Secretary of State for the Home Department

> whether he is aware that certain employees have been dismissed immediately after giving information of breaches of the law; and, if this be true, whether he will give directions to the Public Prosecutor to take proceedings in order to punish such an attempt to defeat the ends of justice by terrorising witnesses?[17]

Donations continued to swell the hardship fund, with one supporter reported as having sent 200 pink roses for the strikers to wear as badges.[18] Sympathy for the workers was not universal, however. On 13 July *The Times* reported in somewhat fatalistic tones that:

> The strike of the employees of Messrs Bryant and May has assumed another phase. Yesterday morning the usual outdoor meeting on the Mile-end waste was finally abandoned, Mr Charrington having placed his small hall at the disposal of the girls … Many of them appear to look upon the chance of being taken on again at the works as hopeless … The managers of the company remain firm, and there seems but little hope of terms being arranged.[19]

The next day it continued on the same theme, describing how the women would eventually have to find work elsewhere,

> a dismal prospect, but such as this almost certainly the end of a strike entered upon with inadequate resources and at the instigation of agitators who make it the business of their lives to sow discord between employers and employed.[20]

*The Times* put the blame for the match-workers' action squarely on the Fabian Society – 'those pests of the modern industrial world' – for bringing the quarrel to a head and egging the women on to strike.[21]

In fact, although undoubtedly encouraged by Besant, it was the women's own solidarity and forthrightness which led to the strike and which would eventually force the employer to make significant improvements at work. Over the course of around 16 days, the women organised large rallies and protests in parks around London.

On 18 July 1888 the strike came to an end, following intervention by the London Trades Council (LTC),[22] which had met with the Bryant and May directors alongside the Match

[15] 'The match girls on strike. Bryant and May interviewed', *The East London Observer*, 14 July 1888, 5.
[16] HC Deb, 6 July 1888, vol 328 cols 563–565.
[17] ibid.
[18] *East London Advertiser*, 14 July 1888.
[19] *The Times*, 13 July 1888.
[20] *The Times*, 14 July 1888.
[21] ibid.
[22] The willingness of the LTC to do this is notable. As a body which represented skilled craftsmen, it was usually reluctant to support the endeavours of unskilled workers.

Girls Strike Committee.[23] The company made a number of concessions, agreeing to abolish deductions for paints, brushes and stamps and to provide separate eating facilities, and that no employee would be dismissed for taking part in the strike. Most importantly, in a move to try and prevent further damaging strikes by permitting the workers the opportunity to negotiate peacefully in future without the glare of publicity, it was agreed that 'the firm will view with satisfaction the formation of an organised trade union among the employees in order that any just grievances they may have in future be represented directly to the heads of the firm'.[24] The Union of Women Matchmakers was quickly established, with Besant as its secretary.[25]

The speed of the employers' capitulation caught some by surprise. On the same day, *The Times* published a letter written by the directors of Bryant and May the day before (the same day as the meeting with the LTC), refuting all allegations of poor wages and unfair deductions.[26] The resolution of the strike is testimony to the good work of the LTC and the willingness of the workers to accept the concessions.

However, the strike had clearly drawn public attention to working conditions of factory workers and other 'sweated labour' in Victorian Britain as well as the power of collective resistance. A couple of days later, the LTC published a letter warning

> The moral outcome of the dispute … will be poor indeed unless the matchmakers and all of us keep in view the labour question as a whole … There is a line of cheapness below which nothing but degradation to the workers is a result without advantage to the consumers … the insatiable demand for the lowest price, irrespective of methods or consequences, is the curse of the modern industrial life.[27]

Clementina Black, Secretary of the Women's Protective and Provident League (WPPL), who had 'helped with the heavy work' supporting the strike,[28] wrote to *The Times* emphasising 'the importance of promoting among these match-makers trade organization of an efficient nature' and that the WPPL was to be instrumental in helping them to set up a union which would ensure that the position of the match-makers would be 'materially and permanently improved'. She was in no doubt that the public was now convinced 'that the want of a proper trade organization among them inevitably tends to the existence of conditions of employment in every respect unjust and oppressive'.[29]

## III. What Happened Next

An early victory for the Bryant and May match-workers was the abolition of the system of fines. Just 13 days after the publication of her white slavery article, Besant reported that a factory inspector had visited the factory to enforce the Truck Act 1831, which declared such fines to be illegal.[30]

[23] *The Times*, 18 July 1888.
[24] ibid.
[25] The union changed its name to the Matchworkers' Union by the end of 1888 and admitted male workers and continued until 1903.
[26] *The Times*, 18 July 1888.
[27] *The Times*, 20 July 1888.
[28] Besant, *Annie Besant: An Autobiography*, n 12 above, chapter XIV.
[29] *The Times*, 23 July 1888.
[30] Besant, n 14 above.

Following the strike, the first women factory inspectors were appointed. The position of Factory Inspector had been established by the Factories Act 1833. The (feminist) Society for Promoting the Employment of Women (SPEW) and, later, the WPPL 'lobbied sporadically for the appointment of female inspectors to enforce protective legislation regarding women workers'.[31] Gertrude Tuckwell, the first woman magistrate in London, also lobbied on behalf of the Women's Trade Union League for women factory inspectors,[32] while the Trades Union Congress had supported the appointment of women inspectors since 1878. In 1893 Kensington Vestry took 'a very bold decision' to advertise to take on two Women Inspectors of Workrooms to ensure compliance with the factory legislation, which at this time covered 'over-crowding, lighting, ventilation and sanitary conditions'.[33] Lucy Deane Streatfeild, a civil servant and member of the National Union of Women's Suffrage Societies, and Rose Squire were the first two women to hold such positions.

As for the use of the dangerous white phosphorus, which had played no small part in propelling the match-workers into strike action, the Berne Convention banned the use of the toxic chemical in 1906, although it was not until the end of 1910 that it finally became illegal to use in Britain.

Finally, the match-workers' strike acted as an – often under-acknowledged – catalyst for the Great Dock Strike the following year, which mobilised thousands of male dock-workers bringing the docks of London to a standstill. John Burns, the strike's leader, urged a mass meeting of tens of thousands of strikers to 'stand shoulder to shoulder. Remember the match women who won their fight and formed a union'.[34]

## IV. Significance

Sidney and Beatrice Webb described the match-workers' victory as the turning over of 'a new leaf in Trade Union annals'; that 'it was a new experience for the weak to succeed' and that 'the lesson was not lost on other workers'.[35] Although for many years trade unions remained a predominantly male preserve – in 1914 just 10 per cent of women workers were unionised[36] – the strike stands out as a watershed in the evolution of feminist organisation, campaigning and solidarity. It demonstrated that women too could be successful in bargaining with their employers for improved conditions, and sparked a radical change in the way that unions formed. Through the combined efforts of the match-workers and the socialists, most notably the Fabian Society, the Social Democratic Federation and the Socialist League, it realised the power of collective organisation, demonstrating that uniting together in a common cause could bring about improvements in the workplace, a revolution in trade unionism and, in time, legislative action.

[31] Ruth Livesey, 'The Politics of Work: feminism, professionalization and women inspectors of factories and workshops' (2004) 13(2) *Women's History Review* 233.

[32] **First Women Justices of the Peace, 1919.**

[33] Pat Pleasance, 'Lucy Deane Streatfeild' in *These Dangerous Women, 1915–2015* (Women's International League for Peace and Freedom, 2015) 55.

[34] Raw, n 1 above, 15.

[35] Beatrice Webb and Sidney Webb, *The History of Trade Unionism* (Longmans, Green & Co, 1898).

[36] 'Setting the workers alight: the East End Match Girls' Strike' (BBC Legacies, no date).

The strike also impacted on the parliamentary landscape. Speaking in the 2013 House of Commons debate on the Bow Match Women's Strike, Diana Johnson MP declared:

> The match women's strike has never been given the prominence that it deserves. Their self-organisation has been overlooked and their bravery has never been properly recognised, but if it had not been for them winning their strike in 1888, it is possible that many of us here today, especially the Labour women MPs, would not be Members of Parliament and speaking in the House of Commons.[37]

## Further Reading

- Mary Drake McFeely, 'The Lady Inspectors: Women at Work 1893–1921' (1986) 36 *History Today* 11.
- Louise Raw, *Striking a Light: The Bryant and May Matchwomen and their Place in History* (Continuum, 2011).
- *Pall Mall Gazette*, 16 July 1888, issue 7279; 17 July 1888, issue 7280.
- Christine Wheeldon, '"Pioneers in the Corridors of Power": Women Civil Servants at the Board of Trade and the Factory Inspectorate, 1893–1919' (Unpublished thesis, Goldsmiths College, University of London, 2014).

[37] 'Bow Match Women's Strike', n 4 above, 28WH.

# 12

## *R v Jackson* (1891)

TERESA SUTTON

Edmund Jackson was a spurned and desperate man. After his wife, Emily, refused to live with him, Jackson violently abducted her and imprisoned her in his home in order to forcibly persuade her to change her mind. Emily Jackson's family obtained a writ of habeas corpus as a means of releasing her. Before the Court of Appeal, Edmund Jackson justified his actions claiming that

> if a wife refuses to live with her husband, he has the right by law to take possession of her person by force, and keep her, not imprisoned, but confined, till she consents to do so in order to prevent her from permanently withdrawing her society from him.[1]

The Court of Appeal held that there was no such right. No English subject had the right to imprison another person regardless of whether they were their wife or not.[2]

*R v Jackson* has long been recognised as a Victorian landmark case for married women. In legal terms the case turned on a writ of habeas corpus, whereby the court requires a party who has detained someone to bring that person before the court so the legality of the detention can be examined. In everyday terms *Jackson* involved a private domestic dispute. It began with an unhappy and abusive marriage. It ended as a landmark for all married women and authority for the – now perhaps obvious – proposition that a man cannot abduct and detain a woman simply because she is married to him.

## I. Context

*Jackson* may be seen as an outworking of the concept of marital unity during which a wife was under coverture or subordinate to her husband. One of the starkest historical spectacles of married women being regarded as the property of their husbands was the practice of wife-selling. This was fictionalised in Thomas Hardy's *Mayor of Casterbridge* in which a drunk husband declares; 'I don't see why men who have got wives and don't want 'em, shouldn't get rid … Why shouldn't they put 'em up and sell 'em by auction to men who are in need of such articles?'[3] The practice of wife-selling continued into the nineteenth

[1] *R v Jackson* [1891] 1 QB 671, 674.

[2] ibid 681.

[3] Thomas Hardy, *The Mayor of Casterbridge* (revised edn, Macmillan, 1964 [1886]) 8.

century, aided, in part, by the common law legal fiction of coverture; that is that in the eyes of the law 'the very being or legal existence of the woman is suspended during the marriage, or at least is incorporated and consolidated into that of the husband'.[4]

There was little practical legal escape for a woman like Emily Jackson, who wished to end a violent or unsatisfactory marriage. The **Divorce and Matrimonial Causes Act 1857** had established a new Court for Divorce and Matrimonial Causes. But given the costs and huge difficulties in doing so, it is no surprise that Emily Jackson did not attempt to formally end her marriage even after her abduction. Emily Jackson's upper middle class status, her independent means and the support of her family enabled her to simply refuse to live with her husband. Her last will described herself as married to Edmund Jackson.[5]

The new legislation offered no solution for Edmund Jackson either. He initially tried to rely on the remedy of a decree of restitution of conjugal rights. When his wife ignored this there was no formal way forward for him. The Matrimonial Causes Act 1884 had abolished any punitive powers of the courts for contempt of such an order. Edmund Jackson was focused on enforcing his own rights within the marriage as he perceived them. In so doing, he has been described as 'exhibiting classic batterer behaviour', motivated by a determination to have his wife 'by any and all means'.[6]

The story of the Jackson marriage is far from the romanticised Victorian ideal. Both parties were in their forties when they met. Emily Jackson was living with her unmarried sister and suffering from ill-health. Edmund Jackson was an older gentleman of limited means and enigmatic career. Against the backdrop of the normality of marriage for women at this time, for Emily Jackson to be of this age – without the prospect of marriage and without a chosen reason to be a spinster – would have signified failure.[7] However, even at the time, the case was somewhat of a cause célèbre. After the legal case had concluded both parties published their own accounts or personal defences. Emily Jackson's consisted of a series of published newspaper articles and letters. Edmund Jackson wrote and published a book, titled *True Story*.[8] Both records show that the courtship was far from a whirl-wind romance. Their relationship appears to have been uncertain, faltering and lacking commitment, and was discouraged by Emily Jackson's sisters.

## II. The Landmark

Edmund and Emily Jackson were married on 5 November 1887 at St Paul's Church in Blackburn. Emily Jackson's family were unaware of the wedding until she returned home that evening. Edmund Jackson left her that day to prepare to travel to New Zealand to make a new home for them both. Emily Jackson agreed to follow on and join her husband in New Zealand once he had things in order. The increasingly agitated correspondence

[4] William Blackstone, *Commentaries on the Laws of England* vol 1 (Oxford, Clarendon Press, 1765) 430.

[5] Emily Jackson died on 21 March 1898 and probate was granted on 2 December 1898.

[6] Kristin Kaslem, 'Looking for Law in All the Wrong Places: Outlaw Texts and Early Women's Advocacy' (2004) 13(2) *Southern California Review of Law & Women's Studies* 273, 289.

[7] Jane Lewis, *Women in England* (Harvester Wheatsheaf, 1984) 3.

[8] Edmund Jackson, *The True Story of the Clitheroe Abduction or Why I Ran Away With My Wife* (North-East Lancashire Printing and Publishing Co, 1891).

between them shows that relations gradually soured as Emily Jackson reflected on her own position, changed her mind about travelling to New Zealand and grew in resentment at her husband's unexpected requests for financial help. By the time that Edmund Jackson had returned from New Zealand in 1888 she had decided that she would not live with him. Describing a meeting with her husband, Emily Jackson writes: 'I said I wished him to hear from my own lips that I had made up my mind, uninfluenced by my friends, not to live with him in consequence of his conduct to me.' She told him that she would 'afraid to live with him.'[9]

Edmund Jackson took matters into his own hands on Sunday 8 March 1891. In his *True Story* account he writes:

> Was I going quietly to submit to the extraordinary course which she had elected to take? No! … I was advised at the time – and this I still assert – that I was perfectly within my rights in carrying my wife off so.[10]

As Emily Jackson left the Sunday service at Clitheroe Parish Church, Edmund Jackson and his companions seized her, forced her into his carriage and abducted her. It was a very public and humiliating display of control by violence made worse by that fact that Emily Jackson held the position of patron of that Church. In her story, *Vindication*, Emily Jackson writes:

> He seized me very roughly by the arm and said 'You are my wife, come with me'. I said that I would not, and clung to my sister as well as I could, calling her to hold me fast and prevent him from taking me away. The struggle that ensured was very violent … From the rough handling I received in the struggle I felt sore all over my body for several days; my chest was very painful, my arms were very much bruised and swollen, and were black and blue from the shoulders to the elbows and discoloured, and finger marks and swelling were seen by the doctor a month afterwards.[11]

Emily Jackson feared she was being taken to an asylum, but instead the carriage travelled to Rover Street in Blackburn where Emily Jackson was detained and guarded until produced in court in response to the writ of habeas corpus. During the detention she was not allowed any contact with her family, doctor or lawyer. In the early stages of the detention there was further intimidation and violence. Emily Jackson writes that she was threatened with having her neck screwed round 'like a chicken's' if she did not do as her husband said and was told that he would detain her 'for ever if necessary'.[12]

However, Edmund Jackson had underestimated the legal background of his wife's family. They immediately began criminal proceedings for assault, and their physical protests and the police presence drew fervent press attention. Emily Jackson's family's application for a writ of habeas corpus came before the High Court on 16 March 1891 and was rejected. Mr Justice Cave said that to allow the application would

> tend to unsettle the lady's mind, and make her believe that the Court was going to do what the Court will not do – remove her from her husband's custody – upon no ground whatever, except that she does not like to live with him.[13]

[9] *The Times*, 23 April 1891, 12.
[10] Jackson, n 8 above, 26.
[11] *The Times*, n 9 above, 12.
[12] ibid.
[13] Law Report, High Court of Justice, Queen's Bench Division, 16 March (*The Times*, 17 March 1891).

The Jackson family appealed to the Court of Appeal on 17 March 1891. The Court of Appeal issued the writ and in response Edmund Jackson bought his wife to the Court on 19 March 1891 to justify her detention. The case was decided by the Lord Chancellor, Lord Halsbury, Master of the Rolls, Lord Esher and Lord Justice Fry – no woman could possibly ever sit as a judge in any Victorian court. That said, Lois Bibbings has highlighted a fascinating and powerful detail of female presence in the courtroom from the newspaper accounts.[14] Just before the case started three extra chairs were brought into Court for Lady Halsbury, Lady Esher and another female companion, presumably so that they could keep a watch on proceedings. All three judges agreed that there was no right to detain a married woman in this way. In the High Court Mr Justice Jeune (who sat with Cave J) had held that forcible detention by a husband was not illegal. However, Lord Halsbury saw no merit in Edmund Jackson's case at all:

> The return seems to me to be based on the broad proposition that it is the right of the husband, where his wife has wilfully absented herself from him, to seize the person of his wife by force and detain her in his house until she be willing to restore to him his conjugal rights. I am not prepared to assent to such a proposition.[15]

Lord Halsbury and Lord Esher both condemned the force used in the case. Lord Esher observed that if Parliament had created a problem by making it 'impossible effectively to enforce' in such circumstances a decree for the restitution of conjugal rights, then Parliament should address that rather than it being addressed privately by individuals.[16] Lord Justice Fry agreed that there was no 'rag of authority' for a right of a husband to capture a wife and that after the Matrimonial Causes Act 1884 and the changes which that introduced, personal detention could not have been envisaged.[17]

Releasing Emily Jackson from imprisonment in her husband's home was presented as the obvious outcome on the part of the Court of Appeal. A husband could not abduct or control and detain a wife. Whilst the Court of Appeal constructed this decision in terms of an application of the current law rather than a change to or development of the law, it is plain that previous practice under common law and customary law had not always taken this approach.

## III. What Happened Next

In the immediate aftermath of the case there was an initial furore; letters to newspapers, calls for an appeal, a subscription list to raise funds for Edmund Jackson, but it came to nothing. The criminal assault charges against Edmund Jackson were withdrawn with an order for Emily Jackson to pay the costs.[18] Emily Jackson faced hostility both in the press

[14] Lois S Bibbings, *Binding Men: Stories about violence and law in late Victorian England* (Routledge, 2014) 161.
[15] [1891] 1 QB 671, 680.
[16] ibid 684.
[17] ibid 685, 686.
[18] 'The Clitheroe Abduction Case – At Clitheroe', *The Times*, 24 March 1891, 10; 'The Clitheroe Abduction', *The Blackburn and Standard Weekly Express*, 28 March 1891, 7.

and in person. When she tried to return home on 28 March 1891 she was met with violent crowds. Demonstrations continued outside her home. Local people built an effigy of her and sang for 'he's a jolly good fellow' in praise of her husband.[19] Wider consequences included reports of local copycat abductions and concerns that the decision would impede efforts to protect women from domestic violence.[20] The Jacksons remained married but living apart in Blackburn and Clitheroe respectively until Emily Jackson's unexpected death of blood poisoning seven years later. Newspaper accounts tell of Edmund Jackson being informed of her illness by an anonymous letter but being unable to reach her before she died.[21] With huge irony, he became patron of the Clitheroe Parish Church from which he abducted her.[22]

In terms of divorce and domestic violence, the law developed further in small steps. Victorian feminists continued to campaign against the oppression of married women with limited success. The Summary Jurisdiction Act 1895 extended separation and maintenance allowances where there was persistent cruelty on the part of the husband. In the longer term the Royal Commission on Divorce and Matrimonial Causes of 1910–12 and then the **Matrimonial Causes Acts of 1923** and 1937 and the Divorce Reform Act in 1969 would completely change the picture of divorce law.

## IV. Significance

*Jackson* was a hugely controversial case that created contemporary debate on the nature of marriage and has continued to intrigue legal historians and academics. The audacity of the kidnap in full view of the church congregation and the tension of the siege played out in the national press hold a fascination for modern audiences.

*Jackson's* first landmark significance for Victorian married women was to finally and definitively rule out the possibility of being subject to any lawful abduction and detention imposed by their husband. Married women benefitted from the controls imposed on the behaviour of married men. In the most recent detailed analysis of the significance of the case, *Jackson* was considered in the context of a study of men, violence and law in late-nineteenth-century England. *Jackson* was one of five case studies that Lois Bibbings used to consider attempts to restrict the behaviour of men and 'legally bind men by delineating the parameters of unacceptable and unlawful violence.'[23] In *Jackson* this was in the context of domestic abuse.

*Jackson's* second landmark significance is as a case where a Victorian married woman was able to be 'heard'; was able to put her side of the story, despite of having no formal voice in the legal proceedings. Whilst Emily Jackson's free will was at the very centre of the case the High Court was anxious to prevent her from thinking, let alone speaking, and before the

[19] 'The Clitheroe Case – Since the proceedings', *The Times*, 28 March 1891, 5; 'The Clitheroe Abduction Case', *The Times*, 30 March 1891, 4.

[20] 'Imitating Mr Jackson', *The Blackburn Standard and Weekly Express*, 28 March 189, 11.

[21] Cumberland and Westmorland Newspaper Archives, 26 March 1898.

[22] 'Townships: Clitheroe' in W Farrer and J Brownbill (eds), *A History of the County of Lancaster* vol 6 (Victoria County History, 1911) 360.

[23] Bibbings, n 14 above, 190.

Court of Appeal she only spoke in private. Kristin Kalsem argues that when Emily Jackson's voice is eventually heard through her 'outlaw text', *Vindication*,[24] she speaks to the place of Victorian marriage, marital unity and coverture more generally, and 'provides a clear example of what injustices the law was failing to protect against'.[25]

Despite its longer-term significance, *Jackson* made little practical difference to the day-to-day lives of married women. It may even be viewed as a realignment of obstacles before married women. Maeve Doggett has considered *Jackson* in the context of the legal history of wife-beating, coverture and the fiction of marital unity.[26] She has no doubt that the decision is a 'legal landmark', '[s]weeping away centuries of judicial authority', but does not regard it as straightforward progress for women.[27] Doggett argues that, rather than reflecting the improvement in women's status at law, the *Jackson* decision was a 'reaction' to it. The law was adapting to support more subtle ways of entrenching male and female roles in late Victorian society.[28]

Whilst she technically remained legally married, Emily Jackson was physically able to leave her husband. Edmund Jackson was unable to force her to return despite his most spectacular efforts. Notwithstanding the difficulties of financial provision and practical arrangements for children of a marriage, it is now taken for granted that a married partner may leave the marriage if they wish to do so. In 2013 there were nearly 115,000 divorces.[29] However, as is shown elsewhere in this collection, the issue of violence within domestic relationships continues to be a problem of enormous significance.[30] According to the End Violence against Women Coalition, in 2016, over one million women were victims of domestic violence in England and Wales.[31] By finally categorically removing the possibility of a man having any right to abduct and detain a woman because she was married to him, *Jackson* is clearly just one landmark along a long continuing road.

## Further Reading

- Lois S Bibbings, *Binding Men. Stories about violence and law in late Victorian England* (Routledge, 2014).
- Maeve Doggett, *Marriage, Wife-Beating and the Law in Victorian England* (University of South Carolina Press, 1993).
- Kristin Kalsem, 'Looking for Law in All the Wrong Places: Outlaw Texts and Early Women's Advocacy' (2004) 13(2) *Southern California Review of Law & Women's Studies* 273.

[24] Emily Jackson's own account was published in instalments in *The Times* on the 18 April, 20 April, 21 April, 22 April and 23 April 1891 and is referred to as her *Vindication*.

[25] Kaslem, n 6 above, 281 and 276.

[26] Maeve Doggett, *Marriage, Wife-Beating and the Law in Victorian England* (University of South Carolina Press, 1993).

[27] ibid 142.

[28] ibid 148.

[29] Office for National Statistics, *Divorces in England and Wales: 2013* (ONS, 2015).

[30] eg **First Women's Refuge, 1971; *Davis v Johnson* (1978); Violence Against Women, Domestic Abuse and Sexual Violence (Wales) Act 2015**.

[31] EVAW, evidence submitted to the Fawcett Society's *Sex Discrimination Law Review* (January 2018), 52.

# 13

# *A Pageant of Great Women*, Cicely Hamilton, 1909–12

KATHARINE COCKIN

*A Pageant of Great Women* was one of the most successful plays of the British women's suffrage movement.[1] Written by Cicely Hamilton, an accomplished actor and dramatist, and directed by Edith Craig, who also designed the costumes, the play foregrounded the legal arguments for the vote by creating a court setting in which 'Woman' and 'Prejudice' presented the case for and against women's enfranchisement before 'Justice'. This dramatisation of the political arguments for legislative change empowered female political activists to create their own court at a time when women were excluded from the legal profession. The play took an innovative, informative and entertaining approach which captured the imagination and enthusiasm of audiences. It complemented the many other strategies by women's suffrage activists and their supporters to disseminate their alternative perspective on justice.

Written at a time of heightened intensity in the suffrage campaign, the play rehearsed the principal arguments on the topic of women's enfranchisement and gave women practice in public speaking and debate. The spectacular dramatisation of these arguments raised awareness of women's history. By gathering over 50 'great women' of the past from many countries on stage as evidence that women deserved the vote, the play had a visually stunning impact and a didactic function. It created opportunities for local women's suffrage activists and supporters to perform as these 'great women' alongside leading figures of the suffrage movement such as Lady Constance Lytton. All of those assembled, the performers and the audience, effectively acted as witnesses to the successful prosecution of the case before Justice. The play was staged across Britain between 1909 and 1912 and in other countries including the USA and South Africa.[2]

[1] *A Pageant of Great Women* was first performed on 12 November 1909 at the Scala Theatre, London. It was first published in 1910 and remains in print: Naomi Paxton (ed), *The Methuen Drama Book of Suffrage Plays* (Methuen, 2013); Katharine Cockin, Glenda Norquay and Sowon S Park (eds), *Women's Suffrage Literature. Volume III Suffrage Drama* (Routledge, 2007).

[2] See Naomi Paxton (ed), n 1 above, xi.

# I. Context

During the nineteenth century, the suffrage movement was dominated by the lobbying of members of parliament and by publications which aimed to counter the arguments against women's enfranchisement based on claims for women's biologically determined subordinate role to men and the sexes' occupation of separate, complementary, spheres. With presumed superior strength and intellectual abilities, men claimed the public sphere of politics and work as their own, whereas women were regarded as biologically weaker and destined for motherhood and domesticity. These separate spheres were ideological and rendered invisible the alternative reality in which a vast number of women worked in both physically gruelling, manual jobs in factories and domestic service as well as intellectually challenging roles as doctors and writers. Women were nevertheless expected to pay income tax and were able to vote in local elections, and they could act as Poor Law Guardians. The majority political movement for women's enfranchisement demanded the vote on the same basis that men held it, which, at the time, would have extended it to a middle-class constituency of propertied women. Some activists argued for wider equality and consistency in the treatment of women, and included children as the beneficiaries of this social reform. The involvement of children in the women's suffrage movement, in street processions and attending plays, demonstrates the strategic education in feminist thinking of the next generation.

The increasing frustration after decades of campaigning gave rise to new, militant methods in the twentieth century. These were co-ordinated by the Women's Social and Political Union (founded 1903), led by Emmeline Pankhurst and her daughters. The militancy which developed included a variety of law-breaking activities and indeed the strategy of law-breaking became a distinguishing feature of the twentieth-century 'suffragettes' that was eschewed by the broadly law-abiding suffragists. The destruction of property, civil disobedience and resistance to prison regulations (which did not acknowledge women's suffrage activists as political prisoners) are actions which have come to dominate the cultural representations of the women's suffrage movement. The more spectacular law-breaking activities have become particularly memorable. These included the breaking of shop windows and disruption of the peace at public party-political meetings and various means of obstruction, including activists chaining themselves to railings. These actions became increasingly dangerous and, although the militant leadership advocated only the destruction of property and not people, some individuals did come to harm. The strategy of hunger-striking during imprisonment was effective in that it achieved swift legislative change, but not the intended extension of the franchise. In order to prevent the embarrassment of death in prison of a hunger-striking suffrage activist, the dubious practice of forcible feeding and acts of torture were introduced, and in turn the Prisoners (Temporary Discharge for Ill-Health) Act 1913.

Women's suffrage militancy then took a cultural turn. Innovative publicity stunts and spectacular public interventions using graffiti, street marches and processions were part of the developing repertoire of militants. The Women's Freedom League, which had formed in reaction to the autocracy of the WSPU, particularly supported these methods, although the street march was instigated by the National Union of Women's Suffrage Societies (NUWSS). The dissemination of persuasive responses to the anti-suffrage arguments was an effective means of influencing the male electorate at large, whose members of parliament would need to vote in Parliament to bring about the legislative change to extend the franchise. The newspapers produced by the various women's suffrage organisations were sold on the street to reach a wider public. They featured political essays and commentary, notices of forthcoming events and reports as well as short stories, poems and plays.

The effective use of the literary, visual and dramatic arts emerged as a significant force at the time of increased militancy in the campaign for women's enfranchisement in Britain after 1905. In particular, these cultural interventions attracted the attention of the press as well as readers and theatre-goers. Theatrical performance was a means of reaching a theatre-going public. It was also used as a recruitment and training strategy during the more militant phase in the early twentieth century. Performers had experience of sexual harassment, unequal pay and precarious working conditions. The costumes they wore and the roles they played on stage were an influential part of the cultural construction of gender. Their expertise in public speaking and managing an audience were invaluable.

The production of Elizabeth Robins's play *Votes for Women* in 1907 at the Royal Court Theatre, London, led to the founding of the Actresses' Franchise League (AFL) in the following year and a very productive period of play-writing and production. Edith Craig was a freelance director for the AFL and founded the Pioneer Players theatre society (1911–25), which promoted women's writing for the stage and for which she directed numerous plays implicitly related to the campaign for women's suffrage. Craig lived with her female partner, Christopher St John (Christabel Gertrude Marshall), at 31 Bedford Street, Covent Garden, London which became a base for suffrage activism, housing the International Suffrage Shop – described as 'The Only Feminist Bookshop' – before it found permanent premises.[3] It was Craig who suggested the idea of *A Pageant of Great Women* to Cicely Hamilton, whose facility with writing and developing persuasive arguments was in great demand. In 1911 she had engaged in a public debate with GK Chesterton and she collaborated with composer Ethel Smyth to write the lyrics to 'The March of the Women', which became the anthem of the women's suffrage movement. The International Suffrage Shop later acted as publisher for *A Pageant of Great Women*.[4]

Women's suffrage theatre was at the heart of London's newly developing art theatre. The breadth of the topics and examples used by dramatists contributed significantly to the creative and imaginative engagement employed to inspire and influence the audience. The issue of prostitution, for instance, was controversially taken up as one which affected all women. This feminist perspective had informed Josephine Butler's earlier campaigns to repeal the Contagious Diseases Acts in the 1860s.[5] Other relevant topics exposed the prevailing assumption that marriage was somehow compulsory and provided scenarios in which women were shown resisting or rejecting marriage. Such dramatic plots shared the political arguments set out by Cicely Hamilton in *Marriage as a Trade* (1909). Role models and historical precedents, from Joan of Arc to Queen Caroline, were identified to lend authority to the campaign and inspire supporters.

[3] Katharine Cockin, *Edith Craig and the Theatres of Art* (Bloomsbury Methuen Drama, 2017) 133–38.
[4] ibid 135–38.
[5] See **Section 5(1) of the Criminal Law Amendment Act 1885**.

## II. The Landmark

*A Pageant of Great Women* located the legal system and legislative change at the heart of the women's suffrage movement. The 'Great Women' appeared ceremonially in thematic groups and remained on stage, eventually creating a large body. The selection of great women demonstrated women's differing contributions to society, summarised in a series of two- or three-line biographical portraits of the figures who appeared in historically accurate costumes. The 'Learned Women' emphasised women's intellectual abilities: Hypatia, St Teresa, Lady Jane Grey, Madame de Stael, Madame de Scudery, Jane Austen, Georges Sand, Caroline Herschell, Madame Curie, Madame Roland. The 'Artists' included performers as well as painters – Sappho, Vittoria Colonna, Angelica Kaufmann, Vigée le Brun, Rosa Bonheur, Margaret van Eyck, Nance Oldfield, Mrs Siddons, Mari-Anne de Cupis de Camargo – while the 'Saintly Women' – Saint Hilda, Elizabeth Fry, Elizabeth of Hungary and Saint Catherine of Siena – were accompanied by attendants (in the case of Fry, these were a group of prison children).[6] The small group of 'Heroic Women' provided a diverse range of examples of women's courage, distinction and excellence and included Marat's assassin, Charlotte Corday, together with Flora Macdonald, Kate Barlass and Grace Darling. The much larger group of 'Rulers' consisted of Victoria, Elizabeth, Zenobia, Philippa, Deborah, Isabella, Catherine the Great, Tsze-His-An and Maria Theresa, accompanied by attendants. The final group to appear on stage was the 'Warriors' who embodied the physical strength and courage of women in battle: Joan of Arc, Boadicea, Agnes of Dunbar, Emilie Plater, Ranee of Jhansi, Maid of Saragossa, Christian Davis, Hannah Snell, Mary Ann Talbot and, perhaps unexpectedly, Florence Nightingale.

There were many cultural interventions in the political suffrage campaigns, seeking to create or co-opt spaces for the voice of the unenfranchised women to be heard. The suffragists often used women's history as a means of empowerment, drawing on relevant and less obvious role models and events to support their arguments. Lectures were given at political events on various topics such as inspirational women in ancient Egypt or in Shakespeare's plays. Similarly the newspapers published by women's suffrage organisations and widely read by supporters regularly featured biographical articles about women 'pioneers' and their achievements.

What was distinctive about the play, however, was its unorthodox but effective strategy of emphasising that the obstacle to women's enfranchisement – and to justice and equality more generally – was *prejudice* rather than men as a group. (In the political debates about legislative change and women's enfranchisement the arguments tended to draw on gender stereotypes). This strategy was embodied by the character of Prejudice, who presented the anti-suffrage arguments before Justice and in response to the case presented by Woman. The use of characters as abstract entities or types – as Justice, Woman and Prejudice – drew on the ancient forms of the mediaeval morality plays, providing an underpinning aesthetic precedent to lend authority to the performance. The play presented the arguments for enfranchisement in a clear and memorable way by means of concise dialogue, relying on the familiarity of the audience with the kinds of introductory history text books which used lists and the encyclopaedic format to provide memorable figures of the past. Audiences

[6] See **Gaols Act 1823**.

would also be familiar with the pageant form. The Edwardian period saw the popularity of civic pageantry, with towns and cities organising historical pageants involving local participants. These pageants served an educational purpose but they also fostered a sense of local community as well as reinforcing social hierarchies.

In *A Pageant of Great Women*, the majority of the huge cast of over 50 performers was silent. This apparently contradictory mode of performance nevertheless enabled amateur performers from the ranks of the suffrage activists to take part on stage and directed attention to their physical presence as their powerful gaze was directed outwards to the audience. Their silence also complemented their historical location, as great women *of the past*, while the three speaking parts – Woman, Prejudice and Justice – occupy *the present moment* of urgent political action, and Woman tells their stories.

The play was advertised in the women's suffrage newspapers and one of these focused on the impact of the experience on the audience and possibly the actors in attending the play. It was promoted as an experience which would transform and empower: 'Come to [the] public hall in Beckenham. Women have been great. Come and realise your beliefs'.[7] It was staged at least five times in London, including at the Royal Albert Hall, as well as across Britain in Swansea, Eastbourne, Beckenham, Sunderland, Sheffield, Ipswich, Cambridge, Bristol, Nottingham, Middlesbrough and Liverpool, often at the invitation of local women's suffrage societies. It took nearly two weeks to rehearse and its inclusion of local suffrage activists as performers (often as local 'great women') and huge cast meant its staging was a large-scale celebratory political event. It was reported in the national and women's suffrage press. It also had a global reach. *A Pageant of Great Women* was produced in the USA, South Africa and Ireland as well as being considered for production at the Congress of the International Women's Suffrage Alliance in Budapest in June 1913.[8] The play, produced by Craig, attracted significant international attention and through its inclusion of great women from different countries – including Russia, China, France and Poland – emphasised the shared experiences of women across the world. The international dimension of women's suffrage was particularly acknowledged by the Women's Freedom League, an organisation which supported productions of the play at Swansea, Beckenham, Sunderland, Ipswich Sheffield and London.

## III. What Happened Next

At the outbreak of the First World War, political efforts were reassessed in light of the rapidly changing events and priorities. Many women redirected their time and energy to charity work in support of the war and others were actively engaged in pacifist organisation. The militant WSPU encouraged its supporters to support the war. Hamilton spent nearly three wartime years in France where she supported the Scottish Women's Hospitals at the Abbey at Royaumont from November 1914. Women formerly involved in women's suffrage

[7] *The Vote*, 10 September 1910, 231.

[8] See Katharine Cockin, 'Cicely Hamilton's Warriors: Dramatic Reinventions of Militancy in the British Women's Suffrage Movement' (2005) XIV(3) *Women's History Review* 527–42.

theatre, such as Lena Ashwell and Cicely Hamilton, applied their skills to organising theatre to entertain troops in France.

After the war the extension of the franchise to some women in the **Representation of the People Act 1918** was a timely measure to respond to the upheavals in experience of returning veterans and women who had been actively replacing them in various fields of employment. The most visible and immediate impact of enfranchisement was the candidacy and election of women members of parliament. The failure to secure election by leaders of the women's suffrage campaigns was significant; the first woman elected member of parliament, Constance Markiewicz, was prevented from taking her seat by a point of political principle as she would not pledge allegiance to the monarch. Markiewicz had played Florence Nightingale in a production in Ireland likely to have been *A Pageant of Great Women* or an adaptation of it.[9] Nevertheless, the need for continuing vigilance in order to achieve the wider transformations of society which the vote for women had promised ensured that former suffrage activists focused their attention on local government, the civil service and other organisations in the fields of social services, education and the arts.

Hamilton also continued to be active in the campaigns for social reform and justice both nationally and internationally. She was a regular contributor to Lady Rhondda's[10] feminist journal *Time & Tide*, writing articles such as those on 'The Commonsense Citizen' which reflected on women's role in society. She supported legal abortion and contraception and rights for women workers and was critical of socialism, fascism and nationalism generally. Craig continued to support political campaigns after the enfranchisement of women and directed a play by the American dramatist, Upton Sinclair, *Singing Jailbirds*, in 1930 for the Independent Labour Party's Masses' Stage and Film Guild in London. She was actively involved in the interwar reconstruction of theatres and other cultural organisations and was one of the national leaders of the British Drama League, which promoted amateur theatre nationwide as a means of rebuilding communities.[11]

## IV. Significance

*A Pageant of Great Women* was a very successful political play. It reached several thousand spectators at a time all over Britain, promoting the activity of women's history-making as much as women's suffrage. It normalised the idea of women's achievements. When the campaigns for women's enfranchisement in Britain became more militant, some activists rejected the polite letter-writing and lobbying tactics that seemed to have been unproductive, in favour of a range of eye-catching, spectacular and subversive interventions. Supporters in the arts were encouraged to use their expertise, resources and contacts to help spread the word. Authors, artists and theatre workers in particular were invaluable. *A Pageant of Great Women* was one of the many cultural interventions in the political suffrage campaigns

[9] See Rosemary Cullen Owens, *Smashing Times: A History of the Irish Women's Suffrage Movement 1889–1922* (Women's Press, 1984) 80.

[10] See further **Life Peerages Act 1958**.

[11] See Cockin, *Edith Craig and the Theatres of Art*, n 3 above, ch 6.

which created or co-opted spaces for the voice of the un-enfranchised women to be heard. It had an enormous impact on the campaign, successfully raising awareness, informing the audience, building communities, empowering and educating women.

The story of *A Pageant of Great Women* is remarkable. Great women of the early twentieth century combined to find out about great women of the past and many of the names in the play have again become forgotten. This kind of feminist historical recovery project is more often associated with the women's theatre movement of second-wave feminism of the 1970s – and indeed, the play and its creators were rediscovered and their work republished at this time – but it is clear that it was a feature of First-Wave feminism too. The *Pageant of Great Women* is reminiscent of Judy Chicago's *The Dinner Party* and has some affinity with Caryl Churchill's *Top Girls* and Eve Ensler's *The Vagina Monologues*. These are the inheritors of the women's suffrage theatre legacy.[12]

## Further Reading

- Katharine Cockin, *Edith Craig and The Theatres of Art* (Bloomsbury Methuen Drama, 2017).
- Julie Holledge, *Innocent Flowers: Women in the Edwardian Theatre* (Virago, 1981).
- Lis Whitelaw, *Cicely Hamilton* (Women's Press, 1990).

[12] Cockin, *Edith Craig and the Theatres of Art*, n 3 above; and Cockin, 'Cicely Hamilton's Warriors', n 8 above.

# 14

# Representation of the People Act 1918

MARI TAKAYANAGI

The Representation of the People Act 1918 gave the Parliamentary vote to all men aged 21 and over, and all women aged 30 and over who met (or whose husband met) the minimum property qualification for the local government franchise, meaning occupation of land or premises of a yearly value of not less than five pounds or of a dwelling-house. The Act also gave women the university franchise, a second Parliamentary vote for university graduates, provided they were 30 years old and would be entitled to be so registered if they had been men. Women campaigned for a further 10 years before they got the vote on the same terms as men by virtue of the Representation of the People (Equal Franchise) Act 1928.

## I. Context

Before 1832, the right to vote in Parliamentary elections differed widely across Great Britain and Ireland. The electorate was a tiny proportion of the population. Only men could vote, although this restriction came from common law rather than statute law.[1] Women were formally excluded from the Parliamentary franchise in England, Wales and Ireland by the 1832 Reform Acts, which made many reforms to the electoral system and enlarged the electorate, but also defined a voter as a 'male person' for the first time.[2]

Mary Wollstonecraft was an early advocate of political rights for women (in ***A Vindication of the Rights of Woman*, 1792**), and in the first half of the nineteenth century many women were involved in election campaigning, exercising patronage, campaigns for Parliamentary reform, and in the Chartist movement. Following early efforts by women such as Mary Smith, the first woman to present an individual petition for the vote to Parliament in 1832, and the anti-slavery feminist Quaker Anne Knight, the formal national organised

[1] It possible that some women may have voted on a small scale in counties and boroughs, and in local elections; Neil Johnston, *The History of the Parliamentary Franchise* (House of Commons Library research paper RP13/14, 2013).

[2] Representation of the People (England and Wales) Act 1832; Representation of the People (Ireland) Act 1832, The Representation of the People (Scotland) Act 1832, simply refers to 'Persons' and so the exclusion of women from the Scottish electorate continued to be based on custom. The 1868 case *Chorlton v Lings* (1868) LR 4 CP 374 subsequently established that the word 'man' only included men in relation to the Parliamentary franchise. See further ***Edwards v Attorney General of Canada* (1930)**.

movement for 'Votes for Women' began with a mass petition in 1866.[3] The Kensington Society, a discussion group for middle-class women, barred from higher education at this time, debated the issue in 1865 and subsequently set up a small informal committee to organise a petition. Participants included Barbara Bodichon,[4] Elizabeth Garrett and Emily Davies, who used family and friendship networks to gather 1500 signatures from women all over the country. Although many signatories were women of the leisured classes, some worked as teachers, dressmakers and shopkeepers, and others were the wives of butchers, greengrocers and blacksmiths.[5] On 7 June 1866, John Stuart Mill MP presented the petition to the House of Commons and the following year he initiated the first Parliamentary debate on women's suffrage. This was unsuccessful, and women were excluded from the enormous expansion of the vote in the Second Reform Act 1867, which gave the vote to working-class men in boroughs for the first time.[6]

Women sought the vote for a variety of reasons; many women claimed that they owned or rented property, ran businesses, were subject to the law and paid taxes, but without the right to representation that men in the same position had. Others argued that laws were made that especially affected women and children, and that without the vote women had no way of pressurising MPs to attend to women's issues or look after their interests. In the decades following 1866, women continued to petition and lobby, resulting in a number of private members' bills and almost annual debates in Parliament, particularly around the passage of the Third Reform Bill in 1884 which established a uniform franchise across the UK for the first time and extended the vote to working-class men in counties.[7] Women did gradually achieve the right to vote in local elections through various pieces of legislation, culminating in the Qualification of Women (County and Borough Councils) Act 1907.[8]

By the early twentieth century, the vote had become the most pressing issue for feminists, a prerequisite to tackling other inequalities. In 1897, the National Union of Women's Suffrage Societies (NUWSS) was formed, bringing together a wide variety of suffrage groups under the leadership of Millicent Fawcett. Then in 1903, the Women's Social and Political Union (WSPU) was founded by Emmeline Pankhurst and others who were impatient with the lack of progress and sought to use more direct methods of campaigning. In 1905, Christabel Pankhurst and Annie Kenney initiated the first militant action, disrupting a Liberal Party meeting in Manchester. Over the next nine years militancy grew and took many forms, such as stone throwing, window breaking, and chaining themselves to railings, though not violence against people. These actions were, however, frequently met with violence by the police. The militant campaigners became known as

[3] The literature on women's suffrage is vast. See eg Elizabeth Crawford, *The Women's Suffrage Movement: A Reference Guide, 1866–1928* (Routledge, 1999).

[4] See ***A Brief Summary of the Most Important Laws Concerning Women*, Barbara Leigh Smith Bodichon, 1854.**

[5] Ann Dingsdale, '"Generous and lofty sympathies": the Kensington Society, the 1866 women's suffrage petition and the development of mid-Victorian feminism' (Unpublished PhD thesis, University of Greenwich, 1995). Also '1866 Suffrage Petition Women': http://1866suffragepetitionwomen.blogspot.co.uk/.

[6] Representation of the People (England and Wales) Act 1867, followed by the Representation of the People (Scotland) Act 1868 and the Representation of the People (Ireland) Act 1868.

[7] Representation of the People Act 1884.

[8] Patricia Hollis, *Ladies Elect: Women in English Local Government 1865–1914* (Clarendon Press, 1987).

the 'suffragettes', while the peaceful constitutional campaigners were known as the 'suffragists'. Although much smaller in number than the suffragists, the suffragettes were more successful in gaining press and public attention. Divisions in the WSPU led to the formation of other suffragette organisations including the Women's Freedom League, led by Charlotte Despard, and Sylvia Pankhurst's East London Federation of working-class suffragettes.

In 1909, Marion Wallace-Dunlop became the first suffragette to go on hunger strike in prison, and subsequently suffragettes were forcibly fed, a horrific procedure. Women were held down by force and had a rubber tube inserted, sometimes through the mouth but usually through the nose (and occasionally via the rectum or vagina), into the stomach, into which a mixture of milk and bread were poured. There was such public revulsion that the Government was eventually forced to adopt an alternative method of dealing with such women. The 'Cat and Mouse' Act 1913[9] enabled authorities to release weakened hunger strikers temporarily and re-arrest them later to continue their sentence; this was an alternative form of torture which effectively meant such prisoners would never reach the end of their sentence. In the same year, Emily Wilding Davison died after she attempted to disrupt the Epsom Derby by throwing herself at the King's horse. Her funeral was attended by thousands of women from both the militant and constitutional sides of the movement. Later that year the Suffrage Pilgrimage took place, a mass NUWSS march of women from all over the country culminating in a rally of 50,000 women in Hyde Park, London.

Unfortunately, none of this campaigning bore fruit in Parliament. Despite numerous attempts, no suffrage Bill was able to progress. Although the rhetoric focused on women's lack of capacity and interest in politics, the failure was largely due to the fact that the Liberal government was unwilling to back a Bill which would enfranchise only middle- and upper-class women who would be likely to vote Conservative, while the Conservative opposition was unwilling to support any broader working-class enfranchisement since they would be likely to vote Liberal or Labour. The Labour Party supported universal suffrage, but had very few MPs in this period. It should be remembered that approximately 40 per cent of men were also unable to vote before 1918, since they lacked the necessary residential and property qualifications.

At the outbreak of war in 1914, militancy was suspended and all suffragette prisoners released. Suffrage campaigners differed in their approach to the war. Emmeline and Christabel Pankhurst turned their energies into supporting the mobilisation of women for war work. Sylvia Pankhurst, a pacifist, opposed the war and worked to relieve the grave plight of working-class women in the East End. Charlotte Despard, also a pacifist, supported the Women's Peace Crusade. The NUWSS was split on the issue, but Millicent Fawcett chose to support the war effort, with some anti-war suffragists leaving the movement as a result. However, although the public campaign may have been suspended, none of the suffrage campaigners abandoned their cause during the war. Emmeline Pankhurst saw her war work as a means to this end, and Millicent Fawcett continued to write letters, request meetings and lobby the Government.

[9] Prisoners (Temporary Discharge for Ill-Health) Act 1913.

## II. The Landmark

The 1918 Act came about as a result of the recommendations of the Speaker's Conference on Electoral Reform during 1916–17.[10] The last General Election had taken place back in 1910, so another was overdue. It was clear that the next election could not possibly take place using the same residential and property qualifications as in 1910, because men on military service would not be able to vote, which was not politically acceptable in wartime. Attempts to introduce a temporary register also failed, and so at the suggestion of Walter Long, President of the Local Government Board, a conference was set up to consider the issue. It was chaired, at the request of the Prime Minister, HH Asquith, by the Speaker of the House of Commons, James W Lowther, and met between October 1916 and January 1917. Asquith's Government was replaced by a Coalition led by David Lloyd George in December 1916, but the Conference continued its work.

The Speaker's Conference's terms of reference were to examine, and if possible submit agreed resolutions on, four matters: franchise reform; redistribution of seats; electoral registration reform; and method and cost of elections. It had 32 members: five from the House of Lords and 27 from the House of Commons. The 27 MPs were made up of 11 Unionist (Conservatives), 10 Liberal, three Irish Nationalist and three Labour MPs. Among them were at least 15 women's suffrage supporters and 11 anti-suffragists (with others undecided or unclear) as well as a mix of supporters of 'one man one vote' and those keen to safeguard the plural vote (which protected university and business interests). Perhaps surprisingly, given the diversity of its opinions, 34 of its 37 resolutions were unanimous; however, one of the resolutions which were not unanimous was on women's suffrage. Following the efforts of sympathetic members such as Willoughby Dickinson MP, the Conference recommended the franchise be conferred on all women who were on the local government register, or whose husbands were on the register, provided they had reached a certain age 'not agreed upon'.

Led by Walter Long, now Colonial Secretary, and Home Secretary Sir George Cave, the Government introduced the Representation of the People Bill in May 1917, embodying all the Conference's resolutions, but leaving women's suffrage and proportional representation to a free vote of the House of Commons. The Act as passed introduced a vast array of sweeping reforms. The expansion of the male franchise enabled any man aged 21 years or older to register if he occupied a residence (regardless of the value of the premises or rates paid, as had previously been the case). Men on military or naval service were allowed to vote from the age of 19 (women on military or naval service had to be aged 30 like their civilian counterparts), while conscientious objectors (who had not performed other war services or alternative work of national importance) were disqualified from voting for five years. Proportional representation and alternative voting were the subject of much debate, but were eventually rejected.

The women's suffrage aspect was one of the most controversial parts of the Bill. Significant levels of suffragist lobbying such as letter writing and deputations had resumed

[10] Homer Lawrence Morris, 'Parliamentary Franchise Reform in England From 1885 to 1918', no 2 vol XCVI in *Studies in History, Economics and Public Law* (Columbia University, 1921), chapter ix; Martin Pugh, *Electoral Reform in War and Peace 1906–18* (Law Book Company of Australasia, 1978).

from mid-1916, and the negotiations of Millicent Fawcett were crucial in ensuring that the Government included some measure of women's suffrage in the Bill. The 30-year age limit was chosen in order that women should not comprise the majority of the electorate. The local government franchise eligibility requirement ensured the vote went to the head woman of the household, in a property worth at least £5 annually. These compromises were accepted by virtually all women's suffrage campaigners except for Sylvia Pankhurst, who never wavered from her support of full adult suffrage.

While some MPs continued to oppose women's suffrage implacably at every stage, others who had previously opposed it now announced their support – either, like Asquith, because they had changed their minds or, like FE Smith, because they were pragmatic about its success, and did not want to risk losing the entire Bill. In the House of Lords, the President of the League for Opposing Woman Suffrage, Lord Curzon, chose to abstain in the crucial division, and the long battle for votes for women was finally won. The Representation of the People Act received Royal Assent on 6 February 1918.

## III. What Happened Next

The first election after the Representation of the People Act 1918 was the General Election of December 1918. Held under unusual conditions only weeks after the end of the First World War, it was called by Lloyd George, ostensibly to give himself a mandate for the peace negotiations in 1919, and his Coalition Government duly won an overwhelming victory. Women voted for the first time, and not, apparently, very differently from men either in terms of numbers or party affiliation.[11] There were 8,479,156 women on the electoral register, ie who were over the age of 30 and met the property qualification, just under 40 per cent of a total of 21,221,615 electors.

A separate Act, the Parliament (Qualification of Women) Act 1918, allowed women to become MPs. It was more radical than the Representation of the People Act in that women could stand without any restrictions as to age or property. Seventeen women stood, but the only one to be elected was Constance Markievicz who, as a member of Sinn Féin, did not take her seat at Westminster.[12] Markievicz went on, however, to take her seat as a member of the first Dáil Éireann in Ireland. Christabel Pankhurst stood unsuccessfully for The Women's Party, the former WSPU, which subsequently disbanded.

Feminist organisations continued to campaign on a wide variety of issues including property inheritance, marriage and divorce, legitimacy and adoption, and pensions for widows and orphans. The NUWSS became the National Union of Societies for Equal Citizenship, and new organisations formed included Viscountess Rhondda's Six Point Group,[13] which campaigned for legal equality for women in various areas including equal pay. Following

[11] Martin Pugh, *Women and the Women's Movement in Britain 1914–1999* (2nd edn, Macmillan, 2000) 145–54.

[12] Sinn Féin is an Irish Republican party whose members (to this day) stand in elections to the Westminster Parliament but refuse to take their seats, as they do not recognise the legitimacy of that body to legislate for Ireland.

[13] See further **Life Peerages Act 1958**.

a further 10 years of campaigning by feminist groups, with pressure brought to bear by a large number of private members' bills and Parliamentary questions from sympathetic male MPs and the few early female MPs, the Representation of the People (Equal Franchise) Act was finally passed by Stanley Baldwin's Conservative government in 1928, giving women the vote on the same terms as men.

## IV. Significance

The significance of the suffrage campaign has been downplayed, many MPs at the time and historians subsequently preferring to give credit for the achievement of the vote to women's war effort rather than their campaigns, which have often been presented as damaging rather than advancing the cause. In truth, however, many of the women who contributed the most to the war effort in terms of their work in munitions factories, farms and other industry were aged under 30 and many more did not qualify for the local government franchise due to the property restrictions, and so were also not entitled to vote. In addition, women on military and naval service were still subject to the age qualification, even though their male colleagues were able to vote at age 19.

The significance of the 1918 Act is that it was a huge concession of principle: women could now vote in Parliamentary elections, and as constituents were able to put pressure directly on MPs to look after their interests. As such, it is undoubtedly a legal landmark. It was also a compromise, as legislation so often is; the age and property qualifications ensured that its actual significance, in terms of the numbers and proportion of women allowed to vote, was limited for a decade until the 1928 Act. Having the vote did not bring about all the changes that suffrage campaigners had hoped for; further reforms continued to be resisted. But as a fundamental right, that women count in a democracy, its achievement was a prerequisite for further advances.

## Further Reading


- Elizabeth Crawford, *The Women's Suffrage Movement: A Reference Guide, 1866–1928* (Routledge, 1999).
- Nicoletta F Gullace, *The Blood of Our Sons: Men, Women and the Renegotiation of British Citizenship During the Great War* (Palgrave Macmillan, 2002).
- Homer Lawrence Morris, *Parliamentary Franchise Reform in England from 1885 to 1918*, no 2, vol XCVI in *Studies in History, Economics and Public Law* (Columbia University, 1921), chapter ix.

# 15

# Maternity and Child Welfare Act 1918

HAZEL BIGGS

The Maternity and Child Welfare Act 1918 aimed to improve the provision available for the health of mothers and young children. Under its auspices local authorities in England and Wales (Scotland and Ireland were explicitly excluded) were to make arrangements for attending to the health of expectant and nursing mothers, and for children under five years of age who were not attending schools recognised by the Board of Education at the time. The services provided included maternal and child welfare clinics, day nurseries and health visitors, none of which had previously been routinely available.

## I. Context

Political pressure had been building for the government to take action to improve the health of the nation, including children, since long before the enactment of the 1918 Act.[1] The advent of the Boer War (1899–1902) had revealed the very poor state of the nation's health, with approximately 20–30 per cent of potential recruits being physically unfit, largely due to inadequate nutrition and sanitation.[2] For the same reasons infant mortality rates were very high and the birth rate was falling. Maternal mortality had also been unacceptably high for many years, such that 'maternal mortality was the yardstick for assessing maternity services and was carefully examined by obstetricians'.[3]

Also at this time debates were surfacing about the causes of poor public health, child and infant mortality and the nature of childhood itself. Opinions were frequently divided on the relationship between poverty and poor child health, often questioning whether it was due to poverty or more related to good or bad motherhood. Poverty was undoubtedly the major cause of poor infant health and maternal outcomes, but politically that was difficult to overcome since prevailing opinions among those in power until the early twentieth century regarded poverty as often being the result of fecklessness and low moral fibre. Consequently, it was not until the liberal reform agenda of the Liberal Government elected in 1906 that the focus shifted to social welfare. Labour Exchanges for the unemployed and sickness benefits

[1] Report of the Inter-Departmental Committee on Physical Deterioration: volume I. Parliamentary Papers, Session 1904, Vol XXXII (HMSO, 1904) 1.

[2] ibid 8 (evidence of General Borrett, 9 December 1903, [167]).

[3] Geoffrey Chamberlain, 'British maternal mortality in the 19th and early 20th centuries' (2006) 99 *Journal of the Royal Society of Medicine* 559–63, 559.

for workers were introduced and, in relation to children, the emphasis was on improving mothering, primarily through education about hygiene, nutrition and the provision of sterilised milk and health visitors.[4]

The First World War which ended in 1918 is inextricably connected to the enactment of the Maternity and Child Welfare Act the same year. By the end of the war 500,000 children were fatherless at a time when state support for the welfare of families was virtually non-existent. Women who had been widowed in the war would have to work to support themselves and their children, as there was little or no state assistance available.

> It was most difficult of all for war widows, who had to get by on a meagre army pension. Some remarried, often for the sake of the children. But the loss of so many men in the war meant that competition for their hand in marriage was fierce.[5]

Prior to the war, social and welfare support consisted only of limited provision made under the Poor Law. Numerous charitable and voluntary initiatives had been implemented to try to address the issues by providing necessities such as clothing, milk and meals to those in particular need,[6] but these were in short supply and tended to be confined to specific geographical locations.

In the early 1900s milk clinics, fashioned on a successful model tried in France, were introduced to provide guidance on infant feeding problems and safe milk. Numerous brands of infant feed were available by the late nineteenth century to help supplement mothers' milk, with condensed milk being readily available. Consequently the milk clinics should have helped alleviate some of the issues central to the high rate of infant mortality, but the scheme quickly faltered. Poor maternal attendance was blamed for the failure, but it seems more likely that mothers were deterred by the cost of the milk, the provision of which, unlike in France, was not means tested or subsidised. In 1906 the first publically funded provision for health and welfare outside of the Poor Law was implemented for school-age children, in the form of the Education (Provision of Meals) Act 1906. It allowed, but did not compel, local authorities to provide free school meals for children, with the meals being funded from charitable donations. In 1914 it became compulsory for free school meals to be made available for needy children, paid for by government subsidy.

These measures would have assisted families where there were older children, but did little to alleviate the problem of infant and maternal mortality. In 1907 what is thought to have been the first infant welfare centre in England was established at the St Marylebone Dispensary in London.[7] The centre was founded by Dr Eric Campbell Pritchard, an early pioneer of infant feeding, and offered consultations to advise on infant feeding and child welfare more generally. Other clinics followed, and by 1912 the National Association for the Prevention of Infant Mortality was formed, based on the work of the numerous voluntary agencies working in the field, including the National Society for the Prevention of Cruelty to Children.

[4] See further Deborah Dwork, 'The Milk Option: an aspect of the history of the Infant Welfare Movement in England 1898–1908' (1987) 31 *Medical History* 99–119 and Deborah Dwork, *War is Good for Babies and Other Young Children: A history of the infant and child welfare movement in England, 1898–1918* (Routledge, 1987).

[5] Denise Winterman, 'Children of the Great War', *BBC News Magazine*, 9 November 2007.

[6] Benjamin Seebohm Rowntree, *Poverty: A study of Town Life* (Macmillan, 1901).

[7] Wellcome Trust, Medical Officer of Health reports 1848–1972: Report of the Medical Officer of Health for St Marylebone, Metropolitan Borough, 1–68, 55.

## II. The Landmark

Women campaigned on numerous social welfare issues throughout the war, including working with the Fabian society to establish a system for fixing minimum wages, and were particularly active in campaigning for social change to improve maternal and child health.[8] They were also instrumental in setting up voluntary child welfare clinics as an exemplar for government to follow as a means of helping to help maternal death rates and infant mortality.

The Maternity and Child Welfare Act 1918 effectively provided government subsidies for local authority and voluntary welfare services to support pregnant women, nursing mothers, and children below school age. Women had campaigned throughout the war as well as in the pre-war period due to concerns about death rates and the health of mothers and infants, and the campaigns resonated with government anxiety about the health and physical fitness of the population.[9] This Act was part of a raft of legislation promoting health and social welfare introduced by the Liberal Government led by Lloyd George that, de facto, made up the beginnings of the welfare state. The introduction of these measures signalled a move away from the patchy support available through the voluntary sector, to a more systematic form of state support. Alongside this Act, a Ministry of Health was also established in 1918, which took over the administration of the Poor Law and general health policies in order to address the generally poor state of public health and the high infant mortality rates.

To oversee and administer these arrangements local authorities were required to establish Maternal and Child Welfare Committees whose members must be 'persons specially qualified by training or experience in subjects relating to health and maternity'.[10] The Act specified that not less than two-thirds of the committee members must be members of the council and that at least two of them must be women. William Hayes Fisher, who was President of the Local Government Board at the time, had made it clear that working women should be represented on these committees.[11] Women councillors had sat on Parish Councils for some time prior to this, largely to carry out sanitary inspections of workshops employing women and to report any public health breaches. At the time it was regarded as inappropriate, and 'contrary to English conceptions of decency', for men to conduct such inspections, so it was necessary to appoint women councillors. Women had also been members of School Boards and had long been associated with Boards of Guardians for the administration of the Poor Law.[12]

The Act operated in conjunction with the Notification of Births Acts 1907 and 1915, which had been introduced to ensure that all births were registered, enabling more accurate records to be kept so that infant mortality rates could be tracked. Outside of London the expenses associated with these Acts could generally be claimed from the relevant district councils, and in the capital under mechanisms provided for within the Public Health (London) Act 1891, which enabled local authorities to provide the services without having

[8] Dwork, n 4 above.
[9] Pat Thane, 'The Liberal Party and Family Welfare, 1906–1922' (2011) 21 *Cercles* 1–10, 8.
[10] Section 2(2) of the Maternity and Child Welfare Act 1918.
[11] 'Maternity and Child Welfare', *The British Journal of Nursing Supplement: The Midwife*, 24 August 1918.
[12] Fabian Tract No 93, 'Women as Councillors', Fabian Municipal Programme (second series) no 4 (1900).

to raise taxes. It placed the onus on the County Councils to charge the related expenses as 'general County Council expenses' as part of the burgeoning public health initiatives of the time. Under this Act grants were payable in respect of the salaries of inspectors, midwives, health visitors and nurses engaged in all aspects of maternity and child welfare work. The costs of doctors attending women during pregnancy and childbirth, and any necessary hospital treatment, were also covered, which was important at a time when medical attention had to be paid for. In addition, the expenses associated with centres to provide the education and advice for expectant and nursing mothers, medical supervision and, if needed, convalescent accommodation, were also met under the Act. The costs of providing food to the women and their children under five would also be catered for if the Medical Officer deemed this to be necessary. Day nurseries or crêches were also funded to enable mothers to go out to work.

## III. What Happened Next

The First World War was a great driver for social health and welfare reform, not least because of concerns about the fitness of any future fighting force and the need for a robust workforce to support the economy. The raft of Liberal post-war legislative health and welfare provision reforms soon began to take effect. By 1920 all but seven local authorities had made arrangements under section 1 of the Act.[13] Rates of infant mortality, which had been a major concern for the administration, began to fall and the health of mothers and children also improved. The birth rate was stabilised and various Education Acts were implemented, raising the school leaving age and including the introduction of school medical services so that health and vitality continued to be assessed even after children started school.[14] Better ante-natal and post-natal care, facilitated through the provisions of the Maternity and Child Welfare Act, combined with better medical care, also led to a decline in maternal mortality, meaning that fewer children were left without mothers. As a further consequence more pregnancies were carried to term and resulted in live births. This, however, also tended to result in larger families and there were soon calls for the welfare clinics to be permitted to provide advice about birth control.[15]

Alongside the health and welfare reforms, a number of social and cultural changes also had a profound influence on the lives of women. Many of the women who had worked to support the war effort were contracted only for the duration of the war, and so were required to return to the domestic environment when it ended. After the experiences of working in factories and in clerical positions during the war, many women sought employment outside of domestic service so that middle-class women often found themselves without the domestic servants they had previously relied upon. Reforms like the Maternity and Child Welfare Act 1918 undoubtedly helped to facilitate women's ability to take paid work, although single women and widows, especially those with children to support, claimed

[13] Dr Christopher Addison MP, HC Deb, 09 November 1920, vol 134 col 1007.
[14] John Stewart, 'The Dangerous Age of Childhood' (*History and Policy*, 2012).
[15] 'Birth Control Review: Fewer Babies Better Born', June 1926: https://lifedynamics.com/app/uploads/2015/09/1926-06-June.pdf; **Abortion Act 1967**.

priority over paid employment. Both aspects were criticised, as reflected in comments to the *Daily Herald* letters page in October 1919:

> No decent man would allow his wife to work, and no decent woman would do it if she knew the harm she was doing to the widows and single girls who are looking for work ... Put the married women out, send them home to clean their houses and look after the man they married and give a mother's care to their children. Give the single women and widows the work.[16]

# IV. Significance

The Maternity and Child Welfare Act 1918 was a landmark legislative reform that over time helped to fundamentally change women's experience of pregnancy, childbirth and child rearing. State support for the welfare of mothers and their children, while not without criticism,[17] has certainly improved infant and maternal mortality rates. The care of pregnant women in Britain, combined with employment rights and benefits, has been beneficial for women generally, and more recent innovations with regard to paternity leave are also to be welcomed. The Act represents a turning point in the law's response to lives and lived experiences of women and children in England and Wales in the early twentieth century and beyond, and can be seen as the forerunner of the provision of medical and social support provided to pregnant women and new mothers, and their babies, today under the National Health Service.

## Further Reading


- Gwendoline M Ayers, *England's First State Hospitals and the Metropolitan Asylums Board 1867–1930* (Wellcome Institute of the History of Medicine, 1971).
- Deborah Dwork, 'The Milk Option: an aspect of the history of the Infant Welfare Movement in England 1898–1908' (1987) 31 *Medical History* 99–119.
- Deborah Dwork, *War is Good for Babies and Other Young Children: A history of the infant and child welfare movement in England, 1898–1918* (Routledge, 1987).
- Frank K Prochaska, *Philanthropy and the Hospitals of London: The King's Fund, 1897–1990* (Clarendon Press, 1992).
- Pat Thane, 'The Liberal Party and Family Welfare, 1906–1922' (2011) 21 *Cercles* 1–10.


[16] Cited in Joanna Bourke, *Working-Class Cultures in Britain: Gender, Class, and Ethnicity* (Routledge, 1994). See also Joanna Bourke, 'Women on the Home Front in World War One', *BBC History online*, 3 March 2011.

[17] Angela Davis, 'Choice, Policy and Practice in Maternity Care Since 1948' (*History and Policy*, 2013); Ank de Jonge, Jeanette AJM Mesman, Judith Manniën, Joost J Zwart, Jeroen van Dillen, Jos van Roosmalen, 'Severe adverse maternal outcomes among low risk women with planned home versus hospital births in the Netherlands: nationwide cohort study' (2013) 346 *British Medical Journal* 3263; Philippa Roxby, 'Making childbirth safer and easier for women', *BBC News online*, 28 April 2013.

# 16

# Article 7 of the Covenant of the League of Nations, 1919

AOIFE O'DONOGHUE

Article 7 of the Covenant of the League of Nations stated that its Secretariat – an international civil service – would be open to both women and men.[1] Male domination of the formal worlds of diplomacy and international law had, prior to the First World War, ensured that women were excluded, just as they were in the national sphere, from formally engaging in public international law. The Paris Peace Conference in 1919, which created the League of Nations, was the first occasion when women officially addressed delegates and, for a few women, took part in negotiations. As a direct result of women's lobbying at the 1919 Peace Conference, women-led non-governmental organisations (NGOs) including the Women's Peace Party, the International Women's Congress for Peace and Freedom and the Inter-Allied Suffrage Conference (IASC), were at the forefront of pushing for legal and political change at the domestic and international levels. In Paris, these organisations held meetings (the first international NGO parallel conferences) and sent petitions and representatives to push for changes on key issues such as women's suffrage, employment rights, citizenship, and women's roles in the new, and at the time novel, international organisation, the League of Nations.

Article 7 of the Covenant of the League of Nations was a stupendous achievement for those women who were heard in Paris. By new and innovative methods of lobbying they were at the forefront of a new form of transnational political engagement and the fruit of their endeavours was the first acknowledgment that by right women had a place alongside men in the halls of diplomacy. At the point when new forms of governance at the international level, such as the League of Nations, were being formed these women ensured that women were part of the landscape of international organisations, that they had a right to be there and that they must be in the League of Nations' Secretariat.

## I. Context

While women always played a significant role in the salons, receptions and dinners of informal, albeit still critical, diplomacy, they were entirely excluded from the formal world

[1] Article 395 of the Constitution of the International Labour Organization also mandated that a certain number of its Secretariat be women.

of diplomats. For some public international law academics in the nineteenth century, this exclusion extended to a right of states to refuse to accept female diplomats should another state send such an emissary.[2] The rejection of an ambassador has serious consequences; thus, the right to reject a diplomat on the basis of gender was significant. But this right of refusal was questioned by other academics. Robert Phillimore, writing in 1854, declared that '[a] state cannot reasonably refuse to receive an ambassador on the grounds of sex', giving examples such as Margaret of Austria, Louisa of Savoy and the Duchess of Orleans (who negotiated as plenipotentiary in a Treaty between France and England under Charles II) as examples of women holding diplomatic office.[3]

Most commentators ignored examples of women's international agency. But such instances are significant within international law where state practice can form new law. Writing women out of state practice and not recognising them as potential diplomats meant excluding them from the creation of public international law. However, women were present as wives and daughters and thus an important part of diplomatic efforts particularly in the organisation of receptions and balls. Such was the importance of that role that the UK Foreign Office until the 1970s officially recognised it and preferred wives not to hold alternative employment while their husbands were on mission abroad so they could devote time to this unpaid labour.[4] The influence of women through these unofficial channels ought not to be ignored, but it was partial, class-based and usually conservative. It was also not considered part of international law.

The first international organisations emerged in the nineteenth century. Most were technical institutions, but others possessed political and advocacy aims. These first organisations helped to set the template for twentieth-century governmental and non-governmental organisations and amongst these, and among the most influential, were women's organisations. Most were Euro-American and campaigned on issues such as suffrage, women's right to retain citizenship upon marriage to a foreigner,[5] abolition of trafficking of women, women's education, women's working conditions and peace.[6] International treaties on laws of war were becoming more common, as was the creation of permanent institutions such as the Permanent Court of Arbitration (an organisation that women were significant in establishing).[7] These internationally networked organisations recognised that in order to put pressure on governments for domestic and international legal change, taking a global perspective mattered. However, women were confined to the non-governmental sector and even here organisations that had not been specifically created by women side-lined them. Only within the women-led organisations such as, the International Women's Congress for Peace and Freedom and the IASC, could women maintain their role as leaders in campaigning activities.

[2] Robert Philimore, *Commentaries upon International Law*, Vol II (T & JW Johnson, 1855) 170.

[3] ibid.

[4] Helen McCarthy, *Women of the World: The Rise of the Female Diplomat* (Bloomsbury, 2014).

[5] **British Nationality Act 1948**.

[6] Jill Liddington, *The Road to Greenham Common: Feminism and Anti-militarism in Britain Since 1820* (Syracuse University Press, 1989) 13–59.

[7] Jane Addams, *Peace and Bread in a Time of War* (Hail & Co, 1922) 53–55.

The IASC, the International Women's Congress for Peace and Freedom and the Women's International League for Peace and Freedom[8] emerged in the decades before 1919 as national campaigning organisations that built alliances across continents to push for both legal and political reform recognising that some issues, such as peace and trafficking of women, of necessity required international responses. Most of these organisations were feminist in outlook with a wide geographical spread. Across decades activists such as Josephine Butler,[9] feminist Huda Sha'arawi,[10] trade unionist Margaret Bondfield[11] and Nobel Peace Prize winner Jane Addams pressed for domestic and international law reform.[12] Jane Addams, a significant figure in the women's movement in the United States on both social reform and suffrage, founded the American Civil Liberties Union after 1919. At the international level, she was a leading figure in the Peace Movement and her book *Newer Ideals of Peace* was influential in the years prior to the First World War.

Women were absent from the formal delegations of states but the new world of international organisations, both governmental and non-governmental, saw the first access points for women in decision-making positions. In the latter case, women formed, sustained and achieved success in lobbying as the first modern NGOs. Women-led organisations set the template on how international NGOs could co-ordinate their work and have success in pressing for reform. Women showed how to move grass-roots campaigns from the local to the national and international levels, assisting each other across campaigns to achieve success at each level including on suffrage, access to employment and social care amongst others.[13] One of the next steps was to open the field of official diplomacy to women.

## II. The Landmark

The Paris Peace Conference in 1919 is an extremely significant moment in modern international legal history. It not only established the League of Nations, the precursor to the United Nations, but also created several new states in Eastern Europe and set the template for de-colonisation. Over the months from January to August 1919 some of the fundamental structures of international law in the twentieth century were established. It is here that the first international inter-governmental organisations, in the contemporary

[8] Liddington, n 6 above.

[9] Josephine Butler was a feminist campaigner who fought for women's suffrage, education, and the end of human trafficking and child prostitution (see Jenny Daggers, Diana Neal and Josephine Elizabeth Grey Butler (eds), *Sex, Gender, and Religion: Josephine Butler Revisited* (Peter Lang, 2006)).

[10] Huda Shaarawi founded the Egyptian Feminist Union and fought against the restrictions on women living public lives in Egypt (Sania Sharawi Lanfranchi, *Casting off the Veil. The Life of Huda Shaarawi, Egypt's First Feminist* (IB Tauris, 2014)).

[11] Margaret Bondfield was the first woman cabinet member in the UK (excluding Countess Constance Markievicz during the Irish War of Independence who, while being the first women elected to the UK Parliament and to sit on a cabinet in the UK, did not take up her seat) and a lifelong trade unionist who fought to improve the working lives of women (June Hannam and Karen Hunt, *Socialist Women: Britain, 1880s to 1920s* (Routledge, 2012)).

[12] Margaret E Galey, 'Forerunners in Women's Quest for Partnership' in Anne Winslow (ed), *Women, Politics, and the United Nations* (Greenwood Publishing Group, 1995) 4.

[13] Liddington, n 6 above, 13–59.

sense of the term, were established, with one, the International Labour Organization (ILO), still operating today. Ensuring women's recognition as having a legitimate role within these organisations was essential if women were to have a voice in the development of international law in the twentieth century and beyond. As such, the need to recognise the right of women to form part of the secretariats of both the League of Nations and the ILO was an essential component of the lobbying of women's organisations at Paris and their most notable success.

Article 7 of the Covenant of the League of Nations states that 'All positions under or in connection with the League, including the Secretariat, shall be open equally to men and women'. Alongside the League of Nations, the ILO also states in its Constitution under Article 9.3 that 'A certain number of these persons shall be women' and, under Article 3.2 on Meetings and Delegates, that

> Each delegate may be accompanied by advisers, who shall not exceed two in number for each item on the agenda of the meeting. When questions specially affecting women are to be considered by the Conference, one at least of the advisers should be a woman.

The Second International Congress of Women (ICW) was held in Zurich at the time of the Paris Conference, as German delegates would not have been able to obtain visas to travel to France.[14] Jane Addams described how the ICW decided that groups going to Paris to lobby would bring 'certain issues which had hitherto been inarticulate in international affairs' to the fore.[15] This would prove difficult; the public/private divide associated with the sovereign equality of states meant that issues relating to women were rarely considered to be of importance to international law but were, rather, domestic law issues. For instance, one of the great successes of the women's organisations was the reception of the Women's Suffrage Organisation by then US President Woodrow Wilson. They suggested that the conference ought to address the conditions of women and children across the world. Following the meeting Wilson brought a proposal to the Supreme Council of Five (the victorious powers after the First World War: the UK, the US, France, Italy and Japan) to form a Commission on the issue. The proposal was withdrawn, however, after Wilson was unable to find further support, with Japan and Italy declaring that such issues were private domestic matters. There was still some success for the Women's Suffrage Organisation, though: lobbying of the French and Italian delegations ensured that the IASC testified before the Commission on Labour, which directly resulted in the re-wording of its recommendations.[16]

Critically, the International Council of Women and the IASC, after lobbying, could appear before the Commission on the League of Nations.[17] In their presentation they made several recommendations including an agreement to suppress traffic in women, recognition of the principle of women's suffrage and the right of women to vote in independence plebiscites, amongst others. Most particularly they recommended that women be eligible for positions in the new League's Secretariat. While these groups did not achieve all their aims, such as universal suffrage, they succeeded in two significant areas. First, they secured

[14] Steve Charnovitz, 'The Emergence of Democratic Participation in Global Governance (Paris, 1919)' (2003) 10 *Indiana Journal of Global Legal Studies* 45–77.

[15] Addams, n 7 above, 62.

[16] Charnovitz, n 14 above, 68.

[17] ibid 68.

the vote for women in several state independence plebiscites and their eligibility to work at the League of Nations. Second, these women established the terms on which NGOs would lobby and influence international conferences and agreements, which continue today.

Some women did have official roles in Paris. Gertrude Bell played a very prominent role in the creation of the settlements in the Middle East and the establishment of countries such as Iraq and Syria.[18] Queen Marie of Romania, as a representative of what would become a state, succeeded in negotiations to establish Romania in its modern form.[19] Other women held key roles on scientific bodies leading up to the Conference. In particular, a number of women geographers and lawyers took part in Conference preparation.[20] Yet these women were seen as exceptions rather than the norm. Article 7 of the League of Nations Covenant would change that.

## III. What Happened Next

After 1919 the story of women working within international law is mixed. International organisations took the lead in appointing women. However, it would take a long time for states to incorporate women into their diplomatic services on an equal footing. It was 1951 before the first women joined the UK Foreign Office as equal diplomats, while the marriage bar survived until 1973; and it was 1976 before the first female UK ambassador, Anne Warburton, was appointed.[21] Other countries were more forward-looking. Armenian Diana Abgar, generally recognised as one of the first woman diplomats, was appointed in 1918 (although Armenia was not recognised by other countries at that point), and the USSR appointed the feminist Alexandra Kollontai as Soviet Ambassador to Sweden in 1923.[22] Nonetheless States remained rather reluctant to use women as diplomats and delegates to international organisations. Of State appointments to the League of Nations, at each League Assembly barely 20 of the 250 delegates were women and they were normally assigned to women's questions, with none serving on the most senior political body, the League's Council or the Permanent Court of Justice.[23] At the San Francisco Conference that established the United Nations some women were present, including British MPs such as Ellen Wilkinson and Florence Horsburgh and diplomats Bertha Lutz and Wu Yi-Fang, but they were vastly outnumbered by their male colleagues in State delegations.

The League of Nations Secretariat fared better and it is here where the lobbying of 1919 had most impact. While most women held supporting or administrative roles within the Organisation, others began to hold more obviously political roles:[24] 'Women were included

[18] McCarthy, n 4 above, 65–74.

[19] ibid 84.

[20] 'War Services of Members of the Association of American Geographers' (1919) 9 *Annals of the Association of American Geographers* 53.

[21] McCarthy, n 4 above, 297.

[22] Cathy Porter, *Alexandra Kollontai: A Biography* (Haymarket Books, 2014).

[23] Francine D'Amico, 'Women workers in the United Nations: from margin to mainstream?' (1999) *Gender Politics in Global Governance* 19–40; Mary K Meyer and Elisabeth Prügl (eds), *Gender Politics in Global Governance* (Rowman & Littlefield, 1999) 20.

[24] ibid 20.

in the Conference on the Codification of International Law, the Disarmament Commission and two of the Permanent Mandates Commissions'.[25] From 1919 to 1930 Rachel Crowdy headed the League of Nations' Social Section, which in turn influenced the work of the Advisory Committee on Traffic in Women and Children, and she was involved in the drafting of the Convention on the Traffic of Women and Children and the Convention on the Suppression of and Circulation of Obscene Publications.[26] Gabriella Radziwell from the UK was a senior figure in the League of Nations Information Section.

While the relatively small numbers of women within the League were disappointing, they were trailblazers in establishing women as significant voices in the formation of international law to the extent that the League's successor organisation, the United Nations, had (again with lobbying) within its Charter a commitment to equality among men and women in its Secretariat. While progress has been extremely slow, the presence of women in the Secretariats in Geneva and New York made it impossible for states to deny that women could serve as diplomats and, further, that women made essential contributions to the development of international law. The women's organisations that lobbied in 1919 morphed into a variety of feminist movements that led the way in lobbying for several Conventions on Women's Working Conditions in the inter-war period and after 1945 in the passage of the Convention on the Elimination of Discrimination Against Women and the Women's Conferences in Mexico, Beijing and New York.

## IV. Significance

The women's organisations that attended the Paris Peace Conference established modern non-governmental lobbying and ensured the role of women in international organisations. They demonstrated that uniting through transnational organisations and consistent, persistent lobbying could bring about legal change and that women's presence and voices could change international agendas and establish new legal structures. Article 7 of the League of Nations Covenant established that women had a place in international diplomacy and thus in the creation of international law. The women who went to Paris in 1919 and lobbied for Article 7 showed the type of change that could happen if women's voices are heard. While this was insufficient to break the patriarchal grip on international law, women's presence pushed debates on gender equality into the mainstream of international law.

Gender inequality remains a critical issue at the international level. In 2016 the UN Secretary General admitted that 83 per cent of its entities have failed to hit gender targets, with no overall progress since 2012 and only 33 per cent possessing a gender unit or equivalent to aid in achieving gender equality.[27] While progress remains slow, the women in Paris in 1919 made certain that women were part of the operation of international law as a right, guaranteeing that their voices would only become louder.

[25] Galey, n 12 above, 5.

[26] ibid 5.

[27] Status of Women in the United Nations System 2016: http://www.unwomen.org/-/media/headquarters/attachments/sections/library/publications/2016/status-of-women-in-the-united-nations-system-2016-en.pdf?vs=2511.

## Further Reading

- Jane Addams, *Peace and Bread in a time of War* (Hail & Co, 1922).
- Helen McCarthy, *Women of the World: The Rise of the Female Diplomat* (Bloomsbury, 2014).
- Leila J Rupp, *Worlds of Women: The Making of an International Women's Movement* (Princeton University Press, 1997).

# 17

# Sex Disqualification (Removal) Act 1919

MARI TAKAYANAGI

The Sex Disqualification (Removal) Act 1919 is a short statute that begins:

> A person shall not be disqualified by sex or marriage from the exercise of any public function, or from being appointed to or holding any civil or judicial post, or from entering or assuming or carrying on any civil profession or vocation.

It enabled women to become barristers, solicitors, jurors and magistrates, to enter other professions such as accountancy and, with some caveats, to enter the higher ranks of the Civil Service. It allowed women to be admitted to incorporated professional societies, and gave universities the power to admit women to membership or degrees (which they all did already, except for Cambridge and Oxford). However, its impact was not as great as feminist campaigners and supportive MPs hoped. Specifically, it did not eliminate the marriage bar – the practice of requiring women to leave paid employment on getting married – in occupations such as teaching, while provisos included in the Act ensured that women could still be barred from some parts of the Civil Service including the Foreign and Diplomatic service, and that judges could exclude women from juries.[1] In fact the Act did not abolish discrimination on the grounds of sex or marriage, which had to wait for the **Sex Discrimination Act 1975** to be achieved.

## I. Context

Discrimination against women in education, the professions and public life had been the object of feminist campaigning for decades before the achievement of the vote for some women in the **Representation of the People Act 1918**. For example, women had long campaigned to enter the legal profession, with a Court of Appeal test case and several Bills in Parliament attempting to overcome the opposition of both the Law Society (solicitors) and the Bar Council (barristers).[2] Individual women had also tried to enter the other professions and been refused entry by professional societies, such as Mary Harris Smith (the Institute

[1] Mari Takayanagi, 'Parliament and Women, c 1900–1945', (unpublished PhD thesis, King's College London, 2012), chapter 2.

[2] Rosemary Auchmuty, 'Whatever happened to Miss Bebb? *Bebb v The Law Society* and women's legal history' (2011) 31(2) *Legal Studies* 175–343; **Women's Legal Landmarks: An Introduction**.

of Chartered Accountants), Aleen Cust (the Royal College of Veterinary Surgeons), and Hertha Ayrton (the Royal Society). Suffrage campaigners had also long argued that women magistrates were needed, especially in new children's courts, and women jurors to hear cases on issues such as sexual assault and rape.[3]

By 1919, now that some women had finally been given the vote, women's entry to professions was largely uncontroversial in Parliament. It has been argued that women would have been allowed to enter the legal profession even if the 1919 Act had not been passed, through more specific legislation, since both professions had finally come around to the idea and a Barristers & Solicitors (Qualification of Women) Bill had already passed in the House of Lords with almost no opposition. Likewise, a Justices of the Peace (Qualification of Women) Bill was passed in the Lords later in 1919. Both Bills were rendered unnecessary by the passage of the Sex Disqualification (Removal) Act.

## II. The Landmark

The Sex Disqualification (Removal) Bill was introduced by the Government in response to the Parliamentary success of a more radical Private Member's Bill, the Women's Emancipation Bill, introduced by Benjamin Spoor MP on behalf of the Labour Party on 21 March 1919. Spoor's Bill was aimed at 'remov[ing] certain restraints and disabilities imposed on women'. It contained three clauses:

- to remove the disqualification of women for holding civil and judicial appointments;
- to include women on the franchise on the same terms as men;
- and to allow women to sit and vote in the House of Lords.

In this period, immediately after the First World War, Labour were in opposition against a Conservative-dominated Coalition Government led by the Liberal David Lloyd George. As today, backbench MPs had the opportunity to enter a ballot to introduce bills (called Private Members' Bills). Though such Bills were often primarily aimed at attracting publicity and discussion (then, as now, they stood little chance of becoming law without Government support), some successfully made their way through the legislative process.[4] Labour used their second place on the ballot that year to introduce the Women's Emancipation Bill. It had its second reading debate on 4 April 1919, moved by William Adamson MP, and the little opposition there was among MPs was all about the franchise clause; virtually nothing was said against the civil and judicial appointments clause, or women and the Lords. There was cross-party support from men of diverse parties and backgrounds, and particularly strong support from Labour mining MPs: Benjamin Spoor represented the mining constituency of Bishop Auckland, and William Adamson had been a miner for 27 years. It is perhaps ironic to find these MPs promoting a Bill for gender equality when at the same time they were also pushing for the Restoration of Pre-War Practices

[3] Anne Logan, *Feminism and Criminal Justice: A Historical Perspective* (Palgrave Macmillan, 2008).

[4] Peter A Bromhead, *Private Members' Bills in the British Parliament* (Routledge & K Paul, 1956). See also **Abortion Act 1967**.

women to be allowed into the Administrative Class (1st Division) of the Home Civil Service, and following efforts by Major Hills (the MP for Ripon) this did happen, although numbers were small. The first women entered in 1922, with women competing in open examinations on equal terms with men from 1925.[11] But the principle of equal pay in the Civil Service was not achieved until 1954 and more generally not until the Equal Pay Act 1970.[12]

Campaigning efforts by feminist organisations continued, and indeed the Sex Disqualification (Removal) Act 1919 was only one of many pieces of legislation passed during the inter-war period. Other Acts of Parliament between 1918 and 1939 enabled women to become MPs (Parliament (Qualification of Women) Act 1918); equalised property inheritance rights (Law of Property Acts 1922 and 1925); provided better conditions for pregnant women and children (**Maternity and Child Welfare Act 1918**); improved training for nurses and midwives (Midwives Act 1918, Nurses Registration Act 1919); improved affiliation, separation and maintenance orders and reformed marriage and divorce law, including equalising the right for women to sue for divorce (**Matrimonial Causes Acts 1923** and 1937); removed the automatic death penalty for infanticide and created the offence of child destruction (Infanticide Act 1922, Infant Life (Preservation) Act 1929); raised the age of marriage to 16 (Age of Marriage Act 1929); introduced equal guardianship (Guardianship of Infants Act 1925); allowed women to sit in courts of arbitration (Industrial Courts Act 1919); introduced widows' and orphans' pensions (Widows', Orphans' and Old Age Contributory Pensions Act 1925); reformed legitimacy law and adoption law (Legitimacy Act 1926, Adoption of Children Act 1926); and equalised the franchise (Representation of the People (Equal Franchise) Act 1928).

## IV. Significance

The Sex Disqualification (Removal) Act 1919 was a Government replacement for a more radical Private Member's Bill, and as such it was a compromise. The two really radical clauses from the Women's Emancipation Bill on equal franchise and woman peers were lost. The Act has been called 'a broken reed in the face of the resurrection of obstacles such as the bar on married women and further protective legislation',[13] and cited as evidence in a wider historical judgement that feminist achievements in the inter-war period were insignificant; that the reforms which were achieved were 'guided by non-feminist forces' and therefore channelled women into maintaining their more traditional place in society.[14]

However the negative verdict from some historians and commentators obscures the positive spirit in which the Women's Emancipation Bill was debated and underestimates the tremendous advance the Sex Disqualification (Removal) Act represented. Passed only a year after the end of the Great War and the granting of votes to some women, the Act managed

[11] Hilda Martindale, *Women Servants of the State, 1870–1938: A History of Women in the Civil Service* (George Allen & Unwin Ltd, 1938).

[12] **Dagenham Car Plant Strike, 1968**.

[13] Martin Pugh, *Women and the Women's Movement in Britain 1914–1999* (2nd edn, Macmillan, 2000) 90.

[14] Harold Smith, 'Sex Versus Class: British Feminists and the Labour Movement 1919–1929' (1984) 47 *The Historian* 19–37.

to get through Parliament at a time when the peace settlement was still ongoing, there was trouble in Ireland and returning soldiers were in need of employment and rehabilitation. Clearly the Government had many other priorities and it is surely remarkable that such a Bill was able to progress at all. It was only now that women in Parliament were recognised as voters and MPs, and not potential trouble-makers capable of violence. Feminists well recognised that the Act did not bring gender equality and continued to try to make it work, campaigning against professional discrimination in the Civil Service, teaching and elsewhere.

## Further Reading


- Cheryl Law, *Suffrage and Power: the Women's Movement 1918–1928* (IB Tauris, 1997).
- Mari Takayanagi, 'Parliament and Women, c 1900–1945' (unpublished PhD thesis, King's College London, 2012).
- Pat Thane, 'What Difference Did the Vote Make?' in Amanda Vickery (ed), *Women, Privilege and Power: British Politics 1750 to the present* (Stanford University Press, 2001) 253–88.

# 18

# First Women Justices of the Peace, 1919

ANNE LOGAN

On 24 December 1919, immediately after the Royal Assent to the **Sex Disqualification (Removal) Act 1919**, the Lord Chancellor announced the appointment of the first seven women Justices of the Peace (JPs) in Great Britain and Ireland.[1]

Sometimes referred to as 'magistrates', JPs – who performed their tasks voluntarily – presided in petty sessional courts where they dealt summarily with minor criminal charges and referred more serious cases to higher courts. JPs were not required to have any legal training. At the beginning of the twentieth century only London (and a few other places where the volume of criminal charges was especially high) had salaried, legally qualified magistrates. In total, JPs handled over 90 per cent of criminal charges.

## I. Context

The office of JP had existed in England since the twelfth or thirteenth century, when members of the gentry were charged by Parliament to keep the peace and to pursue, restrain, arrest and punish offenders. This system was extended to Wales in 1536. For several hundred years the role of the JPs expanded as they were given additional administrative tasks, but the establishment of a comprehensive system of local government in the late nineteenth century narrowed the focus of JPs' work to judicial tasks.[2]

The admission of women to the magistracy – indeed the 1919 Act as a whole – was a natural consequence of the admission of (some) women into the parliamentary franchise in 1918 (by virtue of the **Representation of the People Act 1918**) and the subsequent legislation which permitted women to stand as candidates in parliamentary elections. However, it should not be assumed that there was an absence of agitation for the appointment of women as JPs. Although women's suffrage organisations had naturally focused their campaigns on winning the vote, the inclusive notion of citizenship which lay behind their demands encompassed the duties of a citizen as well as rights.[3] In fact, however, demands for women

[1] 'Women in the Seat of Justice', *Daily Express*, 24 December 1919, 1. Although appointments were made for Scotland and Ireland, this entry is concerned with England and Wales only.

[2] Anne Logan, 'Magistrates' in Jo Turner, Paul Taylor, Sharon Morley and Karen Corteen (eds), *A Companion to the History of Crime and Criminal Justice* (Policy Press, 2017) 137–39.

[3] Anne Logan, 'Making Women Magistrates: Feminism, Citizenship and Justice in England and Wales' (Unpublished PhD thesis, University of Greenwich, 2002).

JPs were rarely made on grounds of abstract principle: rather they arose from practical situations in which feminists believed a woman's perspective was needed. The first and most significant of these scenarios was the courts' handling of male violence towards women and children. As early as 1910, the journal of the National Union of Women's Suffrage Societies (NUWSS) printed a letter from the organisation's Shropshire president advocating that women JPs be appointed in order that they might be present 'in all cases brought before police courts in which girls and children are the victims and men the offenders'.[4] The second main feminist argument for women JPs focused upon the contribution they might make to the country's new juvenile courts which had been established in the wake of the Children Act 1908. Indeed, the suggestion that women magistrates be appointed for children's courts began to be made around the time of the report of the Royal Commission on Justices of the Peace in 1910, only four years after the property qualification for JPs had been abolished.[5]

The Women's Freedom League (WFL) was the most vocal suffrage organisation when it came to campaigning for women JPs. In the years immediately before the First World War, the WFL paper, *The Vote*, contained a regular feature ironically entitled 'How Men Protect Women' which reported on the light sentences given to men who had committed violent offences towards women, sometimes contrasted with seemingly harsh treatment for female offenders.[6] The WFL soon added the appointment of women JPs to its demands and in 1918 its Secretary called for at least one woman to be appointed to every magistrates' bench.[7] Other women's organisations, notably the NUWSS and the National Council of Women (NCW), were also vocal in backing this cause, to the extent that it was clear it had widespread support from a broad section of organised womanhood. The appointment of women magistrates was also urged by members of the labour movement and by penal reform groups, including the Penal Reform League (PRL) which had been formed in 1907 as a response to the imprisonment of suffragettes. Together these elements made up a broad coalition of support for the measure, although, in truth, the majority of Labour politicians were likely more interested in the effective and adequate staffing of juvenile courts than matters of justice for women.

## II. The Landmark

Although the King's Speech which set out the Government's agenda in 1919 contained no mention of women's rights, no fewer than three Parliamentary Bills were introduced in the session with the intention of admitting women to the lay magistracy. The first was the Labour-Party-backed Women's Emancipation Bill which, despite being proposed by an Opposition Party, received both a second and a third reading in the House of Commons, prompting the Government to introduce its own, less radical, Sex Disqualification (Removal) Bill. Although much was made in speeches of women's work during the recent war and the

[4] *Common Cause*, October 1910.

[5] Anne Logan, '"A Suitable Person for Suitable Cases": The Gendering of Juvenile Courts in England, c.1910–39' (2005) 16(2) *Twentieth Century British History* 129–45.

[6] See, for example, *The Vote*, 17 February 1912, 197.

[7] Florence Underwood, 'Portia on the Bench: a plea for women magistrates', *Reynold's Newspaper*, 16 June 1918.

proof it offered of feminine fitness for the public sphere, the support of a majority of MPs for the Women's Emancipation Bill is perhaps better attributed to their awareness that women now formed a part of their electorate. Even those who voted against the proposals paid lip service to women's rights, albeit while suggesting (among other things) that the House had more pressing issues to deal with. The specific proposal to allow women JPs received little attention in the debates and appears to have been largely uncontroversial, being generally regarded as a natural corollary to women's suffrage. While the two Bills mentioned above were more wide-ranging than merely allowing for the appointment of women JPs, the third Bill, introduced in the House of Lords, was very specific. The Justices of the Peace (Admission of Women) Bill was proposed by Liberal Peer Lord Beauchamp, in May 1919 and passed its second reading unopposed. During the debate Lord Beauchamp received an assurance from the Lord Chancellor, Lord Birkenhead, that the Bill or one like it would soon become law and that women would be made JPs with full powers, not merely to deal with children's cases:

> Lord Halsbury made the observation that in his view there were many causes to which women could contribute much, but that it would not be desirable to make women magistrates with limited functions. To that view, I confess, I assent. If your Lordships, and Parliament generally, are prepared to sanction so great an innovation you must do so with a full consciousness that the choice is being taken for all purposes, and that no distinction must or can be drawn between the case of female and male magistrates.[8]

In the event, Lord Beauchamp's Bill was also superseded by the Government's Sex Disqualification (Removal) Bill, later the Sex Disqualification (Removal) Act 1919.

On Christmas Eve 1919, the names of the first seven women JPs were announced. The women were Lady Crewe, daughter of the former Prime Minister Lord Rosebery; Margaret Lloyd George, the Prime Minister's wife and the first woman JP to be sworn in in Wales; Elizabeth Haldane, a Liberal who represented Scotland on the committee; a women's trade union leader, Gertrude Tuckwell; the prominent novelist and anti-suffragist Mary Ward; Lady Londonderry, who was known for her voluntary war work as well as being a political hostess; and the Fabian Society activist Beatrice Webb. This group had been chosen to balance both political and geographical interests and it is noteworthy that many of them were related to leading politicians: Haldane, for example, was the sister of a former Lord Chancellor.[9] However, in fact, it was another woman, Ada Summers, who became the first woman to preside in a magistrates' court on New Year's Eve in 1919 by virtue of her office as Mayor of Stalybridge, which entitled her sit as an ex officio JP.[10]

In addition to their work in the courts, the first seven women JPs were tasked, under Lady Crewe's leadership, with producing a list of other women who might also be recommended to become JPs.[11] This was a deviation from the normal method of appointment, which usually followed local recommendations to the Lord Chancellor or the Chancellor

[8] HL Deb, 20 May 1919, vol 34 col 737.

[9] Logan, n 3 above, 149–55.

[10] *The Times*, 1 January 1920, 9.

[11] Mary Ward died before the Committee had done much work and was replaced by Violet Markham, a Liberal and former anti-suffragist.

of the Duchy of Lancaster. The so-called 'Lord Chancellor's Women's Advisory Committee' was a unique body. It was disbanded in July 1920 after it had produced a list of 172 names. Subsequent women JPs were chosen in the conventional manner (as they had been throughout in the parts of north-west England which came under the Duchy of Lancaster for judicial appointments, rather than the Lord Chancellor).[12]

Most of the women on the Lord Chancellor's Women's Advisory Committee's list accepted appointment and were sworn in at their local courts. However, their number was tiny in relation to the total number of JPs (although the exact proportion is unknown) and fell very far short of the 'one woman on every bench' standard desired by the WFL. It is clear that neither the Lord Chancellor, Lord Birkenhead, nor many other politicians expected there to be large numbers of women appointed to the magistracy. Before the 1919 Act was passed, Lord Birkenhead had told the Lords and 'the many women in the country who may be aspirants in the near future to a seat on the Bench' that JPs' benches were already 'tolerably full' and that he would not make unnecessary additions 'merely in order' that women might be accommodated.[13] Even Lord Buckmaster, a friend of the women's movement, claimed that only 'exceptional' women would be suitable for appointment.[14]

## III. What Happened Next

Even after the first appointments there continued to be comment in the press about women lacking 'judicial qualities' – of being over-sentimental, irrational, incapable of dispassion – and/or lacking the legal knowledge or experience to be JPs (although the latter was not a requirement for male JPs). The passage of legislation was not sufficient in itself to challenge or change such attitudes or to ensure women's appointment. It was left to women's organisations to keep up the pressure for the appointment of women and to urge that women were worthy and did possess the essential qualities for judicial decision-making. The need for more women JPs was argued by a broad, well-networked group of women's organisations, acting together with penal reform pressure groups and the Labour Party. Prominent organisations included the NCW's Public Service and Magistrates' Committee, the Howard League for Penal Reform (HLPR) and the Magistrates Association (MA). The Public Service and Magistrates' Committee, led by Florence Keynes JP, undertook valuable research, for the NCW, into the numbers and location of women JPs at a time when no systematic national records were kept.

The developing specialism of juvenile courts continued to be used as a key argument for the appointment of women JPs. Statistics suggest that the Juvenile Courts (Metropolis) Act 1920, which reconfigured London's children's courts by introducing a team of two lay justices (one man and one woman) to sit alongside a stipendiary magistrate on young

[12] For a full discussion of the Advisory Committee and list it compiled, see Logan, n 3 above, 143–76. The list can be found in the papers of the National Council of Women, London Metropolitan Archives, ACC/3613/03/002/B and is reprinted, with some omissions, in Thomas Skyrme, *History of the Justices of the Peace*, vol 3 (Barry Rose, 1991) 1292–322.

[13] HL Deb, 20 May 1919, vol 34 col 738.

[14] *Daily Dispatch*, 9 November 1919.

people's cases, and the Children and Young Person's Act 1933 both prompted a wave of appointments. The former, passed in the teeth of fierce opposition from London's legally qualified magistrates, helped to push the number of women JPs in the capital to over 100 by 1927.[15] Elsewhere progress was slower, and the NCW were still trying to ensure that there were sufficient women to cover juvenile courts in the late 1930s.

The new women JPs used networks not only to lobby for appointments but also to train themselves and induct them into modern, progressive, so-called penal-welfare methods. A key network was the Magistrates Association. Margery Fry, who had been appointed a JP in London in 1919 and was Secretary of the HLPR, arranged for that body to pay the salary of the Association's first organiser, Cecil Leeson. Together Fry and Leeson wrote to all the women JPs appointed in 1920 encouraging them to join the HLPR and thereby establishing the beginnings of an important network.[16] It is likely that this initiative accounts for the disproportionately high number of women MA founding members (one-third of individual subscribers in 1922). Fry and Tuckwell (one of the first seven JPs) both served on the MA's executive committee for many years and the MA held women-only meetings at its annual conferences throughout the inter-war years. As well as national organisations, there is evidence that women magistrates formed their own clubs or associations in many parts of the country. Leading figures across the network of women's organisations, penal reform groups and magistrates' societies promoted training, policy discussion, and sharing of good practice at a time when new JPs received no formal training whatsoever. They proclaimed the virtues of probation and of medical and psychological reports on offenders, and promoted discussion of alternatives to short prison sentences. One particularly active group, the Gloucestershire Women Magistrates Society, inspired a male JP in 1935 to set up a JPs' discussion group in Oxfordshire.[17] In this way, the women JPs transformed the lay magistracy, deflecting criticism of the 'amateur', and helped to ensure its survival in the twentieth century.

Feminist campaigning, together with developments such as legislation aimed at protecting children, ensured a steady growth in the number of women magistrates. In 1948, the first-ever official survey of JPs in England and Wales was responded to by 3,700 women and 13,100 men, which suggests that women made up over 20 per cent of JPs at that time.[18] By then, the presence of women on the bench was no longer a cause of very much comment and the 1948 feature film, *Good Time Girl*, even featured a woman JP as chairman [note: not chair*woman*] of the juvenile court.

The proportion of women JPs continued to rise steadily in post-war decades to just over 4000 in 1962 and just over 10,300 in 1983. This figure has remained relatively stable, with the result that in 2016 women made up 53 per cent of the lay magistracy.[19] The greater availability and willingness of women to do voluntary work than men is one of the reasons

[15] Logan, n 5 above.

[16] HLPR archive, Warwick University Modern Records Centre, MSS16C/4/21.

[17] Anne Logan, 'Professionalism and the impact of England's first women justices, 1920–1950' (2006) 49 *The Historical Journal* 3.

[18] Report of the Royal Commission on Justices of the Peace (Cmd 7463, 1948) 6.

[19] Judicial Office, 'Judicial Diversity Statistics 2016' (*Judicial Office Statistical Bulletin*, July 2016, revised December 2016), 16.

behind this increase. Women represented a new pool of voluntary labour for the justice system to draw upon, especially in the decades before the 1980s when middle-class, married women were less likely than more recently to be in paid employment.[20] The availability of well-educated women willing to volunteer for magisterial duties is also likely to have slowed the move toward professionally-qualified justices. In 2001 it was claimed that lay JPs saved the state at least £30 million a year.[21]

While there is no evidence that women JPs judged or decided cases in any fundamentally different way from men, there was plenty of discussion in the 1920s that this could be the case. Much of this comment was based on stereotypical views about women, who were (confusingly) accused of being both tougher and softer on criminals than their male counterparts. However, there were some early women JPs who had been active in the suffrage movement and who brought feminist sensibilities to their work. Importantly the infanticide legislation of 1922 (which introduced the separate offence of infanticide by a mother against her own child of under one month old) has been ascribed at least in part to the lobbying of policy networks of new women JPs.[22]

## IV. Significance

After centuries of all-male law courts, the introduction of women JPs was not merely a legal landmark but a revolution. Over the first 600 years since the office of JP originated it is unlikely that more than a tiny number of women had held it and none had done so since the early sixteenth century. In contrast, in the hundred years since the 1919 Act many thousands of women have served as JPs.

Moreover, it was a change which had immediate impact. Whereas aspiring women lawyers took years to qualify professionally, women JPs could (for good or ill) sit in court immediately. So whereas the proportion of the legal professions who were women grew only slowly after the 1919 legislation, the number of women magistrates enjoyed steady growth from the very beginning and women became a significant presence upon JPs' benches within a generation. Today just over half of all JPs are women.

Without doubt, the introduction of women JPs enabled women to establish quickly a presence in the summary courts. However, the impact of women JPs went beyond mere numbers; they also inaugurated a transformation of the lay magistracy – who still handle the vast majority of criminal cases in England and Wales – in unexpected ways. But it was the work of the women JP's associated organisations and networks which had the most profound effect, pushing the lay magistracy towards modernisation through enhanced training and education opportunities and thus greater professionalism, laying the foundations for the Magistrates Association and magistracy today.

[20] For the role of voluntary work in the careers of educated women, see Pat Thane, 'Girton Graduates: Earning and Learning, 1920s to 1980s' (2004) 13(4) *Women's History Review* 347–61.

[21] Letter to the editor from the Chairman of the Magistrates Association published in *The Guardian*, 23 January 2001.

[22] Daniel JR Grey, 'Women's Policy Networks and the Infanticide Act 1922' (2010) 21(4) *Twentieth Century British History* 441–63.

## Further Reading

- Anne Logan, '"A Suitable Person for Suitable Cases": The Gendering of Juvenile Courts in England, c.1910–39' (2005) 16(2) *Twentieth Century British History* 129–45.
- Anne Logan, 'Professionalism and the impact of England's first women justices, 1920–1950' (2006) 49 *The Historical Journal* 3.
- Anne Logan, 'In Search of Equal Citizenship: the campaign for women magistrates in England and Wales, 1910–1939' (2007) 16(4) *Women's History Review* 501–18.

# 19

# First Woman to be Admitted to an Inn of Court, Helena Normanton, 1919

JUDITH BOURNE

Helena Normanton (1882–1957) was the first woman to be admitted to an Inn of Court on 24 December 1919, immediately after the **Sex Disqualification (Removal) Act 1919** received royal assent. Until Normanton's admission women had been refused entry, thus preventing women from becoming barristers. She was also the first woman to be briefed in both the High Court[1] and the Central Criminal Court[2] and was, with **Rose Heilbron**, one of the two first women King's Counsel in England and Wales.[3]

## I. Life

Normanton was born on 14 December 1882 in West Ham, then in Essex, now in East London.[4] Her father was a pianoforte maker who died in mysterious circumstances on the Metropolitan Line when Normanton was four years old. The census records that her mother was successively a milliner, publican and boarding-house keeper. Normanton's parents had separated, which would have attracted great social stigma at the time, and perhaps as a result her early life was full of change and upheaval: the family moved frequently and her sister was sent to a boarding school for fatherless girls.

Normanton trained as a pupil-teacher, one of the only professional careers open to women at this time, whilst living at home in Brighton between 1895 and 1903. She enrolled at Edge Hill, an all-female teacher training college, where according to the principal, Sarah Hale, the students demonstrated 'a healthy interest in feminism'.[5] Indeed, this may have been one of the reasons Normanton chose to study there. In 1905, Normanton began work as a history teacher. Her archives contain references praising her performance as a teacher: she was 'possessed of ability much above average … [who] brings to bear on any question

[1] *Searle v Searle*, High Court of Justice (Divorce) in papers held at the Women's Library, LSE (WL: 7HLN/A/09).
[2] The case of *R v* Eyles, reported in the *Daily Express*, 'First Woman in the Old Bailey', 7 February 1924.
[3] **First Woman Member of the Faculty of Advocates, Margaret Kidd, 1923**.
[4] This landmark draws on the research contained in Judith Bourne, *Helena Normanton and the Opening of the Bar to Women* (Waterside Press, 2016).
[5] Fiona Montgomery and Mark Flinn, *A Vision of Learning: Edge Hill University 1885–2010* (Third Millennium Publishing, 2010) 38.

under discussion a lucidity and sanity of judgment too infrequently found in those of her sex'.[6] In 1912, while working full time, she was awarded a first class degree in History from the University of London external programme.[7] In 1915 she left school-teaching to take up a controversial choice of employment, that of tutor to the sons of the Baron de Forest, a Liberal MP, and twice divorced man of Austrian origins, who had converted from Judaism to Roman Catholicism. A year later she became an extension lecturer in history at the University of London, a position she stayed in until she joined the Bar.

Normanton was a prominent member of a number of influential women's groups and networks. In 1914, she joined the Women's Freedom League, a suffragette organisation, and was the guest speaker at their Magna Carta celebrations in 1915,[8] where she argued that Magna Carta was the source and basis of women's legal rights. The same year she produced a pamphlet for the National Federation of Women Teachers, arguing for equal pay for equal work. After some women obtained the vote,[9] including Normanton herself, in 1918, she shifted her attention to ensuring the extension of the vote to *all* women, through her membership of the Union of Women Voters, and women's participation in civic society, as the first secretary of the National Women's Citizen Association. In 1921 she was an early member of Lady Rhondda's Six Point Group.[10]

Normanton claimed to have fostered an ambition to become a lawyer from the age of 12 when she visited a solicitor with her mother.[11] Her mother could not understand the advice proffered, but the solicitor could see that Normanton understood and made her recite the advice, which she did, leading him to remark that she was 'quite the little lawyer'. She felt her mother was the victim of sex inequality because she lacked rudimentary legal knowledge that Normanton supposed men had.

Normanton joined the Committee for the Admission of Women to the Legal Profession, a network of women campaigning for women's entry to the bar, possibly founded in 1904 by Christabel Pankhurst after her application to Lincoln's Inn was rejected.[12] Membership of an Inn of Court was (and still is) crucial to a career at the Bar, for without eating the correct number of dinners at an Inn, a student could not and still cannot be called as a barrister. In the glare of publicity, Normanton applied for admission to Middle Temple in February 1918 and was rejected. The following June, Normanton appealed against her rejection. This was also rejected. In November 1919, when it was clear that the (then) Sex Disqualification (Removal) Bill would become law, Normanton rang the Under Treasurer at Middle Temple and requested to be admitted as a student and was told that her application must 'stand over until the Bill' became law. A month later they wrote to her explaining that they had received her references, but that the Treasury Office would be closed between 24–31 December.

[6] Women's Library, LSE: WL: 7HLN/A/01.

[7] She was awarded her LLB from the University of London in 1930.

[8] Antoinette Burton, *Burdens of History: British Feminists, Indian Women, and Imperial Culture* (University of North Carolina Press, 2000).

[9] See **Representation of the People Act 1918**.

[10] See **Life Peerages Act 1958.**

[11] Helena Normanton, *Everyday Law for Women* (1st edn, Richard Clay & Sons 1932) 6.

[12] There is little archival material surrounding this group, however see *Evening News*, 9 March 1920; Elizabeth Crawford, *The Women's Suffrage Movement: A reference guide 1866–1928* (UCL Press, 1999); Rosemary Auchmuty, 'Whatever Happened to Miss Bebb? *Bebb v The Law Society* and women's legal history' (2013) 31 *Legal Studies* 199, 209–12; Elsie Lang, *British Women in the Twentieth Century* (T Werner Laurie, 1929).

It was clear that they would not be rushed into admitting her. The Bill was due to receive Royal Assent on 23 December 1919. On that day the Treasury Office wrote to Normanton explaining that the Bill was due to receive assent at 3pm and they would wait for her until 4.05pm in case she 'should call'. Further, in the event of her not calling, they supplied her with a telephone number and address, as they wished to cause her (ironically) as 'little delay as possible'. She must have gone to the Treasury Office on Christmas Eve, the day the office should have been closed, as her archives contain a library card in her name (the 'Mr' scrubbed out and 'Miss' written in) and a membership fee receipt.

Normanton passed her Bar Finals with a third in October 1921, the same month she married Gavin Watson Clark. She retained her maiden name. She was called to the bar at Middle Temple in November 1922, alongside eight other women[13] (and one at Inner Temple).[14] They were not the first women to be called: that honour went to Ivy Williams,[15] called to the Bar at Inner Temple, in May 1922.[16] Normanton held her first brief on 21 December 1922. In 1949 she was made a King's Counsel.

After joining the Bar, Normanton continued to be involved in a number of women's campaigns including arguing for the separate assessment of married person's tax[17] – becoming, in 1929, Chair of the Married Person's Income Tax Reform Council – and as a member of the National Council for Equal Citizenship and President of the Married Women's Association in 1952. Her practice was largely limited to poor persons and lower court work (though she was the first woman to prosecute in a murder case in 1948). She practised successfully until her retirement in 1951. She died in Beckenham in 1957.

## II. Context

Normanton was not the first woman to demand entry to the legal profession. Women had been forming networks for the right to enter the legal profession since 1873 when Maria Grey[18] unsuccessfully[19] organised a petition signed by 92 women to attend lectures given by the Council of Legal Education.[20] Thirty years later, in 1903 Bertha Cave[21] applied to join Gray's Inn and was again refused. She appealed as a litigant in person to the House of Lords and was heard before a formidable group of judges, including the Lord Chancellor, Lord Halsbury, who unanimously rejected her appeal. There was no precedent which

[13] Monica Geikie Cobb, Auvergne Doherty, Ethel Bright Ashford, Naomi Wallace, Sybil Campbell, Elise Wheeler, Lillian Dawes and Beatrice Honor Davy.

[14] Theodora Llewellyn Davies.

[15] Hazel Fox, 'Williams, Ivy (1877–1966)' in *Oxford Dictionary of National Biography* (OUP, 2004).

[16] Her academic achievements had allowed her to shorten the period of call. In 1920 she had become the first woman to teach law in a British university when she became a tutor to the Home Students at Oxford.

[17] **Section 32 of the Finance Act 1988**.

[18] Philippa Levine, 'Grey, Maria Georgina (1816–1906)' in *Oxford Dictionary of National Biography* (OUP, 2004).

[19] Mary Jane Mossman, *The First Women Lawyers: A Comparative Study of Gender, Law and the Legal Professions* (Hart Publishing, 2006) 116.

[20] Established in 1852 by the Inns of Court to supervise the education of Bar students. It employed professors to lecture. See the Council of Legal Education archive held at the Institute of Advanced Legal Studies, University of London.

[21] MT. 1/MPA/22.

allowed women such entry. In 1904 Christabel Pankhurst's application was rejected (no doubt for the additional reason that her suffragette behaviour was 'disgraceful').[22] Undeterred, the Committee for the Admission of Women to the Legal Profession went on to assist Miss Bebb, and three others in their landmark (but unsuccessful) case to force open the solicitor's profession in 1913.[23] In 1914, the Committee to Open the Legal Profession to Women was established and campaigning continued until the outbreak of the First World War. It was only after the war that the Law Society had a change of heart, voting to admit women in 1918. However, the Bar stood firm, refusing to open its doors until forced to do so by the 1919 Act, and only then doing so grudgingly.

Normanton's admission happened during a time of great social and global change. It is no coincidence that Normanton made her application to Middle Temple in the same month that some women had finally obtained the vote. The extension of the franchise gave women confidence, not simply in their legal status but in the fact that they had won a major campaign for equality. Further afield, Europe had been irreversibly changed during and by the First World War; there had been a revolution in Russia and there was conflict in Ireland and India. Women were already able to practise law in many other countries, including the United States and former British colonies like Australia, New Zealand and Canada. Clara Brett Martin had joined the Law Society of Upper Canada in 1867; Arabella Mansfield had been admitted to the Iowa Bar in the US in 1869, followed by Ethel Benjamin, who had been admitted as a barrister and solicitor of the Supreme Court of New Zealand in May 1897 and Flos Greig, who was admitted to the Victorian Bar in 1905.

## III. What Happened Next

In England and Wales, the initial round of appointments was followed, in 1923, with the call of a further 10 women. In 1924, the number of women called rose to 18, but in 1925 this had fallen to nine.[24] These figures were typical until the mid-1940s, with the result that by 1970 women accounted for just 8.2 per cent of those called to the Bar. This increased to 37 per cent by the mid-1980s,[25] and by the early 1990s 42.7 per cent of those called to the Bar were women.[26] In 2016, 616 women were called to the Bar (47 per cent) – though in recent years they have exceeded the 50 per cent mark. However, despite making up almost half of those joining the profession for over a quarter of a century, women's occupation in and progression through the legal progression has been painfully slow. Current figures reveal that women make up just 36 per cent of the practising Bar and a mere 14 per cent of QCs.[27]

[22] Auchmuty, n 12 above, 214.
[23] *Bebb v Law Society* [1914] 1 Ch 286. See further **Women's Legal Landmarks: An Introduction**.
[24] Richard Abel, *The Making of the English Legal Profession 1800–1988* (Beard Books, 1988) 330 (Table 1.12).
[25] Bar Council figures (on file with editors).
[26] Bar Council figures (on file with editors).
[27] Bar Council, 'Called to the Bar and tenancy statistics' (*Bar Council*, no date): https://www.barstandardsboard.org.uk/media-centre/research-and-statistics/statistics/called-to-the-bar-statistics/.

## IV. Significance

> To all Edge Hill suffragists I give this advice – it takes no moral courage whatever to walk in procession.[28]

In her lifetime, Normanton attracted much negative comment from legal contemporaries affronted by her feminism. She was, according to one,

> a war horse from the old feminist days and the terror of her male colleagues … a comic character quite without fear, and physically unattractive. She can only be described as large and blowsy … incredibly common not to say vulgar … a menace to the movement for she was always trying to organise the women into forming separate groups from the men.[29]

These kinds of comments are, of course, the classic response to pioneer women. We can conclude from this that Normanton represented a challenge to the established order: a woman determined to practise at the Bar at whatever personal cost; a woman determined to challenge men's monopoly on the legal profession; a woman not afraid of rivalry; a woman competing for substantive equality. Nor was she unaware of the impact of her gender on her lawyering:

> [W]omen often say that they cannot get a man lawyer to understand what their real grievance is. Something has gone wrong with their marriage and they are not able to convince a man as to the cruelty of the case.[30]

Though she was quick to add that she did not wish to be confined to 'women's cases'.[31]

Normanton's admission as the 'first' woman to enter an Inn of Court symbolised – and was in fact – the end of men's unchallenged control of the legal profession. It was a ground-breaking step in itself, and her fortitude in remaining in practice despite the negative narrative and constant allegations of self-publicity that grew up around her demonstrates her continuing determination to break down discrimination against women at the Bar.

## Further Reading


- Rosemary Auchmuty, 'Whatever Happened to Miss Bebb? *Bebb v The Law Society* and women's legal history' (2013) 31 *Legal Studies* 199–230.
- Judith Bourne, *Helena Normanton and the Opening of the Bar to Women* (Waterside Press, 2016).
- Patrick Polden, 'Portia's Progress: Women at the Bar in England, 1919–1939' (2005) 12 *International Journal of the Legal Profession* 293–338.


[28] Normanton writing in the *Edge Hill Magazine* in 1908.
[29] Women's Library, LSE, WL: LOCKET.
[30] As reported in *The Vote*, 20 February 1920.
[31] ibid.

# 20

# Committee on the Employment of Women on Police Duties, 1920

COLIN R MOORE

In 1920 the Report of the Committee on the Employment of Women on Police Duties (the 'Baird Committee') recognised that women could be sworn in as constables in the police forces of England, Wales, and Scotland. It also acknowledged the valuable role that women police fulfilled when undertaking police work. Such recommendations were built on the success and usefulness of the various, sometimes competing, voluntary private women police services established during the First World War.

However, the Baird Committee was only a qualified success for the recognition and extensions of the rights of women: women police came close to being abolished entirely a few years later, as a result of austerity-type pressures, and the numbers of women police did not increase significantly until the Second World War. Furthermore, women police tended to fill specialist roles in specialist departments within the Police, until the **Sex Discrimination Act 1975**, over 50 years later, which achieved apparent, but perhaps not actual, equality. Nevertheless, the Baird Committee was an important first step in facilitating the careers, and improving the prospects, of women entering the Police Service.

## I. Context

Police forces employed some women for limited purposes prior to the First World War but any calls to deploy women police officers, following the American example, were resisted by the Home Office. On the outbreak of hostilities, arguments that policemen were otherwise engaged, just as their duties began to increase because of the war, began to hold a greater sway.[1] Voluntary groups of women police began to form during the war under a variety of different group identities. The first key group was the Women Police Service (WPS),

[1] See John Carrier, *The Campaign for the Employment of Women as Police Officers* (Gower Publishing Company, 1988) 2, who refers to National Archive, Home Office, HO45/10806/309485/71 and Home Office, *Report of the Commissioner of Police for the Metropolis* (Cd 8188, 1914). See generally: Dorothy Peto, *The Memoirs of Miss Dorothy Olivia Georgina Peto, OBE* (Metropolitan Police Museum, 1993) and Chloe Owings, *Women Police* (Frederick H Hitchcock, 1925) in relation to American Women Police.

formed by Margaret Damer-Dawson and Mary Allen, both of whom had links with the militant suffragette Women's Social and Political Union.[2] The second, and ultimately more successful, were the less radical Women Patrols established by the National Union of Women Workers (NUWW), in consultation with a number of moral welfare groups, and led by Mrs MG Carden.[3] Recognising the need for proper training, the NUWW opened a training school in Bristol in January 1915, followed by schools in Liverpool and Glasgow. These became known collectively as the Federated Training Schools and operated under the directorship of Dorothy Peto.

In terms of work undertaken, the WPS was keen to carry out 'rescue work', warning vulnerable women of the dangers of 'immoral behaviour', as well as having a contract to police women working in munitions factories, while both the WPS and NUWW spent a large amount of time monitoring the behaviour of working-class women, carrying out patrols in parks and other public spaces, and 'moving on "dangerous" women'.[4] Most of these voluntary women police were not attested or sworn in as police officers, and therefore lacked the power of arrest, although a few were sworn in as constables. The first of these was Edith Smith (WPS) in Grantham in August 1915, although prior to the **Sex Disqualification (Removal) Act 1919**, the effectiveness of these swearing in procedures was a matter of some doubt.

The women police patrols were initially voluntary in nature with the majority of costs paid for by local funds. However, at least part-payment from the Exchequer was facilitated by section 4 of the the Police, Factories, etc. (Miscellaneous Provisions Act) 1916, which allowed half of the cost of women police to be met by central funds in the same manner as male police. Initially, the Metropolitan Police paid for some of the NUWW patrols, but when Sir Nevil Macready replaced Sir Edward Henry as Metropolitan Police Commissioner, he clearly felt that having an outside organisation running women patrols was unsatisfactory. On 22 October 1919 Macready submitted a proposal to the Home Secretary, Edward Shortt, for the formation of an experimental formal Women Police service. Approval in principle was given by the Sir John Baird, Under-Secretary of State for the Home Department, a month later, although it was emphasised that the women were not to have the status of constable or be full members of the force, but to act as an auxiliary service.

While formally the new organisation was independent of the NUWW, Sofia Stanley, a member of the NUWW, was appointed as Superintendent of the 'Metropolitan Police Women Patrol', and Carden was appointed as a member of the selection panel. Indeed, many of the first recruits were former members of the NUWW patrols (the WPS were almost entirely excluded from the new official patrol).[5] One of the first women to be appointed was Lillian Wyles. Writing in 1952, she commented:

> We twenty-five women were not unaware of the hostility we were to meet. We already had experience of what lay in store for us: but of the downright malice and vindictive spirit to be shown by

[2] Louise Jackson, *Women Police: Gender, Welfare and Surveillance in the Twentieth Century* (Manchester University Press, 2006) 21.

[3] Carrier, n 1 above, 11.

[4] 'The First World War and Women Patrols': www.open.ac.uk/Arts/history-from-police-archives/Met6Kt/WomenPolice/wpWW1.html.

[5] Carrier, n 1 above, 81–86.

some of the men towards us we were, as yet, blissfully ignorant. Had we known how rough was to be our passage, how severe the gales and storms that would rage around us until we reached calm waters it would have made not one whit of difference to our determination to pilot our tiny band of one hundred women to success and security in the Metropolitan Police.[6]

## II. The Landmark

While the Metropolitan Police Women Patrol laid the foundations for full attestation and constable status for the women police, the Women Patrol members themselves, which were limited to London, lacked powers of arrest. The Desborough Committee on the Police Service, established in March 1919, declined to consider the issue of Women Police.[7] Peto lobbied the Home Office in July 1919 on behalf of the Federated Training Schools to campaign for a similar Committee on women police. She argued that questions of the status of women police, as well as pay and pensions, needed urgent consideration, though it was also clear that she hoped that the London scheme would be extended nationwide. Similar lobbying was carried out by Carden, and the Home Office agreed to meet a deputation from the NUWW, now renamed as the National Council of Women (NCW), as well as delegates from the Federated Training Schools. On 8 August 1919, the delegation met with Sir John Baird, Under-Secretary of State for the Home Department, who promised consideration of conferring a power of arrest or similar power on members of the Women's Patrol.[8] Nancy Astor MP also proved to be an important ally in the House of Commons, pressing the Home Secretary, Sir William Joynson-Hicks, by methods as bizarre as reserving his favourite seat in the House of Commons using a pink prayer card bearing the words 'Committee on Women Police'.[9] The contribution of this action is unclear, but a Committee was appointed on 11 February 1920, chaired by Baird.[10]

The Baird Committee was tasked with inquiring into the 'nature and limits of the assistance which can be given by Women in the carrying out of Police duties', as well as examining the appropriate 'status, pay and conditions' of women employed on those duties.[11] Women's views were represented directly on the Committee itself by Lady Astor and Dame Helen Gwynne-Vaughan, former commander of the Women's Royal Air Force. Twenty of the 47 witnesses examined by the Committee were also women. These included representatives from the WPS, NCW, the Federated Training Schools, and the National Council for Combating Venereal Disease. Several serving policewomen, including Wyles, gave evidence.

The Committee unequivocally concluded that the war had proved the advantage in deploying women to carry out certain aspects of police work, and that these duties could

[6] Lilian Wyles, *A Women at Scotland Yard: Reflections on the Struggles and Achievements of Thirty Years in the Metropolitan Police* (Faber and Faber, 1952) 12.
[7] Home Office, *The Committee on the Police Service* (Cmd 874, 1920).
[8] Carrier, n 1 above, 93–96.
[9] ibid 96 and Christopher Skykes, *Nancy, the Life of Lady Astor* (Panther, 1979) 219.
[10] Home Office, *Committee on the Employment of Women on Police Duties* (Cmd 877, 1920) [15].
[11] ibid [3].

be performed efficiently provided that the women concerned were appropriately qualified, trained, paid, and integrated into the police force: 'We are of the opinion that in thickly populated areas, where offences against the law relating to women and children are not infrequent, there is not only scope but urgent need for the employment of policewomen'.[12] It recommended that there were to be no more voluntary patrols. Instead local police authorities would decide if women police would be employed in a given area.[13] While most witnesses, and the Committee itself, agreed with the Home Office and Scottish Office that women could not be regarded as substitutes for men in a police force – women police were to be an addition to the male strength of the force, not a replacement – nearly all witnesses accepted that women had demonstrable value in relation to the investigation of offences committed by, or against, women and children. Other witnesses affirmed that women were physically capable of carrying out police duties. Dr Letitia Fairfield, for example, gave evidence that women could be on their feet for eight hours, and Wyles emphasised that drilling improved walking.[14]

Crucially, the Committee recommended that all women should be sworn in as constables if they were employed by a police force to carry out police duties beyond that of a police matron or routine administration.[15] It was of the view that any legal bar to this step had been extinguished following the enactment of the Sex Disqualification (Removal) Act 1919. In terms of duties, the Committee reported that women police would be specifically suitable for custody and escort of women and minors, as well as administrative tasks – the latter usually seen as useful training for men seeking promotion, police widows, and police officers injured in the line of duty. However, the Committee proposed that the exact deployment of women police should remain a matter for local Watch Committees in consultation with the Chief Constable, albeit on specific standardised pay and conditions for women. The Committee recommended that conditions for policewomen should be the same as those of men – with the exception of pay and working hours – although their shorter working life (because the retirement age for women was lower) meant that a slightly modified pension scheme would be necessary.[16]

## III. What Happened Next

Although the Baird Report was seen generally as a policewomen's charter,[17] in the early 1920s the number of employed policewomen actually decreased. The British economy was clearly in difficulty in the early 1920s, but it is also clear that this position was capitalised upon by opponents of the women police. They were among the multitude of public functions targeted by the 'Geddes Axe'. The Geddes Committee, which had been tasked with

[12] ibid [15].
[13] ibid [13]. With the result that 142 of a total 241 Chief Constables, particularly those heading up County and Borough forces, felt that the employment of women police was unnecessary in their districts.
[14] ibid [9]–[10], [12] and [13]. Home Office, *Committee on the Employment of Women on Police: Minutes of Evidence* (Cmd 1133, 1921) [1535] and [1160]. See Carrier, n 1 above, 102.
[15] This did not happen until 1923.
[16] *Committee on the Employment of Women on Police Duties*, n 10 above, [26]–[28], [31], [33]–[36] and [79]. See Carrier, n 1 above, 103.
[17] Carrier, ibid.

saving £100 million from the government budget,[18] proposed that the women police should be abolished entirely, as their impact on policing was 'negligible' and the expenditure, in a time of austerity, could not be justified.[19] This position was supported by the Police Federation, who represented rank-and-file police officers – though not, until 1948, women police – as well as by the Home Secretary and the new Metropolitan Police Commissioner, Sir William Horwood.

The NCW, along with Nancy Astor and others, met officials from the Home Office to argue that the work of women police was both important and actually reduced public expenditure in other areas.[20] Many of the arguments emphasised women police's different skills and insights compared to their male colleagues, particularly in relation to women criminals. There were further protest speeches on the matter by Lord Aberdeen and the Archbishop of Canterbury, in the House of Lords, and by Lady Astor in the House of Commons.[21]

> I wish to draw the attention of the House to the dismissal of the Metropolitan women police patrols … The ['Baird'] Committee … said that the women patrols should form part of the police force and should have power of arrest. Why did not the Home Secretary act upon that recommendation? In spite of the Sex Disqualification (Removal) Act, the women patrols in London never had power of arrest, and they would have been much more useful if they had had that power … Sir Nevil Macready, the head of the London Police, said that, not only would he have women police, but he would give them full powers of arrest the same as constables, and he wanted to put the whole question of solicitation in their hands, because he felt they could do it better than the men … [The] Committee said that women needed to be specially qualified and highly trained for the work, yet the Home Secretary says a great deal of it will still be done by policemen's wives. No doubt policemen have delightful and charming wives, highly cultivated and qualified, but I do not believe they marry them because they will be able to deal with girls and women in a skilled way … As a matter of fact, I think policemen select their wives on the same line as lawyers and politicians; they select them because they like them, they do not select them because they may be of use to them in police work any more than a lawyer selects his wife in order she may prepare a brief for him.[22]

Nevertheless the proposal to reduce the number of women police in the Metropolitan Police to 20 was approved by the Home Secretary, and only 20 women were retained,[23] although the established number was increased to 50 in 1924.[24] By the time the next Committee on the Employment of Policewomen reported (the 'Bridgeman Report') in 1924, the total strength of women police nationally was 110.[25]

By 1939, policewomen still represented less than one per cent of the total police force, despite the fact that the Royal Commission on Police Powers and Procedures in 1929

[18] ibid 116–117.
[19] *Second Interim Report of the Committee on National Expenditure* (Cmd 1582, 1921) 62.
[20] Carrier, n 1 above, 118–21.
[21] HL Deb, 8 March 1922, vol 49 cols 393–404 and HC Deb, 28 March 1922, vol 152 cols 1259–81, respectively.
[22] HC Deb, 28 March 1922, vol 152, cols 1260–1263.
[23] *Report of the Commissioner of Police of the Metropolis for the Year 1923* (HMSO, 1924) 8.
[24] ibid.
[25] Home Office, *The Report of the Committee on the Employment of Policewomen* (Cmd 2224, 1924) (the 'Bridgeman Report') 4.

had recognised the value of women police and suggested that their numbers should be increased.[26] However, although small in number, a significant number of women carved out successful careers, including several of those who had campaigned for the inclusion of women in the formal police force. Wyles became first woman to serve as a fully-attested, ranking officer in the Metropolitan Police CID and the first to be promoted to Chief Inspector, serving with the CID until her retirement in 1949. Peto was appointed as the Metropolitan Police's first woman staff officer in April 1930, retiring in 1946. Damer-Dawson was awarded an OBE in 1918 but died two years later.[27] She was succeeded as Commandant of the WPS, now known as the Women's Auxiliary Service, by Mary Allen, who founded the *Policewomen's Review*, which ran from 1927 until 1937.[28]

Separate policewomen's departments were maintained until the 1970s, at which point women were fully integrated into the main police force. The demise of these departments and integration of women police can be attributed to their success and effectiveness in carrying out 'specialist' or 'welfare' work, as well as the unsustainability of separate forces in the face of equal opportunities frameworks which were a prerequisite for European Economic Community (EEC) membership.[29] However, it was clear that well into the 1980s the Metropolitan Police had an unofficial policy of keeping levels of women police at around 10 per cent of the total force, and thus unlawfully discriminating against women applicants.[30]

Women are still underrepresented in the police generally and face inequality in relation to promotion opportunities.[31] Currently women represent 29 per cent of the total police strength in England and Wales and just under 23 per cent of Chief Constables (or equivalent). A survey in 2012 revealed that 42 per cent of women police officers had given serious thought to leaving. Their reasons for doing so point to a general lack of consideration for the particular difficulties faced by many women police officers, including refusals of flexible working and lack of support during pregnancy and following maternity leave.[32] This was doubtless compounded by the institutional masculinity of the police,[33] expressed within police cultural values of aggression, competitiveness, obsession with conflict, hyper-heterosexuality, and 'rigid in-group/out-group distinctions'.[34] Encouragingly, Cressida Dick became the first woman Commissioner of the Metropolitan Police (the most senior police officer in the country) in 2017, a landmark in itself. But this

[26] Home Office, *Royal Commission on Police Powers and Procedures* (Cmd 3297, 1929); Arthur L Dixon, *Home Office Between the Two World Wars* (unpublished, 1966).

[27] Louise A Jackson, 'Wyles, Lilian Mary Elizabeth (1885–1975)' in *Oxford Dictionary of National Biography* (OUP, 2010); RM Douglas, 'Peto, Dorothy Olivia Georgiana (1886–1974)' in *Oxford Dictionary of National Biography* (OUP, 2006); and David Doughan, 'Dawson, Margaret Mary Damer (1873–1920)' in *Oxford Dictionary of National Biography* (OUP, 2004).

[28] Mrs Albert Broom, 'Allen, Mary Sophia (1878–1964)' in *Oxford Dictionary of National Biography* (OUP, 2004).

[29] Jackson, n 2 above, 201–02.

[30] David Smith and Jeremy Gray, *Police and People in London* (Avebury, 1985) 507–09.

[31] Home Office, *Police Workforce: England and Wales*, 2016. See also Allen, Grahame and Noel Dempsey, *Police Service Strength* (House of Commons Library Briefing Paper 00634, 2016).

[32] Toby Helm, 'Four in 10 female police officers have considered quitting the force', *The Guardian*, 14 July 2012.

[33] Tom Cockcroft, *Police culture: Themes and Concepts* (Routledge, 2012) 61.

[34] Nigel G Fielding, 'Cop Canteen Culture' in Tim Newburn and Elizabeth A Stanko (eds), *Just Boys Doing Business: Men, Masculinities and Crime* (Routledge, 1994) 46, 47, quoted by Cockcroft, ibid 62–63.

smashing of this glass ceiling, as Louise Jackson has suggested, also serves to highlight what remains to be done if police officers are truly to reflect the diverse nature of the United Kingdom.[35]

## IV. Significance

Despite the ongoing lack of gender equality in the police force in England and Wales, the Baird Committee represents an important legal landmark for women generally, and women police in particular. Without it women would probably have been driven out of the force altogether as the Geddes Axe fell. The strategy adopted by feminists, of emphasising gender differences, created a space and opportunity for women to become police officers after the First World War and gain constable status. Social maternalism, emphasising 'women's innate' qualities as mothers and carers, was used to justify women's involvement in policing, just as it was in a similar manner in relation to medicine and social work. However, as Jackson emphasises, it was only in policing that such gender differences were institutionalised into a separate career structure, until the 1970s.[36] Perhaps only the Church of England saw worse discrimination than the British Police[37] in relation to limitations placed on women building a professional career equivalent to men.

It is difficult to see how any more could have been gained at the time of the Baird Committee, given the opposition to women police from Chief Constables as well as from within the Home Office. This is evidenced by the side-lining of the WPS, motivated by a desire, voiced by Macready, to 'eliminate any women of extreme views – the vinegary spinster or blighted middle-aged fanatic'.[38] While conservatism, both political and social, is typical in the aftermath of war,[39] such views make the achievements of the first women police even more remarkable.

## Further Reading

- John Carrier, *The Campaign for the Employment of Women as Police Officers* (Gower Publishing Company, 1988).
- Home Office, *Committee on the Employment of Women on Police Duties* (Cmd 877, 1920).
- Louise Jackson, *Women Police: Gender, Welfare and Surveillance in the Twentieth Century* (Manchester University Press, 2006).

[35] Louise Jackson, 'Why haven't we had a female Commissioner of the Metropolitan Police before now?' (*History & Policy* 2017).

[36] Jackson, n 2, 200–201.

[37] **Bishops and Priests (Consecration and Ordination of Women) Measure 2014 and Canon C2, 'Of the Consecration of Bishops', 2014.**

[38] Carrier, n 1 above, 85.

[39] Margaret and Patrice Higonnet, *Behind the Lines: Gender and the Two World Wars* (Yale University Press, 1987) 41.

# 21

# First Woman Law Agent, Madge Easton Anderson, 1920

ALISON LINDSAY

Madge Easton Anderson (1896–1982) was the first woman to qualify as a Law Agent in December 1920, following a successful petition to the Court of Session (Scotland's highest civil court),[1] although the decision was not formally registered until January 1921. She was also the first woman solicitor in the UK, the first woman Law Agent (in Scotland) and the first woman to practise law professionally in both Scotland and then England, as well as being a partner in the first UK law firm to be run exclusively by women.

## I. Life

Anderson was born in the district of Kelvin, in the north of Glasgow, on 12 August 1896; the youngest of three daughters of Robert Anderson and his wife, Anne Chisholm. Her father began his career as a cutlery salesman but by the time of the 1901 census had his own business selling surgical instruments. The family's growing prosperity was reflected in a move across the city to the newly-established suburb of Pollokshields, where Anderson attended Hutchesons' Girls' Grammar School from 1904 to 1913. The school emphasised academic excellence and was established around the same time, and with the same aims, as the Girls' Public Day School Company in England. It offered non-boarding education for a modest fee to growing numbers of middle-class parents. As there were no sons in the Anderson family, there was perhaps an added interest in giving their daughters the best possible education. Anderson's sister Ellen studied medicine and became a noted bacteriologist, so she had a close example before her of the opportunities open to educated young women.

At that time, it was necessary to obtain an undergraduate Arts degree before going forward to study law. Scottish universities award these as Master of Arts (MA) degrees, equivalent to the English Bachelor of Arts (BA). Anderson began her studies at Glasgow University in 1913 at the age of seventeen, and graduated in 1916 with an ordinary MA; that is, not specialising in any particular subject. Although she did not attend university in the academic year 1916–17, Anderson was nevertheless working towards a legal career.

[1] *Anderson, Petitioner* 1921 1 SLT 48.

She was fortunate to have had the support of Glasgow lawyer John Alexander Spens, whose son was one of the University's examiners. He arranged for her to be taken on as an apprentice in his own firm, Maclay, Murray and Spens in 1917, at a time when there was no prospect of women being admitted as law agents, as he was of the opinion that such disqualification must soon be removed.

In 1917 Anderson entered the Faculty of Law at the University of Glasgow. She was an excellent student: she was joint winner of a prize in Jurisprudence and Public International Law in her final year, and during her course received first class certificates of merit in Evidence and Procedures, International Private Law and International Public Law.[2]

All this meant that when the **Sex Discrimination (Removal) Act 1919** was passed on 23 December 1919, Anderson had already served two years as an apprentice solicitor and was studying for a Bachelor of Laws degree, which she was awarded on 20 April 1920. In May 1920, her apprenticeship was concluded and discharged. This gave her every qualification for recognition as a Law Agent (as solicitors in Scotland were then called) save the requirement to pass an examination on Forms of Process set by the Incorporated Society of Law Agents. In her petition to the Court of Session (standard procedure for male Law Agent candidates, although Anderson had to have hers typed since the printed version referred to 'him' and 'his'), she explained that the Society's Registrar had declined to accept her intimation of this apprenticeship, since it had begun prior to the 1919 Act. After examining the facts, and supported by a report to the President of the Court of Session by Lord Ashmore (one of the Senators of the College of Justice in Scotland), the Court directed that the intimation should be accepted and Anderson be permitted to sit the required examination. She passed it in October 1920, and by the end of the year had been admitted as a Law Agent.

It is not clear where Anderson was working in 1920 and 1921, but by 1922 she was with another Glasgow law firm, John Steuart and Gillies.[3] She remained there for five years before setting up on her own in Giffnock, a suburb of Glasgow, to which her parents had moved. Her father's death in 1932 may have been one of the drivers behind her move to London with her mother and aunt. In 1937, after passing the final examination of the English Law Society, she was qualified to practise as a solicitor in England. Her legal partners in London were both women: Edith Annie Berthan and Beatrice Honour Davy. They practised together until the partnership was dissolved in 1951.

Very little is known about Anderson's work for clients, and nothing after she exchanged Scotland for London. Private practice is, by its very nature, private. Likewise, there is no information as yet identified to say whether she was involved in any wider fight for women's suffrage and equality, or whether she was simply fortunate in being able to take advantage of developments concurrent with her own career.

In 1949, Anderson purchased a large house near Dunkeld in Perthshire. For a number of years she ran this as a private hotel. From 1952 to 1963 her name appears in various Scottish law directories as a practitioner, though no evidence has yet been traced of any legal work. She gave up the hotel in 1963 and moved to a cottage near Crieff, before settling at the Whyte Cottage, Bankfoot, near Perth. She died on 9 August 1982. Apart from minor bequests, her estate, valued at around £20,000, was left to her only niece, Anne, daughter

[2] Information from Glasgow University Archive Services.
[3] Scottish Law List 1922.

of her sister Ellen. A neighbour remembers 'Miss Anderson' (never 'Madge') as a fiercely independent lady, fond of cats and gardening, and daunted by nothing.

## II. Context

The first woman in Scotland to attempt a legal career was Margaret Howie Strang Hall who, in 1900, at the age of 18, petitioned the Court of Session to be allowed to sit the first examination of the Incorporated Society of Law Agents.[4] She had the promise of an apprenticeship if she was successful, but the Court concluded that the legislation of the time, despite referring to 'persons', related only to men.

> Whatever power the Court may have had formerly of admitting persons to practise as law-agents in the Courts of Scotland,[5] we think that the power of the Court … is now limited and defined by the Act of 1873 … The Court is authorised to admit 'persons', a term which, no doubt, is equally applicable to male and female. But in the case of an ambiguous term, that meaning must be assigned to it which is in accordance with inveterate usage. Accordingly we interpret the meaning 'male persons' as no other has ever been admitted as a law-agent. If females are now to be admitted as law-agents, that must, in our view, be authorised by the Legislature.[6]

*Hall* was one of several cases in England and Scotland in which courts responded to challenges by women by holding that the word 'persons' must be defined according to 'inveterate usage' rather than the normal rules of statutory interpretation.[7] No further petition was made until Anderson's in 1920.

Women had for several years been able to take a law degree at one of the (then) four Scottish universities; the earliest graduates were Eveline MacLaren and Josephine Gordon Stuart who graduated as Bachelors of Laws from Edinburgh University in April 1909.[8] Over 10 years later, Anderson was the first woman to obtain the same degree from Glasgow University

Early attempts by suffragettes to obtain access to professional opportunities for women largely ceased during the First World War, but the issue did not go away and was returned to at an early stage after the Armistice. Lord Buckmaster, Liberal Lord Chancellor early in the war, was a keen advocate for women solicitors and presented the Barristers and Solicitors (Qualification of Women) Bill in the House of Lords in February 1919. This was debated in March and remitted to a committee of the whole House, but progressed no further. At the end of that year, on 23 December, the Sex Disqualification (Removal) Act 1919 was passed and women were at last enabled to follow their chosen profession. Women had earlier been legally permitted to conduct their own defence if involved in a legal case;[9] now they were entitled to do so professionally.

[4] *Hall v The Incorporated Society of Law Agents* (1901) 3 F 1059; 1901 9 SLT 150.

[5] The Law Report in *Hall* refers to a report in Justiciary records from June 1563, in which Lady Crawford appeared as an advocate in the High Court of the Justiciary for a prisoner who was eventually acquitted ((1901) 3 F 1059, 1062).

[6] ibid 1065.

[7] ***Edwards v Attorney General of Canada* (1929)**, and see the **Introduction** for a discussion of *Bebb v Law Society.*

[8] Hector L MacQueen, 'Scotland's First Women Law Graduates: An Edinburgh Centenary' in Hector L MacQueen (ed), *Miscellany VI* (Stair Society vol 54, 2009) 221–65.

[9] ibid 225.

The different system of law which operated in Scotland, and which had been confirmed by the Act of Union in 1707, meant that Anderson's path to successful entry into the profession was speedier than that of her English contemporaries such as Maud (Ingram) Crofts or **Helena Normanton**. Thus, by the time of the 1919 Act she was ahead of aspiring women lawyers in England, who could not start their formal training until the Act had been passed.

## III. What Happened Next

It is striking how little was made of Anderson's achievement, particularly in comparison to the degree of fame, even notoriety, enjoyed by similar pioneers in England. Anderson's career was not widely reported in Scottish legal publications, although one newspaper reproduced a photograph of her in her graduation robes following her successful petition.[10] Nor does there appear to have been any publicly-voiced opposition to Anderson or to the idea of women working in the field of law; she managed to secure a position in another Glasgow firm before setting up her own practice.

Following Anderson's success, the rate of application by women to be law agents in Scotland did not immediately increase. The second woman to make the same petition, Isabella Burt, had graduated from Edinburgh University in 1911 and gone to work for her father, William Burt, a lawyer in Dunfermline. Burt submitted her petition to the Court of Session in April 1921, but the determination was not given until July 1922. A third application was made in 1923 and a fourth in 1924; but even by the end of 1930 only 21 women had qualified to work as solicitors in Scotland. England and Wales had around 100 women solicitors by this point; however, with a population eight times the size of Scotland, there were proportionately more women in law in Scotland than elsewhere in the UK. But when Anderson's name reappeared in Scottish law lists in the 1950s, she was still part of a very minor order; at the time only around three per cent of lawyers in Scotland were women. In 2015, it was reported that over 51 per cent of practising solicitors in Scotland were women (compared to 48 per cent in England and Wales).[11]

## IV. Significance

In comparison with her near contemporary, **Margaret Henderson Kidd**, Anderson has been greatly neglected in literature. Many jurisdictions, often with legal systems based on the United Kingdom model, already had women lawyers but Anderson was the first British woman to achieve this success. She did not lead the way as a single standard bearer, since quite a number of women in England who already held LLB degrees or their equivalent, such as Ivy Williams, were poised to launch themselves into the legal profession as soon as

[10] *The Daily Record and Mail*, 16 December 1920.

[11] Severin Carrell, 'Number of female solicitors in Scotland overtakes male for the first time', *The Guardian*, 23 December 2015.

the disqualification was lifted; but for two years she held the title of the only woman qualified to work as a lawyer in Britain.

In an article written the year after her failed petition, Margaret Hall wrote, 'many women, if they had the opportunity, would much prefer to consult a member of their own sex more particularly in matters pertaining to social relationships'.[12] With Anderson and her later colleagues, that option was now open to women, although in many cases – then and now – it led women lawyers to an involuntary specialisation in family law.

## Further Reading

- Angus McLean, 'Women in Law' (1994) 62 *Scottish Law Gazette* 10–14.
- Hector L MacQueen, 'Scotland's First Women Law Graduates: An Edinburgh Centenary' in Hector L MacQueen (ed), *Miscellany VI* (Stair Society vol 54, 2009).
- Mary Jane Mossman, *The First Women Lawyers: A Comparative Study of Gender, Law and the Legal Professions* (Hart Publishing, 2006).

[12] Margaret Hall, 'Women as Lawyers' (1901) 1 *New Liberal Review* 222, 226.

# 22

# Foundation of the Association of Women Solicitors, 1921

ELIZABETH CRUICKSHANK*

The Association of Women Solicitors (AWS) was the first organisation in England and Wales whose purpose was to represent women in the legal profession. Initially it was an informal grouping of six or seven women articled clerks (trainee solicitors) who came together on an unrecorded date in 1920 or 1921 for mutual support and companionship. They called themselves 'The 1919 Club' in recognition of the **Sex Disqualification (Removal) Act 1919**, which had opened the solicitors' profession to women.[1] For several decades the 1919 Club was the only, if very tenuous, contact some women solicitors had with other women legal practitioners, but in the later years of the twentieth century it grew into a powerful support and lobbying association, before coming to an end as an indirect consequence of the deregulation of legal services. In 2013, it was absorbed into the much less effective Women Lawyers Division of the Law Society of England and Wales.

## I. Context

From the start, the training requirements of barristers and solicitors were very different. Barristers' training was centred on one of the four Inns of Court situated in London, where formal study was undertaken for the Bar examinations, and where aspirant barristers attended 12 formal dinners as part of an arcane socialisation process. By contrast there were no dining conditions for articled clerks. In addition to passing the Law Society Intermediate and Final Examinations they served a prescribed period of apprenticeship or 'articles' with any established solicitor anywhere in England and Wales. Barristers were thus forced to meet each other on a social level, but solicitors were not. Although local Law Societies existed in many towns, qualified solicitors were not required to become members, nor were they required to become members of the Law Society itself.

* Chairwoman of the Association of Women Solicitors (2004–05).

[1] The name 'Association of Women Solicitors' was not formally adopted until 1969. The name 'the 1919 Club' is used before that date and the abbreviation 'AWS' from 1969 onwards.

In 1903 the Law Society set up a School of Law to prepare articled clerks for their examinations,[2] at which attendance was not compulsory. On the enactment of the 1919 Act women were permitted to attend the Law Society's classes and lectures. The Solicitors Act 1922 set out a mandatory tripartite set of training provisions. First, the undertaking of an 'academic year' for articled clerks who were neither university graduates nor '10-year men' (that is, those who had been employed as clerks in a solicitor's firm for at least 10 years); secondly, passing the Law Society's Intermediate Examination; and, thirdly, passing the Law Society's Finals Examination. Attendance at lectures run by the Law Society School of Law or at a recognised institution (usually a university) became a pre-requisite of sitting the Intermediate Examination.[3] On 19 March 1920 the Law Society resolved that all admission conditions appertaining to male articled clerks should apply equally to women, who were thus able to take equal advantage of any exemptions or concessions. Many of the first women articled clerks elected to attend the Law Society's classes in Chancery Lane, some probably being in London for that sole purpose.

## II. The Landmark

The earliest surviving record of the 1919 Club's history is contained in an undated set of notes written by Sybil Warren, Chairwoman of the 1919 Club in 1935 and later its President. In 1920–21 very few women were articled and two of those who were, and were attending the Law Society's classes, found after some time that there were other women attending other classes, none of them knowing of each other's existence and all of them feeling rather isolated.[4] These first two unnamed articled clerks may have been **Carrie Morrison**[5] and Maud Ingram (later Crofts), contemporaries at Girton College, Cambridge. Other founder members who lived in London were Ulrica Ann Hastie, Miriam Rose and Katherine Elizabeth Chambers, the first woman to register her articles with the Law Society. On being asked for permission to invite other women articled clerks to a meeting in a vacant classroom, Dr Jenks, the Head of the Law School, felt that he could not accede to 'such a revolutionary proposal without reference to a higher authority and accordingly, the permission of the Council of the Law Society was obtained in solemn form'.[6]

Those present at the meeting decided to call themselves 'The 1919 Club'. Although a few photographs and dinner menus from the period before the Second World War have survived, the only extant minutes date from 1945 and Sybil Warren's is the only surviving record of the Club's formation.

[2] Harry Kirk, *Portrait of a Profession: A History of the Solicitor's Profession, 1100 to the Present Day* (Oyez Publishing, 1976) 61.

[3] ibid 63.

[4] Notes in the author's possession.

[5] See **First Woman Solicitor in England and Wales, Carrie Morrison, 1922**. Carrie Morrison was Vice-chairman of the AWS at the time of her death in 1950.

[6] Notes in the author's possession.

## III. What Happened Next

For 50 years (1920 to 1970), membership of the 1919 Club grew slowly, reflecting the snail's-pace growth in the numbers of women solicitors. The Club recorded 48 members in 1945, but over 200 in 1970 (out of a total of 750 practising women solicitors). Nearly all Club meetings were held in London, and subscription levels were set at different rates for 'Town' and 'Country' members to reflect the often substantial distances some members travelled to meetings. Meetings were infrequent and not all women solicitors wished to belong to the Club, giving a variety of reasons for their decision. Anna Amphlett stated that 'my only purpose in joining any club was to acquire clients', which fellow solicitors were unlikely to become, and Daphne Glick did not join because she regarded most 1919 Club members as 'formidables'. Patricia Tipper did not feel that she was a pioneer: 'I just get people out of their knotty problems.' Peggy Mason saw 'little point in having an association of women solicitors. I see no difference between women and men solicitors. We all do the same job'.[7]

However, Warren was adamant that the 1919 Club was never intended to be a 'women's movement' as 'members have always regarded themselves as "solicitors" and not as "women solicitors"'. It was just a support group, intended, she said, to provide an opportunity for members to meet 'for their mutual help and comfort' and to provide encouragement to those who were struggling with their articles. Members met for 'a chat' or to play various games.

> Then as numbers increased they had debates and lectures on subjects of general interest, preceded by dinner in a room above a small restaurant (the Ariston restaurant) in Essex Street … the arts of companionship and entertainment are among the graces of life and the 1919 Club exists to encourage them.

These observations reflect the secure middle-class origins of most of the Club's first members.[8] In July 1930, with probably fewer than 30 members, they entertained a group of American women lawyers and four years later held their first annual dinner at the Trocadero Restaurant, with a six-course dinner (described in French) with speeches from the President of the Law Society and Lady Pentland, the wife of the erstwhile Governor of Madras.

As time went on, the 1919 Club appears to have become a (small) part of the legal establishment. In January 1936 Sir Claud Schuster, Permanent Secretary to the Lord Chancellor's Office, conveyed Judge Tobin's outrage that a woman solicitor had appeared before him in a 'a rather florid hat' to the Secretary of the Law Society. Its President immediately sought the views of 'the 1919 Club, which is a society of women solicitors' and accepted their recommendation that women solicitors in court should have uncovered heads rather than the mortar boards desired by Tobin.[9]

During the Second World War and its immediate aftermath Club meetings were less frequent and less lavish. As bombed-out and understaffed law firms struggled to survive, the

[7] From interviews by the author with retired women solicitors (on file with author).

[8] See Elizabeth Cruickshank, '"Follow the Money": The First Women Who Qualified as Solicitors 1922–1930' in Judith Bourne (ed), *First Women Lawyers in Great Britain and the Empire Record*, vol1 (St Mary's University, 2016) 76–90.

[9] National Archives LCO2/1580.

Club began to show symptoms of a failing organisation. Annual general meetings became occasions for continued apologies from Club secretaries for failure to arrange activities, and in 1946 members considered whether the Club should be wound up. This was not only rejected but, crucially, members voted in that same year to adopt a significant amendment to Rule 2 of the Club's constitution, which now stated that:

> The objects of the Club shall be to (a) bring together women solicitors and articled clerks by means of debates, dinners, meetings and such other social functions as shall be authorised by the Club in General Meeting and (b) *to support the interests of women in the solicitors' profession* (emphasis added).

Even though the concept of proactive representation was now constitutionally enshrined, the Club's support of its members' right to be considered as equals within their male-dominated profession was essentially reactive. In November 1954, acting on a complaint from Sylvia Kemp, joint author of *Kemp and Kemp on Damages*, the Club succeeded in causing a notice designating the Solicitors Room at the West London County Court as being for 'Gentlemen Only' to be removed. However, such successes did not of themselves encourage membership loyalty. In 1960 and 1969, Club attendances were so diminished that members again debated a winding-up followed by a grand dinner; on both occasions it was decided that the Club's initial raison d'être of 'providing social and instructional meetings' while encouraging professional companionship was still valid.

At the 1969 AGM, the explanatory strapline 'The Association of Women Solicitors' was added to the traditional 'The 1919 Club' and a new, younger committee was formed including Juliet Becker, Eva Crawley and Rosalind Bax, all of whom were to become future AWS Chairwomen. The Association began to look beyond the merely social to providing tangible services to members and other women solicitors. Its reorganisation coincided with an accelerating increase in the number of women solicitors. The Companies Act 1967, which enabled partnerships consisting of more than 20 members, led to larger partnerships with the consequence, foreseen or not, that firms were more willing to take on women articled clerks. Soon the Association of Women Solicitors, as the Club was now called, had a sufficient pool of volunteer members to provide a widening range of member services.

Eva Crawley set up a Returner Course in 1977 at Lucy Cavendish College, Cambridge, to bring solicitors who had not practised for a number of years up to date with legal developments and to prepare them for the contemporary workplace. She also developed a mentoring scheme – a consultancy service rather than a long-term guidance and supervision programme – to provide confidential advice to those considering changing specialisms, entering into partnership, moving between private practice and governmental or commercial enterprises, or even moving to another region or country. For 15 years Judith Willis ran a maternity helpline giving basic information on the employment rights surrounding pregnancy and motherhood. This was renamed the Maternity and Paternity Helpline in 2007, when new legislation gave parental leave rights to fathers as well as mothers.

From 1954, there was a regular Newsletter. This became increasingly sophisticated, expanding from a Roneoed sheet for 100 members to a glossy publication called LINK, running from 2001–13, and which, at its height, was sent to 18,000 AWS members. In 2007 LINK recorded that, for the first time, women solicitors had a voice on the Law Society Council through Alison Parkinson's election as the AWS-nominated Council member. In 2006 Fiona Woolf, a former AWS chairwoman, became the second woman President of the Law Society.

The AWS Working Party (later the AWS Law Reform Committee) prepared papers and responses on the Elimination of Sex Discrimination and Equality of Opportunity to the Equal Opportunities Commission (1981) and amendments to the Equal Pay Act (1983), and presented proposals on Tax Reform (1983).[10] It successfully campaigned for a reduced Practising Certificate Fee for those practising part-time (1993) and, in 2004, against a drastic increase in Continuing Professional Development requirements, which would have seriously disadvantaged this same group. In 1992, it published a model clause on maternity leave arrangements for equity partners and, more ambitiously, a rapidly sold-out *Guidelines to Part-time Working*.

Expansion was aided by the provision from 1972 onwards of an annual grant from the Law Society; in 1973 the value of subscriptions amounted to £153.19, against a Law Society grant of £100. Instead of spending time on administration and time-consuming subscription collection, the energies of some very able women solicitors, among them future law partners and a future Lord Mayor of London (Fiona Woolf), could more positively be devoted to supporting other women solicitors. In 1987 the AWS became a Representative Group of the Law Society, entitling it to more substantial administrative support and in 1990 became fully-funded by the Law Society, while retaining autonomy and control.

The additional funds enabled the mother organisation, based in London, to assist in the setting up of regional AWS groups and for almost 20 years the AWS operated in a similar way to the Law Society itself, with local groups, of which there were 12 in 2013, performing social, networking and support functions under a central umbrella organisation, whose views on women's position were increasingly sought. The Law Society grant had generously increased on an annual basis to reflect the increase in membership, probably peaking in 2003 at £81,000 per annum.

However, the Law Society's attitude to its constituent groups changed with the passing of the Legal Services Act 2007 which assigned professional regulation to the Solicitors Regulation Authority. Forced to focus mainly on representation and professional support, the Law Society looked increasingly for commercial means of enhancing its own income.

The impact of the Legal Services Act on the AWS was vast and almost immediate. Its committee members' time was now consumed in drawing up papers in support of Law Society grant applications and attending meetings where an embattled Law Society frequently changed its stance on its relationship with the AWS. Simultaneously, the Law Society gradually withdrew its financial support for its representative groups such as the Young Solicitors' Group and the AWS. By 2010 the Law Society had reduced its grant by more than half, which was then insufficient even to pay for production costs relating to LINK. Finally, in 2013, with the complete withdrawal of Law Society funding and having used up all its reserves, the AWS had little option but to be absorbed into the new Women Lawyers Division of the Law Society (WLD). This latter organisation is run from and by Law Society staff with input from a committee of women solicitors. The Law Society has now acquired complete financial control at the expense of losing many volunteers who provided formal and informal support to other women solicitors. Although it now runs a truncated Returner Course as a money-making operation, there is no longer a maternity helpline or a mentoring scheme and LINK has been replaced with a Law Society information site.

[10] **Section 32 of the Finance Act 1988.**

Going forward, several groups of women solicitors have formed regional groups; some, such as Bristol and Merseyside, adopting the WLD name while others, such as Surrey and London, continue to style themselves as AWS. The latter are self-financing through realistic subscriptions and income from events open to women solicitors and trainees in their local areas. In effect they are returning to the objects set out in the Rule 2 Amendment above. The London branch, for example, offers access to maternity advice, disseminates an informative e-Newsletter to members and responds to consultation documents.

## IV. Significance

The AWS and its forerunner, the 1919 Club, were important as the first (and for many decades only) professional support organisation for women solicitors in England and Wales. By contrast the Bar Council not only did not support, but had actively discouraged the creation of a separate women barristers' association. At its Annual General Meeting in 1933, in response to **Helena Normanton's** proposal that women barristers would like 'to have a small committee to entertain foreign women barristers … and to pursue certain educational studies together', the Chairman of the Bar Council replied firmly that 'the proposal was opposed by a large majority of practising women barristers'.[11] Indeed, the **Association of Women Barristers** was only formed in 1991.

In truth, for at least the first 40 years of its existence the 1919 Club was of marginal importance for its members, who came for the most part from a small section of society, comfortably off and aided by servants, with a strong likelihood that if married they would give up work on becoming mothers, if not on marriage itself. For much of that time their public energies would have been channelled into other professional women's organisations such as the Soroptimists.

By the 1960s an increase in numbers brought the confidence to act as a representative group. The AWS changed from being a 'non-campaigning' organisation to one which publicly promoted the interests of its members as working mothers, or as members of ethnic minorities, as well as arguing for the legal and social rights of women generally. It also provided and publicised positive ways of assisting women solicitors over the life-time of their careers. In 2006 it adopted a new strapline: 'Essential for Success'. For a time, it appeared to be a highly-valued part of the legal hierarchy. It was consulted, invited to participate in Law Society Conferences and, crucially, entitled to Law Society funding and administrative services. AWS volunteers provided the Mentoring Scheme, the Maternity Helpline and the Law Reform Committee at no cost to members and at minimal cost to the AWS itself. Only two services were heavily subsidised by the Law Society: the Returner Course offered an intensive week-long residential experience for women returning to the profession; and LINK was disseminated free to all AWS members.

However, the history of the AWS should serve as an inspiration and a warning. An impressively small cohort of women solicitors had succeeded in founding an organisation to support each other, had maintained it through economic recessions and war and, in more

[11] *The Times*, 19 January 1933.

benign economic circumstances, had expanded into the twenty-first century. But its subsequent gradual demise demonstrates how an organisation can all but disappear through a laudable desire for expansion coupled with an unrealistic reliance on income which was not self-generated.

## Further Reading

- Elizabeth Cruickshank, 'Follow the Money' in *First Women Lawyers in Great Britain and the Empire Record*, vol 1 (St Mary's University, 2016) 76–90.
- Elizabeth Cruickshank and Katherine Southby (eds), *LINK AWS* (PZ Publishing 2001–13) Issues 1–2 and 4–49 held by The Law Society Library, Chancery Lane, London.
- Harry Kirk, *Portrait of a Profession: A History of the Solicitor's Profession, 1100 to the Present Day* (Oyez Publishing, 1976).

# 23

# First Woman to Practise as a Barrister in Ireland and the (then) United Kingdom, Averil Deverell, 1921

LIZ GOLDTHORPE

Averil Deverell was the first woman to practise as a barrister in Ireland and the (then) UK.[1] She was not the first woman to be called to the Bar; that honour went to Frances Kyle who was called alongside Deverell in November 1921.[2] But Deverell negotiated the unique challenges of practice as the only woman barrister in Ireland for several months after her call. Over long career of nearly 40 years, she had several other milestones to her credit: first woman to be admitted to read for the Irish Bar;[3] first woman law reporter; first to get a coveted 'red bag' as a junior; first 'Mother of the Bar' (in recognition of her seniority after a lengthy practice); and first secretary of the Dublin University Women Graduates Association (DUGWA).[4]

## I. Life

Born a twin into a comfortable Dublin Anglo-Irish Unionist family in 1893, Averil Deverell lived for most of her life in Greystones, County Wicklow. Her family background provided

[1] The Anglo-Irish Treaty was signed on 6 December 1921 and provided for the establishment of the Irish Free State within a year as a self-governing dominion within the 'community of nations known as the British Empire', a status 'the same as that of the Dominion of Canada'. It also provided Northern Ireland, which had been created by the Government of Ireland Act 1920, an option to opt out of the Irish Free State. Deverell entered the Law Library almost a year before the Irish Free State came into existence on 6 December 1922 (the day its Constitution was enacted by the British parliament) and at a time when Ireland was still part of the UK.

[2] 'First Irish Portias', *Daily Sketch*, 3 November 1921, 4.

[3] Deverell's memorial for admission as a student is dated 8 January 1920, a few days before that of Kyle, but both are shown to have paid the duty for admission as students on the same date (11 February 1920). Oddly, when it came to completing Deverell's memorial for admission to the degree of barrister-at-law, it was written in the appropriate blank space on the printed form that she had been admitted a student in Michaelmas term 1919 (King's Inns MS, Kyle and Deverell Memorials). See also Colum Kenny, '"You just have to get on with it" – the advance of women in the legal profession, 1901–2011' in Daire Hogan and Colum Kenny (eds), *Changes in practice and law: A selection of essays by members of the legal profession to mark twenty-five years of the Irish Legal History Society* (Four Courts Press, 2013).

[4] Founded 25 April 1922; see Susan Parkes (ed), *A Danger to The Men? A History of Women in Trinity College Dublin 1904–2004* (Lilliput Press, 2004) 110.

much inspiration for a legal career, with several lawyers on her mother's side and a solicitor father who was Clerk of the Crown and Peace for County Wicklow. She also had close connections to her English paternal uncle, a London barrister and Middle Temple Bencher, whose daughter, Naomi Constance Wallace, was later to be one of the first women to be called to the English Bar in 1922.

Deverell's early education and her social and family life were typical of her class and background, including attendance at a Protestant girls' school and presentation, in July 1911, at the last Royal Court to be held in Ireland. But sleepy Greystones did not escape its share of political incidents: a protest was staged there by Irish suffragettes in 1910 and a prominent nationalist was arrested at the station in 1918. Strong family connections to Unionist politics and an almost exclusively loyalist social circle aside, Deverell's personal papers show some identification with suffrage issues: she took a leading role in a 1911 play 'How The Vote was Won', first performed in London in 1909 as a campaigning vehicle for the Women's Social and Political Union and the Actresses' Franchise League (AFL).[5] A friend contributed the full text of Laurence Housman's suffrage poem 'Woman This and Woman That' to Deverell's autograph book and a family friend and neighbour, Mrs Caroline West, hosted Irish Women's Reform League (IWRL) events, including a visit by Housman to Greystones in 1912. But little is really known about what Deverell thought of the range of constitutional changes that Ireland was undergoing.

Having graduated from Trinity College Dublin[6] with a law degree in 1915, and done extensive war service as a member of the Voluntary Aid Detachment, Deverell finally managed to persuade the authorities to allow her to serve as an ambulance driver during the First World War in France and Flanders in 1918. In 1919, with Frances Kyle, she gained admission to King's Inns, Dublin. The latter's academic success was hailed as signalling 'women's invasion of the law … We are a liberal-minded people, as our universities have shown, and a large accession of women to the law would be quite consistent with the adventurous spirit of the age'.[7] Deverell and Kyle were 'excused' some aspects of their legal training by the King's Inns' Benchers (the senior members of Inn). In Deverell's case, this was in recognition of her war service,[8] a concession also made to several men. They were both called to the Bar on 1 November 1921 amongst a group of 18 men, including Deverell's twin brother, William.[9]

In January 1922, several months before **Helena Normanton** was called to the Bar in London, Deverell became a member of the Law Library in Dublin, the essential start to her career. She was noted as: 'An interesting figure … [in] the regulation wig and gown'.[10]

[5] Suffragette one act ensemble piece by Cicely Hamilton about an all-woman general strike, directed by Edith Craig, Ellen Terry's daughter, featuring AFL members and colleagues of Housman.

[6] By way of comparison, her cousin, Naomi Constance Wallace, who studied at Trinity College, Cambridge, was not able to be awarded a degree. Cambridge University did not admit women to full membership until October 1948.

[7] *Irish Times*, 26 October 1921.

[8] Kenny, n 3 above. All Bar details are from Kenneth Ferguson (ed), *King's Inn Barristers* (King's Inns Dublin, 2005).

[9] The group also included John Clarke MacDermott and Paddy McGilligan, future Irish Lord Chief Justice and Attorney General respectively.

[10] *Irish Law Times*, 1 April and 22 April 1922. See also Ferguson, n 8 above, 81, 97. Ireland seemed less troubled about dress code for women barristers than England, although Kyle said in an interview to *The Vote* in January 1922 that she and Deverell had (unsuccessfully) petitioned the Lord Chief Justice to be allowed not to wear wigs.

She was also called soon afterwards in Belfast, where Kyle only practised very briefly as a probationer. (Prior to the foundation of the Irish Free State later that year it was, for a while, unclear whether barristers would be able to continue to practise in both cities).[11]

Like Normanton, Deverell initially had to supplement her earnings. In Deverell's case, she established dog kennels in Greystones.[12] Naming these 'The Brehon Kennels' ('Brehon' referring to the ancient Gaelic system of law) may be evidence of her reputation for a provocative wit. However, based on available cases reported in press and law reports, it seems Deverell had regular work. Her first court appearance, a hearing before the Lord Chief Justice on 21 April 1922, was followed by a steady flow of instructions. She also undertook law reporting, and her first law report appeared in the *Irish Law Times* in 1922.[13] DUGWA was founded in 1922, with Deverell as its first secretary. Through the Irish Federation of University Women, of which **Frances Moran** was later to become President, DUGWA was affiliated with the International Federation of University Women (IFUW), founded in the wake of the First World War, and sent delegates to the regular international conferences held by IFUW on such subjects as the education of women. (Moran was to become IFUW President in the 1950s).

Undertaking mainly a range of Chancery work, Deverell appeared in court in personal injury and employment disputes and 'gave numerous written opinions on tangled legal subjects'.[14] Her archive shows a longstanding connection to one firm, Charles BW Boyle & Sons of Dublin, which specialised in trade union cases. They also acted for Jim Larkin, the trade unionist leader in the 1913 Lockout, and Deverell's caseload included instructions that related to the Larkin family. In 1928, she scored a major success by appearing as a junior before the Judicial Committee of the Privy Council (JCPC), led by Alfred Dickie, KC.[15] The case was a leading constitutional law challenge by a group of Irish civil servants to the interpretation of their terms of employment in the transfer provisions of the 1921 Anglo-Irish Treaty. Deverell had been briefed from 1927 when her father had been an early litigant, but it was the 1928 appearance that got her the customary, and coveted, red brief-bag presented to a junior appearing for before the JCPC the first time. This was an increasingly rare trophy after 1933 when such appeals were abolished by the Irish government, and eventually Deverell's historic symbol was the only one left in Ireland.

In later life, she was proud of becoming 'Mother of the Bar' in recognition of her seniority. She mentored a number of women lawyers from a very wide range of backgrounds (including the daughter of an IRA commandant, the daughter of a Cherokee Indian and the niece of Jenny Wyse Power, leading suffrage campaigner, President of Cumann na mBan

[11] Barristers did not choose between Dublin and Belfast in 1921. The Bars stayed united until 1922–23 and the creation of separate Inns of Court in Belfast. The two Bar Councils have had an annual joint meeting since 2013.

[12] *Irish Independent*, 26 July 1928; *Irish Times*, 14 December 1922; *Irish Times*, 24 July 1928.

[13] Marion Duggan was formally appointed by the Law Reporting Council of Ireland as the first woman law reporter in 1928, but was pressured into resigning in 1934. See Eamonn G Hall, *The Superior Courts of Law 'Official' Law Reporting in Ireland 1866–2006* (Incorporated Council of Law Reporting for Ireland, 2007) 150. As a law graduate, she had reported on court cases for the IWRL in the *Irish Citizen* and initiated public debate about the need for women lawyers as the anonymous author of the IWRL pamphlet 'Women's Need of Women Lawyers'. See Louise Ryan, *Winning The Vote for Women, the Irish Citizen newspaper and the suffrage movement in Ireland* (Four Courts Press, 2018).

[14] 'Averil KS Deverill, an appreciation', *Irish Times*, March 1979.

[15] *In re Payment of Compensation to Civil Servants* [1929] AC 242 (PC), [1927] 1 IR 285; *Wigg and another v Attorney General of the Irish Free State* [1927] UKPC 45, [1927] AC 674.

and a founder member of Sinn Fein). She also instigated a campaign for a return of the women's robing room in the 1930s complete with a sign reading 'Women Barristers' (rather than 'Lady' Barristers).

She died in Greystones in 1979, leaving a bequest to Trinity Law School.[16] Her gravestone in the family plot is simply marked 'barrister-at-law'. Her portrait, over the entrance to the Law Library's Averil Deverell Room, bears a small plaque stating her Call 'prior to the admission of any lady to [the] English Bar', and her legacy is commemorated in the Trinity Averil Deverell Scholarship. From March 2018 her name will be on a dedicated seating space for Junior Counsel in the Law Library.

## II. Context

Deverell's achievements are all the more remarkable when set against the contemporary background of a very difficult period in Irish–English and international history. She lived, studied and practised not only during two world wars, but also throughout years of nationalist rebellion, the fight for suffrage, an Anglo-Irish War of independence 1919–21, Ireland's partition and civil war from 1922, as well as major constitutional and professional upheaval.

Although Brehon law had allowed for women brehons (or lawyers) such as Brigh Brugaid (c. 50 AD), from the 1700s onwards women's legal status – both as lawyers and generally – was greatly diminished under the common law which replaced it.[17] However, Irishwomen pursued legal careers with the same determination as elsewhere; their path to university education and training and entry to the profession blighted by similar prolonged battles to those of their foreign counterparts. Isobel Weir Johnston exemplified this. Refused entry at 16 years-old to the Bar in England and Wales,[18] and to King's Inns in Dublin in 1901 – the Under-Treasurer to the Irish Benchers informing her that 'it was not competent for a lady to enter this Inn as a student, or become a member of the Irish Bar'[19] – she was one of three women undergraduates admitted to Trinity College Dublin when it first opened its doors to women in 1904.[20]

Madeline Collins entered in 1908 and was the first woman law graduate – LLB in 1909 and LLD in 1912, but she did not enter the profession. Deverell followed in 1911. Both Kyle sisters were also amongst a very small group of Trinity law graduates: Kathleen in 1914 and Frances in 1916.

Trinity was a rarefied environment, captured by one woman in the 1950s:

> cut off from the rest of Dublin … largely composed of a staff and student body of the Old Anglo-Irish, Unionist, ascendancy, with fossilised pre-1922 ideas. Life was still orderly, snobbish and conservative, good-mannered … fun for those who fitted in.[21]

[16] Ferguson, n 8 above, 173.

[17] See generally, Máiréad Enright, '"Involuntary Patriotism": Judges, Women and National Identity on the Island of Ireland' in Máiréad Enright, Julie McCandleless and Aoife O'Donoghue (eds), *Northern/Irish Feminist Judgments: Judges' troubles and the gendered Politics of Identity* (Hart Publishing, 2017) 27.

[18] *Irish Times*, 13 October 1951.

[19] Minute Book of the Council, 25 October 1901 (King's Inns MS, 6).

[20] Letitia Alice Walkington was the first woman law graduate in either Ireland or Britain – from the Royal University of Ireland in 1888.

[21] Parkes, n 4 above, 188.

The very small group of women, curtailed by strict rules that forced them to leave the campus by 6pm and refused them membership of student societies, used Trinity as the bedrock of future successes and friendships.

But external events were to penetrate complacent isolation: the 1913 Dublin Lockout (a major industrial strike lasting seven months), the 1914–18 war which devastated student ranks, the 1916 Easter Rising and, just eight months after Deverell was called to the Bar, civil war. In April 1922, Irish anti-Treaty forces occupied the Four Courts, as they had done during the 1916 Easter Rising.[22] Substantial and prolonged disruption ensued. After fire and explosions had destroyed the major law buildings forming Dublin's legal centre, the legal machinery was in need of reconstruction 'out of the scanty materials that were left'.[23] Court work, legal offices and the Law Library were moved to improvised accommodation at King's Inns until 1923, before returning (via Dublin Castle) to the Four Courts in 1932.[24]

Many of the legal practices returned too. Without the English system of sets of chambers, the Law Library was, and still is, the central source of work. After robing in the Four Courts cellars, barristers climbed the stairs to the large but cramped Library and waited for briefs to arrive. It offered consultation rooms, and formal customs offering valuable opportunities to consult other more senior colleagues, but its layout required a physical proximity that is a surprise even today.

In 1919 the **Sex Disqualification (Removal) Act 1919** made possible the appointment, after a long battle, of Georgina Frost as Petty Sessions Clerk in 1920, and the first (unnamed) woman magistrate was appointed in Dublin.[25] But the Irish Free State brought limited rewards for women, despite their prominent participation in revolution. Although the 1922 Constitution guaranteed equal rights for women, a ban on women working after marriage in areas such as the civil service was not removed until 1973,[26] while controversial articles contained in the 1937 Constitution specifically recognising women's place in the home remain in place.[27] It also signally failed to capitalise on the talents of women who served in the Dail Courts – a grassroots civil war court structure aimed at replacing British-appointed courts, which operated from 1920–24 – including Marion Duggan, the fifth woman to be called to the Bar (in 1925).[28]

## III. What Happened Next

The first woman solicitors in Ireland, Mary Dorothea Heron and Helena May Early, were appointed in 1923.[29] In 1924 King's Inns held a dinner for over 250 guests in honour of

[22] *Irish Law Times*, 29 April and 6 May 1916, cited by Ferguson, n 8 above, 87–88, 99.

[23] Sir Thomas Maloney, last Lord Chief Justice of Ireland, *Irish Law Times*, 24 October 1924, cited in Ferguson, n 8 above, 50, 100.

[24] Ferguson, n 8 above, 99–102, 101–107; *Irish Law Times*, 7 April 1923; *Irish Law Times*, 14 April 1923; *Irish Law Times*, 14 June 1924; *Irish Law Times*, 17 October 1923.

[25] *Irish Law Times & Solicitors Journal*, 21 February 1920.

[26] **Education Act 1944**.

[27] Subject to a proposed referendum in 2018.

[28] Mary Kotsonouris, *Retreat from Revolution: The Dáil Courts*, 1920–1924 (Irish Academic Press, 1994) 38, 45, 126.

[29] Ivana Bacik, Cathryn Costello and Eileen Drew, *Gender Injustice: Feminising the Legal Professions?* (Trinity College Dublin Law School, 2003) 63.

a large party of visiting American and Canadian judges and lawyers. There were men on the table of women lawyers, but the women included early American pioneers such as Mary O'Toole, the Irish-born first woman US municipal judge, as well as Frances Kyle, Averil Deverell, and Helena Mary Early.[30] But progress was slow. Mary (Mollie) Dillon Leetch was called in 1924, followed by Marion Duggan and Antonia McDonnell in 1925.[31] Just 12 women in total were called to the Bar between 1921 and 1950. Frances Moran became the first woman Senior Counsel in 1941, although she did not practise as such. Mella Carroll became the first practising woman Senior Counsel in 1976, and later first woman elected Chair of the Irish Bar. By the mid-1970s, the accumulated total of women called to the Bar stood at 38.[32] Most were from comfortable backgrounds, often with family legal connections.[33] By the early 2000s, this had increased to 482.[34] As in other jurisdictions, the number of women solicitors increased more rapidly. By 1936, 16 women had been admitted as solicitors.[35] And in 2015 it was reported as a 'world first' that there are now more women solicitors than men in Ireland.[36]

Despite a long wait to appoint the first two Irish woman judges (Eileen Kennedy as a district judge in 1963 and Mella Carroll to the High Court in 1980), in 2014 women made up a third of the Irish judiciary.[37] There have also been a number of women judges on the Irish Supreme Court, including Susan Denham, appointed in 1993 and first woman Chief Justice between 2001 and 2017. At present there are two women Supreme Court judges.

## IV. Significance

Although Deverell never achieved the further formal recognition of some of her contemporaries, her achievements are remarkable – even more so in the contemporary political and professional circumstances. Her personality and energy enabled her not only to survive, but to succeed, within the parameters set by the prevailing circumstances, and her full inspiration deserves greater recognition. For her groundbreaking contribution in the opportunities she seized and the support she gave to others, she stands as an important landmark in the history of women lawyers in Ireland and beyond.

## Further Reading


- Ivana Bacik, Cathryn Costello and Eileen Drew, *Gender Injustice: Feminising the Legal Professions?* (Trinity College Dublin Law School, 2003).


[30] Mary Dorothea Heron was the first woman solicitor, but Early the first to practise; both were admitted in 1923.

[31] ibid 62.

[32] ibid 71.

[33] Margaret Ó hÓgartaigh, *Far From Few: Professional Women in Ireland: 1880–1930* (Unpublished PhD thesis, University College Dublin, 1999) 320–21; see also Bacik et al, n 29 above, 59.

[34] Bacik et al, n 29 above, 72.

[35] ibid 63.

[36] Michelle Hennessy, 'A world first: There are now more female than male solicitors in Ireland', *thejournal.ie*, 13 February 2015.

[37] Christine Bohan, 'The number of female judges has hit a record high', *thejournal.ie*, 2 December 2014.

- Richard Noel Cooke, 'A Portrait of Averil KS Deverell, the first woman to practise at the Irish Bar' (Women and Law Conference, unpublished paper, 2000).
- Colum Kenny, '"You just have to get on with it" – the advance of women in the legal profession, 1901–2011' in Daire Hogan and Colum Kenny (eds), *Changes in practice and law, A selection of essays by members of the legal profession to mark twenty-five years of the Irish Legal History Society* (Four Courts Press, 2013).
- Susan Parkes (ed), *A Danger to The Men? A History of Women in Trinity College Dublin 1904–2004* (Lilliput Press, 2004).
- King's Inns Library and Archives.

# 24

# First Woman Solicitor in England and Wales, Carrie Morrison, 1922

ELIZABETH CRUICKSHANK

On 18 December 1922, Carrie Morrison (1888–1950) became the first woman to be admitted as a solicitor of the Supreme Court of England and Wales. She went on to use her skills as a solicitor to argue for equality between the sexes and through organisations such as the Women and Children's Protection Society and the Divorce Law Reform Union for changes to family law legislation and procedure. She was one of the founding members of the 1919 Club, which became the Association of Women Solicitors.[1]

## I. Life

Morrison was born in Richmond, Surrey, in 1888. Her parents were Judith Wakefield Shepherd (1856–1924), the third daughter of an illiterate Lincolnshire labourer, and Thomas Morrison (1834–1901), a comfortably-off City of London metal broker of Scottish ancestry. Because of the peripatetic nature of her father's occupation, Morrison attended five different schools in four different countries by the age of 15. She was awarded exhibitions from both Manchester High School for Girls and Girton College, Cambridge, where she achieved First Class Honours in the Modern and Medieval Languages Tripos in 1910. In June 1915 after two uncongenial attempts at teaching, in Penarth, South Wales, and at East Putney High School in London, Morrison worked in various departments of MI5, including a secondment in 1919 to the Army of the Black Sea in Constantinople.

She 'dropped into (legal) work by accident' through assisting solicitor Alfred Baker with a travel permit application at MI5's Military Permit Office (MPO). Baker offered her a clerical position at his firm 'after the War is over'.[2] When the **Sex Disqualification (Removal) Act 1919** opened the legal profession to women, Baker not only offered her articles (training contract), but also unusually waived the customary training premium and paid her a small salary.[3]

After qualification Morrison gave free or low-cost legal advice as a Poor Man's Lawyer at Toynbee Hall in London's East End,[4] where she met Ambrose Appelbe, a fellow volunteer,

[1] See **Foundation of the Association of Women Solicitors, 1921**.
[2] *Evening Telegraph*, 31 October 1922.
[3] ibid.
[4] JAR Pimlott, *Toynbee Hall: Fifty Years of Social Progress 1884–1934* (Dent, 1935).

whose non-conformist and socialist beliefs were similar to her own. In 1928 Morrison and Appelbe established their own law practice (Appelbe and Morrison) in Whitechapel and, despite his being 15 years younger, they married in 1929.[5] In the 1930s, they both came to the 'notice' of MI5 – Appelbe because of his suspected membership of the Communist Party and Morrison (curiously, since she had worked for MI5) because of her 1932 defence of the so-called 'Becontree rioters', who demonstrated against the eviction of an RAF officer's widow by the London County Council.

In 1937 Morrison divorced Appelbe on the grounds of adultery. The circumstances surrounding the divorce, particularly the carefully worded petition, suggest that the divorce was a generous act of collusion on her part. Although Appelbe remarried, she did not, but unusually, and to the horror of her friend Maud Crofts, continued to practise in partnership with him until her death in 1950. Like **Helena Normanton**, Morrison was a persistent advocate of a woman's right to an independent professional persona, refusing to use her married surname[6] and successfully petitioning the President of the Probate, Divorce and Admiralty Division to be permitted to use a professional rather than a marital status descriptor in official documents.[7] In reply to the question, 'Do you suffer from any physical difficulty?' on an official form Morrison replied, 'No, except being a woman.'[8]

## II. Context

Although women had been employed as clerks in solicitors' offices since at least the 1880s,[9] some acquiring substantial legal skills and knowledge, their status and earnings were constrained by lack of formal qualifications. For several decades campaigners had attempted, first through legislation (several private member's bills) and then through litigation in *Bebb v Law Society*,[10] to have the Law Society admit women to the profession. All were unsuccessful, in part, no doubt, due to a fear that competition from women might reduce profitability in an overcrowded and frequently badly remunerated profession. Women were, it was argued, 'conspicuously unfitted' to be solicitors because they had 'no idea of relevance or analogy or evidence'.[11]

The First World War changed the situation, and also attitudes. 565 solicitors and 341 articled clerks were killed and hundreds more retired through age or stress, leaving 3,000 fewer solicitors in 1919 than at the beginning of the war. To hasten the qualification of new solicitors, the Solicitors (Articled Clerks) Act 1918 provided that the articles of those who had performed 'essential war work' could be reduced by a year, a concession extended to women articled clerks by a Law Society Resolution on 19 March 1920.[12] Qualification as

[5] The civil ceremony was performed at Stepney Register Office on 4 April and 'blessed' two days later by noted woman preacher Maude Royden. Later Morrison and Appelbe both became Executive Committee members of the Society for the Ministry of Women.

[6] *Girton College Register 1869–1946* (Cambridge, 1948) 187.

[7] *The Law Society Gazette*, 1950, 238.

[8] *The Law Society Gazette*, 1960, 304.

[9] 2,519 in 1911 (1911 Census General Report), including Eliza Orme, who ran her own office with the assistance of some qualified men. See Leslie Howsam, 'Eliza Orme' in *Oxford Dictionary of National Biography* (OUP, 2004).

[10] *Bebb v Law Society* [1914] 1 Ch 286.

[11] Elsie M Lang, *British Women in the Twentieth Century* (Northumberland Press, 1929) 157.

[12] Law Society Minutes, 19 March 1920.

a solicitor required passing the Law Society Finals examinations and successful completion of articles, usually over a period of three years for university graduates, after which the training firm must certify the articled clerk/trainee is a fit and proper person to be admitted. Once the Sex Disqualification (Removal) Act 1919 cleared the way for the admission of women to both the solicitors' and barristers' professions, Morrison's articles were reduced from three years to two by virtue of her Constantinople secondment. As none of the other three women (Maud Crofts, Mary Elizabeth Pickup and Mary Elaine Sykes) who also passed their Finals in December 1922 qualified for the reduction in articles, Morrison was the only woman whose training could be completed by the end of 1922.

## III. What Happened Next

Despite Morrison's admission as a solicitor attracting copious coverage in the national (but not the legal) press, the profession was not immediately swamped by women. The numbers of women holding practising certificates rose slowly, to 116 in 1931 and to 356 (out of 19,000 practising solicitors) in 1957, the first year the Law Society enumerated women solicitors separately. The high cost of usually unsalaried training (a £300 to £500 training premium plus £80 stamp duty to register articles with the Law Society) made it difficult for anyone, man or woman, to qualify without the benefit of family money and/or family connections. In consequence, the majority of 1920s women qualifiers were closely related to male solicitors, their entry into and continuation in the profession often being dictated by their fathers.[13]

Nevertheless, women fared better as solicitors than as barristers. Helena Normanton, one of the first women barristers, observed in 1934 that no more than 18 out of the 200 women called to the Bar since 1922 worked 'hard, continuously and seriously at the active part of the profession'.[14] In contrast, Morrison considered that 50 per cent of qualified women solicitors 'found the profession sufficiently worthwhile to renew their practising certificates'.[15] Admission as solicitors gave women a geographically portable and flexible qualification, enabling them to set up as sole practitioners (Charlotte Beatty, 1925), join established practices (Winifred Lewis, 1924) and family firms (Mary Sykes, 1923), or to create new partnerships (Crofts with her husband and brother, 1923); the first all-women partnership was formed by Edith Berthen and Beatrice Davy in 1931.[16] 31 women solicitors were trained by other women between 1922 and 1960.

But continuing male prejudice often resulted in the rejection of aspirant women solicitors and lower salaries once qualified. In 1956 Law Society prize-winner Rosalind Bax had to accept 80 per cent of the salary of contemporary male colleagues.[17] In 1951 Linklaters refused 'even to consider having a girl',[18] echoed in the 1970s by the 'we are prejudiced

[13] Elizabeth Cruickshank, '"Follow the Money": The First Women who Qualified as Solicitors' in *First Women Lawyers in Great Britain and the Empire Record*: vol 1 (St Mary's University, 2016) 76.

[14] DW Hughes, *Careers for our Daughters* (A&C Black, 1936) 134.

[15] ibid 135. Issued by the Law Society, a practising certificate indicates that the holder is a qualified solicitor.

[16] See **First Woman Law Agent, Madge Easton Anderson, 1920**.

[17] First woman equity partner in a major City firm in 1972.

[18] Rosemary Vaughan, 1990 (author's notes).

against female articled clerks'[19] of another firm. In 1975, with increasing educational opportunities for women and the disappearance of the training premium, the number of women holding practising certificates increased to 1,563 out of 29,850 solicitors,[20] and in 2015, almost 100 years after Morrison's admission, women almost achieved parity in numbers: 65,147 women or 48 per cent of the total, held practising certificates. Yet, in the same year, only 19 per cent of women were listed as partners in law firms, compared with 43 per cent of men.[21]

Morrison had a surprisingly significant impact on a number of substantive legal issues. With Appelbe she contended before her professional peers for substantial changes in family and divorce law which have subsequently been implemented. In 1933 she argued that 'housekeeping money given to a wife by her husband should be the wife's own property'[22] and 10 years later she acted as solicitor to Mrs Dorothy Blackwell when the latter unsuccessfully appealed the decision that a woman has no right to savings made from housekeeping.[23] Just over 30 years later, the **Married Women's Property Act 1964** established that housekeeping money belonged jointly to husband and wife.

Often regarded as 'an eccentric whose occasional abrupt manner hid a very generous nature',[24] Morrison was representative of many women solicitors in combining remunerative practice with pro bono legal advice in her local Hertfordshire community. Her experiences of London's East End and war-time Constantinople as well as living with the distress of her younger sister's nervous ill-health and subsequent suicide in 1924 gave her emotional resilience and a practical sympathy for the disadvantaged. In 1938 she decried the inadequacies of the Poor Persons' Defence Act 1930 and supported the extension of state aid to poor litigants; 11 years later this was provided for by the Legal Aid and Defence Act 1949.[25] In 1939 Morrison and Appelbe asked the Law Society to oblige solicitors to contribute to a compensation fund for members of the public disadvantaged by the defalcations of errant members of the profession.[26] Two years later, the Solicitors Act 1941 established the Solicitors' Compensation Fund, into which each solicitor paid an annual £5.[27] Perhaps not at the forefront of any movement to procure such changes, she advocated them strongly at Law Society meetings where, as a woman, she was in a conspicuous minority.[28]

However, Morrison's main public focus was on social fairness and equality, particularly in relation to the laws governing families and marital relationships. She was the first 'lady solicitor' who defended a 'woman petitioner' under the Poor Persons Rules[29] and was recognised by her contemporaries as the 'senior woman solicitor of England'.[30] Together with

[19] Elizabeth Cruickshank, *Women in the Law* (Law Society, 2003) 119.
[20] Richard L Abel, *The Legal Profession in England and Wales* (Blackwell Publishing, 1998) 415.
[21] Law Society, 'Trends in the Solicitors Profession: Annual Statistics Report April 2016' (Law Society, 2016).
[22] *Law Society Gazette*, 1933, 6.
[23] *Blackwell v Blackwell* [1943] 2 All ER 579.
[24] *Hertfordshire Mercury*, 24 February 1950, 1.
[25] *Law Society Gazette*, 1938, 230.
[26] *Law Society Gazette*, 1939, 188.
[27] Harry Kirk, *Portrait of a Profession: A History of the Solicitor's Profession, 1100 to the Present Day* (Oyez Publishing, 1976) 105.
[28] She was the first woman to present a paper at a Law Society Provincial Meeting (1931).
[29] Lord Merrivale, *The Daily Telegraph*, 26 May 1928.
[30] Lang, n 11 above, 168.

May Seaton-Tiedeman of the Divorce Law Reform Union, Morrison advocated the creation of Courts of Domestic Relations to deal with matrimonial difficulties and family quarrels 'but with powers to dissolve a marriage'.[31] She was acknowledged by Helena Normanton as being the only other woman lawyer in any way involved in working for the passing of the Matrimonial Causes Act 1937 which liberalised the divorce law.[32]

## IV. Significance

Millicent Fawcett predicted that women's admission to the legal professions would have a double benefit: 'first the advantage to women themselves in following an honourable profession, and secondly to the general mass of women, who would have the opportunity of having a trained legal adviser of their own sex'.[33]

Morrison is significant because she demonstrated how a woman could combine a professional career with a public persona, and yet, even while arguing for the extension of women's rights, could also contend that a better society involved treating men with equal fairness in terms of marital and inheritance rights. She hoped any legislation brought in to change English law inheritance provisions, for example, 'would be made fair to men, and that it would be made compulsory not only for the widow to inherit part of the estate of her husband, but also for the widower where the wife had the money'.[34] Indeed, she was highly critical of women who took advantage of their husbands and, in an unusual role reversal, tried to protect her young (male) articled clerk from some of the more salacious matters that she was involved in, while herself fighting hard for prostitutes brought before the magistrates.[35]

At root, Morrison believed in justice and fairness. Not all women lawyers have concerned themselves with the betterment of society, but it is noteworthy how often Morrison's name appears in accounts of campaigns and litigation, and how often she attracted the admiration of clients and colleagues of both sexes for her determination that the law should be used as an instrument of fairness and not oppression.

## Further Reading

- Harry Kirk, *Portrait of a Profession. A History of the Solicitor's Profession, 1100 to the Present Day* (Oyez Publishing, 1976).
- Mary Jane Mossman, *The First Women Lawyers: A Comparative Study of Gender, Law and the Legal Professions* (Hart Publishing, 2006).
- Hilary Sommerlad and Peter Sanderson, *Gender Choice and Commitment* (Ashgate, 1998).

[31] Carrie Morrison, 'Courts of Domestic Relations', A paper presented at a meeting of the Solicitors Benevolent Association (1931).

[32] **Matrimonial Causes Act 1923**.

[33] *The Solicitors Journal*, 4 April 1914.

[34] *The Times*, 6 October 1932.

[35] Sandy Alexander interviewed by the author, 24 April 2008.

# 25

# Matrimonial Causes Act 1923

PENELOPE RUSSELL

Prior to the Matrimonial Causes Act 1923, women in England and Wales found it harder than men to get a divorce. This was because the grounds for men and women petitioners were different: under section 27 of the **Matrimonial Causes Act 1857**, a husband divorcing his wife only had to prove one ground to obtain a divorce, whereas a wife divorcing her husband had to prove two. A husband could obtain a divorce on the basis of his wife's adultery alone, whereas a wife could not: her husband's adultery had to be aggravated by incest, bigamy, rape, sodomy, bestiality, cruelty or desertion of two years. The Matrimonial Causes Act 1923 removed this double standard and equalised the grounds for divorce so that a wife could now obtain a divorce on the basis of her husband's adultery alone.

This equalising measure was brought about by the clear-sighted and prompt actions of the post-war feminist campaign group, the National Union of Societies for Equal Citizenship (NUSEC). Concerned that previous divorce Bills[1] had been mired in controversy because they had been side-tracked into seeking to liberalise the grounds for divorce, NUSEC introduced a simple Bill addressing the equality of the grounds only, which minimised potential opposition. The Bill received Royal Assent on 18 July 1923, establishing the principle of equality in divorce.

## I. Context

The unequal grounds for divorce set out in the Matrimonial Causes Act 1857 were symbolic of the moral double-standard prevalent in Victorian society at that time, in that it was considered worse for a woman to commit adultery than a man. A man's adultery, unlike a woman's adultery, was not viewed as serious enough to justify ending a marriage. Indeed, the 1871 Royal Commission on the Contagious Diseases Act 1866 reported that there was 'no comparison to be made between prostitutes and the men who consort with them. With the one sex the offence is committed as a matter of gain; with the other it is an irregular indulgence of a natural impulse'.[2] Women were responsible for maintaining the stability of

[1] Divorce Bill 1892, Divorce Bill 1902, Matrimonial Causes Bill 1914, Separation and Divorce Bill 1918, Matrimonial Causes Bill 1920 and Matrimonial Causes Bill 1921.

[2] *Report of the Royal Commission upon the Administration and Operation of the Contagious Diseases Acts 1866–69, Parliamentary Papers* (1871), [60].

the family by upholding the highest standards of morality. Their adultery and any resulting illegitimate offspring threatened men's property rights. Ursula Vogel has commented that

> The idea that a wife's (but not a husband's) adultery strikes at the order of property and, as a direct consequence, at the foundations of civil society itself, reflects a near-unanimous consensus of legislators, jurists, moralists echoed over many centuries of European legal history.[3]

The campaign for divorce reform gathered momentum at the turn of the twentieth century when growing concerns about the need for divorce reform led to the establishment of pressure groups, such as the Society for Promoting Reforms in the Marriage and Divorce Laws of England, set up by Earl Russell in 1902, which later merged with the Divorce Law Reform Union (DLRU), set up by May Louise Seaton-Tiedemann in 1906. Most of the members of the DLRU were lawyers (and therefore men), concerned with the operation of the Matrimonial Causes Act 1857. For example, collusion and fraud were encouraged by the statutory framework: wives often applied for a decree of restitution of conjugal rights as a precursor to divorce because this enabled them to avoid waiting for two years to prove the aggravating factor of desertion under the 1857 Act.[4] Another difficulty was that there was only one court (the Court for Divorce and Matrimonial Causes[5]) and it was located in London. The cost of travel and overnight accommodation for parties and witnesses meant that divorce was out of reach to large sections of society.

The DLRU went on to have over 1000 members,[6] including high-profile figures such as Sir Arthur Conan Doyle and Thomas Hardy. The group employed paid staff to write pamphlets, hold public meetings and publish draft parliamentary Bills. The objective of the DLRU was to campaign for the establishment of a Royal Commission to consider the operation of the law and potential reform,[7] an objective in which it was ultimately successful. Former President of the Divorce Court and member of the DLRU, Lord Gorell, brought a motion in the House of Lords in 1909 saying:

> Poverty prevents large numbers of people – what those numbers may be it is quite impossible to say – from having access to the Court in London … For there is still practically one law for those who can afford to bring a suit in the Divorce Court and another for those who cannot, and the latter embraces a very large portion of the population.[8]

It was agreed that a Royal Commission would be appointed to investigate the issue, sitting under Lord Gorell's chairmanship.

The Royal Commission on Divorce and Matrimonial Causes lasted for two years and heard from 246 witnesses, finally reporting in 1912. Most witnesses were asked 'Do you think that the grounds for divorce should be the same for both men and women?' and, of the 94 who replied, 76 said that they should be the same.[9] The principle of equality of

[3] Ursula Vogel, 'Whose property? The double standard of adultery in nineteenth-century law' in Carol Smart (ed), *Regulating Womanhood: Historical Essays on Marriage, Motherhood and Sexuality* (Routledge, 1993) 148.

[4] See the statistics unearthed by Colin S Gibson, *Dissolving Wedlock* (Routledge, 1994) 85, which show a large drop in applications for restitution after 1923.

[5] Section 6 of the Matrimonial Causes Act 1857.

[6] Stephen Cretney, *Family Law in the Twentieth Century* (OUP, 2005) 216.

[7] DLRU, 'The Causes and Objects of the Divorce Law Reform Union' (The National Labour Press Ltd, 1914).

[8] HL Deb, 14 July 1909, vol 2 col 477.

[9] See calculation in Ann Sumner Holmes, 'The Double Standard in the English Divorce Laws, 1857–1923' (1995) 20 *Law and Social Inquiry* 602, based on *Royal Commission on Divorce and Matrimonial Causes: Minutes of Evidence* (3 vols) (HMSO, 1912).

grounds was uncontroversial but views were divided about whether the grounds for divorce should be extended, necessitating the production of both minority and majority reports. The minority report recommended equality but opposed any extension of the grounds, on the basis that making divorce easier would open the floodgates; the majority report recommended equal extended grounds, to include desertion, cruelty, incurable insanity, habitual and incurable drunkenness and imprisonment under commuted death sentence.[10] Both reports recommended that the grounds, whether extended or not, should be the same for both men and women.

The DLRU sought the implementation of the recommendations of the majority report. However, opposition to the liberalisation of divorce was powerful and wide-ranging, from religious groups such as the Church of England and the Catholic Church, to women's groups such as the Mothers' Union[11] (with 278,000 members)[12] and even some prominent feminists. For example, Nancy Astor, a Conservative Member of Parliament with close ties to NUSEC,[13] believed that easier divorce in her home country, the United States of America, had not been in the interests of women. She argued in the House of Commons debate in April 1920 that the Bill for divorce reform should not be supported:

> Get back to the principle. Shall we help women and children and men by making divorce easier? I think the world is too loose altogether. What we need is tightening up. I want to tighten up the men as well as the women.[14]

There were concerns that extension of the divorce grounds would be of more benefit to men than women, making it easier for husbands to end marriages and abandon their financially dependent wives.

Whereas DLRU sought to improve the fairness and effectiveness of the law, the campaign for equality was driven by post-war feminist groups such as NUSEC and the Six Point Group. The additional hurdle of proving aggravating factors meant that women found it harder to obtain a divorce and remarry: either leaving them trapped in abusive marriages or destitute if living separately. Some feminists wanted equality as an end in itself; others thought that it would bring about an improvement in male behaviour. When giving evidence to the Royal Commission in 1910, Millicent Fawcett said

> I urge most strongly that the difference between the sexes which now exists in divorce law should be put an end to … The law sanctions a lower standard for men, and I think that this has an injurious effect upon them.[15]

NUSEC was one of a number of post-war feminist campaigning groups and was large and well-organised, having the benefit of a national office based in London, supported by a network of local societies (220 in 1920).[16] NUSEC was the reincarnation of the non-militant National Union of Women Suffrage Societies, having succeeded in winning votes for women

[10] *Report of the Royal Commission on Divorce and Matrimonial Causes* (HMSO, 1912).

[11] Griselda Rowntree and Norman H Carrier, 'The Resort to Divorce in England and Wales, 1858–1957' (1958) 11(3) *Population Studies*, 188, 198.

[12] Dorothy E Stetson, *A Woman's Issue. The politics of family law reform in England* (Greenwood Press, 1982) 103.

[13] Nancy Astor MP was the first woman to take her seat in the House of Commons. See **Representation of the People Act 1918**.

[14] HC Deb, 14 April 1920, vol 5 col 1794.

[15] *Minutes of evidence taken before the Royal Commission on Divorce and Matrimonial Causes*, Vol II, 371.

[16] Martin Pugh, *Women and the Women's Movement in Britain 1914–1959* (MacMillan Education Ltd, 1992) 242.

in 1918. Elected president Eleanor Rathbone was a prolific writer and determined activist for social reform.[17] The activities of NUSEC included monitoring parliamentary Bills, mobilising public support and applying pressure for reform by using personal contacts and letters.[18] Rule II of the NUSEC Constitution sought 'real equality of … status … between men and women' and their 1919 programme for reform included promoting equality in the divorce laws.

The NUSEC journal *The Common Cause of Humanity* published in October 1919 displayed a full-page poster launching a £10,000 appeal, with the headline 'The vote is won. Equality is not yet won'. It listed the NUSEC demands which included: 'the immediate reform of the Divorce Law … An equal moral standard must be established'. Another NUSEC poster exhorted women to 'use your vote' and 'to use it intelligently' and listed what women wanted, including 'An Equal Moral Standard between Men and Women'. NUSEC was appealing to those wanting to raise male sexual standards to the level expected of women, a strategy linked to the social purity movement which had arisen from increasing concerns about male promiscuity, viewed as threatening family stability, causing illegitimacy and spreading venereal disease.[19]

Other post-war feminist campaigning groups included the Six Point Group, established in January 1921 by Lady Rhondda to campaign for law reform in six areas.[20] Although its membership was less than 300, the group was influential. Its periodical *Time and Tide* commented on contemporary political developments from a feminist perspective and was widely read, being distributed across the country to libraries. The periodical was entirely run by women and independent of the mainstream press. As well as including theatre reviews, short stories and satirical pieces, it used articles, editorials and letters pages to comment on new legislation. For example, when monitoring the voting practices of MPs, the periodical placed the name of Dennis Herbert on their Black List because of his opposition to divorce reform. The *West Herts Post* and *Watford Newsletter* subsequently reported that Dennis Herbert was chased by women at a packed and lively Six Point Group meeting in his constituency in July 1923.[21]

Other campaigners for divorce reform included the women's labour movement. Non-contributory old age pensions and welfare benefits had been introduced by the Liberal Government in 1908 and 1911 respectively but there was concern that large numbers of women would miss out on benefits because their new marital relationship could not be legally recognised.[22] Margaret Llewelyn-Davies, General Secretary of the Women's Co-operative Guild representing 26,000 artisans' wives, gave evidence to the Royal Commission in 1910 that

> feeling was extremely strong – unanimous as regards an equal standard for men and women, and equal facilities for rich and poor – and all except about five and six were of the opinion that serious incompatibility should be a ground for divorce.[23]

[17] **Family Allowances Act 1945**.
[18] Stetson, n 12 above, 107.
[19] Holmes, n 9 above, 611.
[20] Dale Spender, *Time and Tide Wait for No Man* (Pandora Press, 1984) 172. See **Life Peerages Act 1958**.
[21] Spender, ibid 140.
[22] Gibson, n 4 above, 81.
[23] *Minutes of evidence taken before the Royal Commission on Divorce and Matrimonial Causes* Vol III, 150 (Cd 6478–6482, 1912).

## II. The Landmark

A Bill for divorce reform was presented in 1914 but withdrawn because of the start of the First World War. After the war, further Bills to extend the grounds were presented in 1918, 1920 and 1921 but did not succeed despite being supported by a petition of over 100,000 signatures obtained by the DLRU in 1920.[24] It was only when NUSEC decided to separate the issues and present their own single-clause Bill for equality that the principle was enacted. Eva Hubback, the parliamentary secretary of NUSEC, found an MP to sponsor the Bill (Major Cyril Entwistle) and arranged for members across the country to lobby their MP in support of the principle of equality.[25] Cyril Entwistle tried to minimise debate on the second reading by saying 'The sole object of this Bill is to give equality to the sexes in the matter of divorce, and it has no other purpose whatsoever'.[26] His words were echoed by Lord Buckmaster who, introducing the Bill for its second reading in the House of Lords, stated that '[i]t has this purpose and this purpose alone: to secure that whatever may be the grounds of divorce they shall be the same for both women and men'.[27] The Bill had a smooth reading and passed its third reading with a clear majority in the House of Commons of 257 to 26.[28]

## III. What Happened Next

The Matrimonial Causes Act 1923 provided that it was lawful for a wife to obtain a divorce by relying on the ground that her husband had been guilty of adultery. The statute meant that women no longer had to prove any additional aggravating offence and could rely on adultery alone. As a consequence of reform, it was easier for women to obtain a divorce and the proportion of petitions filed by wives rose from 41 per cent in 1921 to 62 per cent in 1924.[29]

Subsequent divorce reform did not take place for another 15 years, with the extension of the divorce grounds on an equal footing in the Matrimonial Causes Act 1937. The 1937 Act's extended grounds for divorce of adultery, cruelty and desertion are still recognisable in today's system of divorce: a petitioner in England and Wales can establish irretrievable breakdown of the marriage by proving one of five facts which include adultery, unreasonable behaviour and desertion.[30] Although no-fault facts are also available (separation for two years with consent and separation for five years without consent),[31] the current statutory framework encourages the use of fault because doing so avoids postponement of proceedings for two or five years. In fact, figures suggest that almost half of all petitions are based on unreasonable behaviour,[32] which according to the Law Commission increases

[24] Cretney, n 6 above, 220.
[25] Stetson, n 12 above, 110.
[26] HC Deb, 2 March 1923, vol 160 col 2355.
[27] HL Deb, 26 June 1923, vol 54 col 573.
[28] HL Deb 26 June 1923, vol 54 cols 573–610; HC Deb, 8 June 1923, vol 164 col 2658.
[29] Gibson, n 4 above, 85.
[30] Sections 1(2)(a), (b) and (c) of the Matrimonial Causes Act 1973.
[31] Sections 1(2)(d) and (e) of the Matrimonial Causes Act 1973.
[32] Co-Op Legal Services press release, 'Almost half of all divorces due to unreasonable behaviour' (20 September 2013).

feelings of bitterness and hostility on marriage breakdown.[33] Historically, the judiciary have tried to minimise conflict by approving particulars that are mild.[34] However, in a recent case a woman was forced to wait five years for a divorce after her husband defended the proceedings and the Court of Appeal dismissed her appeal, upholding the judge's ruling that the particulars (including ones that the husband had refused to speak during a meal) were 'minor altercations of a kind to be expected during marriage'.[35] Calls for reform of divorce law are being led by senior figures in the judiciary (including **Lady Hale**), family law solicitors and campaign groups such as the Marriage Foundation, all arguing for a new simplified no-fault system.

# IV. Significance

The Matrimonial Causes Act 1923 is a landmark statute that established the principle of equality in divorce. Even if the legislators' motivations for reform were pragmatic rather than ideological,[36] the enactment of the statute marked a significant success for post-war feminist campaigning groups. The all-female NUSEC recognised the importance of equality in law for women, and achieved their objective by refusing to be distracted by male demands for an extension of the divorce grounds. The decision of NUSEC to present an uncontroversial simple Bill was the catalyst that brought about equality for women in divorce.

## Further Reading


- Ann Summer Holmes, 'The Double Standard in the English Divorce Laws, 1857–1923' (1995) 20 *Law and Social Inquiry* 601–20.
- Rebecca Probert, 'The Controversy of Equality and the Matrimonial Causes Act 1923' (1999) 33 *Child and Family Law Quarterly* 1.
- Dorothy Stetson, *A woman's issue. The politics of family law reform in England* (Greenwood Press, 1982).


[33] Law Commission, *Family Law: the Ground for Divorce*, (Law Com No 192, 1990) [2.16].

[34] *Livingstone-Stallard v Livingstone-Stallard* [1974] 2 All ER 766.

[35] *Owens v Owens* [2017] EWCA Civ 182, [46].

[36] Rebecca Probert, 'The Controversy of Equality and the Matrimonial Causes Act 1923' (1999) 33 *Child and Family Law Quarterly* 1, 6.

# 26

# First Woman Member of the Faculty of Advocates, Margaret Kidd, 1923

CATRIONA CAIRNS

Dame Margaret Henderson Kidd KC's life was a series of firsts: first woman member of the Faculty of Advocates (the Scottish Bar) in July 1923, first woman advocate (barrister) to appear before the House of Lords and a parliamentary select committee, first woman King's Counsel in the United Kingdom in 1948, and, as sheriff-principal, first woman member of the Scottish judiciary in 1960. In short, she was a remarkable woman and it comes with a fair degree of astonishment to note that her life has never been the subject of a full biography. The only physical mark left by her achievements appears to be a portrait hanging in the Faculty of Advocates (in the Advocates' reading room), where she was the first, and to date only, woman 'Keeper of the Library'.

## I. Life

Margaret Kidd was born on 14 March 1900 in Bo'ness, Linlithgowshire, the eldest of nine children. Her mother was a teacher and her father a solicitor and Unionist MP for Linlithgowshire.[1] She graduated with an MA and an LLB from the University of Edinburgh in 1922 and, pursuing her legal training with the firm of Mitchell and Baxter, was admitted to the Faculty of Advocates a year later.[2] In fact, becoming an advocate may well have been a 'back up' option – her preferred career in the Diplomatic Corp was not open to women – though it appears that she received encouragement in her choice of profession from her father who suggested she go to the Bar and 'have fun'.[3]

Kidd had a long and very successful career as an advocate, although not much appears to have been done to accommodate her arrival. The ladies' robing room was situated opposite the condemned cell in Parliament House, and hot water was only put in after the Second World War.[4] Though her legal practice was wide, she focused on family law, as was often

[1] When her father died in 1928, Kidd sought to contest his seat. She was unsuccessful, but it is worth bearing in mind that women MPs remained an anomaly, the first having been elected to Parliament less than 10 years earlier.

[2] Isobel Anne Poole, 'Kidd, Dame Margaret Henderson (1900–1989)' in *Oxford Dictionary of National Biography* (OUP, 2004).

[3] ibid.

[4] ibid.

typical for women, where her contemporaries recognised that she brought fresh eyes to old problems, such as her (unimplemented) recommendation that a family sheriff court would be more responsive to family law issues.[5]

By the time she became King's Counsel in 1948 she had been standing junior counsel for the Post Office and the then Ministry of Works. Her pioneering appointment was a popular one. *The Scotsman* commented:

> As the only woman in a hitherto masculinely exclusive and exclusively manly fraternity, and a naturally conservative one at that, her presence might have led to a certain amount of perturbation or even resentment ... The fact that she is one of the most popular and well-liked members of the Faculty is a tribute to her character and personality.[6]

In 1960 Kidd became the first woman sheriff-principal, a part-time judicial position with responsibility over various sheriff courts in her jurisdiction. She was appointed first to Dumfries and Galloway and then in 1966 to Perth, at time the most prestigious of sheriff-principaldoms, a post she held until her retirement in 1974. She was editor of the Court of Session law reports of the *Scots Law Times* (the oldest and best known Scots law reports) from 1942 until 1976.

Outside the courtroom, Kidd was assistant lecturer in public international law at the University of Edinburgh and a founding member of the Stair Society (established in 1934 to promote knowledge of the history of Scots law). In 1950, she served as a member of the Royal Commission on Betting, Lotteries and Gaming. She received honorary doctorates from the Universities of Dundee and Edinburgh. She was vice-president of the British Federation of University Women and of the Electrical Association for Women and was involved with a number of other charities. She was made a Dame of the British Empire in 1975.[7]

In 1930 Margaret Kidd married Donald MacDonald, a solicitor; they had a daughter, Anne. Margaret died in 1989.

## II. Context

Without doubt, Margaret Kidd's appointment came at a time of enormous change in the legal profession – and other professions. Although women had been able to study law and graduate since 1909,[8] it was not until the **Sex Disqualification (Removal) Act 1919** opened up many professions to women, that they were able to practise as lawyers. Soon after, in 1920, **Madge Easton Anderson** became the first Scottish woman solicitor in Scotland and the UK. Three years later, Kidd became one of a number of pioneering women barristers, following Frances Kyle and **Averil Deverell** in Ireland and Ivy Williams and **Helena Normanton** in England and Wales.

[5] ibid.

[6] 21 December 1948, cited in 'Scotland's History: Dame Margaret Henderson Kidd QC' (*Scotland's People*, 14 March 2017): https://www.scotlandspeople.gov.uk/article/scotlands-history-dame-margaret-henderson-kidd-qc.

[7] Poole, n 2 above.

[8] The first Scottish women law graduates were Eveline MacLaren and Josephine Gordon Stuart. Neither went on to become professional lawyers, though they did retain 'close connections' with the legal profession (First Women LLBs centenary', *Scots Law News*, 4 April 2009).

## III. What Happened Next

The inescapable conclusion is that Margaret Kidd becoming the first woman advocate did not open the floodgates and lead to a rush of other women becoming advocates. Incredibly, Kidd was the only woman advocate for 25 years until Isabel Sinclair's appointment in 1948. Sinclair was also only the second woman to take silk in 1964. This stands in contrast to the progress of women in the solicitors' profession, following **Madge Easton Anderson's** ground-breaking appointment. In 1949, Kidd commented:

> Much excellent work is being done steadily and faithfully by many able women solicitors in town and country districts throughout Scotland. The general public know too little of the service which they give … In the nature of things it is more constructive than that of the advocate, and there can be no doubt that in the administrative sphere the balanced judgment which ought to be the outcome of legal training combined with feminine intuition can play an important part in shaping things to come.[9]

The Bar in Scotland was and remains relatively small (both in comparison to the Bar in England and Wales and the solicitors' profession in both jurisdictions). This may have played a part in the slow pace of change. However, the Scottish legal profession was and is less divided than its English and Welsh counterparts. Solicitors (historically called agents) were usually the ones pleading in sheriff courts, not advocates, meaning that once a number of women became solicitors, there were a number of women pleading before judges. In higher courts, however, advocacy remained for a long time an almost exclusively male preserve.[10]

Some insight into the reasons for this is provided by Isabel Sinclair during an interview in 1996.

> It seems to me that my generation of legal women lacked a bit of confidence and the attitude of society at the time put many women off … Nowadays women have lots of confidence and know they can do a good job.[11]

Her view was that it was the attitude of clients, rather than the legal establishment, which caused the most problems for women advocates.

> The difficulties faced by women advocates like me in the early days can be summed up by an incident which happened soon after I became a QC. Like everybody else I got some criminal work from the Crown Office. However two men, Charles Johnston and Ian Stewart, who were called the same day as me, were getting big criminal cases and I wasn't. I went up to the Crown Office and asked about this and was told there were a couple of Glasgow men up for slashing people with razors who had to be represented separately. The Crown Office representative told me about the case and I expected him to give me the papers but instead he said he had to ask if the accused would have me first. So here I was, a well qualified advocate as good as the men, having to be scrutinised by this little Glasgow thug who maybe would condescend to be defended for free by a woman! I was downcast and as I headed for the door the Crown Office chap, obviously having a

[9] 'Dame Margaret Kidd, pioneer of women in law, dies aged 89', *The Herald*, 27 March 1989.
[10] Lord Rodger of Earlsferry, 'Rights of Audience – A Scottish Perspective' (The Child & Co Lecture, 1993).
[11] 'Approaching the bench', *The Herald*, 23 December 1996.

> change of heart, tried to make me feel better by saying, 'don't worry, no doubt he'll take you, after all beggars can't be choosers.'[12]

After all, if women advocates struggled to obtain work, why would other bright women law students follow in their footsteps? Becoming a solicitor would have appeared the better option, especially given that it also offered the possibility of carrying out advocacy work.

More recently, while progress remains slow – just 30 of the 142 permanent sheriffs are women[13] – a number of other firsts have fallen by the wayside. In 2005 Valerie Stacey QC was elected as the first woman Vice-Dean of the Faculty of Advocates, and the second woman to be elected as an office bearer after Margaret Kidd's tenure as Keeper of the Library. Elish Angiolini became the first female Solicitor General for Scotland in 2001 and the first female Lord Advocate in 2006 (the most senior legal positions in the Scottish government).

## IV. Significance

Without doubt, Margaret Kidd opened the door to the Scottish Bar for women and, more importantly, demonstrated that women could succeed and reach the very top of the legal profession. Typically for her generation, Margaret Kidd denied having faced any discrimination at work during her career, though she did later admit that 'if I'd been a man I might have built up a bigger practice.'[14] While Kidd – repeating the mantra of many pioneering women lawyers – put her ground-breaking achievements down to 'a lot of luck in happening to be at the right place at the right time',[15] the assessment of Lord Hope, former Deputy President of the UK Supreme Court, is likely to be closer to the truth:

> Her success was won by strength of character, courage and integrity and it is a mark of her true qualities that, despite what might seem to be the revolutionary nature of her achievement, she always held the affection and respect of those around her.[16]

### Further Reading

- Judith Bourne, *Helena Normanton and the Opening of the Bar to Women* (Waterside Press, 2016).
- Mary Jane Mossman, *The First Women Lawyers: A Comparative Study of Gender, Law and the Legal Professions* (Hart Publishing, 2006).
- Isobel Anne Poole, 'Kidd, Dame Margaret Henderson (1900–1989)' in *Oxford Dictionary of National Biography* (OUP, 2004).

[12] ibid.
[13] Andrew Ticknell, 'No disguising the lack of women leading our judiciary', *The Scotsman*, 22 January 2012.
[14] n 9 above.
[15] ibid.
[16] Poole, n 2 above.

# 27

# First Woman Professor of Law in Ireland, Frances Moran, 1925

EMMA HUTCHINSON

The life of Frances Moran was one of firsts. Appointed Reid Professor of Law at Trinity College, Dublin (TCD) in 1925, she was the first woman law professor in Ireland, pre-dating her UK counterpart by 45 years.[1] She was also the first woman to hold a Dublin University chair in any subject. In 1924 she was only the fourth woman to be called to the Irish Bar and, in 1941, she became the first woman Senior Counsel in Ireland.

## I. Life

Frances Elizabeth Moran was born on 6 December 1893, the fourth child and second daughter of Senator James Moran and Elizabeth Faulkiner. Her father was an hotelier by trade who later became a Justice of the Peace and a member of the first Seanad. Her older brother William was a graduate student at Trinity College, Dublin (TCD) and later a solicitor.[2]

Raised in a Catholic family in Hollybrook Park in the north Dublin coastal suburb of Clontarf, following a secondary education at Dominican College, Eccles Street and in Belgium,[3] Moran entered TCD in 1911. In 1915 she graduated with a BA in Modern Languages (French and English) followed by a LLB in 1918 and LLD in 1919. When she was called to the Bar in 1924 she came first in her class.[4] She was appointed Reid Professor of Law at TCD in 1925 and held that position until 1930. In 1932 she became Professor of Property Law at the Honorable Society of King's Inns, the principal place of training for all barristers in Ireland. She held this post until 1968. From 1934 to 1944 she was also Professor of Laws at TCD, during which time she was effective head of the law school.[5] A motion

[1] The first woman law professor in the UK was **Claire Palley**, appointed Professor of Public Law at Queen's University, Belfast in 1970.

[2] Census of Ireland 1911, 7 Hollybrook Park, Clontarf West, Dublin.

[3] Louis McRedmond (ed), *Modern Irish Lives, Dictionary of 20th Century Biography* (Gill & Macmillan, 1996) 218.

[4] 'University Women Leader to Be In Houston for Two-Day Visit', *The Houston Chronicle*, (November 1953).

[5] RB McDowell and DA Webb, *Trinity College Dublin 1592–1952: An Academic History* (Cambridge University Press, 1982, 453).

to advertise the chair of Professor of Laws externally was defeated at the college council.[6] In 1944 she stepped up to the Regius Professorship.[7] These chairs are unique to the British Isles and are established by royal appointment; the Regius Professorship, for example, was founded by Charles II in 1667 and is one of the oldest chairs at TCD.[8] Their rarity invests them with a significant level of prestige.[9]

Throughout this period Moran was also in practice at the Bar, specialising in conveyancing.[10] She was called to the English Bar at Gray's Inn in 1940 and in 1941 to the Inner Bar in Ireland, becoming the first woman Senior Counsel in Ireland. She attended the Nuremburg trials[11] and in 1947 she toured Canada, speaking about this experience.[12]

Her position at King's Inns meant that all future lawyers were her students, almost all of them male.[13] Described by students as a 'formidable academic',[14] she taught real property, equity and torts, which even RFV Heuston, in his otherwise disparaging obituary, conceded took some skill.[15] Her lectures were delivered with sharp precision, and 'sloppiness in the law or in the use of English was not tolerated'.[16]

In 1957 she was awarded an honorary LLD from Queen's University, Belfast. The following year she became the first woman elected to the board of TCD, representing non-fellow professors. (Women were not permitted at that date to become fellows.) She retired in 1963, but became the first woman honorary fellow when fellowship was opened to women in 1968. She was made Honorary Bencher of the King's Inns in 1969.

In addition to her academic and legal careers, Professor Moran was a strong advocate for women's education. She was president of the Dublin Association of University Women Graduates from 1950 to 1952, of the Irish Federation of University Women from 1949 to 1951 and of the International Federation of University Women from 1950 to 1953. In the latter role she addressed the American Association of University Women (AAUW) at their conference in Atlantic City in 1951[17] and embarked on a well-received tour of their branches in November 1953. Although Moran had by now been in post in Ireland for almost three decades, 'it was unlikely that a student attending law school in New York in the 1950s and early 1960s would ever have seen a woman professor'.[18]

Frances Moran never married. Described as a woman who talked and dressed with style,[19] she was active in the social life of TCD, a popular luncheon guest who would breeze from tea party to tea party on Trinity Wednesday wearing what was described as an

[6] ibid.
[7] ibid.
[8] John V Luce, *Trinity College Dublin, The First 400 Years* (Trinity College Dublin Press, 1992) 92.
[9] ibid. It should be noted, however, that the Crown has never exercised the right of appointment in Ireland.
[10] RFV Heuston, 'Frances Elizabeth Moran' (1989) 11 *Dublin University Law Journal* 1.
[11] Paul Gallagher, 'An Irishman's Diary', *The Irish Times*, 2 April 1997.
[12] 'Famous Woman Lawyer to Lecture in Tacoma', *News Tribune*, 11 November 1953.
[13] Ronan Keane, *Equity and the Law of Trusts in the Republic of Ireland* (2nd edn, Bloomsbury Professional, 2011) [9.01].
[14] Susan M Parkes (ed), *A Danger to the Men? A History of Women in Trinity College Dublin 1904 to 2004* (Lilliput Press, 2004) 195.
[15] Heuston, n 10 above, 5.
[16] 'Professor Frances Moran Obituary' (1978–80) 2 *Dublin University Law Journal* 76.
[17] Frances Moran, 'The IFUW in the World Today' (1951) 45 *American Association of University Women Journal* 9.
[18] Cynthia Fuchs Epstein, *Women in Law* (Basic Books, 1981) 226.
[19] McDowell and Webb, n 5 above, 453.

Ascot hat.[20] From a pro-Treaty nationalist background,[21] RB McDowell and DA Webb assess her as 'a strange mixture of progressive feminism and strong conservatism in the fields of politics, morality and social behaviour'.[22] She addressed the AAUW on how the United States could lead the way on freedom for women,[23] but on the topic of Irish politics she spoke of her opposition to the Gaelic revival.[24] She did not speak with an 'Irish brogue', preferring, in her words, to speak English in the way it is spoken in England.[25] Noted for her wit, she told members of the AAUW's Los Angeles branch that the study of law had become a 'serious thing' for her when she purchased law texts from a friend and decided to actually read them before turning an honest profit on their resale.[26] To her students she said that becoming a trustee was one of the 'three roads to ruin in life' and the least enjoyable at that.[27] She described the Nazi war criminals at the Nuremburg trials as looking like 'men who had sat up all night in a third-class railway carriage'.[28]

She took an active interest in the lives of her students and in turn was held in considerable esteem by them, chairing a debate with Sir Norman Birkett in the Graduates Memorial Building[29] before women were even admitted to membership of the college debating societies and being nominated to be the first woman to dine in the junior common room.[30] In 1964, one year post retirement, she returned to the college once more to fill the place of the late Dr VTH Delany who had succeeded her.[31]

She died on 7 October 1977 at the age of 83, leaving a large bequest to TCD school of law in her will.[32] This bequest led to the establishment of the Frances E Moran Memorial Studentship for postgraduate students, which exists to this day. The first Frances E Moran student, Deirdre Curtin, is currently Professor of European Union Law and head of department at the European University Institute, Florence. TCD has also hosted an annual memorial lecture since 1980.[33]

## II. Context

Trinity College, Dublin was founded in 1592. For four centuries its students were male but, in 1904, it became the first of the 'ancient' British universities to admit women students to lectures and degrees. It was not, however, the first institution in Ireland to grant degrees to

[20] Heuston, n 10 above, 2.
[21] Heuston describes Professor Moran's upbringing in a home where the *Freeman's Journal* was read. During the time of the Irish Civil War this newspaper took a pro-Treaty nationalist stance (ibid).
[22] McDowell and Webb, n 5 above, 453.
[23] Moran, n 17 above.
[24] Norma H Goodhue, 'AAUW Hears Talk by Dublin Professor', *Los Angeles Times*, 25 November 1953.
[25] ibid.
[26] Jean Ward, 'University Women Hear Dr Moran, Irish Visitor', *Los Angeles Examiner*, 25 November 1953, 2.
[27] Keane, n 13 above.
[28] Heuston, n 10 above, 7.
[29] 'Prof goes to Queen's', *Trinity News*, 16 May 1957.
[30] 'Fellows' Resolution', *Trinity News*, 10 February 1955, 2.
[31] 'Prof Moran Returns', *Trinity News*, 6 February 1964, 1.
[32] Heuston, n 10 above, 6.
[33] JCW Wylie, *Irish Land Law in the Next Century, First Frances E Moran Memorial Lecture* (Trinity College, Dublin, 1980).

women. In 1879 the Royal University of Ireland had been created to act as an examining body and, following representations by feminists, women (taught in a range of institutions) were able to take its examinations and graduate from 1884 onward. Women's admission to higher education was not easily won: all manner of objections were raised, including their delicate physical constitution,[34] their perceived lack of interest in intellectual study or a career,[35] and the danger they posed to the male students. Fears were expressed about distracted undergraduates, fortune-hunters, and scandals.[36] As a result, advocates were careful to couch their arguments in acceptable terms: educating women, they said, served to introduce a 'higher tone' to family life.[37]

By 1914, women made up 15 per cent of the annual intake into TCD,[38] rising to 26 per cent in 1920–23,[39] but at the time Moran was appointed they still remained subject to the Rules for Women Students 1905,[40] which substantially restricted their movements and participation in college. Women staff were barred from the comfortable senior common room and the Board of the College and could not be fellows. One former student recalls the 'demeaning' sight of eminent female staff clustered upon tiny stools in the ladies' coffee room.[41] Another recalls that 'all the women academics were marginalised, existing to some extent on the fringe of college life, and regarded by some as rather a joke'.[42] Nowhere is this marginalisation and trivialisation more shamefully evident than RFV Heuston's obituary of Frances Moran, in which he questions her qualifications, achievements and teaching but praises her for not being too strong a feminist: 'nobody was hit with her handbag'.[43]

It is remarkable then, given the resistance of TCD to the participation of women, that the first woman law professor should come from that institution. It is equally remarkable that the first woman professor should be in the field of law. The legal profession had been as resistant as academia, if not more so, to the entry of women and it was only after the enactment of the **Sex Disqualification (Removal) Act 1919** that the first two women Irish women were called to the Bar, Frances Kyle and **Averil Deverell** in 1921.

## III. What Happened Next

No other woman to date has held the chair of Regius Professor of Law at TCD and by 2003 there were only three full-time female law professors in Ireland.[44] Ivana Bacik has, however, been Reid Professor of Criminal Law, Criminology and Penology at Trinity College since 1996. Statistics released by the Irish Higher Education Authority in 2014 revealed that less

[34] Parkes, n 14 above, 23.
[35] McDowell and Webb, n 5 above, 342.
[36] ibid 347.
[37] Judith Hartford and Claire Rush (eds), *Rethinking Education, Volume 3, Have Women Made a Difference? Women in Irish Universities 1850–2010* (Peter Lang, 2010) 17.
[38] McDowell and Webb, n 5 above, 349.
[39] ibid 501.
[40] Parkes, n 14 above, Appendix D.
[41] ibid 267.
[42] ibid 196.
[43] Heuston, n 10 above, 7.
[44] Ivana Bacik, Cathryn Costello and Eileen Drew, *Gender Injustice: Feminising the Legal Professions?* (Trinity College Dublin Law School, 2003) 86.

than a third of senior academic posts were held by women and across all third-level institutions there were only 19 women professors.[45] Chief among the reasons for this lack of representation at senior level appears to be the 'care ceiling', that is the restrictions placed on women's advancement by their actual or assumed position as primary carers.[46]

In legal practice, too, progress was slow. Ireland would not see the appointment of another female senior counsel until Mella Caroll in 1976,[47] and Northern Ireland, shamefully, not until Eilish McDermott's appointment in 1989. Despite the fact that women have outnumbered men as practising solicitors in Ireland since 2014,[48] there exists what Ivana Bacik refers to as the 'sticky floor' where women find themselves concentrated at the lower levels of the profession. In her 2003 collaborative work on women's equality in the law[49] she identified the same problems of male social networks that exclude women from vital professional contacts and the assumption that women will be responsible for childcare, which persist as they did in Moran's era, together with negative perceptions of women. Indeed responses to a Bar of Ireland consultation in 2016 indicated that there is a simple preference among instructing solicitors for male counsel.[50] It is unsurprising then that women counsel make up just 38 per cent of the membership of the Law Library in Dublin, and only 16 per cent of senior counsel.[51]

At the same time, having had two women Presidents,[52] Ireland is in the unique position of having a significant concentration of women holding senior appointments in law and justice. The first woman Garda Commissioner, Nóirín O'Sullivan, third woman Minister for Justice, Frances Fitzgerald, Chief Justice Susan Denham, Attorney General Máire Whelan, Director of Public Prosecutions, Claire Loftus, Chief State Solicitor, Eileen Creedon, and President of the District Court, Rosemary Horgan, all carry on the tradition, begun with women like Frances Moran, Averil Deverell and Frances Kyle, of stepping into roles it was thought women could not do.

## IV. Significance

The significance of what Frances Moran achieved cannot be understated. As a pioneering professor in a university and a profession that were particularly resistant to the inclusion of women, she 'dominated Irish legal education'[53] at time when women at any level in the legal profession were rare. She set an example to male and female students alike of what women

[45] Pamela Duncan, 'Women under-represented in senior university posts HEA finds', *The Irish Times*, 3 December 2014.

[46] John Holden, 'The everyday reality of gender imbalance at professor level at third level', *The Irish Times*, 18 March 2014.

[47] Caroll was the first woman to practise at the Inner Bar in Ireland and became the first woman Superior Court judge when she was appointed to the High Court in 1980.

[48] Aine McMahon, 'Scales of justice tip in favour of women but more needs to be done', *The Irish Times*, 23 February 2015.

[49] Bacik, Costello and Drew, n 44 above.

[50] The Bar of Ireland, 'Submission by the Council of the Bar of Ireland to the Gender Equality Division, Department of Justice and Equality on measures to tackle the gender pay gap' (The Bar of Ireland, 2017).

[51] ibid.

[52] **First Woman President of Ireland, Mary Robinson, 1990**.

[53] Obituary, n 16 above.

could achieve, and stifled before the argument could even be raised the idea that women were incapable of fulfilling these roles. She went on to play an important part in changing attitudes to professional women. We see the long-term effect of this today with the strong representation of women in the upper echelons of the Irish legal and justice systems.

Frances Moran's situation was, however, exceptional in that she was an unmarried woman from an influential family with legal connections. Had she married or come from a different background she might not have ended up where she did. The first woman eligible to be called to the Bar in Ireland, Madelline Collins,[54] did not pursue her career because she got married; the third woman called to the Bar, Mary Dillon-Leech, also gave up her career on marriage.[55] The reception was no better for the married woman in academia. AA Luce, leading the opposition to women fellows at Trinity College in 1964, made the point, which RB McDowell and DA Webb considered still valid in 1980, that for a married woman domestic duties would increase to such an extent as would prevent her from 'conscientiously carrying out the duties of a full time post'.[56] His comment 'Imagine "Mrs Quiverful FTCD"[57]?' brought down the house.

It is clear from research conducted by Ivana Bacik, Cathryn Costello and Eileen Drew in the early 2000s that marriage and children, or the potential thereof, continue to act as a bar to women's advancement within the legal profession.[58] While Article 41.2 of the Irish Constitution continues to provide constitutional protection to the woman's place in the home, there is still work to be done to lift women's feet off the 'sticky floor'.

## Further Reading


- Ivana Bacik, Cathryn Costello and Eileen Drew, *Gender Injustice: Feminising the Legal Professions?* (Trinity College Dublin Law School, 2003).
- Judith Hartford and Claire Rush (eds), *Rethinking Education, Volume 3, Have Women Made a Difference? Women in Irish Universities 1850–2010* (Peter Lang, 2010).
- Susan M Parkes (ed), *A Danger to the Men? A History of Women in Trinity College Dublin 1904 to 2004* (Lilliput Press, 2004).


[54] Parkes, n 14 above, 59.

[55] Bacik, Costello and Drew, n 44 above, 57.

[56] McDowell and Webb, n 5 above, 353.

[57] Fellow of Trinity College Dublin. Mrs Quiverful is a character in Anthony Trollop's *Barchester Towers* (1857), wife of a poor clergyman who has 14 children.

[58] Bacik, Costello and Drew, n 44 above.

# 28

# *DPP v Jonathan Cape and Leopold Hill* (1928)

CAROLINE DERRY

In November 1928, Radclyffe Hall's novel *The Well of Loneliness* was found to be criminally obscene: liable to 'deprave and corrupt' those likely to read it. What makes the case significant is that the 'obscenity' of the book resided in its subject-matter, lesbianism. For the Chief Magistrate, its harm lay not in graphic sexual depictions of 'sexual inversion' (there were none), but in its plea for tolerance of 'inverts'.

This was not the first mention of lesbianism in the legal context, although overt discussion was a rare and recent phenomenon. However, the 1928 trial marked a high point of legal and social visibility, with discussion extending beyond the courtroom into daily newspapers. The specific version of lesbian relationships described in the book, with its reliance on sexological discourses, would thus colour public perceptions within and beyond the legal system for much of the twentieth century.

## I. Context

Sex between women has never been explicitly prohibited in English criminal law, although it has been within the ambit of other laws governing, for example, indecent assault, age of consent, and public decency,[1] as well as wide-ranging social, economic and medical policing mechanisms. The reason for this legal silence was made explicit in 1921 during parliamentary debates on a proposal to criminalise 'gross indecency between women'. As Conservative MP John Moore-Brabazon argued, the English approach to lesbians was 'to leave them entirely alone, not notice them, not advertise them. That is the method that has been adopted in England for many hundred years'.[2]

The subject of sex between women was only articulated in the context of a spoiling amendment designed to be controversial enough to kill the Criminal Law (Amendment) Bill 1921, which would have strengthened age of consent laws, in particular by increasing

[1] eg indecent assault on a female contrary to section 52 Offences Against the Person Act 1861 (*R v Mourez* (1885) 49 *Justice of the Peace* 745), later section 14 Sexual Offences Act 1956 (eg *R v Allen* [1996] 2 Cr App R (S) 36), now sections 2 and 3 Sexual Offences Act 2003 (*R v Newland*, unreported, *The Guardian*, 12 November 2015). Two men were convicted of 'insulting behaviour' under s 5 Public Order Act 1986 for kissing at a bus stop (*Masterson v Holden* [1986] 3 All ER 39).

[2] HC Deb, vol 145(8) cols 1802–1803.

the age of consent for indecent assault from 12 to 16. However, lawmakers were also being drawn into other confrontations: not only between the growing movement for tolerance of female and male 'inverts' and those who saw them as a threat to society, but also between the feminist movement and traditional ideals of womanhood.

Victorian ideologies of female sexual passivity continued to inform the criminal law: notoriously, the Punishment of Incest Act 1908 criminalised men *having* and women *permitting* sexual intercourse with certain family members. They also supported the notion that if the possibility of sex between women were kept secret from respectable ladies,[3] it would never occur to them to try it. How could someone who simply permitted sexual activity engage in it with another passive being?

Feminists had long condemned the sexual double standard, notably in opposing the Contagious Diseases Acts 1864–1869 which criminalised prostitutes while tacitly endorsing their male clients. By the turn of the twentieth century, some feminists identified the power of refusing heterosexual relations in radical terms: Lucy Re-Bartlett argued that women should not marry until men righted their wrongs against women, while Cicely Hamilton condemned 'marriage as a trade'.[4] At the same time, women's opportunities for independence and engagement in the public sphere were growing. It was unsurprising that the role of women in both public and private spheres was a topic of urgent debate.

Meanwhile, eugenic ideas emphasised women's sexuality and motherhood as vital to the development of the race: those who deviated from the ideal of white, middle-class womanhood potentially threatened the nation itself. 'Inversion' as just such a threat had been the theme of dancer Maud Allen's action for criminal libel against Noel Pemberton-Billing MP.[5] In the closing months of the First World War, the right-wing Independent MP for East Herts had published an article in his journal *Vigilante* accusing Allen of belonging to the 'Cult of the Clitoris' and thus associated her with 47,000 homosexual men and women whom he claimed were being exploited by German agents. Allen lost her case following a number of defence arguments, including that her very knowledge of the word 'clitoris' implicated her as a lesbian. Newspaper reports kept the precise allegation unclear, leaving most readers unaware of its nature.[6]

Such sexual ignorance was challenged by the new discipline of sexology. While many feminists were involved in the sexological movement, it was not itself necessarily feminist: for leading British sexologist Havelock Ellis, the movement for female emancipation had involved an increase in female homosexuality, allied to increases in female criminality and insanity.[7] Nonetheless, 'inverts' such as Hall were able to mould such discourses into an argument for rights and recognition: Hall saw herself as a 'propagandist' for inverts,[8] and the

[3] For further discussion of their race- and class-specific nature, see Catherine Hall, *White, Male and Middle-Class: Explorations in Feminism and History* (Routledge, 1992); Lucy Bland, *Banishing the Beast: English Feminism and Sexual Morality 1885–1914* (Penguin, 1995).

[4] Lucy Re-Bartlett, *Sex and Sanctity* (Longmans, 1912); Cicely Hamilton, *Marriage as a Trade* (Moffat, Yard & Co, 1909). See further ***A Pageant of Great Women*, Cicely Hamilton, 1909–12**.

[5] See Lucy Bland, *Modern Women on Trial: Sexual Transgression in the Age of the Flapper* (Manchester University Press, 2013) chapter 1; Michael Kettle, *Salome's Last Veil: The Libel Case of the Century* (Granada Publishing, 1977); Jodie Medd, '"The Cult of the Clitoris": Anatomy of a National Scandal' (2002) 9(1) *Modernism/Modernity* 21–49.

[6] Bland, ibid, 36–37.

[7] Havelock Ellis, *Studies in the Psychology of Sex Vol. 1: Sexual Inversion* (The University Press, 1897) 100.

[8] Radclyffe Hall, letter to Gerard Manley Hopkins, 13 August 1928, cited in Richard Dellamora, *Radclyffe Hall: A Life in the Writing* (University of Pennsylvania Press, 2011) 193.

*Well* drew upon sexological theories which cast inversion as innate in order to argue it was neither immoral nor unnatural. In keeping with Hall's appeal to scientific authority, Ellis provided the novel's foreword. However, as the *Well* case demonstrated, there was strong resistance to this argument among many parliamentarians, judges, and newspaper editors.

## II. The Landmark

Raclyffe Hall was a middle-brow author who had won the Prix Femina and the James Tait Black Prize for her 1926 novel *Adam's Breed*. That literary success encouraged her to write *The Well of Loneliness*, which she described as the first 'long and very serious novel entirely upon the subject of sexual inversion'.[9] It portrays 'congenital invert' Stephen Gordon, her upbringing as a boy and First World War service as an ambulance driver, and her relationships with other women. Gordon sacrifices the last of these so that her lover can marry a man, and the novel concludes with the plea: 'Acknowledge us ['inverts'], oh God, before the whole world. Give us also the right to our existence.'

Initially, the book enjoyed a muted but largely positive reception, thanks partly to Hall's efforts to control its advertising and to seek out sympathetic reviewers.[10] That changed dramatically on 19 August 1928, when James Douglas's *Sunday Express* editorial thundered 'I would rather give a healthy boy or a healthy girl a phial of prussic acid than this novel. Poison kills the body, but moral poison kills the soul.' Douglas demanded that the Home Secretary take legal action to prevent the novel's distribution if its publishers did not withdraw it. It was no coincidence that the attack came from a newspaper in the middle of a circulation war.

Nonetheless, the next day publisher Jonathan Cape submitted the book to the Home Secretary, Sir William Joynson-Hicks, for his view on whether it might breach the Obscene Publications Act 1857, which provided for the seizure and destruction of obscene material held for sale or distribution. This Conservative MP is described in the *Oxford Dictionary of National Biography* as 'the most prudish, puritanical, and protestant home secretary of the twentieth century', who also sought to censor publications on birth control, DH Lawrence's novels and a translation of the *Decameron*.[11] Predictably, his verdict was that the *Well* should be withdrawn.

Cape therefore ceased publication – but took casts of the type to Paris for publication there. The *Well* was thus soon back in print and being imported into England. When copies were seized by Customs on 4 October, officials expressed 'considerable doubt whether the book can properly be regarded as indecent or obscene'.[12] However, the Director of Public Prosecutions took a different view and proceedings were brought in Bow Street Magistrates' Court, with the publishers summoned to show cause why the books should not be destroyed as an obscene libel.

[9] Letter to Newman Flower, 10 April 1928, quoted in Laura Doan and Jay Prosser, 'Introduction: Critical Perspectives Past and Present' in Laura Doan and Jay Prosser (eds), *Palatable Poison: Critical Perspectives on the Well of Loneliness* (Columbia University Press, 2001) 1–31, 1.

[10] Doan and Prosser, 'Introduction', ibid; Dellamora, *Radclyffe Hall: A Life in the Writing*, n 8 above, 192–95.

[11] FML Thompson, 'Hicks, William Joynson-, first Viscount Brentford (1865–1932)' in *Oxford Dictionary of National Biography* (OUP, 2004; online edn, September 2010).

[12] HO144/22547, reproduced in Dellamora, n 8 above, 196.

In his judgment (*Director of Public Prosecutions v Jonathan Cape and Leopold Hill* (1928), unreported) on 16 November 1928, the Chief Magistrate, Sir Chartres Biron, relied upon *R v Hicklin*,[13] which defined as 'obscene' material which tended 'to deprave and corrupt those whose minds are open to such immoral influences, and into whose hands a publication of this sort may fall'. The *Well* would not do so by explicit sexual content, since there was none. However, Biron identified a different source of corruption: the book glorified 'unnatural practices between women … which between men would be a criminal offence, and involve acts of the most horrible, unnatural and disgusting obscenity'.[14] Had lesbianism been presented as 'a tragedy' then the novel might not have been obscene.[15] Instead, it was

> a plea for existence in which the invert is to be recognized and tolerated, and not treated with condemnation, which they are at present, by all decent people. This being the tenor of the book, I have no hesitation whatever in saying that it is an obscene libel, that it would tend to corrupt those into whose hands it should fall, and that the publication of this book is an offence against public decency, an obscene libel, and I shall order it to be destroyed.[16]

## III. What Happened Next

An appeal to the Quarter Sessions (a local court, held four times a year, which heard criminal cases as well as criminal and civil appeals) was dismissed after five minutes' deliberation.[17] In 1929, however, the US edition was the subject of another trial in New York, whose Court of Special Sessions ruled that its treatment of a 'delicate social problem' was *not* obscene. Pegasus Press continued to print the novel in France, and was never prosecuted. The US and France thus became sources of illicitly-imported copies for readers in Britain, where the *Well* remained out of print until 1949. Hall would publish several more, uncontroversial, novels before her death in 1943.

While the legal response reflected a wish to enforce silence upon the subject of lesbianism, reporting of the trial had carried the subject into the nation's homes.[18] That uneasy tension between visibility and silencing was apparent a year later, in the prosecution of Colonel Barker. He had married Elfrida Haward in 1923; but when imprisoned for bankruptcy in February 1929, it was discovered that Barker was physically female. In fact, Valerie Barker had been living as male since ending a violent relationship with a man. Barker was prosecuted at the Old Bailey for perjury, having made a false entry in the marriage register.[19] Although Barker pleaded guilty, the judge Sir Ernest Wild chose to question Haward about their sexual relations before passing a sentence of nine months' imprisonment for

[13] *R v Hicklin* (1868) 3 QB 360.

[14] Sir Charles Biron, 'Judgement' in Doan and Prosser (eds), n 9 above, 39–49, 41–42.

[15] ibid 42. On this basis, he later advised against prosecuting Compton MacKenzie's *Extraordinary Women*, which 'draws a most distasteful and detestable picture of practitioners in vice' (HO45/15727, reproduced in Dellamora, n 8 above, 198).

[16] Biron, n 14 above, 48–49.

[17] Diana Souhami, *The Trials of Radclyffe Hall* (Weidenfeld, 1998) 214–18.

[18] See in particular Souhami, ibid.

[19] Inspector Walter Burmby, *Central Officer's Special Report*, 6 May 1929, PRO MEPO 3/439, 1.

'perverted conduct' which had 'profaned the House of God … outraged the decencies of nature, and … broken the laws of man'.[20]

Wild J had participated in the 1921 parliamentary debates around criminalising gross indecency between women, but must also have been influenced by the recent *Well* trial: Barker, like Stephen Gordon, claimed to have been 'brought up as a boy' and had driven ambulances in wartime France.[21] Yet Barker felt obliged to vigorously deny 'perversion' and would later claim an essential femininity despite having continued to live as a man after leaving prison.[22] Barker's case was a manifestation of the newly-developing concern with 'perversion' amongst the middle and upper classes which followed the *Well* trial. Nonetheless, silencing was by no means abandoned: Wild questioned Haward about her sexual relationship with Barker largely by showing her relevant passages of her written statements and asking if they were true.[23] His concern both to find out about sexual behaviour and to keep it secret from the public is a graphic illustration of the contradictory pressures of silencing and social concern.

Legal silence then fell once again and remained intact for most of the century, even when sexuality was otherwise in the spotlight. When the Wolfenden Committee sat in 1957, its terms of reference on homosexual offences included indecent assault against women[24] and the evidence heard included a number of references to lesbianism[25] (the *Well* was published in paperback in Britain in the 1950s). However, the report itself simply dismissed acts between women as lacking 'the libidinous features that characterise sexual acts between males',[26] a distinction which witnesses had often refused to make. Similarly, the 1981 final report of the Policy Advisory Committee on Sexual Offences failed to mention sexual activity between women.[27]

Lesbianism would not return to the centre of legislative attention until the debate over section 28 of the Local Government Act 1988, introduced by the Thatcher government, which prohibited local authority 'promotion' of homosexuality as a 'pretended family relationship'. Primarily targeted at schools, it was a response to the growing visibility of lesbians and gay men, including radical feminists.[28] Ironically, in standing as a symbol of oppression, the section prompted political activism and increased lesbian visibility. As women defined their own sexuality publicly, and the law moved towards recognition of lesbian and gay rights, so we finally moved out of the shadow of the *Well*.

[20] 'Judge on Crime of "Col Barker"', *The Evening News*, 25 April 1929
[21] 'Colonel Barker', *Sunday Dispatch*, 10 March 1929, 1 and 5, 5.
[22] Rose Collis, *Colonel Barker's Monstrous Regiment: A Tale of Female Husbandry* (Virago, 2001); James Vernon, 'For Some Queer Reason: The trials and tribulations of Colonel Barker's Masquerade in Interwar Britain' (2000) 26(1) *Signs: Journal of Women in Culture & Society* 37–62.
[23] Insp Burmby, n 19 above
[24] Matthew Waites, 'Inventing a "Lesbian Age of Consent"? The History of the Minimum Age for Sex between Women in the UK' (2002) 11(3) *Social and Legal Studies* 323–42, 333.
[25] Public Record Office, HO 345/13.
[26] Committee on Homosexual Offences and Prostitution, *Report of the Committee on Homosexual Offences and Prostitution* (Her Majesty's Stationery Office, 1957) 38.
[27] Policy Advisory Committee on Sexual Offences, *Report on the Age of Consent in Relation to Sexual Offences* (Her Majesty's Stationery Office, 1981).
[28] Davina Cooper, *Sexing the City: Lesbian and Gay Politics within the Activist State* (Rivers Oram Press, 1994); Lynn Alderson, 'Clause 29: radical feminist perspectives' (1988) 13 *Trouble and Strife* 3–6, 6.

## IV. Significance

In offering a brief moment of visibility to relationships between 'sexual inverts', the *Well* trial would have a legal and cultural impact extending for decades. It is unfortunate that its reliance upon sexological models made these the lens through which lesbian relationships were viewed, while the lack of open discussion left them largely unchallenged in legal and popular contexts. The notion of pseudo-inversion proved particularly dangerous. While Hall had hoped that the innate nature of congenital inversion would make it a cause for sympathy, courts judging lesbian women saw themselves as protecting pseudo-lesbians, who might choose heterosexual relationships if not corrupted. These notions of corruption fed into such diverse legal areas as the sentencing of women in the criminal courts[29] and custody debates in the family courts.[30]

The *Well* helped to shape perceptions of lesbianism in popular culture, too. Most bookshops would sell sexological texts only to doctors, lawyers and scientists, but the theories became more widely known through this trial.[31] The response of 'invert' readers demonstrated the isolation, and thirst for information and validation, experienced by many at this time. However, visibility through the lens of congenital inversion was double-edged. While feminist critiques of sexuality had denied the naturalness of existing sexual behaviour and demanded that male behaviour should change,[32] the sexologists' work re-naturalised sex roles and undermined women's moral claims. A refusal of heterosexuality might be no more than a front for lesbianism.[33] The 'spinster' was thus an object of suspicion.

But it is undeniable that the trial gave visibility to lesbianism, and that the book remained the one novel on the subject that everyone knew about. By the 1970s, it was both recognised as a milestone and criticised for the way in which it treated the subject: Jane Rule described it as '*the* lesbian novel, a title familiar to most readers of fiction, either a bible or a horror story for any lesbian who reads at all'.[34] Some recent readings have gone further and debated whether the *Well* is best understood today not as a lesbian but as a transgender text.[35] While the *Well* may seem like a historical relic, the use of 'born that way' arguments as a basis for seeking rights remains prominent.[36] In a time of unprecedented legal advances, we still risk conceptualising same-sex relationships as something inferior which no one could choose, and tying appeals for rights to appeals to apparent scientific authority.

[29] See eg *R v Allen* (n 1 above) where the defendant was described as a 'malign influence'.

[30] Lynne Harne and Rights of Women, *Valued Families: The Lesbian Mothers' Legal Handbook* (The Women's Press, 1997).

[31] Margaret Jackson, *The Real Facts of Life: Feminism and the Politics of Sexuality c 1850–1940* (Taylor and Francis, 1994) 129.

[32] ibid, chapter 3.

[33] See further Lillian Faderman, *Surpassing the Love of Men: Romantic Friendship and Love Between Women from the Renaissance to the Present* (The Women's Press, 1985) 237.

[34] J Rule, 'Radclyffe Hall' (1975), reproduced in Doan and Prosser (eds), *Palatable Poison*, n 9 above, 77–88, 78.

[35] Jay Prosser, '"Some Primitive Thing Conceived in a Turbulent Age of Transition": The Transsexual Emerging from *The Well*' in Doan and Prosser, *Palatable Poison*, n 9 above, 129–44; Judith Halberstam, '"A Writer of Misfits": "John" Radclyffe Hall and the Discourse of Inversion' in Doan and Prosser (eds), *Palatable Poison* (n 9 above) 145–61.

[36] For a concise and critical overview, see Simon Copland, 'Born this way? Society, sexuality and the search for the "gay gene"', *The Guardian*, 10 July 2015.

## Further Reading

- Laura Doan and Jay Prosser (eds), *Palatable Poison: Critical Perspectives on the Well of Loneliness* (Columbia University Press, 2001).
- Radclyffe Hall, *The Well of Loneliness* (Penguin Classics, 2015).
- Diana Souhami, *The Trials of Radclyffe Hall* (Weidenfeld, 1998).

# 29

## *Edwards v Attorney General of Canada* (1929)

SARAH MERCER

In *Edwards v Attorney General of Canada*[1] the Judicial Committee of the Privy Council decided that women were 'persons' within the meaning of the British North America Act 1867. The reasoning in this case brought to an end the line of 'persons' cases dating from the mid-nineteenth century, in which women had been debarred from a range of public roles on the ground of 'inveterate custom' and insistence that the legislation had never been intended to include them. Through the doctrine of precedent, each of these cases had drawn on those that went before as authorities for the exclusion of women, courts claiming that only specific new legislation could change the position. In many of the preceding cases, legislation was eventually passed to admit women, but *Edwards* changed the law through a court decision at such a high level (though technically Privy Council judgments only have persuasive effect, and *Edwards* was a Canadian case) that it became impossible for future courts to argue that women were not 'persons' in law for any purpose.

## I. Context

The origins of the 'persons' cases lay in the feminist response to the passage of the Representation of the People Act 1867, which lowered the property qualification required to vote in the borough elections for men 'of full age, not subject to legal incapacity'. During the debates, John Stuart Mill MP had made a speech in favour of women's suffrage and moved an amendment to the bill 'to leave out the word "man" in order to insert the word "person"'.[2] Though the amendment was defeated,[3] a number of feminists who fulfilled the property qualification decided to capitalise on the ambiguity of the word 'man' and try to register to vote. When the revising barrister for the borough of Manchester refused to place the women's names on the register, an appeal was made and the case was heard under the name of *Chorlton v Lings*.[4] The argument for the women had two main prongs. First, there had been originally no distinction between men and women in exercising the parliamentary franchise, and no subsequent legislation had altered that. Second, even if women had not

[1] *Edwards and Others v Attorney General of Canada* [1930] AC 124, [1929] UKPC 86.
[2] HC Deb, 20 May 1867, vol 187 cols 844–845.
[3] The amendment 'that the word "man" stand part of the clause' was approved by 196 votes to 73 (ibid).
[4] *Chorlton v Lings* (1868) LR 4 CP 374.

possessed the vote before the Representation of the People Act 1867, that Act, as interpreted by Lord Brougham's Act of 1850 which provided that words implying the masculine gender should be deemed and taken to include females unless the contrary was expressly provided, gave them the right. The evidence of women exercising the franchise in historical times was scanty but the point about Lord Brougham's Act was more substantial. The respondents argued that 'if the Court can see that it was the intention of the legislature not to enfranchise women, they must give effect to that intention notwithstanding the previous statute' and that 'such an intention, if it had existed, would undoubtedly have been expressed in distinct words'.

The judges rejected the women's case, considering both that there was insufficient evidence to argue usage and that the interpretation of Lord Brougham's Act was a 'strained one'. Bovill J said that it was 'unnecessary to consider … whether it is desirable that women should possess the franchise' and cited Coke as authority.[5] Byles J also pointed out that

> though we are not at liberty to construe an Act of Parliament by reference to the debates upon it in the legislature, yet it is impossible to suppose that Parliament … intended to admit to the poll another half of the population.[6]

Other cases followed. In 1873, the Scottish courts held in *Jex-Blake and others v Senatus of the University of Edinburgh and the Chancellor thereof*[7] that women were not allowed to be admitted as students and to attend (separate) classes with a view to being examined and then graduating as doctors. In *Beresford Hope v Lady Sandhurst*,[8] following the re-organisation of local government, the Court of Appeal agreed that women, while persons for the purpose of electing councillors, were not persons for the purpose of *being elected* a councillor. In *De Souza v Cobden*,[9] the Court of Appeal, however, decided that, having been elected and acted as councillors, they were persons for the purpose of suffering a penalty.[10] In *Hall v The Incorporated Society of Law Agents in Scotland*[11] the Court of Session considered that women were not persons for the purpose of being admitted to the examinations for law agents.[12] In 1908 the House of Lords in *Nairn and others v University of St Andrews and others*[13] decided that women, having by now gained the right to attend university and to graduate, were not entitled, as graduates, to participate in the franchise for the Scottish university seats. In *Bebb v Law Society*,[14] Miss Bebb's attempt to sit the Law Society's examinations with a view to becoming a solicitor were again frustrated when the Court of Appeal agreed that women were not persons for the purposes of the Solicitors Act 1843. And in 1922, even after the passage of the **Sex Disqualification (Removal) Act 1919**, when the question of whether a peeress in her own right was entitled to be summoned to the House

[5] ibid, 382.
[6] ibid, 393.
[7] *Jex-Blake and others v Senatus of the University of Edinburgh and the Chancellor thereof* (1872–73) 10 Sc L Rep 549.
[8] *Beresford Hope v Lady Sandhurst* (1889) 23 QBD 79.
[9] *De Souza v Cobden* [1891] 1 QB 687.
[10] **First Woman Prospective Parliamentary Candidate, Helen Taylor, 1885.**
[11] *Hall v Incorporated Society of Law Agents in Scotland* (1901) 3 F 1059, 1901 9 SLT 150.
[12] **First Woman Law Agent, Madge Easton Anderson, 1920.**
[13] *Nairn and others v University of St Andrews and others* [1909] AC 147.
[14] *Bebb v Law Society* [1914] 1 Ch 286.

of Lords was considered, the Committee for Privileges by a majority of 22 to 4 decided that she was not.[15] In all these cases the (male) judges justified their decisions by suggesting that they were bound by precedent. As Phillimore LJ in *Bebb* noted, 'we are not here to say what should be the law … [O]ur function is to declare the law'.[16]

In Canada, meanwhile, a similar struggle for votes for women had resulted in the achievement, by 1919, of the right for all women (except those excluded by race) to vote in federal and most provincial elections.[17] From 1919, too, women could stand for the federal House of Commons. Women, however, could not serve as Senators in Canada's upper house.[18]

## II. The Landmark

Five Albertan women (Henrietta Edwards, Nellie McClung, Louise McKinney, Irene Parlby and Emily Murphy, later known as the Famous Five) decided to challenge this. They were part of what has been described as the maternal feminist movement.[19] They were all middle class, white and Protestant, and were involved in temperance, purity and eugenics movements.

Emily Murphy had campaigned since 1919 for the appointment of a woman to the Senate, sending letters to the press and government ministers and lobbying both Conservative and Liberal governments. The problem was the British North America Act of 1867 (effectively (then) Canada's constitution) which required a 'person' to be qualified for appointment and – as we have seen – women were not (legally) people. The only solution appeared to be a constitutional amendment, but the politics of 1920s Canada made this hard to achieve. By 1927, Emily Murphy had given up hope of achieving her goal through political means and turned instead to the courts. She was not confident but believed that

> if … the tradition-bound judges could not be convinced to break with the past and refused to declare women to be 'persons' in the eyes of the law, she could reactivate the political campaign by ridiculing the constitution's deplorable failure to recognize the legal personhood of women.[20]

However, appointment to the Senate was discretionary, so she had no standing to challenge her non-appointment. Murphy decided to use a distinctive feature of Canadian law and petition the Government to direct a reference to the Supreme Court of Canada. The petition was signed by all five of the women and submitted in August 1927. The question referred was 'Does the word "persons" in section 24 of the British North America Act, 1867, include female persons?'

[15] *Viscountess Rhondda's claim* [1922] 2 AC 339; see Life Peerages Act 1958.

[16] [1914] 1 Ch 286, 297.

[17] In Quebec women only gained the right to vote in 1940.

[18] Under the Military Voters Act 1917 and the Wartime Elections Act 1917 nurses and women in the armed services, and women with husbands, sons or fathers serving overseas were allowed to vote. All women over 21 were allowed to vote from 1 January 1919.

[19] See further Christina Hoff Sommers, *Who Stole Feminism?: How Women have Betrayed Women* (Touchstone, 1994) and Nancy F Cott, *The Grounding of Modern Feminism* (Yale University Press, 1987).

[20] Robert J Sharpe and Patricia J McMahon, *The Persons Case: The Origins and Legacy of the Fight for Legal Personhood* (University of Toronto Press, 2007) 104.

The case – *Edwards v Canada (Attorney General)*[21] – came before the Supreme Court of Canada in March 1928. The province of Alberta supported the women's position; the province of Quebec strongly opposed it. The Court unanimously rejected the women's arguments. Anglin CJ adopted a strict formalist approach: 'If the phrase "qualified persons" in section 24 includes women today, it has so included them since 1867'.[22] He doubted whether the Imperial Parliament would have made clear its intent to render 'women eligible for appointment to the Senate at a time when they were neither qualified to sit in the House of Commons nor to vote for candidates for membership in that House.' Instead, he suggested,

> [had] it not rather, by clear implication, if not expressly, excluded them from membership in the Senate? Such an extraordinary privilege is not conferred furtively, nor is the purpose to grant it to be gathered from remote conjectures deduced from a skilful piecing together of expressions in a statute which are more or less precisely accurate.[23]

Moreover, he continued 'when Parliament intends to overcome a fundamental constitutional incapacity it does not employ such an equivocal expression as is the word 'persons'.[24] He concluded that '*Chorlton v Lings* is conclusive against the petitioners'.[25] Duff J and Mignault J agreed, viewing the words of the constitutional provision as having a meaning that was 'fixed' in time.[26] Mignault J went further

> the contentions which the petitioners advanced at the hearing are not new. They have been conclusively rejected several times, and by decisions by which we are bound … It appears hopeless to contend against the authority of these decisions.[27]

The outcome of the case divided public opinion in Canada, many accepting that the judges had decided correctly on the law but considering the result absurd. Emily Murphy was determined to keep going: 'We must not give up the fight … It may not be for a while, but ultimately we are going to succeed'.[28] The Canadian Justice Minister announced that 'means will be taken to secure an amendment to the BNA' but Murphy was concerned that such an amendment might not pass the Senate and, following a meeting with the other women, petitioned the government to permit an appeal to the Judicial Committee of the Privy Council (JCPC).

The Judicial Committee of the Privy Council, created in 1833 to advise the monarch, was, in the grandiose words of then Lord Chancellor, Lord Haldane, 'the supreme tribunal of the Empire and every subject of the King-Emperor is entitled to go in'.[29] It gives a single advisory opinion which can then be implemented by the monarch by Order in Council. Its decisions are binding on overseas jurisdictions and persuasive in the UK (but given the similarity in the composition of the JCPC and the Supreme Court, unlikely to be at odds). The case was heard in London in July 1929 before Lord Sankey, the Lord Chancellor – newly

[21] *Edwards v Canada (Attorney General)* [1928] SCR 276.
[22] [1928] SCR 276, 282.
[23] ibid, 285.
[24] ibid.
[25] ibid, 290.
[26] ibid, 301.
[27] ibid, 303.
[28] Sharpe and McMahon, n 20 above, 137.
[29] Lord Haldane cited in Sharpe and McMahon, n 20 above, 143.

appointed by the Labour Government – Lord Darling, Lord Merrivale, Lord Tomlin and Sir Lancelot Sanderson.

Despite Mignault J's fears, the JCPC were early able to dispense with the earlier case law – mostly by ignoring and distinguishing it. Lord Sankey, giving the opinion of the Council, looked at two areas: first, the 'extraneous circumstances such as previous legislation and decided cases', and second, 'the internal evidence derived from the Act itself'. In relation to the first he considered that, although the respondents had placed 'great reliance' on *Chorley v Lings*, it was 'clearly distinguishable'. The appeal to history, the Council considered, was far from conclusive; they noted that 'customs are apt to develop into traditions which are stronger than law and remain unchallenged long after the reason for them has disappeared'. In relation to the second area, Sankey stated:

> His Majesty the King in Council is the final Court of Appeal from all these communities and this Board must take great care therefore not to interpret legislation meant to apply to one community by a rigid adherence to the customs and traditions of another.

He went on to note that two provisions in the Act made reference to 'males' rather than to persons and another provision using 'persons' referred to the use of English or French in court proceedings and must therefore have applied equally to men and women. He concluded:

> their Lordships have come to the conclusion that the word 'persons' in section 24 includes members both of the male and female sex and that, therefore, the questions propounded by the Governor-General must be answered in the affirmative and that women are eligible to be summoned to and become members of the Senate of Canada, and they will humbly advise His Majesty accordingly.

## III. What Happened Next

None of the 'famous five' were ever appointed to the Canadian Senate. Emily Murphy had wanted a Senate seat, but sadly, within three years of the decision, Murphy, Edwards and McKinney had died. Neither Parlby nor McClung wanted to go to the Senate but both continued to write and campaign on political issues. McClung was appointed a governor of the Canadian Broadcasting Commission and was a delegate to the League of Nations, as was Parlby. All five women were named as honorary senators in 2009 and there are statues of them in Calgary and Ontario. As of January 2018, the Canadian Senate has 45.7 per cent female representation and Canada ranks 59th in the world for women's participation in national politics.[30]

## IV. Significance

*Edwards* demonstrates how 60 years of legal precedent embodying one form of ideology can be overturned to embrace a new ideology when the time is apparently right. Right up to

[30] Figures from 'Women in National Parliaments' (Inter Parliamentary Union, 1 January 2018): http://archive.ipu.org/wmn-e/classif.htm.

this case, judges had shown themselves unsympathetic to women's claims and had used all the legal techniques at their disposal to reject them. Indeed, the cases, it has been argued,

> provide a clear example of the way in which words … may be manipulated to further particular interests. The judges appealed to custom in their efforts to exclude women from certain areas of public and professional life … Their arguments regarding the meaning of the word person are extraordinarily devious.[31]

But those very techniques – of adherence to precedent and long usage, of deference to the legislature – were just as easily dispensed with when the courts wished to reach a different conclusion. In the view of Albie Sachs and Joan Hoff Wilson,

> the only inference that can be drawn … from the [Privy Council] judgment is that Lord Sankey … thought it absurd that women should be debarred from public office solely on the grounds of sex, and even more absurd that the word person should be the instrument for achieving this result. Having arrived at that conclusion or rather having started off on that premise it was not difficult for them to write a judgment that paid conventional respect to all the earlier decisions while totally ignoring their effect.[32]

They go on to suggest that it would also have been hard for Lord Sankey to demur, since he was at the same time sitting in Cabinet with the first woman Cabinet Minister and Privy Councillor, Margaret Bondfield.[33] The view that this was a political decision is reflected also in **Lady Hale's** comment that 'despite all the historical learning deployed this looks more like political than black letter reasoning.'[34]

This may all be true. But the social and political climate would not have changed, and ideologies about women within it, had not feminists campaigned long and vigorously to influence public opinion and mobilised forces to challenge the law. Women employed different strategies for achievement of their goals: organising protests, lobbying politicians to introduce legislation, and, finally, bringing legal challenges in court. The persons cases generally, and *Edwards* in particular, demonstrate the effective use of all three.

## Further Reading

- Albie Sachs and Joan Hoff Wilson, *Sexism and the Law: A Study of Male Beliefs and Judicial Bias in Britain and America* (Wiley-Blackwell, 1978).
- Robert J Sharpe and Patricia I McMahon, *The Persons Case: The Origins and Legacy of the Fight for Legal Personhood* (Toronto University Press, 2007).

[31] Wade Mansell, Belinda Meteyard and Alan Thomson, *A Critical Introduction to Law* (3rd edn, Cavendish Publishing, 2004) 93.

[32] Albie Sachs and Joan Hoff Wilson, *Sexism and the Law: A Study of Male Beliefs and Judicial Bias in Britain and America* (Wiley-Blackwell, 1978) 42.

[33] ibid.

[34] Brenda Hale, 'Confessions of a Lady Law Lord' (Bentham Club Lecture, London, 2005).

# 30

# Education Act 1944

HARRIET SAMUELS

The Education Act 1944 restructured the education system in England and Wales.[1] It is a landmark for women for two reasons. First, it raised the school leaving age (referred to as ROSLA) from 14, and provided for free full-time education for children between 5 and 15 years of age (section 35).[2] Second, it abolished the so-called marriage bar – a practice that had been an obstacle to the employment of married women teachers – setting a precedent for other employers (section 24(3)). The Act also occasioned a spirited, but ultimately unsuccessful, struggle for equal pay for women. In addition, although the Education Act 1944 was steered through Parliament by Richard Austin 'Rab' Butler MP, a Conservative Minister, it was implemented by Labour's first woman Education Minister, and committed feminist, Ellen Wilkinson MP.

## I. Context

The Education Act 1944 was one of a number of pieces of legislation intended to regenerate the country in the aftermath of the Second World War. It was precipitated by the need for a skilled workforce to drive the post-war economy, a recognition of the poverty and poor education of city children who had been evacuated to the countryside, inconsistencies in educational provision across the country, the poor literacy of conscripts, and the new-found presence of Labour Ministers anxious to improve the conditions of the working class.[3] The policy embodied in the Education Act 1944 was drafted by a group of male civil servants in the early 1940s.[4] When Butler was appointed President of the Board of Education in 1941 he and his Labour Parliamentary Secretary, Chuter Ede, were determined to press ahead with the proposals in the form of a Bill, overcoming then Prime Minister Winston Churchill's initial hostility.[5] The result was a complex law that reflected different political and other interests.

[1] It was followed a year later by the Education (Scotland) Act 1945.

[2] Education Act 1944, s 35.

[3] Michael Barber, *The Making of the 1944 Education Act* (Cassell, 1994) 2–4.

[4] Board of Education, *Education after the War* (HMSO, 1941) ('The Green Book').

[5] Barber, n 3 above, 38. See also Ray Cocks, 'Ram, Rab and the Civil Servants: A Lawyer and the Making of the Education Act 1944' (2001) 21 *Legal Studies* 15.

The marriage bar, which excluded married women from certain professions including teaching, had become widespread after the First World War. Men returned home from the front and there was a shortage of work.[6] In response, many local education authorities refused to hire married women and dismissed married teachers. Feminists saw the removal of the marriage bar as a part of the wider struggle for equality. It symbolised women's function as a reserve army of labour normally dependent on their husbands' wages, whose main occupation was home and family.[7] The bar had been the subject of several unsuccessful parliamentary Bills and legal challenges throughout the 1920s. Most notably, it had been found by the courts to be lawful and compatible with the **Sex Disqualification (Removal) Act 1919**.[8] Women teachers were especially active in promoting equality and often had a strong feminist sensibility.[9] Lobbying by the National Union of Women Teachers (NUWT) had continued through the war years and had also been largely – though not completely – unsuccessful: the bar was abolished by the London County Council in 1935 after some skillful NUWT campaigning and the election of women councillors.[10] For feminists

> the introduction of the Bill provided an excellent opportunity to press for women's rights. The decision to abolish the marriage bar was not included in the original Bill, but was added as an amendment after lobbying by feminists.[11]

The debate over the marriage bar occurred at a time when the Second World War had raised the profile of women conscripted into the workforce.[12] By September 1943, 46 per cent of women between 14 and 59 were doing some sort of national service, including 80 per cent of women who were married with no children.[13] Women's groups, women MPs and some women trade unionists mobilised to pressure the Government to maximise women's work for the war effort.[14] This feminist energy spilt over into attempts to amend the Education Bill. An amendment providing for equal pay for teachers was introduced by Conservative MP Thelma Cazalet-Keir.[15]

> In this Amendment, all we ask the President [Butler] to do, is to say in this Clause that he accepts the principle that the basic rate of pay shall not be decided on sex, but on the worth of the job … I will take a London school, a mixed central school … where boys and girls, from 11 to 16, are taught side by side by a mixed staff – five men and eight women, with a headmistress in charge, all at their maximum salaries. The teachers specialise in all subjects. There is no difference in the

[6] Alison Oram, *Women Teachers and Feminist Politics 1900–39* (Manchester University Press, 1996) 26.
[7] Jane Lewis, *Women in England 1870–1950: Sexual Divisions and Social Change* (Wheatsheaf Books, 1984) 200.
[8] *Short v Poole Corporation* [1926] Ch 66; *Price v Rhondda Urban District Council* [1923] 2 Ch 372.
[9] Oram, n 6 above.
[10] Oram, n 6 above, 169.
[11] Harold L Smith, 'The Womanpower Problem in Britain During The Second World War' (1984) 27 *The Historical Journal* 925, 942.
[12] See Penny Summerfield, 'Women, War and Social Change: Women in Britain in World War II' in Arthur Marwick (ed), *Total War and Social Change* (Macmillan Press, 1988) 95–183.
[13] Ministry of Labour and National Service, *Report for the Years 1939–1946*, Parliamentary Papers 1946–47 (Cmd 7225, 1946–47) as cited in Smith, n 11 above, 934.
[14] Harold L Smith, 'British Feminism in the Second World War' in Phillipa Levine and Susan Grayzel (eds), *Gender, Labour, War and Empire: Essays on Modern Britain* (Palgrave Macmillan, 2009) 93–115, 94.
[15] HC Deb, 28 March 1944, vol 398 cols 1355–1396.

> work of the men and the women and all take equal shares in the exchange of duties, such as in the provision of meals and milk. The men receive £84 a year more than the women …[16]

Although it passed initially, Churchill made the amendment a vote of confidence and the amendment failed.[17]

The Government was also unenthusiastic about amending the Education Bill to remove the marriage bar, fearing it would build momentum for feminist demands for equality and set a precedent for the civil service. However Chuter Ede, Butler's Parliamentary Secretary, reluctantly agreed to the removal of the bar. Government backing for the amendment introduced in May 1944 meant that there would be majority support for change in the House of Commons.[18] Ede calculated that married women would help with the teacher shortage and that other feminist demands for equality could be contained. He commented that, unlike in the civil service, married women were needed as role models for their women students: it was unhealthy for schools to have too many spinsters, whom he described as thwarted, sex-starved and repressed, a common image of unmarried women in a period when marriage was considered women's only proper role.[19]

## II. The Landmark

The Education Act 1944 created a national system of education overseen by the Minister of Education but administered locally (sections 1, 8(1)(b)).[20] Many local authorities introduced the tripartite system as a result of the influence of the Norwood Report.[21] This report, on the secondary school curriculum, was written by educationists during the war. The tripartite system was premised on the notion that children fell into three groups, each with varying abilities and talents, and should accordingly be allocated to three categories of school: grammar, secondary modern and technical. The 1944 Act did not mention selection or prescribe particular types of school. It was sufficiently flexible to allow local authorities to create a comprehensive system or, more usually, to impose selection at 11. In fact, few technical schools were established, essentially producing a bipartite system of grammar and secondary modern schools, whose contribution to social mobility was dubious.[22] This system remained in place until 1964 when there was a move towards introducing comprehensive education nationally.[23] Parents had a duty to ensure that their child received an 'efficient full time education suitable to his [or her] age, ability, and aptitude, either by

[16] HC Deb, 28 March 1944, vol 398 cols 1357–1358. In an earlier debate Thelma Cazalet-Keir MP had urged local authorities to follow the example of the London County Council and introduce paid maternity leave (HC Deb, 10 March 1944, vol 397 col 2384).

[17] See Barber, n 3 above, 88–96.

[18] HC Deb, 9 May 1944, vol 399 col 1806.

[19] See Public Records Office, Kew, ED 136/467, 6 March 1944, as quoted in Cocks, n 5 above, 32.

[20] Ken Jones, *Education in Britain: 1944 to the Present* (Cambridge University Press, 2003) 19.

[21] Report of the Committee of the Secondary School Examination Council, *Curriculum and Examinations in Secondary Schools* (HMSO, 1943) ('The Norwood Report').

[22] Jones, n 20 above, 16 and 30.

[23] See Department of Education and Science, *The Organisation of Secondary Schools*, Circular 10/65 1965.

regular attendance at school or otherwise' (section 36) until he or she was 15 (section 35).[24] The legislation left open the possibility of the school leaving age being raised from 15 to 16 by Ministerial Order, which occurred in 1972.[25]

The re-organisation of the school system meant that local authorities assumed control of the appointment and dismissal of teachers at state schools. The marriage bar was removed by section 24(3), which stated that 'No woman shall be disqualified for employment as a teacher in any county school or voluntary school, or be dismissed from such employment, by reason only of marriage'. The absence of any reference to, or use of, the language of equality was deliberate. Unlike feminists, who had seen the removal of the marriage bar as a matter of principle, the Government was motivated by pragmatic concerns. As Ray Cocks notes, the Government wanted to ensure that the law would be interpreted as narrowly as possible and did not want to be seen to endorse broader ideas of equality between men and women.[26]

## III. What Happened Next

### A. Implementation of Raising of the School Leaving Age (ROSLA)

Implementing the 1944 Act required the Labour Government, elected in July 1945, to find 13,000 additional teachers and 5,000 additional classrooms at a time when money was in very short supply. The Minister for Education, Ellen Wilkinson MP, applied in August 1945 to postpone the rise until April 1947 as permitted by the legislation. Time was needed to recruit staff, provide facilities and find school buildings for an extra 200,000 students.[27] Despite real pressure from the Treasury and others, Wilkinson pressed on and secured ROSLA, arguing that any further delay would adversely affect working-class children whose education had been the most disrupted by the war.[28] In her speech to the Labour Party conference in 1946 she said:

> When I went to the Ministry of Education I had two guiding aims, and they come largely out of my own experience. I was born into a working-class home, and I had to fight my own way through to the University. The first of those guiding principles was to see that no boy or girl is debarred by lack of means … the second one was that we should remove from education those class distinctions which are the negation of democracy.[29]

Her view was that educational reform was an electoral promise and should not be dropped yet again because of economic policy.[30] She regarded implementing the 1944 Act as a 'job for

[24] Section 36 of the Education Act 1944.
[25] Raising of the School Leaving Age Order 1972.
[26] Cocks, n 5 above, 32.
[27] Matt Perry, *Red Ellen Wilkinson: Her Ideas, Movements and World* (Manchester University Press, 2014) 381 and Nigel Middleton and Sophia Weitzman, *A Place for Everyone: A History of State Education from the End of the 18th Century to the 1970s* (Victor Gollanz, 1976) 324.
[28] Perry, ibid 382–83 and Middleton and Weitzman, ibid 324–25.
[29] Labour Party Annual Conference Report 1946 as cited in Perry, n 27 above, 373.
[30] Perry, n 27 above, 382.

a generation'.[31] Her tenacity in overcoming opposition to ROSLA during a time of austerity, after so many failed attempts by others, is widely acknowledged as her greatest achievement as a minister. She was also responsible for increasing spending on education, the provision of free school milk for all children, ensuring a school lunch was supplied and a new scholarship scheme to enable pupils to attend university.[32]

## B. The Impact of the Tripartite System

Most local authorities opted for a system that selected between 7 and 30 per cent of students passing the 11-plus exam to go to grammar schools depending on the area. However, the system discriminated against girls. More girls passed the 11-plus than boys – and this was seen as unfair to boys who were said to mature later. To equalise the number of places between the sexes, boys were given places over girls who had higher scores. In short, girls had to do better than boys to get a place at a selective school. This practice continued until a House of Lords decision held that it contravened the **Sex Discrimination Act 1975**.[33]

In truth, the overall impact of the Education Act 1944 on girls' education depended on their social class. In general the middle classes dominated grammar schools whilst working-class children usually attended secondary modern schools.[34] Until 1962 the majority of children who went to secondary modern schools left at 15 without qualifications.[35] The consequence was that the professions were only open to those children who had attended grammar schools.[36] Even at grammar school, girls, particularly those from working-class backgrounds, tended to leave school as soon as they could, which was usually before taking public exams.[37] Boys' education was prioritised by families, as it was thought that girls were likely to waste their education by marrying and giving up work.[38]

Despite these institutional and cultural disadvantages (usually but not only) middle-class grammar school girls often did very well.[39] Access to such schools produced a steady supply of girls taking science and maths,[40] as well as the skills, qualifications and aspirations to enable them to gain entry to university and the professions, from which they shattered

[31] Billy Hughes, 'In Defence of Ellen Wilkinson' (1979) 7 *History Workshop and Journal* 157, 159.

[32] Hughes, ibid and Perry, n 27 above.

[33] See *Birmingham City Council v Equal Opportunities Commission* [1989] AC 1155. See further on academic selection at age 11, Deborah Thom, 'Better a Teacher than a Hairdresser? "A Mad passion for Equality" or Keeping Molly and Betty down?' in Felicity Hunt (ed), *Lessons for Life: The Schooling of Girls and Women, 1850–1950* (Basil Blackwell, 1987) 124–44.

[34] Rosemary Deem, *Women and Schooling* (Routledge, 1978); Gary McCulloch, *Failing the Ordinary Child?: Theory and Practice of Working Class Secondary Education* (Open University Press, 1998) 77–78 and Stephanie Spencer, *Gender, Work and Education in Britain in the 1950s* (Palgrave, 2005) 51.

[35] This was because the public exams were taken at 16 and compulsory education ended at 15. See Deem, n 34, above, 58–59.

[36] When working-class children attended grammar school they were apt to underachieve, or leave early with no qualifications (Ministry of Education, *Early Leaving: A Report of the Advisory Council for Education (England)* (HMSO 1954) paras [90]–[93]) ('The Gurney-Dixon report').

[37] The Gurney-Dixon report, ibid [27] and [103] and Deem, n 34 above, 59.

[38] The Gurney-Dixon report, ibid [103].

[39] Phillida Bunkle, 'The 1944 Education Act and Second Wave Feminism' (2016) 25 *Women's History Review* 791.

[40] Madeline Arnot, Miriam David and Gaby Weiner, *Closing the Gender Gap: Postwar Education and Social Change* (Polity Press, 1999) 108.

the myth that women were not capable of high achievement and acted as role models for future generations. Nevertheless, it was some time before the opportunity to gain these transformative qualifications was open to a wider pool of girls, including the majority of working-class girls attending secondary modern schools.

### C. The Marriage Bar

The 1944 Act was more positive for adult women because the removal of the marriage bar enabled married women to apply for teaching positions and remain in post after marriage. The shortage of teachers and the increase in the birth rate meant there was a demand for teachers to work in infant schools. After the war the Government simultaneously promulgated an idealised vision of family life whilst needing women's labour to achieve the necessary economic regeneration.[41] The Government therefore encouraged married women teachers to return to work by promoting part-time work, working near home and relieving them of extra duties.[42] At the same time, however, a number countervailing factors inhibited married women's ability to undertake paid work, including the dominant cult of domesticity, the double burden of employment and 'running' a family, and the reduction in childcare facilities. Nursery schools that had been provided during the war to enable women to work shrank in number.[43]

Equal pay for teachers was implemented in stages between 1956 and 1961 and for all workplaces by the Equal Pay Act 1970, which came into force in 1975.[44] The marriage bar was removed by the BBC and for civil servants in 1946, following a review by the National Whitley Council.[45]

## IV. Significance

Free universal secondary education introduced by the 1944 Act was premised on the egalitarian notion that success should be on merit rather than family background, and that there should be parity of esteem between the different types of school.[46] However, this impulse for equality, as far as it went, was only concerned with class and social levelling. It did not extend to gender equality. There was little, if any attempt to produce a more gender-neutral curriculum.[47]

Nevertheless the Education Act 1944 was a step forward in improving girls' life chances. It ensured that secondary education was freely available and made it unlawful for parents to remove girls from school early, as had been common practice in the past. Attending school might not result in leaving with a qualification, but for the first time a generation of young

[41] Elizabeth Wilson, *Halfway to Paradise: Women in Post War Britain: 1945–1968* (Tavistock Publications, 1980).
[42] See Ministry of Education, *Report of the Working Party on the Supply of Women Teachers* (HMSO, 1949).
[43] Summerfield, n 12 above, 107.
[44] **Dagenham Car Plant Strike, 1968; *Birmingham City Council v Abdulla* (2012).**
[45] Whitley Council Committee, *Marriage Bar in the Civil Service* (HMSO, Cmd 6886, 1946).
[46] The Green Book, n 4 above, chapter 1, para [2].
[47] Thom, n 33 above, 125.

people, including the working classes, had an automatic right to free secondary education until the age of 15.[48] This created a generation of women who came of age in the dynamic atmosphere of the 1960s, many of whom became active in second-wave feminism.[49]

The removal of the marriage bar for teachers was of real significance – especially for *married* women. While the teacher shortage provided an opportunity for the removal of the marriage bar, the accompanying disavowal of feminism by the Government – the purported need for the influence of married women in schools and deliberately misogynistic denigration of single teachers – is indicative of a familiar backlash in response to the success of feminist arguments. It would be a long and uneven path towards equality. Nor had the removal of the marriage bar happened overnight. It was one of a number of demands, including equal pay, made by the teachers' unions, and by concerted cross-party activism by a group of women MPs and their allies during the war years.[50] It was a hard-won victory, but one that laid the groundwork for future campaigns on equal pay, maternity leave and childcare. And that had significant consequences for the education of girls, who were able to complete their education and gradually populate the workplace, universities and professions in greater numbers than ever before.

## Further Reading

- Laura Beers, *Red Ellen: The Life of Ellen Wilkinson, Socialist, Feminist, Internationalist* (Harvard University Press, 2016).
- Alison Oram, *Women Teachers and Feminist Politics 1900–39* (Manchester University Press, 1996).
- Deborah Thom, 'Better a Teacher than a Hairdresser? "A Mad passion for Equality" or Keeping Molly and Betty down?' in Felicity Hunt (ed), *Lessons for Life: The Schooling of Girls and Women, 1850–1950* (Basil Blackwell, 1987)

[48] Deem, n 34 above, 58.
[49] Middleton and Weitzman, n 27 above, 383.
[50] Oram, n 6 above, 172–74.

# 31

# Family Allowances Act 1945

LUCY VICKERS

The Family Allowances Act 1945 introduced the first systematic payment of welfare support to women for the support of children. It provided payment of an allowance for the second and subsequent children in any family under the age of 16 while in education or serving an apprenticeship.[1] The 1945 Act had three distinctive features which were understood to be key to its effectiveness. It was not means-tested; it was paid direct to the mother; and payment was not linked to family size. It has since been replaced by Child Benefit, which has recently become means-tested and paid only in respect of a maximum of two children per family.

The architect of the Act was Eleanor Rathbone MP, one of the first women MPs. She campaigned for family allowances throughout her career and the introduction of the Act is generally attributed to her.

## I. Context

The introduction of the Family Allowance Act in 1945 is best understood within the context of longstanding debates on how to tackle poverty, although the Act can also be seen as part of a feminist agenda to give women a level of financial control for their families. In terms of poverty relief, the aim of earlier laws such as the Poor Laws had been to address poverty by providing money only to the very poorest families. The approach taken by the start of the twentieth century included the introduction of tax allowances for children in 1909.[2] This tackled the problem of how to help larger families, but only benefited those who paid tax, still leaving many in poverty.

One remedy for child poverty was to increase wages, a suggestion largely supported by the Left and the labour movement. However, work undertaken by Eleanor Rathbone demonstrated that increasing wages can be an inefficient way to tackle poverty, as no wage can be identified which is both high enough to support larger families and yet fair and affordable. For example, a wage set to support a family with three children will leave workers with fewer

[1] See Rupert Cross, 'The Family Allowances Act, 1945' (1946) 9(3) *Modern Law Review* 284–89.

[2] Child tax allowances were first introduced in 1798 and abolished again in 1805. In 1909 allowances of £10 per child were introduced for those with incomes of under £500 per year.

children well-off, but those with more than three children will still not have enough. By linking payment directly to family size, family allowances overcome this problem.

The case for family allowances was not only based on the need to address child poverty. It also had strong underpinnings in the women's movement: child poverty was caused in part because women and children were dependent on men using their wages to support the family.

Eleanor Rathbone, the main campaigner for family allowances, was born in Liverpool in 1872. In 1909 she became the first woman to be elected to Liverpool City Council. In 1918 Rathbone's experience of administering separation allowances during the First World War led her to found the Family Endowment Society to campaign for their universal introduction. In 1919 Rathbone took over the presidency of the National Union of Women's Suffrage Societies (renamed the National Union of Societies for Equal Citizenship) on the retirement of Millicent Fawcett.[3] Her campaign for family allowances was based both on her concern for women's political and economic equality and her understanding of the experience of women who lived in poverty.[4] Her experience of social work in Liverpool had shown that there were direct causal links between poverty and gender, due both to women's wages being low, and also the fact that women were dependent on men, some of whom did not spend their wages on supporting their wives and children.[5]

In Rathbone's view, the answer to children's and women's poverty was a system of social security payments to be paid to mothers in respect of their children, building on the experience of separation allowances paid to women while men were away fighting, based on the number of dependent children in the family. Separation allowances resulted in better health for women and children and increased women's independence[6] and so it was clear that this system could be effective to reduce both child poverty and women's dependence on men's wages.[7] Rathbone's book *The Disinherited Family*[8] set out in detail the case for endowment in the UK, as well as reviewing the development of similar schemes in Europe, the US, Canada, Australia and New Zealand. As a form of poverty reduction, family allowances are clearly more effective than either tax allowances or minimum wages, and the logic of the case as set out by Rathbone seems unassailable. Indeed, Rathbone garnered some key converts such as William Beveridge, then Director of the London School of Economics, who included a system of family allowances within his 1942 Beveridge Report.

Despite the strength of the case in favour of family allowances in terms of women's and children's poverty, the campaign was not universally supported by the Left or by the feminist movement. One area for debate related to the relationship between family allowances and campaigns for increased pay. Trade unionists argued that men needed additional pay to support a family. If family allowances were to be introduced, the state would provide for some of the costs of children, and the argument for increased wages would be undermined.

[3] Susan Pedersen, *Eleanor Rathbone and the Politics of Conscience* (Yale University Press, 2004) 177. **Representation of the People Act 1918**.

[4] John McNicol, *The Movement for Family 1918–1945* (Heinemann, 1980).

[5] Pedersen, n 3 above, chapter 6.

[6] Joya Misra, 'Mothers or Workers? The Value of Women's Labor: Women and the Emergence of Family Allowance Policy' (1998) 12(4) *Gender and Society* 376, 382; Hilary Land, 'The Introduction of Family Allowances: an Act of Historic Justice?' in Clare Ungerson (ed), *Women and Social Policy, A Reader* (Macmillan, 1985).

[7] Eleanor Rathbone, 'The Remuneration of Women's Services' (1917) 27(105) *The Economic Journal* 55, 67.

[8] Eleanor Rathbone, *The Disinherited Family* (E Arnold & Co, 1924).

The potential for family allowances to drive down men's wages meant that the Labour Party did not originally support the idea of family allowances.[9] In contrast, many feminists argued that family allowances were necessary to remove this argument in favour of differentiation in wages between the sexes: pay should be based on individual merit, rather than men's need for a family wage.[10]

Despite strong feminist arguments in favour of family allowance, the feminist movement was in fact split over the campaign.[11] Fawcett felt that family allowances would remove the incentive for men to work, and Ada Nield Chew believed women should be encouraged to work outside the home.[12] For many, equality was to be achieved by creating a gender-neutral world, with a focus on civil and political rights such as suffrage and equal pay, and removing barriers to women's full participation in the labour market.[13] In contrast, family allowances could be seen to encourage the expectation that a woman's place was in the home, and could hamper the movement for equal citizenship.

Rathbone, a key player in the suffrage movement and strong supporter of equal citizenship, argued that her family allowance policy could equally serve feminism's ends. Family allowances could encourage women to work and could help achieve equal pay; equally they would help value women's caring work for those who chose to stay at home to care for children. Ascribing value to this work could be just as important in progressing the cause of women's equality.[14] Moreover, Rathbone's project was primarily fuelled by a desire to promote women's independence from men. Although for tactical reasons the focus of much of the campaign was on child poverty, for Rathbone, the need to enhance women's status and independence was also key.[15] Rathbone's 'New Feminism', included the belief that feminism needed to move beyond winning access to jobs and activities that had been the preserve of men. It should also include taking account of motherhood, not just as a temporary event, but as a form of labour that would absorb much of women's adult lives. Feminism would be a failure, in her view, if becoming a mother meant giving up independence and political participation. This was not part of a 'return to hearth and home' rhetoric, but instead was based on her knowledge, gained during her social work in Liverpool, of the lived experience of working-class women, and of the harsh realities their lives.[16]

One key part of Rathbone's case for family allowances was that it should be paid to the mother. This was partly a practical concern, based on her experience of seeing men fail to use their earnings to provide for their families. But payment to the mother was not only pragmatic; it was underpinned by Rathbone's feminist thinking. It was designed to recognise the importance of women's caring work and remove women's dependency on men. As she put it, payment to the father would lower the status of motherhood 'because it treats the wife as a mere appendage, which means literally a hanger on, of her husband'.[17] Although it is arguable that dependency on a man was to be replaced by dependency on the state, nonetheless, state provision was preferable as it could be enforced and allowed control over

[9] Misra, n 6 above, 383.
[10] Rathbone, n 7 above, 68.
[11] See Pedersen, n 3 above, chapter 10.
[12] Pedersen, ibid 183.
[13] See Misra, n 6 above.
[14] Pedersen, n 3 above, 59.
[15] H Land, 'The Family Wage' (1980) 6 *Feminist Review* 55.
[16] Pedersen, n 3 above, 180.
[17] HC Deb, 8 March 1945, vol 408 col 2276.

the money once it was received.[18] Moreover, it was believed that payment to the mother would ensure that the funding reached the children who depended on it.

## II. The Landmark

After decades of campaigning, governmental support was finally given for a Family Allowances Bill in 1945, forming part of a package of social reform including maternity services, the **Education Act 1944** and the National Health Service.[19]

The Act was widely seen at the time as Rathbone's personal achievement.[20] However, Susan Pedersen sets this milestone in the context of other social and welfare reforms which were introduced at the time. She argues that child poverty concerns had become more pressing during the Second World War and that the Government recognised that what was predicted to be years of post-war austerity could be softened by the payment of universal child allowances.[21]

Although Rathbone had long argued that allowances should be paid to the mother, the initial Bill proposed that the allowance would belong to the father. In a heated debate[22] Rathbone stated that, despite it being 'one of the bitterest disappointments of my political life if the Bill did not go through', she would vote against the Act unless her original plan that the allowance be paid to the mother was implemented.[23] The House of Commons debate on the issue included considerable support for payment to be to the mother, and the Bill was eventually amended. Arguments were based on feminist principles as well as more pragmatic considerations such as the fact that in practice the maintenance of the children falls upon the mother.[24] Rathbone's influence on the debate was significant, and the fact that she was prepared to jeopardise the Bill in order to achieve this outcome demonstrates her commitment not only to a system of family allowances, but also to the details of the scheme that she had devised.

## III. What Happened Next

One of the interesting matters that emerges from the debates in the first half of the twentieth century on family allowances is how many of the issues are still debated today. The key features on which Eleanor Rathbone was so insistent were that the allowance should be paid to the mother; that it was non-means tested; and that payment was related to family size.[25]

[18] Ruth Lister, 'Women, Economic Dependency and Citizenship' (1990) 19(4) *Journal of Social Policy* 445, 453.

[19] HC Deb, 8 March 1945, vol 408 col 2261. See also Pedersen, n 3 above, 359.

[20] See for example the tributes to Rathbone in Cross, n 1 above. See also her obituary in *The Times*, 3 January 1946.

[21] Pedersen, n 3 above, 361.

[22] HC Deb, 8 March 1945, vol 408 cols 2259–2370.

[23] ibid, col 2283.

[24] ibid, col 2293.

[25] Eleanor Rathbone was my grandmother's second cousin and I was brought up with the story of her role in the introduction of family allowances. The importance of the fact that the allowance was paid to the mother and was non-means tested was firmly part of that narrative.

The reason for payment to the mother was both practical and symbolic. Practically, it was the mother who would most usually need the money as she would be undertaking the care; more importantly for Rathbone, family allowance was designed to raise the status of women, and recognise the importance of child-care in the nation's life. The reason for not means testing was to remove any stigma attached to accepting 'welfare' help with family finances;[26] it would also help to sell the idea to the middle classes as they too would benefit. In Rathbone's view, the allowance was a restitutionary benefit, recognising the right of families to a share in the nation's wealth, and the fact that it was paid to everyone would result in higher uptake. Payment per child was also fundamental to ensuring that larger families did not live in poverty.

Between 1945 and 2013, some elements of the family allowance system were changed. Between 1977 and 1979 it was decoupled from the tax system and renamed Child Benefit. Yet the fundamental characteristics of a non-means-tested payment, usually paid to the mother, paid regardless of family size remained in place.

However, since 2013, fundamental aspects of the allowance system have been unpicked. Child Benefit became means-tested for the first time in 2013. More serious in terms of its impact on child poverty has been the move to limit Child Benefit and Child Tax Credits to only the first two children from April 2017. It is said that this will encourage personal responsibility for birth control.[27] However, family allowances were introduced in the form chosen explicitly because a one-size family income (at the time set through minimum wages) will always fail to provide for the poorest larger families. Moreover, one of the levers for introducing family allowance was to alleviate the impact of post-war austerity measures on the poorest. Seventy years later, austerity arguments have been used instead to limit payments to many of society's most vulnerable.

## IV. Significance

The case made for family allowances was closely linked to Rathbone's feminism. She believed that payment of an endowment to mothers would increase women's independence and recognise the economic value of the work of child rearing. The fact that so many women and children lived in poverty, due to the very poor wages for women, also motivated the move to family allowance.

Evidence from the 1970s showed how many women relied on family allowance to give a measure of financial independence or indeed to allow them any money of their own at all. Women reported valuing family allowance as they did not have to beg their husbands for money, but could use it to provide food for the family and budget for longer-term costs. Family allowance also provided a financial lifeline in times of family breakdown.[28]

Feminist debates about the role of men and women in the home and in the labour market[29] are still continuing today, as is the link between poverty and gender. Child poverty

[26] Pedersen, n 3 above, 289.

[27] 'Tories consider limiting child benefit to three children', *BBC News Online*, 5 March 2015.

[28] See written evidence of the Family Allowance Campaign to the House of Commons Select Committee on Tax-Credit, 17 April 1973 (House of Commons, 1973, Vol II) 380–90, cited in Land, n 6 above, 30.

[29] Land, ibid 76.

has increased since the 1990s,[30] with 28 per cent of children living in poverty in the UK in 2014–15, and children in large families being at greater risk of living in poverty: 34 per cent of children in poverty live in families with three or more children.[31] Yet, the changes introduced in 2013 and 2017 represent a direct return to the arguments in the lead up to the introduction of the family allowance, with their eugenic overtones, that provision of funding for an unlimited number of children encourages irresponsibility in family planning and might encourage larger families among the poor. In addition to placing limits on the payment of Child Benefit, an overall benefits cap was introduced in 2013 which includes Child Benefit, and applies regardless of family size. This has the potential to cause further serious financial hardship for families, with children being disproportionately affected.[32]

Whatever the rights and wrongs of having children without the means to provide for them, few would deny that the responsibility is not that of the children themselves, and so the cost should not be borne by them. The move to capping benefits without regard to need results in a complete undermining of the main achievements of the Family Allowances Act 1945. It also represents a willful refusal to learn from the past. The painstaking research undertaken by Eleanor Rathbone in the studies which underpinned the campaign for family allowances made clear the effect of any attempt to impose a single size of welfare payment: either the payment must be over-generous to the majority or it will be dangerously inadequate for the poorest. The fact that women often head up households in poverty means that this shift away from the universal family allowances achieved by Eleanor Rathbone remains a pressing matter of concern for feminists today.

## Further Reading


- John McNicol, *The Movement for Family Allowance 1918–1945* (Heinemann, 1980).
- Susan Pedersen, *Eleanor Rathbone and the Politics of Conscience* (Yale University Press, 2004).
- Eleanor Rathbone, *The Disinherited Family* (E Arnold & Co, 1924).


[30] Robert Joyce, *Child poverty in Britain: recent trends and future prospects* (Institute of Fiscal Studies, 2014).

[31] An analysis of the income distribution 1994/95–2015/16, Table 4.5db (Department for Work and Pensions, 2016).

[32] Children are seven times more likely than adults to lose out (The Children's Society, no date): http://www.childrenssociety.org.uk/.

# 32

# British Nationality Act 1948

HELEN KAY AND ROSE PIPES

The passing of the British Nationality Act in 1948 marked a significant moment for women in the history of their long struggle for equal citizenship. One short paragraph in the Act, section 14, is all it took to allow a British woman the right to retain her nationality when she married a foreign man, a right lost in 1870. The section was retrospective, allowing those who had lost their British nationality on marriage before the Act to get it back. It conferred on women the same right as men to retain or change their nationality and signified the end of years of campaigning by women to claim the right to British nationality, irrespective of their marital status.

## I. Context

Until 1844, the position in Britain was that those born on British soil and (after the British Nationality Act 1730) to a British father would have British nationality. Under the Naturalization Act 1844, foreign-born wives of British men were automatically granted British nationality, while British wives of foreign men retained their British nationality. The Naturalization Act 1870 changed this; thenceforth, for the first time in history, British women lost their British nationality on marrying an 'alien' or non-British person. By this action, they would become aliens themselves and, it was assumed, would automatically be granted the nationality of their husband's country, though this did not always happen. The British Nationality and Status of Aliens Act 1914 confirmed that 'the wife of a British subject shall be deemed to be a British subject and the wife of an alien shall be deemed to be an alien'. The 1914 Act did, however, permit a woman to make an application to regain her British nationality: if her husband renounced his British nationality after the marriage; or on widowhood or divorce from a foreign husband.

In drafting the 1914 Act, the main concern of British Home Office officials had been to achieve uniformity of nationality legislation across the Commonwealth. The Secretary for the Colonies, Lewis Harcourt, informed Parliament that a 'British subject anywhere is a British subject everywhere'.[1] Beneath this express rationale, however, lay other considerations. Many men still clung to the ideal of coverture, under which a woman's legal

[1] HC Deb, 13 May 1914, vol 62 col 1201.

personality was subsumed in her husband's. While many aspects of coverture had been discarded by the turn of the twentieth century – notably, married women's property no longer passed to their husbands following the Married Women's Property Acts 1870 and 1882[2] – the fear that independent rights would lead to dissension within the family and a direct challenge to the husband's authority stood in the way of further advances, such as votes for women.[3] Indeed, many felt there had been enough reforms for women already. Racism was also a factor, and a series of Aliens Acts were passed in the early decades of the twentieth century aimed at reducing Jewish and other non-British immigration. Thus the 1914 Nationality Act could be seen as discouraging women from marrying aliens and 'diluting' or 'polluting' British stock.[4]

A handful of MPs raised objections to the 1914 Bill on behalf of women. Sir Willoughby Dickinson MP raised the issue: 'A man does not become a foreigner because he marries a foreigner, and why should a woman?'[5] But, as so frequently happens, concessions to women were characterised both as less important, because they only affected a small number of women, and as a potential impediment to the wider goal. Leo Amery MP warned against endangering the common citizenship of the whole British Empire 'merely for the sake of removing some small local grievance, or for a further step in the theoretical position of women'.[6] When a deputation of women delegates from the British Dominions Woman Suffrage Union met with Lord Harcourt, the Minister for the Colonies, to state their strong objections to the clauses affecting the status of women in the Bill, the Minister replied 'that it is of far more consequence that British law should be in conformity with international law than that it should afford protection to women'.[7]

In fact, the legislation had a significant effect on women's status as citizens. Some women were left stateless when their husband's country did not automatically confer nationality, as happened with women who married US citizens after 1922, while others lost their rights of citizenship including access to welfare benefits and, later, the right to vote.[8] Many of them had been quite unaware of this consequence of marriage to a non-British man.

Feminist organisations quickly took up the issue, including the International Council of Women, made up of feminist organisations from 25 countries, which had been campaigning on this issue since 1905. In June 1914, the National Union of Women Workers (NUWW) Executive Committee urged that the Government 'should make adequate provision to safeguard the nationality of British women who marry foreigners'. As Lady (Laura) Aberconway contended,

> When Ministers say that they think it is 'beneficial' for women in every case to be forced to assume the nationality of their husbands, our rulers show a deplorable ignorance of the advantages of

[2] **Married Women's Property Act 1882**.
[3] **Representation of the People Act 1918**.
[4] Women, Immigration and Nationality Group (WING), *Worlds Apart: Women under Immigration and Nationality Law* (Pluto, 1985) 14; Page Baldwin, 'Subject to Empire: Married Women and the British Nationality and Status of Aliens Act' (2001) 40(4) *Journal of British Studies* 538.
[5] HC Deb, 13 May 1914, vol 62 col 1208.
[6] HC Deb, 29 July 1914, vol 65 col 1500.
[7] *Jus Suffragii*, August 1914, 8(12), 157.
[8] Jacqueline Bhabha and Sue Shutter, *Women's Movement: Women under Immigration, Nationality and Refugee Law* (Trentham, 1994) 21.

> individual freedom … The assertion that this Bill has been considered and agreed to by officials in every part of the British Empire is no reason for this deplorable neglect of the interests of women.[9]

The Act passed into law in August 1914, just as war was breaking out. For women married to enemy aliens, the nationality issue became one of great importance. In September 1914 Chrystal Macmillan, the organiser of relief work with women in London on behalf of the International Woman Suffrage Alliance (IWSA), reported to the Executive Committee of the NUWW on the destitution of British-born wives of enemy aliens: their husbands had been interned, and as 'enemy aliens' the wives were sacked from their employment. But neither they nor their children were eligible for public relief. The Committee duly passed a resolution urging 'the Government to instruct the local Distress Committees, in making regulations to reduce unemployment and in administering relief, to treat British-born wives of aliens as British subjects'.[10]

The women of the British Dominions Woman Suffrage Union joined with the National Council of Women to organise a petition to the British Government. The National Union of Women Suffrage Societies (NUWSS) called upon

> the Imperial Government to introduce a measure to provide that a woman on marriage with an alien shall not be deprived of her nationality against her will, but that she will be given the same choice of nationality as a man, including the right to naturalise independently of her husband: and further, it urges the Government to instruct its delegates to the next Imperial Conference to vote in favour of recommending the adoption of similar laws throughout the Empire.[11]

In the summer of 1918, Chrystal Macmillan sent out questionnaires from the IWSA to women's organisations throughout the Empire, requesting information on each country's laws relating to women's nationality. In that same month, a Government Amending Bill on the British Nationality and Status of Aliens legislation was introduced to the House of Commons and the NUWW intensified their campaign to have the Bill further amended to give married women equal nationality rights with men. Dickinson was willing to move an amendment but gave way when the Home Secretary proposed to set up a sub-committee of experts to deal with the question of nationality. The women felt that some progress had been made, as their campaign 'was doubtless partly responsible for the fact that the question of married women's nationality was discussed more thoroughly than ever before'.[12] As a result of their lobbying, women married to enemy aliens were allowed to keep their British nationality, but could lose it for 'bad character'.[13]

When the promise made by the Home Secretary to set up the committee to study the question of nationality had still not been honoured by 1921, the NUWW asked Chrystal Macmillan to prepare a draft Bill, to be entitled 'British Nationality, Married Women Bill 1921', and they appointed a sub-committee of women and sympathetic MPs to prepare the Bill to be introduced into the House of Commons. Sir John Butcher MP introduced the Bill, the Nationality of Married Women Bill (1922), into the House of Commons, but a dissolution of Parliament brought its passage to an end.

[9] *Jus Suffragii*, July 1914, 8(11), 141.
[10] Minutes, NUWW Committee, 8 September 1914.
[11] *Jus Suffragii*, April 1918, 12(7), 108.
[12] *Jus Suffragii*, August 1918, 12(11), 179.
[13] WING, n 4 above, 15–17.

A Joint Select Committee of the House of Commons and the House of Lords was appointed the following year, 1923, 'to examine the British Law as to the Nationality of Married Women; to consider in their legal and practical aspects the questions involved in the possession by husband and wife of the same or of different Nationalities'.[14] The Select Committee composed of 10 men and one woman took evidence from 10 people, of whom only one, Chrystal Macmillan, was a woman: the majority of witnesses were male senior civil servants. Although most Committee members were sympathetic to the women's claim for independent nationality, they were swayed by the view of the male witnesses who emphasised the importance of having unity of nationality within the family unit and maintaining the British character of a man's family.[15] Several witnesses suggested that British women brought hardship on themselves by marrying foreign men. The British legal position was stated firmly and somewhat anachronistically by Sir Cecil Hurst, Legal Adviser to the Foreign Office: 'Our law in this country … is founded on the principle that husband and wife are one, and that one is the husband'.[16]

In contrast, Chrystal Macmillan argued in her evidence that 'a woman is as attached to her nationality as a man is', and that depriving a British woman of her nationality or imposing British nationality on an alien woman because of the nationality of her chosen husband, is not treating the woman or her nationality with respect'.[17] However, she was hopeful of legislative change in 1925, when a resolution sponsored by the National Union of Societies for Equal Citizenship (NUSEC) was passed by the House of Commons without opposition:

> that, in the opinion of this House, a British woman shall not lose or be deemed to lose her nationality by the mere act of marriage with an alien, but that it shall be open to her to make a declaration of alienage.[18]

Still the law remained unchanged. The Private Members' Bills introduced in 1928, 1929 and 1930 were not sponsored by the Government and ran out of Parliamentary time. To get a Bill successfully through Parliament, the National Council of Women agreed to form a new committee, the Nationality of Married Women Pass the Bill Committee (NMWPBC), to consolidate planning of their campaign to change British and Commonwealth law to give women independent personal nationality. Three years later, Parliament was given a choice of two Bills on the nationality of married women, one promoted by the Pass the Bill Committee, and the other, a Government-sponsored Bill, which would bring British law into line with international law. The main purpose of the Government-sponsored Bill was to prevent women's statelessness and did not remove the requirement that the nationality of a married woman would normally be dependent on that of her husband or the law of her husband's country. Only if marriage to an alien would render her stateless would she be allowed to keep her British nationality.

The NMWPBC took a deputation to Parliament, supported by 30 nationally organised societies, and organised a petition from 118 British and Dominion organisations to be

[14] Select Committee of House of Commons & House of Lords, *Report on The Nationality of Married Women* (HMSO, 1923).
[15] ibid 14.
[16] ibid 38.
[17] ibid 127.
[18] Referred to by Sir John Sandeman Allen (HC Deb, 27 June 1933, vol 279 col 1335).

presented to the Imperial Conference meeting in Ottawa, to protest that the Bill continued to deny a woman's political right to her British nationality independent of her husband's nationality. The women MPs, with one exception, overcame party allegiance to vote against the Bill, but despite these strong protests by women, the Government Act was passed which only permitted women who would otherwise become stateless to remain British, but did not extend that right to all women who married aliens.[19]

Although the debates in the British Parliament from 1925 to 1933 showed a majority in favour of independent nationality for women, agreement was needed from all countries represented in the Imperial Conference. South Africa and the Irish Free State vetoed all suggestions in the Conference debates that husband and wife could have separate nationalities, although, surprisingly, the Irish Free State granted women independent nationality shortly afterwards, under the Irish Nationality and Citizenship Act 1935.

In 1937, with the death of Chrystal Macmillan who had led the drive for women's independent nationality for over 20 years, the campaign became more subdued. With the onset of the Second World War, the NMWPBC agitated for the right of British-born wives of Germans to resume their original nationality. This resulted in the introduction of Home Office regulations that were less restrictive than those imposed in 1914, but British women married to foreign men still had to submit to war-time restrictions on their place of residence and travel.

## II. The Landmark

The immediate impetus for the British Nationality Act 1948 was the large number of British women who had married American servicemen during the Second World War and then discovered that they had lost their British nationality. At the same time, the argument that there should be unity of nationality rights throughout the former Empire was losing its traction as increasing numbers of former colonies were permitting women to retain their nationality upon marriage. In 1946, Canada, followed by New Zealand and Australia, enacted national legislation giving women equal nationality rights with men.

The main clauses in the 1948 Act dealt with issues relating to citizenship rights of people born in the colonies and former colonies, who became British subjects, able to live, work and vote in the UK. Section 14 granted British women the right to retain their British nationality when they married foreigners. At last they had regained their right to independent nationality and were able to maintain or change their nationality in the same way as men.

The Act also removed the automatic access of foreign wives to British citizenship when they married a British man and substituted an entitlement to register as a British citizen. Foreign men who married British women, however, had to apply for naturalisation, a slower and more expensive process. Another gendered difference was that children born abroad to British mothers married to foreigners still had to take their father's nationality whereas those born to British fathers were automatically British.

[19] British Nationality and Status of Aliens Act 1933.

## III. What Happened Next

Labour shortages in the 1950s and 1960s led to a Government-sponsored wave of immigration from former colonies, especially those in the West Indies, Asia and Africa. The racist backlash that followed led to the imposition of immigration controls under which, again, women were particularly disadvantaged. While Commonwealth husbands who were admitted could be accompanied by their wives and children, and even 'common-law' wives in some instances, women could not automatically bring their husbands and children. The reasoning behind this differential treatment was partly the presumption in English law that husbands should choose the family's place of residence and partly the perception that wives were men's dependants, supported and controlled within the family unit, whereas foreign husbands threatened the stability of both workforce and home. The notorious 'primary purpose' rule was employed, most often against non-white applicants, to keep out of Britain those men who the assessors concluded had married not for 'love' but to gain entry into the country.[20] Under the Commonwealth Immigrants Act 1962, the entry into the UK of British subjects not of British ancestry was restricted and a special quota scheme for those who fell into this group was introduced, under which vouchers were given to 'heads of households', who were almost always men.

The Nationality Act 1981 aimed to reconcile the increasingly complicated immigration rules with nationality law by making the latter more restrictive. Along with new rules designed to limit still further who could become British citizens, the automatic right of women married to British men to become British was removed. Non-British wives and husbands of British citizens would now both have to apply for naturalisation. A positive equality measure, however, was that children born abroad to British women could now take their mother's nationality.

## IV. Significance

By granting women the right to hold or change their British nationality as men had always done, the British Nationality Act of 1948 gave women the legal right to equal citizenship with men, a major step forward in acknowledging women's rights as human rights in UK law: 'Nationality is a basic human right, not because it is a precondition for participation in self-government but because it offers territorial identity, security, harbour and, in a most fundamental sense, home: in other words, protection'.[21]

The British Nationality Act 1948 removed one more area of law and society in which women were regarded as appendages of their husbands and reproducers of the next generation. The arguments used to delay the reform over more than 40 years of feminist campaigning concealed the strongest motivation: to keep women in their place. The 'common code' in nationality law across the Empire was more of an imperial illusion than

[20] Sue Shutter and Spare Rib Collective, 'Racism and Sexism in the New Nationality Act' (April 1983) *Spare Rib* 129, 32.

[21] Helen Irving, *Citizenship, Alienage and the Modern Constitutional State: A Gendered History* (Cambridge University Press, 2016) 250.

actual practice, but women's political and legal right to independent nationality had to be sacrificed in the negotiations between the Parliaments of the Empire. The notion that a difference in the nationality of parents would lead to divisions of loyalty within the family, capable of destroying family unity and harmony, ignored situations where the woman and her foreign husband, both deemed to be foreign, had children born in Britain who were deemed to be British. The British Nationality Act 1948 granted all British women the right to British nationality but the right of women to transmit their nationality to their children was not resolved until 1981.

## Further Reading


- Mervyn Jones, *British Nationality Law* (Clarendon Press, 1956).
- Chrystal Macmillan, 'Nationality of Married Women: Present Tendencies' (1925) *Journal of Comparative Legislation and International Law* 142–54.
- Chrystal Macmillan, *The Nationality of Married Women* (The Nationality of Married Women Pass the Bill Committee, 1931).
- Dorothy Page, 'A Married Woman, or a Minor, Lunatic or Idiot: The Struggle of British Women against Disability in Nationality, 1914–1933' (Unpublished PhD Thesis, University of Otago, Dunedin, 1984).

# 33

# Married Women (Restraint Upon Anticipation) Act 1949

ROSEMARY AUCHMUTY

The Restraint Upon (or more usually 'On') Anticipation was an equitable device, imposed in a settlement on a married woman, which ensured that she could not touch the capital property that had been settled on her or any future income under the settlement. The purpose was to prevent her husband from forcing her to give it to him. By the mid-twentieth century, the restraint had become a serious encumbrance on married women's ability to meet their financial obligations, to the annoyance both of the women themselves, who resented the suggestion that they were not competent to handle their own money, and of their creditors who could not get their hands on it. One of the last remaining gender-specific protective devices of equity, the restraint was finally abolished by the Married Women (Restraint Upon Anticipation) Act 1949.

## I. Context

The Industrial Revolution wrought huge changes in women's lives. Urbanisation and the factory system brought about the separation of home and work; home became women's sphere, work men's; men became 'breadwinners', aiming to earn a 'family wage' sufficient to support wife and children; women were de-skilled and lost the opportunity to contribute to the family income. A new capitalist middle class emerged with increasing wealth to manage. Keen to model himself on upper-class ways, the industrialist *paterfamilias* prided himself on his ability to maintain his wife and daughters in idleness, neither labouring for a living nor soiling their hands with domestic chores. Marriage became the only acceptable 'career' for a woman of this class. The result was a kind of infantilisation of these women, correctly perceived by **Mary Wollstonecraft** in ***A Vindication of the Rights of Woman* (1792)** as a direct result of their lack of education, useful occupation, and legal power.

A second effect of the Industrial Revolution was the weakening of old forms of social control within the family. Now that men went out to work, leaving 'their' women at home, they were no longer able to exert the same degree of *private* power in the household. As a result, Sheila Rowbotham argues, new *public* restrictions were introduced, so that 'patriarchal control was actually strengthened among the dominant class'.[1] As Erna Reiss explained in her 1934 account of women's legal history, 'Women were thought of as helpless creatures who would certainly get into trouble if left to look after themselves'.[2]

Under the system of coverture which defined married women's legal position at the time, a wife's legal personality was subsumed into that of her husband, and her property, broadly speaking, belonged to him in common law. Wealthy fathers wishing to ensure that a daughter's property was not squandered by a rogue husband developed the practice of settling property on her for her separate use. However, there was nothing to stop her giving the property to her husband. The relative powerlessness of married women made them easy prey for husbands who might persuade or force them to part with their assets in pursuit of some imprudent scheme or simply for their own benefit. This was the impetus for the restraint on anticipation, which prevented a married woman from touching the settled capital or any future income. The corpus of settled property remained intact however hard the husband or creditors tried to get at it.

Although, like most legal and equitable innovations, the restraint on anticipation could trace its roots back to early case law such as *Butler v Duncombe*,[3] the story recounted in later litigation was that Lord Thurlow LC was inspired to invent it following a case in 1791, *Pybus v Smith*,[4] in which a ward of Chancery was prevailed upon by her new husband, who had married her for her money, to convey her separate estate as security for his debts. Thus, 'while the wax was still warm on the deed', as Lord Thurlow put it, 'the creditors got a claim on it'. Unable to help her, the Lord Chancellor suggested that 'such improvident acts might be prevented in future by the introduction of words *positively restrictive of such sweeping alienation*'.[5] Acting as trustee for the marriage settlement of a Miss Watson, he devised a suitable clause to insert into the deed in order to protect her, he said, from a husband who might 'kick or kiss' her out of it. This became the recognised formula:

> The trustees shall from time to time pay the income to such person or persons and for such intents and purposes as the married woman shall, notwithstanding her coverture, direct, but so as the same be not by way of anticipation.[6]

The enthusiasm of another Lord Chancellor, Lord Cottenham, whose authoritative statement of the law was given in *Tullett v Armstrong*,[7] ensured that the restraint on anticipation became a standard feature of settlements on married women in the nineteenth century and into the twentieth, even after the passing of the **Married Women's Property Act 1882**. It is clear from this case that the restraint was indeed beneficial to women who might otherwise

[1] Sheila Rowbotham, *Hidden from History: 300 Years of Women's Oppression and the Fight Against It* (Pluto, 1973) 55.

[2] Erna Reiss, *Rights and Duties of Englishwomen: A Study in Law and Public Opinion* (Sherratt & Hughes, 1934) 150.

[3] *Butler v Duncombe* (1718) 2 Vern 761, 1 P Wm 448.

[4] *Pybus v Smith* (1791) 3 Bro CC 341; 1 Ves Jun 189.

[5] CS Kenny, *The History of the Law of England as to the Effects of Marriage on Property and on the Wife's Legal Capacity* (Reeves & Turner, 1879) 104; WG Hart, 'The Origin of the Restraint upon Anticipation' (1924) 40 *Law Quarterly Review* 221.

[6] Kenneth R Swan, 'Restraint on Anticipation under the Married Women's Property Acts' (1905) 21 *Law Quarterly Review* 233.

[7] *Tullett v Armstrong* (1838–40) 1 Beav 48; 4 My & Cr 377.

have lost their property to a greedy or persuasive husband. This was certainly how it was viewed by legal men: Dicey, for example, boasted that a woman subject to a restraint was 'absolutely guarded against the possible exactions or persuasions of her husband, and received a kind of protection which the law of England does not provide for any other person except a married woman'.[8] This was, of course, because no other person needed it, as first-wave feminists recognised. Caroline Cornwallis commented:

> Indeed, so hazardous is it thought by fathers in general, to leave their daughter's property in the hands of the husband ... that none who can afford to pay any legal expenses, trust their property on so frail a foundation as the husband's prudence and integrity.[9]

In truth, however, the real policy consideration was not the protection of married women but the protection of family property; and the real beneficiaries were her heirs and next-of-kin rather than the married woman herself.[10] William McCurdy explained:

> By the beginning of the eighteenth century the legal position of a husband in respect to his wife's property and his uncontrolled use of his rights and powers therein were becoming increasingly intolerable to persons who desired to convey, devise or bequeath interests therein to, or settle them upon, daughters or other female relatives.[11]

The problem was, therefore, not incompetent wives but their scheming husbands, and the vulnerability that the marriage laws facilitated. The restraint on anticipation was born of a struggle between two groups of men, propertied fathers and their daughters' husbands: as Mary Poovey puts it, 'the woman was merely the representative or carrier of property, and even her love for her husband imperilled her father's goods'.[12]

## II. The Landmark

The movement for abolition of the restraint on anticipation began in the late nineteenth century. The large body of litigation on the subject, reviewed in *Pike v Fitzgibbon*,[13] reveals the extent to which upper- and middle-class men had come to employ this device in settlements on their daughters, but also how often claimants went to court to get round it. A typical situation was where a husband had lost all his money and his wife was desperate to use hers for the family's benefit. But the courts stood firm until 1881 when, under section 3 of the Conveyancing and Law of Property Act (subsequently re-enacted in section 169 of the Law of Property Act 1925), they were empowered to remove a restraint

[8] AV Dicey, *Lectures on the Relation Between Law and Public Opinion in England During the Nineteenth Century* (Macmillan, 1914, 2nd edn 1962) 379.

[9] Caroline Cornwallis, 'The Property of Married Women: Report of the Personal Laws Committee on the Laws relating to the Property of Married Women' (1856) 66 *Westminster Review* 331, 344.

[10] Otto Kahn-Freund, 'Inconsistencies and Injustices in the Law of Husband and Wife' (1952) 15 *Modern Law Review* 34.

[11] William E McCurdy, 'Property Torts Between Spouses and Use During Marriage of the Matrimonial Home Owned by the Other' (1957) 2 *Villanova Law Review* 450.

[12] Mary Poovey, *Uneven Developments: the Ideological Work of Gender in Mid-Victorian England* (Virago, 1989) 72.

[13] *Pike v Fitzgibbon* (1881) 17 Ch D 454.

when this would be to the benefit of the woman concerned. Even then, their reluctance to do so was legendary: as Kekewich J explained,

> Regarding the restraint on anticipation as intended for the protection of the wife, I view these applications with extreme jealousy; and when they are occasioned, as is often the case, by the husband's extravagance, I never grant them unless satisfied that the wife's happiness will be seriously endangered by refusal or will really be advanced by such order as is asked.[14]

For feminists, however, the imposition of a restraint on a married woman's separate property was problematic for two reasons. First, it meant she could not use her capital for her own purposes, such as setting up a business, or, as in the case above, to assist her family to recover from some financial disaster. Secondly, the differential treatment of married women perpetuated the idea of women's inferiority and subordinate status. 'The very fact that such a doctrine as the restraint against anticipation came into existence', Erna Reiss concluded, 'shows us how little the Legislature or the Courts trusted a woman to look after her interests'.[15]

By the inter-war years of the twentieth century, equal-rights feminists were campaigning for the abolition of all forms of legal 'protection' for women. Lady Rhondda (founder of the Six Point Group and herself a successful businesswoman)[16] pointed out that the restraint on anticipation, in denying married women access to their capital, prevented them from embarking on large-scale investments and turned them into poor credit risks. The National Union of Societies for Equal Citizenship drafted a Removal of Coverture Bill which would not only abolish husbands' responsibility for their wives' debts and torts, the concept of separate property, and the restraint on anticipation, but also guarantee wives without income of their own a share in their husband's. Though Lord Buckmaster, a former Lord Chancellor and a good friend of the feminists,[17] agreed to introduce a re-drafted version of the Bill, he died in 1934 before he could do so. The Law Revision Committee, however, recommended in that year that the restraint on anticipation be abolished as it was 'no longer consistent with the present position of married women'.[18]

If women wanted this reform, by now men wanted it even more. Husbands resented the fact that if wives whose capital was subject to a restraint ran up debts beyond their incomes, it was the husband who had to pay. Creditors likewise resented their inability to touch that capital, even in cases of fraud by the woman. 'We have heard about the rights of wives for some years, but in this case we ought to consider the rights of husbands', declared the Lord Chancellor, Viscount Cave. *The Times* leader of 21 December 1934 pointed out that men, not women, suffered under property laws that gave differential treatment to women. 'Indeed there is almost no limit to the loss that a vindictive wife equipped with a modicum of law might inflict on an unoffending and helpless consort', the writer complained. So powerful was the impression created by the men's rights lobby that the only question asked about the

[14] *Paget v Paget* [1898] 1 Ch 47 55.
[15] Reiss, n 2 above, 150.
[16] **Life Peerages Act 1958**.
[17] He had been Counsel for Miss Bebb in *Bebb v Law Society* [1914] 1 Ch 286; **Women's Legal Landmarks: An Introduction**.
[18] Dorothy M Stetson, *A Woman's Issue: The Politics of Family Law Reform in England* (Greenwood, 1982) 132–33.

restraint on anticipation in parliamentary debate during the passage of the Bill that became the Law Reform (Married Women and Tortfeasors) Act 1935 revealed the questioner to be under the impression that the restraint had been introduced for the purpose of defrauding a married woman's creditors![19]

The Law Reform (Married Women and Tortfeasors) Act 1935 abolished the concept of 'separate property' created by the Married Women's Property Acts 1870 and 1882. Under section 1, married women could acquire, hold and dispose of any property, sue and be sued, make contracts and be liable for them, and be subject to bankruptcy law, exactly as if they were single women. Under section 3, husbands' liability for their wives' debts and torts, whether acquired before or during the marriage, immediately ceased. Section 2 abolished the creation of future restraints on anticipation. But what the Act did *not* do was to abolish restraints already in existence. The legislators of 1935 may well have imagined that the device was going to be allowed to die out gradually, but this was not to be.

When the Countess Mountbatten of Burma returned from India after the second world war, she faced debts of tens of thousands of pounds. Edwina Mountbatten (1901–60) was the wife of the last Viceroy of India and one of the richest women in Britain, having inherited millions from her financier uncle Sir Ernest Cassel. Her fortune, however, was tied up in trusts, as was customary in the wealthy classes, from which she derived an income unequal to the demands of vice-regal hospitality in India, her charity work world-wide, and expensive living generally. With higher taxes eating up an increasing proportion of that income – under the Labour government which came to power in 1945, income tax was levied in the top band at 19s 6d [97½p] in the pound – Lady Mountbatten's pre-war after-tax income had been reduced tenfold, from £45,000 to £4,500 a year.[20]

Unfortunately for Lady Mountbatten, when Sir Ernest had settled money on her he had imposed a restraint on anticipation on her interests, which prevented her from using her capital to meet her debts. Desperate for cash, on legal advice she brought a Private Bill (a Bill that only applies to a particular individual or organisation, not to be confused with a Private Member's Bill) in Parliament to enable her restraint to be lifted. In this she had the Prime Minister's tacit approval since, if she could not find the funds to pay her debts, the Government would have had find the money to cover them. An additional incentive for the Government was the recognition that the great properties of England and Wales were increasingly passing from private hands into public and charitable ownership, and public policy was to facilitate this. The House of Lords was sympathetic, but a hostile group of Conservatives in the Commons forced the withdrawal of the Bill. Public opinion was also against it; as one newspaper commented, 'It is a bad principle when the law is pointedly altered in one case'.[21] The Government thereupon introduced its own Bill, of general application, which was passed in the Commons by 180 votes to 47. Thus, under the Married Women (Restraint Upon Anticipation) 1949, all existing restraints were abolished.

[19] ibid 129, 134–35, 139.
[20] Philip Ziegler, *Mountbatten: The Official Biography* (Collins, 1985) 488.
[21] Madeline Masson, *Edwina: The Biography of the Countess Mountbatten of Burma* (Robert Hale, 1958) 229.

## III. What Happened Next

In terms of a direct consequence of this Act, nothing really happened. Lady Mountbatten cleared her debts, and life went on much as before for most married women. As property ownership spread further down the social scale, the absence of the restraint on anticipation became irrelevant, since the women involved would never have had trusts created in their favour in the first place. But equal property rights did not mean, in the absence of anti-discrimination legislation, that married women were treated equally in practice. Male guarantors were routinely required for women's commercial undertakings up to the 1970s, and homes were normally conveyed to the husband alone, even where the wife had contributed to the purchase. Nor did men stop pressuring their wives to use their money to back their business deals or cover their debts. Practising lawyers, noting that they knew of several instances where a restraint had 'almost certainly saved the whole family, including children, from destitution', predicted that its abolition would render many wives, 'whose interests the Legislature seems wholly to have forgotten', vulnerable to men's exploitation and financial loss.[22] The truth of this prediction was borne out in later cases like ***Williams & Glyn's Bank v Boland, Barclay's Bank v O'Brien*** and ***Radmacher v Granatino***.[23]

## IV. Significance

While the abolition was largely driven by commercial considerations, and even though only a very few very wealthy women were subject to a restraint by this time, the symbolic significance of the Married Women (Restraint Upon Anticipation) Act 1949 was high, for it brought to an end one of equity's last remaining gender-specific protections and signalled that (in principle anyway) married women could be trusted to manage their finances independently.

The story of the restraint on anticipation is a textbook case of the development of English property law with respect to women. First, it was introduced to counter the oppressive effects of laws which facilitated patriarchal power: the common-law rule that a married woman's property belonged to her husband and the limited protection offered by the concept of 'separate property' under a trust. Second, it came to be used as an *instrument* of patriarchal power, a means of restricting married women's access to money. Third, the campaign for its abolition shows how first-wave feminists recognised the need for married women to have equal property rights with men as a pre-condition to their material emancipation. But it was only because the restraint came to be seen as a burden on *men* that it came to be abolished. Finally, the problem that had led to its introduction – men's exploitation of women's assets in the context of an intimate relationship – did not go away. Men just found different ways to go on doing it in a different social and legal context.

[22] FE Farrer, 'Beneficial Trusts in Marriage and Other Settlements' (1936) Conv (NS) 102, 111–12. See also JW Cocks, 'The Rise and Fall of the Restraint on Anticipation' (1936) *The Woolsack* 10, 10–11.

[23] ***Williams & Glyn's Bank v Boland*** [1981] AC 487; ***Barclay's Bank v O'Brien*** [1992] 3 WLR 593; ***Radmacher v Granatino*** [2010] UKSC 42.

## Further Reading


- Otto Kahn-Freund, 'Inconsistencies and Injustices in the Law of Husband and Wife' (1952) 15 *Modern Law Review* 34.
- CS Kenny, *The History of the Law of England as to the Effects of Marriage on Property and on the Wife's Legal Capacity* (Reeves & Turner, 1879).
- Dorothy M Stetson, *A Woman's Issue: The Politics of Family Law Reform in England* (Greenwood, 1982).

# 34

# Life Peerages Act 1958

SUPUNI PERERA

The Life Peerages Act 1958 enabled life peerages – peerages appointed by the Government for life rather than on a hereditary basis – to be granted for the first time. Prior to this the only people allowed to sit in the upper chamber were hereditary peers, a limited number of judges known as 'Lords of Appeal in Ordinary' (or 'law lords'), and bishops. Significantly, the Act also specifically provided for the appointment of women as life peers (section 1(3)). Given that women hereditary peers were not permitted entry to the House of Lords until the enactment of the Peerage Act 1963, and there were no women law lords until 2004[1] or bishops until 2015,[2] the conferment of a life peerage was the only way for women to be able to sit in the second chamber of the UK parliament.

The 1958 Act was thus a vital landmark in the progression of women toward full political representation. However, it also had a political purpose – to ensure a (more) balanced representation of the different political parties by allowing people to enter the House based on what they had achieved in their career rather than an accident of birth. Without doubt, the addition of life peeresses has, over the years, introduced differing perspectives which inform and enhance the constitutional role of the House of Lords, specifically its making and shaping of laws and checking and challenging the Government more effectively.[3]

## I. Context

While there is evidence that women had been hereditary peers 'in their own right' for centuries, they were explicitly excluded from Parliament. Even in medieval times, 'although women were sometimes summoned to attend medieval parliamentary assemblies, they never actually attended in person or sat in Parliament. Contemporary doctrines of Roman law and canon law effectively precluded women from participating in public life'.[4]

[1] **Lady Hale** was the first woman to be appointed to the Appellate Committee of the Houses of Lords in January 2004.

[2] The Right Reverend Rachel Treweek was the first woman bishop to take a seat in the House of Lords in October 2015. See further **Bishops and Priests (Consecration and Ordination of Women) Measure 2014 and Canon C2, 'Of the Consecration of Bishops', 2014**.

[3] House of Lords Briefing, 'Role and Work' (2011).

[4] Gavin Drewry and Jenny Brock, 'The Impact of Women on the House of Lords', *Studies in Public Policy* (Strathclyde, Centre for the Study of Public Policy, 1983) 4, quoted in Dorothy Hughes, *Women in the House of Lords* (HL Library Note LLN 2015/017, 30 June 2015).

In 1918, after long campaigns, women over the age of 30 were given the right to vote following the enactment of the **Representation of the People Act 1918**. In the same year, the Parliament (Qualification of Women) Act 1918 permitted women to be elected to the House of Commons. A year later, the **Sex Disqualification (Removal) Act 1919** allowed women to become senior civil servants, magistrates and judges. But it would be another 40 years until women were able to sit in the House of Lords. This was not for want of trying. Amendments tabled to include provisions relating to women hereditary peers in both the 1918 and 1919 Acts were unsuccessful. While the admission of women to the House of Lords did not have the same prominence in suffragist and suffragette campaigns for the extension of the franchise as the extension of the vote, a number of women peers were suffragettes, and they provided the campaigns with 'legitimacy and authority'.[5]

One such woman was Viscountess Rhondda. Margaret Haig Thomas (1883–1958), later Viscountess Rhondda, was the only child of Viscount Rhondda, a businessman, Liberal politician and member of the House of Lords. Viscount Rhondda had no sons and therefore had received permission for his title to pass on to her daughter on his death, but any entitlement to sit in the House of Lords was explicitly excluded. Lady Rhondda was a former suffragette who had, in 1920, founded *Time and Tide*, a feminist weekly political and review magazine, and, in 1921, the Six Point Group, an equal-rights pressure group for women. In 1913 she had been jailed for refusing to allow her husband to pay a £10 fine for setting a post-box on fire. She was released following five days on hunger strike. In 1918, after her father's death, she announced her intention to claim 'the right to have, hold, and possess a seat, place, and voice' in the House of Lords.

In 1920 she petitioned the Crown to take up her seat,[6] relying on the Sex Disqualification (Removal) Act 1919, which provided that a person should not be prohibited by sex from exercising any public function (section 1). This, she argued, secured her ability to sit in the House of Lords. Her case was referred to the House of Lords Committee for Privileges in 1921, and was heard the following year. The Committee initially ruled in her favour. However, following objections from the Lord Chancellor, Viscount Birkenhead, the case was referred back to the Committee, which subsequently voted against her petition. This time the Committee argued that the 1919 Act did not confer upon women the right to exercise a public function. Rather it simply removed a disability preventing them from doing so. Thus women could only be admitted on the enactment of legislation specifically allowing for it.[7] The reasoning for the decision was grounded in a mixture of paternalism and fear. While Lord Birkenhead believed that women, protected by men, did not need to engage in national politics,[8] others, such as George Bernard Shaw, suggested that a successful business woman like Lady Rhondda would put the male peers to shame, stating the House saw her as a 'terror'.[9]

[5] Mari Takayanagi, 'A Changing House: The Life Peerages Act 1958' (2008) 27(3) *Parliamentary History* 383.

[6] You can read Viscountess Rhondda's petition on the UK Parliament website (Parliamentary Archives, HL/PO/DC/CP/4/153).

[7] Hughes, n 4 above, 2; Duncan Sutherland, 'Peeresses, Parliament and Prejudice: The Admission of Women to the House of Lords, 1918–1963' (2000) 20 *Parliaments, Estates and Representation* 215, 221–22.

[8] Angela V John, *Turning the Tide: The Life of Rhondda* (Parthian, 2013) 451.

[9] Ivett Császár, 'Orwell and Women's Issues – a Shadow over the Champion of Decency' (2010) X *Eger Journal of English Studies* 39, 44.

Subsequently, the Parliament (Qualification of Peeresses) Bill 1924 was introduced in the Lords by Viscount Astor, husband of Nancy Astor, the first woman MP to sit in the House of Commons. This was the first of many – failed – Bills proposing that hereditary women peers should be able to sit in the upper chamber presented between 1924 and 1929 in the aftermath of the Rhondda case.[10] In 1932, Conservative peers and MPs suggested a reduction in the number of hereditary peers and the creation of life peers, removing the bar on women's entrance to the House.[11] However, despite the acknowledgement of the importance of the matter, the feeling at the time was that the House had more pressing issues to consider – notably, in the words of the then Solicitor General, Boyd Merriman, 'a supreme national crisis'.[12]

Following the Second World War there was a renewed concern both about the admission of women and the hereditary principle. In 1948 a petition asking for a seat, place and voice, which included the signatures of Lady Rhondda and Baroness Ravensdale (later to be one of the first life peers), was presented to the House of Lords. This was followed in 1949 by a vote in the House of Lords on its composition, which established for the first time that the upper chamber was in favour of admitting women.[13] Viscount Jowitt, the then Lord Chancellor, expressed his view in favour of the equality of the sexes, but against allowing women life peers according to the hereditary principle.[14] He continued

> With regard to the matter of the competence of women, it seems to me, with the greatest respect, that those who doubt the competence of women to play their part in this House are regarding women as they used to be regarded in Jane Austen's days, as clinging females who have the vapours from time to time. It bears no relation whatever to the facts as we know them to-day. Anybody who knows the services that women rendered during the war will realise that. I am quite unable to bring myself to approve any intellectual test being applied to women that is not applied to men. I deny entirely that the presence of women in your Lordships' House would have any adverse effect upon its deliberations. I have seen women come into my own profession, I have seen women sitting on the Bench, and I have no doubt at all in saying that what they have done has improved things; and so they have … I have no shade of a doubt but that women have a distinctive contribution which they might make in your Lordships' House.[15]

Although the motion was agreed by 45 to 27, the matter once again took a back seat until the Conservative Government came to power in the early 1950s.[16] The timing of this renewed interest should not be overlooked – Elizabeth II had become Queen in 1952 – a (hereditary) appointment, which added a further argument to be deployed by those agitating for the admittance of women peers. In 1953, Viscount Simon introduced a Bill to create up to 10 life peers of both sexes.[17] Again the Bill failed, this time because the Labour Government was ambivalent about the creation of new peerages in light of its desire to push for more comprehensive reform of the House of Lords.[18] Indeed, Duncan Sutherland argues that the

[10] HL Deb, 16 July 1930, vol 78 cols 198–536.
[11] Glenn Dymond, *The Life Peerages Act 1958* (HL Library Note LLN 2008/011, 21 April 2008) 18.
[12] HC Deb, 30 November 1932, vol 272 cols 928–930.
[13] HL Deb, 27 July 1949, vol 164 cols 581–624.
[14] ibid col 611.
[15] ibid col 607.
[16] Dymond, n 11 above, 18; ibid col 622.
[17] Dymond, n 11 above, 7.
[18] ibid; Donald Shell, *The House of Lords* (Manchester University Press, 1993) 13–14.

reason why the admission of women peers took so long was because it became 'entangled with the more controversial question of the wider reform of the Lords' composition and powers'.[19] Ann Oakley makes the same point more bluntly: 'Gender got mixed up with the issue of constitutional reform; most people who wanted to do something about the House of Lords did not want to do anything about women'.[20]

## II. The Landmark

In 1957, the Macmillan Conservative Government introduced the Life Peerages Bill which empowered the Crown to create men and women life peers, who would sit and vote in the House of Lords and whose peerages would dissolve upon their death.[21] During the Bill's second reading in the House of Lords, the Earl of Home, Leader of the House of Lords, exposed a substantial consensus towards the introduction of women to the House in order to keep it 'up to date':[22]

> The need to keep this House up to date is perhaps the most powerful argument for the introduction of women. There are some of your Lordships who may contend – indeed, some have – that women have not made the mark on the political life of this country that was expected of them. Some of our instincts against surrendering this, one of the last sanctuaries of the male, may be very strong. Some may say that women do not understand how golden is silence, particularly when seven o'clock in the evening is approaching. My trouble is that I cannot see any argument in logic or in reason, why, if women are in another place, they should not be here.[23]

Not everyone was in favour of the reform. An amendment was introduced by the Earl of Airlie, for example, to omit women peers on the basis that changes to the composition of Parliament should be made step by step and a fear the country was not ready for such drastic alteration. He continued:

> I should make it quite plain from the start that I speak in no anti-feministic vein – and I have taken great trouble to make quite certain I use the right word … Nearly all of us work with [women] in local government and on local committees, and often they are not only as good as, but better than, many of the men. Nevertheless, I personally am inclined to feel that it will be extremely difficult for them to fit into your Lordships' House as we know it. The great function which this Chamber has now to perform – and it is one of the few left to it – lies in the revision of hasty and ill-conceived legislation. I, for one, submit, though I may be wrong, that that is not the particular métier of the female sex.[24]

His amendment failed.

When the Bill returned to the House of Commons in 1958 Jennie Lee, a Labour MP, proposed the exclusion of clause 1(3) (allowing for the conferment of a life peer on women)

[19] Duncan Sutherland, 'Peeresses, Parliament and Prejudice: The Admission of Women to the House of Lords, 1918–1963' (2000) 20 *Parliaments, Estates and Representation* 215, 216.
[20] Ann Oakley, *A Critical Woman: Barbara Wootton, Social Science and Public Policy* (Bloomsbury, 2011) 14.
[21] Dymond, n 11 above, 18; Life Peerages Bill, clause 1(3).
[22] HL Deb, 3 December 1957, vol 206 col 611.
[23] ibid.
[24] ibid 658.

arguing that the upper chamber required deeper restructuring.[25] Her amendment was also defeated.[26] Despite receiving general support there was an underlying feeling that this change was relatively small in the context of the overall substantive reform the House required. The Bill passed the third reading stage in the House of Commons by 292 votes to 241. The Life Peerages Act came into force on 30 April 1958.

On 24 July 1958, the first 14 life peers were announced, including four women.[27] Baroness Wootton, an academic and public figure, was the first to be created a life peer and also the first woman to chair proceedings of the Lords as Deputy Speaker. The first to take her seat was Baroness Swanborough, founder of the Women's Voluntary Service, which had worked with refugees, war victims and armed forces and also effectively contributed in the evacuation of thousands of city children during the war. Baroness Elliot of Harwood was the first woman to speak in the Lords as a member. She was granted life peerage for her outstanding work towards prison reform and childcare, and also had an interest in international affairs. The fourth, Baroness Ravensdale, was recognised for her voluntary work with young people.[28] Ann Oakley notes that although Wootton's background was 'rather different' to that of the three titled co-entrants,

> there were also some strange similarities between the four new Ladies of the House: all four had been born within nine years of one another; … all had a reputation for begin fearlessly outspoken; all were childless; one had never married and three were widows.[29]

Lady Rhondda lived to see the passing of the 1958 Act, but died before she could see the first women take their seats.

## III. What Happened Next

Debates about the membership of the House of Lords – and its reform more generally – continued. While women could now be appointed life peers, women hereditary peeresses were still excluded. Despite a resolution moved by the Marquess of Reading in January 1959, and the House agreeing in principle that women hereditary peers should be allowed in their own right to sit and vote, they were not admitted until the Peerage Act was passed in July 1963.[30] The first hereditary woman peer was Baroness Strange, admitted in November 1963.[31]

More fundamental reform followed in the late 1990s during a period of significant constitutional reform led by the Labour Government. The House of Lords Act 1999 excluded most of the hereditary peers from the upper chamber. Its bold statement, in section 1, that 'no-one shall be a member of the House of Lords by virtue of a hereditary peerage' was tempered

[25] Lee accepted a life peerage in 1970.

[26] Takayanagi, n 5 above, 387; HC Deb, 25 March 1958, vol 585 col 354; Dymond, n 11 above, 20–21.

[27] Takayanagi, n 5 above, 391.

[28] Baroness Ravensdale was also a hereditary peer in her own right, though of course was not appointed on this basis.

[29] Oakley, n 20 above, 16. Although Wootton was a widow, she had remarried and her second husband was still very alive – claiming the title 'peeress' following his wife's appointment!

[30] HL Deb, 21 January 1959, vol 213 cols 612–644.

[31] HL Deb, 19 November 1963, vol 253 col 207.

by a compromise provision in section 2, allowing for 90 hereditary peers and the holders of the offices of Earl Marshal and Lord Great Chamberlain to remain, alongside the Bishops and (then) law lords.[32] The 90 hereditary peers are elected by their fellow Lords by means of a by-election.[33] In 1999, just five women were so elected. Today only one female hereditary peer, the Countess of Mar, sits in the chamber.

However, although women hereditary peers are now able to sit in the upper chamber, not all peerages can be inherited by women. There have been various attempts to legislate on this matter. Lord Diamond introduced Bills in 1992 and 1994 to allow peerage titles to pass to the eldest legitimate child, regardless of gender. Both Bills failed.[34] In March 2013, Mary Macleod MP introduced the Succession to Hereditary Peerages and Estates Bill in order to remove the principle of male preference primogeniture, which also failed.[35] During the 2015–16 session, Lord Trefgarne introduced the Succession to Peerages Bill intended to allow daughters to inherit a peerage, although sons would still take priority over their sisters in the line of succession. This Bill was re-introduced in June 2017, and, at the time of writing, is awaiting its second reading.[36]

Inevitably perhaps, despite the various attempts to strengthen women's presence in the House of Lords, they are still significantly under-represented. In part this is the result of the over-representation of Conservative Parties traditionally led by men.[37] While prime ministers and party leaders from across the political spectrum have actively sought to improve the number of women in the House of Lords,[38] in 2018, 208 of the current members of the Lords are women.[39]

## IV. Significance

It may be – as Sutherland suggests – that the admission of women to the House of Lords was simply a 'by-product' of wider constitutional reform aimed at making the upper chamber 'more effective, addressing the issue of low attendance, and more representative'.[40] Certainly, the introduction of life peers, and the expertise they brought with them, strengthened the House of Lords as an institution.

However, the Life Peerages Act 1958 is an important legal landmark for women as the first step toward equality between men and women peers. It challenged – and ultimately

[32] House of Lords, *Register of Hereditary Peers* (18 May 2016) 3.

[33] Section 2(4) of the House of Lords Act 1999 and Standing Order 10.

[34] Hughes, n 4 above, 14; HL Deb, 26 November 1992, vol 540 cols 1118–1166; HL Deb, 7 March 1994, vol 552 cols 1283–1330.

[35] HC Deb, 25 March 2013, vol 560 cols 1303–1306.

[36] Hughes, n 4 above, 14; Lord Trefgarne, Succession to Peerages Bill [HL] 2016–17.

[37] 25% of women peers are Conservative, compared to 33% and 32% of Labour and Liberal peers. See further, Adrian Vatter, 'Bicameralism and Policy Performance: The Effects of Cameral Structure in Comparative Perspective' (2005) 11 *Journal of Legislative Studies* 194.

[38] Hughes, n 4 above, 12.

[39] UK Parliament, *Members of the House of Lords*: http://www.parliament.uk/mps-lords-and-offices/lords/.

[40] Hughes, n 4 above, 7.

conquered – narrow-minded sexism, such as that of the Earl of Glasgow who commented in a debate on the composition of the House of Lords that

> [t]he main point is that many of us do not want women in this House. We do not want to sit beside them on these Benches, nor do we want to meet them in the Library. This is a House of men, a House of Lords. We do not wish it to become a House of Lords and Ladies.[41]

While there is disagreement as to the 'difference' of women peers,[42] what is clear is that women peers have spoken with authority on a wide range of topics,[43] including issues which might not otherwise have been considered and issues considered to be 'women's issues'.[44] Further, as Gavin Drewry and Jenny Brock have noted, 'one striking characteristic of women Peers is their success in obtaining frontbench office'.[45] Indeed, six of the past nine Leaders of the House have been women, as is the current Leader of the Opposition. So too were the first two Lord Speakers. Indeed, there is something quite gratifying in the comment of Baroness Hayman, the first woman to hold this position, that: 'it gives me some quiet satisfaction that, should a man break through the glass ceiling to succeed me, he will be known as the first male Lord Speaker'.[46]

I wonder what the Earl of Glasgow would have made of that.

## Further Reading

- Christina Eason, 'Women Peers and Political Appointment: Has the House of Lords Been Feminised Since 1999?' (2009) 62(3) *Parliamentary Affairs* 399–417.
- Mari Takayanagi, 'A Changing House: The Life Peerages Act 1958' (2008) 27(3) *Parliamentary History* 380–92.
- Duncan Sutherland, 'Peeresses, Parliament and prejudice: the admission of women to the House of Lords, 1918–1963' (2000) 20 *Parliaments, Estates and Representation* 215–31.

[41] HL Deb, 31 October 1957, vol 205 col 690.
[42] Hughes, n 4 above.
[43] ibid 19.
[44] Joint Committee on the Draft House of Lords Reform Bill, *Draft House of Lords Reform Bill* (2010–2012, HL Paper 284-III, HC 1313-III) 61.
[45] Gavin Drewry and Jenny Brock, 'The Impact of Women on the House of Lords', *Studies in Public Policy*, 1983, 12 in Hughes, n 4 above, 3.
[46] Baroness Hayman, *Women in the Lords: The Life Peerages Act – Women and Change in the House of Lords since 1958*, 6 December 2007 in Hughes, n 4 above, 5.

# 35

# First Woman to Hold Regular Judicial Office in England and Wales, Rose Heilbron, 1964

LAURA LAMMASNIEMI

Dame Rose Heilbron QC, barrister and judge, became the first woman to hold regular judicial office in England and Wales when she became Recorder of Burnley in 1964. She was also the first woman to try a murder trial at the Old Bailey and, before that, one of the first two women barristers (with **Helena Normanton**) to be appointed King's Counsel in England and Wales.[1]

## I. Life

Rose Heilbron was born in 1914 in Liverpool, the younger daughter of Max and Nellie Heilbron who ran a boarding house for Jewish immigrants. After attending the local grammar school, the Belvedere School, she studied law at the University of Liverpool, graduating in 1935 with a first-class honours degree, one of the first two women to do so at that university in law. She was awarded the Lord Justice Holker scholarship to join Gray's Inn and in 1937 obtained an LLM, again one of only two women holding such a degree. She faced explicit sex discrimination in trying to obtain a pupillage and was turned down on at least one occasion because she was a woman.[2] In 1939, however, she finally joined chambers at 43 Castle Street in Liverpool, and during the Second World War she launched her career as a criminal barrister. In 1945, she married Nathaniel Burstein, a medical consultant, and their daughter, Hilary Heilbron, was born in 1949.

A few months after Hilary's birth, aged only 34, Heilbron became one of the first two women King's Counsel in England and Wales (**Helena Normanton** was the other). She was the youngest KC since 1783. Her standing was such that in 1955 the *Manchester Evening Standard* asked: 'Will Rose Heilbron one day became Britain's first woman judge?'.[3] Many in the legal profession believed she would eventually achieve this goal, and the *Daily Telegraph*

[1] **Margaret Kidd** of Scotland was the first woman to be appointed KC in the UK, in 1948.

[2] Hilary Heilbron, *Rose Heilbron: The Story of England's first Woman Queen's Counsel and Judge* (Hart Publishing, 2012) 20.

[3] *Manchester Evening News*, June 1955.

argued that, if Heilbron became a judge, it would be the first time a judge could be called 'charming'.[4] Following a great deal of speculation, on 26 November 1956 it was announced that Heilbron was to become Recorder of Burnley, the first woman to hold regular judicial office.[5] She went on to become the second woman High Court judge in 1974, after **Elizabeth Lane** in 1962.

Throughout her career, Heilbron led a number of high-profile criminal trials which gave her a celebrity status in the local and national press.

> Miss Heilbron has impressed me on scores of occasions … She has brought a refreshing sparkle into the most wearying of assize civil actions. Her admirable air of confidence, her twinkling eyes, and – more often than not – the tilt of her wig with just that slight suggestion of rakishness, make her presentation of a case an affair of interest no matter how dull its content.[6]

As was usual with professional women, Heilbron practised under her maiden name, and when appointed a judge, she was known as Mrs Justice Heilbron. In 1975, Heilbron was appointed to chair an Advisory Committee on rape following the infamous *DPP v Morgan*,[7] dubbed the 'rapists' charter' because it allowed a defendant's honest belief in the victim-survivor's consent to absolve him of liability.[8] Drawing on years of experience on criminal trials, the committee argued that criminal trials differed from other trials because they allowed complainant's sexual history be brought out in the trial, which they described as a 'reprehensible feature of trials of rape'.[9] Their recommendations included anonymity for complainants (and not defendants) in order to 'protect the victims from hurtful publicity' and to encourage reporting of rape[10] as well as limitations on sexual history evidence.[11]

In 1985, Heilbron was elected treasurer at Gray's Inn, the first woman to hold that position, and retired in 1988. In addition to her accomplishments in law, she was also an active member of Soroptimist International, a professional women's organisation. She died in 2005.

## II. Context

As a daughter of Jewish small-business-owners from Liverpool, Heilbron was exceptional in the legal profession in the 1950s. Access to the Bar and obtaining tenancy was difficult for women and for those outside of the middle and upper classes; family connections were particularly important for women.[12] Although anecdotal evidence would suggest that the absence of men during the war gave space for women like Heilbron to enter the profession, statistics do not support this. Throughout the 1920s and 1930s women constituted just

[4] 'The Woman Who Might Be a Judge', *Daily Telegraph*, September 1955.

[5] A Recorder is a part-time judge who was formerly assigned to a particular city's Quarter Sessions. Quarter sessions were abolished when the Courts Act 1971 replaced them with Crown Courts, and Heilbron became the Recorder of the Crown Court.

[6] Norman Cook of the *Daily Post*, quoted in Rachel Cooke, *Her Brilliant Career: Ten Extraordinary Women of the Fifties* (Virago Press, 2013) 279.

[7] *DPP v Morgan* [1976] AC 182.

[8] See further **Section 1 of the Sexual Offences Act 2003**.

[9] Home Office, *Report of the Advisory Group on the Law of Rape* (Cmnd 6352, 1975) [153]–[157].

[10] ibid. See further **Section 4 of the Sexual Offences (Amendment) Act 1976**.

[11] **Section 41 of the Youth Justice and Criminal Evidence Act 1999**.

[12] Richard Abel, *The Making of the English Legal Profession* (Beard Books, 1998) 68.

two to six per cent of those called to the Bar.[13] In 1957, a year after Heilbron was appointed Recorder of Burnley, only 68 women were nominally at the Bar and out of those, only 45 were actually practising.[14] After Normanton's death in that year, Heilbron was the only QC among them.

Moreover, while Heilbron's judicial appointment was no great surprise, given the high regard in which she was held, it was by no means a certainty. The women who had paved the way for Heilbron's judicial career – Sybil Campbell, who was the first stipendiary magistrate (what we would now call a District Judge in the Magistrates' Courts),[15] as well as Dorothy Dix (deputy Recorder of Deal) and Edith Hesling (the first woman to sit in the County Courts) – had faced a great deal of prejudice both publicly and privately. When Heilbron made an application to become a Recorder, the former Attorney-General, Hartley Shawcross, wrote to her expressing his support but conceding that her sex might prove an obstacle with the Conservative Lord Chancellor, Lord Kilmuir.[16]

Following Heilbron's first appearance as a judge at the Old Bailey, the *Daily Mail* wrote that it 'would be misleading to compare her appearance at the Old Bailey with Nancy Astor entering the Commons, or Margaret Bondfield, the Cabinet. Hers has been a steady, if determined, climb up the legal ladder.[17] Heilbron's climb was certainly determined, but it was not without difficulties: she had to overcome a great deal of prejudice from colleagues and clients, especially at the start of her career.[18] George Kelly, the defendant in her perhaps most famous murder case, is reported to have initially said he wanted a 'fella' because 'whoever heard of a judy defending anyone?'.[19] Although convicted, Kelly later praised Heilbron, and the high-profile case, known as the Cameo case, launched her career as a KC and led to Heilbron being named 'Woman of the Year' by the *Daily Mirror* in 1949.

## III. What Happened Next

Considering Heilbron's achievements, first as a KC in 1949 and then as a Recorder in 1956, it took a long time for Heilbron to be appointed a High Court judge in 1974. Many felt that she should have been the first woman appointed, rather than **Elizabeth Lane**, and that, had she been a man, she would have been appointed earlier.[20] While happy for Lane's advancement, Heilbron was naturally disappointed not to be the first woman High Court judge.[21] By the time she was finally appointed to the High Court, she was 60 years old and so unlikely to be appointed to the Court of Appeal. It took another 14 years for the first woman – **Elizabeth Butler-Sloss** – to be appointed to the Court of Appeal.

[13] ibid 80.

[14] LCB Gower and Leolin Price, 'The Profession and Practice of the Law in England and America' (1957) 20 *Modern Law Review* 317.

[15] Patrick Polden, 'The Lady of Tower Bridge: Sybil Campbell, England's first woman judge' (1999) 8 *Women's History Review* 202.

[16] Sir Hartley Shawcross, quoted in Heilbron, n 2 above, 191.

[17] Vincent Mulchrone, 'My Lady of the Old Bailey', *Daily Mail*, 5 January 1972.

[18] Heilbron, n 2 above, 20–22.

[19] Heilbron, n 2 above, 78; some newspapers have reported the words as: 'I want no Judy defending me', see 'Dame Rose Heilbron', *The Telegraph*, 10 December 2005.

[20] Cherie Blair in Heilbron, n 2 above, vii.

[21] Heilbron, n 2 above, 265.

It was symptomatic of gender bias at the time that, despite being one of the leading criminal lawyers in the country, Heilbron was appointed to the Family Division of the High Court. In fact, the first four women High Court judges – Elizabeth Lane, Rose Heilbron, Margaret Booth and Elizabeth Butler-Sloss – were all appointed outside their area of expertise to the Family Division, at the time the least prestigious of the specialisms but considered women's natural place. It was not until 1992 that the first woman, Ann Ebsworth, was appointed to the Queen's Bench Division. Mary Arden was appointed to the Chancery Division a year later.

Of the 122 women called to the Bar in the 1930s with Heilbron, only five were still practising in the 1960s.[22] Although more women joined the bar in the 1950s and 1960s, only 20 per cent were still in practice a decade later. The low retention rate among women barristers has undoubtedly had an impact on judicial appointments with the result that, even in 2017, only 22 per cent of High Court and 24 per cent of Court of Appeal judges were women.[23]

## IV. Significance

> I am no bluestocking ... The general impression of a woman lawyer seems to be a sober old maid. I have not adopted the law as a hobby. I am serious about my career, but that does not mean I shall give up dancing, swimming, golf or tennis.[24]

It is said that Rose Heilbron never intended to be a pioneer for women.[25] Yet undoubtedly she was. In addition to her landmark appointments, her work as both a lawyer and a judge had a significant impact on women's legal rights.[26] As a judge, Heilbron presided over important cases dealing with gender and women's rights such as *C v S*,[27] in which she denied a man the right to prevent his wife from having an abortion. Thanks to her role in the Advisory Committee on rape, she was influential in shaping the use of evidence in sexual offences trials.

Heilbron also was a role model for women due to her visibility.[28] The press reported every trial. She was affectionately, if patronisingly, called Heilbron the 'woman judge pin-up girl'[29] and the 'housewife who is Britain's Portia'.[30] Others commented that 'Success has not spoiled Rose Heilbron QC ... She is charming, unaffected, modest and likes nothing better in her spare time than doing her own shopping'.[31] These representations, possibly due to the fact that she fitted conventional notions of feminine beauty and presentation and was very careful not to appear overtly feminist, might have been the key to

[22] Abel, n 12 above, 83.

[23] Judiciary of England and Wales Diversity Statistics 2017 (20 July 2017).

[24] Rose Heilbron talking to the *Daily Express*, quoted in Cooke, n 6 above, 275.

[25] Heilbron, n 2 above.

[26] Though not just for women. It is said that when she successfully defended three Liverpool dockers against charges that they had unlawfully gone on strike, crowds of Liverpool workers lined the platform at Liverpool Lime Street to salute her return (Cooke, n 6 above, 281).

[27] *C v S* [1988] QB 135.

[28] Heilbron, n 2 above, vii.

[29] 'Woman Judge Pin-up Girl of British Courts', *Rockhampton Morning Bulletin*, 1957.

[30] 'Housewife Who is Britain's Portia!', *Durban Sunday Tribute*, June 1955.

[31] *Liverpool Post* in Cooke, n 6 above, 286.

her mainstream popularity but they were in stark contrast to how other women in law had been represented. Sybil Campbell, for example, was labelled the 'Beast of Belsen' in the press (just two months after the liberation of the Bergen-Belsen concentration camp) for her tough line dealing with petty thieves in the Police Court in Tower Bridge.[32] Heilbron showed that a woman could combine a highly successful career and happy family life without being pilloried by the press, but only if observing the correct decorum.

> It would be difficult to overstate how well know and admired – loved, even – Rose Heilbron was in her day. Partly, this was the nature of her business. Thanks [to] the death penalty, murder trials were followed far more avidly than now ... But even among the famous lawyers ... [she] was in a class of her own.[33]

Queues of mainly women and girls waited to see the first opening of Burnley Quarter Sessions after her appointment.

But it was not just the press that made Heilbron a role model. She actively mentored other women: in the words of **Lady Hale**, she enabled others to 'follow where she had led'.[34] It is notable that the majority of the first women High Court judges were from the Northern Circuit.[35] She performed the same role for other aspiring professional women through her work with the Soroptimists and other organisations. Without doubt, she was and is an inspiration for women (and men) lawyers across the generations – many of whom, like Vera Baird QC (who named her as her 'legal hero' for *The Guardian* newspaper in 2010) are 'still fighting the legal battles Heilbron began'.[36]

Her positive treatment in the press and by her legal colleagues did not, however, translate into either the immediate or long-term breaking down of barriers for women in the legal profession and access to the judiciary. Women have remained disadvantaged not only in terms of progression but also in terms of access to power and judicial positions. While the exclusion of women from the barristers' mess or from dining at judicial lodgings was commonplace for Heilbron and her contemporaries (when she was away from home she would eat alone), it was not until August 2017 that women barristers were able to use the large male-only locker-room at Southwark Crown Court.[37]

## Further Reading

- Rachel Cooke, *Her Brilliant Career: Ten Extraordinary Women of the Fifties* (Virago Press, 2013).
- Brenda Hale, 'Rose Heilbron' in *The Oxford Dictionary of National Biography 2005–2008* (OUP, 2013)
- Hilary Heilbron, *Rose Heilbron: The Story of England's first Woman Queen's Counsel and Judge* (Hart Publishing, 2012).

[32] Polden, n 15 above, 514–16.
[33] Cooke, n 6 above, 286.
[34] Brenda Hale, 'Rose Heilbron' in Lawrence Goldman (ed), *The Oxford Dictionary of National Biography 2005–2008* (OUP, 2013).
[35] ibid.
[36] Vera Baird, 'My Legal Hero: Rose Heilbron', *The Guardian*, 11 August 2010.
[37] Jonathan Prynn, 'Female barristers win right to use all-male locker room at London court', *Evening Standard*, 21 August 2017.

# 36

# Married Women's Property Act 1964

SHARON THOMPSON

Contemporaneous commentators on the Married Women's Property Act (MWPA) 1964 described it as 'one more example of an atomised reform of one isolated aspect of the law'.[1] At first glance this appears correct; section 1 comprises only 71 words. Its effect was simple: it enabled a wife to share housekeeping money (and any property derived from that money) equally with her husband, when previously it was legally considered to be her husband's money only and so reverted back to him. Yet in spite of its brevity and apparently narrow scope, the Act was hugely significant, as for the first time, it enabled married women without independent income to acquire their own money.

## I. Context

The MWPA 1964 was a landmark in married women's economic independence, because it brought the problems associated with the principle of separation of property into focus. Whilst the **Married Women's Property Acts** (MWPAs) of 1870 and **1882**[2] made it a *possibility* for married women to be financially independent by enabling them to legally own property in their own right, the *reality* for most married women throughout most of the twentieth century prevented this possibility from being realised.[3] In the mid-twentieth century, most women gave up paid employment on marriage, and those who did work tended to occupy low-paid jobs.[4] These material inequalities were in many ways reinforced as a result of the sexual division of labour within the family.[5] Work in the home was almost exclusively the wife's domain and was unpaid. Although this work did not directly produce the household earnings, it was crucial to the generation of this income because it enabled the breadwinning husband to work in the public sphere. However, this contribution was not recognised in law. The principle of separate property meant that only the husband could have a legal interest in the money and property he earned. Though money earned by a wife would also belong to her outright, the little money she could earn was generally spent

[1] Olive Stone, 'Married Women's Property Act 1964' (1964) 27 *Modern Law Review* 576, 576.
[2] **Married Women's Property Act 1882.**
[3] **Married Women (Restraint Upon Anticipation) Act 1949.**
[4] Ferdynand Zweig, *Women's Life and Labour* (Gollancz, 1952).
[5] Sandra Fredman, *Women and the Law* (Clarendon Press, 1997) 108.

on food, clothing and other consumables for the family.[6] This also left married women economically vulnerable on divorce, as until 1970[7] they would be dependent on maintenance from their ex-husbands, and this was not always paid. In short, married women had no claim to property directly earned by their husbands and little opportunity to accumulate property in their own right.

The hardship resulting from the economic position of married women in the mid-twentieth century was striking in cases concerning ownership of housekeeping money. In particular, the situation of Mrs Blackwell[8] became a popular narrative for advocates of reform. Mrs Blackwell had approximately £103 of housekeeping savings standing to her credit in the Oxford and District Co-operative Society, but was not permitted by the court to keep any of it when she separated from her husband. Even though she had brought in lodgers to help her husband pay off the mortgage on their home and had shopped at the Co-op in order to receive dividends, Mrs Blackwell was left no money of her own. As Labour MP Edith Summerskill wrote in her memoirs:

> Mrs Blackwell after sixteen years of unremitting toil on behalf of her family was not entitled to a penny for her services. She was a pathetic little figure in her basement room when I visited her in London … She was helpless and hopeless, a victim of a legal system which still in the twentieth century treats the wife as a chattel of her husband.[9]

Thus, though the MWPAs in 1870 and 1882 might have formally bestowed on a married woman individual legal personality on marriage, she was by no means equal to her husband because, even if she managed household finances that enabled the mortgage on the family home to be repaid, that home could not belong to her unless she was named on the documents of title, and wives rarely were. She could act only as her husband's agent and in no other capacity.[10] Mrs Blackwell's counsel argued that the law had left her worse off than a paid housekeeper.[11] Summerskill also noted that the wife could have spent the housekeeping money on herself instead of having the prudence to invest it.[12] In fact, Goddard LJ, one of the judges in the case, was worried the opposite would happen: that if women were permitted to save out of their housekeeping allowance, and then keep the proceeds, 'women would be tempted to give their husbands tinned meat rather than roast meat'.[13]

Perhaps the most shocking aspect of Mrs Blackwell's case was that the hardship she experienced was by no means exceptional.[14] As Summerskill observed, 'different versions of the Blackwell case [appeared] in our newspapers every day'.[15] Put simply, the judiciary made it clear in *Blackwell* that the MWPA 1882 could not and would not be interpreted to recognise the value of married women's unpaid work in the home.[16] Significantly, the MWPA 1964

[6] ibid 48.

[7] The Matrimonial Proceedings and Property Act 1970 widened the scope of financial provision for the non-moneyed spouse on divorce.

[8] *Blackwell v Blackwell* [1943] 2 All ER 579.

[9] Edith Summerskill, *A Woman's World* (Heinemann, 1967) 145.

[10] Mrs Blackwell's solicitor was **Carrie Morrison**, the first woman admitted as a solicitor in England and Wales.

[11] 'Mrs Blackwell and Mrs 1964', *The Catholic Citizen* (London, 15 June 1964).

[12] Summerskill, n 9 above.

[13] ibid 144, referring to Goddard LJ's comments in *Blackwell v Blackwell* (n 8 above).

[14] See *Preston v Preston* 1950 SLT 196; *Hoddinott v Hoddinott* [1949] 2 KB 406 (where the wife was held to have no legal interest in winnings from a joint investment of husband and wife).

[15] HL Deb, 19 November 1952, vol 507 col 1874.

[16] Fredman, n 5 above, 3.

was the first time such work could be legally recognised as having economic value. But, as Rosemary Auchmuty has remarked, the feminist activism behind such reform, particularly during the first half of the twentieth century, does not feature in contemporary accounts and has instead been 'deliberately erased or reconstructed in safe, non-radical forms with the feminist agency removed'.[17] Such reconstruction is clear in the context of the MWPA 1964. Indeed, the impetus behind the Act is often documented as being the Report of the Royal Commission on Marriage and Divorce in 1956 alone,[18] with no mention of the Married Women's Association (MWA), which provided evidence crucial to the Royal Commission's report, raised consciousness (inside and outside Parliament) about the plight of women such as Mrs Blackwell, and even financed Mrs Blackwell's (unsuccessful) appeal.

The MWA was formed in 1938 to promote the rights of housewives and mothers and included prominent post-first-wave feminists such as **Helena Normanton**, Vera Brittain, Helen Nutting, Edith Summerskill and Juanita Frances (who founded the Association). One of the specific aims of the Association was to promote legislation to regulate the financial relations between husband and wife as between equal partners,[19] and so it sought to challenge the court's narrow view of wives as mere agents of their husband's money, with no legal entitlement to it. Their strategy was to make women aware of how the law affected them and, in particular, of women's economic vulnerability as a result of being unable to save housekeeping money. In addition, the Association alerted the wider public to the urgent need for legal reform in its magazine *Wife and Citizen*, and by political lobbying. Undoubtedly, however, the Association's most powerful ally in driving the introduction of the MWPA 1964 was Labour MP and self-identified feminist Edith Summerskill, who was its first president.

## II. The Landmark

The first legislative attempt to reform the issue of married women and housekeeping money was the Women's Disabilities Bill 1952. Edith Summerskill moved the second reading of the Bill, viewing it as an attempt 'to remedy the injustice suffered by women in the position of Mrs Blackwell'.[20] Wider in scope than the eventual MWPA 1964, it comprised three clauses addressing issues affecting married women on relationship breakdown and unmarried mothers when maintenance orders were not observed.[21] The second clause was similar to the MWPA finally enacted, providing that housekeeping savings could be divided equally between husband and wife, or in any proportion the court considered just.[22]

[17] Rosemary Auchmuty, 'Feminists as Stakeholders in the Law School' in Fiona Cownie (ed), *Stakeholders in the Law School* (Hart Publishing, 2010) 35–64, 49.

[18] Law Commission, *Transfer of Money Between Spouses – the Married Women's Property Act 1964* (Law Com Working Paper No 90, 1985) [4.1].

[19] Records of the Married Women's Association: http://discovery.nationalarchives.gov.uk/details/rd/9d19c2e7-12c7-44ab-b73a-abfd80593390.

[20] ibid.

[21] Specifically, clause one of the Bill stated that if a man defaulted in payment of a maintenance order, and was employed, the court could make an order requiring his employer to make payments to the court in respect of the money due to the applicant.

[22] Clause 2 also provided that if forced to leave the family home, the wife could have use of household goods and furniture, and in some cases the court could grant tenancy rights to the wife in respect of the family home.

It would be an understatement to say that the Women's Disabilities Bill did not receive a warm reception during its second reading in the House of Commons. There was significant resistance to the prospect of a wife having a share in housekeeping money. Summerskill's perspective on this debate, as recounted in her memoirs, is particularly interesting. In her view the suspicion in respect of this Bill was not dissimilar to the attitudes of those opposed to the MWPAs 1870 and 1882. The battle against coverture might have been fought in a different era, but the prejudice surrounding reform of women's rights 70 years later was much the same. As she incisively stated: 'I have found nothing more calculated to catch a prejudiced man off his guard than a speech advocating the further emancipation of women'.[23] Her Bill was called 'ultra-feminist', 'grossly unpractical', and anticipated to 'introduce strife and disharmony into the home'.[24] Indeed, it is farcical that, like those in opposition to the MWPAs 1870 and 1882, there appeared to be more concern for the husband's meals than for advancing women's rights,[25] as Members commented that reform would lead to unpleasant dinners and displeasing breakfasts if the family business could be 'thrashed out before a bench of magistrates'.[26] Yet even though, as Summerskill observed, 'the anti-feminists had gathered in force against [her]',[27] she was not without support on this matter. Fifty-four Members voted in favour of the Bill, and in the public gallery members of the MWA filled almost every seat.[28]

Though the Bill did not pass, it was a precursor to the Report of the Royal Commission on Marriage and Divorce led by law lord Fergus Morton, four years later. The Commission proposed that 'savings made from money contributed by either the husband or the wife or by both for the purpose of meeting housekeeping expenses'[29] should belong to each spouse in equal shares. Importantly, the Commission stated that its recommendation was based on witnesses' evidence, provided in part by the MWA, that exposed the 'real hardship' for wives who had saved housekeeping money for years only to have this money belong in law to the husband.[30]

The Royal Commission's report undoubtedly led to more widespread public consciousness of the plight of married women like Mrs Blackwell. This encouraged Summerskill to make another attempt at reform, and she drafted one of the shortest Bills in history. Titled the Married Women's Savings Bill,[31] it consisted of 25 words: 'If a wife makes savings out of what her husband gives her for housekeeping, half of any money so saved shall belong to her absolutely'. The change in temperature in the House of Lords towards this Bill was plain, and 11 years after the Women's Disabilities Bill, the Married Women's Savings Bill passed its second reading in the House of Lords.[32] It could not progress further because the Parliamentary session ran out of time, but before reintroducing the Bill in the new session

[23] Summerskill, n 9 above, 148.

[24] HC Deb, 25 April 1952, vol 499 col 922 (Mr Bell).

[25] Summerskill, n 9 above.

[26] HC Deb, 25 April 1952, vol 499 col 975 (Mr Doughty).

[27] HL Deb 19 November 1952, vol 507 col 1874.

[28] Summerskill, n 9 above, 150.

[29] Royal Commission on Marriage and Divorce, *Royal Commission on Marriage and Divorce: Report 1951–1955* (HM Stationery Office, 1956) [701].

[30] ibid [645] and [700].

[31] If the wording of this particular Bill had been introduced it would have been the shortest English statute in history. This is currently the Parliament (Qualification of Women) Act 1918, which consists of 27 words.

[32] Summerskill, n 9 above, 156.

of Parliament, Summerskill had it redrafted as the Married Women's Property Bill 1964 to incorporate the language of the Royal Commission's report, so that the housekeeping money would belong to the husband and wife in equal shares instead of granting the wife a one-half share absolutely. However, the wording differed from the report because it was not gender-neutral, only granting the wife an equal share in housekeeping money derived from the husband, and not vice versa.

The Bill passed successfully through the House of Lords and was moved by Douglas Houghton MP in the House of Commons. Procedurally, Private Members' Bills only require one dissenting member of the House in order to obstruct them. The first time the Married Women's Property Bill was called it was defeated by a single, anonymous objector. Therefore the following week, Summerskill described bracing herself 'waiting for the fatal word [object] like some poor unfortunate creature waiting for the executioner's axe, with an iron determination not to wince when the blow fell'.[33] But no one objected and the Bill was passed. Summerskill was successful in introducing reform that would enable married women to save in their own right.

## III. What Happened Next

One of the major criticisms of the MWPA in 1964 was that it discriminated against men, because it only applied to housekeeping money received by the wife, and therefore differed from the recommendations of the Royal Commission in 1956.[34] But one of the powerful aspects of the MWPA was that it was *not* gender-neutral, because the issue it addressed was an issue that affected married women in a way that it *did not* affect married men. It was almost exclusively women who were responsible for the unpaid work in the home, and who were financially vulnerable as a result of this. Thus, the MWPA's discriminatory focus was arguably *crucial* in highlighting the sexual division of labour and the limitations of separate property. Though the Act did not protect housewives who did not receive any allowance from their husbands,[35] the spirit of the legislation – that *both* spouses are entitled to the financial fruits of the marital partnership – paved the way for the evolving divorce law reform in the next decade.

Not all feminists agreed that a focus on married women's rights to housekeeping allowance was an appropriate response to the question of economic equality between husband and wife. Some members of the MWA contended that all property in marriage should be divided equally, as they believed marriage to be a joint enterprise comprising equally important financial and non-financial contributions. Helena Normanton, however, submitted evidence on the Association's behalf to the Royal Commission of Marriage and Divorce[36] arguing that wives should be paid an allowance from the family income for their work in the home but should not be entitled to the resources of their husband, and could be

[33] Stone, n 1 above, 158.

[34] John Dewar, *Law and the Family* (Butterworths, 1989) 119.

[35] Otto Kahn-Freund, 'Matrimonial Property – Some Recent Developments' (1959) 22(3) *Modern Law Review* 241–72, 249.

[36] She later withdrew this evidence and submitted it independently. Following this, the Married Women's Association resubmitted a different memorandum of evidence to the Commission.

penalised if their housekeeping was wilfully negligent.[37] This angered members who felt that Normanton's evidence portrayed the wife as an 'employed subordinate, and not a partner' in marriage.[38] This caused irreparable tensions in the MWA and led to Normanton resigning and establishing the Council of Married Women in 1952. Interestingly, Normanton's view that wives should be provided with a housekeeping allowance was reflected in the Wages for Housework campaigns of the 1970s and continues to divide feminists today.

## IV. Significance

The MWPA 1964 was a 'major triumph'[39] for the MWA. Twenty years after *Blackwell*, married women had a legal right to a half-share of housekeeping money, thus recognising that this money had often been generated through wives' own efforts anyway.[40] But the members of the Association were clear that the Act represented only slight progress towards economic equality in marriage.[41] In the words of Olive Stone (lecturer in law at the LSE and campaigner for married women's property rights), the amount of money wives could acquire under the Act would likely have been very little.[42] Nevertheless, she recognised that the Act was important because it had established a principle based on equality. As a result, it would be short-sighted to criticise the MWPA 1964 for not doing enough to address the financial position of married women. The strategy for reform adopted by the MWA was *necessarily* incremental, because the prospects of further legislation at that time were unrealistic.[43] Edith Summerskill's attempts to achieve broader reform for women in the Women's Disabilities Bill 1952 had been met with considerable resistance, but this resistance decreased substantially when she drafted the Married Women's Property Bill, because it was short, pragmatic, and sought to erode only one cause of women's economic inequality in marriage.[44]

The significance of this incremental reform cannot be overstated, because it led to more radical discussions of automatic equal division of property between husband and wife (a central aim of the Married Women's Association). For instance, in 1985 the Law Commission produced a Working Paper centred on dramatically extending the principle of equal division in the MWPA 1964, by proposing a rule whereby any money transferred by either spouse would immediately belong jointly to husband and wife.[45] Although this rule was never implemented, the Paper triggered a broader conversation around financial equality between spouses at this time, and this was directly facilitated by the MWPA 1964.

[37] 'Not Properly Understood: Mrs Normanton Defends Her Report', *Beckenham Advertiser*, 13 March 1952.

[38] 'Wives hope ex-officials will return', *Daily Dispatch*, 3 April 1952.

[39] '"Only slight progress" in the fight for equality', *Hampstead Highgate Express*, 11 December 1964.

[40] For instance, some of the money invested by Mrs Blackwell comprised profits from her work taking lodgers into the home.

[41] n 39 above.

[42] Stone, n 1 above, 580.

[43] Law Commission, n 18 above, [4.4].

[44] Indeed, the Royal Commission's 1956 recommendation on housekeeping savings was the furthest extent to which it would go to improve economic equality in marriage: Carol Smart, *The Ties that Bind* (Routledge, 1984) 38.

[45] Law Commission, n 18 above.

As a result, the MWPA 1964 forms an important, albeit unrecognised part of the historical context surrounding current principles of financial provision on divorce.[46]

## Further Reading

- Sandra Fredman, *Women and the Law* (Clarendon Press, 1998).
- Olive Stone, 'Married Women's Property Act, 1964' (1964) 27 *Modern Law Review* 576–80.
- Edith Summerskill, *A Woman's World* (Heinemann, 1967).

[46] The MWPA 1964 was repealed in Scotland by the Family Law (Scotland) Act 1985. The Act remains in force in England and Wales. The Equality Act 2010, s 200 (not currently in effect) amends the MWPA 1964 prospectively to make it gender neutral. The Family Law (Property and Maintenance) Bill 2005 sought to extend the Act's provisions to civil partners but was not passed. The Act was never introduced in Northern Ireland.

# 37

# First Woman High Court Judge in England and Wales, Elizabeth Lane, 1965

JUDITH BOURNE AND FRANCES BURTON

Elizabeth Lane (1905–88) was the first woman to be appointed as a county court judge and as a High Court judge in England and Wales. In 1945 Sybil Campbell had become the first judge of a lower court[1] – a stipendiary magistrate – but the higher courts remained wholly male until Lane's appointment to the High Court in 1965.

## I. Life[2]

Elizabeth Lane (nee Coulborn) was born in 1905, to (as she described it) an upper-middle-class family. She had a conventional, if rather old-fashioned, education for a girl of her class, being educated at home by a governess until she was 11 or 12 years old before being sent to Twizzletwig School in Hindhead. At 15 she attended Malvern School for two years, where her only 'interest in life' was hockey. Having passed the 'Higher Oxford' (an examination that allowed entry into UK universities), she gave up on education, determined to 'have a good time'. Thus, she never went to university. In 1924 she journeyed to Canada to keep house for her brother and it was there she met her future husband, (Henry Jerrold) Randall Lane. They married in 1926. When her husband decided to study for the Bar, he suggested that she join him. At the time, a university degree was not a prerequisite for becoming a lawyer. She was convinced, she said, that she would never pass, and that if she did it would be a 'miracle' and that she would be 'no good' at it. However, she did and she was.

She was called to the Bar in 1940. A pupillage was arranged with Geoffrey Howard (who would also become a county court judge). She was told in no uncertain terms that she would not be able to remain in Howard's chambers after her pupillage (although they would be able to find a tenancy for her elsewhere) as the Clerk would not wish to have a woman in chambers and as women were not considered a good 'financial proposition'. In the event, however, she was asked to stay on. Immediately she joined the Midland Circuit and, encouraged by Paul Sandlands KC, the Bencher at Inner Temple who had arranged her pupillage,

[1] Sybil Oldfield, 'Campbell, Sybil (1889–1977)' in *Oxford Dictionary of National Biography* (OUP, 2004).
[2] Details of her life are taken from her autobiography: Elizabeth Lane, *Hear the Other Side* (Butterworths, 1985).

set to work as a barrister. The Midland Circuit was seen as a launch pad for any barristers who did not think they were likely to be able to make a career at the Bar in London, but it also suited her, coming as she did from Cheshire. Like others who have taken that route she took any work that was available, such as poor prisoners' defences, divorces, and other basic poorly-paid work, but quickly built up a practice.

Her first official appointment came in 1948 as a member of the Home Office Committee of Enquiry into the Use of Depositions in Criminal Cases. She applied to become QC in 1959 and on her second attempt, in 1960, she was appointed. This was testament to her work ethic, energy and drive as it was unusual even for men to be appointed so quickly. She was only the third woman Silk in England, the other two being **Helena Normanton** and **Rose Heilbron**, both appointed KC in 1949. This ethic can be seen in her work not just as a barrister but her roles as Chairman of the new Mental Health Tribunals (1960) and Commissioner of the Crown at Manchester (1961), the equivalent of today's Deputy High Court judges. At the end of 1961, she was appointed Recorder of Derby.

In 1965 she was appointed to the Probate, Divorce and Admiralty Division of the High Court where most of the work was in Family Law, clear evidence of gender stereotyping as she was an expert in criminal law. In February 1971 she chaired the review of the working of the **Abortion Act 1967** and, somewhat to everyone's surprise, the working group's report on this controversial topic offered the legislation its unanimous support.[3]

On her appointment to the High Court, Lane became a Dame of the Order of the British Empire and, after some discussion about her admissibility because of her sex, a Bencher of Inner Temple, which made her one of the select group of senior leading members of the Inn which governs the Inn's affairs. She retired in 1978 and died in Winchester in 1988.[4]

## II. Context

Mrs Justice Lane's appointment in 1965 came in a decade of social change for both men and women. Precedent for women judges was limited: apart from Sybil Campbell, the only women judges of any kind were Dorothy Dix[5] who, as deputy Recorder of Deal, became the first woman to preside over a jury trial in 1946, and Rose Heilbron, who became the Recorder of Burnley in 1956.[6]

Since the Judicature Acts of 1873–75, the High Court has been considered the first rung of the higher courts' judicial ladder. It was, and still is, quite unusual for a High Court judge to be appointed first to the county court. The usual route for advancement was via a part-time Recorder and/or a deputy High Court judicial appointment (then called a 'Commissioner of the Crown'). In fact, Lane had taken on both of these roles in 1961, and

[3] National Archives SA/ALR Papers of the Committee on the Working of the Abortion Act (The Lane Committee), 1971–74.

[4] Elizabeth Butler-Sloss, 'Lane, Dame Elizabeth Kathleen (1905–1988)' in *Oxford Dictionary of National Biography* (OUP, 2004).

[5] Patrick Polden, 'Portia's progress: women at the Bar in England, 1919–1939' (2005) 12 *International Journal of the Legal Profession* 293–338.

[6] Brenda Hale, 'Heilbron, Dame Rose (1914–2005)' in *Oxford Dictionary of National Biography* (OUP, 2009); Hilary Heilbron, *Rose Heilbron: The Story of England's First Woman Queen's Counsel and Judge* (Hart Publishing, 2012).

so it was her appointment to the county court in 1962 that marked a diversion from the usual route. Patrick Polden suggests that the county court role may have been made so that the Lord Chancellor's officials, who dominated appointment processes, could see how (as a criminal law specialist) she would handle a level of civil justice above her existing Recorder's experience in small civil cases.

In any event, her elevation was clearly an experiment, since no woman had attained such an appointment before. Lane had won the admiration of George Coldstream, the Lord Chancellor's Department's permanent secretary, who wrote of her to the Lord Chancellor (Lord Gardiner) that 'she was so inherently capable that she would do almost any second row judicial job thoroughly competently'.[7] He apparently rated her above Rose Heilbron, who waited rather longer for her appointment. Polden speculates as to whether, in these circumstances, Gardiner made a personal decision on her appointment to the High Court, or whether that too was also the outcome of the usual process which was heavily influenced by the permanent staff.[8]

Lane was the only woman High Court judge for nine years until Heilbron's appointment in 1974. She was never promoted to the Court of Appeal. Perhaps this was a step too far for the establishment, but (as was usual for men who retired from the High Court Bench) she occasionally sat there after her retirement.

## III. What Happened Next

Lane's appointment appeared to represent the beginning of equality in the legal profession. However, the 2017 statistics on judicial diversity show that 50 years after Lane became the first woman on the High Court Bench women's progression in the judiciary has been slow. In 2017, only 9 of the 38 Court of Appeal Judges were women; 21 out of 97 High Court judges; and 28 per cent of all judges.[9] Currently there are only two women Supreme Court Justices Of (court) judges who declared their ethnicity, the percentage who identify as Black, Asian and Minority Ethnic is seven per cent.[10] The 2012 House of Lords Constitution Committee looking at diversity in judicial appointments lamented: 'the judge inhabiting a court room in England and Wales is stereotypically a white male from a narrow social background.'[11]

## IV. Significance

Elizabeth Lane is important as the first woman High Court judge and as Chair of the 1971 committee to examine the working of the 1967 Abortion Act. But her significance is much greater than this: she represents a woman's distinctive contribution to 'justice' or, rather (in view of the statistics), the lack thereof. We know very little about her motivations or

[7] Polden, n 5 above, 305.

[8] Polden, n 5 above, 305–06.

[9] Courts and Tribunals Judiciary, Judicial Diversity Statistics 2017: https://www.judiciary.gov.uk/about-the-judiciary/who-are-the-judiciary/diversity/judicial-diversity-statistics-2017.

[10] ibid.

[11] House of Lords Select Committee on the Constitution, *Judicial Appointments* (HL Paper 272) [68].

approach to judging, perhaps because she feared accusations of self-publicising (a disciplinary offence for barristers). Her autobiography relates that she did not intend to be a pioneer of any sort, unlike many other women of her time in the law who set out to cut ice, or crack (or preferably breach) 'glass ceilings', and generally to push the boundaries of what women could do. She claimed only to be a fairly ordinary upper-middle-class girl from Cheshire who stumbled into a legal career because she married a lawyer. She suggested that her success at the Bar was down to good health and stamina, a capacity for hard work, a good temper, her ability to conceal her true feelings, not becoming emotionally involved, a pleasing voice, and good luck.[12] But there must have been more to it than that.

## Further Reading


- Hilary Heilbron, *Rose Heilbron: The Story of England's first woman Queen's Counsel and Judge* (Hart Publishing, 2012).
- Elizabeth Lane, *Hear the other side: Audi alteram partem: The autobiography of England's first woman judge* (Butterworth, 1985).
- Patrick Polden, 'Portia's progress: women at the Bar in England, 1919–1939' (2005) 12(3) *International Journal of the Legal Profession* 293–338.


[12] Lane, n 2 above, 60–62.

# 38

# Abortion Act 1967

NICKY PRIAULX AND NATALIE L JONES

The Abortion Act 1967 transformed a procedure performed clandestinely, and at huge physical risk to women, into one that was lawful when performed by the medical profession. Section 1(1) of the 1967 Act, which applies to England, Wales and Scotland, provides for abortion if two registered medical practitioners are of the opinion, formed in good faith, that to continue the pregnancy would involve risk to the life of the pregnant woman, or endanger the physical or mental health of the pregnant woman or any existing children of her family, greater than if the pregnancy were terminated; or that there is a substantial risk that if the child were born it would 'suffer from such physical or mental abnormalities as to be seriously handicapped'. The law also permits doctors to take into account the woman's 'actual or reasonably foreseeable environment' (section 1(2)).

## I. Context

> I once knew a woman who had a backstreet abortion and died; a married woman, already the mother of three young children, who just could not afford another child. I was absolutely shocked. It was the first time I had come across abortion. I was in my early twenties, working at St Bartholomew's Hospital doing research, and I mentioned it to a group of doctors one lunch time. They looked at me in amazement, and said words to the effect: 'Well, where have you been all your life? Stay behind on Friday.' I discovered that Bart's and all the other London hospitals put wards aside every Friday and Saturday night for women who were brought in as a result of backstreet abortions – Friday being pay day. Bleeding, septic, sometimes dying. This was accepted everywhere.[1]

*Prior* to the 1967 Act – with the exception of Scotland – the governance of abortion in the United Kingdom consisted of section 58 of the Offences Against the Person Act 1861, which made abortion an offence, carrying a maximum penalty of 'penal servitude for life'.[2] The only exception to this was via the Infant Life (Preservation) Act 1929 which made it lawful

[1] Diane Munday, Women's rights campaigner and former General Secretary and Vice-chair of the Abortion Law Reform Association, in British Pregnancy Advisory Service, *Pioneers of Change: Interviews with People who made the Abortion Act 1967 possible* (BPAS, 2007).

[2] It provided that the pregnant woman herself, as well as those performing abortions, could be held guilty of the offence.

for a doctor to perform a termination in order to *save the woman's life*. While the judiciary played a role in broadening the circumstances by which a termination could be performed in *R v Bourne*, the law seemed both fragile and ambiguous.[3] By virtue of the chilling effect of the criminal law[4] and a 'strong tradition against the operation within their profession', few doctors were willing to terminate openly in the National Health Service (NHS) on *Bourne* grounds.[5] As such, 'the spirit of the old law still had a wide deterrent effect. Tens of thousands of women who wanted their abortions either could not get them or dared not ask their doctors for them'.[6]

The effect of law was to bar the way to most women who wanted *lawful and safe* abortions and to leave women dependent upon a clandestine industry which responded to their need for reproductive control. Discursive notions of abortion as matters of 'women's choice' or 'reproductive control' are relatively modern ones. Instead, abortion continued to be typified as the 'illegal operation' in being the 'only operation specifically prohibited by law'.[7] From stories of women, commonly among the working classes, sharing information and assisting each other in procuring abortion, a range of techniques emerged as a private network of interventions to address 'female irregularities': termination by use of 'slippery elm' (a bark that expanded with moisture), applying hot douches, consuming abortifacients intended for use on domestic animals, inserting hat pins, knitting needles or skewers, or the use of pills and potions advertised by a rising industry of medical manufacturing 'to 'restore regularity' or to 'remove obstructions'. The effect of the law was not to prevent such interventions; rather, its effect was to withhold the opportunity for care, safety and expertise in respect of procedures that were commonly performed, with results that were 'generally undesirable and often appalling'.[8]

Feminists had campaigned for abortion law reform for decades. Stella Browne who, with Janet Chance and Alice Jenkins, founded the Abortion Law Reform Association (ALRA) in 1936, had lectured on 'The right to abortion' as early as 1929 at the World Sexual Reform Congress in London. In the years before the Second World War, ALRA toured the country addressing women's organisations, and even the Co-operative Women's Guild, representing working women well aware of the horrors of illegal abortions, offered support to what remained a controversial issue.[9] During the Second World War they continued their public education but the 1950s marked a turning-point, when ALRA lobbied Parliament for legislation that would provide lawful access to termination of pregnancy on therapeutic grounds, where pregnancy was the result of sexual offences, for women with too many children and

[3] *R v Bourne* [1938] 3 All ER 615. Note that in Scotland the situation was different. The Offences Against the Person Act, Infant Life (Preservation) Act and the *Bourne* judgment did not apply. Abortion was a common law offence but as Keith Hindell and Madeleine Simms note, 'its limits were not strictly defined' or, it would appear, frequently enforced (*Abortion Law Reformed* (Peter Owen, 1971) 14). Some within the Scottish medical profession regarded the Abortion Act 1967 as a reform affording England and Wales some of the freedoms that Scottish doctors had thus far enjoyed in this field.

[4] Despite the fact that doctors were rarely arrested (by contrast with lay women abortionists), and in practice there were few convictions for unlawfully procured abortions (see Kate Gleeson, 'Persuading Parliament: Abortion Law reform in the UK' (2007) 22 *Australasian Parliamentary Review* 23–42).

[5] Hindell and Simms, n 3 above, 14.

[6] ibid 16.

[7] Barbara Brookes, *Abortion in England 1900–1967* (Routledge, 1990).

[8] Hindell and Simms, n 3 above, 25.

[9] See *Sheila Rowbotham, A new world for women: Stella Browne, social feminist* (Pluto Press, 1977).

in respect of 'abnormal' foetuses. A 'eugenic clause' proved quite central to ALRA's lobbying efforts, and also helped to strongly align ALRA to the British Medical Association (BMA), which had long advocated eugenic terminations and sought law reform for that purpose.

## II. The Landmark

Noted as being the first systematic attempt to 'lobby' support, ALRA convinced a number of Parliamentarians whose names had been drawn in the annual Private Members' Ballot to sponsor an Abortion Bill. Bills introduced to Parliament in 1954 and 1960 failed to progress, but the Thalidomide tragedy, which resulted in hundreds of babies being born with congenital disabilities as a result of their mothers consuming a pill intended to deal with morning sickness, provided a dramatic new rallying point for lobbying. An international rubella epidemic in the mid-'60s also helped to reinvigorate ALRA. With the BMA concerned about legal ambiguity in respect of doctors' criminal liability for providing abortions for women who had contracted rubella, a fresh agenda for law reform was set. ALRA courted the medical profession to legitimate its position and help convince politicians and the public at large. The BMA, asserting its authority on the matter of abortion, formed a special committee to direct reform in 1965. For the BMA, as with ALRA, the styling of abortion reform was not in the name of 'abortion on demand'. The BMA argued for law reform in order to clarify the position of doctors and to provide protection for doctors. In this respect, the BMA sought the full medicalisation of abortion and to 'protect clinical autonomy and discretion of doctors on abortion'.

In May 1966, ALRA's latest sponsor, Liberal Party MP David Steel, introduced the Medical Termination of Pregnancy Bill that, after a series of amendments, became the Abortion Act 1967. In course of the passage of the Bill, David Steel strategically manoeuvred between parliamentarians and the BMA and the Royal College of Obstetricians and Gynaecologists (RCOG), making a considerable number of compromises, by which to encourage the greatest support for the Bill.[10] Most notably, for an Act that has become so crucial for women, the various legislative architects never advocated affording women the freedom to determine what happens to their bodies. Indeed, for the large medical associations, that was the specific fear. The BMA and RCOG were resistant to any provision that was fashioned by reference to 'non-medical criteria' that could lead patients 'to believe that abortions would be carried out automatically'. It is in this sense that the language of the debate leading up to the 1967 Act is at odds with a feminist agenda. As Sally Sheldon notes in her analysis of the passage of the Abortion Act, on either side of the debate the aborting woman was characterised as a 'marginal and deviant figure who stands against a wider norm of women who neither need nor desire abortion' so that the

> decision to abort is not seen as an intrinsically acceptable one, as a choice which a woman could face at some time in her life. Rather, it is an option which may be justified only in certain cases by the individual circumstances (or inadequacies) of individual women, in the opinion of two doctors.[11]

[10] The Bill took what was then a record time of 18 months for its Committee stage. See further Gleeson, n 4 above.

[11] Sally Sheldon, *Beyond Control: Medical Power and Abortion Law* (Pluto Press, 1997) 42.

The two doctors provision was – and remains – controversial. As Diane Munday, former General Secretary and Vice-chair of the ALRA, notes:

> None of us were happy that it would be in doctors' rather than women's hands, but it was the price that had to be paid for legislation at all … I can remember being in a basement room in the Commons with David Steel, Vera Houghton [then Chair of the ALRA], a representative from the Royal College of Obstetricians and Gynaecologists (RCOG) and somebody very high up in the Church, almost horse-trading clauses, 'We'll let this go if you'll put that in' … I have been attacked by some in the women's movement who say 'You sold us down the river, you gave the power to doctors, you've really stitched women up.' It wasn't like that. If we had held out for anything broader we would have been left with nothing.[12]

The Abortion Act 1967 came into operation in England and Wales and Scotland on 27 April 1968. The Act has never applied to Northern Ireland. At the time of its enactment, the Parliament of Northern Ireland had little appetite to follow the rest of the UK's lead. Since then politicians in Northern Ireland – and sometimes at Westminster – have resisted all efforts to extend it.[13]

## III. What Happened Next

Immediately following the enactment of the Act, described as having a greater immediate impact than its supporters had anticipated, NHS hospitals saw a dramatic increase in the number of abortions performed. Women who had once turned to backstreet abortionists or sought clandestine terminations from doctors in private now consulted their GPs and were referred to gynaecologists. In 1967, fewer than 10,000 NHS abortions were carried out officially. Twelve months after the 1967 Act came into effect, that number increased to 22,000, in 1969 to 33,000 and by 1970, just under 50,000.[14] In the year following reform, some disparities in provision appeared between 'the liberal and the illiberal regions', with patients seeking treatment by liberal providers. In response to an even sharper rise in demand some hospitals refused to treat patients outside of their catchment areas. Meeting this demand, and perhaps more ably having anticipated it, pregnancy advisory services emerged, with the British Pregnancy Advisory Service, opening up on the first day the 1967 Act came into operation.

The growth of this sector, composed of non-profit-making organisations and commercial organisations, spurred a backlash, largely driven by concerns that women were not accessing abortions as had been envisaged (through the NHS) and of the potential for the abuse of women. While second-wave feminists continued to campaign for abortion on

[12] Munday, n 1 above.

[13] When Direct Rule returned to Westminster in 1972, successive Governments were reluctant to grasp the political hot potato of abortion law in Northern Ireland. In 2008, a move to extend the 1967 Act to Northern Ireland was blocked by the then leader of the House, Harriet Harman, purportedly because she feared there may be 'unintended consequences' for existing abortion laws (Nicolas Watt, 'Harman to block Commons votes on liberalising abortion laws', *The Guardian*, 21 October 2008). In 2017, Arlene Foster, leader of the Democratic Unionist Party and the first woman First Minister of Northern Ireland, promised to prevent the extension of the 1967 Act to Northern Ireland (Henry McDonald, 'No extending abortion act to Northern Ireland, first female leader says', *The Guardian*, 6 January 2016).

[14] Hindell and Simms, n 3 above, 214.

demand ('Free Contraception and Abortion on Demand' was one of the first four demands of the Women's Liberation Movement, issued in 1970), in the same year David Steel MP formed part of a working party to consider the operation of the Act in the private sector. They recommended a system of notification by abortion providers to the Department of Health of key statistics, as well as the signatures from the two doctors confirming they had examined the patient and formed their opinion in good faith. At the same time, there was a series of unsuccessful attempts to 'destroy the Abortion Act before it had time to prove itself'. These attacks, they highlight 'came thick and fast', including numerous attempts in the House of Commons to 'curtail and restrict the new legislation'.[15] But one year later, such attempts to unravel dimensions of the Abortion Act looked less likely to command support. MPs were much impressed by figures showing the reduction in abortion-related deaths and abortion emergencies, and were now cognisant of the strong support for the 1967 Act within the medical profession.

In the 50 years elapsing since the enactment of the Abortion Act 1967, despite a reported 50 or 60 abortion Bills seeking to restrict access to abortion treatment, there have been few revisions to its central terms.[16] One exception is section 37 of the Human Fertilisation and Embryology Act 1990, which revised the 1967 Act to impose a time-limit of 24 weeks' gestation except in circumstances where there was a serious risk to the pregnant woman's life or health, or where there was a substantial risk of foetal handicap. Nevertheless, with the exception of the latter which now stands for around one per cent of all terminations performed annually, these changes were largely cosmetic, reflecting existing law and clinical practice. The 1967 Act has also withstood challenges brought via the courts. In *Paton v BPAS*,[17] a husband's attempt to seek an injunction to restrain the defendants from terminating his estranged partner's pregnancy, failed at domestic level and before the European Commission of Human Rights (*Paton v United Kingdom*[18]). As Sheldon notes, 'abortion has become entrenched as a normal part of routine healthcare, with the A[bortion] A[ct] offering a platform for the provision of safe, high quality, state-funded services, typically provided in the first trimester of pregnancy'.[19]

Increasingly, however, the regulation of abortion across the United Kingdom appears ever less unified. The Scottish Parliament, now enjoying new legislative powers over a range of areas, including abortion, following the Scotland Act 2016, has recently announced its decision to make the abortion drug misoprostol available for women to use at home.[20] While this does not involve the creation of new law, but instead makes greater use of existing powers under the 1967 Act (that is, subsections 1(3) and (3A)), the approach highlights a more liberal and enabling approach to women's reproductive rights that pro-choice campaigners have welcomed.

In Northern Ireland, however, the freedoms women enjoy in the regulation of their reproductive bodies stand in stark contrast to the rest of the United Kingdom. Abortion

[15] ibid 219.

[16] Zoe Williams, 'Why, 50 years after the Abortion Act, it's time to abolish the law altogether' *The Guardian*, 25 October 2017.

[17] *Paton v British Pregnancy Advisory Service* [1979] QB 276.

[18] *Paton v United Kingdom* (1980) 3 EHRR 408.

[19] Sally Sheldon, 'The Decriminalisation of Abortion: An Argument for Modernisation' (2016) 36 *Oxford Journal of Legal Studies* 334–65.

[20] Libby Brooks, 'Women in Scotland will be allowed to take abortion pill at home', *The Guardian*, 26 October 2017.

provision remains extremely limited, governed by some of the most restrictive laws in Europe.[21] In practice, what this means is that women living in Northern Ireland who wish to have a termination, and who have the financial and other means to do so, will usually travel to England.[22] In 2016, more than 700 women made this journey.[23]

## IV. Significance

> No choice has a more profound impact on a woman's life than her decision whether or not to become a mother. Bound up with sexuality and gender identity, choices about childbearing and motherhood are emotionally gripping and socially pivotal. They affect one's attitude towards oneself – self-esteem may be enhanced, or it may suffer.[24]

The significance of the Abortion Act 1967 as a 'Women's Legal Landmark' then, may appear to be largely self-explanatory. The 1967 Act constitutes a significant step forward for women's rights in providing a secure legislative footing explicitly for abortion. Given the legal uncertainties running up to the 1967 Act, where abortion stood as 'a dirty and potentially lethal secret',[25] the Act's existence affords women beneficiaries and providers alike with certainty and clarity as to when a termination of pregnancy will be lawful. The 1967 Act, at least to some extent, went some way to addressing this institutional resistance and tendency towards secrecy. It moved towards countering the notion of abortion as an illegitimate medical procedure. As such, its importance is not that abortion happens (for it happens irrespective of the law), but it transforms the conditions of how abortions happen and who performs them, and in large measure remedies some of the hypocrisy inherent in pre-1967 law.

The Abortion Act 1967 provided the medical profession and women with greater certainty around when, and under what circumstances termination of pregnancy would be legally permissible, something that should unequivocally be acknowledged and valued. More broadly however, the provision of lawful abortion has been critical for the emergence of other medical technologies, including prenatal screening, foetal imaging and other diagnostic technologies commonly used to detect foetal abnormalities. In the absence of lawful abortion, a good part of contemporary pregnancy 'care' or 'reproductive choice' as we know it, becomes fairly redundant. But when evaluating the broader social significance of the Act to *women*, much more needs to be said.

[21] In October 2017, the UK Supreme Court heard a challenge to Northern Ireland's abortion laws, specifically the denial of abortions to women who had become pregnant through rape (*In the matter of an application by the Northern Ireland Human Rights Commission for Judicial Review (Northern Ireland), Reference by the Court of Appeal in Northern Ireland pursuant to Paragraph 33 of Schedule 10 to the Northern Ireland Act 1998 (Abortion) (Northern Ireland)* [2018] UKSC 27). In 2015, the High Court in Belfast held that this was a breach of British and European human rights laws, this was overturned on appeal ([2017] NICA 42). See further: ***In the matter of an Application for Judicial Review by the Northern Ireland Human Rights Commission* [2015]**.

[22] From December 2017, following a campaign led by Labour MP, Stella Creasy, women living in Northern Ireland will be able to apply for 'hardship' grants to travel to England for a (free) NHS abortion.

[23] UK Government, 'Report on abortion statistics in England and Wales for 2016' (Office of National Statistics, 13 June 2017, updated 13 October 2017).

[24] Diana Meyers, 'The Rush to Motherhood: Pronatalist Discourse and Women's Autonomy' (2001) 26 *Signs: Journal of Women in Culture & Society* 735, 735.

[25] Marge Piercy, 'Foreword' in Ellen Messer and Kathryn E May, *Back Rooms: Voices from the Illegal Abortion Era* (Prometheus Books, 1994).

Critically, the 1967 Act is a living instrument. The language of the 1960s does not define the meaning of abortion provision today. While the Act is strict on its face and affords women no right to demand an abortion, in practice doctors interpret the Act liberally, and beyond what reformers had intended. And that attitudinal shift is significant. In this sense, the symbolic effect of the Abortion Act 1967 lies in the everyday acceptance that a woman's identity *can* be separate from her reproductivity. The impact of the 1967 Act reaches beyond the creation of a space where abortion can be represented as both 'lawful' and 'legitimate', to a more critical transformation of the politics of women's identities.

Despite a recent campaign, supported by the BMA, the Royal College of Gynaecologists and the Royal College of Midwives, to move abortion regulation out of the criminal domain entirely,[26] it would seem that a wide-scale review of the Abortion Act 1967 in terms of reducing access to abortion, looks unlikely. In large measure, the 1967 Act at some level is working well, with an abortion rate that corresponds with other Western countries, extremely low mortality rates, and with the majority of terminations taking place early in pregnancy. However, akin to any physical landmark, the Abortion Act 1967 is fragile, incomplete, and valued in conflicting ways and as such, is often contested. It remains a deeply contested and politicised landmark, but one without which our biographies as women would look very different indeed. It stands to remind us of an unfinished journey – an 'unfinished revolution'. We need to be prepared to defend and maintain its very existence, as well as to fight for others to enjoy the same basic liberties the 1967 Act provides.

## Further Reading


- Barbara Brookes, *Abortion in England 1900–1967* (Routledge, 1990).
- Kate Gleeson, 'Persuading Parliament: Abortion Law reform in the UK' (2007) 22 *Australasian Parliamentary Review* 23–42.
- Keith Hindell and Madeleine Simms, *Abortion Law Reformed* (Peter Owen, 1971).
- Sheila McGuinness, 'A guerrilla strategy for a pro-life England' (2015) 7 *Law, Innovation and Technology* 283–314.
- Sally Sheldon, *Beyond Control, Medical Power and Abortion Law* (Pluto Press, 1997).


[26] See Sally Sheldon, 'The Decriminalisation of Abortion: An Argument for Modernisation' (2016) 36(2) *Oxford Journal of Legal Studies* 334 and Williams, n 16 above.

# 39

# National Health Service (Family Planning) Act 1967

LEONORA ONARAN

The National Health Service (Family Planning) Act 1967 secured the National Health Service (NHS) provision of family planning services. It had a transformative effect on the lives of many women as, for the first time, they were able to obtain contraceptive advice and services freely on the NHS, regardless of their marital status, and whether for social or medical reasons.

## I. Context

The Family Planning Act 1967 had a long and troubled gestation. Birth control was considered by many to be a controversial and taboo subject. For much of its history it has been caught between (sometimes) overlapping – but distinct – motivations and arguments relating to equality, the alleviation of poverty, eugenics, religion and morality. Throughout history, in every corner of the world, the absence of accessible, affordable contraceptive services has meant that women in their childbearing years, particularly those from lower socio-economic groups, have faced often insurmountable difficulties in attempting to limit the size of their families. Moreover, the consequences of a population that was growing without any control had wide-ranging consequences for all, as campaigners emphasised:

> The social and personal evils emanating from the population explosion are frightening: chronic over-crowding in an already difficult housing situation: illegal abortion: enormous burdens upon the social security services imposed by the problem families and unwanted children, leading to public hostility to the concept of social security itself; the enhanced crimogenic risk; marital discord, anxiety, frigidity and ill-health; the battered baby syndrome; the evils are innumerable.[1]

For a good century before the Act there had been attempts to educate the wider population about steps that could be taken to avoid unwanted pregnancies. In 1877, Charles Bradlaugh – a London publisher and founder of the Malthusian League, a group whose

[1] Alec Samuels, 'The National Health Service (Family Planning) Act 1967' (1967) 7(4) *Medicine, Science and the Law* 177–80.

mission was to educate the public about population limitation – and Annie Besant, the estranged wife of a Lincolnshire vicar, were prosecuted for obscene libel for distributing an illustrated pamphlet, 'Fruits of Philosophy', which outlined and recommended certain checks on the increase of population.[2] While the jury found the publication to be obscene, they found the defendants not guilty, on the basis that their motives in publishing it were not corrupt.[3] The 'lewd, filthy book'[4] in question had been written in 1832 by an American physician, Charles Knowlton, who himself had been fined and imprisoned in the USA for distributing such information. The publicity surrounding Bradlaugh and Besant's prosecution did, however, achieve the wider dissemination of information about various artificial methods to prevent pregnancy.[5] Besant's conviction was later quashed on a technicality,[6] though she did not escape unscathed; she subsequently lost custody of her seven-year-old daughter for the dual reasons of 'publication of the obscene book and the refusal of religious instruction to the child'.

By the early 1920s, there were a number of birth control societies operating clinics throughout England under the slogan 'children by choice, not chance'.[7] The first clinic was opened by Marie Stopes in 1921. Stopes also published a number of books on birth control including the influential *Married Love* in 1918. However, in 1924 she too fell foul of libel law when she lost her action against Dr HG Sutherland and his publishers, who had criticised her 'monstrous campaign of birth control' in a book called *Birth Control: A Statement of Christian Doctrine Against the Neo-Malthusians*.[8]

In February 1926, Ernest Thurtle, Labour MP for East London, presented a 10-minute Bill, the Local Authorities (Birth Control) Enabling Bill, to the House of Commons. Its aim was to 'authorise local authorities to incur expenditure, when deemed expedient, in conveying birth control knowledge to married women who desire it'.[9] Thurtle was apparently driven by a desire to 'remove one of the disabilities of poverty'. He was acutely aware that affluent women were already able to access such information, as evidenced by the fact that the birth rate in Westminster at that time was 11.2 per 1000, whereas in Shoreditch, a deprived area within Thurtle's constituency, it was 25 per 1000. For Thurtle, the statistics demonstrated that those with limited resources, who lived in the most unsuitable conditions in which to raise children, were often the most fecund. However, he did not see these children as inferior stock, as many did:

> It is said we are breeding from the wrong stock. I am not prepared to accept that. There is no reason to assume that the children of the working classes are one whit inferior, either physically or mentally, to the children of the better-off classes. What is true is that as soon as they come into life they never get anything like equality of opportunity with the other classes.[10]

[2] *R v Bradlaugh (Charles) and Besant (Annie)* (1877) 2 QBD 569.

[3] *Re Besant* (1878) 11 Ch D 508, 509.

[4] *Charles Bradlaugh and Annie Besant v The Queen* (1878) 3 QBD 607 (CA).

[5] See more detail on the increase in sales of the pamphlet in *R (on the application of Smeaton) v Secretary of State for Health* [2002] EWHC 610 (Admin) [178].

[6] See n 4 above.

[7] Family Planning Association, *A history of family planning services factsheet* (FPA, October 2011): www.fpa.org.uk/sites/default/files/a-history-of-family_planning-services-october-2011.pdf.

[8] *Sutherland v Stopes* [1924] All ER 19.

[9] HC Deb, 9 February 1926, vol 191 cols 849–857, 849.

[10] ibid col 850.

And his concern for the women who had to bear the children was in marked contrast to that of those who argued against birth control:

> These are days of sex equality, and, if the House is honest, it must realise some implications of that sex equality. I submit that one of them is that a woman is entitled so far as practicable to decide what the size of her family should be. There are thousands, hundreds of thousands, of working-class women in this country to-day who have not the necessary knowledge. As a consequence, many of them have very much larger families than they want to have. Many of them spend weary years during their child-bearing period, worrying about the possibility of another child coming to add to their burdens. As a consequence of these anxieties, they are frequently thrown into the aims of quacks and charlatans of all kinds, and in their desperation they frequently resort to all kinds of hazardous and dangerous expedients, with very serious consequences to themselves. I submit that it is time a helping hand was held out to these women and that the book of knowledge was made open to them.[11]

Although Thurtle's Bill merely sought statutory permission for local authorities to be allowed to offer contraceptive advice – it did not suggest they should be compelled to do so – it was defeated by 167 votes to 81 after James Barr, a Presbyterian minister and the MP for Motherwell, Scotland, led an impassioned debate against the introduction of 'a national policy of birth control and propaganda'.[12]

Despite this setback, a significant breakthrough occurred two months later, when former Lord Chancellor Lord Buckmaster, who was Vice-President of the Malthusian League, presented a House of Lords motion in which he requested that the Government consider allowing all local authority welfare centres to offer married women, particularly those who were the 'poorest … most ignorant … destitute … shiftless, hopeless'[13] women, information about family limitation. The resolution narrowly passed, and Britain's parliament became the first 'to define responsible parenthood as a legitimate and essential concern of public service'.[14]

In 1930, the various family planning organisations combined to form the National Birth Control Council. The same year the Lambeth Conference of the Church of England, while promoting complete abstinence as 'the primary and obvious method' for limiting parenthood, acknowledged that there might morally sound reasons for using an alternative methods 'provided this is done in light of Christian principles'.[15] 1937 saw more progress when disquiet about increases in maternal mortality levels resulted in further guidance to local authorities to offer family planning advice to married women whose health would be endangered by further pregnancies. This was often facilitated by the Family Planning Association – now the FPA – which was founded in 1939.[16]

However, despite these incremental parliamentary advances, as late as 1941 judges in the family courts continued to plead ignorance about birth control use. In *Firth v Firth*

[11] ibid cols 852–853.

[12] ibid col 854.

[13] HL Deb, 28 April 1926, vol 63 col 997.

[14] HC Deb, 17 February 1967, vol 741 cols 935–1020, 935 (Edwin Brooks MP).

[15] Anglican Communication Office, *The Lambeth Conference: Resolutions Archive from 1930*, Resolution 15: The Life and Witness of the Christian Community – Marriage and Sex (Anglican Consultative Council, 2005): http://www.anglicancommunion.org/media/127734/1930.pdf.

[16] FPA, n 7 above.

unreported,[17] Langton J refused to agree with counsel for the wife that it was 'common knowledge that young people, for a period … after their marriage, had intercourse only with the intervention of contraceptives'.[18] Judicial scrutiny of such matters continued in *Cowen v Cowen*,[19] when a wife succeeded in getting her marriage dissolved as a consequence of her husband's refusal to carry out his conjugal duties without either using condoms or by practising coitus interruptus. The Court of Appeal found that Mr Cowen's 12-year refusal to have sex without birth control meant that that the marriage had never been truly consummated and, accordingly, could be annulled.[20]

*Cowen* was quickly followed by *Baxter v Baxter*.[21] Mr Baxter petitioned for annulment of his 10-year marriage. The Court heard that Mrs Baxter wished to remain childless and so, throughout the marriage, she refused to have sexual relations unless her husband wore a condom. While sympathetic to his claim – unlike the lower courts, the House of Lords did not see his willingness to comply with his wife's request as acquiescence in the decision not to procreate but rather as a pragmatic alternative to not having any marital sex – the Lords unanimously held that the marriage had been fully consummated. *Cowen*, which had precipitated Mr Baxter's and others' similar applications, was no longer considered good law.

Not surprisingly, the *Baxter* decision aroused a lot of interest throughout the establishment and amongst the general public. Questions about the purpose of marriage, and the appropriate legal response to any failure to fulfil that purpose, were widely debated.[22] Shortly after, a Royal Commission on Population concluded that 'Control by men and women over the numbers of their children is one of the first conditions of their own and the community's welfare … public policy should assume, and seek to encourage, the spread of voluntary parenthood'.[23] The Commission recommended the lifting of all restrictions on public services offering contraceptive advice to married women. However, family planning and contraception services were not included within the original remit of the National Health Service when it was established in 1948.

## II. The Landmark

The arrival of the 1960s saw attitudes towards sex change radically. In a Britain that was, in the words of Edwin Brooks MP, 'profligate with erotic titillation, yet curiously grudging with sexual instruction',[24] it became increasingly uncommon for women to retain their virginity until the wedding night. In order to safely enjoy sexual liberation, access to affordable contraception was needed. In 1961 the contraceptive pill was made available on the NHS, but only on prescription to married women. It was later offered, again on prescription, to engaged women and young women with irregular or painful periods. It was also

[17] *Firth v Firth*, 25 June 1941, unreported, cited in *Baxter v Baxter* [1948] AC 274, 279.
[18] As described in *Baxter v Baxter* [1948] AC 274, 278.
[19] *Cowen v Cowen* [1946] P 86, [1945] 2 All ER 197.
[20] Nullity retained its roots in ecclesiastical law, unlike divorce.
[21] See n 17 above.
[22] LCB Gower, '*Baxter v Baxter* in Perspective' (1947) 11(2) *Modern Law Review* 176.
[23] Royal Commission on Population (Cmnd 7695, 1945) [427], [434] and [657].
[24] n 14 above, col 946.

possible to purchase condoms and other contraceptive devices via mail order, from barber's shops, pharmacies, vending machines in public conveniences, and from specialist clinics – for married women – run by the Family Planning Association and Marie Stopes. The first contraception service for unmarried women was opened in 1960 by Helen Brook in a Marie Stopes Clinic in East London. She went on to found the Brook Advisory Centre for Young People in 1963. Nonetheless, increased rates of illegitimacy and illegal abortions were amongst the unwanted consequences of the sexual revolution.[25]

There was also growing recognition that many young women wanted to avoid the 'treadmill of motherhood'.[26] In November 1966, the Ken Loach play 'Cathy Come Home' had brought into the nation's homes glimpses of the difficult reality of life on the breadline for many families with children.[27] Population growth in some cities was outstripping the availability of decent affordable housing, and it was people like Cathy, Reg and their children – living in the 'ghettoes of the under-privileged'[28] – who were bearing the brunt. Some measures were put in place to attempt to alleviate the situation. In February 1966, the Minister for Health, Richard Crossman, sent all local health authorities a circular requiring them to urgently put in place services offering free contraceptive advice and treatment for women whose wellbeing would be put at risk by further pregnancies.

However, many felt the Government was being too slow to act on the issue. In the end, the 1967 Act – like its unofficial companion the **Abortion Act 1967** – was introduced as a Private Member's Bill. The Bill, introduced by Edwin Brooks, provided for a universal birth control service, available to all, regardless of marital status or whether family planning was required for social or medical reasons:

> The problems are deep-seated and inter-related, but no one today can surely doubt that the characteristically very large families are both a symptom and a cause of social privation. It is amongst these families that the hoary distinction between medical and social need is so futile.[29]

It quickly garnered cross-party support. The MPs recognised that it was time to give people better support in managing their fertility and, in turn, hoped that the difficulties arising in their constituencies would improve as a result. There was also acknowledgment by some that in 'striking a blow to relieve women of uncontrolled maternity or the tyranny of their own fertility which has bound women ever since life began',[30] the Act would have a significant impact on the lives of women.

> I must say quite clearly that my sympathy is all with the women … Those hon Members who are not too far removed from childhood will remember the nursery rhyme which begins, 'There was an old woman who lived in a shoe, She had so many children she didn't know what to do' That puts the problem very well. The mother with too many children is old before her time. She becomes prematurely aged. Generally, she lives in overcrowded and very difficult circumstances. She brings up her enormous family on a shoe-string. She often gives up the unequal struggle and

[25] As per the House of Lords debate on the National Health Service Act 1967, 68,000 illegitimate children were born in England and Wales in 1965.

[26] n 14 above, col 939 (Brooks MP).

[27] See further **Housing (Homeless Persons) Act 1977**.

[28] n 14 above, 938 (Brooks MP).

[29] ibid cols 938–939.

[30] n 14 above, col 983 (Renee Short MP).

> subsides in a morass of apathy and carelessness because she is so disheartened. This is the situation which we want to change.[31]

The Act received its Royal Assent on 28 June 1967.[32]

## III. What Happened Next

Without doubt, the National Health Service (Family Planning) Act 1967

> swept away … the remaining institutional restraints on the provision of contraception for social rather than purely medical reasons and the remaining distinction between the provision under the NHS of contraceptive to the married and unmarried.[33]

However, the provisions of the Act were permissive rather than mandatory. Local authorities were not *obliged* to provide such facilities. Nevertheless, the powers were widely taken up, often through agencies such as the Family Planning Association. During the 1970s, these powers increased to include free vasectomies (National Health Service (Family Planning) Amendment Act 1972), the provision of all forms of birth control free of charge on the NHS irrespective of age or marital status (National Health Service Reorganisation Act 1973) and the incorporation of general practitioners within the NHS family planning services.

However, social ambivalence at the role played by contraception in encouraging youthful promiscuity continued into the 1980s. Victoria Gillick's (ultimately unsuccessful) efforts to prevent doctors from prescribing contraception to under-16s garnered the support of 250–500,000 members of the public and over 200 MPs.[34] Fifty years after the enactment of the Act, there is a growing concern that 'women's hard-won access to contraception is under threat'.[35] The Advisory Group on Contraception, reporting in 2017, found that over a third of councils had closed, or planned to close, services delivering contraceptive care since 2015.[36] At the same time, a YouGov survey commissioned by the FPA found that many women are struggling to access contraception.[37]

## IV. Significance

Explaining her motivation for her ground-breaking work and clinics, Helen Brook commented that 'I felt that, until women were free of the fear of unwanted pregnancy, they would not be able to take up the equal opportunity of work'.[38] Today family planning and the

[31] ibid col 985.

[32] A similar provision came into force in Scotland via section 15 Health Services and Public Health Act 1968.

[33] Sir James Munby, President of the Family Law Division, 'Marriage from the 18th to 21st Century', *The Incorporated Council of Law Reporting Annual Lecture*, 25 April 2013.

[34] ***Gillick v West Norfolk and Wisbech Area Health Authority* (1986)**.

[35] Jayne Kavanagh, Medical Director for the Campaign for Contraception quoted in '35,000 people demand government action to prevent contraception crisis in the UK' (FPA press release, 2 November 2017).

[36] Advisory Group on Contraception, *Cuts, Closures and Contraception: An audit of local contraceptive services in England* (November 2017) 1.

[37] FPA press release, n 35 above.

[38] Ann Furedi, 'Obituary: Helen Brook', *The Independent*, 8 October 1997.

use of contraception in England and Wales are widespread. In 2015–2016, over 1.2 million individuals contacted dedicated sexual and reproductive health services for reasons relating to contraception.[39] The introduction of a universal family planning service in the 1967 Act helped women gain greater control over their fertility. With good family planning provision, it was no longer an automatic assumption that women would marry, become pregnant, and remain at home to bring up children, whilst husbands took on the role of sole breadwinner. Women could now plan their futures with more certainty and make choices about whether to remain in education, climb the corporate ladder and when to start a family. This has had positive benefits not only for women, but also for society as a whole.

## Further Reading

- Clare Debenham, *Birth Control and the Rights of Women: Post-suffrage Feminism in the Early Twentieth Century* (IB Tauris, 2014).
- Gillian Douglas, *Law, Fertility and Reproduction* (Sweet & Maxwell, 1991).
- Emily Jackson, *Regulating Reproduction: Law, Technology and Autonomy* (Hart Publishing, 2001).

[39] NHS Digital Statistics on Sexual and Reproductive Health Services England 2015/16 (19 October 2016).

# 40

# Dagenham Car Plant Strike, 1968

DAWN WATKINS

The Dagenham car plant strike involved 187 women who were employed as sewing machinists by the Ford Motor Company in Dagenham, Essex. Ford had carried out an extensive review of its wages structure, under which both male and female job roles were allocated a grade. The women argued that the Grade B that had been allocated to their role failed to take into account the level of skill involved in their work, and that they should be allocated Grade C, which was more in line with the grade allocated to men for work involving similar levels of skill.

Because they voiced their complaints only after the new structure had been formally agreed between Ford and their Union representatives, the women were required to follow a formal grievance procedure in order to seek redress. Sensing that this would be futile, the women took strike action. The strike lasted for three weeks and it resulted in the closure of the entire plant until a settlement was reached.

The women achieved a pay rise and although this was not yet equal to the pay assigned to male workers, the strike is widely considered to represent an important step towards the introduction of the Equal Pay Act 1970, a statute designed 'to prevent discrimination, as regards terms and conditions of employment, between men and women'. The strike has since been dramatised in the film *Made in Dagenham* in 2010 and *Made in Dagenham the Musical* in 2014.

## I. Context

Examples of equal pay claims date back to the 1830s[1] and as far back as 1888 the Trades Union Congress (TUC) adopted a motion put forward by Clementina Black, a prominent feminist campaigner and honorary secretary of the Women's Trade Union League, that 'in trades where women do the same work as men they shall receive the same wages'.[2] However, the motion was never acted upon and prior to the First World War, feminists such as Millicent Fawcett, President of the National Union of Women's Suffrage Societies, had even argued *against* trade unions on this point, suggesting instead that the appropriate focus for

[1] Mary Davis, *An Historical Introduction to the Campaign for Equal Pay* (Trades Unions Congress, Winning Equal Pay: the value of women's work, no date): www.unionhistory.info/equalpay/roaddisplay.php?irn=820.

[2] TUC Equal Pay Resolution, 1888.

reform was on securing equal job opportunities and training for women, and not equal pay. It was suggested that by insisting on equal pay, trade unions could in fact be operating to limit women's job opportunities; an outcome that suited members of the male-dominated trade unions who feared that the entry of women into more highly-skilled and traditionally male forms of labour could threaten men's job security.[3] After the First World War, however, Fawcett changed her position and urged that 'the best chance of women preserving … the industrial freedom which the war has brought them lies in the earnestness and sincerity with which industrial women maintain the principle "equal pay for equal work"'.[4]

It was during this same initial post-war period that the supposed first ever 'Equal Pay strike' in England occurred,[5] when in August 1918 women tramway and bus workers in London and other towns and cities went on strike in response to being offered a war bonus of 20 shillings per week, as compared to the 25 shillings per week offered to their male counterparts.[6] The women were successful, but a government inquiry, prompted by the strike, concluded that no action should be taken concerning the issue of equal pay more generally.[7] During the inter-war years, many trade unions stopped demanding equal pay, with some even pursuing policies that exaggerated pay inequality. But during the Second World War, when women had, through necessity, taken on more highly-skilled and traditionally 'male' work but for much lower pay, demands for equal pay became an increasingly prominent political issue. There were instances of equal pay disputes occurring in the munitions and engineering industries during this time.[8]

Related to this, concerns were expressed regarding the unequal rates of compensation that were allocated to women under wartime legislation. For example, a woman civilian was entitled to less compensation for injury arising from 'war operations' than a man, under the terms of the Personal Injuries (Emergency Provisions) Act 1939. This prompted the formation of a pressure group called the Equal Pay Campaign Committee, chaired by Conservative MP, Mavis Tate. In what has been described as 'one of the greatest victories of the feminist movement in World War II',[9] this group successfully persuaded the Government to change its policy on the issue in 1943. The group then began to focus its activities on securing equal pay, but its ambitions were stunted by Prime Minister Winston Churchill's announcement in May 1944 that there was to be a Royal Commission, tasked with investigating and reporting on the relationship between the remuneration of men and women and 'to consider the social, economic and financial implications' of introducing equal pay. In its lengthy report issued in October 1946, the Commission acknowledged the apparent injustice of unequal pay, but justified it as necessary for economic reasons. It also drew on evidence concerning women's lack of physical strength and their apparent

[3] James P Henderson, 'Equal Pay vs Equal Job Opportunity for Women: The Debate in Great Britain from 1891 to 1923' (1992) 19 *International Journal of Social Economics* 296, 298.

[4] Millicent G Fawcett, 'Equal Pay for Equal Work' (1918) 28 *The Economic Journal* 1.

[5] Davis, n 1 above. Earlier strikes such as the Match-worker Strike in 1888 had focused on conditions rather than wages.

[6] 'Traffic Strike Spreading', *The Times*, 20 August 1918, 7.

[7] *Report of the War Cabinet Committee on Women in Industry* (Cmd 135, 1919).

[8] Davis, n 1 above.

[9] Harold Smith, 'The Problem of Equal Pay for Equal Work in Great Britain during World War II' (1981) 53 *Journal of Modern History* 663.

inability to deal with 'surprise situations'. These points were strongly disputed by three of the Commission's female members, Anne Loughlin (former chair of the General Council of the TUC), Janet Vaughan (later Principal of Somerville College, University of Oxford) and Lucy Frances (Nancy) Nettlefold (a company director, and one of the four Oxbridge women who challenged the Law Society's refusal to permit them to sit their examinations in what became known as *Bebb v The Law Society*).[10] In a memorandum of dissent included within the report, they questioned the credibility of some of the evidence the Commission had received, and challenged the view that 'it is necessary to make a choice between "exact justice" and "oiling the wheels of economic progress"'.[11]

By the mid-1950s, the principle of equal pay had been endorsed by each of the political parties, as well as the TUC, and conditions for women working in the public sector began gradually to improve. However, attempts to bring about the general implementation of the principle continued to stall. For example, amidst fears that 'the British economy would collapse if women obtained pay parity with men',[12] a Private Member's Bill introduced in 1954 by Labour MP Douglas Houghton, 'to establish the principle of equal pay' failed to progress past a second reading in the House of Commons. Nevertheless, the trade unions persisted and when the Labour Government came into power in 1964, it had committed to introducing equal pay legislation in its manifesto.[13] Added pressure for reform came from the new Government's desire to join the European Economic Community (EEC), established under the Treaty of Rome in 1958. Under Article 119 of this treaty, all Member States would be required to 'ensure and subsequently maintain the application of the principle that men and women should receive equal pay for equal work'. Nevertheless, by the time that the dispute arose at Dagenham in 1968 there had been no practical implementation of the Government's commitment and it was still accepted practice for employers to discriminate openly between men and women when allocating rates of pay.

## II. The Landmark

At the time of the strike, Ford employed over 30,000 workers at its two main UK plants in Dagenham, Essex and Halewood, Merseyside. Of these, just 900 were women and approximately 450 of them were involved in the cutting and sewing of seat covers and internal facia pads for vehicles. This was skilled work, and the sewing machinists had to pass a stringent test before they were taken on. They argued that Ford had failed to recognise this when grading the role at level B. In addition, they pointed out that wherever a man was required to take a test prior to employment, then his post was automatically given a higher grade of C or above.

Prior to the company undertaking its wages review, all women workers at Ford had been employed at a set grade, regardless of their role. This was around 80 per cent of the rate paid to men. Under the new grading system, the pay differential remained but was set

[10] *Bebb v Law Society* [1914] 1 Ch 286. See further **Women's Legal Landmarks: An Introduction**.
[11] *Report of the Royal Commission on Equal Pay* (Cmd 6937, 1944–1946) 187–93.
[12] Davis, n 1 above.
[13] Steven Fielding, *The Labour Governments 1964–1970, Volume 1* (Manchester University Press, 2003) 127.

at 85 per cent, as demonstrated in the table below.[14] Looking at this table today, it seems remarkable that the women were *not* complaining about this very obvious injustice at the onset of the strike. However, Ford considered this lower rate to be justified on a number of grounds, including the fact that women were prevented by legislation from working night shifts or weekend overtime. Ford also emphasised that its approach was in line with industry standards.[15]

| *Grade* | *Standard hourly rate* *Men* | *Women* | *Range of service increments (per hour)* |
|---|---|---|---|
| A ... ... | 7s. 6½d. | 6s. 8½d. | 2d.—1s. 0d. (maximum payable after 4 years' service) |
| B ... ... | 8s. 9½d. | 7s. 5½d. | |
| C ... ... | 9s. 3½d. | 7s. 10½d. | |
| D ... ... | 9s. 9½d. | No jobs in D. or E. | |
| E ... ... | 10s. 9½d. | | |

There were some 20 different trade unions at Ford at the time and the majority of the sewing machinists at Dagenham were members of the National Union of Vehicle Builders (NUVB). The unions had been consulted concerning the company's wage restructure, and had formally agreed it in July 1967. However the sewing machinists disputed the terms of the agreement, prompting the NUVB to complain to Ford that they should have been allocated a higher grade. Despite repeated discussions, Ford refused to make any change to the grading and, since they lacked any faith in the company's internal grievance procedures, the women called a one-day strike on 29 May 1968, followed by a full strike on 7 June. Subsequently the sewing machinists at Ford's Halewood plant also went on strike in support of their Dagenham co-workers. The NUVB declared the strike official on 13 June, as did the Amalgamated Union of Engineering and Foundry Workers (AEF), and it was only at this stage that the argument broadened into one of equal pay. The AEF pressed this issue in particular, emphasising that the women were receiving just 85 per cent of the equivalent rate for men. The strike lasted for three weeks, attracting wide media attention and resulting in thousands of Ford's employees being laid off.[16]

In April 1968, Barbara Castle MP had been appointed as the Secretary of State for Employment and Productivity. Initially she had seemed to continue the trend of supporting equal pay in principle, but showed reluctance to enforce it in practice. However, because of its scale and significance, Castle intervened personally in the Dagenham strike and in the forthcoming months she came to play a significant role in pressing for equal pay legislation.[17] On 28 June Castle chaired a meeting between representatives of Ford and the unions, as well as many of the women on strike. A settlement was reached and the women returned to work on 1 July. It is notable that under the terms of this settlement, the striking women's roles were not regraded and they were *not* awarded equal pay. Rather they remained on Grade B and received a pay increase that resulted in them receiving 92 per cent of the equivalent rate for men.

[14] Extracted from the *Report of a Court Inquiry under Sir Jack Scamp into a dispute concerning sewing machinists employed by Ford Motor Company Limited* (Cmnd 3749, August 1968) [14].

[15] Henry Friedman and Sander Meredeen, *The Dynamics of Industrial Conflict: Lessons from Ford* (Croom Helm, 1980) 88.

[16] '9,000 Ford workers now laid off because of strike', *The Guardian*, 26 June 1968.

[17] Fielding, n 13 above, 127–35.

# III. What Happened Next

The strike acted as a much-needed catalyst for action on the issue of equal pay. Later in 1968 the TUC formally agreed to support all equal pay strikes, and in 1969 a new pressure group called the National Joint Action Campaign Committee for Women's Equal Rights organised a high-profile march through London, demanding immediate action.[18] Given the potential for further unrest, Castle was able to successfully persuade her fellow government ministers that legislation was now a necessity[19] and a Bill 'to establish the principle of equal pay' was introduced into Parliament in December 1969.

In its initial form, the Bill required that equal pay 'for equal work and work of equal value' be introduced within 12 months of the passing of the legislation, and it envisaged that this would be achieved through collective agreements made between employers and employees, or via external regulation.[20] However, these terms were drastically amended and rather than securing equal pay for work of equal value, the complex terms of the Equal Pay Act 1970 placed a more limited obligation on employers to 'give equal treatment as regards terms and conditions of employment to men and to women' where they were employed in 'like work' or in work that has been rated by the employer as 'equivalent'. In addition, rather than placing this obligation collectively on employees and employers, it placed the responsibility of securing equal treatment on the individual employee (male or female) to bring a claim against their employer to an industrial tribunal. Continuing the pattern of stalling activity on this issue, the Equal Pay Act 1970 did not come into force until December 1975 and this time-lag meant that employers had time to re-classify jobs and to maintain the pay differential between men and women, albeit now in a more covert way.[21] It was some years later, in 1983, that the Equal Pay Act 1970 was amended to include work of 'equal value' in line with changes made to European Law.

# IV. Significance

Whilst it did not immediately achieve equal pay for Ford's sewing machinists, the Dagenham car plant strike is nevertheless a significant landmark for women. Coming just prior to the onset of the women's movement, it stands out as an early example of women organising themselves separately from male workers and leading a highly-effective campaign. Notable too is the fact that these were working-class women. As Huw Benyon describes, they were 'solid middle-aged women with round faces and brown coats with small fur-trimmed collars. Slight girls with short cropped hair, short green leather coats, lace-up shoes and small square handbags. Not your Chelsea girls'.[22]

As well as improving the women's immediate circumstances, the strike acted as a catalyst for wider, positive change, especially for women working in industry. Demands for equal pay had been voiced many years before but attempts to bring about practical change were

[18] '1,000 women march for equal pay', *The Times*, 19 May 1969, 2.
[19] Fielding, n 13 above, 131.
[20] Bill to establish the Principle of Equal pay (Equal Pay) 1968–69, Paper No 141.
[21] **Susan Atkins and Brenda Hoggett, *Women and the Law*** (Basil Blackwell, 1984) 21.
[22] Huw Benyon, *Working for Ford* (2nd edn, Penguin Books, 1984) 178.

continually stalled, even when the notion of equal pay had been agreed in principle. This highly-publicised action by the Ford sewing-machinists, and the further unrest that ensued, meant that the issue of equal pay was brought with some sense of urgency to the attention of government – prompting Parliament to legislate.

Of course, we also know that the implementation of the legislation was stalled for a further five years and, perhaps more importantly, we know that the Equal Pay Act 1970 (now incorporated into the Equality Act 2010) did not achieve the long-awaited equal pay for women. There has continued to be inequality between men and women's wages, with recent figures released by the Office for National Statistics indicating that the gender pay gap for all employees (both full-time and part-time) is currently 18.1 per cent.[23] In light of this the Fawcett Society maintains that 'the difference in pay between men and women remains the clearest and most dramatic example of inequality for women'.[24]

So can we *still* claim this as a landmark? Yes. The legislation sets out the principle that men and women should be paid equally; something that had proved impossible to achieve throughout the decades that preceded it. But there is clearly more to be done. In the Equality Act 2010, a provision was added that requires all employers (both public and private sector) with 250 or more employees to publish information to show the differences in the pay between their male and female employees. This requirement for gender pay-gap reporting came into effect in April 2017 and it is a welcome development, since it will encourage employers to take responsibility for implementing and monitoring equal pay among their workforce; rather than placing the onus on individual employees to take action.[25]

For Ford's sewing machinists, they finally achieved a successful outcome for their original complaint, when their roles were regraded to Grade C in 1984, following further strike action.[26]

## Further Reading

- Huw Benyon, *Working for Ford* (2nd edn, Penguin Books, 1984).
- Steven Fielding, *The Labour Governments 1964–1970, Volume 1* (Manchester University Press, 2003).
- Henry Friedman and Sander Meredeen, *The Dynamics of Industrial Conflict: Lessons From Ford* (Croom Helm, 1980).

[23] See Office for National Statistics (online), 'The gender pay gap – what is it and what affects it?', 26 October 2016: https://www.ons.gov.uk/employmentandlabourmarket/peopleinwork/earningsandworkinghours/articles/thegenderpaygapwhatisitandwhataffectsit/2016-10-26.

[24] See Fawcett Society, 'Close the Gender Pay Gap': www.fawcettsociety.org.uk/policy-research/the-gender-pay-gap/. The Fawcett Society is a charity campaigning for gender equality and women's rights; named in honour of Millicent Fawcett (1849–1929).

[25] The Equality Act 2010 (Gender Pay Gap Information) Regulations 2017.

[26] Sabby Sagall and Sheila McGregor, 'When History was Made in Dagenham' (October 2010) *Socialist Review* 351.

# 41

# First Woman Professor of Law in the UK, Claire Palley, 1970

FIONA COWNIE

In 1970, Claire Palley became the first woman to become a Professor of Law in any university in the United Kingdom when she was appointed to a Chair in Public Law at Queen's University Belfast. Her academic career had begun in South Africa and subsequently continued in Southern Rhodesia, but the political views held by Claire Palley and her husband, as strong opponents of Apartheid and white minority rule, led to social ostracisation, which also affected the lives of their sons. For that reason the Palleys decided to educate their children in the UK. Claire Palley took up a lectureship at Queen's in 1966. She was promoted to Reader the following year and to a Chair in 1970.

## I. Life

Claire Palley was born in South Africa in 1931 and grew up in Durban. She had one younger sister, Anne, who as Anne Routier became a Nationalist MP in South Africa. Educated at Durban Girls' College, she graduated from the University of Cape Town with a BA and an LLB. She became a lecturer at Cape Town in 1953, a post she held until she and her husband, Ahrn Palley, left South Africa in 1956 because of their opposition to Apartheid policy. They settled in the then Federation of Rhodesia and Nyasaland, where Ahrn Palley was Rhodesia's only Independent MP from 1962 to 1970, opposing the white led Rhodesian Government. The couple had five sons. Before resuming her career as an academic, Claire Palley gained her PhD from the University of London, which was published in 1966 by Oxford University Press as *The Constitutional History and Law of Southern Rhodesia 1888 to 1964*. That same year, she moved to Belfast to take up a lectureship in law, gaining rapid promotion and becoming a professor in 1970.

Claire Palley specialised in constitutional law and during her time in Belfast, in addition to her academic writing, she wrote numerous articles in *The Times* about the 'Troubles', criticising the actions of the British Government, and also appeared regularly on BBC radio.[1] In 1973, she moved to the University of Kent, and shortly thereafter became Master of Darwin College there, a post she held for eight years. During this time she acted as

[1] Interview with Claire Palley (CP Interview) November 2013, on file with the author.

an adviser to the African National Congress (ANC) in the talks which led in 1979 to the Lancaster House Agreement, which in turn led to the revocation of Rhodesia's Unilateral Declaration of Independence and paved the way for the birth of the state of Zimbabwe.

In 1984 Claire Palley became Principal of St Anne's College, Oxford, a post she held until 1991. From 1994 to 1998 she was the UK's member on the United Nations Sub-Commission on Prevention of Discrimination and Protection of Minorities, and was awarded an OBE in 1997 for services to human rights. She was also Constitutional Adviser to the Government of Cyprus from 1980–94 and was re-appointed in 1999, finally retiring in 2004. Her well-received monograph, *An international relations debacle: the UN Secretary-General's mission of good offices in Cyprus, 1999–2004*, was published by Hart Publishing in 2005.

## II. Context

Claire Palley was appointed to her Chair at a time when universities still benefited from a favourable funding regime which allowed them to appoint additional staff. At Queen's University Belfast, 13 new professors were appointed during the quinquennium 1968–73.[2] Claire Palley was one of these. Yet across the sector the number of women academics in universities remained stubbornly low and they continued to obtain promotion much less frequently than men.[3] The dominant position of men in universities at the time is clearly reflected in contemporaneous analyses of higher education. Women are hardly mentioned at all in Halsey and Trow's seminal work on academic life, *The British Academics*, published in 1971.[4] In *Dons and Students: British universities today*, published in 1973, the author, an academic publisher, aims 'to explain the academic world to a larger circle'.[5] In order to do this, he invents the University of Bolderdale, which is populated by numerous academics – all of them men except for three, all of whom are married to male dons. Thus it is no surprise that when Claire Palley was appointed at Queen's, of the 24 academics in the Law School, only three others were women.[6]

In relation to Claire Palley's own appointment, Professor William Twining, a member of the panel which appointed her, recalls that she applied for a Chair which was widely advertised and attracted a number of candidates, from Queen's and elsewhere. 'She was certainly not appointed because she was a woman. She was very strong on research. We didn't think we were making history, we just thought it was the right thing to do', he said in retrospect. 'The panel was more concerned about whether she was Protestant or Catholic. Which it turned out didn't apply in her case because she was Jewish'.[7] Twining also remembers that when the question of whether a woman could be a law professor was raised outside the panel, members of the panel pointed to **Frances Moran**, who had been a law professor at Trinity College, Dublin from 1934 to 1963.

[2] Brian M Walker and Alf McCreary, *Degrees of Excellence: The Story of Queen's, Belfast, 1845–1995* (Institute of Irish Studies, 1994) 138.

[3] Margherita Rendel, 'How Many Women Academics 1912–76?' in Rosemary Deem (ed), *Schooling for Women's Work* (Routledge & Kegan Paul, 1980).

[4] Albert H Halsey and Martin Trow, *The British Academics* (Faber and Faber, 1971).

[5] John MacCallum Scott, *Dons and Students: British Universities Today* (The Plume Press, 1973) 7.

[6] *Commonwealth Universities Yearbook 1971.*

[7] Interview with William Twining, 2014, on file with author.

The Commonwealth University Yearbook for 1971 records that in 1970 women constituted just under 10 per cent of full-time UK legal academics, and only four of them, in addition to Claire Palley, had been promoted: two were Senior Lecturers and two were Readers. Yet, however much disquiet there may have been among women academics about this state of affairs, there was no major campaign to appoint more women professors, either at Queen's or elsewhere. At the time, the Society of Public Teachers of Law (SPTL), the largest learned association of academic lawyers (of which Claire Palley was a member), was more concerned with its internal politics – especially its refusal to admit as members law teachers who worked in polytechnics – than with the promotion prospects of its women members.[8] Feminism, while growing in influence during the 1970s, did not have a particularly high profile in legal academia. Palley's view was that while she was not unsympathetic to feminism, her activism in terms of the advancement of human rights (including work for the Minority Rights Group and the Citizens' Advice Bureaux as well as the ANC) was more of a priority to her at the time.[9] She was, however, very aware of the significance of her appointment, and its importance in terms of women's emancipation. 'At the time, I was very excited and proud, and hoped soon to be followed by others'.[10]

## III. What Happened Next

In fact, it took until 1990 for the number of women law professors in the UK to reach double figures. Until 1988 only another eight women had joined Claire Palley as professors of law in the UK. But in 1990 four more were appointed, bringing the total to 13.[11] The continuing low numbers of women law professors reflected the slow progress made in the general advancement of female academics in universities, with Ann Brooks reporting that by 1991 just 4.7 per cent of the professoriate were women.[12] Brooks's research, which examined the position of female academics and the reasons for the continuing male dominance of universities, resulted in an acknowledgement that the under-representation of women in leadership positions within universities arose from 'a mixture of power, patronage and prejudice which resulted in the promotion of the white academic male to positions of control and leadership in the academy'.[13] Current data suggests that the situation remains much the same in contemporary academia. While women are entering the academy as students in ever-greater numbers, there is no evidence to suggest that this is having a significant effect on the position of female academics, who remain largely in the lower ranks, only 23 per cent of professors being women.[14]

Celia Wells's research, published at the end of the 1990s, provides useful insights into the working lives of the women who had followed Claire Palley as professors of law.[15]

[8] Fiona Cownie and Ray Cocks, *A Great and Noble Occupation: The History of the Society of Legal Scholars* (Hart Publishing, 2009) 122.

[9] CP Interview.

[10] Personal communication (on file with author).

[11] *Commonwealth Universities Yearbooks 1971–1981.*

[12] Ann Brooks, *Academic Women* (SRHE & Open University Press, 1997) 21.

[13] ibid 59.

[14] HESA, 'Staff at Higher Education Providers 2014–15': www.hesa.ac.uk/sfr225.

[15] Celia Wells, 'Women Law Professors – Negotiating and Transcending Gender Identities at Work' (2002) 10 *Feminist Legal Studies* 1.

She found that promotion had generally come more slowly for these women than for their male counterparts, and most believed that their gender had affected their career. From the way they dressed to the lack of role models and the effects of caring responsibilities both domestic and professional, there is plenty of evidence in Wells's research to suggest that women's experience of performing a senior role in law schools is significantly different to that of the (white, male) 'norm'. Indeed, the strongest theme in the interviews she conducted was the strongly held belief that women take on more pastoral work in universities, which is not valued in terms of promotion. Women, said one interviewee 'are not frankly as ruthless [as men] about keeping their time for research free'.[16]

My own research on legal academics, published in 2004, revealed that gender remained an issue into the twenty-first century and was acknowledged as such by the majority of both men and women working in university law schools.[17] Yet despite this, women have come to play increasingly significant roles in the public life of legal education, both within universities, as Heads of School, Deans and Pro Vice-Chancellors, and on the national stage, as chairs of the Law Panel of the last three university Research Assessment Exercises and chairs of all three academic legal associations, as well as in giving plenary addresses at prestigious national and international conferences.

## IV. Significance

It is now nearly 40 years since Claire Palley became a Professor of Law. Her appointment demonstrated that it was possible, in a field stereotypically associated with men and masculinity, with rationality, logic and an absence of emotion, for a woman successfully to achieve the highest academic rank. Claire Palley's career also demonstrated that it was possible for a woman not only to succeed in academia, but at the same time to be a mother and to play a leading role in public life as a political activist, concerned with the effects of her research on the society in which she lived. In that regard, she was far ahead of her time. The fact that progress has been slow, in terms of the numbers of women following in her footsteps, should not detract from the importance of that first step towards the promotion of gender equality among legal academics, which remains a landmark moment.

## Further Reading

- Fiona Cownie, *Legal Academics: culture and identities* (Hart Publishing, 2004).
- Celia Wells, 'Ladies in Waiting; the Women Law Professors' Story' (2001) 23 *Sydney Law Review* 167.
- Celia Wells, 'Working Out Women in Law Schools' (2001) 21 *Legal Studies* 116.

[16] ibid 18.
[17] Fiona Cownie, *Legal Academics: Culture and Identities* (Hart Publishing, 2004) 168.

# 42

# First Women's Refuge, 1971

FELICITY KAGANAS

In 1971, the members of the Chiswick women's liberation group formed a new group, Women's Aid, to offer help to women. They began with protests against food prices and then about the withdrawal by the Government of free milk from schools. Five hundred mothers, children, and some fathers, marched down the High Road led by a cow. The so-called 'Milk March' drew more women to join the group. After meeting for some time in one another's houses, they decided they needed a community house and acquired from the council, at a peppercorn rent, a derelict house.[1]

It was during the group's meetings that it emerged that some of the women were suffering violence at the hands of their male partners. The group gave them shelter. Word spread and the house, with four bedrooms and an outside toilet, was soon 'inundated' with women and children.[2] It was at this community meeting place that the first refuge for abused women in Britain and the world opened its doors. It was here that 'violence against women began to be defined as a problem of epic proportions … Here that the inspiration for a social movement began'.[3]

## I. Context

Before the Chiswick refuge, explains Jenny Smith, a former resident, there was nowhere for abused women to find safety. She describes unsuccessfully seeking help; she was told to return home by her priest and her doctor prescribed tranquilisers and sent her for electroconvulsive therapy.[4] Many of the women coming to the refuge were referred by organisations that could not themselves offer help or shelter: 'Citizens' Advice Bureaux, probation officers, the Samaritans, doctors, magistrates and social workers'.[5] Erin Pizzey, who became the 'figurehead' of Chiswick Women's Aid,[6] summed up the plight of the abused woman:

> [S]he can limp to her GP, stagger to the casualty ward, drag herself to the social worker, cry out to the police, beseech the Marriage Guidance Council, implore the Family Service Unit, plead with

[1] Caroline Charlton, 'The First Cow on Chiswick High Road' (1972) 1 *Spare Rib* 24.
[2] Jenny Smith, *The Refuge* (Simon & Schuster, 2014) 178–79.
[3] Rebecca Emerson Dobash and Russell P Dobash, *Women, Violence and Social Change* (Routledge, 1992) 26.
[4] Smith, n 2 above, 212, 128, 165.
[5] Erin Pizzey, *Scream Quietly or the Neighbours Will Hear* (Penguin Books, 1974) 23–24.
[6] Dobash and Dobash, n 3 above, 26.

> Dr Barnardo's, beg the NSPCC and come away, through the swish of hands being compassionately washed in all directions, with only a babble of conflicting advice and not one jot of practical help.[7]

Women who fled their homes could not get rehoused as they were deemed intentionally homeless and they also risked having their children taken into care.[8] Social security payments were refused. Women were admitted to mental hospitals for depression. Police practice was not to intervene and they did not arrest perpetrators.[9] The policy was to advise the woman to initiate proceedings herself for common assault, although there was no legal aid for private prosecutions and there was also a risk of further violence because of the delay before the hearing.[10] If the police did act, the woman might not press charges because the perpetrator would, in many cases, be released on bail. And, in any event, sentencing in the magistrates' court was often derisory.[11]

The family justice system did not help either. It was possible to apply for an injunction to restrain a violent spouse and even to exclude a husband from the home,[12] usually owned by him, although exclusion was seen as draconian by the courts. However these remedies were available only to *married* women and only if the victim had filed a petition for divorce, nullity or judicial separation. No petition for divorce could, at that time, be presented before three years had elapsed since the date of the marriage,[13] but injunctions were sometimes granted if the victim undertook to file a divorce petition after the three-year period had passed.[14] Also, the three-year requirement did not apply if the petitioner could prove exceptional hardship on her part or exceptional depravity on the part of the respondent. The grounds for divorce included cruelty and, after the Divorce Reform Act 1969[15] became the law, the only ground, irretrievable breakdown of the marriage, could be evidenced by behaviour that the petitioner could not reasonably be expected to live with. Once there was a decree absolute or an order for judicial separation, the court had no jurisdiction to exclude husbands from the home and could only grant non-molestation injunctions.[16]

Unmarried cohabitants or wives who did not petition for divorce, nullity or judicial separation could only seek a non-molestation injunction, and then only if they brought a claim for damages for assault, battery or trespass to person or land.[17] It seems that the courts seldom granted these injunctions.[18] In any event, enforcement was a problem.[19]

## II. The Landmark

Erin Pizzey was the central figure in the refuge and an accomplished publicist. As a result of newspaper articles as well as television and radio interviews with her, letters began arriving

[7] Pizzey, n 5 above, 91.
[8] ibid 19, 93ff.
[9] ibid 98; Susan Maidment, 'The Law's Response to Marital Violence in England and the USA' (1977) 26 *International and Comparative Law Quarterly* 403, 407–08.
[10] Maidment, ibid 409–10.
[11] Pizzey, n 5 above, 117.
[12] *Silverstone v Silverstone* [1953] P 174.
[13] Section 1 of the Matrimonial Causes Act 1937.
[14] Maidment, n 9 above, 418.
[15] Now Matrimonial Causes Act 1973.
[16] See ***Davis v Johnson* (1978)**.
[17] Maidment, n 9 above, 424.
[18] *Report from the Select Committee on Violence in Marriage* Vol 2, Session 1974–75 HC 553-11 (HMSO, 1975) 65.
[19] Maidment, n 9 above, 422–24.

from all over the country.[20] Some women simply turned up at the door. By 1973 there were nearly 100 telephone calls a day and there were so many women and children in the house that some had to sleep on mattresses on the floor in the hallway.[21] A much larger house was secured and this, too, filled up quickly. It was licensed for 36 people but was often occupied by 130.[22] More houses followed and these filled up too. Since Pizzey operated an open-door policy,[23] refusing to turn any woman away, she was taken to court for breaching rules about overcrowding.[24]

Initially, funding came from donations and jumble sales. Then Hounslow Council began to provide funding. Social security payments covered the living expenses of the women and children. Later, funding came from the Greater London Council. Conditions in the house, especially in the early years, were poor and that women were willing to live there with their children was testament to their need. Other Women's Aid groups were formed in England, Scotland, Wales and Ireland, and they too set up refuges.[25]

There have been critical accounts of the way the Chiswick refuge was run. Observers commented that the staff were controlling, created a chaotic environment and fostered dependency on the part of the women. The women were pathologised and violence was seen as something transmitted inter-generationally.[26] In contrast, staff in other Women's Aid refuges prioritised self-help and respected the women's autonomy.[27] Nevertheless, some women thrived in the Chiswick house. Smith describes her time there as 'the best time of my life' and says she regained her self-respect. She considers the women in the refuge as pioneers for abused women and recalls that it was the women who answered the phones, made the rules and made decisions.[28]

## III. What Happened Next

The issue of domestic violence was raised for the first time in Parliament in 1971 by Jack Ashley MP after he heard about the work of Chiswick Women's Aid.[29] Public awareness of domestic violence and of the refuge grew with the publication in 1974 of Pizzey's book, *Scream Quietly or the Neighbours Will Hear*, and the broadcast of a Thames Television documentary filmed at the refuge, with the same title, in the same year.[30] Reporters from different countries came to the house and Pizzey, together with some of the women, travelled around Europe to speak to groups opening refuges.[31] American observers visited British refuges seeking to transfer knowledge to the United States, where the refuge movement was also growing.[32] In the UK, women began joining together to set up refuges on a national scale.[33]

[20] Pizzey, n 5 above, 20.
[21] ibid 43.
[22] ibid 44.
[23] Smith, n 2 above, 196.
[24] ibid 236.
[25] ibid 65–66.
[26] Dobash and Dobash, n 3 above, 85–86, 114–18.
[27] ibid 88.
[28] Smith, n 2 above, 203, 279.
[29] 'About Refuge': http://archive.li/xl0vT.
[30] Smith, n 2 above, 228.
[31] ibid 245, 248.
[32] Dobash and Dobash, n 3 above, 26–27, 84–85.
[33] Pizzey, n 5 above, 25.

The National Women's Aid Federation (NWAF) (subsequently renamed Women's Aid) began in 1974 with a gathering of Women's Aid groups wishing to set up a more egalitarian organisation.[34] They saw their task not as changing *women* but as changing the social context and conditions in which they lived.[35] Chiswick Women's Aid was not part of the NWAF; Pizzey wished to dominate the public stage and to maintain access to funding. She wrote to social work and housing departments in an attempt to ensure that no other refuge would get funding without her approval. The split was 'fraught with conflict',[36] but campaigning continued.

In 1975 a House of Commons Home Affairs Select Committee on violence in marriage was set up. It took evidence from many individuals and organisations, including Chiswick Women's Aid and Women's Aid groups from the Federation. It concluded that the 'most insistent evidence we have received has been that specialised refuge facilities should be available very readily and rapidly'.[37] Other recommendations of the Committee included changes in the way homelessness was construed. It called for changes in police practice and increased use of arrest. It also recommended the removal of the need to institute divorce proceedings to obtain an injunction, changes to the law to better provide for the exclusion of the abuser from the matrimonial home, better remedies for cohabitants and better remedies in the magistrates' courts.

These recommendations led to the **Domestic Violence and Matrimonial Proceedings Act 1976**. This was the first statute in the UK to provide for stand-alone civil law orders aimed at protecting both married and cohabiting victims of domestic violence. These orders were non-molestation injunctions and injunctions excluding abusers from the family home or part of it, and even from the area in which it was situated. Section 2 made provision for judges to attach a power of arrest which enabled the police to arrest without warrant a person suspected of being in breach of an order. Further legislation followed. The Domestic Proceedings and Magistrates' Court Act 1978 gave limited powers to magistrates' courts to make personal protection orders and exclusion orders and the Matrimonial Homes Act 1983 dealt with occupation of the marital home. The **Housing (Homeless Persons) Act 1977** recognised that victims who fled violence or threats of violence should be classified as homeless.

So the role of the refuge movement had grown to include campaigning, lobbying and education. Chiswick Women's Aid became Chiswick Family Rescue and, in 1993, it was renamed Refuge.[38] It was as a result of its campaigning calling for police action to combat abuse that the first Domestic Violence Unit was established and that, in 1987, the Metropolitan Police Service issued a Force Order instructing officers to take domestic violence seriously.

Campaigners' criticism of the Government, as well as of the criminal and family justice systems, has continued over the years[39] and some problems persist. For example, in 2014

[34] Dobash and Dobash, n 3 above, 33.
[35] ibid 120.
[36] ibid 33–34.
[37] Select Committee Report, n 18 above, x, [21].
[38] '35 years of Refuge': http://www.webcitation.org/5mXlJ2XBi.
[39] For an overview see Alison Diduck and Felicity Kaganas, *Family Law, Gender and the State* (3rd edn, Hart Publishing, 2012) 564–72; 599–603.

an inspection report by HM Inspectorate of Constabulary concluded that '[t]he overall police response to victims of domestic abuse is not good enough'.[40] And a follow-up report noted 'a number of causes of concern'.[41] In addition, there is some evidence that sentencing by the courts remains lenient.[42] New problems have emerged. Family courts have become increasingly ready to order that children have contact with fathers despite evidence of domestic abuse. And legal aid has been withdrawn from private family law cases unless there is proof of domestic violence through the production of specified types of evidence, many of which are difficult for victims to produce.

Nevertheless, the response of the criminal and family justice systems to domestic abuse has changed and campaigns by Refuge and Women's Aid have been instrumental in many of the changes. For instance, as a result of the efforts of Women's Aid and others, Part IV of the Family Law Act 1996[43] includes an automatic power of arrest where violence has been used or threatened. Common assault and breach of non-molestation orders have been made arrestable offences. Because of the efforts of Women's Aid and its partners, the law has changed to make coercive control a criminal offence. In 2016, Practice Direction 12J *Child Arrangements and Contact Order: Domestic Violence and Harm* was reviewed[44] in response to the publication by Women's Aid[45] of a report on child homicides, examining cases involving children killed by fathers who had been allowed contact with them, despite being known perpetrators of domestic abuse. The legal aid regulation dealing with domestic violence has been declared invalid[46] in a case initiated by Rights of Women and the gateways again came under review.[47]

As far as the job of running refuges is concerned, funding has remained a problem. For example, in 2015, 92 women and 75 children seeking refuge were turned away and, in nearly half of these cases, they were turned away because 'the refuge did not have capacity to support them'.[48] However, in 2017, the Government, which has a *Violence against Women and Girls* strategy, pledged to provide £20 million for domestic abuse services.[49]

## IV. Significance

The opening of the Chiswick Women's Aid refuge was something that happened almost by chance and on a very small scale. Yet the sheer weight of the need that was revealed when

[40] HM Inspectorate of Constabulary, *Everyone's Business: Improving the Police Response to Domestic Abuse. Executive Summary* (2014) 6–7.

[41] HM Inspectorate of Constabulary, *Increasingly Everyone's Business: A progress Report on the police response to domestic abuse* (2015) 6.

[42] Louise Tickle, 'Why is domestic abuse still not taken seriously in UK courts?', *The Guardian*, 8 March 2016.

[43] This replaced the 1976, 1978 and 1983 Acts.

[44] Mr Justice Cobb, *Review of Practice Direction 12J FPR 2010: Child Arrangement and Contact Orders: Domestic Violence and Harm* (Report to the President of the Family Division).

[45] Women's Aid, *Nineteen Child Homicides* (2016). See also Women's Aid Press Release, 'Twenty Child Homicides. Child First Goes to Downing Street' (23 January 2017).

[46] *R (Rights of Women) v Secretary of State for Justice* [2016] EWCA Civ 91.

[47] Owen Bowcott, 'Legal aid shakeup hands lifeline to domestic violence victims', *The Guardian*, 23 February 2017; Owen Boycott, 'MoJ Scraps Legal Aid Restrictions for Victims of Domestic Violence', *The Guardian*, 4 December 2017.

[48] Women's Aid, *Annual Survey 2015: The Findings* (2015) 14.

[49] See 'Women's Aid Statement on £20 million Fund for Domestic Abuse': https://www.womensaid.org.uk/womens-aid-statement-20-million-fund/. But see, for more recent developments, Jamie Grierson, 'Council Funding

its existence became known, and the events that followed, make it very significant. The refuge uncovered not only the pressing need for safe places for victims but also the wider issues detrimentally affecting women, such as financial dependence.[50]

At the time the refuge took in its first occupant, domestic violence was not constructed, either in law or in society generally, as a serious problem. Even a few years later, the House of Commons Select Committee referred to 'the ignorance and apathy of some government departments', remarked that little was known about the prevalence of domestic violence and observed that some people believed it was a husband's right to beat his wife.[51] The Committee praised the 'pioneering role' played by Chiswick Women's Aid[52] and said: 'One of the achievements of Chiswick Women's Aid has been to publicise a problem which can now be much more openly and realistically discussed'.[53] Not only did the existence of the refuge mean that the women who went there found safety and support, it meant that domestic violence made its way onto the legislative, policing and policy agenda. That is not to say that this would not otherwise have happened or that it would not otherwise have happened in the 1970s. However, Pizzey was particularly adept at publicising the problem.

Pizzey and Chiswick Women's Aid did not espouse the feminist approach taken by Women's Aid and, now, Refuge. Nor did they see changing the law or the status of women as central to their concerns. Indeed, in her evidence before the Select Committee, Pizzey said that although the law had a part to play, the problem was a medical one, and that the men were psychopaths who needed treatment.[54] In her book she referred to herself as a feminist, albeit one put off by the publicity surrounding 'women's lib',[55] and set out to refute the arguments that women 'provoke, deserve or enjoy being beaten'.[56] However, in 1982, she published a book entitled *Prone to Violence* arguing that victims of abuse sought out violent men and were addicted to pain. She has also frequently denounced feminism. She has, for example, written that she was never a feminist, that she 'always knew that women can be as vicious and irresponsible as men' and that the 'the [feminist] movement, which proclaimed that all men are potential rapists and batterers, was based on a lie that, if allowed to flourish, would result in the complete destruction of family life'.[57] She has sought to publicise the issue of violence against men, and is patron of the Mankind Initiative.[58] Had the refuge movement not gone on to develop on very different lines and within the context of feminist activism,[59] it would not have become the force it is today, campaigning to promote women's safety and their wider interests as well as offering shelter.

for Women's Refuges Cut by Nearly £7m Since 2010', *The Guardian*, 23 March 2018: https://www.theguardian.com/society/2018/mar/23/council-funding-womens-refuges-cut-since-2010-england-wales-scotland (last accessed 18 June 2018).

[50] Dobash and Dobash, n 3 above, 60.

[51] Select Committee Report, n 18 above, vi–vii.

[52] ibid xii [25].

[53] ibid xxiv [59].

[54] ibid Pizzey's evidence, [7]–[8].

[55] Pizzey, n 5 above, 9.

[56] ibid 43.

[57] Erin Pizzey, 'Why I loathe feminism … and believe it will ultimately destroy the family', *Mailonline*, 24 September 2009.

[58] Mankind Initiative: Helping men escape from domestic abuse, 'About Us': http://new.mankind.org.uk/about-us/about-us/.

[59] See eg Women's Aid, 'Our History': https://www.womensaid.org.uk/about-us/history/.

It has been estimated that Refuge's interventions save the state £5.9 million a year in criminal justice and healthcare costs.[60] The charity supports more than 4,500 women and children every day.[61] In 2012–13 it was providing emergency accommodation for 722 women and 658 children in 42 refuges.[62] It also runs outreach services and makes independent domestic violence advocates available to assist women through the legal process.[63] In 2003, Refuge and Women's Aid launched a national freephone helpline,[64] a service described by users as 'essential' or 'very important' in changing their lives.[65] Women's Aid now consists of 220 organisations running 300 services[66] and has an important campaigning role.

These large and significant organisations differ from Chiswick Women's Aid in their adherence to strong feminist agendas. But they grew out of a movement that started in a small rundown house in Chiswick where a decision was made to offer sanctuary to women who could get no help elsewhere.[67] They continue to provide help and safety and to expose the gaps in policy and law that place women and children in harm's way.

## Further Reading

- Rebecca Emerson Dobash and Russell P Dobash, *Women, Violence and Social Change* (Routledge, 1992).
- Marianne Hester, *Who does what to whom? Gender and Domestic Violence Perpetrators* (University of Bristol in association with the Northern Rock Foundation, 2009).
- Erin Pizzey, *Scream Quietly or the Neighbours will Hear* (Penguin, 1974).

[60] NEF Consulting, *National Domestic Violence Charity Refuge: Social Return on Investment. Summary Paper* (November 2016) 1.

[61] Refuge, 'Refuge saves the health service and the criminal justice system £5.9 million a year': http://www.refuge.org.uk/2016/11/22/refuge-saves-the-health-service-and-criminal-justice-system-5-9-million-a-year/.

[62] NEF Consulting, *Social Valuation of Refuge Services for Survivors of Domestic Violence* (May 2013) [2.1].

[63] ibid.

[64] Women's Aid, n 59 above.

[65] Cath Gregory Consulting, *National Domestic Violence Helpline Impact Study* (2008) 1.

[66] Women's Aid, n 59 above.

[67] It has been suggested that the Lambeth refuge opened before or around the same time as the Chiswick refuge (communication to editors by Elizabeth Woodcraft) but the author has not found any record of this.

# 43

# Section 25 of the Criminal Justice Act 1972

ANNE LOGAN

More than 50 years after the **Sex Disqualification (Removal) Act 1919** had first admitted women to the jury-box, Parliament finally legislated to remove all remaining statutory gender discrimination from the rules for jury qualification. Under section 25 of the Criminal Justice Act 1972, every person aged between 18 and 65 and registered as a parliamentary or local government elector, with a few non-gendered exceptions, would henceforth qualify for jury service.

## I. Context

Under the 1919 Act, only women who individually satisfied the Juries Act 1825 rules on property qualification were eligible to be called for jury service. The requirements were helpfully summarised for readers of the feminist paper, *The Vote*, in 1919, namely that jurors were primarily holders of property assessed to be worth over £30 in London and £20 elsewhere in England and Wales.[1] Since women were less likely than men to be designated as householders or property occupiers (married women particularly, as their husbands were usually classified as such), far fewer women than men were called for jury service between 1920 and 1974, when the 1972 Act came into force.

However, this was not the only source of sex discrimination against women where juries were concerned. A proviso to the 1919 Act which permitted judges to order single-sex juries on account of the likely nature of the evidence in a case was only repealed in 1971.[2] Moreover, the rules of peremptory challenge, whereby defendants were entitled to challenge potential jurors and get them removed without giving a reason, were sometimes used by barristers to exclude women jurors. It is also likely that there was additional, informal discrimination against women; for example, in 1952 someone in the office of the Sherriff of Middlesex claimed he only summoned 14 women in every 100 potential jurors as they were less 'reliable' than men.[3]

The practical effect of the 1919 legislation was that until the 1970s it was common for juries to contain only one or two women at most. Feminist campaigning in favour of

[1] *The Vote*, 16 April 1920, 20.
[2] Section 35(7) of the Courts Act 1971.
[3] TNA HO45/24917, memorandum dated 11 February 1952.

equality in jury qualification began as soon as the 1919 Act was passed. In 1921, *Woman's Leader*, the newspaper of the National Union of Societies for Equal Citizenship (NUSEC), noted with concern that 'the vast majority of married women living with their husbands' did not qualify for jury service.[4] In the late 1920s Florence Keynes JP, convenor of the National Council of Women (NCW)'s Public Service and Magistrates Committee, launched a vigorous campaign to amend the law. Keynes enlisted the support of sympathetic members of Parliament, including George Wilfrid Holford Knight MP, a long-term supporter of women in the legal profession. In June 1933 he introduced a draft Juries (Amendment) Bill to make spouses of existing jurors eligible for jury service, but the measure failed to proceed.[5] It would seem that that the strongest opposition faced by this and other similar measures came from the still male-dominated legal profession.[6]

Organised feminist campaigning on this issue ceased in the 1940s but was revived towards the end of the 1950s. A coalition of women's organisations, including not only the NCW but also the National Union of Townswomen's Guilds (NUTG), the 'Six Point Group'[7] and the Status of Women Committee, mobilised in support of MPs who were willing to take up the issue. As a result, in 1962 Judith Hart MP introduced a Bill under the 'Ten Minute Rule' to make the electoral register the basis for jury qualification. Although Hart's Bill was narrowly defeated, the Government set up a committee of enquiry into the question of eligibility for jury service. The committee, chaired by Lord Morris, reported in 1965, having heard evidence from – among other groups and individuals – an impressive array of women's organisations ranging from the Suffragette Fellowship to the National Federation of Women's Institutes (NFWI). The Morris Report recommended the replacement of the existing property-based rules with a system in which jurors were drawn from the electoral register.[8]

Alongside the long and impressive list of women's organisations lobbying for change by the 1960s there was increasing dissatisfaction in legal and political circles regarding the (by then) archaic laws on jury service.[9] Judges were frustrated by a shortage of jurors caused by the lengthy list of professions whose practitioners won automatic exemption from jury service: indeed the Morris Report estimated that only 22.5 per cent of the names on the electoral register were eligible for jury service, of which just 11 per cent were women.

At the same time, social and cultural attitudes towards gender were changing with the increasing entry of women into paid employment and public life in the 1960s. Where in the past there had been strong objections to mixed-sex juries dealing with cases involving sexual evidence, particularly homosexual offences, these appear to have been on the wane especially after the decriminalisation of homosexual acts between consenting adult men in private under the Sexual Offences Act 1967. According to the NUTG journal, 'women share with men the unpleasant aspects of life presented by the press and the BBC',[10] so there was

[4] *Woman's Leader*, 11 February 1921, 35.
[5] HC Deb, 20 June 1933, vol 279 cols 647–649.
[6] Anne Logan, '"Building a new and better order"? Women and Jury Service in England and Wales, *c* 1920–1970' (2013) 22(5) *Women's History Review* 701–16.
[7] See further **Life Peerages Act 1958**.
[8] Lord Morris, *Report of the Departmental Committee on Jury Service* (Cmnd 2627, 1965) (Morris Report).
[9] Logan, n 6 above, 712.
[10] (February 1962) XXIX(2) *The Townswoman* 32.

no reason why they should not discuss these together on a jury. Single-sex juries seemed at odds with the cultural zeitgeist.

However, there continued to be resistance by some judges to mixed juries and to the presence of women even in the era of the so-called 'permissive society'. In 1967 a judge used the proviso in the 1919 Act to order an all-male jury in the case of the prosecution under the Obscene Publications Act 1959 of the English publishers of a controversial American novel, *Last Exit to Brooklyn*, even though the prosecution's counsel argued that both men and women should be able to decide whether or not the book was obscene.[11]

Peremptory challenge too was still used to purge women jurors at this time, most notoriously in the infamous 'moors murders' trial of 1966. But the notion of single-sex juries was definitely under attack. When an all-female jury was empanelled under the 1919 proviso in *R v Sutton* (1968)[12] counsel for both the prosecution and the defence objected to the judge's order. A (male) civil servant observed that there were no valid arguments at all for all-female juries and the one for all-male ones – 'that some cases might be too shocking for women' had 'little validity in 1968'.[13] Three years later the proviso allowing judges to order single-sex juries was repealed as a result of an amendment to the Courts Act 1971 proposed by the former Lord Chancellor Lord Gardiner, who was sympathetic to feminist issues, and supported by Lady Wootton, an academic and JP.[14]

## II. The Landmark

It was some years before the Morris recommendations were implemented. No attempt was made to legislate while the 1966–70 Labour Government was in power, despite requests for action from the Conservative MP Joan Vickers.[15] In the early 1970s, MPs from both sides of the House, including Edward Gardner QC (Conservative) and Jack Ashley (Labour), began to step up the pressure once again, in the form of parliamentary questions.[16] It is clear from their statements that they were in receipt of considerable amounts of correspondence from members of women's organisations concerned about the lack of action. Despite the emergence of second-wave feminism in the 1970s, those campaigning for the change remained the old-style feminist organisations such as the NCW and the NFWI, who retained their focus on institutional change and increased participation by women. They were still powerful forces, having memberships of hundreds of thousands of women, and they were much more likely to be listened to by the establishment than the newer feminist groups.

Yet the Government still procrastinated, with spokesmen merely conceding that jury qualification was a 'possible subject' which they would tackle 'when time permits'. In 1971 several amendments were tabled to the Courts Bill to enact the Morris Report proposals. Two MPs who had served on the Committee – one Conservative and one Labour – introduced one such amendment in the Bill's committee stage. The proposer, Edward Gardner QC,

[11] *The Times*, 14 November 1967, 11.
[12] *R v Sutton* (1968) 53 Cr App R 128, a case involving the manslaughter of a baby.
[13] TNA HO291/1192 Brennan to Chadwell, 12 July 1968.
[14] HL Deb, 8 December 1970, vol 313 cols 901–902.
[15] HC Deb, 28 April 1966, vol 727 col 42W.
[16] HC Deb, 18 March 1971, vol 813 col 367W; 15 July 1971, vol 821 col 134W.

pointed out that the Juries Act 1825 was clearly obsolete and 'hopelessly out of date'. Pointedly, he told the Government that action was needed, not promises for the future.[17] He withdrew his amendment after assurances that the Government was considering the matter. The following year, the Home Secretary, Reginald Maudling, announced that the Government planned to replace the property qualification for jury service with a qualification based on citizenship as evidenced by inclusion in the electoral register, as part of the new Criminal Justice Bill.[18] The Criminal Justice Act was passed in 1972 and the new system of jury qualification finally came into force in 1974.

## III. What Happened Next

The removal of gender discrimination in the rules for jury qualification brought about a profound change in the administration of justice, by at last removing the link between jury service and property occupation. The 1972 Act paved the way for increased diversity on juries, not only in gender terms but also with the likelihood of more young people undertaking jury service, the voting age for men and women having been reduced to 18 in 1969.

However the change did not arouse very much comment at the time, perhaps because public – and even (some) legal – opinion had run ahead of the legislation. With the proviso for single-sex juries gone, and jury qualification now based upon the electoral register, the only practical method of discriminating against women jurors was through the right of peremptory challenge, which had been notoriously used by defence barristers in the 'moors murders' trial. In its evidence to the Morris Committee the feminist society, the Six Point Group, had argued that any woman juror removed as a result of a peremptory challenge should be replaced by another woman, but the Committee rejected that proposal on the grounds that it would not be necessary once jury qualification depended on the electoral register and the supply of potential women jurors was thereby greatly increased.[19] It is probably significant that the right to make peremptory challenges to jurors did not last for long after the 1972 Act, and was eventually abolished by the Criminal Justice Act 1988. The right to trial by jury remains in this country, and jury service is still an important part of a citizen's duty.

## IV. Significance

The change in the rules for jury qualification in 1972 was without doubt a necessary and somewhat overdue modernisation of a thoroughly archaic law. As was pointed out during the parliamentary debates, the 1825 Act was nearly a century and a half old when it was finally replaced, and the property values and terminology were thoroughly out of date. Yet its survival on the statute book not only precluded the vast majority of women from eligibility for jury service, but also many men who were not ratepayers in their own right, particularly

[17] HC Deb, 7 April 1971, vol 815 cols 502–524.
[18] HC Deb, 11 May 1972, vol 836 col 410W.
[19] Morris Report, n 8 above, 105, [330].

younger citizens. For women, the significance of the reform was the removal of an indirect but powerful, symbolic form of gender discrimination; one which women's organisations had long lobbied against, not only because of its symbolism but also because they believed that the country would be better served if women played an equal part in the administration of justice. No longer would juries contain (at most) two or three women. Moreover, they became much more representative of the population at large, albeit dependent upon the thoroughness of the electoral registration process. Arguably this increased diversity has aided the survival of the jury system into the late-twentieth and early-twenty-first centuries.

However, the question should be asked why it took so long for this seemingly uncontroversial and logical reform to take place. The main reasons seem to lie in the deep antipathy towards and prejudice against women of much of the legal profession in general, and judges in particular. From the 1920s until the 1960s judges had taken advantage of the power to order single-sex juries and indulged barristers who made gender-biased challenges on their clients' behalf. Myths about women's unsuitability, unreliability, emotionalism and unworldliness lingered long after the 1919 Act had ensured the presence of at least a few women on most jury panels. Young women were especially suspect. In 1929 the Director of Public Prosecutions, Sir Archibald Bodkin, expressed horror at the prospect of a '"flapper" voter in a murder case'.[20] It was only in the 1960s that there was a noticeable shift in attitudes, yet as late as 1961 Charis Frankenburg JP of the NCW argued that lawyers remained prejudiced against jurywomen.[21] As explained above, changing social attitudes in the 1960s, coupled with the general shortage of jurors, led to the suggested overhaul of the system in the Morris Report. Even then, another decade passed before the reform was implemented.

## Further Reading

- Anne Logan, '"Building a new and better order"? Women and Jury Service in England and Wales, c 1920–1970' (2013) 22(5) *Women's History Review* 701–16.
- Anne Logan, *Feminism and Criminal Justice: a Historical Perspective* (Palgrave Macmillan, 2008) 86–95.
- Kevin Crosby, 'Keeping women off the jury in 1920s England and Wales' (2017) 37(4) *Legal Studies* 695–717.

[20] TNA HO45/24917.
[21] 'Ladies of the Jury' *Manchester Guardian*, 13 December 1961.

# 44

# Sex Discrimination Act 1975

ANNE MORRIS*

It would seem axiomatic that a collection of Women's Legal Landmarks would include the Sex Discrimination Act 1975. The Act is undoubtedly of symbolic and legal significance for women but it is not without its critics. Indeed, even the White Paper that preceded the Act, *Equality for Women*, cautioned against expecting too much:

> It is important to recognise the inevitable restraints on what can be achieved by legislation, so that it is seen in proper perspective, without arousing false expectations or encouraging a sense of complacency.[1]

Despite its limitations, the Sex Discrimination Act 1975 (SDA) deserves its place as a landmark both as a valuable measure in its own right and as an important marker on the road to modern anti-discrimination laws. It is, moreover, another example of what can be achieved when campaigners and law-makers are united in the desire to produce social change.

## I. Context

When the Sex Discrimination Act was passed in 1975 it was intended to counteract the pervasive and blatant discrimination that women faced in all aspects of their lives including employment, education, finance and housing. In employment, discrimination against women extended through pay, recruitment, training, promotion, and dismissal.[2] The number of women (particularly married women) in employment had been steadily increasing, but they remained concentrated in lower-paid occupations and most worked part-time with all the adverse consequences that had for pay and pensions.[3] The expectation that men were the breadwinners persisted, and a woman could be refused a job simply because the employer would prefer a man.[4] There were still laws that restricted women's permissible occupations and hours of work,[5] while the professions remained hostile to women: *Equality*

* The author would like to thank Susan Atkins for her insightful comments on an earlier draft.

[1] Home Office, *Equality for Women* (Cmnd 5724, 1974) [21].

[2] ibid [8]–[9].

[3] Gill Court, *Women and the labour market: two decades of change and continuity* (Institute of Employment Studies, 1995).

[4] For an example of this after the Act see *Whitehouse v Highland Regional Council*, S/4479/77.

[5] See eg section 86 of the Factories Act 1961.

*for Women* noted that there had been little improvement in the proportion of women in the professions since the **Sex Disqualification (Removal) Act 1919**.[6]

Outside of paid work, a woman seeking financial independence would discover that if she was single it was difficult to get a loan because of the assumption that she did not have long-term job prospects. If married she would find that she needed her husband's signature to guarantee even minor hire purchase payments[7] and her income was unlikely to be considered equally with her husband if they were seeking a mortgage.[8] The attitude that women were subordinate to men in financial affairs – indeed, hardly to be trusted – is evident in a decision made just before the Sex Discrimination Act 1975 came into force. In a case concerning a property purchase, the judge, Caulfield J (as summarised by the *Times Law Reports*), held that

> Even in present times, when there was a movement by women for equality with men, a sensible wife did not generally make the major decisions. Most wives sensibly left such decisions to their husbands. A solicitor should not take instruction from a wife where a husband was available.[9]

It was against this background that demands grew for legislation to combat sex discrimination. Although not everyone was (or is) convinced by the usefulness of legislation to achieve equality,[10] the 1960s witnessed new attempts at using law to prohibit discrimination. The initial focus was race discrimination[11] and in some ways this worked to the advantage of those campaigning for sex equality laws. Lessons were learned from the shortcomings of the earlier race legislation and some of the prime movers in the political sphere, such as Roy Jenkins (Home Secretary 1965–67 and 1974–76) and Anthony Lester (Jenkins' special adviser at the Home Office with responsibility for equality legislation), were able to capitalise on that experience. A number of factors contributed to the willingness to legislate. The imminent entry of the United Kingdom into the European Economic Community (EEC) meant, for example, that the campaign for the Equal Pay Act 1970 was helped on its way by the need to comply with Article 119 of the Treaty of Rome, requiring pay equality between the sexes.[12] The Equal Pay Act did not, however, address the inequalities arising outside contractual terms of employment, and the EEC was turning its attention to a broader Directive calling for equal treatment between the sexes in areas including employment and training, promotion and working conditions.[13] Quite apart from the European influence, pressure for legislation wider in scope than the Equal Pay Act was growing, not least from the Women's Liberation Movement (WLM). Two of the four initial demands of the first WLM conference in 1970 were for equal pay and equal educational and employment opportunities.[14] In March 1971, in what was described as the first national women's

[6] n 1 above, [11].

[7] See eg 'Sex Discrimination in practice' (1974) 28 *Spare Rib* 20.

[8] n 1 above, [15].

[9] *The Times*, Law Report, 21 November 1975, 14.

[10] For a contemporary view see Elizabeth Vallance, 'Equality for Women: a note on the White Paper' (1975) 46(2) *Political Quarterly* 201.

[11] Race Relations Acts 1965 and 1968.

[12] See further **Dagenham Car Plant Strike, 1968**.

[13] Eventually, Council Directive 76/207/EEC (Equal treatment of men and women).

[14] See British Library, 'Women's liberation: a national movement' (Sisterhood and after, 8 March 2013): https://www.bl.uk/sisterhood/articles/womens-liberation-a-national-movement.

demonstration since the suffragettes, 4,000 WLM supporters marched through London and presented a petition to Downing Street, outlining their demands.[15]

In Parliament, Private Members' Bills were unsuccessfully attempted by Joyce Butler, William Hamilton and Baroness Seear, but the referral to a House of Lords Select Committee of Baroness Seear's Bill meant that the then Conservative Government was presented with compelling evidence of widespread sex discrimination, and the Government drew up its own proposals in 1973.[16] The Labour Government that came to power in 1974 took up the proposals and widened them. In 1974 it produced the White Paper, *Equality for Women*. Between its publication and the introduction of the Sex Discrimination Bill the proposals had been widened further in response to public consultation and, crucially, included reference to 'indirect' discrimination. Introducing the second reading of the Bill, the Secretary of State for the Home Department, Roy Jenkins, stated: 'The unequal status of women in our society is a social evil of great antiquity. Its causes are complex and rooted deeply in tradition, custom and prejudice'.[17] In seeking to address that evil, the Sex Discrimination Act was, clearly, an ambitious measure.

## II. The Landmark

The Sex Discrimination Act 1975 came into force along with the Equal Pay Act 1970 on 29 December 1975. Within its scope were employment, education, goods, facilities, services and premises. In the employment context, it extended to employers and to bodies such as trade unions, employment agencies and vocational training bodies. It outlawed certain discriminatory practices such as advertisements using job descriptions with a sexual connotation (such as waiter, salesgirl or stewardess).[18] The Act also set up mechanisms for enforcement of the law. These included the right of an aggrieved individual to take a complaint to an Industrial (now an Employment) Tribunal. Significantly, however, enforcement was also to be in the hands of a new body, the Equal Opportunities Commission (EOC). The Commission's duties included working towards the elimination of discrimination and the promotion of equality between men and women. In order to fulfil those duties, it was given a number of powers including providing assistance to those bringing a complaint, but the power that initially appeared to offer a real opportunity for the promotion of sex equality was the ability of the EOC to conduct formal investigations and where appropriate to issue legally enforceable non-discrimination notices.[19] The Act thus relied on a two-pronged approach: individual complaints and institutional enforcement.

In pursuit of equality, the Act set out the kind of behaviour that would be unlawful. It applied equally to men and women, making it unlawful to discriminate against either sex 'on the ground of' sex. It extended its coverage to 'marital status' but only in the employment field and only to those who were married, not those who were single.[20] It established

[15] (1978) 69 *Spare Rib* 41.
[16] See WB Creighton, *Working Women and the Law* (Mansell, 1979) 152.
[17] HC Deb, 26 March 1975, vol 889 col 511.
[18] SDA 1975, s 38.
[19] SDA 1975, ss 57–61.
[20] SDA 1975, s 3. Thus in *Bick v Royal West of England School for the Deaf* [1976] IRLR 326, it was not unlawful to discriminate against a woman who was about to be married.

three statutory forms of discrimination which came to be known as direct and indirect discrimination and victimisation. Direct discrimination occurred where a person treated a woman less favourably than he treated or would treat a man, on the ground of her sex.[21] A person would *indirectly* discriminate against a woman if he applied to her a requirement or condition which applied equally to a man but which was such that the proportion of women who could comply with it was considerably smaller, which could not be justified, and which was to her detriment.[22] Victimisation occurred where a person treated another less favourably because the victim had alleged a breach of the Act, brought proceedings under the Act or assisted someone else to do so.[23] Having set out the meaning of discrimination, the Act then went on to set out when it would be unlawful in the different areas covered by the law. In employment, for example, section 6 made it unlawful to treat women less favourably in recruitment, terms of employment, and opportunities for training. It was unlawful to refuse to employ someone because she was a woman, or to dismiss her for that reason.

It seemed that the Act had the potential to make a real difference. It must be borne in mind, however, that it contained a number of important exceptions. It excluded, for example, employers with fewer than five employees.[24] More significantly it did not cover employment benefits relating to death and retirement meaning that sex discrimination in social security benefits and pensions was, for the time being, untouched.[25] The Act also contained an exemption where it could be shown that being a man was a 'genuine occupational requirement' for the job.[26] This included jobs restricted to men because of laws regulating the employment of women. In other words the SDA left in place, for the time being, the 'protective' legislation that restricted the job opportunities of women.[27]

## III. What Happened Next

Nobody would expect the Sex Discrimination Act to have had an immediate effect. Prejudices were too deeply ingrained to expect that they would vanish with Royal Assent. Nevertheless, the pace of change was still a disappointment to many. The Act's shortcomings also became apparent. Its underlying principle was that women should be treated in the same way as a man in the same circumstances,[28] an approach that ignores the systemic inequalities in education and in family structures which prevent women competing on equal terms with men. It also ignores that fact that only women experience pregnancy and childbirth. The SDA had no provisions dealing specifically with pregnancy and the courts initially held that a woman who was dismissed because she was pregnant could not bring a sex discrimination claim because there was no man with whom she could be compared.[29]

[21] SDA 1975, s 1(1)(a).
[22] SDA 1975, s 1(1)(b).
[23] SDA 1975, s 4.
[24] SDA 1975, s 6(3)(b). This was subsequently repealed in the SDA 1986.
[25] SDA 1975, s 6(4).
[26] SDA 1975, s 7.
[27] This was not addressed until the Sex Discrimination Act 1986.
[28] SDA 1975, s 5.
[29] *Turley v Allders Department Stores* [1980] IRLR 4. But see: Case C-177/88 *Dekker v VJV Centrum* [1992] ICR 325; *Webb v EMO Air Cargo (UK) Ltd* [1995] ICR 1021. See now section 18 of the Equality Act 2010.

Another omission was that the Act did not refer to sexual harassment and so it was necessary to bring a complaint within direct discrimination: that is, less favourable treatment on the ground of sex. This could be problematic, as seen in a case where a woman objected to a display of 'pin-ups'. It was held that a man might have been equally offended and therefore there was no sex discrimination.[30] Perhaps, however, one of the greatest disappointments in the aftermath of the legislation was the ineffectiveness of the legal powers of the EOC to conduct formal investigations.[31] There are many reasons why the EOC failed to seize the opportunity granted by the SDA, including the complexity of such investigations, although that complexity was largely foisted on them by the procedural requirements imposed by judges who were hostile to the idea of institutional enforcement,[32] preferring to leave the implementation of the law to individual claimants who were subjected, without legal aid, to the vagaries of the tribunal and courts system.[33]

Despite these problems, however, the Sex Discrimination Act, in conjunction with European Law,[34] began to make a real difference. Indirect discrimination cases in particular had an impact that extended far beyond the particular complainant and her place of work. Although proving indirect discrimination was complex and the courts unpredictable, decisions had far-reaching effects. Moreover, they emphasised that discrimination does not always stem from the intentional prejudice of those guilty of sexism: it can result from the unthinking application of long-standing practices that can no longer be justified. Unlawful indirect discrimination was found, for example, in relation to age limits for jobs in the civil service (applicants had to be aged between 17½ and 28), a condition that adversely affected women who may have been out of the job market because of child-care responsibilities; and in cases where part-timers (the majority of whom were women) were treated less favourably than full-timers.[35] A particularly significant case brought by way of judicial review by the EOC successfully challenged legislation that required part-timers to have worked longer than full-timers in order to qualify for statutory redundancy pay and protection from unfair dismissal.[36]

Cases involving direct discrimination, though often difficult to prove,[37] helped to underline the message that women were now entitled to demand equal treatment. Successes were not confined to employment. In a ground-breaking case concerning education, the House of Lords held that it was unlawful sex discrimination to demand higher scores from girls applying to selective schools. One of the crucial aspects of this case was the statement by Lord Goff that unlawful direct discrimination does not depend on motive:

> if [it did] it would be a good defence for an employer to show that he discriminated against women not because he intended to do so but (for example) because of customer preference, or to save money, or even to avoid controversy.[38]

[30] *Stewart v Cleveland Guest Engineering Ltd* [1996] ICR 535. See now section 26 of the Equality Act 2010.

[31] For a critique of the EOC generally, see Vera Sacks, 'The EOC ten years on' (1986) 49 *Modern Law Review* 560.

[32] Lord Denning compared the formal investigation to the Spanish Inquisition: *Science Research Council v Nassé* [1979] 1 QB 144 at 172. See also George Appleby and Evelyn Ellis, 'Formal Investigations: The CRE and EOC as Law Enforcement Agencies' [1984] *Public Law* 236.

[33] Alice Leonard, *Judging Inequality: The Effectiveness of the Industrial Tribunal System in Sex Discrimination and Equal Pay Cases* (Cobden Trust, 1987).

[34] Especially the Equal Treatment Directive 1976, 76/207/EEC.

[35] *Price v Civil Service Commission* [1978] ICR 27; *Clark v Eley (IMI) Kynoch Ltd* [1983] ICR 1.

[36] *R v Secretary of State for Employment, ex parte Equal Opportunities Commission* [1995] 1 AC 1.

[37] Susan Atkins, 'The Sex Discrimination Act 1975: The End of a Decade' (1986) 24 *Feminist Review* 57.

[38] *R v Birmingham City Council, ex parte Equal Opportunities Commission* [1989] AC 1155, 1194.

Bearing in mind that sex discrimination is often based on unthinking stereotypical assumptions about what women should do, how they should look, and where they should work, such cases were instrumental in signalling the need for changing attitudes.

## IV. Significance

For all the criticisms levelled at it, the Sex Discrimination Act 1975 was immensely significant for a whole generation of women who needed no longer to accept that sexism was just the way of the world. They could point to the Sex Discrimination Act and challenge the discrimination they faced. It is important to remember that decided cases, however numerous, are the tip of the iceberg: some complaints settle before getting to court and sometimes the mere existence of a law is enough to provoke changes, not simply because of any deterrent value (although there is that) but rather because it indicates how society is supposed to operate. Cases decided after the Act came into force illustrate the ways in which women had routinely been treated in all walks of life. When Belinda Shortt unsuccessfully applied for a job as a painter and decorator she was told that her application had been 'a "brave" venture into the usually male-dominated place of work.' The fact that a building site was not women-friendly was 'of course sexist, but that is how they are run.' It was suggested that she might like to consider interior design instead. Because it was 1995 and not 1975, Ms Shortt succeeded in showing unlawful discrimination.[39]

Despite the daunting prospect of a court case, many women faced the challenges and secured victories not only for themselves but for many others who benefited from the changes that came along, slowly but surely. Sex discrimination has not been eradicated – far from it – but the Sex Discrimination Act did alter the landscape for the better. Over the years there was a series of amendments, many necessitated by European Law (which played a crucial part in achieving improvements for women), until finally, the Act was repealed and the laws on sex discrimination were included with other 'protected characteristics' in the Equality Act 2010. On 29 December 1975, as the Sex Discrimination Act came into effect, Ronald Bell, QC, Conservative MP for Beaconsfield said of it that it exposed Parliament to ridicule: 'The good it will do will be microscopic and the harm will be immense'.[40] History proves him wrong on both counts.

## Further Reading


- **Susan Atkins and Brenda Hoggett, *Women and the Law* (Blackwell, 1984)**.
- WB Creighton, *Working Women and the Law* (Mansell, 1979).
- Bob Hepple, *Equality: The New Legal Framework* (Hart Publishing, 2011).


[39] *Shortt v Shaylor* Case No 5926/95, Equal Opportunities Review Case Law Digest No 28, Summer 1996.
[40] Anon, 'Cinderella outlawed from today', *The Guardian*, 29 December 1975, 18.

# 45

# First Rape Crisis Centre, 1976

ALISON DIDUCK

> In November 1974 a group of approximately 40 women met to discuss rape with a view to 'doing something about it' ... In the weeks that followed the group roughly split into two – those who wanted to form a political group and those who wanted to set up a Rape Crisis centre.[1]

The early work of these remarkable homemakers, lawyers, journalists, doctors, students, nurses and unemployed women was difficult. They needed first to secure premises, charity status and funding. They then invited counsellors from other organisations and speakers from the legal and medical professions to help them realise their goal. On 15 March 1976 they opened in North London, the first Rape Crisis Centre (LRCC) in Britain. Its aims were to offer 'sympathetic non-judgemental support, advice and information on police and legal procedures for those women who chose to report', and ultimately, 'to help raped women regain their strength as individuals'.[2] The original LRCC collective of about 10 women maintained a 24-hour telephone line and offered face-to-face support and medical referrals. They engaged in research, public education and training of new support workers. In the first 19 months of operation they received 84 calls[3] and by 1978 were receiving about 25 calls per week.[4]

The significance of the achievement of this small collective of women, and the anti-rape movement of which they were a part, is difficult to overestimate. Not only did the LRCC provide an essential and unique service for survivors at a time when the social and legal culture of rape was extremely hostile to them, it paved the way for Rape Crisis Centres across the UK. Further, and crucially, it did all of its work in a way which was true to its beliefs: it merged 'theory and practice'[5] by operating as a feminist collective committed to eliminating hierarchies of power from the ground up.

## I. Context

Prior to the Sexual Offences (Amendment) Act 1976, the substantive law of rape was contained in section 1(1) of the Sexual Offences Act 1956, which stated only that 'It is a

[1] Rape Counselling and Research Project, First Annual Report, 1977, 2.
[2] Victoria Green, 'Crisis Centre Opens' (1976) 46(17) *Spare Rib* 17.
[3] Rape Counselling and Research Project, n 1 above, 12.
[4] Romi Bowen and Bernadette Manning, 'Writing Our Own History' (1987) 10 *Trouble and Strife* 49, 50.
[5] Helen Jones and Kate Cook, *Rape Crisis Responding to Sexual Violence* (Russell House Publishing, 2008) 3.

felony for a man to rape a woman'.[6] The actual definition of the offence, unlawful sexual intercourse with a woman without her consent, was derived from common law. Like all criminal offences, rape consisted of an actus reus (a guilty act) and a mens rea (a guilty mind). Like now, the difficulty with prosecuting rape usually lay in establishing mens rea. In 1975 that difficulty was exacerbated by the House of Lords decision in *DPP v Morgan*,[7] which established that a man might be acquitted of rape if he honestly believed his victim was consenting, regardless of the reasonableness of his belief. Further at this time, because complainants were not granted anonymity in court proceedings, many were named in the press.[8] Cross-examination on their character, reputation and previous sexual history was freely permitted. Estimates of the number of rapes actually reported to police ranged from one in three to one in 99,[9] and of those that were prosecuted, the conviction rate was poor. Perhaps for these reasons, and also because few women talked about their experiences because being a victim of rape was stigmatising, rape was assumed to be rare. When it did occur, it was assumed always to be graphically violent and to be committed by strangers.[10] The newspaper reports in the 'sexually liberated' 1960s and 1970s from which much of the public received its information offered florid accounts of rape and sexual humiliation, often as a means of titillation.[11]

The legal and social situation for women was much the same in other western countries. Indeed, the anti-rape movement in the UK began in the United States. From around 1967 women involved in the Women's Liberation Movement in the US began to meet to talk about their experiences in what became consciousness-raising groups. Women spoke of their own violations and came to discover the personal was indeed political. From consciousness raising came the first public 'speak out' on rape in New York in 1971. Its effect was powerful. It galvanised women's activism and organisation around rape. Women began to talk about and, importantly, to write about and study rape: Susan Brownmiller's ground-breaking work[12] showed that rape was not a rare psychologically aberrant act; Louise Armstrong brought to light the reality of child sexual abuse;[13] and Diana Russell gave us the politics of rape from survivors' perspectives.[14] From feminist consciousness raising, 'speak outs' and women's writing came the anti-rape movement and a new theory and politics of rape. The first Rape Crisis Centre in the US opened in Washington DC in 1972. The idea spread quickly. By 1973 15 other centres had opened in the US[15] and the UK anti-rape movement was not far behind. As the women involved in the original London Rape Crisis collective demonstrated, it too grew out of consciousness raising and the commitment not only to offering support for victims of rape, but also to their feminist politics.

[6] See further **Section 1 of the Sexual Offences Act 2003**.
[7] *DPP v Morgan* [1976] AC 182; (1975) 61 Cr App R 136.
[8] Keith Soothill and A Jack, 'How Rape is Reported' (1975) *New Society*, June 19, 702. See further **Section 4 of the Sexual Offences (Amendment) Act 1976**.
[9] Sylvia Walby, Alex Hay and Keith Soothill, 'The Social Construction of Rape' (1983) 2 *Theory Culture and Society* 86, 91–92.
[10] Jones and Cook, n 5 above, 5.
[11] Walby, Hay and Soothill, n 9 above, 95.
[12] Susan Brownmiller, *Against Our Will: Men, Women and Rape* (Simon and Shuster, 1975).
[13] Louise Armstrong, *Kiss Daddy Goodnight: A Speak out on Incest* (Hawthorn Books, 1978).
[14] Diana Russell, *The Politics of Rape: The victim's perspective* (Stein and Day, 1975).
[15] Jones and Cook, n 5 above, 7.

## II. The Landmark

The London Rape Crisis Centre was feminist and it said so. Its feminist method of collective working and consciousness raising came together to create a vital and radical form of support for women who had experienced rape. Its core values included believing women, working with women's rather than the law's understanding of rape, not offering 'counselling' in the therapeutic sense,[16] but rather providing non-directional support and respecting women's confidentiality and autonomy. For the first few years it maintained a 24-hour telephone service, often with unpaid workers sleeping overnight in the office. Workers took calls from women who had just been raped, women who had been raped years ago and women who had been raped as children. They saw women face to face at the Centre and at the women's own homes. All workers received training for the support work they engaged in. And these early anti-rape workers were clear that they were providing 'support work' and not counselling or therapy. The ethos was that women who had been raped were not 'ill' and did not require healing; they wanted support and information outside of a medical model. Indeed, Rape Crisis Centre workers were reluctant to use the word 'victim' at all.[17]

As a result of their roots in feminist consciousness raising, which understood rape as only one form of violence experienced by women on an everyday basis, the LRCC made links with other organisations devoted to combatting all forms of violence against women. They engaged with Women's Aid, the new refuge movement which worked with survivors of domestic violence,[18] with anti-porn and anti-street harassment campaigns, and with 'incest survivors' groups. Sometimes this work took the form of direct campaigns and sometimes public education. Indeed, both were as important a part of the LRCC's mission as survivor support work.

Public education took the form of speaking to different lay groups.[19] Unlike the early relationships US Rape Crisis Centres built with police, prosecutors and medical professionals, however, LRCC's collaboration with professional groups was less successful in these early days. While some discussions were fruitful with forensic medical practitioners, the London Rape Crisis Centre faced open hostility from the police. The Metropolitan Police refused to recognise Rape Crisis and instructed its officers not to refer women who had been raped to the LRCC. Indeed, the LRCC was informed formally by the Commissioner that there would be 'no useful purpose served' to arrange a meeting between the Met and the LRCC to discuss the possibility of establishing a working relationship between them.[20]

Notwithstanding LRCC's difficult early relationship with law enforcement and with government, however, it carried on its campaign to reform the law and procedure. It submitted written evidence, for example, to the Advisory Group on the Law of Rape, chaired by **Rose Heilbron**, the first woman judge to sit at the Old Bailey, to the Criminal Law Revision Committee in 1977 and to the Royal Commission on Criminal Procedure in 1978.

[16] Rape Counselling and Research Project, n 1 above; Bowen and Manning, n 4 above, 52–53.

[17] Rape Counselling and Research Project, ibid.

[18] See further **First Women's Refuge, 1971**.

[19] Rape Counselling and Research Project, n 1 above, 15; London Rape Crisis Centre, *Second Annual Report* (1978) 10.

[20] Rape Counselling and Research Project, ibid, Appendix 7; London Rape Crisis Centre, ibid, Appendix III.

## III. What Happened Next

Shortly after it began, the London group offered assistance to other groups around the UK and Ireland who wished to start Rape Crisis Centres and the movement grew quickly. Glasgow Rape Crisis opened in 1976, the Kent Rape Counselling and Research project started in 1977, Tyneside Rape Crisis and Edinburgh Rape Crisis opened in 1978 and Birmingham Rape Crisis and Dublin Rape Crisis[21] in 1979. By 1988 there were 62 rape crisis groups across the UK and Ireland.[22] Most of these groups relied primarily upon charitable and local government funding, although Irish centres have always received state funding. Many UK groups were reluctant originally to accept central government funding for fear it would necessitate a change in organisational structure from their non-hierarchical ethos. As demand for their services grew, however, some groups abandoned their women's liberation focus in favour of a model of partnership-based service provision. Some changed their names from Rape Crisis to Sexual Assault Support and began to offer services for men. Some local centres began to enjoy good relationships with the police, but an edgy relationship with the police remained for others.

Difficulties with the police were highlighted in 1982 after the BBC broadcasted a fly-on-the-wall documentary supported by the Home Office and the Thames Valley Police who wished to demonstrate to the public their everyday work and procedures. In an episode entitled 'A Complaint of Rape' police officers were shown subjecting a complainant to extreme bullying and hostile questioning. To the surprise of the police, the public were shocked and public outrage led directly to changes in police and forensic medical procedures. Rape Crisis Centres, however, were not a part of many of these changes and relations with the Home Office remained difficult, exemplified by Ian Blair's 1985 report in which, unlike in the US, he saw no possibility of a cooperative relationship developing in the UK between the police and Rape Crisis Centres.[23]

Another result of the BBC documentary was the establishment by Dr Raine Roberts of the first Sexual Assault Referral Centre (SARC) in Manchester in 1986. The St Mary's Sexual Assault Referral Centre provided coordinated forensic, counselling and medical aftercare service to survivors of rape or sexual assault. The now 36 SARCs in the UK continue this service, for both men and women. SARCs, primarily funded by the police and the NHS, are based on a medical model of rape and work closely with the police. Perhaps because of these differences in their philosophies and service delivery, the early relationship between the original Manchester SARC and Manchester Rape Crisis was difficult. The Manchester Rape Crisis collective was not invited to be a part of the set-up of the SARC and they, like many SARC/RCC relations, continue to operate separately.

SARCs appear now to be the government's preferred targets of funding for 'victim-centred services'. SARCs are aimed at improving criminal justice. 80 per cent of their 'clients' come from police or criminal justice referrals. These users are more likely to be the victims of recent sexual violence, to be assaulted by strangers and to be assaulted in public places. In contrast, the number of RCCs has fallen over the years. RCCs have twice the number of

[21] See further **Section 5 of the Criminal Law (Rape) (Amendment) Act 1990**.
[22] London Rape Crisis Centre, *Sexual Violence, the Reality for Women* (The Women's Press, 1984) 136–39.
[23] Ian Blair, *Investigating Rape: A New Approach for Police* (Croom Helm, 1985).

self-referrals as SARCs. These women are twice as likely to be assaulted in domestic settings and by family members or partners.[24] Further, RCCs' woman-centred focus and independence from statutory agencies is both an advantage and a disadvantage when seen beside SARCs. On the one hand, RCCs are seen as a non-mainstream space where survivors can tell their stories, yet on the other, their non-alignment with other agencies means they suffer from lack of or late referrals, to the detriment of some women. The existence of SARCs has affected the work that some RCCs are able to do, but despite the variable relationship between individual SARCs and RCCs, most will cross-refer, as it is clear there is a need for the work done by both. And, while government funding and expansion is focused now on SARCs, it is probably true to say that RCCs laid the foundation for the victim-led work that SARCs now do.

## IV. Significance

Despite a sometimes rocky road, UK RCCs navigated their first 40 years more or less successfully, working through different philosophical and political challenges to ensure their crucial work continues. In 1993, for example, after much negotiation, a Rape Crisis Federation was created with Home Office funding, bringing together 35 Centres. Not all centres were agreed on the benefits of federating, however, and indeed London Rape Crisis did not participate. In 2003 the Home Office withdrew its funding, but the RCF's website continued and with a small grant, again from the Home Office, Rape Crisis England and Wales was created. Today, there are 45 independent member RCCs in Rape Crisis England and Wales, which, according to its website, is 'proud to call itself' a 'feminist organisation'.[25]

And so, in the 40 years since London Rape Crisis opened its doors, much has changed. Organisational and structural changes, changes in funding and partnership collaborations have meant that only a few RCCs have maintained the original LRCC collective model, for example. Another change is that unlike in 1976, it would be almost unthinkable today for consultations on police procedure, criminal justice or law reform to proceed without Rape Crisis involvement. On the other hand, some things remain the same. Funding for rape crisis remains perpetually uncertain. Many centres are facing closure, despite the number of calls and referrals for service which show that the incidence of sexual violence remains stubbornly and depressingly high. In 2016–17, Rape Crisis England and Wales reports statistics from the Ministry of Justice, Office of National Statistics and Home Office that:

- Approximately 85,000 women and 12,000 men are raped in England and Wales every year; roughly 11 rapes (of adults alone) every hour;
- 1 in 5 women aged 16–59 has experienced some form of sexual violence since the age of 16;
- Only around 15 per cent of those who experience sexual violence choose to report to the police; and

[24] Amanda Robinson and Kirsty Hudson, 'Different yet complementary: Two approaches to supporting victims of sexual violence in the UK' (2011) 11(5) *Criminology and Criminal Justice* 515, 530.

[25] Rape Crisis England and Wales, 'Why women & girls?': https://rapecrisis.org.uk/whywomengirls.php.

- Approximately 90 per cent of those who are raped knew the perpetrator prior to the offence.[26]

Rape Crisis England and Wales is the legacy of the London Rape Crisis Centre. It exists 'to promote the needs and rights of women and girls who have experienced sexual violence, to improve services to them and to work towards the elimination of sexual violence'.[27] Each of its member centres still provides specialist counselling, advocacy and information services in a women-only safe space. They will refer men to other services with which they coordinate. Rape Crisis England and Wales publish their own reports, respond to other reports, and continue their pioneering work of campaigning, educating, research and consultation. Similar work continues among Rape Crisis Scotland's 14 member centres and the Rape Crisis Network Ireland's 11 centres. Most importantly, RCCs across the UK and Ireland are there for women. Member centres of Rape Crisis England and Wales alone respond to an average of over 3000 calls per week providing essential help to thousands of rape survivors, 95 per cent of whom are female. In 2015–16 over 58,000 individuals in England and Wales received an on-going Rape Crisis service of more than 350,000 sessions of specialist support, including advocacy, emotional support and counselling.

The Women's Liberation Movement, and the anti-rape movement and Rape Crisis Centres around the world to which it gave birth, changed the way rape was understood socially and legally. These centres helped to influence police, medical and criminal justice procedures and substantive law. They have assisted and supported millions of individual women. They are a truly remarkable example of women working together to improve women's lives. The commitment of the original London Rape Crisis Collective and the thousands of women it has continued to inspire to do this work are both moving and powerful.

## Further Reading


- Susan Brownmiller, *Against Our Will: Men Women and Rape* (Simon and Shuster, 1975).
- Helen Jones and Kate Cook, *Rape Crisis, Responding to sexual violence* (Russell House Publishing, 2008).
- Liz Kelly, *Surviving Sexual Violence* (University of Minnesota Press, 1988).


[26] Rape Crisis England and Wales, 'Statistics': http://rapecrisis.org.uk/statistics.php.
[27] Rape Crisis England and Wales, 'Who we are and what we do': https://rapecrisis.org.uk/historyofrapecrisis.php.

# 46

# Section 4 of the Sexual Offences (Amendment) Act 1976

CLARE McGLYNN AND JULIA DOWNES

Anonymity for rape complainants, that is shielding the identity of the complainant in the press, was established in 1976 by section 4 of the Sexual Offences (Amendment) Act: 'after a person is accused of a rape offence no matter likely to lead members of the public to identify a woman as the complainant in relation to that accusation shall … be published in England and Wales'. The provision was gender-specific and worked by making it a criminal offence for the media to reveal the complainant's identity or any information that might lead to the complainant being identified. The law did not prevent complainants from being named in court, nor is there any restriction on their being named in discussions other than in the media.

This legal landmark was an important turning point for women, as it recognised the harmful stigma and scrutiny that rape complainants experience when their identities become publicly known. Since 1976, the law has been strengthened so that it now applies to women and men, to complainants of all sexual offences, and anonymity lasts for their lifetime. This legal landmark continues to protect the privacy rights of rape complainants, with the aim of encouraging complainants to report sexual offences and support prosecutions without fear of being blamed and shamed in public.

## I. Context

During the 1960s and 1970s, women began to gather and discuss how their own experiences of being a woman were connected and structured by wider systems of oppression known as 'patriarchy' and 'male supremacy'. These small and local consciousness-raising groups made up the backbone of the Women's Liberation Movement (WLM), an ambitious movement that, from 1970 until 1978, met annually at the National Women's Liberation Movement Conference to make key demands for women's rights. It was within the spaces and publications of the WLM where women discussed and made sense of their own experiences of rape, and the harmful impacts that myths, stereotypes and double standards had on them and other women who had experienced rape. Rape Crisis England and Wales was established in 1973 to support women who had experienced rape and to campaign for an end to sexual violence.[1] As more women came forward to report rape to the police and seek justice, the media and the legal system became targets of debate. In the media, sensationalised headlines and reporting focused on the complainants' personal lives and sexual histories, effectively shaming victims of rape in public. The now notorious House of Lords judgment in *DPP v Morgan*[2] highlighted the injustice that victims of rape encountered in the courtroom.

This case involved a defendant, Morgan, who had invited his three friends home to have sex with his wife based on Morgan's claim that she would consent to 'kinky' sex with all four men and that any violent resistance from her was a sign of her pleasure. Three men were convicted of rape and Morgan was convicted of aiding and abetting (as marital rape was not yet unlawful – this later changed following the House of Lords judgment in *R v R*).[3] The men appealed against their convictions and while the House of Lords upheld the convictions, it confirmed 'mistaken belief in consent' as a defence. Subsequently labelled the 'rapist's charter',[4] this defence meant that if a man honestly believed that a woman consented to sex (no matter how unreasonable that honest belief), he could not be found guilty. The public outcry that resulted from this decision led to the establishment of the Advisory Group on the Law of Rape chaired by the first woman High Court judge, **Mrs Justice Heilbron**.

As well as examining the law of rape, including a review of laws on the use of sexual history evidence, the Heilbron Committee considered how to encourage more complainants to come forward to report rape and whether any legal protections were necessary. The Heilbron Report recommended a number of reforms including granting anonymity to rape complainants.[5] The Report stated:

> Public knowledge of the indignity which [the complainant] has suffered in being raped may be extremely distressing and even positively harmful, and the risk of such public knowledge can operate as a severe deterrent to bringing proceedings … Nor is it generally the case that the humiliation is anything like as severe in other criminal trials: a reprehensible feature of trials of rape … is that the complainant's prior sexual history … may be brought out in the trial in a way which is rarely so in other criminal trials.[6]

The Report concluded, therefore, that rape complainants should be granted anonymity in order to encourage more victims to come forward and make reports of rape, give evidence in court and to improve conviction rates. The Report also recommended restrictions on the use of sexual history evidence in rape trials.[7]

## II. The Landmark

The section 4 of the Sexual Offences (Amendment) Act 1976, as amended, provides lifelong anonymity for rape complainants. This condition of anonymity worked by making it a

[1] **First Rape Crisis Centre, 1976**.
[2] *DPP v Morgan* [1976] AC 182; (1975) 61 Cr App R 136.
[3] *R v R* [1991] 3 WLR 767. See further **Section 5 of the Criminal Law (Rape) (Amendment) Act 1990**.
[4] Jennifer Temkin, *Rape and the Legal Process* (Sweet & Maxwell, 1987) 79.
[5] Home Office, *Report of the Advisory Group on the Law of Rape* (Cmnd 6352, 1975).
[6] ibid 27.
[7] **Section 41 of the Youth Justice and Criminal Evidence Act 1999**.

criminal offence for the media to reveal the complainant's identity or any information that might lead to the complainant being identified. This prohibition comes into action when a person is accused of rape, in practice a report to the police, and lasts for the whole of the complainant's lifetime. To be clear, the law does not prevent the defendant knowing the name of their accuser or the complainant's name being used in court proceedings. Therefore the anonymity granted is primarily protection from the media identifying the complainant to the public. This entitlement can only be lifted in certain circumstances, for example if the complainant chooses to reveal his or her identity, or if, following an application by the defendant, the court orders that anonymity should be lifted in order to encourage defence witnesses to come forward or if it is in the public interest.

## III. What Happened Next

The 1976 Act represented a significant 'win' for feminists campaigning for change. However, it was limited in scope. In 1986 Ms Saward was raped by burglars in her own home whilst her father and boyfriend were violently beaten.[8] As her attackers were unknown to Saward, and the police were yet to arrest anyone, newspapers discovered they could print her name and address without any legal repercussions, *The Sun* going so far as to publish a photo of Saward. This revealed a legal loophole in that the Act would only apply once a specific individual suspect had been identified. Section 158(2) of the Criminal Justice Act 1988 rectified this anomaly, stating that a rape complainant would be awarded anonymity as soon as 'an allegation that a woman has been the victim of a rape offence has been made by the woman or by any other person'.

Only providing complainant anonymity in cases of rape was also questioned. Other sexual offences also attract stigma, yet there were no restrictions to prevent complainants being named in the media. In response, the Sexual Offences (Amendment) Act 1992 further increased the scope of complainant anonymity with section 2(1) extending the protections to complainants of all sexual offences. The Youth Justice and Criminal Evidence Act 1999 further amended these provisions, removing any distinction between the type of material which can be published between allegation and charge, and charge and trial.

Since anonymity for rape complainants was introduced, there has been continued debate as to whether this protection facilitates or indeed encourages women to make so-called false allegations. *The Times* editorial that accompanied the publication of the Heilbron Report referred to the risk of allegations 'with no basis in fact brought by women for vindictive and malicious reasons'.[9] More recently, Helen Reece, a critic of complainant anonymity, argued that 'we should not facilitate the small number of women who make malicious allegations of rape by granting them anonymity – we should know their names, and if removal of anonymity discourages them, so much the better'.[10] This fear of 'false allegations' has continued to be debated despite evidence that only three per cent of reported rapes constitute false

[8] Julie Bindel, 'Rape campaigner Jill Saward on why she is standing against David Davis' *The Guardian*, 2 July 2008.

[9] Editorial, 'Reforming the Law on Rape' *The Times*, 11 December 1975.

[10] Helen Reece 'Rape Trials Should Be Completely open', *Spiked online* (18 February 2013).

allegations.[11] This institutional culture of disbelief is not lost on women and may be some of the reason behind the persistently low numbers of women coming forward to report rape and sexual assaults to the police.[12]

As well as discussion over the propriety of the anonymity provisions, they are also proving more and more difficult to enforce with the ease of mass communications via the internet and social media. Section 5 of the Sexual Offences (Amendment) Act 1992 criminalises 'the person publishing the matter' for 'publication in any other form'. This means that any member of the general public can be liable for breaching complainant anonymity if they post personal information, including names, addresses, photos and videos, about rape complainants on social media.

A few high-profile prosecutions have been brought against some who named the victim. For example, in 2012, after the footballer Ched Evans was convicted of rape, nine people were ordered to pay £624 in compensation to the victim after directly identifying her on social media.[13] As well as naming her, the posts vilified the victim, calling her a 'money grabbing slut', a 'dirty slapper', and threatening to post her address online. The court criticised the behaviour of the defendants, stating that their actions had 're-victimised this woman'.[14] Despite this public condemnation, the victim's name was still easily available through a Google search online. Further, during a news report about the convictions, *Sky News* accidentally used an image of the Tweets including the victim's name in the background of a broadcast.[15] The new identity of the victim has since been revealed online numerous times; most recently her photo was published on a foreign news website.[16] Overall it has been reported that she has been forced to change her identity and relocate five times.[17] This chain of events demonstrates that the concerns alive when the 1976 Act was first adopted have intensified. Women still risk public humiliation, condemnation and abuse for reporting and being victims of rape.

Accordingly, Alison Saunders, the Director of Public Prosecutions, has announced that as social media continues to undermine the law, new 'preventative laws' are needed to protect rape complainants.[18] Chief Constable Kavanagh (Essex Police), of the National Council of Police Chiefs, agreed with Saunders in a House of Lords Select Committee inquiry, suggesting that preventative legislation would 'assist in keeping people more safe in

[11] Liz Kelly, Jo Lovett and Linda Regan, *A Gap or Chasm? Attrition in Reported Rape Cases. Home Office Research Study 293* (Home Office, 2005); Liz Kelly, 'The (In)credible Words of Women: False allegations in European rape research' (2010) 16 *Violence Against Women* 1345–55.

[12] Home Office and Ministry of Justice, *An Overview of Sexual Offending in England and Wales* (January 2013).

[13] 'Footballer rape trial: Ched Evans jailed five years, Clayton McDonald cleared', *BBC News online*, 20 April 2012.

[14] James Orr, 'Police to arrest Twitter users who revealed name of Ched Evans rape victim', *The Telegraph*, 25 April 2012.

[15] 'Sky News accidentally identifies Ched Evans rape victim while reporting Twitter row', *The Telegraph*, 24 April 2012.

[16] Martin Evans, 'Ched Evans's victim's new identity revealed online', *The Telegraph*, 20 October 2014.

[17] Ched Evans has subsequently had his conviction for rape quashed and he was acquitted at a re-trial: *R v Ched Evans* [2016] EWCA Crim 452. The complainant remains a victim of serious public and media intrusion, as well as suffering the humiliation of having her sexual history revealed in court: see further Clare McGlynn, 'Rape Trials and Sexual History Evidence: reforming the law on third party evidence' (2017) 81(5) *Journal of Criminal Law* 367.

[18] Lydia Smith, 'Rape victims named and abused on social media as anonymity protection "too weak"', *International Business Times*, 10 July 2014.

the online environment and provide a framework … that gives oversight and accountability to police when they do venture into this sensitive area'.[19]

While these arguments to strengthen anonymity receive widespread support, others have questioned whether complainant anonymity is paternalistic and is actually responsible for constructing, rather than challenging, the social stigma that rape victims experience in society. For feminist critic Naomi Wolf, anonymity for rape victims perpetuates 'Victorian era' stereotypes of women's sexuality as fragile and pure, in which rape victims can only be seen as 'damaged goods' who have endured a 'fate worse than death'.[20] For Wolf, upholding complainant anonymity makes rape prosecutions more difficult by allowing officials to evade responsibility for transparent reporting of assaults and shielding their obligation to prosecute rape systematically. However, Katha Pollitt has responded vigorously to this critique, drawing attention to the commonplace attacks on the credibility of those who make accusations of rape. Pollitt defends complainant anonymity as the best way to encourage and help real-life rape victims to report assaults:

> if what women see all around them is that those who come forward have their lives shredded and their reputations, thanks to the Internet, forever linked to their most traumatic life event, they will decide, in greater numbers now that coming forward just isn't worth it.[21]

## IV. Significance

The granting of anonymity to complainants of sexual offences represents a significant legal landmark for women, albeit one that has had its limits tested by the ease of social media communications. It enables women and men to report sexual offences to the authorities without fear of being named (and therefore shamed) in the media. The continuing reality of shame and victim blaming means that we continue to require this law. Women and men still do not report rape and sexual assault very often. Statistics have revealed that only 15 per cent of female victims of serious sexual offences reported the crime.[22] As Rosa Knight, a helpline coordinator at Rape Crisis, says: 'the main reason women don't go to the police is the shame. Anonymity when they do is absolutely crucial'.[23] Women fear being ostracised by their family and friends: they fear being blamed for the rape, and they fear reprisals from their alleged attacker.

Complainant anonymity, therefore, sends a signal that the legal system recognises the difficult social contexts in which women and men report rape, and helps to encourage victims to come forward and access justice. Justice demands that allegations of criminal offences need to be made, investigated, and where appropriate result in convictions. This is necessary to ensure just punishment of those who have breached society's moral code that is the criminal law, as well as seeking to prevent future crimes.

[19] Select Committee on Communications, *Social Media Offences* (HL 2014, QQ 11–24), 20.

[20] Naomi Wolf, 'Julian Assange's Sex-crime Accusers Deserve to be Named', *The Guardian*, 5 January 2011.

[21] Katha Pollitt, 'Naomi Wolf: Wrong Again on Rape', *The Nation*, 10 January 2011.

[22] Home Office and Ministry of Justice, n 12 above.

[23] Quoted in Jane Martinson, 'Let's Not Hide Behind the Argument that Anonymity isn't Possible on the Web', *The Guardian*, 6 November 2012.

Nonetheless, in an ideal world, we would not require a law granting anonymity. We would not need this law because stigma would not attach to those who report a sexual offence. Shame would not be felt by those who had been raped. We would also not need such a law because there would be fewer incidents of sexual assault. In fact, therefore, the legal landmark we should seek is repeal of these provisions, safe in the knowledge that women and men will continue to report rape, as well perhaps, as there being less rape or sexual offending to report. But we are not there yet.

## Further Reading


- Helen Boyle, 'Rape and the Media: Victim's Rights to Anonymity and Effects of Technology on the Standard of Rape Coverage' (2012) 3 *European Journal of Law and Technology*: http://ejlt.org/article/view/172/262.
- Clare McGlynn, 'Rape, Defendant Anonymity and Human Rights: adopting a "wider perspective"' (2011) 3 *Criminal Law Review* 199–215.
- Jennifer Temkin, *Rape and the Legal Process* (OUP, 2002).

# 47

# Housing (Homeless Persons) Act 1977

LAURA BINGER AND HELEN CARR

The Housing (Homeless Persons) Act 1977 provided the first legal definition of homelessness and imposed a duty on all local authorities to provide long-term housing for homeless people who met particular conditions. The passing of the Act was significant because, for the first time, women were able to make a direct and legally enforceable claim upon the state when they were facing a housing crisis, rather than being reliant upon the discretionary and often arbitrary policies of local authorities. Moreover, because the Act gave priority to pregnant women and those responsible for children, it put an end to the cruel practice of taking the children of homeless women into care in order to avoid having to house their families, and provided statutory recognition of the needs of non-traditional families. Equally significant was the definition of homelessness set out in section 1(2)(b) of the Act, which included people who had accommodation but were at risk of domestic violence if they continued living there. For those who had fled from violence, section 5(1)(iii) provided an exception to local connection rules for people who ran a risk of domestic violence if they returned to the area where they had local connection.

The Act was important, as it addressed the failures of the state to recognise the particular vulnerabilities of women in connection with housing. However, it did so in a way which perpetuated notions of women as dependent and victimised, and created a complex legal apparatus which is often extremely remote from the day-to-day experiences of women facing housing crises.

## I. Context

Prior to the implementation of the Housing (Homeless Persons) Act 1977, homeless women who needed accommodation were reliant upon the powers given to local authorities under the National Assistance Act 1948 (NAA 1948). The NAA 1948 was one of the foundational statutes of the post-war welfare state. One of its primary purposes was to replace the discredited and despised Poor Laws, which had relied upon the workhouse to provide for and simultaneously discipline the destitute. Although the destruction from Second World War bombings had precipitated a housing crisis, the state anticipated that council house building would alleviate that crisis and that couples would delay starting families until they were allocated housing or that they and their children would live with their parents until housing became available. The problem of homelessness, and particularly family homelessness, commonly triggered by relationship breakdown, eviction from private rented accommodation, or the unaffordability of relatively costly council housing, had not been anticipated. As a result of families bunking in together, putting up with domestic violence, or renting inappropriate accommodation in the private rented sector, the problem was frequently hidden from public view.

The NAA 1948 reflected contemporary policy priorities, which saw homelessness as a health and welfare issue rather than a housing problem and placed responsibility for responding first with the Department of Health and later with the re-organised Department of Health and Social Services. Local government under the NAA 1948 was only required to provide temporary accommodation to homeless families, and homeless people who were refused assistance under the legislation were not able to go to court to challenge local decisions. Meanwhile, central government was constrained in its approach to local authorities taking only limited action to influence local practices, even where it disagreed with local government implementation of the NAA 1948.

The inadequacy of the provision for homeless families was slowly recognised, particularly as it became clear that council house building was not going to be able to solve the housing crisis and the consequences were becoming visible. Ken Loach's 1966 BBC television play *Cathy Come Home* vividly told the story of a family torn apart by homelessness and caused national outrage. The charity Shelter was founded around the time that the play aired and it campaigned vigorously for reform.

Government appeared to be more ambivalent about actually doing something. During the 1950s, '60s and '70s a number of national government circulars were issued with the intent of persuading local authorities to change how they implemented the NAA 1948. The case for action to recognise and provide for the long-term needs of homeless families was buttressed by two government-commissioned reports, the Greve Report on homelessness in London, and Glastonbury's report on homelessness in the southwest.[1] However, the Local Government Act 1972 watered down the NAA 1948 by reducing the *duty* of local authorities to provide temporary accommodation to a *power*.

The pendulum swung back in February 1974 when Joint Circular 18/74 was issued. The circular directed local authorities unable to accommodate all homeless people to house the most vulnerable homeless people who made it into one of the specified 'Priority Groups' –

> families with dependent children living with them, or in care, adult families or people living alone who either became homeless in an emergency such as fire or flooding or are vulnerable because of old age, disability, pregnancy or other special reasons.

The circular, issued by the Department of the Environment and the Department of Health and Social Security, also addressed the housing needs of those suffering domestic violence, instructed local authorities not to separate families when providing accommodation, and urged housing authorities to take the primary role in responding to homelessness. The latter was important to campaigners because it would give homeless families a route to more permanent housing in council housing, rather than only temporary housing in hostels or bed-and-breakfasts. It was also, however, important conceptually in that it indicated a shift

[1] John Greve, Dilys Page and Stella Greve, *Homelessness in London* (Edinburgh, 1971); Byran Glastonbury, *Homeless Near a Thousand Homes: A Study of Homeless Families in South Wales and the West of England* (London, 1971).

from thinking about homelessness as a problem of individual fecklessness and problematic and dysfunctional families to a problem caused by inadequate and unaffordable housing.

However, many local authorities did not respond to the national circulars. Indeed, prior to the 1977 Act both a Department of the Environment survey and research by Shelter had found that large numbers of local authorities were not following their directions. Charities publicised stories of people, including pregnant women and women leaving abusive relationships, who clearly fell within the defined priority groups, being refused accommodation by local authorities. In many areas, the local authorities responsible for housing refused to take primary responsibility for housing homeless people. The problem only worsened when homeless people went to the courts. When the Roberts family was refused even temporary accommodation by Dorset County Council, Shelter assisted them in challenging the decision in the courts and argued that the local authority had not followed Circular 18/74, but the High Court found that the local authority was not bound by the circular.[2]

The result was that homeless women continued to face a very hard time. Many were refused accommodation entirely. Even if provided with accommodation, women with children in many local authority areas would be offered only short-term accommodation, which was often little better than workhouse conditions – at times the accommodation was provided in former workhouses and at times families were split up due to rules that, for example, excluded men from temporary accommodation.[3] If the family had not found alternative accommodation before their eviction date, then the women would be evicted and their children taken into care. Finding alternative accommodation was problematic. Single-parent families were generally excluded from council housing waiting lists. Women fleeing domestic violence with their children were frequently refused help by local authority housing departments who did not consider them to be homeless or told to return to the local authorities where their abusers lived. Women without children, including pregnant women, were refused even temporary accommodation in many areas. Private rented accommodation was scarce and often unsuitable, and private landlords were reluctant to house single mothers. So the situation for women in housing crisis was dire.

On the heels of the erosion of local authorities' duties in the 1972 amendments to the Local Government Act, the campaign for national and legally-binding obligations towards the homeless was energised. A number of prominent charities concerned with homelessness formed an alliance and created the Joint Charities Group (JCG). The Group included Shelter, the Catholic Housing Aid Centre (CHAC), the Shelter Housing Aid Centre (SHAC), the Campaign for Homeless and Rootless (CHAR, an organisation representing various homelessness charities), the Child Poverty Action Group (CPAG) with the National Council for One Parent Families, and Public Health Advisory Service. The aim of the JCG was to create an effective parliamentary lobby for legislative change.

The role of women in the campaign has been invisibilised, so even the work of those who played important roles in housing, like Audrey Harvey, an adviser, researcher, writer, and activist, is rarely mentioned in the history of homeless persons legislation. Women's organisations, in particular, the National Women's Aid Federation, were clearly involved

[2] Campaign for the Homeless and Rootless, *Jubilee Year for the Homeless?* (Campaign for the Homeless and Rootless (CHAR) 1977). The case is reported as *Roberts v Dorset County Council* (1976) 75 LGR 462.

[3] Ron Bailey and Joan Ruddock, *The Grief Report: A Shelter Report on Temporary Accommodation* (Shelter, 1972).

in campaigning for the legislation, but are not credited in most historical narratives of this time period. Moreover, the actions of homeless women themselves, such as those involved in the Kings Hill Hostel Campaign, who campaigned against Kent County Council's inhumane treatment of homeless families, have been all but forgotten.

## II. The Landmark

By the mid-1970s it was clear to reformers that only national legislation could provide the necessary safety net for the homeless. A telegram sent from an organisation supporting the proposed Act to an MP and read aloud during parliamentary debates succinctly demonstrates the priorities and hopes of its supporters: 'Legislation imperative to safeguard rights of children and families in danger of separation. Establish basic responsibility by statute. Then code of practice for guidance'.[4] Central government attempts at persuasion had failed to change local authority mindsets and, although local campaigning had resulted in some local authorities extending provision, this was limited and ad hoc. The Labour Party, as part of its manifesto commitments in 1974, had pledged to implement homelessness legislation. However, its tenuous hold on power following the 1974 election and its commitment to drastic and divisive public expenditure cuts during the 1976 IMF crisis led to it avoiding the political hot potato of legislating on homelessness. Nor did it want to alienate local authorities, many of whom were strongly opposed to attempts to curtail their discretion through new legislation on homelessness.

The JCG had begun laying the groundwork for a push for legislation in 1973, focusing on building relationships with MPs and key civil servants. They had already gained the support of a number of MPs when in 1977 one of these MPs, Stephen Ross, the Liberal MP for the Isle of Wight, came fourth in the private member's bill ballot. Within hours the JCG approached him and persuaded him to sponsor a bill they had drafted. Relatively quickly, the government took over the bill with the Department of the Environment producing a more professional and arguably more radical draft. The bill was amended many times before it was passed. Its final form included major concessions to the concerns of local authorities and the fears of Conservative politicians, some of whom described the legislation as a scroungers' charter.[5]

Although based on the core provisions of Circular 18/74, the bill went further, and in so doing developed the framework that remains at the core of today's homelessness legislation. This revolves around the definition of homelessness, the scope of priority need, tests of intentionality, and the significance of 'local connection'. Campaigners hoped that enacting the provisions of the circular as legislation would finally compel local authorities to follow its provisions, but they also used the bill to address issues that had not been addressed in the circular and attempted to build into it the ability to expand its scope. The local connection provision was seen by campaigners to be a step forward from what had preceded it.

[4] Andrew Welsh MP reading a telegram sent to Stephen Ross from the British Association of Social Workers in Scotland (HC Deb, 18 February 1977, vol 926 col 920).

[5] Lorraine Thompson, *An Act of Compromise: An Appraisal of the Effects of the Housing (Homeless Persons) Act 1977 – Ten Years on* (SHAC and Shelter, 1988).

It directed local authorities not to immediately turn away people who did not have a connection to their area. It did, however, retain the concept of local connection by providing that if applicants have a local connection to an authority other than the one to which they have applied, then, in most circumstances, it is that local authority which owes them a duty.

The JCG continued to work with government on the Code of Guidance issued alongside the Act. Because it contained important advice to local authorities, it was considered to be the best way to ensure a liberal interpretation of legislative requirements.

Just as important as what the Act did is what it did not do. MPs emphasised that it required no additional funding. Though it mentioned the funding of charity groups, that funding was to be allocated from an existing funding stream in the budget. Local authorities were directed to ensure that particular people be housed, but were not given funds to build housing for these people. Ross had at first hoped to tie the bill to measures aimed at bringing empty houses into use, but this was quickly dropped. The effect was to direct local authorities to allocate existing housing differently rather than to build or purchase additional housing to meet unmet housing need. The other problem of the legislation was that it left single people, including those who were victims of domestic violence, with very little statutory protection. This was because, although single people could fall within the categories of 'in priority need' if they were vulnerable, the category of vulnerability was narrowly drawn and, in particular, excluded references to domestic violence.

## III. What Happened Next

The Act, once implemented, immediately provoked litigation, reflecting local authorities' reluctance to accept homelessness responsibilities and homeless people's utilisation of the new powers to challenge local authority decision-making in the courts. The most significant of the early challenges was that of the Puhlhofers.[6] Mr and Mrs Puhlhofer were living with their two young children temporarily in bed-and-breakfast accommodation in a guest house. They had one single bedroom with no means of washing clothes or cooking. They applied to the local authority for accommodation as homeless persons because the room was inadequate for their needs. The council decided that they were not homeless or threatened with homelessness within the meaning of the Act. The House of Lords, in a shockingly literal interpretation of the legislation, upheld the decision of the local authority, refusing to impose any duty to consider whether the accommodation was reasonable or appropriate. This led to an amendment to the legislation in 1986, adding to the definition of homelessness the requirement that accommodation available to a person had to be suitable for them. This was significant for women fleeing domestic violence as it meant that being accommodated in a refuge would not enable local authorities to exclude them from homelessness provisions. However, the *Puhlhofer* litigation had another consequence. It enabled local authorities to ignore the more liberal requirements of the Code of Guidance in favour of the statutory provisions.

The problem of single people who become homeless because of experiencing or fearing violence was not effectively tackled until the 2002 Homelessness (Priority Need for

[6] *R v Hillingdon London Borough Council, ex parte Puhlhofer* [1986] AC 484.

Accommodation) (England) Order, which extended the vulnerable category of priority need to include 'a person who is vulnerable as a result of ceasing to occupy accommodation by reason of violence from another person or threats of violence from another person which are likely to be carried out'.

## IV. Significance

Supporters of the Act recognised that it was a compromise but celebrated it as a first step towards a long-term goal of housing all homeless people. This vision for the future was not just an amorphous hope for slow changes over the long term but an anticipation that there would be specific changes coming soon. In particular, campaigners hung their hopes on the anticipated Code of Guidance for clarifying and expanding its provisions. In this regard, the Act did not meet expectations. It did, however, include meaningful changes that meant many homeless women were able to live in temporary accommodation without having to separate their families, were provided with long-term housing in the social rented sector, and could challenge decisions they disagreed with. These important changes were accompanied by new problems that were not always anticipated by those who campaigned for the Act. Due in part to its complexity and in part to it having provided rights while neglecting to provide the resources needed for local authorities to meet the duties imposed on them, the Act has been the subject of a constant flow of litigation out of which lawyers have perhaps benefitted most.

Moreover the Act, perhaps because of the way it perpetuated notions of women as dependent and victimised, has not protected women from the privatisation and precaritisation of housing which began with the election of Thatcher in 1979. The 'Right to Buy' depleted social housing stock, and houses sold were not replaced. Security of tenure was first dismantled in the private rented sector by the Housing Act 1988 and, since the Housing and Planning Act 2016, is slowly being phased out of the social sector. Since 1996 local authorities have been able to discharge their duties to homeless people by offering them housing in the private rented sector. Insecurity is increased because rapid rises in rents have not been matched by wages or benefits. Measures in response to austerity – the benefit cap, which places an upper limit on the amount of benefits payable to someone, and the 'bedroom tax' which reduces benefits paid to people deemed to be under-occupying their homes – are making people homeless and disproportionately affect women because of their economic and social situation.

The impact of these measures is stark. Figures produced by the Public Accounts Select Committee in December 2017 indicate that in 2017 there were over 78,180 households, including 120,170 children, who were in temporary accommodation, and 9,100 people sleeping rough in the UK. As the Committee points out, the problem is greater than even these figures suggest, as '[t]here is also an unknown number of people who are neither sleeping on the street nor in temporary accommodation but are housed by friends and family in shifting circumstances'.[7] The Act, which started life as an important charter of housing rights for women, has morphed into a flimsy welfare safety net, which, although it prevents

[7] House of Commons Committee of Public Accounts, *Homeless Households* (HC 462, 13 December 2017).

children sleeping on streets, does little to guarantee a sufficient supply of decent, secure and affordable housing, and condemns women and children to months and even years in bed and breakfast or other unsuitable temporary accommodation.

## Further Reading

- Ken Loach, *Cathy Come Home* (BBC, 1966).
- Ellen Malos and Gil Hague, 'Women, housing, homelessness and domestic violence' (1997) 20 *Women's Studies International Forum* 343.
- Paula Mayock and Joanne Bretherton (eds), *Women's Homelessness in Europe* (Palgrave Macmillan, 2016).
- Sophie Watson and Helen Austerberry, *Housing and Homelessness: A Feminist Perspective* (Routledge and Kegan Paul, 1986).

# 48

## *Davis v Johnson* (1978)

SUSAN EDWARDS

*Davis v Johnson*[1] resolved once and for all the correct interpretation of the Domestic Violence and Matrimonial Proceedings Act (DVMPA) 1976, which had up until then been construed in different ways. The House of Lords held that the proprietorial right of a husband to occupy the matrimonial home in the event of his physical abuse of a wife (section 1(1)(c)) or partner (section 1(2)) could be suspended, thereby excluding the husband or male partner from the property or part of it (section 1(1)(c)). The five judges (Lords Diplock, Kilbrandon, Salmon and Scarman and Viscount Dilhorne) were unanimous that the DVMPA provided a wife or partner with a remedy for protection which allowed for interference with a husband or male partner's proprietorial right in cases where her life was in serious or grave danger. For the first time, the law provided protection for wives and cohabitants living in the same household. Lord Salmon stated:

> In my view Parliament in passing this Act, was not concerned with the preservation of proprietary rights but with affording protection to 'battered wives'. … I am certain that the Act of 1976 was not intended to deprive him of his proprietary rights … but only to interfere for a fairly short period … whilst his former mistress had the opportunity to look for accommodation.[2]

## I. Context

In 1976, few women shared rights in the matrimonial home and few, if any, were the sole owner, sole tenant or occupier. However, prior to the enactment of the DVMPA that year the legal remedies available to a wife or unmarried partner seeking protection from domestic violence were extremely limited. A wife could apply under the Matrimonial Homes Act 1967 for injunctive relief against a husband's violence but only where proceedings for divorce or judicial separation had been initiated. For many women, divorce or separation was not an option; financial dependency, need for housing, support to children, shame, and fear of further violence were just some of the factors compelling women to remain in violent relationships and often in silence. Unmarried partners, referred to by the Lords in *Davis v Johnson* as 'mistresses' or 'cohabitees', were in a different (worse) position.

[1] *Davis v Johnson* [1979] AC 264; [1978] 2 WLR 553.
[2] ibid, 575D–H.

There was no protection except to report the incident to the police and seek any remedy that the under-enforced criminal law might offer.

Yet the risk of violence behind closed doors was very real. One-fifth of all recorded homicides, irrespective of the relationship of victim to suspect, were committed against female spouses and cohabitants. Robert Chester and Jane Streather's study on cruelty and divorce in 1972 found that, of 8,800 English divorces granted for cruelty in 1967, 94 per cent were granted to wives. Indeed cruelty accounted for just under a third of wives' decrees (compared to under three per cent of husbands'). In 90 per cent of these cases repeated physical violence was reported.[3] The police were reluctant, moreover, to proceed with charges for criminal assault against men as the ideology of the privacy of the home prevailed, allowing men's woeful conduct within it to continue unfettered, even in the face of brute violence against women. Perpetrators when proceeded against, if at all, faced the puny charge of breach of the peace and were subsequently fined.[4] Mrs X who gave oral evidence to the *Select Committee on Violence in Marriage* in 1976 confirmed this use of breach of the peace even in circumstances of the most serious violence.

> I have had ten stitches, three stitches, five stitches, seven stitches, where he has cut me. I have had a knife stuck through my stomach; I have had a poker put through my face; I have no teeth where he knocked them all out; I have been burnt with red hot pokers; I have had red hot coals slung all over me; I have been sprayed with petrol and stood there while he has flicked lighted matches at me … I have been to the police … and they held him in over the weekend and he came out on Monday. He was bound over to keep the peace … On the Tuesday he gave me the hiding of my life.[5]

There was evidence too of derisory sentences imposed by judges upon conviction of the perpetrator. Jo Richardson MP, presenting the Bill that was to become the DVMPA for its second reading in the House of Commons, reported a case where a husband even with two previous convictions for assaulting his wife evaded appropriate punishment:

> During one attack, he tied a flex so tightly round her throat that her larynx was damaged and she had to be fed through a tube in hospital. The man was taken to court, fined £2 and told to behave himself.[6]

Domestic violence was not, as is so often imagined, only 'discovered' by second-wave feminists. First-wave feminists like Frances Power Cobbe had campaigned vigorously for the authorities to take it more seriously (for example, in her influential article 'Wife Torture in England')[7] and to increase penalties against men who beat their wives. Their efforts led to the enactment of the Matrimonial Causes Act 1878, which enabled women to leave their violent husbands and get maintenance. In 1949, Renee Duffy, a battered wife, was convicted of the murder of her violent husband.[8] Though her appeal against conviction was

[3] Robert Chester and Jane Streather, 'Cruelty in English Divorce: Some Empirical Findings' (1972) 34(4) *Journal of Marriage and Family* 706, 708–09.

[4] Susan Edwards, *Policing Domestic Violence* (Sage, 1989).

[5] *Select Committee on Violence in Marriage. Together with the Proceedings of the Committee*, Session 1974–75, Vol 2 (HMSO, 1975) 25.

[6] HC Deb, 13 February 1976, vol 905 col 862.

[7] Frances Power Cobbe, 'Wife Torture in England' (1878) *Contemporary Review*, reprinted in Susan Hamilton (ed), *'Criminals, Idiots, Women, & Minors': Nineteenth-Century writing by women on women* (Broadview Press, 1995) 132–69.

[8] *R v Duffy* [1949] 1 All ER 932.

refused, overwhelming public sympathy resulted in a petition (organised by her solicitor, Frank R Johnson), supported by 12,000 signatures ensured her reprieve from a death sentence.[9]

But the Women's Liberation Movement can take credit for starting to bring about real change in the treatment of domestic violence. In 1971 Erin Pizzey published *Scream quietly or the Neighbours will hear*, which detailed the testimonies of women who had fled domestic abuse.[10] In 1974 she founded Chiswick Family Aid in 1974 and the National Women's Aid Federation was set up in the same year to provide support to victims of domestic violence, the first national domestic violence organisation. The burgeoning sexual politics of the 1970s also provided the political articulation of the specificities of women's oppression.[11] One of the seven demands of the Women's Liberation Movement called for an end to domestic violence.[12] In 1975, following the *Select Committee on Violence in Marriage*,[13] Jo Richardson introduced a Private Member's Bill on Domestic Violence which was later supported by the Government. At 2.10pm on 13 February 1976, moving the Bill for the second time she addressed the House of Commons:

> At about this time on a Friday afternoon thousands of women are dreading the thought of Friday night. To them Friday night can often mean a night of strife with the man in the house. It can mean a night that ends in injury and battering, yet relatively few people, possibly not even the neighbours, may know about it. To many women it is something that they feel they should keep within the family, so they continue to suffer it. Some women are injured on week nights, and at any time, but Fridays and weekends, when father is at home, are times to be dreaded in many families.Wife beating is as old as the hills. Unfortunately there are many who believe it is their right to beat their women and that any interference from outside is an unwarranted intrusion.[14]

The enactment of the DVMPA in 1976 was enormously important for all women, but especially those living in and through abusive relationships. It gave the county courts power to grant non-molestation injunctions against the abusive spouse or cohabitee and also allowed for the making of orders to exclude them for a period from the family home.

## II. The Landmark

So how did this eminently sensible piece of legislation just two years later come to be considered by the House of Lords?

[9] Susan Edwards, 'Justice Devlin's legacy: Duffy – a battered woman "caught" in time' (2009) 12 *Criminal Law Review* 851–69. Women were labouring under other difficulties too. In *R v Millar* [1954] 2 QB 282 it was decided that a husband could not be guilty of rape on a wife but only guilty of common assault. This legal position persisted until it was overturned in *R v R* [1991] UKHL 12. See further Section 5 of the Criminal Law (Rape) (Amendment) Act 1990.

[10] Erin Pizzey, *Scream Quietly or the Neighbours will hear* (Penguin, 1974). See further First Women's Refuge, 1971.

[11] Kate Millet, *Sexual Politics* (Doubleday, 1970), Sheila Rowbotham, *Woman's Consciousness, Man's world* (Penguin, 1973); Del Martin, *Battered Wives* (Pocket Books, 1976); Rebecca Emerson Dobash and Russell P Dobash, *Violence Against Wives* (Open Books, 1980).

[12] See Finn Mackay, 'The 7 Demands of the UK Women's Liberation Movement' (no date): https://finnmackay.wordpress.com/articles-i-like/the-7-demands-of-the-uk-womens-liberation-movement/.

[13] Select Committee on Violence in Marriage, n 5 above.

[14] HC Deb, 13 February 1976, vol 905 col 857.

Nehemiah Johnson and Jennifer Davis were unmarried cohabitants living together as joint tenants in a council flat at 13, Nisbet House, Homerton High Street, East London. Jennifer Davis was the victim of violence inflicted by Nehemiah Johnson which the Court of Appeal described as 'extreme', forcing her to leave with their daughter of two and a half and seek refuge in a Women's Refuge in Chiswick on the other side of London (one of the few refuges in the city). Johnson threatened to kill Davis, and said he would dump her in the river or chop her up and put her in the freezer. The case, which was legally protracted, no doubt further compounding her mental anguish, commenced with a hearing in Brentford County Court on 18 October 1977, almost a year to the day since the enactment of the DVMPA, and concluded on 9 March 1978.

Davis was initially successful. District Judge Paulusz, in Brentford County Court, granted her the relief she sought, restraining Johnson from assaulting or molesting her or their child and ordering him to vacate the flat. Six days later, the Court of Appeal, in a different case, *Cantliff v Jenkins*,[15] determined that the DVMPA did not permit exclusion of a perpetrator where parties were joint tenants, since each had equal interest in the property (by virtue of the Law of Property Act 1925). In other words, the remedy was only available in the relatively rare circumstances where the victim of violence was the sole owner or sole tenant of the property. A companion case, *B v B*,[16] also ruled that the DVMPA did not apply to unmarried cohabitants.

On October 26 Mr Johnson appealed the original order to another county court, where District Judge Lewis now found himself bound by the decision in *Cantliff* and rescinded that part of the original order which had required Johnson to vacate the property. Ms Davis subsequently appealed this decision to the Court of Appeal where, because of the reservations over the interpretation of the law, a court of five members instead of three was (unusually) constituted.

Lord Denning in the Court of Appeal set down in plain narrative the problem and what needed to be done 'to protect the weak and as Parliament intended'.[17] In his opening statement, he told it exactly as it was:

> Battered wives is a telling phrase. It was invented so as to call the attention of the public to an evil. Few were aware of it. It arose when a woman suffered serious or repeated physical injury from the man with whom she lived. She might be a wife properly married to her husband; or she might only be a woman called, falsely, a 'common law wife'.[18]

The Court found for Ms Davis by a bare majority. Delivering the majority judgment, Denning LJ restored the original order of District Judge Paulusz requiring Mr Johnson to vacate the flat. In the course of his judgment, he held that the interpretation of statute allowed for consideration of, in this case, the findings of the *Select Committee on Violence in Marriage*:

> Some may say – and indeed have said – that judges should not pay any attention to what is said in Parliament. They should grope about in the dark for the meaning of an Act without switching on the light. I do not accede to this view.[19]

[15] *Cantliff v Jenkins* [1978] 1 All ER 836.
[16] *B v B* [1978] 1 All ER 821.
[17] *Davis v Johnson* [1979] AC 264, 283; [1978] 1 All ER 841 (CA).
[18] ibid 270–71.
[19] ibid 276–77.

Mr Johnson then appealed to the House of Lords, contending that section 1 of the 1976 Act did not confer on a county court the jurisdiction to exclude a person from premises in which he had a proprietary interest, and that the Court of Appeal could not depart from its earlier decisions or look to other documents which had not been relied upon by counsel, in finding the intention of Parliament. In the House of Lords, Lord Diplock recognised that the provisions in the Act had led 'to a conflict of judicial opinion'.[20] Lord Scarman said the section was difficult and obscure.[21] Nevertheless, their Lordships were in (different shades of) agreement regarding the interpretation of section 1. Lord Diplock asserted that

> under the existing substantive law a mistress is entitled to protection against the tort of assault, and if, as in the instant case, she is a joint tenant with her paramour of the premises in which she is living with him, she has a legal right to continue in peaceful occupation of them.[22]

Lord Scarman added that the intention of Parliament was to strengthen remedies and protect life and limb. Lord Dilhorne said that, whilst the Act made 'drastic inroads into common law property rights of spouses',[23] he accepted that it applied to cohabitants or partners. It was conceded by all that the Act intended to 'over-ride a property right, if it be thought to be socially necessary'.[24] The original order of District Judge Paulusz was reinstated once and for all.

## III. What Happened Next

Despite the victory won in *Davis v Johnson*, in the post-*Davis* period judges were reluctant to oust a man from the matrimonial home even for a short period of time; the 'grave and serious violence' threshold trigger to the remedy was rarely met. Statistics showed depressingly that few such ouster injunctions were granted.[25] On 1 October 1997, almost 20 years to the day since Davis went to the Brentford County Court, the DVMPA was repealed. Section 33(7) of the Family Law Act 1996 introduced a new creature for interpretation by the courts: the 'balance of harm' test. This required that the significant harm suffered by the applicant had to be established as being as great as or greater than the harm to the other party from being excluded before an ouster injunction could be made. The human rights of both parties were set against each other. Moreover, in balancing her need for safety and protection against his right to residence, consideration had to be given to the housing needs, financial resources, and the likely effect of any order on the health, safety or well-being of the parties (section 33(6)). Thus in *Chalmers v Johns*,[26] refusing an occupation order for exclusion, Thorpe LJ asserted, '[t]he order remains draconian, particularly in the perception of the respondent. It remains an order that overrides proprietary rights and

[20] *Davis v Johnson* [1978] 2 WLR 553, 557 (HL).
[21] ibid 579
[22] ibid 564–65.
[23] ibid 565.
[24] ibid 591.
[25] Susan Edwards, 'Domestic Violence and Harassment' in Julie Taylor-Browne (ed), *What works in Domestic Violence* (Whiting and Birch, 2001) 199, 201.
[26] *Chalmers v Johns* [1999] 1 FLR 392.

it seems to me that it is an order that is only justified in exceptional circumstances'.[27] More recently, the 1996 Act has been amended by the Domestic Violence, Crime and Victims Act 2004, which among other things removed the distinction between married and cohabiting couples (section 2) and extended the provisions of the 1996 Act to same-sex (section 3) and non-cohabiting couples (section 4).

Unduly lenient sentences for domestic violence and domestic violence manslaughter persisted, prompting Labour MP Harriet Harman, when Solicitor General, in December 2002, to refer lenient sentences in domestic violence manslaughter back to the Court of Appeal with a view to 'encourage judges to impose stiffer terms of imprisonment'.[28] They did not.[29]

## IV. Significance

Without doubt *Davis v Johnson* was a turning point both in law and in judicial understanding of domestic violence. The problem of domestic violence, despite these changes, remains a significant problem in its extent and in the failings of the criminal justice response. Over a quarter of women have experienced domestic abuse since the age of 16.[30] On average two women in England and Wales are killed by their current or former partner every week.[31] Cuts to Legal Aid are making it significantly harder for women to access the courts to protect themselves and their family.[32] The position adopted by the House of Lords in *Davis* appears to be in retreat. The significant gains for battered women introduced and made possible by Lord Denning in the Court of Appeal and approved by the House of Lords have been realigned through the lens of 'rights' which, together with the 'balance of harm' test to be applied in applications involving a condition of exclusion (section 33(6) and (7) of the Family Law Act 1996), introduces a notional level playing-field in a land of unequals.

In February 2017 the Prime Minister, Theresa May, announced a 'major programme of work leading towards bringing forward a Domestic Violence and Abuse Act'. This was later confirmed in the Queen's Speech. The Act will establish a Domestic Violence and Abuse Commissioner, as well as consolidate existing protection orders. It remains to be seen whether this ambition survives the Brexit landscape, but if it does *Davis* teaches us that there will be a new generation of judges and practitioners who require continuous enlightenment and understanding of the prevalence and seriousness of domestic violence, both in the effects of violence on its victims and also the consequent homelessness which follows when women are forced to leave in order to protect their lives.

[27] ibid 397.

[28] Attorney General's References (Nos 74, 95 and 118 of 2002) [2002] EWCA Crim 2982.

[29] See also Susan Edwards 'Injustice that puts a low price on a woman's life', *The Times*, 2 September 2003.

[30] Crime Survey for England and Wales 2015–16, cited in Pat Strickland and Grahame Allen, *Domestic Violence in England and Wales* (HC Briefing Paper 6337, 21 June 2017).

[31] Refuge, 'The facts': http://www.refuge.org.uk/our-work/forms-of-violence-and-abuse/domestic-violence/domestic-violence-the-facts/.

[32] Louise Tickle, 'How the UK's legal system is failing victims of domestic violence', *The Guardian*, 29 November 2014.

## Further Reading

- Nicola Groves and Terry Thomas, *Domestic Violence and Criminal Justice* (Routledge, 2013).
- Rebecca Dobash and Russell Dobash, *Violence against Wives: A Case against the Patriarchy* (Open Books, 1980).

# 49

# Health (Family Planning) Act 1979

MÁIRÉAD ENRIGHT

Before the Health (Family Planning) Act 1979, selling contraceptives and importing them for sale were criminal offences in Ireland.[1] Importing contraceptives for personal use was also prohibited. This Act legalised those activities in certain circumstances, allowing married couples, and people with relevant medical needs, to access condoms and other contraceptives on a doctor's prescription. The Act began a slow de-coupling of Irish law from absolutist interpretations of Catholic social teaching, and marked an important legal acknowledgment of the public health costs of restricting access to contraception. It also provided a legal avenue of access to contraceptives, confirming growing public support for the principle that women should be able to determine the number and spacing of their children.

## I. Context

In 1935, the fledgling Irish state legislated to restrict contraceptive access. Two inquiries had contributed to a moral panic around contraception. The Evil Literature Committee (1926) documented widespread availability of British 'contraceptive propaganda' in Ireland.[2] The Carrigan Commitee (1931) found that women both used home-made contraceptives and bought them from English mail order services and some chemists. This Committee recommended that doctors should retain discretion to prescribe and supply contraceptives on grounds of religious conviction or medical need. However, the Pope, responding to the newly liberal Anglican stance on contraceptives announced at the Lambeth Conference of 1930, had forbidden Catholics to use them, even on health grounds. In the encyclical *Casti Conubii* he proclaimed that 'God alone can reward' the mother who risks her life in

[1] It is worth noting that restrictive contraceptive laws existed elsewhere in Europe at this time, often motivated by ethno-nationalist projects designed to reverse population decline. France legislated to restrict access to all methods of contraception except condoms in 1920, only repealing this law in 1967. In Germany, the Nazi regime banned the importation, sale and manufacture of all contraceptives except condoms. This law was only repealed in West Germany in 1961. Italy's fascist anti-contraception laws were not repealed until 1971; Spain's in 1977. The law forbidding advertising of contraceptives in Portugal was repealed in 1976. In the United States, some 'Comstock' condom distribution laws remained in force until the Supreme Court decision in *Eisenstadt v Baird* 405 US 438 (1972). Part of what is unusual about Ireland is that some legal restrictions remained in place until the 1990s.

[2] See also **National Health Service (Family Planning) Act 1967**.

pregnancy 'for the fulfillment of the office allotted to her by nature'. At the time, the Catholic Church not only held great institutional and material power in Ireland, but was fundamental to the politics of respectability which had become central to Irish nationalism.[3] As such, there was no shortage of parliamentarians willing to enact Church teaching as law. *Fianna Fáil* (FF) duly legislated for the Catholic position.

Section 17(1) of the Criminal Law Amendment Act 1935 made the sale of contraceptives, and importation for sale, crimes attracting punishments greater than those imposed for prostitution. Under section 17(3) customs officers seized and destroyed contraceptives imported for personal use. Few protested against the legislation at the time. Senior Catholic doctors maintained that they could never prescribe contraception in good conscience, and leading maternity hospitals prohibited sterilisation until the 1970s.[4] It is testament to the controversy attached to the idea of contraception that active women's organisations such as the Irish Housewives' Association and the Joint Committee of Women's Societies and Social Workers raised no objections either.

The prohibition had a severe impact on women's private and family lives. Without access to reliable artificial contraception, married women – particularly rural and working-class women – were condemned to frequent pregnancies and large families, and so often to poor health, poverty, and overcrowded housing. Single women faced another burden. In Ireland, as elsewhere, pregnancy outside marriage was evidence of grave social transgression. Social disapproval was reinforced by state supported Church-run institutions for the management of 'illegitimate' pregnancy. These institutions – the Magdalene Laundries[5] and the Mother and Baby Homes[6] – are today the subject of state transitional justice mechanisms. Amongst other abuses, they are associated with the forced adoption of children and the incarceration of women. Some women who could do so sought escape by travelling to England, at first to give birth and have their children adopted under the auspices of Catholic organisations there. Later, they travelled to obtain abortions under the **Abortion Act 1967**. The effective ban on contraception can be read as one of several structures which set out and enforced a strict Catholic code of sexual conduct for women, and punished those who resisted.

By 1968, this rigid connection between law and religion was dissolving. Catholics had expected a change in Church teaching on contraception, following the recommendations of the Vatican's Special Commission on Family Problems. They were disappointed. The papal encyclical *Humanae Vitae* affirmed that, although the use of artificial contraception was a minor sin, it was wrong to entrust reproduction to individual reason. Despite liberal Catholic dissent, the formidable Archbishop McQuaid of Dublin maintained this status

[3] See further Tom Inglis, *Moral Monopoly: The Rise and Fall of the Catholic Church in Modern Ireland* (UCD Press, 1998).

[4] A direct impact of the prohibition on contraception on medical practice was the development in Ireland of symphysiotomy – an obstetric operation which severs the labouring woman's pubic ligament. This operation was intended to make multiple vaginal deliveries easier by permanently widening the pelvis, and was developed on the assumption that women should not or would not be able to use contraceptives. Many women who underwent the operation suffered lifelong injuries. See further Marie O'Connor, *Bodily Harm: Symphysiotomy and Pubiotomy in Ireland 1944–1992* (Evertype, 2011).

[5] See further James Smith, *Ireland's Magdalene Laundries and the Nation's Architecture of Containment* (Notre Dame, 2007); **Concluding Observations of the UN Committee against Torture, Recommendation to Ireland regarding the Magdalene Laundries, 2011**.

[6] See further Mother and Baby Homes Commission of Investigation: http://www.mbhcoi.ie/MBH.nsf/page/index-en.

quo, pronouncing contraception 'evil', and banning the pill in maternity hospitals under his control. By 1974, however, with McQuaid gone, the Church hierarchy largely accepted that they could not expect the state to legislate their teaching. Conservative lay organisations succeeded them, thriving in the space provided by political ambivalence. Liberal Catholic politicians did not provide an effective opposition to these movements; indeed, many rural backbenchers firmly supported them.

A new family planning movement formed in the midst of this political ambivalence. In 1971 Senator **Mary Robinson** introduced the first of seven unsuccessful contraception reform Bills in the Seanad.[7] She was active in the Irish Family Planning Rights Association (IFPRA) and the Irish Women's Liberation Movement (IWLM). While IFPRA framed contraceptive access as a civil rights issue, the IWLM facilitated autonomous women's groups which organised around the contraceptive access issue, and protested at religious services, at the Archbishop's palace and outside Parliament in support of Robinson. Robinson's reform campaign drew on growing awareness of engrained habitual avoidance of the contraceptive law among Irish Catholics. By 1978, 48,000 women were taking the pill. It had been introduced into the country in 1963, but doctors prescribed it as a 'cycle regulator' rather than as a contraceptive: indeed the Government licensed it as such.[8] Access to the pill was possible, therefore, but depended on women's ability to find and pay a suitable doctor. Because women could not ask to access contraceptives as of right, the encounter with a doctor might be humiliating and intrusive. Some women travelled to Northern Ireland, smuggling contraceptives back in personal luggage. In May 1971, the IWLM dramatised the state's unwillingness to enforce the law by staging the Contraceptive Train – a group performance of this established cross-border practice. They bought contraceptives in Belfast, and returned to Dublin, teasing the waiting customs officers and chanting 'The law is obsolete: We have enforced the Constitution'. They were not arrested and their purchases were not confiscated.

The Contraceptive Train, and the story of Mary Robinson, are well known in Ireland. It is less often remembered that some groups also organised long-term mass resistance to the law. The Fertility Guidance Company, later the Irish Family Planning Association (IFPA), established a clinic in Dublin in 1968. It operated within the law: it did not attempt to sell contraceptives or import them in bulk because members felt vulnerable to prosecution and attack. Instead supporters imported small quantities of contraceptives on return from abroad. Some clients received free contraceptives; others used mail order forms to buy them from the International Planned Parenthood Federation in England, with the client bearing the risk of confiscation. One group went further. In 1972, some IFPA members established Family Planning Services Ltd (FPS) to meet clients' needs and to challenge the existing law by distributing contraceptives nationwide. FPS began as a mail order service, primarily for condoms, run from volunteers' homes, sometimes with the assistance of their children. FPS ordered condoms from London Rubber (now Durex) for delivery to Northern Ireland, importing vanloads over the border. Customers sent orders to a PO box number advertised in the national press, enclosing £1. In time, FPS produced order forms and 'price lists'.

[7] **First Woman President of Ireland, Mary Robinson, 1990.**

[8] This was also the position in Canada for a time; the Pill was approved for use as a hormone regulator in 1960 but its sale as a contraceptive was not decriminalised until the Criminal Law Amendment Act 1968–69.

FPS insisted it was supplying contraceptives in exchange for donations rather than selling them, thus avoiding the criminalisation of sale under the 1935 Act. Despite occasional brushes with police and customs services, they were never prosecuted. By 1973, sales funded a small staffed office and shop, followed shortly afterwards by a new Dublin family planning clinic.

In 1973, the Supreme Court heard the case of May McGee, a married mother of four whose health was at serious risk from further pregnancies.[9] She had ordered spermicidal jelly from England using a prescription provided by family planning activist Dr Jim Loughran. The Court found that the prohibition on importation of contraceptives for personal use violated married couples' constitutional right to privacy. Mary Robinson immediately re-introduced her 1971 Bill, but *McGee* had no immediate official effect on the law. In 1974 the Fine Gael-Labour coalition proposed the Control of Importation, Sale and Manufacture of Contraceptives Bill, which would only have licensed pharmacists to import contraceptives, for supply to married couples. The Minister for Justice maintained that unmarried people had no entitlement to 'fornication'. But even this Bill could not attract conservative support; seven *Fine Gael* members voted against their party's legislation and the Bill collapsed.

The courts had opportunities to constrain the family planning movement's activities, but did not take them. In 1974, the Catholic activist John O'Reilly complained to police that FPS and IFPA sold contraceptives to children in breach of the legislation, and a prosecution commenced. He could not prove sale in court, and was humiliated when he admitted to ordering contraceptives in his children's names. In 1976, in *Irish Family Planning Association v Ryan*[10] the Supreme Court emphasised the authors' medical expertise, in overturning the decision to censor the IFPA's booklet *Family Planning*. The movement was attaining new respectability.

These positive experiences of legal challenge, and the flexible legal position inaugurated by McGee, emboldened family planning activists. FPS's growing income helped build a nationwide family planning network: they assisted and supplied clinics and mail order services in Cork (1974), Limerick (1975), Galway (1977), the for-profit Well Woman in Dublin (1978) and student unions. These organisations adopted FPS's 'supply for donation' strategy, and operated very much in the open. Throughout, their strongest opposition was not the local police force, but religious groups, who would occasionally picket some clinics, and denounce their activities in various public forums. As their customer base grew, so did the gap between law's claim to enforceability and women's lived reality.

## II. The Landmark

FF regained power in 1977. As Health Minister, Charles Haughey promised family planning legislation reflecting 'our community, our beliefs, our sense of values'. His Bill became the Health (Family Planning) Act 1979: an attempt to grant some legal access to contraception, while mollifying those who associated it with rejection of religion, morality and Irish cultural distinctiveness.

[9] *McGee v Attorney General* [1974] IR 284.
[10] *Irish Family Planning v Ryan* [1979] IR 295.

The family planning movement argued for free state-funded public health services, available to all who needed them.[11] Although lack of support within the governing party meant that they were effectively closed out of formal law reform discussions, the family planning movement continued to engage in protest. The Contraception Action Programme (CAP), founded in 1976, encompassed a radical feminist group, founded the previous year, called Irishwomen United, as well as FPS, socialists and students' unions. CAP defied the restrictive contraceptive laws, repeatedly framing them as elitist and hypocritical. A CAP campaign poster from the time depicts male politicians, including Haughey, with swollen bellies under the caption 'If They Got Pregnant Would We Have This Bill?'. They picketed one of Haughey's public speeches carrying placards suggesting that the Minister himself did not obey the existing law: 'Where Do You Get Your Condoms Charlie?'. CAP also openly sold contraceptives without pretence of 'donation', seeking out places where working-class women would gather, including shopping centres, street markets and housing estates. In late 1978, to protest Haughey's Bill, CAP opened a shop in Dublin, called Contraceptives Unlimited, which sold condoms. It was typical of CAP's disruptive and de-stigmatising humour that the shop featured a Christmas tree decorated with inflated condom 'balloons'. Despite police presence, there were no arrests.

The Act that was passed in 1979 rejected the CAP model of open sale. Contraceptives could not be sold in ordinary shops, in vending machines or by mail order. They were available only in pharmacies, with a doctor's prescription. The doctor's role was to check that the client had a bona fide family planning or medical need for contraception. Although sale of contraceptives was no longer illegal as such, family planning clinics could not sell them without employing pharmacists and doctors. Doctors could not sell contraceptives independently. Free supply was also prohibited. Permissible informal importation of contraceptives was confined to small quantities in travellers' personal luggage. Contraceptives ordered from commercial services abroad remained vulnerable to seizure. Organisations importing in bulk required a licence. FPS and the IFPA had struggled for women's right to regulate their own fertility, free of medical tutelage. Now their poorer clients, who might struggle to use the personal importation provision, were subjected to unjustified expense and scrutiny. Few Irish pharmacists stocked contraceptives, and doctors could conscientiously object to prescribing them. The legislation also marked an attempted retrenchment of Catholic power. The movement's clinics received no funding under the Act: it was designed to divert contraceptive sales away from them. By contrast, natural family planning clinics went unregulated, and became entitled to additional funding. All clinics were required to provide advice on natural as well as artificial methods of contraception.

## III. What Happened Next

The clinics immediately announced their intention to defy the Act. In remaining open, they risked prosecution: sale and importation of contraception except as permitted under the Act remained offences attracting a fine of £500, or a period of six months' imprisonment,

[11] See eg Cork Women's Health Group leaflet: https://s3-eu-west-1.amazonaws.com/corklgbtarchiveomeka%2Foriginal%2F3e5b5411e177dbeb53ca2aefff283c75.jpg.

both rising on subsequent offences. Yet continued criminalisation had little effect. There were two reasons for this. First, a combination of customer loyalty and pharmacists' and GPs' lack of support for the legislation meant that family planning clinics retained their majority share of the contraceptive market. Second, as before, the law was not enforced. In 1983, Dr Andrew Rynne, in a planned act of civil disobedience, breached the Act by selling contraceptives at the weekend when pharmacies were closed. His fine was lifted on appeal because it was his first offence.

Steps were taken to reconcile law and practice when, in 1985, the Labour Minister for Health, Barry Desmond, proposed an amendment to the Act, permitting sale of contraceptives to adults in family planning clinics. The Act still prevented sale from vending machines or in ordinary shops, and prohibited sale to teenagers. Despite heated debates reflecting law-makers' efforts to grapple with the relationship between secular law and the demands of Catholicism, the legislation passed. In part, these changes were made possible by shifts in conservative attention from contraception to abortion. Following the effective constitutional prohibition of abortion in 1983, right-wing campaigners focused on policing women's efforts to access abortion information and care, and contraception largely slipped below the radar. In 1984, police investigated the Well Woman Clinic for vending machine sales. The prosecution collapsed, but it seems clear that the interest in Well Woman had more to do with their potential connection to abortion activism than with contraception itself.

## IV. Significance

The 1979 Act was hardly progressive. It sought to 'secure the orderly organisation of family planning services'. It did this in part by excluding egalitarian family planning activists from legitimate public health networks, law-making and service provision. The legislation reinforced the idea that contraceptive access was a privilege to be granted only to married couples, overseen by doctors as gatekeepers. It foreshadowed and partly legitimised habits of bargaining with conservative social forces, and liberal incrementalism, which dog Irish reproductive rights advocacy to this day. At the same time, it failed to suppress the family planning movement – through direct action and disobedience, they were able to maintain the resistant health networks they had spent so long establishing. They were able to ensure women's access to contraception through the most mundane form of political resistance: the private, low-cost purchase of packets of condoms.

This is not to say that the 1979 Act was a simple failure on all possible counts. It is important to look beyond its formal enforcement to its wider life; to the political relations enabled by the struggles over its terms. The 1979 Act was a watershed precisely because it marked the point at which formal legislation could no longer claim a complete hold over Irish women's reproductive agency, at least as far as contraception was concerned. In the 1970s, family planning volunteers had effectively normalised and institutionalised alternative reproductive health services despite state interference; services which were more accessible, empowering and compassionate, and more in keeping with international best practice than anything the state was ready to officially countenance. The Act was unable to dismantle their work, and indeed, in many respects, the illegal purchase of condoms was much more an everyday experience for Irish people than the enforcement of the law itself.

Thus, the struggle around the 1979 Act paradoxically marked the point at which Church and state ceased to be the primary arbiters of reproductive morality in Ireland, particularly at street level. At the same time it marked a new confidence in the reproductive rights movement – today very visible in abortion rights campaigning[12] – around the possibility of one day establishing women as sole decision-makers in matters of their own health.

## Further Reading

- Máiréad Enright and Emilie Cloatre, 'Commentary on *McGee v Attorney General*' in Máiréad Enright, Aoife O'Donoghue and Julie McCandless (eds), *Northern/Irish Feminist Judgments* (Hart Publishing, 2017).
- Emilie Cloatre and Máiréad Enright, 'On the Perimeter of the Lawful: Enduring Illegality in the Irish Family Planning Movement 1972–1985' (2017) 44(4) *Journal of Law and Society* 471–500.
- Chrystel Hug, '*Contraception: To A Responsible Sexuality for All*', *The Politics of Sexual Morality in Ireland* (Palgrave, 1998).

[12] **Protection of Life During Pregnancy Act 2013; Thirty-sixth Amendment to the Irish Constitution, 2018.**

# 50

## *Williams & Glyn's Bank v Boland* (1980)

ROSEMARY AUCHMUTY

Prior to *Williams & Glyn's Bank v Boland*[1] a married woman was not legally considered to be in actual occupation of a house owned in law by her husband, even when she lived there and was physically present at the time he mortgaged or sold the property to a third party who now claimed possession. *Boland* established that wives *could* have overriding beneficial (also known as equitable) interests that bound third parties and thus that those third parties would in future, to avoid being caught by such interests, be obliged to make inquiries of the woman in the house as well as the man – to acknowledge, in fact, that women might have separate interests in land from their home-owner husbands.

### I. Context

Before the 1980s, the matrimonial home was normally conveyed into the husband's name only. This practice dated back to the rise of home ownership between the wars – before that, most people rented – when husbands were expected to be breadwinners and wives home-makers. For a man's wife to 'have to' work was considered socially demeaning and a formal or informal marriage bar operated in many occupations. The consequence was that most women had no income with which to purchase property or make mortgage repayments. Those who had worked before marriage would have earned less than men – no Equal Pay Act then – so, unless they had independent means, they could safely be ignored by lenders and conveyancers.[2]

The 1960s saw a rise in the number of owner-occupied homes and also in the number of wives who, with the influx of married women into the paid workforce, could and did contribute to the purchase of the matrimonial home. Old habits die hard, however, and properties were still normally conveyed to the husband, who alone was responsible for the mortgage. The problem with this arrangement was that the wife, not being party to the legal transactions, could lose her home if her husband sold it or defaulted on the mortgage. The case of *Caunce v Caunce*[3] raised this issue when a wife applied to High Court for a

[1] *Williams & Glyn's Bank v Boland* [1981] AC 487.

[2] See eg Jane Lewis, *Women in England 1870–1950* (Wheatsheaf Books, 1984); Sue Bruley, *Women in Britain since 1900* (Macmillan, 1999).

[3] *Caunce v Caunce* [1969] 1 WLR 286.

declaration that she had a beneficial interest in the property that was in her husband's sole name, and further that the lender was prevented from repossessing the property when her husband defaulted on the repayments by virtue of her prior interest.

The property in this case was unregistered. In unregistered land, there are no overriding interests – these are excusive to registered land – but third parties take land subject to the interests of those in occupation *provided they have notice (actual, constructive or imputed) of them.*[4] In *Caunce*, Stamp J accepted that Mrs Caunce had an interest in the property proportionate to her financial contributions but, even though her earnings were paid into her account at the same bank, refused to accept that this meant the bank must have known about it. To insist that it should have made inquiries, he judged, would be 'to place upon a bank *an intolerable burden*' (emphasis added).[5] He further held that a wife could not be considered to be in occupation, even when she was physically present, since, to all appearances, she was only there because she was the legal owner's wife:

> the plaintiff, unlike the deserted wife, was not in apparent occupation or possession. She was there, ostensibly, because she was the wife, and her presence there was wholly consistent with the title offered by the husband to the bank.[6]

Mrs Caunce thereupon lost her home.

In registered land, a person with an interest in the land who is 'in actual occupation' and of whom 'no inquiry has been made' has an overriding interest against a purchaser or mortgagee, provided the latter had not paid the money to two legal owners.[7] In the earliest disputes, the courts followed Stamp J's reasoning in defining 'actual occupation'. In *Hodgson v Marks*, for example, Counsel for the defendant urged that 'if a mortgagee stands on the doorstep … and sees a lady in the house … he is entitled reasonably to assume that, depending on her age, she is the wife/mother/daughter of the vendor';[8] thus, that she was only there because of her relationship to the legal owner. She could not be in 'actual occupation' herself. The Court of Appeal dismissed this argument and, defining 'actual occupation' in its ordinary sense of physical presence, allowed Mrs Hodgson – who was not in fact the wife, daughter or mother of the vendor – to win her case.

## II. The Landmark

But did the Court of Appeal's sweeping interpretation of overriding interest apply also to *wives* living with their home-owner husbands? This was the issue in *Williams & Glyn's Bank v Boland*. Mr Boland, a building contractor, and Mrs Boland, a nurse, married in 1959 and bought their first house with money contributed by both. It was conveyed into their joint names. In 1969 they sold this house and bought another which was conveyed into Mr Boland's name alone, though his wife assumed it was in joint names as before. Sole legal

[4] Section 199 of the Law of Property Act 1925.

[5] [1969] 1 WLR 286, 291.

[6] ibid, 292.

[7] Section 70(1)(g) of the Land Registration Act 1925, now replaced by Schedules 1 and 3 Land Registration Act 2002; Section 27 of the Law of Property Act 1925.

[8] *Hodgson v Marks* [1971] Ch 892, 927.

ownership enabled him, again without his wife's knowledge, to let the bank place a charge on the family home in return for a business loan. The business went into liquidation, the bank called in its loan, and, since Mr Boland's other assets did not cover the debt, the bank sought possession of the family home.

In the High Court,[9] the case was primarily concerned with whether the bank had sold a different piece of Mr Boland's land at an under-value. Mrs Boland's claim that she had an overriding interest was secondary, and quickly dismissed. Although she clearly had an interest by virtue of her contribution to the purchase price, Templeman J found that it was an interest in the proceeds of sale, not in the land itself. In case this argument was not accepted, however, he held in addition that Mrs Boland was not in actual occupation, since occupation for the purposes of section 70(1)(g) of the Land Registration Act 1925 did not include the wife of the legal owner in occupation. He distinguished Mrs Boland's claim from that of Mrs Hodgson on the ground that *Caunce* was the authority for *wives*.

> The presence on the land of the spouse who has no legal interest is only part of the occupation claimed and enjoyed by the legal owner. Were it otherwise, an *impossible position* would be reached: that where a legal owner proposed to mortgage property, it would be the duty of the mortgagee to inquire not only whether the mortgagor's spouse was actually in the property and, if so, when, but also to inquire from the spouse whether he or she claimed any beneficial interest in the property. I find it neither necessary nor desirable to construe the words 'actual occupation' to have *such wide and almost catastrophic effects* (emphasis added).[10]

Mrs Boland appealed to the Court of Appeal.[11] At that time the Master of the Rolls, who presides over that court, was Lord Denning, whose early experience in the divorce court and as Chair of the Lord Chancellor's Committee on Matrimonial Causes in the 1940s had made him aware of the hardships faced by married women who lost out in property disputes because the law favoured their legal-owner husbands. A characteristic of his judgments was to paint a detailed picture of the facts of the case, as he did here in order to show how out of touch with reality Templeman J's judgment had been. He then traced the developments in equity, most of his own creation, which had improved married women's position vis-à-vis the home, and pointed out the substantial shifts in their *economic* position, to which land law had adapted.[12]

> Nowadays most wives go out to work and their earnings are used – directly or indirectly – for the purchase or improvement of the matrimonial home. By so doing they obtain a beneficial interest in it.

To the idea that Mrs Boland's interest was but an interest in the proceeds of sale, he responded: 'That cannot be right', explaining, in typical mix of common sense and normativity:

> When a married man and his wife buy a house, they do it so as to live in it – so that it should be a home for them both and their children – for the foreseeable future. They do not intend to sell it – at any rate not for many years hence.[13]

[9] *Williams & Glyn's Bank v Boland* (1978) 36 P & CR 448 (Ch D).
[10] ibid, 454.
[11] *Williams & Glyn's Bank v Boland* [1979] 2 WLR 550 (CA).
[12] ibid, 557.
[13] ibid.

Turning finally to Stamp J's and Templeman J's interpretation of actual occupation, he said, 'I profoundly disagree. Such statements would have been true a hundred years ago when the law regarded husband and wife as one: and the husband as that one. But they are not true today'.[14]

Satisfied that the need for conveyancers to make proper inquiries of all occupants should cause no difficulties, Denning drew attention to the injustice caused by the exclusion of wives from the protection of section 70(1)(g). Here his progressive law-making was cleverly (but sincerely) deployed in the service of a conservative ideal:

> It seems to me utterly wrong that a lender should turn a blind eye to the wife's interest or the possibility of it – and then afterwards seek to turn her and her family out – on the plea that he did not know she was in actual occupation. If a bank is to do its duty, in the society in which we live, it should recognise the integrity of the matrimonial home.[15]

The bank appealed to the House of Lords,[16] but the law lords (somewhat to Denning's surprise) merely endorsed the Court of Appeal's decision in even stronger language.

## III. What Happened Next

The immediate response to *Boland* by legal commentators was negative, almost hysterically so. Stephen Freeman in the *Modern Law Review* attacked the decisions in both the Court of Appeal and the House of Lords as 'disturbingly superficial' (thus criticising no fewer than eight senior judges) and contended that they 'seriously misjudged' the impact on conveyancing practice.[17] The prospects of a married woman were linked to her husband, he said: she shared his successes, so she should share his losses too.[18] DJ Hurst in the *Statute Law Review* agreed that *Boland* was wrongly decided, but on different grounds.[19] He claimed that 'actual occupation' had a specialised meaning and that all authorities at the time the statute was passed (1925) agreed that 'a wife was incapable of being in occupation if her husband was'.[20] He deplored the loss of legal meaning occasioned when words were interpreted in lay terms, in contrast to the few other commentators, such as Roger Smith,[21] who welcomed the acceptance of social change. Even the Law Commission called for *Boland* to be reversed.[22]

The courts lost no time, however, in implementing the new interpretation of the statute. One beneficiary was Mrs Chhokar in *Chhokar v Chhokar*,[23] whose husband sold the family home (which was in his name though she had a 50 per cent beneficial share) while she was in hospital having a baby. Her temporary absence was held not to negate her occupation

[14] ibid, 560.
[15] ibid.
[16] *Williams & Glyn's Bank v Boland* [1981] AC 487 (HL).
[17] Stephen Freeman, 'Notes of Cases: Wives, conveyancers and justice' (1980) 43 *Modern Law Review* 696, 692.
[18] ibid 696.
[19] DJ Hurst, 'Palm Trees in the House of Lords – Some further thoughts on Boland's case' (1983) 4 *Statute Law Review* 142, 163–64.
[20] This in spite of the ostensible aim of the Law of Property Act 1925 to do away with distinctions based on sex or marriage in property law.
[21] RJ Smith, 'Overriding interests and wives' (1979) 95 *Law Quarterly Review* 504.
[22] Law Commission, *Property Law: The Implications of Williams & Glyn's Bank v Boland* (Report No 115, 1982).
[23] *Chhokar v Chhokar* [1984] FLR 313 (CA).

and the Court of Appeal ruled that she and her children could continue to occupy the home, while the purchaser, who had been party to her husband's fraud, was forced to wait five years before the property could be sold and he could get his money back. In one of those wonderful passages that make reading reports of judgments a pleasure, Lord Justice Cumming-Bruce explained why he differed from the judge in the family court in not ordering an earlier sale:[24]

> Is there any room for crocodile tears because [the purchaser's] unlawful enterprise did not succeed? I can see no room for giving him any more than the court in an unreported case gave to the money-lender who had rights over a debtor. The proceedings are recorded in a play of Shakespeare.[25]

The longer-term and more significant effect of the *Boland* ruling was that conveyancing practice changed. No longer able to assume that married women had no separate interests from their husbands (or, if they had, that such interests could not stand in the way of efficient conveyancing), lenders and conveyancing lawyers began to insist that homes should be conveyed to both spouses. That way, there was no chance of being caught by an unexpected overriding interest. By joining wives to the mortgage, lenders could make both spouses liable for the repayments, and husbands could no longer re-mortgage the property without their wife's knowledge and agreement. The knock-on effect was that lenders were obliged to address wives directly, which meant that they started to take women more seriously: to grasp that they, too, had money; to offer them loans; and to do away with the need for a male guarantor. The new practice of insisting that properties conveyed to couples should be put in joint names put paid to the Law Commission's proposal for statutory co-ownership of matrimonial homes[26] and to legislative attempts to enact this. There seemed no point in enforcing joint ownership if homes were always put in joint names anyway.

The one unforeseen, but quite foreseeable, negative consequence that *Boland* had for women and the courts was a sudden and distinct rise in cases concerning husbands putting undue influence on their wives to agree to mortgage the home to finance an insecure business deal. Before joint ownership, sole-owner husbands like Mr Caunce and Mr Boland could (and did) mortgage the home for their own purposes without consulting or even telling their wives. With joint ownership, however, both parties' consent must be given. The line of cases from *Barclays Bank v O'Brien*[27] to *Royal Bank of Scotland v Etridge (No 2)*[28] stands in direct succession to *Boland*, demonstrating the way in which legal reforms that benefit women are so often followed by renewed efforts by men to maintain the status quo.[29]

## IV. Significance

*Boland*'s importance for women was both practical and symbolic. In practical terms, it meant that wives living in homes that had been conveyed to their husbands (as was customary at

[24] [1984] FLR 313, 331.
[25] Namely, *The Merchant of Venice*.
[26] Law Commission, *Property Law: Third Report on Land Registration* (Report No 158, 1982).
[27] ***Barclays Bank v O'Brien*** [1992] 3 WLR 593.
[28] *Royal Bank of Scotland v Etridge (No 2)* [1998] 4 All ER 705.
[29] Rosemary Auchmuty, 'Men Behaving Badly: An analysis of undue influence cases' (2002) 11 *Social and Legal Studies* 257–82.

the time) but in which they had an equitable interest could, in the event of the husband's sale to another or default on a re-mortgage, establish their prior right to remain in the home. Even if sale eventually followed, a court could postpone it according to circumstances, and the wife's share of the proceeds of sale was assured.

If the need for protection disappeared once conveyancing practice adapted, the case spelt the death-knell of the custom of putting the matrimonial home in the husband's sole name. Henceforth, lenders and buyers wanted to know exactly what the wife's interest was, and the simplest way to achieve this was to ensure that her name was on the documents of title. The gain for women was their inclusion in decision-making concerning the family home: no longer could their husbands sell or mortgage the property without their knowledge. Moreover, joint legal ownership meant that if the relationship broke down, or in a dispute with a third party, the woman was automatically entitled to the agreed share or (failing an agreement) to a half-share, on the principle that 'Equity follows the law'.[30]

Symbolically, *Boland* reflected a sea-change in the perception of married women, and women generally, which led in turn to a shift in their treatment in property law. The cases are revealing of men's reluctance to give up the privileges that financial control gave them and their inability to imagine, let alone concede, a world in which they must share power with women. It can be no accident that the *Boland* litigation coincided with the rise of the Women's Liberation Movement in the UK, which named and identified instances of sexism, sexual harassment, direct and indirect discrimination and exploitation of women by men; campaigned for legal reforms like the **Sex Discrimination Act 1975** and the Domestic Violence and Matrimonial Proceedings Act 1976;[31] and, through the publicity given to its activities, consistently brought women's issues to society's notice. As a result, not only was the married woman in a different place *materially* by 1980, she was *viewed* very differently. By 1980 even the courts recognised that it was inconceivable that women could *still*, a century after the Married Women's Property Acts,[32] be regarded as mere appendages of their husbands.

## Further Reading

- MDA Freeman, 'Monied might and the matrimonial home' (1981) 1 *Family Law* 37–41.
- Helen McCarthy, 'Women, marriage and paid work in post-war Britain' (2017) 26 *Women's History Review* 46–61.
- Roger Smith, '*Williams and Glyn's Bank v Boland*: The Development of a System of Title by Registration' in Nigel Gravells (ed), *Landmark Cases in Land Law* (Bloomsbury, 2016) 125–53.

[30] *Jones v Kernott* [2011] UKSC 53.
[31] See further ***Davis v Johnson* (1978)**.
[32] **Married Women's Property Act 1882**.

# 51

# Greenham Common Women's Peace Camp, 1981–2000

ELIZABETH WOODCRAFT*

In September 1981 a group of around 35 Welsh women, calling themselves Women For Life on Earth, marched from Cardiff to RAF Greenham Common airbase in Berkshire, a distance of over 100 miles, to present a letter to the commander of the base outlining their concerns about plans to locate Ground Launched Cruise Missiles (GLCM), missiles with nuclear warheads, on the airbase. They then set up a peace camp outside the base and organised a series of actions which led to arrests and appearances in court. The women used these legal hearings in imaginative and innovative ways as part of their campaign against cruise missiles being brought to the United Kingdom.

## I. Context

The Greenham women highlighted a concern that had not really gone away since the Second World War and the first use of an atom bomb. Their protest followed a long line of women arguing for peace. In 1914 opposition to the Great War was supported by a large number of women involved in the suffrage movement, leading in 1915 to the International Peace Congress of Women at The Hague in which more than 1200 delegates discussed proposals to end the War and at which the International League for Peace and Freedom was founded.[1] In 1934, the Women's World Committee against War and Fascism was set up, and the Campaign for Nuclear Disarmament with its powerful Ban the Bomb message of the 1950s and '60s was started by women from the Cooperative Women's Guild.

The airbase at Greenham Common was opened in 1942 and was originally used by both the UK Royal Air Force and United States Army Air Forces. After the war it was used solely by the United States Air Force. At the end of the 1970s, NATO approved plans to deploy nearly 600 nuclear cruise missiles in Western Europe. It was proposed that GLCMs should be installed at RAF Greenham Common airbase by December 1983.

* The author defended Greenham Common campaigners in court.

[1] Women's International League for Peace and Freedom, 'History': http://wilpf.org/wilpf/history/; **Article 7 of the Covenant of the League of Nations, 1919**.

## II. The Landmark

The women marchers were not all feminists. There were young women, single women, married women, mothers, grandmothers, pensioners, feminists, socialists, all concerned about the future. The original aim of the marchers was to present a letter which expressed their fears about the effect of cruise missiles, and fear for the future of their children and the future of the living world, which they described as the basis of all life, but once they arrived at the base some women decided to stay, and so the Greenham Common Women's Peace Camp was born. The women who stayed left behind families and friends. Initially a few supportive men were involved, but after a few months it became women only.

Women and children came from all over the country and from across the world to be part of the protest. Camps were set up at the different gates and given the names of the colours of the rainbow, red, orange, yellow, violet, green. At first the women camped in tents and caravans, which were then removed by the Local Authority invoking ancient local bye-laws. So the women created 'benders' – sheets of plastic spread over a bent branch (and so the word bender to describe a tent-like construction entered the English language). There were then evictions where attempts were made to clear the camp by removing the women's belongings. This was a women-only, peaceful anti-nuclear demonstration, essentially a feminist campaign, and the women's commitment was to collective working, non-violence and non-alignment – the over-arching ideology that formed the basis of the women's movement. Meetings were held at the different gates, decisions were taken democratically, and there were no leaders, although the media attempted to create them.

As well as camping in such an ostentatious and long-running protest outside the base, the women undertook many actions, some of which were dramatic and photogenic and garnered much publicity. In December 1982 an enormous demonstration was organised. The word went out and women from all over the country arrived in their thousands, to Embrace the Base. A few weeks later, in the middle of the night of New Year's Eve 1982–83, women from the camp made their way into the base, throwing blankets and rugs over the fence, and danced in a ring on top of the silos which had been built to house the cruise missiles. This led to an iconic photographic image and mass arrests of the women. They organised a blockade of the base in May 1982 with about 250 women protesting by lying in the road at each of the gates, followed by many arrests. An event was organised to Reflect the Base, where thousands of women held up mirrors so that those inside the base could see themselves and their actions. The women also engaged in less flamboyant activities. They chained themselves to the perimeter fence. They wove baby-clothes into the wire of the fence. They entered the base, making token cuts in the wire of the fence, to demonstrate the lack of security, sometimes dressed in costumes – once to have a teddy-bears picnic. At night they lay down in front of the gates as the US Air Force convoys left the base to do practice runs driving around the country lanes of Berkshire. They put sugar in the petrol tanks of the vehicles. They were a constant irritant in the flesh of the US Air Force and the Ministry of Defence who were policing the base.

There was widespread coverage in the media. The camp caught the imagination of the nation. As time went by the right-wing press became very critical of the women, implying in their articles that the women were men-hating feminist lesbians who had abandoned their children.[2] This did not dent their popularity, nor prevent the media from continuing to avidly report on the women and their life in the camp.

During the period that the camp lasted, some 19 years, the women appeared in cases in almost every level of court in the land, Magistrates' Courts, the Crown Court, the High Court, the Court of Appeal and the House of Lords as it then was. The first time that the women as a group came before the courts was after the night of dancing on top of the silos. They were arrested en masse and approximately 30 of them were required to appear in front of the Newbury Magistrates in the early months of 1983 as a result of 'breaches of the peace' to show cause why they should not be bound over to keep the peace. In England and Wales, a breach of the peace is not an offence. It is not punishable by either a fine or imprisonment, and the proceedings do not give rise to any conviction. The issue can only be dealt with summarily, that is in a Magistrates' Court. If the magistrates are of the view that a woman has breached the peace or her behaviour was such that there was a likelihood that she might, the magistrates must, and can only, decide if she should be bound over to keep the peace in the future. If the court requires a woman to be bound over and she refuses, the only sanction is to send her to prison.

As time went on women faced the criminal charge of criminal damage in the Crown Court as well as the Magistrates' Court, for the symbolic snipping of the wire of the perimeter fence. After the first arrests a conference between the women and their lawyers was held in a small room in the Mary Ward Centre, a legal advice centre in London. The women felt the irony of an attempt by the courts to bind them over to keep the peace since that was the very object of their exercise. They wanted to argue the case.

Most of the women wanted to present their case in ways which were not 'legally' permitted, either because of the law, or because of the rules of the court, such as singing or appealing to moral or religious higher laws. However, they also wanted to present a legal case, with a formal legal argument. Some women, from the outset, wished to represent themselves. Some women would have legal representation during the prosecution case and then represent themselves for the defence case. The lawyers' function was to present in court as far as possible the arguments the women wanted put but within a legal framework. The difficulty was to find a path connecting dancing on the silos to protesting against nuclear destruction. After some research it was clear that the stepping-stones of reasonable force and self-defence to prevent a crime meant that the Genocide Act 1969 could be invoked.

The Genocide Act 1969 codified the Convention on the Prevention and Punishment of the Crime of Genocide, which had been approved by the General Assembly of the United Nations on 9 December 1948.[3] The aim and purpose of the Act was to ensure that the atrocities committed before and during the Second World War, the extermination of the Jews and other groups, could never be deemed lawful. The women argued that the presence of nuclear weapons inside the base, and the threat of their use presented the risk of genocide, because of the very nature of nuclear warfare. By engaging in public demonstrations or making the symbolic gesture of cutting the fence around the base, they were using

[2] 'Greenham: the Inside Story', *The Daily Express*, 9–12 April 1984.

[3] The Genocide Act 1969: An Act to give effect to the Convention on the Prevention and Punishment of the Crime of Genocide.

reasonable force against the greater risk of the annihilation which would be caused by the use of cruise missiles. They were attempting to stop the crime of genocide the only way they could – by alerting the country, and the world, to the issue. It was the first time that this defence had been used in such a way and the women were breaking new ground.

It was often a very fine line: calling someone from South Africa to report on uranium mining there and the conditions of the workers in those mines is not an obvious step in a hearing about a breach of the peace in Berkshire. However, certainly for the first mass-arrest cases the lawyers were not criticised for the way the case was run. Clearly, nothing would be served by the court telling the lawyers that they were in contempt of court and asking them to leave the proceedings. The result could have been chaos in the courtroom – more peaceful protests, more embarrassing arrests, and more women being sent shockingly to jail. As the months went by the lay magistrates who normally presided over the Newbury Magistrates' Court were replaced by a single stipendiary magistrate.

The Genocide Act argument failed, as politically it was bound to do, although logically – and indeed legally – it was an arguable point. The women refused to be bound over or pay any fine. By so doing, they were almost inevitably imprisoned. Day after day the country saw women being transported to prison, reminiscent of the days of the suffragettes. The public was outraged.

The women took a decision after the defeat of this argument in the first round of cases that they would not appeal, as it was clear the argument would be lost on appeal which would mean that any lower court would be bound by the decision, which in turn would mean other women could not use it. Unfortunately a male barrister went off-piste and appealed, unsuccessfully, from the Magistrates' Court to the Oxford Crown Court, thereby denying any protestor who appeared in the court below in that area, the right to use that argument.

The women pursued claims in the civil courts, still using these occasions to generate media interest. Because of the careless and aggressive way the evictions, by removal of the women's possessions, were carried out, sometimes women were injured and they brought actions against the police in the County Court for damages for injury suffered during evictions. There were also appeals in the County Court against injunctions or eviction orders relating to their presence on Greenham Common. In the Court of Appeal they pursued their demand for the right to vote since, for those who lived there, the camp was their main residence. The issue was: could people living in a 'bender' vote? The Court of Appeal said yes.[4] In the House of Lords in the case of *Hutchinson*, the women challenged the local authority's right to remove them from common ground, arguing that bye-laws which had been made to prevent access to common land, namely Greenham Common, were invalid. The House of Lords held that the bye-laws did prejudice the rights of common use.[5]

Every charge, every hearing was used by the women as part of their campaign. The women were aware of the popularity of their cause and the accompanying media interest. The legal proceedings were part of their media campaign. They used each appearance in many ways, as a simple media event, because of the number of them who were arrested. They also took actions during the court case (for example, calling US Air Force personnel to give evidence and then making a citizen's arrest for conspiracy to commit genocide),

[4] *Hipperson and Others v Newbury Electoral Registration Officer* [1985] QB 1060.
[5] *Director of Public Prosecutions v Hutchinson; Director of Public Prosecutions v Smith* [1990] 2 AC 783.

they educated the public through the media which had come to cover the hearing (for example, about how uranium is mined in South Africa, how bombs are made), and they entertained (such as using the court-room to stage a mini Gilbert and Sullivan operetta).

The Greenham women also went to the USA to support an *amicus* brief for a case in the New York Southern District Court.[6] In November 1983 they filed an action to 'enjoin the deployment of ninety-six cruise missiles at Greenham Common'. The claim was brought against President Reagan and others by a number of the women on behalf of themselves and their minor children and two US Congressmen. The women's case was that deployment of cruise missiles contravened international law including crimes against peace, laws of war, and the crime of genocide, that the planned deployment violated their rights to life and liberty under the fifth and ninth amendments to the Constitution and Congress's constitutional rights to declare war. The application failed, the judge finding that the case presented 'a non-justiciable political question'. However the media interest was significant and donations poured in.

## III. What Happened Next

The campaign and the camp were successful. Cruise Missiles proper did not come to the UK. Following the Intermediate Nuclear Forces Treaty 1987, cruise missiles were flown back to the US in 1991–92. The airbase was closed in 1993. In 1997 Greenham Common was designated as public parkland. Women remained at the camp until 2000. The Genocide Act 1969 was repealed in 2001 and replaced by the International Criminal Court Act 2001.

Most of the women involved in Greenham remained in some way connected with peace campaigns. The camp became a haven for women who sought to escape the excesses of male aggression. Some women involved became lawyers, others social workers, teachers and environmental campaigners. All would remain affected by the experience throughout their lives.

The feminist strategies of protest used by the Greenham women have been used by later peace campaigners, environmentalists and green protestors, although the Genocide Act defence, initially used by many peace campaigners, soon became impossible to argue, even beyond the purview of the Oxford Crown Court, as judges grew impatient with the argument. The voting rights case of *Hipperson* is still relied on today. After the US action there was more litigation across Europe, along similar lines. It helped in the development of the politics-via-the-law movement. The extreme strategies used by the Greenham women, however – singing their evidence, calling numerous witnesses on obscure points of environmental or social interest, making citizens' arrests in court – have not been repeated.

## IV. Significance

The unique campaign and the methods used by the Greenham women to inform the public through innovative use of the media (before the ubiquity of online social media) meant that

[6] *Greenham Women Against Cruise Missiles v Reagan*, 591 F Supp 1332 (SDNY 1984).

where before there had been little discussion about the USA's use of England as a barrier or starting point for any future use of nuclear weapons, now everyone in the country knew what the issues were. It was a campaign of women, of mothers and children: those who suffer the effects of war and who often have little power in deciding when wars should occur, but who now were taking part in that discussion and acting effectively against war. The campaign was different, organised in a feminist way. There were no leaders, no stars, the message was the important thing, and throughout it all, the blockades of the base, the arrests, the evictions by police and bailiffs, it was peaceful. The women never responded with violence. Commentator Bea Campbell described the peace camp as 'one of the West's most intoxicating theatres of political protest in the 1980s'.[7]

## Further Reading

- David Fairhall, *Common Ground: The Story of Greenham* (Taurus, 2006).
- Barbara Harford and Sarah Hopkins (eds), *Greenham Common: Women at the Wire* (The Women's Press, 1984).
- Lynn Jones (ed), *Keeping the Peace* (The Women's Press, 1983).
- Ann Pettitt, *Walking to Greenham: How the Peace Camp Began and the Cold War Ended* (Honno, 2006).

[7] Beatrix Campbell, 'The legacy of Greenham Common has outlived Margaret Thatcher', *The Guardian*, 18 April 2013.

# 52

# *Gill and Coote v El Vino Co Ltd* (1982)

ANNE MORRIS

Some landmarks, such as the **Sex Discrimination Act 1975**, are immediately recognisable as major events. Others may at the time have seemed less important and may even have been dismissed by some as the unseemly antics of trouble-making feminists. But sometimes incremental changes herald the start of profound transformations. This is true of *Gill and Coote v El Vino Co Ltd*[1] in which two women, a lawyer (Tess Gill) and a journalist (Anna Coote), successfully challenged the rule in a Fleet Street Wine Bar that women would not be served at the bar. It encapsulates the reality that merely to enact a law requiring women to be treated 'equally' with men cannot, by itself, change attitudes and behaviour; nor does it mean that those called on to implement the law (in particular the overwhelmingly male judiciary) would find it easy to abandon their deep-seated notions of the roles and proprieties required of the sexes. It also illustrates, however, that despite the misgivings of some feminists, the law can prove a mechanism for change in the hands of determined women.

## I. Context

The London thoroughfare of Fleet Street was for many years the hub of the English newspaper industry and in its many pubs and wine bars journalists congregated at all hours to drink, socialise and gossip. Because it runs through London's 'legal quarter', which includes the Royal Courts of Justice and the Inns of Court, journalists would be rubbing shoulders – and exchanging information with – members of the legal profession. In 1975, when the Sex Discrimination Act was passed, this was very much a male world. Although the number of women lawyers was increasing, they were still scarce. Indeed, in the mid-1970s nearly one-half of London chambers did not have a single woman barrister.[2] Overall, women barristers and solicitors made up less than 10 per cent of their separate branches of the profession. Moreover, women who entered the legal profession did not find it welcoming. It was often assumed that women would leave work once they had a child and therefore they were less 'committed' to their careers. This, combined with an old-fashioned paternalism (or deliberate obstruction), meant that women were not expected or encouraged to work in the 'hard' and more lucrative areas of law such as

[1] *Gill and Coote v El Vino Co Ltd* [1983] QB 425.
[2] Helena Kennedy, 'Women at the Bar' in Robert Hazell (ed), *The Bar on Trial* (Quartet, 1978) 148.

corporate and commercial law, nor in the darker reaches of the criminal law. Certainly, they were likely to find it difficult to reach senior positions or to earn as much as their male colleagues.

At the time, women journalists were more numerous than women lawyers, at least in parts of the profession. Roy Greenslade notes that there were plenty of women feature writers, columnists, reporters and sub-editors, but very few at executive level.[3] With some notable exceptions, women were pointed in the direction of what Ann Leslie referred to as the 'girlie ghetto' of 'frocks, gossip and knit-your-own-royals.'[4] When in 1982 Anne Robinson became an assistant-editor at the *Daily Mirror* her achievement was marked by a feature in *The Guardian* on 'the red-headed Liverpudlian, 37'. The piece noted that the *Mirror*'s London office at that time employed 263 male journalists and 22 women. There were no women in its Manchester office.[5] *The Guardian* had no room for smugness, despite giving a platform for feminists such as Jill Tweedie and Polly Toynbee. Liz Forgan, who was *The Guardian*'s women's editor in the late 1970s, noted that 'the macho, heavy-drinking, show-off male culture [was] very strong … The daily banter was openly and crudely sexist.'[6]

Women journalists and women lawyers shared an outsider status: in an aggressively male culture they were routinely excluded from the 'club'. This mattered both symbolically and in practice. In 1982, the year *Gill and Coote* was decided, David Podmore and Anne Spencer noted that

> the advancement of women in the legal profession seems to be inhibited by their deviant status, which makes it difficult for them to participate fully in the intensive formal and informal interaction that lies at the heart of professional life.[7]

Some of their interviewees recognised that the 'camaraderie' among male lawyers, which excluded women, had adverse effects on their careers. This is not simply because women are consequently less visible but also because they miss out on informal contacts, information and the forging of networks, all of which are invaluable.[8] Nowhere was this so apparent as in El Vino's. The wine bar on Fleet Street was a perfect example of what was essentially a 'gentleman's club' for lawyers and journalists and it was renowned as a meeting place for both. In his judgment in *Gill*, Griffiths LJ said: 'El Vino's is no ordinary wine bar. It has become an institution in Fleet Street. Every day it is thronged with journalists, solicitors, barristers exchanging the gossip of the day'.[9]

The venue was also renowned for its long-standing rule that women would not be served at the bar. Instead, they had to sit at one of two tables by the door or at a table in a back room and wait for someone to take their order. Not only did this hamper their ability to get a drink, but it meant that they were also excluded from the socialising that went on amongst the men congregated in the main rooms and around the bar. There had been

[3] Roy Greenslade, *Press Gang: How newspapers make money from propaganda* (Macmillan, 2003) 364.

[4] ibid 366.

[5] Anon, 'New face in the Mirror', *The Guardian*, 13 March 1982, 13.

[6] Kennedy, n 2 above, 366.

[7] David Podmore and Anne Spencer, 'Women lawyers in England: the experience of inequality' (1982) 9 *Work and Occupations* 337, 355.

[8] As to the persistence of the importance of networking and its tendency to exclude some groups, see Jennifer Tomlinson, Daniel Muzio, Hilary Sommerlad, Lisa Webley and Liz Duff, 'Structure, agency and career strategies of white women and black and minority ethnic individuals in the legal profession' (2013) 66(2) *Human Relations* 245.

[9] [1983] QB 425, 431.

women prepared to challenge the rule, although prior to the Sex Discrimination Act 1975 they did not have the law (let alone the clientele) on their side. In 1970 a group of women journalists including Anne Robinson (then at the *Sunday Times*), Unity Hall, Anna Coote and Mavis Davidson demanded to be served, with Davidson pointing out that as their money was equal so were their rights.[10] They were forcibly ejected from the premises, each side blaming the other for the scuffle that ensued. For the time being the status quo survived. Then came the Sex Discrimination Act 1975 (the Act). Section 1 of the Act provided that a person discriminates against a woman if, on the ground of her sex, he treats her less favourably than he treats or would treat a man.[11] That principle applied in various contexts, including, under section 29, to the provision of goods, facilities and services. It was unlawful to discriminate against a woman by refusing to provide her with, for example, services, or by refusing to provide her with services of the like quality, in the like manner and on the like terms as were normally provided to male members of the public. Examples of the services covered included access to and use of any place which members of the public or a section of the public are permitted to enter; and facilities for entertainment, recreation or refreshment. Given that El Vino's refused to allow women to stand at the bar (where men stood) and refused to serve them drinks (where men were served) it might seem as though the establishment had little in the way of a defence to a complaint of sex discrimination. That was not the case, however.

On the day that the Act came into force a challenge to the El Vino's rule was mounted by, among others, Sheila Gray, a photographer on the *Morning Star*.[12] The claimants were supported by the National Council for Civil Liberties.[13] The case was heard in the Westminster County Court in 1978 by Judge Ruttle. In his unreported judgment he appears to have followed the Court of Appeal in *Peake v Automotive Products Ltd*.[14] In that case women employees were allowed to leave work at a car factory five minutes earlier than the men, allegedly in the interest of safety to avoid women being jostled in the 4000-strong rush for the factory gates. A male employee argued that this was sex discrimination. The Court of Appeal held that a rule which differentiated between men and women in the interests of safety and in accordance with established standards of 'right conduct as between the sexes' was not discriminatory under the Act. According to Lord Denning MR:

> Although the Act applies equally to men as to women, I must say it would be very wrong to my mind if this statute were thought to obliterate the differences between men and women or to do away with the chivalry and courtesy which we expect mankind to give womankind … It is not discrimination for mankind to treat womankind with the courtesy and chivalry which we have been taught to believe is right conduct in our society.[15]

Shaw LJ agreed:

> The Sex Discrimination Act 1975 was not, in my judgment, designed to provide a basis for capricious and empty complaints of differentiation between the sexes. Nor was it intended to operate

[10] *The Guardian*, 'Miscellany', 'What the El', 19 June 1970; *The Times*, Diary, 'Ladies Day at El Vino's', 19 June 1970.
[11] Provisions on sex equality are now in the Equality Act 2010 which repealed earlier anti-discrimination laws, including the SDA 1975. The principle of non-discrimination applies equally to men.
[12] David Leigh, 'Wine bar ban on women to be tested in court', *The Times*, 31 December 1975, 2.
[13] The NCCL subsequently changed its name to *Liberty*. It is an independent association that campaigns for civil liberties and human rights.
[14] *Peake v Automotive Products Ltd* [1978] QB 233.
[15] ibid 238.

> as a statutory abolition of every instinct of chivalry and consideration on the part of men for the opposite sex.[16]

Lord Denning MR hammered home the final nail by applying to the facts the maxim *de minimis non curat lex*: the law does not concern itself with trifles.[17]

Against this background Judge Ruttle dismissed the claim (and awarded costs against Gray) deciding that the rule applied by El Vino's could not be construed as hostile or adverse to women but was to prevent them from suffering the indignity of being jostled. It was there for reasons of chivalry and administrative convenience. The reaction to the decision was typified by *The Times* leader column which referred light-heartedly to the case, and then reflected on the fact that the losers might appeal 'in a further attempt to have the law poke its sharp nose where it has no business'.[18] In a riposte, Francis Bennion (one of the drafters of the Act) wrote to the newspaper, pointing out that

> It was the avowed aim of the Sex Discrimination Act to override what Mr Justice Phillips (reversed on appeal in the *Peake* case) described as ingrained social attitudes rendered obsolete by changing values. Is Parliament to sit helplessly by while elderly judges insist on upholding those obsolete attitudes and rejecting the principle of equal treatment clearly laid down by the Act?[19]

## II. The Landmark

Parliament did not stir, but Anna Coote returned to the fray along with Tess Gill. On 2 February 1981, they ordered drinks at the bar and were refused service. They complained of sex discrimination contrary to section 29 of the Act, with the support of the Equal Opportunities Commission. In the City of London Court the judge dismissed their claim on the basis that, as a matter of common sense, a 'reasonable person' would not feel less favourably treated. He added that Coote and Gill had exaggerated their dismay, their reaction being 'somewhat extreme', given that only a handful of people had objected to the rule. Coote later criticised the judge's implication that women's rights activists were not reasonable people and indicated they would appeal.[20]

In the Court of Appeal, counsel for El Vino's argued, amongst other things, that simply to deprive women of a choice that was available to men was not less favourable treatment. Women were simply being spared from being jostled. It was also argued that the Sex Discrimination Act did not, unlike the Race Relations Act 1976, provide that segregation was less favourable treatment – thus to exclude women from a public space was not of itself sex discrimination. The Court of Appeal dealt shortly with these arguments (the judgment was reported to have taken only five minutes)[21] and held unanimously that Gill and Coote had suffered discrimination on grounds of their sex. The judges approached the case as

[16] ibid 240.

[17] In *Jeremiah v Ministry of Defence* [1980] QB 87, the Court of Appeal retreated from its finding that safety and good administration could justify differential treatment but approved the application of the *de minimis* principle.

[18] 'El Vino's Levitas', *The Times*, 27 May 1978, 13.

[19] Printed under the title 'Sex Discrimination', *The Times*, 1 June 1978, 17.

[20] David Nicolson-Lord, 'Court blow to wine bar feminists', *The Times*, 16 July 1981, 5.

[21] Staff Reporter, 'Time, ladies, please, as last bastion of male chavinsim falls', *The Times*, 9 November 1982, 3.

a straightforward 'legal' question of statutory interpretation – what does the Act mean? – rather than as groundbreaking point of principle, although they did show a passing familiarity with social interactions in bars.

Griffiths LJ pointed out that men may choose to sit at a table but most chose to stand among the throng at the bar. Women on the other hand, did not have that choice: 'she may wish, if she is a journalist, to join a group in the hope of picking up the gossip of the day. If male journalists are permitted to do it, why shouldn't she?'.[22] Eveleigh LJ was of the same view:

> [I]n the standing area – which was the male preserve – there was a great manoeuvrability and flexibility for conversation and for social intercourse with others. … There is not … the same ability to join other people if you have to go to a table as there is if you are allowed to be among the men who are standing.[23]

All three judges were of the opinion that it was very straightforward to apply the Act in this situation. Section 29 did not require there to be a 'detriment' (as compared to section 6, in the context of employment), simply to have been refused a service available to men. Moreover, the Court unanimously dismissed the idea that the refusal could be said to be *de minimis*. Eveleigh LJ noted that to apply that maxim here would be to say:

> 'Well, she was less favourably treated but only very slightly'. I find it very difficult to evoke the maxim … in a situation where that which has been denied to the plaintiff is the very thing that Parliament seeks to provide, namely facilities and services on an equal basis.[24]

He pointed out that an area of the premises whose popularity was undoubted was being denied to women. It afforded a unique atmosphere in great demand by men and it could not be assumed that there was no demand for it from women. The fact that there had been few complaints (as noted by the judge, Judge Ranking) did not outweigh the obvious fact that a facility greatly prized by men was denied to the plaintiffs.

## III. What Happened Next

Having won their case the successful claimants repaired – unsurprisingly – to El Vino's for a celebratory drink. There were met by the manager, Paul Bracken, who refused to serve them. Although Mr Bracken was prepared to serve other women, he said he would not serve those 'who want to make trouble or make a feminist point'.[25] In fact, many of the women who crowded into the bar were ignored by the staff. Mr Bracken commented that it was a very sad day for El Vino's, a place 'where old-fashioned ideals of chivalry still flourish'. He believed ladies preferred 'to be treated as such'.[26] He was not alone in his displeasure. It was reported that seasoned customers varied in reaction from rhetorical outrage to a scornful dismissal of the affair as a nine-day wonder (claiming the women were just trying

[22] [1983] QB 425 432.
[23] ibid 430.
[24] ibid 431.
[25] *The Times*, 9 November 1982, 3 (n 21 above).
[26] Perera Shyama, 'Sour Grapes verdict at El Vino's', *The Guardian*, 9 November 1982, 1.

to make a point).[27] An elderly lawyer described his reaction as 'shock'.[28] El Vino's and its clientele had calmed down by the following week. On 16 November 1982 it was reported in *The Times* that one of the directors of the El Vino's company had written to Gill and Coote to tell them that the ban that had been imposed on them had been lifted (although Mr Bracken was still saying he would not serve them).

## IV. Significance

Is the fact that women won the right to buy a drink in a bar in London a significant legal milestone? There are legal and practical reasons to celebrate the victory achieved by Tess Gill and Anna Coote. Legally, the decision signalled that it was impermissible to defend sex discrimination based on notions of 'courtesy' or propriety. The Sex Discrimination Act required men and women to be treated equally and it was no longer acceptable to apply quasi-Victorian notions of women being fragile creatures who needed to be protected in (or kept out of) public spaces. Exclusionary rules and customs applied by an overwhelmingly male elite in the guise of 'chivalry' towards the 'fairer sex' were recognised, implicitly at least, as a ploy to inhibit women's participation. The rejection of the *de minimis* argument in this context was important, showing that, on occasions, the (then as now) male-dominated judiciary is willing to address the sexism that when challenged often provokes accusations of over-reaction and hysteria directed towards 'feminist harridans'.

In practical terms, Coote and Gill struck a blow for women in their respective spheres by showing that women lawyers and journalists were not an aberration, but a fact of life that men were going to have to get used to. It was not, of course, the end of the story. Although young women are choosing in greater numbers to enter both the law and journalism, they remain under-represented at senior levels.[29] Their progress is obstructed by the logistical problems of combining work and family life (a burden still disproportionately borne by women[30]) that can lead to women leaving the professions, and by systemic sexism (conscious or otherwise) that can deny them opportunities for promotion.[31] *Gill* is a reminder that attitudes can be changed by women (and men) prepared to take on the establishment, whether at work or at play.

## Further Reading

- Katherine O'Donovan, *Sexual Divisions in Law* (Weidenfeld & Nicholson, 1985).
- **Susan Atkins and Brenda Hoggett, *Women and the Law* (Blackwell, 1984).**
- Carol Smart, *Feminisim and the Power of Law* (Routledge, 1989).

[27] n 21 above.

[28] ibid.

[29] See eg Tomlinson et al, n 8 above; Suzanne Franks, *Women and Journalism* (IB Taurus & Co Ltd in association with the Reuters Institute for the Study of Journalism, University of Oxford, 2013).

[30] Jacequeline Scott and Elizabeth Clery, 'Gender Roles: an Incomplete Revolution? *British Social Attitudes Survey 30th Report* (2013).

[31] See eg Charlotte Proudman, 'Institutional sexism in the legal profession will only end when lawyers confront its existence', *New Statesman*, 25 September 2015.

# 53

# *Women and the Law*, Susan Atkins and Brenda Hoggett, 1984

BRENDA HALE AND SUSAN ATKINS

We wrote *Women and the Law* as academics at the Universities of Manchester and Southampton in 1984. Its aim was to understand how the law perceived and responded to women. It was the first book in the UK comprehensively to examine the gendered nature of the law itself and the legal inter-relationships between women's private and public lives and between men and women. It took women's experiences in life as its starting point, rather than conventional legal categories. We aimed to show how legal doctrine reflected the definition of issues, habits of thought and approaches to finding solutions of men. As we noted in our introduction,

> Our object is not to give a biased account of the law but to uncover the extent to which the law itself is biased towards a particular view of life. Even today that view can readily be recognised as one reflected in male rather than female eyes.[1]

Although not aiming to be a legal textbook, it helped to legitimise this area of study and was followed by a growth in courses within UK law faculties on gender and the law. It also provided a basis for legal change over the following 30 years.

## I. Context

The 1950s were a period of retrenchment for many women, after the comparative liberation of the Second World War, sending them back into the home or inequality in the workplace. Books such as *The Second Sex* by Simone De Beauvoir (1959) and *The Feminine Mystique* by Betty Friedan (1963) ignited what became known as the Women's Movement in the United States. The movement spread to the UK, with books such as *The Female Eunuch* by Germaine Greer (1970), *Sexual Politics* by Kate Millett (1970) and *The Rights and Wrongs of Women* edited by Anne Oakley and Juliet Mitchell (1976). During the 1970s, the UK Women's Liberation Movement grew, focusing on women's control of their bodies, access to contraception and abortion, freedom from male oppression (particularly domestic violence), rights to equal pay and opportunities. It was a time of grassroots activism and

[1] *Women and the Law* (Blackwell, 1984) 1.

debate. The 1968 strike by women sewing machinists at the Ford car factory in Dagenham for equal pay with male Eastman cutters and paint spray operators, whose jobs were more highly graded, led to a number of other equal pay strikes and the formation of a national joint action group which organised a massive equal pay demonstration in May 1969.[2] Erin Pizzey opened the first refuge in the UK for victims of domestic violence in 1971[3] and wrote the influential book, *Scream Quietly or the Neighbours Will Hear* in 1974. The National Women's Aid Federation, now Women's Aid, brought together 40 independent refuges in 1974. The first Rape Crisis Centre opened in the UK in 1973, developing quickly to become a national support, advocacy and advice movement.[4]

The energy and activism of the period resulted in some legislative change. The Law Commission for England and Wales in 1965 included family law within its programme of law reform and published several important reports on the subject in its first decade, most of which resulted in legislation benefitting women. The Matrimonial Homes Act 1967, the first gender-neutral family law legislation, allowed spouses (husbands OR wives) who were not the legal owners of their homes to register their occupation rights, thus protecting them against the possibility of their owner-spouse selling or mortgaging the property to a third party. Legislation coming into force in 1971 introduced no-fault divorce and greatly increased the courts' powers to share out the couple's assets between them to reflect their needs and contributions to the family. The **Abortion Act 1967** greatly expanded the grounds upon which abortion was legal within Great Britain (but not Northern Ireland), while regulating access to it. Family planning was incorporated into the NHS under the National Health Service Reorganisation Act 1973 and all contraceptive services and supplies, including the contraceptive pill, were made freely available to everyone, regardless of age or marital status from 1 April 1974.[5] The Domestic Violence and Matrimonial Proceedings Act 1976 strengthened the civil remedies available to victims of domestic violence and abuse, at a time when the criminal justice system was often reluctant to protect them.[6]

In the public sphere, Article 119 of the Treaty of Rome 1963 made the principle of equal pay one of the founding tenets of the European Economic Community. In order to join the EEC, the UK passed the Equal Pay Act in 1970, albeit with a five-year deferred implementation date.[7] The Social Security Pensions Act 1975 equalised the rates of contributory benefits, although many married women in practice would receive lower pensions because of time out of the workforce due to family responsibilities. The Employment Protection Act 1975 extended protections for pregnant workers and the **Sex Discrimination Act 1975**, with some exceptions, prohibited sex discrimination by the suppliers of employment, education, accommodation, goods and services. The book set these reforms in an historical and legal context and showed how women's inequality was deep-rooted and interconnected in and by law and that much more change was needed.

With hindsight, it is remarkable how unaffected the discipline of law was by all this activism. Academics in other disciplines, especially sociology, history and psychology, were embracing, researching and participating in the development of feminist scholarship.

[2] **Dagenham Car Plant Strike, 1968.**
[3] **First Women's Refuge, 1971.**
[4] **First Rape Crisis Centre, 1976.**
[5] **National Health Service (Family Planning) Act 1967.**
[6] ***Davis v Johnson* [1979] AC 264.**
[7] ***Birmingham City Council v Abdulla* [2012] UKSC 42, [2012] ICR 1419.**

(*Women and the Law* included references to feminist research from other disciplines). However, until the late 1970s, activism on the ground and in Parliament failed to disturb traditional notions of the law's neutrality or the settled demarcation of areas of law.

## II. The Landmark

In the mid-1970s, Hale (then Hoggett) and another colleague at the University of Manchester were asked by William Twining, editor of the Law in Context series, to write a book on Women and the Law, along similar lines to Anthony Lester and Geoffrey Bindman's ground-breaking *Race and Law* (Penguin Books, 1972). Hoggett was encouraged by Professor Herma Hill Kay of UC Berkeley who was a Simon Visiting Professor at Manchester University in the mid-1970s.[8] The project was delayed for a number of reasons, and eventually Susan Atkins, who had published articles on discrimination against women in welfare law in the *Journal of Social Welfare Law* (of which Hoggett was co-editor), was invited to co-author the book.

The delay proved beneficial. Hoggett had already published books on children and mental health law and was comparatively well-known. Atkins was an early member of a small group of women law academics and some socio-legal academics, with common research interests, who came together in the late '70s/early '80s to exchange ideas, discuss and debate their work.[9] Although their specialist areas of law differed, they approached their research with a feminist analysis. They met informally a few times a year with an annual, more formal conference at which papers were presented and discussed. The group was very influential in developing an understanding of why and how the law itself discriminated against women, in raising awareness and arguing for change. The support the group gave its members was vital as involvement in this area of research was not then seen as career-enhancing and articles were hard to place in academic journals.[10]

Atkins was teaching a course on Discrimination Law at the University of Southampton, introduced two years earlier by Albie Sachs and Judith Mayhew.[11] She had expanded the course to a full year and introduced a mandatory dissertation component. The wide and innovative range of subjects chosen by the students, for example, the law on midwives, childbirth and abortion, informed Atkins' own thinking. Her experience of getting students on a 'Second Chance for Women Course' to respond to the Law Commission's Consultation Paper on Illegitimacy demonstrated to her the influence that ordinary women could have when law-makers were made aware of women's perspectives.[12]

[8] Professor Hill Kay wrote the classic American text on Sex Discrimination (*Sex-Based Discrimination: Text, Cases and Materials* (West Publishing Company, 1974) with Ruth Bader Ginsburg, later the second woman appointed to the US Supreme Court.

[9] Members included Anne Bottomley (Kent), Victoria Fisher (Leicester), Nicola Lacey (LSE), Linda Luckhaus (Southampton), Judith Mayhew (Kings College London), Katherine O'Donovan (Kent), Carol Smart (Sheffield), Betsy Stanko (Brunel), Erika Szyszczak (Kent), Jennifer Temkin (LSE), Vera Sacks (Kingston Polytechnic).

[10] ***Feminist Legal Studies* Journal, 1993.**

[11] Judith Mayhew, who moved to Kings College London, was the instigator of the Women Law Teachers Group and Albie Sachs left a copy of the manuscript of his book, 'Sexism and the Law' with Atkins when he went to Mozambique.

[12] The Law Commission subsequently changed its initial proposition to remove the status of illegitimacy AND give all fathers automatic rights over their children, instead proposing only to change the legal status.

Reform of the law was an explicit aim of *Women and the Law*. We saw the book as contributing to the development of a non-sexist education, which we saw as essential to the liberation of both women and men. Quoting Rosemary Deem,[13] we aimed to raise awareness amongst women to fight for change and persuade men to support those changes. 'Only when women are aware of the extent of the discrimination against them, of how it operates and of how to use the law and to influence law reform to their own ends will further progress be made.'[14]

*Women and the Law* was the first book in the UK to examine comprehensively how the law treated and defined women. Structured around the different aspects of women's lives, in the manner of feminist literature, rather than around legal categories, like most law books, it looked at the position of women in their public lives (as workers, citizens and taxpayers), and in their private and family lives, looking at issues of sexuality, motherhood, power, and domestic violence, and the gendered distribution of roles within the family.

It took an historical approach, tracing essentially three stages of development from subordination, through reforms in relation to specific needs of women (particularly in the private sphere) to the recognition of formal equality. It sought to show how formal equality did not bring substantive equality, especially where family roles followed traditional stereotypes. However, it was a work of legal scholarship, using skills of legal analysis to dissect and expose the gendered construction and interpretation of law. It was written in a straightforward and at times direct manner. We were helped tremendously in this respect by a very skilled editor, Elizabeth Bland, who showed us how the original text could be shortened by a third, achieving a greater impact without sacrificing accuracy or depth.

We exposed how the then law on sexual assaults and rape was shot through with male perceptions, anxieties and interests and failed to take account of women's experiences. Discussing proposals to reform the law on rape, we said:

> Recognising that mistakes of identity invalidate consent reflects an important female dimension of intercourse. To men, intercourse may be satisfying no matter who the woman is. For women, the identity of the person is crucial to the act. Even if the law were concerned only about the risks of pregnancy, as opposed to the serious violation of the woman's integrity and personality, this must be obvious.[15]

However, reintroducing the need for fear of force to invalidate apparent consent would be a backward step: 'Consent involves submission but submission does not necessarily involve consent. … *Force* is a male threat which *men* fear. There are many other less explicit ways in which men can cause women to fear them.'[16]

We rejected the notion of a male conspiracy but exposed how law (legislation and case law) was predicated on the male experience, progress often being made once men realised that if the law treated them as it treated women, they would regard it as unjust. One example was ***Gill and Cootes v El Vino Co Ltd***[17] where the Court of Appeal held that it was unlawful discrimination to refuse to serve women drinks at the bar.

[13] Rosemary Deem, *Women and Schooling* (Routledge and Keegan Paul, 1978) 141.
[14] *Women and the Law*, n 1 above, 5.
[15] ibid 69.
[16] ibid.
[17] ***Gill and Cootes v El Vino Co Ltd***[1983] QB 425.

> Lord Justice Griffiths may have given the explanation: 'El Vino's is no ordinary wine bar; it has become a unique institution in Fleet Street. Every day it is thronged with journalists, barristers and solicitors, exchanging the gossip of the day. No doubt it is the source of many false rumours which have dashed the hopes of many an aspirant to a high court appointment.' As Lord Justice Eveleigh said: 'It affords a unique atmosphere which is clearly greatly appreciated and is *in great demand by men and I cannot therefore assume* that there is no true demand for it by women'. (emphasis added)[18]

Published nine years after the Sex Discrimination Act 1975, the book challenged the notion that equality legislation was the answer to women's inequality with men. Not only was women's legal position in the public sphere directly or indirectly affected by her legal position in the private sphere, but the way lawyers thought could also undermine attempts to reform the law and ameliorate her disadvantage. For example, the higher courts at that time were struggling to make sense of the new equality legislation in terms of more familiar legal concepts such as contract, defamation and negligence, resulting in decisions which undermined the law's intent or limited its effectiveness.[19]

## III. What Happened Next

The book seems to have captured the zeitgeist. It was shortlisted for the non-fiction Fawcett Book Prize, which brought it to the attention of a more general readership. The publishers promoted the book at a large international Feminist Law Conference in New York, which Atkins attended, shortly after it was published. The fact that it was published in English may also account for its spread across the globe. Other academics, like Professor Tove Stang Dahl in Oslo, who invited Atkins to teach at her Institute of Women's Law in the later 1980s, were also taking a woman-centred approach to the analysis of law – but her book was only published in English a few years later.[20]

*Women and the Law* was followed by many other books, especially from academics from within the critical legal studies movement, such as Katherine O'Donovan, Erika Szczyszak and Carol Smart. Some of these later works were critical of the legalistic approach we had taken and felt we had given insufficient recognition to the diversity of women's lives. For example Carol Smart in 1989 said that, in accepting the law's terms to challenge law, feminists like us were conceding too much. There was a need to de-centre law, to think of non-legal strategies and to discourage a resort to law as if it held the key to unlock women's oppression.[21] *Women and the Law* came to be seen as part of a second wave of feminist scholarship, overtaken by the late 1980s by a third wave. Arguably however, *Women and the Law* paved the way. By debunking the myth that law was abstract and gender-free, the book also enabled men to begin to explore the ways the law could set expectations for male behaviour, which equally did not respect or reflect the diversity of men's experiences.

Academically the book helped to legitimise a feminist approach to law. In 1998 Clare McGlynn undertook a comprehensive survey of University Law Schools to establish the

[18] See *Women and the Law* (n 1 above) 43.
[19] ibid, 33–38.
[20] Tove Stang Dahl, *Women's Law: an introduction to feminist jurisprudence* (Universitetsforlaget, 1987).
[21] Carol Smart, *Feminism and the Power of Law* (Routledge, 1989).

extent to which courses focused on considering law from a gender/feminist perspective were represented in the academy.[22] She found that 24 law schools offered such courses and that overall just under half of all law schools offered at least one course which included a gender/feminist perspective, the most common approach being the inclusion of feminist jurisprudence within a legal theory course. In 2002, Joanne Conaghan found that feminist scholarship not only engaged in the core subjects such as tort and property law, but also new fields such as healthcare law.[23]

Coincidentally, just as the book was published, Hoggett became the first woman Law Commissioner and was able to translate some of the book's ideas into practical law reform.[24] Soon afterwards, Atkins joined the civil service as a policy-maker.[25] Both were able to put some of the insights they had gained by working together into practical effect.

## IV. Significance

Individually, many women academics and legal practitioners across the world have pointed to *Women and the Law* as a key book in the development of their thinking.[26] In the years following publication, much of the law which we had analysed critically was changed, for example the law on rape and sexual assault,[27] bringing up children, domestic violence and abuse, ownership of the family home, maternity and parental leave. *Women and the Law* can be seen as a book which caught a moment of transition. There have been huge changes in the last 30 years in many areas of law, which have come about because women's experiences and perceptions have been taken into account. Removing the patriarchal rules and assumptions underlying the law of marriage and childcare paved the way for the introduction, first of civil partnerships and more recently of same-sex marriage, same-sex adoptions and same-sex parentage.

In short, nearly every aspect of the law covered in *Women and the Law* has changed, and for the better.

## Further Reading

- Special Issue: Feminist Perspectives on Law (1986) 14(3/4) *International Journal of the Sociology of Law*.

22 Clare McGlynn, *The Woman Lawyer, Making the Difference* (Butterworth, 1998).

23 Referred to in Fiona Cownie, *Legal Academics: Culture and Identities* (Hart Publishing, 2004).

24 **First Woman President of the UK Supreme Court, Brenda Hale, 2017.**

25 As a civil servant, Atkins was a member of the team that presented the UK's first Report on the implementation of the UN CEDAW convention, liaising across government (and women's NGOs and other bodies) at official level (**UK Ratification of the Optional Protocol to the Convention on the Elimination of all Forms of Discrimination Against Women (CEDAW), 2005**). She drafted the UK's second report, which withdrew or modified many of its derogations, eg in relation to women in the military. She later went to the Equal Opportunities Commission as Deputy Chief Executive and in the early 2000s was Director of the Women and Equality Unit in the Cabinet Office.

26 See eg Helena Kennedy in the foreword to *Eve was Framed: Women and British Justice* (Vintage, 1993) and Brenda Hale and Rosemary Hunter, 'A conversation with Baroness Hale' (2008) 16(2) *Feminist Legal Studies* 237.

27 **Section 1 of the Sexual Offences Act 2003.**

# 54

# Warnock Report, 1984

KIRSTY HORSEY

In 1984, after two years of consultations and deliberation, the Committee of Inquiry on Human Reproduction and Embryology published its report.[1] Dubbed the 'Warnock Report', after the Committee's chairwoman, philosopher Mary Warnock (now Lady Warnock), the report was influential in the UK and beyond in the way it facilitated permissive regulation of fertility treatments and related science. Its recommendations enabled scientific and medical advancement, and allowed the UK to remain at the forefront of the development and delivery of new treatments and in innovation in the field. In so doing, the report has allowed numerous women to have children biologically related to themselves (and/or their partner) when this once would have been impossible. The report also recognised the value of allowing the use of donated gametes. In this, and other respects, it foretold changing social and legal understandings of family and parenthood. The regulatory framework around surrogacy – which also stems from the report's recommendations and is another way by which women may have children, even when unable to carry them – has lasted over 30 years.

## I. Context

In 1978, the birth of Louise Brown, the world's first baby born following in vitro fertilisation (IVF), was celebrated around the world. She was born in Oldham General Hospital to a Bristolian couple who had tried unsuccessfully to have a baby for nine years, later discovering that the reason for this was Mrs Brown's blocked Fallopian tubes. The Browns had subsequently agreed to be part of a trial of an experimental new treatment. For them, Louise's birth marked the end of a long period of involuntary childlessness. Importantly, IVF allowed Lesley and John Brown to have a daughter to whom they were both biologically related.[2] For the rest of the world too, the birth was big news. Robert Edwards, one of the pioneers of IVF (alongside Patrick Steptoe and Jean Purdey), was later awarded the 2010 Nobel Prize in Medicine in recognition of his work.

[1] *Report of the Committee of Inquiry into Human Fertilisation and Embryology* (Cmnd 9314, 1984).

[2] The Browns went on to have another daughter, Natalie, by IVF four years later. Natalie is recorded as the world's 40th IVF baby and was the first IVF baby known to go on to have a naturally-conceived baby, in 1999. Louise Brown has also had children by natural conception.

IVF techniques had been developing in animals and with human cells in laboratories for many years by 1978, and a human baby had been inevitable for some time. The only questions were 'where?' and 'who would get there first?' However, Louise Brown's birth marks a point in a much longer timeline in relation to treatments for infertility. Pre-IVF, what used to be known as 'artificial insemination' (now more commonly 'donor insemination') had been in the spotlight. In 1945 a paper in the *British Medical Journal* had called it 'an offence'; it was condemned by Pope Pius VII in 1949 and deemed 'undesirable' by the Feversham Committee in 1960.[3] In fact, it was not until 1958 that a civil court ruled that the practice did not amount to adultery.[4]

Louise Brown's birth highlighted the incredible potential of IVF to bring happiness to many. In July 2016 it was estimated that over 6.5 million IVF babies have been born worldwide.[5] Equally important is the ongoing research on human embryos that IVF – and the Warnock recommendations and resultant legislation – allows for (not to mention research on sperm and eggs and other matters of reproductive health and fertility). Before and after 1978, embryology continued apace and – as with most scientific developments in history, though perhaps even more starkly, as this newest development was about the very foundations of human life itself – public interest (and concerns) grew. As Mary Warnock put it,

> while there has been a long tradition, at least from Aristotle's time, of the value of the developing human foetus in its mother's womb, there was not, and could not have been any tradition of the value of a live human embryo living outside a woman's body, since such a thing had never existed until 1978.[6]

Debates about embryology had (and still have) similarities to those on abortion, inevitably raising the question about when human life begins and has 'value' in the eyes of the law. However, what was new was the nascent scientific potential that understanding the embryo's early development and its properties could bring – not only for infertile women, but also for their children. The two sides were clearly in tension.

Running alongside IVF's medical and scientific developments was the emerging social issue of surrogacy. Kim Cotton became the UK's 'first' surrogate in 1985.[7] This too became newsworthy, the media stoking fears that wealthy foreigners and American agencies were paying British women to be inseminated and to have babies for them – a 'babies for sale' scandal. Cotton was, in her own words, 'vilified by the press'.[8] Alongside her case, other surrogacy cases were reported. In days when a surrogacy arrangement was unusual enough to send councils and/or hospitals into panic and asking for the children concerned to be made wards of court, judicial language in relation to surrogacy was scathing. In *A v C*,[9] for example, Ormrod LJ described the surrogacy arrangement as 'bizarre and unnatural' and a

[3] *Report of the Departmental Committee on Human Artificial Insemination* (HMSO, Cmnd 1105, 1960).
[4] *MacLennan v MacLennan* 1958 SC 105; 1958 SLT 12.
[5] Simon Brown, '6.5 million IVF babies since Louise Brown', *Focus on Reproduction*, 5 July 2016.
[6] *Dishonest to God: On Keeping Religion out of Politics* (Continuum, 2010) 22.
[7] *Re C (A Minor) (Wardship: Surrogacy)* [1985] FLR 846.
[8] Kim Cotton, 'The UK's Antiquated Laws on Surrogacy: A Personal and Professional Perspective' (2016) 3 *Journal of Medical Law and Ethics* 230.
[9] *A v C* [1985] FLR 445.

'sordid little bargain',[10] Cumming-Bruce LJ called it 'a kind of baby-farming operation of a wholly distasteful and lamentable kind' and a 'guilty bargain which should never have been made'[11] and Stamp LJ referred to the case as 'an ugly little drama'.[12]

The possibility that surrogates could carry babies that were *not* created using their own eggs came with the development of IVF – that is for couples who created embryos by IVF which were later transferred to another woman who would act as a gestational 'host'. Thus, the two areas became inextricably linked. Despite the potential that IVF surrogacy indubitably has for those wishing to have their own biologically-related children, it led to greater concerns about potential exploitation or coercion of vulnerable and/or poor women. Emerging at this time – mainly from America – was a wealth of feminist literature that was anti-IVF, anti-surrogacy, anti-assisted reproduction in totality. Andrea Dworkin, among others, condemned fertility treatments as patriarchal tools designed to control women's bodies and render women eventually unnecessary in the reproductive process.[13] Surrogacy was likened to prostitution and slavery. Works of dystopian fiction emerged as obvious allegories (most famously, perhaps, Margaret Atwood's *The Handmaid's Tale*). Only later were alternative feminist voices heard to highlight the other side of the argument, by championing women's reproductive autonomy. Carmel Shalev went further than most, arguing that to enable women to overcome the constraints of patriarchy 'reproducing woman' should be treated as an autonomous moral *and economic* agent, thus free to enter for-profit contracts for surrogacy.[14]

In this early atmosphere of concern about what reproductive technologies could lead to and how fast they were developing, but also in acknowledgement of the sheer potential of these technologies and the related research for women and families, it became clear in the UK that IVF, surrogacy, and embryology (and related fields of research) needed to be regulated. The UK led the world.[15] It was acknowledged that regulation would have to take into account the concerns of some groups as well as allow for the hopes and progress of others. It needed balance.

## II. The Landmark

In 1982, a committee of inquiry was established by the Conservative Government to consider the new reproductive technologies and draw up the principles that should underpin their regulation. Its terms of reference, according to the report Foreword written by Mary Warnock, were 'to examine the social, ethical and legal implications of recent, and potential developments in the field of human assisted reproduction'. Importantly, the chairperson was not only a respected moral philosopher (as opposed to, for example, a scientist,

[10] ibid, 455, 457.
[11] ibid, 459.
[12] ibid, 461.
[13] Andrea Dworkin, *Right-wing Women: The Politics of Domesticated Females* (The Women's Press, 1983) 187–88.
[14] Carmel Shalev, *Birth Power: The Case for Surrogacy* (Yale University Press, 1989).
[15] Only the US was close in time in terms of IVF birth and it was also having surrogacy scandals – the so-called 'Baby M' case – happening at the same time, but its federal nature made regulation on a nation-wide basis as unlikely then as it is now.

doctor or lawyer) but also, perhaps crucially, a woman and a mother. Mary Warnock had variously been mistress of Girton College, Cambridge, headmistress of Oxford High School for Girls, and member of the Oxford Local Education Authority and of the Independent Broadcasting Authority. She also had already experienced chairing a committee of inquiry, having done so in relation to special educational needs provision, from 1974–78.[16]

Mary Warnock, alongside 15 others, spent two years considering the moral and other issues that human assisted reproduction and embryology raised, considering whether to recommend that they needed to be regulated and, if so, how best to do this. As she stated to the Government in the Foreword:

> The task you set the Inquiry was not an easy one. The issues raised reflect fundamental moral, and often religious, questions which have taxed philosophers and others down the ages. Rightly you chose a membership which encompassed not only the many professions with a concern in these matters but the many religious traditions within society, so that as many view-points as possible could be brought to bear on the morally sensitive issues before us.

Speaking in 2016, Mary Warnock reflected on the great debt of gratitude she owed to the late Dr (later Dame) Anne McLaren.[17] Anne McLaren was – unusually – a female scientist working in mammalian embryology who explained the science and its limits to the rest of the committee so clearly that they were able to understand without the hype. Talking about this time, Mary Warnock described the level of animosity and vitriol she endured for considering embryo research as 'remarkable', and her 'wonderful' secretary separating out the hate mail she received. Her view remained that infertility was a disability that should be remedied by any means possible and that research using embryos was absolutely necessary if IVF was to improve.

The report was published in July 1984. It contained a coherent set of proposals for regulation that has stood the test of time, in principle at least, for over 30 years. It concluded that the human embryo has special status and should be protected, but recommended that embryo research be permitted, given appropriate safeguards, in order to improve success rates of IVF and other treatments. However, no embryo was to be kept alive for more than 14 days.[18] While no exact scientific reason exists for this, she admits, Mary Warnock recognised the importance of an ethical bright-line that (almost) everyone could sign up to (though three members of the committee, believing that life begins at conception, felt unable to support any embryo research) and that everyone – scientists, regulators, the public – would understand. It wasn't, however, 'plucked out of the sky', but was based on the understanding of early embryo development she had been taught by Anne McLaren.[19] Even those who regarded the arbitrary 14-day limit as too low

[16] *Report by the Committee of Enquiry into the Education of Handicapped Children and Young People* (Cmnd 7212, 1978).

[17] At the Progress Educational Trust annual conference, December 2016, and later at the 'Anne McLaren: Science, Ethics and the Archive', public event, organised by the British Library in partnership with the Anne McLaren Memorial Trust Fund, held on 20 July 2017 (see an event review in *BioNews* 912 (http://www.bionews.org.uk/page_870742.asp), which includes comments from Lady Warnock on the value of Anne McLaren's input).

[18] The penalty for going beyond this point is 10 years' imprisonment.

[19] Roger Highfield, 'How long should we grow human embryos in the lab?': https://blog.sciencemuseum.org.uk/how-long-should-we-grow-human-embryos-in-the-lab/.

(such as philosopher John Harris) have recognised its value as a 'useful' cut-off point and acknowledged that all the work done to date and what has been learnt about the embryo, including in terms of stem-cell research, has been able to be done within 14 days.[20]

Naturally, given the controversial nature of embryo research, not everyone agreed with the recommendations. In the wake of the report, and long before the Government would be ready to present draft legislation, the Unborn Children (Protection) Bill was introduced to parliament in 1984 by Enoch Powell MP, proposing a ban on the use of embryos for anything other than to enable the birth of a child. This was the first of many such blocking attempts.

The report also proposed that a regulatory authority be established to oversee, via a licensing system, the use of human embryos outside the body in both treatment and research. This body later became the Human Fertilisation and Embryology Authority (HFEA) which came into being in 1991, is still in operation today, and is a model for other such regulatory authorities in numerous other jurisdictions. The report's recommendations on surrogacy were cautious, the majority of the panel and Mary Warnock herself being largely against the practice but not to the extent that they would recommend a total ban, though they did wish to prohibit commercial aspects.

## III. What Happened Next

Following the publication of the report, the Government acted quickly to regulate surrogacy, in particular commercial surrogacy. The Surrogacy Arrangements Act 1985 (SAA) is still in force. It does not – contrary to widespread belief – make surrogacy illegal; instead it prohibits brokers or agents from making profits from surrogacy arrangements, as well as advertising for or as a surrogate. It also renders all surrogacy agreements unenforceable.[21] The rules on legal parenthood following surrogacy are found in the Human Fertilisation and Embryology (HFE) Acts 1990 and 2008. They recognise the surrogate as the legal mother, contrary to intentions and expectations; though they provide for a 'parental order' transferring parenthood providing certain conditions are met.

The first legislation dealing comprehensively with IVF, embryology, donor gametes and other issues came later than the SAA, in 1990, following years of debate inside and outside of parliament. The HFE Act 1990 was far less a 'knee-jerk' affair than the SAA had been; in part, one suspects, because of the tone of the Warnock Report regarding surrogacy as compared to other forms of assisted reproduction. In 2008, significant amendments were made by a new HFE Act, passed as an updating and amending statute (as opposed to wholesale repeal and replacement of the first). This was an attempt to keep up not only with scientific developments but also changing social understandings about families and genetics. For example, it was the 2008 Act that removed the controversial obligation of clinics to consider a potential child's 'need for a father'[22] when deciding whether or not to offer

[20] Andrew Brown, 'The Practical Philosopher', *The Guardian*, 19 July 2003.

[21] A later addition, inserted by the HFE Act 1990.

[22] Section 13(5) of the HFE Act 1990.

treatment – a provision that had in the past been used to deny lesbian couples or single women access to treatment in some clinics – replacing it with the obligation for clinics to consider the child's need for 'supportive parenting'.[23]

Many developments have occurred in IVF, largely because of the report's forward-thinking recommendations which allowed research to continue in the background of and alongside clinical practice. For example, while freezing sperm was relatively commonplace even before IVF was developed, the first baby born following the use of a previously frozen embryo was not born until 1984, the first in the UK from a previously frozen ovum in 2001, and the first worldwide from previously frozen ovarian tissue in 2004. All were milestones in fertility treatment circles – particularly for women. Female cancer survivors, for example, can now have biologically related children, even after treatment that renders them infertile. It is unlikely that these developments would have happened – or happened so soon – or that the techniques used to do so would be continuously improved (the first baby from frozen pre-pubescent ovarian tissue was born in 2016), had it not been for the cautious permissiveness of the Warnock Report.

Most recently, the UK has pioneered extending the law to allow mitochondrial replacement therapies (which mean mothers with heritable mitochondrial diseases can avoid passing them to their children, thereby averting chronic conditions and often, early and painful deaths). And, of course, the debates continue. UK-based researchers demonstrated in 2016 that an embryo could be kept alive in culture for 13 days – the longest ever achieved – reopening the debate on the '14-day rule', one of the Warnock Report's key recommendations. Mary Warnock has commented publicly about the rule and advocates that the limit should be kept for the foreseeable future, until there is true understanding of what happens up to the 14-day mark.

## IV. Significance

Coupled with numerous significant cultural changes since its publication, what makes the Warnock Report so significant is its foresightedness. It led to two pieces of legislation that have stood the test of time (albeit with major amendments in 2008 to the HFE Act). The HFE Act in particular has been used as a model of the way to legislate in this area in numerous other jurisdictions in the years since 1990. In addition, the findings and recommendations of the committee are still significant today; they will and should continue to inform the basis of future discussions on the way these areas should be regulated. This is important in the context of rising infertility: in 2017, one in six couples had fertility problems.[24]

In the context of changing social attitudes the law on surrogacy is now imperfect and out of date. A later Government reviewed surrogacy in 1998, particularly focusing on payments.[25] Nothing came from that review's recommendations. Surrogacy law increasingly struggles to cope with complex new demands, following a boom in international

[23] Section 14(2)(b) of the HFE Act 2008.

[24] Fertility Network UK, 'Medical Problems': http://fertilitynetworkuk.org/for-those-trying-to-become-parents/information/medical-conditions/.

[25] *Surrogacy: Review for Health Ministers of Current Arrangements for Payments and Regulation* (Cm 4068, 1998) (the 'Brazier Report').

(commercial) surrogacy in the internet age, increasing numbers of gay (male) and other couples – and single people – seeking surrogacy,[26] and changing societal understandings of infertility, parenthood and family. It impacts negatively on women's autonomous choices, on who can achieve legal parenthood and on what people may consider 'reasonable expenses'. International surrogacy has undoubtedly highlighted issues of concern regarding potential exploitation of women from poorer countries, leading to recommendations for domestic law reform. Reform should facilitate domestic surrogacy, which has many examples of good practice, but is relatively inaccessible and hard for people to understand due to the restrictive rules on advertising. Increasingly, academic, expert and practitioner voices have joined in calling for reform. The suggestion is that changing the way parenthood is determined, and reassessing policy on advertising and expenses, would enable domestic surrogacy practices to be more transparent and, crucially, more attractive to those who might otherwise go overseas. An updating reform of the legislation looks potentially possible: questions have been asked and debates taken place in both Houses of Parliament;[27] in December 2017, the Law Commission announced that surrogacy would be included in its 13th programme of law reform; and in May 2018 the Law Commission and Scottish Law Commission were granted the funding by the Department of Health and Social Care for concurrent reviews of surrogacy laws.

The flexibility of the legislation on other fertility treatments and embryology, in place since 1990, and as updated in 2008, means that women and their families continue to benefit. While science will always outpace law in this area, the carefully considered moral and legislative framework from which we started will continue to provide a strong foundation underpinning the current – and any future – law.

## Further Reading


- Kirsty Horsey (ed), *Revisiting the Regulation of Human Fertilisation and Embryology* (Routledge, 2015).
- Kirsty Horsey, 'Surrogacy in the UK: Myth busting and reform', *Report of the Surrogacy UK Working Group on Surrogacy Law Reform* (Surrogacy UK, November 2015).
- Michael Mulkay, *The Embryo Research Debate: Science and the Politics of Reproduction* (Cambridge University Press, 2010).


[26] The rules currently prevent single people from obtaining a parental order, despite the fact they can adopt. In 2016 Munby J declared this incompatible with human rights law (*In the matter of Z (a child) (No 2)* [2016] EWHC 1191); at the time of writing, a Remedial Order is progressing through Parliament to correct the incompatibility.

[27] See eg HC Deb, 7 February 2017, vol 621; HL Deb, 14 December 2016, vol 777 cols 1317–1333.

# 55

## Prohibition of Female Circumcision Act 1985

PHYLLIS LIVAHA

The Prohibition of Female Circumcision Act 1985 made it an offence 'to excise, infibulate or otherwise mutilate the whole or any part of the labia majora or labia minora or clitoris of another person' (section 1(1)(a)), or to aid and abet such practices (section 1(1)(b)), except to treat specific medical purposes. The offence was punishable with up to five years' imprisonment, an unlimited fine or both, but it only covered the practice if performed within the UK. The Act is a landmark in the protection of women and girls from a customary practice upon which opinion remains divided.

## I. Context

Female circumcision – also known as female genital mutilation (FGM), female genital cutting (FGC), or simply 'cutting'[1] – is an ancient procedure that takes various forms, the least severe of which is ritual circumcision or pricking of the clitoral hood. *Sunna*, which means 'tradition', entails the excision of the clitoral prepuce while a clitoridectomy entails the complete removal of the clitoris.[2] Infibulation is the most severe of the surgeries, requiring 'the removal or scraping of the labia minora and labia majora which is the two rounded folds of tissue that control the external boundaries of the vulva'.[3] Controversy continues over the use of the terms to describe the procedure. This landmark will use the term 'female circumcision', which is used in both the 1985 Act and in the Convention on the Elimination of All Forms of Discrimination against Women (CEDAW).[4] Campaigns have tended to adopt a

[1] Jessica Horn, 'Not Culture But Gender: Reconceptualizing Female Genital Mutilation/Cutting' in Wendy Chavkin and Ellen Chesler (eds), *Where Human Rights Begin: Health, Sexuality, and Women in the New Millenium* (Rutgers University Press, 2005) 38.

[2] Khadija F Sharif, 'Female Genital Mutilation, What does the New Federal Law Really Mean?' (1997) 24 *Fordham Urban Law Journal* 409, 413.

[3] Leslye Amede Obiora, 'Bridges and Barricades: Rethinking Polemics and Intransigence in the Campaign against Female Circumcision' in Adrien Katherine Wing (ed), *Global Critical Race Feminism: An International Reader* (New York University Press, 2000). See further World Health Organization, 'Classification of female genital mutilation': http://www.who.int/reproductivehealth/topics/fgm/overview/en/.

[4] Convention on the Elimination of All Forms of Discrimination Against Women 1989, Recommendation 14; See further **UK Ratification of the Optional Protocol to the Convention on the Elimination of all Forms of Discrimination Against Women (CEDAW), 2005**.

zero tolerance approach that equates all acts with the most extreme forms,[5] although similar procedures like female genital cosmetic surgery are not subject to the same scrutiny.[6]

In the early 1970s, Fran Hosken, an American feminist writer and social activist, began covering female circumcision practice in her newsletter, *Women's International Network News*. In 1976, Hosken confronted the Somali delegate at a UN Habitat Conference in Vancouver about what she saw as the 'mutilation' of children,[7] and led a letter-writing campaign to hospitals and health clinics in Africa. Her campaign grew throughout the 1970s, gaining the support of some African women. In different African countries, women's groups led campaigns to educate the population about the effects of the practice and doctors wrote about the clinical complications of the practice in medical journals.[8] In 1979, she published *The Hosken Report: Genital and Sexual Mutilation of Females*. Feminists and others took note. UN sub-committees and agencies, including the World Health Organization (WHO), took up the issue, while (many) feminists came to see the practice as a 'tool of patriarchy and a symbol of women's subordination'.[9] Indeed, by the 1980s, many Western countries had criminalised the practice as a human rights violation.

However, crucially, the transnational campaigns which were so critical of the practice largely failed to include the communities who practise it in their discussions. There was a strong feeling among African feminists – many of whom also opposed the practice – that 'feminists from developed countries' were taking over the issue. In 1978, Marie-Angelique Savané argued that they 'must accept that genital mutilation is a problem for African women who themselves must speak out in favour of the eradication of the practices'.[10] During a female circumcision panel held at the same time as the UN Conference on Women in 1980, the fact that a French woman was chairing the meeting and some western feminists were publicly criticising the practice, shocked the African women, causing them to walk out in protest.[11]

It was pointed out that, although FGM tends to be associated with the countries in the Global South, it had been practised in the West in the nineteenth century and into the twentieth to control 'female deviancy', hysteria, epilepsy and lesbianism, while cosmetic surgery continues to be employed in the West to improve women's appearance to meet cultural norms. These tensions exemplify the ongoing struggle not only between cultural relativism and universal human rights, but also between feminists in this context. Specifically, many international human rights activists argue that the practice is a violation

[5] Moira Dustin, 'Female Genital Mutilation/Cutting in the UK: Challenging the Inconsistencies' (2010) 17(1) *European Journal of Women's Studies* 7.

[6] House of Commons Home Affairs Committee, 'Female Genital Mutilation: The case for a national action plan' (HMSO, HC 201 [Incorporating HC 1091, 2013–14], 3 July 2014).

[7] Jessica Cammaert, *Undesirable Practices: Women, Children, and the Politics of the Body in Northern Ghana, 1930–1972* (University of Nebraska Press, 2016) 214.

[8] Anika Rahman and Nahid Toubia (eds), *Female Genital Mutilation: A Guide to Laws & Policies Worldwide* (Zed Books, 2000) 10.

[9] Fran P Hosken, *The Hosken Report: Genital and Sexual Mutilation of Females* (Women's International Network News, 1979). Early attempts during the 1950s to address the issue on a global scale had been unsuccessful.

[10] Marie-Angelique Savané, 'Why We Are against the International Campaign?' (1978) 40 *International Child Welfare Review* 38. See also Nitza Berkovitch and Karen Bradley, 'The Globalization of Women's Status: Consensus/Dissensus in the World Polity' (1999) 42(3) *Sociological Perspectives* 481, 490.

[11] Scilla McLean, *Female Circumcision, Excision and Infibulation: The Facts and Proposals for Change* (Report No 47, 3rd edn, Minority Rights Group, 1985) 10.

of women's human rights, while others assert cultural and religious defences as a reason to respect the practice.[12] Cultural relativists oppose conforming to 'universal' norms, arguing that majority preference should not dictate what is moral,[13] because there is no particular culture that is superior to another when examining issues of law, politics or morality.[14] Conversely, universalism asserts that everyone is linked together by a common cause that is human rights, which are universal, and there is no cultural value in the practice of female circumcision because values change from place to place, and over time, so some of the rituals of the practice can be changed.[15]

## II. The Landmark

British concern over female circumcision dates to colonial days,[16] but it accelerated in the 1970s as African immigration increased.[17] The London-based Foundation for Women's Health, Research and Development Organisation (FORWARD) was founded in 1983 by Efua Dorkenoo, who had been sparked into action after taking a midwifery course in the 1970s and seeing first-hand the effects of infibulation.[18] FORWARD campaigned against the practice and worked with Lord Kennett, who introduced a Private Member's Bill on female circumcision in the House of Lords in 1983. It had the backing of the British Medical Association, the Royal College of Nursing, the Royal College of Midwives, the National Council of Women as well as a number of feminist organisations including the National Federation of Women's Institutes, the Josephine Butler Society and the Fawcett Society.

The first draft of the Bill made no mention of abuse, which remained an issue of debate for three parliamentary sessions until Lord Kennett reintroduced the Bill, classifying female circumcision as a criminal offence unless performed for physical health. During the second reading of the Bill, several debates ensued. One was whether the Act was necessary. Lord Halisham, speaking in his capacity as Lord Chancellor, stated that the practice was already illegal under the Offences Against the Person Act 1861, which provided for up to life imprisonment for maliciously causing grievous bodily harm.[19] Another focused on the wording 'physical health'. The Royal College of Obstetricians and Gynaecologists, who backed the Bill, had reservations about the inclusion of a requirement that two medical practitioners concurred to the operation, which was subsequently dropped.[20] Others argued for the inclusion of a specific (and controversial) prohibition of the practices for 'ritual or

[12] Allison T Slack, 'Female Circumcision: A Critical Appraisal' (1988) 10 *Human Rights Quarterly* 437.

[13] ibid 463.

[14] Alison Renteln, 'Relativism and the Search for Human Rights' (1988) 90(1) *American Anthropologist* 56.

[15] Dominic Wilkinson, 'Cultural Relativism and Female Genital Mutilation' (*Practical Ethics. Ethics in News*, University of Oxford, 7 February 2014).

[16] Hilary Burrage, *Eradicating Female Genital Mutilation: A UK Perspective* (Ashgate Publishing, 2015) 153.

[17] Karlene Davis and Christine McCafferty, 'Forwards' in Comfort Momoh (ed), *Female Genital Mutilation* (Radcliffe Publishing, 2005) 66.

[18] FORWARD, 'Sharing Actions, Achievements and Aspirations: 30 years safeguarding rights and dignity of African women and girls' (FORWARD: Safeguarding rights and dignity): http://forwarduk.org.uk/wp-content/uploads/2016/01/30th-Anniversary-Booklet-FINAL-Digital.pdf. It built on Dorkenoo's work with FORWARD's predecessor the Woman's Action Group on Excision and Infibulation.

[19] HL Deb, 21 April 1983, vol 441 col 676.

[20] HL Deb, 10 November 1983, vol 444 col 991 (Lord Kennet).

customary reasons'.[21] When the Bill moved to the Committee Stage, discussion continued on an amendment to allow for the performance of an operation where it is 'necessary' for the patient's 'mental health'. Opponents described this as a loophole and, without coming to an agreement, the Bill was passed in the Lords and was sent to the House of Commons where this was never discussed.

The Bill was reintroduced to the House of Lords in January 1984, and the amendment concerning the term 'mental health' was again tabled, debated and put to a vote, with a majority voting to leave it out. In March 1984, the Bill was again passed in the Lords and sent to the House of Commons where it was eventually committed to the Standing Committee in 1985.[22] In May 1985, the Bill, sponsored by Baroness Masham, was read a second time. Much of the debate focused on whether the inclusion of a specific reference to 'custom' and 'ritual', in the context of determining whether the procedure is necessary for the patient's mental health, was discriminatory as argued by the chair of the Commission for Racial Equality and, if so, whether it should be avoided.[23] While some argued that those invested in race relations were in danger of 'going over the top, of over-sensitivity' and defeating their own cause, in the same way as many of the 'more extreme' women's liberationists had done,[24] others suggested that they might 'distance ourselves' from the 'culturally unacceptable' practice, without introducing this provocative and discriminatory suggestion.[25] When the Bill was finally passed in July 1985, the words remained.[26]

## III. What Happened Next

In 1989, FORWARD organised a national conference on 'Female Genital Mutilation: Dilemmas for Professionals in Health, Education and Social Work'. It was the first conference on female circumcision in the UK and led to recognition of the practice as child abuse and bringing it within the scope of the UK child protection framework and local authorities.[27] The Department of Health adopted the recommendations from the conference as blueprints for local authority action. However, tensions continued, and the London Borough of Brent debated a motion to legalise it as a 'right specifically for African families who want to carry on their tradition whilst living in [the UK]'.[28] Anne Brent, one of the councillors who opposed the motion, was threatened and verbally attacked. The motion was defeated, but not before the WHO, UNICEF and Alice Walker urged the councillors to oppose the motion.

[21] HL Deb, 10 November 1983, vol 444 col 1000 (Lord Glenarthur).

[22] Prohibition of Female Circumcision HL Bill (1984) 447 col 72, 1076 and 450; HC Bill (1984) 58, col 1069; HC Bill (1985) 72, col 1298.

[23] HL Deb, 15 May 1985, vol 463 col 1228 (Lord McNair).

[24] ibid.

[25] HL Deb, 15 May 1985, vol 463 col 1232 (Viscount of Falkland).

[26] Section 2(1) states that the operation will not be unlawful if it is '(a) is necessary for the physical or mental health of the person on whom it is performed and is performed by a registered medical practitioner'. Section 2(2) continues 'In determining for the purposes of this section whether an operation is necessary for the mental health of a person, no account shall be taken of the effect on that person of any belief on the part of that or any other person that the operation is required as a matter of custom or ritual'.

[27] FORWARD, n 18 above, 12.

[28] Anna Davis, 'Ann John: I was branded a colonialist for fighting against "barbaric" FGM', *London Evening Standard*, 28 March 2014.

No prosecutions were made under the 1985 Act, in part because it was circumvented by taking girls abroad temporarily to carry out the practice. Activists lobbied to close this loophole, leading to the first all-party parliamentary hearing on female circumcision in 2000. This hearing, the All-Party Parliamentary Group on Population, Development and Reproductive Health, led to the recommendation that an extraterritoriality clause be introduced to address this. Other recommendations included strengthening the law and developing information and media campaigns to target specific groups.

Ann Clwyd MP introduced the Female Genital Mutilation Bill on 11 September 2002. It proposed to repeal and re-enact the provisions of the 1985 Act, replacing 'circumcision' with 'mutilation', which was by now in common usage. The proposed Act would also have extraterritorial effect by making it illegal for female circumcision to be performed on British nationals or permanent residents abroad wherever it took place and would increase the maximum penalty on indictment from five to 14 years imprisonment. The Female Genital Mutilation Act 2003 came into force on 3 March 2004. It replaced the 1985 Act in England, Wales and Northern Ireland. The Prohibition of Female Genital Mutilation (Scotland) Act 2005 replaced the 1985 Act in Scotland.

In 2007 and 2014, reports suggested that the number of girls and women who were victims of female circumcision in the UK was increasing.[29] It was estimated that 65,000 girls aged 13 and under were at risk of female circumcision. Responding to a Parliamentary Inquiry into Female Genital Mutilation, the Bar Human Rights Committee of England and Wales (BHRC) produced a damning report in which it concluded that the UK has been in breach of its international law obligations to protect women and children from genital mutilation. It made 12 recommendations, including a national awareness-raising campaign, emphasising that 'FGM is (i) a gross human rights violation; (ii) a crime and child abuse; (iii) a problem in and for British society, which we have a moral and legal duty to combat'.[30]

The BHRC and others also advocated the introduction of 'FGM protection orders' (FGMPO), which would place (potential) victims under the protection of the court, and include the prohibition of travel, residence reporting and mandatory examination.[31] These were introduced in the Serious Crime Act 2015, along with other measures extending the extra-territorial offences to habitual residents of the UK, a new offence of failing to protect a girl from FGM, lifelong anonymity for victims of FGM and a mandatory reporting duty for known cases in under-18s.[32] Bedfordshire Police secured the first FGMPO on the day the law came into force. The order prevented the travel of two young girls, who police believed might have been at risk of being subjected to circumcision, to Africa.[33] Figures from the Ministry of Justice, from September 2016, show that between 17 July 2015

[29] Efua Dorkenoo, Linda Morison and Alison McFarlane, 'A Statistical Study to Estimate the Prevalence of Female Genital Mutilation in England and Wales' (Summary Report, FORWARD, Safeguarding Rights and Dignity, 2007). See also Dexter Dias, Felicity Gerry and Hilary Burrage, '10 reasons why our FGM law has failed – and 10 ways to improve it', *The Guardian*, 7 February 2014.

[30] Bar Human Rights Committee, Report of the Bar Human Rights Committee of England and Wales to the Parliamentary Inquiry into Female Genital Mutilation (February 2014) 4.

[31] See eg House of Commons Home Affairs Committee, n 6 above.

[32] Sections 70–75 of the Serious Crime Act 2015.

[33] Kevin Rawlinson, 'Police obtain first FGM protection order', *The Guardian*, 17 July 2015.

and 30 June 2016, there were 77 FGMPO applications and 68 orders granted (the remainder being under consideration).

In September 2016, the House of Commons Home Affairs Committee produced a further report, *Female genital mutilation: abuse unchecked*, recommending the improved collection of data on the prevalence of female circumcision as well as better communication between relevant support and police agencies: 'It is a hidden crime and the first step towards tackling it effectively is to measure it properly. Only then can resources be allocated accordingly'.[34] Despite this, to date, there have been no successful prosecutions for FGM in the UK.[35] In July 2017, NHS staff recorded close to 5,500 cases of female circumcision in 2016.[36] Writing in 2016, the Home Affairs Committee suggested that:

> It is beyond belief that there still has not been a successful prosecution for an FGM offence since it was made illegal over 30 years ago. That is a lamentable record and the failure to identify cases, to prosecute and to achieve convictions can only have negative consequences for those who are brave enough to come forward to highlight this crime. In the absence of successful prosecutions, FGM remains a national scandal that is continuing to result in the preventable mutilation of thousands of girls.[37]

## IV. Significance

The 1985 Act was a positive step towards stopping a practice considered a serious violation of human rights. It represented the UK Government's clear condemnation of female circumcision and commitment to preventing girls in the UK from being subject to the practice, as well as its decision to legislate directly, rather than wait on the uncertain outcome of individual cases. Women and feminists played a key role in putting – and continue to play a key role in keeping – the issue on the political agenda.[38] In 2017, 'tackling' female circumcision remains an 'integral part' of the cross-Government Ending Violence Against Women and Girls strategy.[39] A new All-Party Parliamentary Group on FGM was launched in October 2017, co-chaired by Labour's Jess Phillips and Tory MP Zac Goldsmith. Speaking

[34] House of Commons Home Affairs Committee, *Female genital mutilation: abuse unchecked*, Ninth Report of Session 2016–17, (HMSO, HC 390, September 2016) 22.

[35] Two doctors were found guilty by a medical disciplinary tribunal for committing serious professional misconduct in relation to female circumcision in 1993 and one of the doctors was deleted from the medical registry (Renee Kool and Sohail Wahedi, 'European Models of Citizenship and the Fight against Female Genital Mutilation' in Scott Nicholas Romaniuk and Marguerite Marlin (eds), *Development and the Politics of Human Rights* (CRC Press, 2015)). A highly-publicised attempt to prosecute a London doctor in 2015 failed (Sandra Laville, 'Doctor found not guilty of FGM on patient at London hospital', *The Guardian*, 4 February 2015).

[36] Peter Walker, 'Met police still don't know where FGM is happening after 32 years without a conviction', *Independent*, 7 March 2017.

[37] House of Commons Home Affairs Committee, n 34 above, 25.

[38] In 2014, Leyla Hussein and Nimco Ali, founders of Daughters of Eve (a non-profit organisation that works to advance and protect the physical, mental, sexual and reproductive health rights of young people from female genital mutilation-practising communities), were named as two of Britain's most influential women in the BBC Woman's Hour power list.

[39] Secretary of State for the Home Department, 'Government response to the ninth report from the Home Affairs Select Committee Session 2017–16 HC 39' (Cm 9375, December 2016): https://assets.publishing.service.gov.uk/government/uploads/system/uploads/attachment_data/file/522166/VAWG_Strategy_FINAL_PUBLICATION_MASTER_vRB.PDF

in the same month, Nimco Ali, co-founder of Daughters of Eve (a non-profit organisation that works to advance and protect the physical, mental, sexual and reproductive health rights of young people from female genital mutilation-practising communities), said she believed it was possible to eradicate it completely by 2030.[40]

> I always say that my FGM was physically painful, but the most painful thing was constant dismissal … Even when I was doing campaigning everyone told me it was a customary act. I said, 'No it's violence against women and girls', and they said 'it's a cultural act' … I have thought about it for 20 years – I haven't just come to a conclusion that I want to protect vaginas. I realised that what happened to me was because I was a girl.[41]

## Further Reading

- Hilary Burrage, *Eradicating Female Genital Mutilation: A UK Perspective* (Ashgate Publishing, 2015).
- Efua Dorkenoo, *Cutting the Rose: Female Genital Mutilation: The Practice and its Prevention* (Minority Rights Group, 1994).
- Carla Obermeyer, 'The Health Consequences of Female Circumcision: Science, Advocacy, and Standard of Evidence' (2003) 17(3) *Medical Anthropology Quarterly* 394.

[40] Anna Davis, 'When David Cameron spoke on FGM, our time had come. We can banish it by 2030', *London Evening Standard*, 11 October 2017.
[41] ibid.

# 56

# *Gillick v West Norfolk and Wisbech Area Health Authority* (1985)

EMMA NOTTINGHAM

The House of Lords' decision in *Gillick v West Norfolk and Wisbech Area Health Authority*[1] ensured that girls under the age of 16 could lawfully make autonomous decisions regarding medical matters and access advice and treatment from a medical professional confidentially, without their parents' knowledge or consent. *Gillick* is widely considered to be a victory for the increased acceptance of children's rights and children's autonomy.[2] It was influential in shifting understandings of parental rights, from being about exerting control over a child to responsibilities and duties that exist for the child's benefit. However, the case was also important for adult women. It was a vital step toward social recognition not only that women could and would engage in sex outside marriage, but might also delay or even reject motherhood, through the use of the oral contraceptive pill, thereby releasing women (should they wish) from the traditional roles of wife, mother and homemaker.

## I. Context

By the 1980s the post-war 'desirability of domesticity'[3] – with its traditional view of family roles, comprising a male breadwinner and the female homemaker – was increasingly being challenged.[4] So too was the view that children ideally should have been born to married couples and have a subordinate role in the family. The role of women in the family was also beginning to change. Gone was the expectation that a daughter of the family was to find a husband and to become a mother when she entered adulthood. The implementation of

[1] *Gillick v West Norfolk and Wisbech Area Health Authority* [1986] AC 112.

[2] For instance, see John Eekelaar, 'The Emergence of Children's Rights' (1986) 6 *Oxford Journal of Legal Studies* 161.

[3] Lesley A Hall, *Sex, Gender and Social Change in Britain since 1880* (Macmillan Press, 2000) 151.

[4] See further Simon Szreter and Kate Fisher, *Sex before the Sexual Revolution: Intimate Life in England 1918–1963* (Cambridge University Press, 2010); Tim Newburn, *Permission and Regulation Law and Morals in Post-war Britain* (Routledge, 1992); Mary Abbott, *Family Affairs: A History of the Family in Twentieth-Century England* (Routledge, 2003); Hall, *Sex, Gender and Social Change*, ibid.

'permissive' legislation – perhaps most notably the **Abortion Act 1967**[5] – and the wider availability of the oral contraceptive pill in the 1960s had transformed understandings of sex outside marriage or for recreational purposes so that it was no longer widely considered to be a 'hazardous activity'.[6] The passing of the **National Health Service (Family Planning) Act 1967** gave local health authorities power to provide birth-control advice, regardless of marital status, and on social as well as medical grounds. As women gained sexual freedom and greater control over their fertility,[7] the dynamics of traditional family norms changed. Women were no longer confined to the traditional gender roles of wife, mother and homemaker.[8] They now had the option to postpone motherhood, have a career and more freedom to engage in sexual activity, both within and outside of marriage, without the fear of pregnancy, and purely for sexual desire.[9]

For some, however, these societal and related legal changes were less welcome. Family life and traditional 'family values' appeared to be under threat, if not outright attack. Sex outside marriage, illegitimacy, promiscuity and women who eschewing traditional gender roles were all targets of the New Moral Right, which included organisations and pressure groups such as The Responsible Society, which by the time of *Gillick* became known as Family and Youth Concern and is now known as the Family Education Trust.[10] The new Conservative Government, elected in 1979 and led by Margaret Thatcher, was keen to protect 'family values', to control gender norms and keep sex associated with parenthood.[11] The difficulty was that the genie was now well and truly out of the bottle.

The preceding Labour Government had taken a difficult view. In response to concerns about the promiscuity of young people,[12] and fears about increased rates of teenage pregnancy, it had sought to reduce the incidence, and protect women from the risk of unwanted pregnancy through the widespread availability of free contraception and sexual health education.[13] This was extended to women under the age of 16 in 1974, when guidelines were issued by the Department of Health and Social Security (DHSS) which allowed for confidential contraceptive advice and treatment to be available to those under 16 without parental consent.

[5] Tim Newburn has stated that the term 'permissiveness' is generally held to apply either to the 1960s or to some period which includes the 1960s' (Tim Newburn, *Permission and Regulation: Law and Morals in Post-war Britain* (Routledge, 1992) preface). See also Kate Marshall, *Moral Panics and Victorian Values* (2nd edn, Junius, 1986) 19.

[6] Mary Abbott, *Family Affairs: A History of the Family in Twentieth-Century England* (Routledge, 2003) 133.

[7] Cas Wouters, 'Balancing Sex and Love since the 1960s Sexual Revolution' (1998) 15 *Theory, Culture & Society* 187, 190.

[8] See further Szreter and Fisher, n 4 above; Hall, n 3 above.

[9] Jennifer Somerville, *Feminism and the Family Politics and Society in the UK and USA* (Macmillan Press, 2000) 63.

[10] Pamela Abbott and Claire Wallace, *The Family and the New Right* (Pluto Press, 1992) 42; Philip Jenkins, *Intimate Enemies Moral Panics in Contemporary Great Britain* (Aldine De Gruyter, 1992) 39; Graham Wootton, *Pressure Groups in Britain 1720–1970* (Allen Lane, 1975); Geoffrey Alderman, *Pressure Groups and Government in Great Britain* (Longman Group, 1984); Somerville n 9 above, 103, 132; Valerie Riches and Robert Whelan, *Family Bulletin, Family & Youth Concern (The Responsible Society)*, No 46 Winter (Nightingale Press, 1986); Dallas Cliff, 'Religion, morality and the middle class' in Roger King and Neill Nugent (eds), *Respectable Rebels: Middle Class Campaigns in Britain in the 1970s* (Hodder and Stoughton, 1979) 128–29; Newburn, n 5 above, 136–57; Jeffrey Weeks, *Sex, Politics & Society: The Regulation of Sexuality since 1800* (2nd edn, Longman, 1989) 249.

[11] Michael Freeman, *Medicine, Ethics and the Law Current Legal Problems* (Stevens & Sons, 1988) 24; Abbott and Wallace, n 10 above 5–7; Marshall, n 5 above, 2, 10; Somerville, n 9 above, 132.

[12] Newburn, n 5 above, 173.

[13] Sally Sheldon, *Beyond Control Medical Power and Abortion Law* (Pluto Press, 1997) 12; Newburn, ibid 6.

This had not gone down well with some sections of the public. Family and Youth Concern actively campaigned nationally against the so-called 'schoolgirl contraception' and for the withdrawal of the guidelines. It believed that parental involvement in contraceptive matters should be encouraged.[14] It sought the support of prospective parliamentary candidates and Area Health Authorities.[15] The National Viewers and Listeners Association, founded by Mary Whitehouse, also adopted this stance,[16] as did as the Nationwide Festival of Light, a short-lived Christian organisation, which called for national action on this issue in its 1978 Bulletin, and subsequently produced a document to enable parents to take action.[17]

Campaigning also occurred at local level. In Dudley, for example, there was campaign activity, supported by the Society for the Protection of Unborn Children, against plans for the establishment of a local birth-control clinic.[18] Similarly, a public protest took place against Doncaster Area Health Authority after it sought to set up a clinic to provide contraceptives to under-16-year-old girls without informing their parents or their general practitioner.[19] This campaign made national news and sparked concern in other parts of the country, including in Victoria Gillick's then home county of Suffolk.[20]

Having read several newspaper articles about the National Health Service setting up birth-control clinics, Gillick wrote to her local community health council, stating that she sincerely hoped that 'secret schoolgirl contraception' was not being provided in Ipswich, because her own daughters would be attending secondary schools in the town and she did not want them to be exposed to the 'corrupting influence' of such clinics.[21] Gillick was invited to the annual public meeting of the Ipswich Community Health Council,[22] during which she became outraged when a letter was read to the attendees from the Regional Administrator of the Family Planning Association, emphasising the importance of adhering to the 1974 DHSS guidelines.[23] This meeting was the start of Gillick's campaign.[24] Soon after, Gillick became an active member of the pressure group 'Parents in Suffolk' who undertook campaign work against the 1974 guidelines.[25] Although Gillick's initial focus was the 1974 guidelines,[26] it was the updated version issued in 1980 that became the catalyst for Gillick's legal action. Section G of the circular, entitled 'The Young',[27] implied that it would not be unlawful for doctors to provide contraceptive advice and treatment to a child under the age of 16, without her parents' consent.[28] This was the first time the campaign against

[14] Simon Lee, *Law and Morals Warnock: Gillick and Beyond* (OUP, 1986) 59.
[15] Martin Durham, *Sex & Politics: The Family and Morality in the Thatcher Years* (Macmillan, 1991) 40; Olaf Raymond Johnston, *Who Needs The Family?* (Hodder and Stoughton, 1979) 134–35.
[16] Durham, n 15 above, 41.
[17] ibid.
[18] ibid.
[19] Johnston, n 15 above, 135.
[20] Victoria Gillick, *A Mother's Tale* (Hodder and Stoughton, 1989) 150.
[21] ibid.
[22] ibid 150–51.
[23] ibid 156.
[24] ibid 162.
[25] ibid 162.
[26] ibid. Victoria Gillick, *Dear Mrs. Gillick: The Public Respond* (Marshall, 1985).
[27] DHSS, *Family Planning Services for Young People* (HN(81)15, 1981) Section G.
[28] ibid.

'schoolgirl contraception' had successfully reached the courts. Earlier attempts by others had been unsuccessful.[29]

## II. The Landmark

Victoria Gillick, a Roman Catholic, was a mother of four daughters (five by the time of the House of Lords' decision and 10 children in total). Following the issuing of the 1980 revised guidelines, she wrote a number of letters to her local Area Health Authority asking for written assurance that in no circumstances would any of her daughters be given contraceptive treatment or an abortion without her prior knowledge or consent whilst they were under the age of 16. The Area Health Authority refused to give such assurance, maintaining that it was bound by the guidelines in the Department of Health and Social Security (DHSS) circular,[30] and emphasised that the treatment prescribed by a doctor was a matter for the doctor's clinical judgement.[31]

In response, she embarked on what Lord Templeman described as a 'crusade' against the guidelines,[32] including a petition signed by between 250,000 and 500,000 people.[33] It was reported that, by November 1983, 200 MPs were supporting her demands.[34] In the courts, she sought a declaration against the DHSS that the circular not only infringed her rights as a parent, but that – were a doctor to act on it – it would amount to advice to doctors to commit the offence of causing or encouraging unlawful sexual intercourse with a girl under the age of 16,[35] or the offence of being an accessory to unlawful sexual intercourse with a girl under the age of 16.[36] She also sought a further declaration against her local Area Health Authority that no one employed by them could provide such advice and treatment to any of her under-16-year-old daughters without her consent, as this too was inconsistent with her parental rights.

Although Gillick lost in the High Court,[37] the Court of Appeal unanimously granted the declarations sought, holding that, other than by court order or an emergency, it would not be lawful for a doctor to give contraceptive advice and treatment to a girl under the age of 16 without parental consent. In so doing, the judgment emphasised the rights and duties of parents (placing little emphasis on the autonomy of children) and concerns about the social, moral and public policy implications raised by availability of the oral contraceptive pill to under-16-year-olds.[38]

[29] Nationwide Festival of Light Broadsheet, June 1975; Bulletin of the Responsible Society 11 (Spring–Summer 1974) cited in Durham, n 15, above 40.

[30] DHSS, n 27 above.

[31] Letter from Norfolk Area Health Authority to Victoria Gillick, 9 March 1981. See also *Gillick v West Norfolk and Wisbech Area Health Authority* [1986] 1 AC 112, 165 (HL).

[32] [1986] AC 112, 206.

[33] '1983: Mother loses contraception test case' (*BBC News*, On this day 1960–2005, 26 July 1983): http://news.bbc.co.uk/onthisday/hi/dates/stories/july/26/newsid_2499000/2499583.stm.

[34] ibid.

[35] Prohibited by section 28(1) of the Sexual Offences Act 1956 (now governed by sections 8 and 10 of the Sexual Offences Act 2003).

[36] Prohibited by section 6(1) of the Sexual Offences Act 1956 (now governed by section 14 of the Sexual Offences Act 2003).

[37] *Gillick v West Norfolk and Wisbech Area Health Authority* [1984] QB 581. See further Lee, n 14 above, 59–62.

[38] *Gillick v West Norfolk and Wisbech Area Health Authority* [1985] 1 All ER 533 (CA).

A bare majority of the House of Lords overturned the Court of Appeal. Lord Scarman stated that, although it would be 'most unusual' for a doctor to give contraceptive advice and treatment to an under-16- year-old girl without her parents' knowledge, parental rights terminate 'once a child has gained sufficient understanding and intelligence to understand the nature and implications of the proposed treatment'[39] (189). The law lords recognised that parents might not always know what is best for their children, and that may be times when the state needs to step in. This was one such time. In fact, this was technically the situation prior to the litigation. This was what the DHSS guidelines provided for, and was what so troubled Mrs Gillick. She was not alone in this view. Thus the litigation also played an important role as a public forum to hear and settle the debate and make clear to wider society the importance of women's and children's autonomy.

## III. What Happened Next

The House of Lords test, now known as '*Gillick* competence'[40] (a phrase coined by Lord Donaldson in *Re W (a minor) (medical treatment)*[41]), was a significant legal development for children's rights as well as for medical practice. It has since become the central test for children's consent to medical treatment. The case placed children's autonomy into the both the social and legal climate. Undoubtedly the litigation had an impact on later developments including the Children Act 1989 and sex education policy. It is ironic that Mrs Gillick's personal crusade to secure parents' rights had the opposite effect in that it ensured that competent children's rights could be upheld.[42]

Commenting later on the case, Gillick spoke of her devastation at the decision: 'I felt like I had been stamped on by the system'.[43] She subsequently worked as a pregnancy counsellor on behalf of the anti-abortion group Life and continues to campaign on this and other topics. In 2002 she won a libel claim against Brook (a pregnancy advisory service) over a factsheet which, she claimed, alleged that she was responsible for the rise in teenage pregnancies in the 1980s.[44]

## IV. Significance

The *Gillick* litigation is a legal landmark for women. Without doubt the House of Lords' decision was a moral as well as a legal judgment.[45] However, it was an important step toward the recognition of women's sexual autonomy and freedom not only to engage in

[39] [1986] AC 112, 189 (HL).

[40] Sometimes referred to as 'Fraser Competence'.

[41] *Re W (a minor) (medical treatment)* [1992] 4 All ER 627, 633.

[42] Jane Fortin, 'The *Gillick* Decision – Not Just a High-water Mark' in Stephen Gilmore, Jonathan Herring and Rebecca Probert (eds), *Landmark Cases in Family Law* (Hart Publishing, 2011) 200.

[43] Sally Weale, '"I will not let it go"', *The Guardian*, 21 November 2000.

[44] 'Morals campaigner wins damages', *BBC News Online*, 12 December 2002.

[45] Lee, n 14 above 6, 59–62.

sexual activity, but also to be supported by the state to exercise control over their fertility confidentially, including those below the age of 16. Moreover, the series of cases was funded almost entirely by legal aid and thus, unless a party is able find money through independent wealth or crowdfunding, it is unlikely that a similar case will occur again.

## Further Reading

- Jane Fortin, 'The *Gillick* Decision – Not Just a High-water Mark' in Stephen Gilmore, Jonathan Herring and Rebecca Probert (eds), *Landmark Cases in Family Law* (Hart Publishing, 2011).
- Victoria Gillick, *A Mother's Tale* (Hodder and Stoughton, 1989).
- Jane Lewis and Fenella Cannell, 'The Politics of Motherhood in the 1980s: Warnock, Gillick and Feminists' (1986) 13(3) *Journal of Law and Society* 321.

# 57

## *Grant v Edwards* (1986)

JOANNE BESWICK

In *Grant v Edwards*,[1] the Court of Appeal found that an unmarried woman whose male partner was sole legal owner of the house they acquired together, and who had made no direct financial contribution to the property, had nevertheless acquired an equitable share in the home by virtue of a constructive trust based on a broadly-defined 'express agreement' that she would have a share, coupled with detriment on her part: the court found that her partner had only been able to pay the mortgage instalments because she paid for everything else. This marked a shift in judicial thinking about the way in which justice should be done to women in this increasingly common situation, not by changing the law, but by interpreting it more equitably and taking into consideration a wider variety of discussions and contributions regarding the household.

## I. Context

During the 1980s, marriage rates were declining and cohabitation was increasing. Yet the practice among conveyancers was to transfer homes into the sole name of the male partner, since traditionally a husband was responsible for supporting his family and men generally were seen as more reliable sources of mortgage repayments. *Gissing v Gissing*[2] had established that the constructive trust offered the best way for a non-legal owner to claim a share in the home, but the experience of Mrs Burns (in *Burns v Burns*[3]) demonstrated how narrowly the requirement of 'common intention' was interpreted. Mrs Burns had lived with Mr Burns for 19 years. She took his name, as was usual at the time, though they were not married: he was still married to a woman who refused to give him a divorce. Mr Burns was the sole legal owner of their home. Mrs Burns' main role was the care of their children, although as they got older the court heard how she began to earn some money, which she put together with the housekeeping money that Mr Burns gave to her. The evidence as to her earnings was that they amounted to some £60 per week, and that she bought a number of items for the house, including a washing machine, tumble-drier, dishwasher, and all the children's clothes, even completely redecorating the house.

[1] *Grant v Edwards and another* [1986] 1 Ch 638; [1986] 2 All ER 426 (CA).
[2] *Gissing v Gissing* [1970] UKHL 3.
[3] *Burns v Burns* [1981] 1 All ER 244 (CA).

The relationship ended after Mr Burns took up with another woman and Mrs Burns left the home. When she claimed a share in the home they had shared for almost two decades, the court found that she had made no contributions to the home that counted for the purpose of establishing a common intention between them that she should have a share. This decision, which left Mrs Burns with nothing (and forced her to live in her car for a time), caused a public outcry.

*Burns v Burns* showed that the law provided little protection for those whose contribution to the family was primarily work in the home, without payment of a salary with which they could make contributions to the cost of acquiring the property. Yet it was only from direct financial contributions that the court would infer a common intention to acquire an interest. Women are the most likely major providers of domestic labour and care-giving: work roles which are not subject to remuneration, but which are often performed at the expense of seeking paid employment outside of the family home. The concentration on direct financial contributions to the home failed to recognise the value of other non-monetary contributions that might most often be made by women. It was said of the Court of Appeal's decision in *Burns* 'that even the most lukewarm feminist can see the injustice of it'.[4]

## II. The Landmark

In *Grant v Edwards* a couple decided to live together and purchased a house. Mr Edwards told Mrs Grant that her name should not go onto the legal documents because it would prejudice her pending divorce. When the relationship broke down she claimed a share in the property on the ground that she had contributed very significantly to its purchase by means of her contribution to the joint household expenses. The judge dismissed her claim and she appealed. The Court of Appeal held that where a couple lived in a property held in the name of only one of the parties, the other party could establish an interest if they could demonstrate a common intention that they would share the ownership, which they had relied upon to their detriment. The Court found that the excuse as to why her name was not on the documentation amounted to an express agreement that she would have a share, as it implied that, had Mrs Grant not been going through a divorce, the property would have been purchased in joint names. She was therefore entitled to a half-share in the house on the basis of the detriment she had suffered in paying all the household expenses, thus enabling Mr Edwards to pay the mortgage instalments.

The decision was a landmark as the Court found that there was an express agreement between the parties to share ownership of the property, and thus a common intention, without such an intention being declared formally in writing. This increased the possibility of a cohabitant being awarded a share in the property. Previously the courts had confined themselves to inferring intention from an individual's contributions, concentrating on financial contributions to the purchase price and disregarding indirect contributions such as paying for household expenses. This was the reason why Mrs Burns fared so badly in her claim. Whilst the Court in *Grant v Edwards* were not fully convinced of the relevance

[4] Editorial [1984] *Family Law* 4, quoted in Dawn Watkins, 'Recovering the lost human stories of law: Finding Mrs Burns' (2013) 7(1) *Law and Humanities* 68–90.

of indirect contributions, their permissive approach to how expressed common intention could be found to exist between the parties was an important development. Recognition of the discussion as to why the property would not be owned in joint names – the excuse that it would jeopardise her divorce – was held to suffice as express agreement. This was an important step as it ensured that excuses, whether deliberate or not, would not suffice to deprive the claimant of an interest. It broadened judicial recognition of the type of informal discussion that might take place between cohabitants. Interestingly, in view of the arguments still often asserted that wives do better than cohabitants in property settlements, the 50 per cent share which the Court awarded Mrs Grant was probably better than she would have received if the couple had been married, where the court has jurisdiction under matrimonial law, as the equal-sharing principle was not part of divorce law at this time and is still often disregarded.

In *Grant v Edwards*, express or common intentions which were not in writing first came to the fore. The Court were able to interpret conversations about not conveying the legal title to her because of her divorce proceedings as an agreement that she should have an interest in the land, albeit that it would be better for her name not to appear on the legal documentation. It appeared to recognise that this type of excuse was one way in which men have excluded women from property rights, and finding for the claimant in this way was clear recognition of the man's duplicitous behaviour. The Court of Appeal retrospectively treated *Eves v Eves*[5] as being decided on the same basis. There the legal owner had told the claimant her name could not appear on the title documentation as she was under 21. Again, the Court held this indicated an agreement that she should have an interest, but that it could not be on the documentation. In other words, these cases emphasised the substance rather than the form of agreements.

This acknowledgment that differing intentions as to ownership of property could exist, beyond that which appeared in the legal documentation, was an important advance for cohabitants who were not legal owners but had made some contributions to acquisition. Historically, these have usually been women. As Nourse LJ held:

> In a case such as the present when there has been no written declaration or agreement, nor any direct provision by the plaintiff of part of the purchase price so as to give rise to a constructive trust in her favour, she must establish a common intention between her and the defendant, acted on by her, that she would have a beneficial interest in the property. If she can do that, equity will not allow the defendant to deny that interest and will construct a trust to give effect to it.[6]

Where there is an 'express agreement' between the parties the court is not required to look for evidence from which a shared intention of beneficial ownership can be inferred (Browne-Wilkinson VC).[7] Reliance can be demonstrated by a broader variety of activities, as was suggested by Browne-Wilkinson VC: 'any act done by the claimant to her detriment relating to the joint lives of the parties is sufficient … The acts do not have to be inherently referable to the house'.[8] Furthermore such conduct would be relevant even though it might be 'referable to the mutual love and affection of the parties and not specifically referable to

[5] *Eves v Eves* [1975] 1 WLR 1338 (CA).
[6] *Grant v Edwards and another* [1986] 1 Ch 638, 648 (CA).
[7] ibid 655.
[8] ibid 657.

the claimant's belief that she had an interest in the house'.[9] This can be contrasted with the narrower view of Nourse LJ, where only conduct 'on which the woman could not reasonably be expected to embark unless she was to have an interest' would suffice.[10]

## III. What Happened Next

In *Lloyds Bank v Rosset*[11] Lord Bridge approved the decision in *Grant v Edwards* by setting out a clear constructive trust test, which is still law. Mrs Rosset's claim was denied because, according to Lord Bridge who delivered the leading opinion, common intention could only be established in two ways, neither of which she could satisfy. These were the express agreement of the parties accepted by *Rosset*, established by *Grant v Edwards*, and common intention inferred from direct contributions to the purchase price, established by *Gissing*.

The ability to contribute is, of course, affected by the differences in gendered participation in the labour market. Although the difference between men's and women's pay for the under-30s has decreased dramatically since 1975,[12] this applies to an age before many women become mothers, and is not true for older age groups. Other evidence about gendered participation in the labour market over the last 10 years shows that part-time working remains overwhelmingly dominated by women and the reality of childcare arrangements shows that progress towards a more equal division of caring responsibilities between women and men is still very slow.[13] Following the House of Lords decision in *Rosset*, only promises as in *Grant* itself, or payments, could lead to a common intention: as Martin Dixon put it, 'it excluded the inference of common intention (absent those factors) even though the parties had engaged in the joint enterprise of family life and had treated the land as owned jointly'.[14] This approach could still leave women like Mrs Burns potentially vulnerable. On the other hand, since ***Williams & Glyn's Bank v Boland***[15] couples have been much more likely to acquire property in joint names, particularly on re-mortgage or re-purchase, when lenders will normally require it. Moreover, although gendered income differentials persist, there is less likelihood of women being in the precarious position of Mrs Burns.

Later case law has potentially added a third way of establishing common intention. Whilst *Stack v Dowden* and *Jones v Kernott*[16] are technically only persuasive authorities for single-owner claims, since both cases concerned parties who already jointly owned the legal title, the courts clearly stated that their reasoning should also apply in acquisition claims where the property is legally owned by just one partner. The majority in *Stack v Dowden* made it easier for a claimant to establish a common intention and thereby gain an interest in

[9] ibid.

[10] He characterised her contributions as conduct 'on which she could not reasonably have been expected to embark unless she was to have a prior interest in the house' ([1986] 1 Ch 638, 648).

[11] *Lloyds Bank plc v Rosset* [1991] 1 AC 107 (HL).

[12] Office for National Statistics, 'UK Wages over the Past Four Decades – 2014' (3 July 2014).

[13] Equality and Human Rights Commission, 'How Fair is Britain?': https://www.equalityhumanrights.com/en/our-work/how-fair-britain.

[14] Martin Dixon, *Modern Land Law* (9th edn, Routledge, 2014) 181.

[15] ***Williams & Glyn's Bank v Boland*** [1981] AC 487.

[16] *Stack v Dowden* [2007] 2 AC 432; *Jones v Kernott* [2010] 1 All ER 947.

the land belonging to another by holding that it is permissible to infer a common intention as to ownership based upon the parties' entire course of dealings in relation to the property. This, and subsequent extensions of circumstances in which a claimant can claim an equitable share, have established 'a mechanism by which the courts have considerable freedom in determining the beneficial interests of couples who share a family home'.[17] Dixon contends that it is clear that this is a 'deliberate response to the lack of legislation in this area'.[18] Even Mrs Burns would now been better off: Simon Gardner argues that her contributions might have been sufficient to give her a 50 per cent share'.[19]

After *Rosset*, therefore, it might have been argued the more restrictive approach of Nourse LJ in *Grant v Edwards* was preferred. In light of Lady Hale's approach in *Stack v Dowden*, where she was in the majority, it is contended that the view of Browne-Wilkinson VC has gained ascendency.

## IV. Significance

*Grant v Edwards* set in train a gradual liberalisation of the strict rule for claiming an interest under a constructive trust. After *Burns v Burns*, the injustice of confining the category of relevant contributions to the property to *direct financial contributions* had become clear even to the courts; feminist legal scholars, and no less than Lord Denning MR, had repeatedly pointed out that such a narrow definition discriminated against women who, in performing their correct social role at the time as carers and homemakers, were generally not in a position to make major financial contributions, and who had never been expected to, in an era when the man was the breadwinner. *Grant v Edwards* was decided against a backdrop of a rise in cohabitation from the 1980s onwards – a rise that has not abated, with cohabitation the fastest growing family form (29.7 per cent increase in the decade 2004–14)[20] – which led to a spate of cohabitant claims and to calls by many family lawyers (and some property lawyers) for a legislative regime for property distribution on the breakdown of a cohabiting relationship, akin to but different from the rights available to married couples on divorce. A scheme proposed by the Law Commission in 2007 has, however, not been implemented,[21] and the normal legal and equitable rules of land law continue to apply in situations such as those in *Grant v Edwards*.

The advantages to women of leaving the regulation of cohabitants' property rights to property law and the constructive trust, as opposed to a special form of regulation like the matrimonial regime, include certainty of rights (as opposed to the discretionary powers of

[17] Dixon, n 14 above, 183. See eg *Abbot v Abbott* [2008] 1 FLR (broad approach to common intention); *Fowler v Baron* [2008] 2 FLR 831 (what the parties intended rather than express discussions) *Geary v Rankine* [2012] EWCA Civ 555 and *Ullah v Ullah* [2013] EWHC 296.

[18] Dixon, n 14 above, ibid.

[19] Simon Gardner, 'Problems in Family Property' (2013) 72 *Cambridge Law Journal* 301.

[20] Office for National Statistics, *Statistical Bulletin: Families and Households, 2014* (ONS, 2015).

[21] Law Commission, *Cohabitation: the Financial Consequences of Relationship Breakdown* (Law Com No 307, 2007).

the divorce court); formal neutrality to family form, gender and sexuality; flexibility; and party autonomy.[22] Although there is research which supports the notion that couples do not understand their legal position and actually make decisions based on erroneous ideas, for example a persistent belief in the concept of common law marriage or some other notion that merely cohabiting actually attributes rights,[23] there are as many myths about the protections offered by marriage, and ultimately many couples simply do not consider the legal implications of their personal relationships at all.[24] The case law developments following *Grant v Edwards* suggest a more realistic judicial approach to the ways in which couples make their financial arrangements, and thus increase the possibility of justice for women.

## Further Reading


- Rosemary Auchmuty, 'The limits of marriage protection in property allocation when a relationship ends' (2016) 28 *Child and Family Law Quarterly* 303–24.
- Simon Gardner, 'Problems in Family Property' (2013) 72 *Cambridge Law Journal* 301.
- Dawn Watkins, 'Recovering the lost human stories of law: Finding Mrs Burns' (2013) 7(1) *Law and Humanities* 68–90.


[22] Rosemary Auchmuty, 'The limits of marriage protection in property allocation when a relationship ends' (2016) 28 *Child and Family Law Quarterly* 303–24; Rebecca Bailey-Harris, 'Dividing the Assets on Breakdown of Family Relationships Outside Marriage' in Rebecca Bailey Harris (ed), *Dividing the Assets on Family Breakdown* (Family Law, 1997) 57.

[23] Nicola Glover and Paul Todd, 'The Myth of Common Intention' (1996) 16 *Legal Studies* 325.

[24] M Hibbs, C Barton and J Beswick, 'Why Marry? – Perceptions of the Affianced' (2001) 31 *Family Law* 197–207.

# 58

# Section 32 of the Finance Act 1988

ANN MUMFORD

Section 32 of the Finance Act 1988 provides that the income of a woman living with her husband shall not be treated as his income for income tax purposes. Before this, a wife's self-reported income was automatically included with that of her husband for tax purposes. Section 104 affords wives the option to ignore marriage for tax purposes and to be assessed for tax separately. One of the last remaining incidents of coverture (the idea that a married woman's legal and financial personality was subsumed into that of her husband), separate taxation was a longstanding feminist target which finally coalesced with official policy to encourage women's fiscal independence.

## I. Context

Women have long understood the importance of having money of one's own. Women who are dependent on their husbands are restricted in almost every area of their lives – at worst, unable to escape an abusive marriage; at best, limited in their ability to influence financial decisions within the family or to spend money on themselves. The feminists who fought for married women's property rights in the nineteenth century recognised that the ability to keep their own earnings (won in 1870) was of more importance to working women than the ability to keep any other property (won in 1882),[1] which only helped the small minority who had such property.

Anita Monteith noted how extraordinary it was that the definition of an incapacitated person in the Income Tax Act 1918 was: 'Any infant, married woman, lunatic, idiot or insane person'. She pointed out that the reference to married women was not removed until the Finance Act 1950 (section 35).[2] Still, married women were treated as appendages of their husbands for income tax purposes. Mid-twentieth-century women who gave up work on marriage or motherhood (as was usual at the time) suffered the indignity of being categorised as (only a) 'housewife', a heartfelt grievance for those who had previously enjoyed the status associated with gainful occupation and who chafed at the restrictions, psychological as much as physical, that dependency enforced. Joint taxation of married couples provided

[1] **Married Women's Property Act 1882.**

[2] Anita Monteith, 'Tax Treatment of married couples' (*Taxation*, 4 October 2017).

an incentive for higher-earning men to keep their wives unemployed or in low-paid or part-time work, as dependent wives functioned as effective tax deductions. It also enabled, indeed obliged, men to know just exactly how much their wives earned, so there could be no privacy about this.

Research from around the world has established the dramatic impact that tax policy can have on both economic and private choices made by the family. For example, the availability of income splitting can affect the cost of women's part-time employment.[3] Indeed, during the 1980s, in Sweden, there was a marked movement amongst women from part-time to full-time employment, driven in part by tax reform.[4] In the Netherlands, on the other hand, out of all Dutch women in the workforce, two-thirds are employed in part-time jobs.[5] This statistic typically is explained in Dutch society through reference to 'a social norm strongly favouring family values'.[6] In 2008, however, the Organisation for Economic Co-operation and Development (OECD) released a report drawing a strong correlation between the prevalence of women in part-time jobs and Dutch policies for taxing second earners, and the availability of childcare.[7] If you have a joint taxation regime, women are 'encouraged' to stay at home with the children full- or part-time because it is financially efficient for the family to do this. If you add the unavailability of affordable childcare into the equation, you leave women with no choice. They might want to work, they might want a measure of financial independence or to further their career, but it is simply not 'worth it'. Tax policy may also affect a couple's decision if and when to have children – there is substantial evidence of this impact in the US.[8]

These statistics, however, operate on the presumption that it is possible to separate a woman's paid and unpaid labour, and a woman's income from her household, and it is notoriously difficult to do this. The concept of 'engulfment' is useful here, and has implications for both men and women.[9] It is through 'engulfment' that the individual is lost in the notion of the 'household' unit, and it is important 'to be wary of the extremes of isolation and engulfment'.[10] From a feminist perspective, this is particularly important, given that the idea that a family unit is responsible for the well-being of children masks the reality that, in fact, responsibility lies mostly or solely with the woman.[11]

The fifth demand of the Women's Liberation Movement was for legal and financial independence for women. Separate taxation found a place within the campaigning for the achievement of this goal. Second-wave feminists joined with professional women's associations to increase pressure on the government: for example, we know from surviving records

[3] Rosenfeld and Birkelund's 2002 research study concluded that 'policy can affect the cost of women's employment' (RA Rosenfeld and GE Birkelund, 'Women's Part-Time Work: A Cross-National Comparison' (2002) 11 *European Sociological Review* 111, 116).

[4] This is the conclusion of the study detailed in Marianne Sundström, 'The Growth in Full-Time Work Among Swedish Women in the 1980s' (1993) 36 *Acta Sociologica* 139.

[5] OECD, *Increasing working hours: Helping reconcile work and family* (OECD Economic Surveys, January 2008) 109–133, 109.

[6] ibid.

[7] ibid.

[8] See eg Jr-Tsung Huang, 'The Personal Tax Exemption and Married Women's Birth Spacing in the United States' (2008) 36(6) *Public Finance Review* 728.

[9] Julie A Nelson, *Feminism, Objectivity, and Economics* (Routledge, 1996) 27.

[10] ibid.

[11] Mary McIntosh, 'Feminism and Social Policy' in Christopher Pierson and Francis G Castle (eds), *The Welfare State Reader* (Polity, 2006) 120.

that as early as 1970 the **Association of Women Solicitors** (AWS) wrote to the Chancellor of the Exchequer requesting amendment of the law relating to the taxation of married couples; in 1983 the Association's Equal Opportunities Working Party produced a submission on the proposed tax reform; in 1985 the Association wrote again to the Chancellor of the Exchequer advocating a personal tax allowance for everyone and greater privacy to all in their dealings with the Inland Revenue; and in 1987 a submission on the Taxation of Women was sent to the Chancellor of the Exchequer:

> A tax system which presupposes female dependence is grossly out-of-date as the majority of women go out to work. This also suggests the radical step that non-working women should be able to carry-forward their personal allowances which are unused while they are at home to a future date when they return to work. It is even suggested that these carried forward allowances should be index-linked.[12]

Another influential lobby was the Women's Budget Group, a network of leading feminist economists, researchers, policy experts and campaigners which scrutinises all government policies from a gender perspective. Their research was (and is) important in shaping government policy, as the Parliamentary debates on separate taxation revealed.

## II. The Landmark

The provisions relating to separate taxation of married people were introduced in 1988 by Nigel Lawson, Conservative Chancellor of the Exchequer, largely to cross-party support. 'The present system for the taxation of married couples goes back 180 years. It taxes the income of a married woman as if it belonged to her husband', Lawson explained to Parliament. 'Quite simply', he argued, 'that is no longer acceptable'.[13] Movements to tackle independent taxation throughout the (then) EEC had been in progress at least since the European Commission issued a memorandum in 1984, recommending full, independent taxation for women throughout Europe. The UK's efforts did not completely match the recommendations from the EEC but, nonetheless, did place the UK ahead of other Member States. Germany, for example, to this day continues to resist the move which is viewed, by some, as antithetical to family unity.

This is an interesting, comparative point: in the UK, the *absence* of independent taxation, and the potential of a financial penalty for marriage, made it a natural issue for the Conservatives to embrace. As Lawson explained in 1988:

> I [have] … two objectives: first, to give married women the same privacy and independence in their tax affairs as everyone else; and, second, to bring to an end the ways in which the tax system can penalise marriage.[14]

Independent taxation appealed to *both* feminist (financial independence for women) and pro-marriage (reduce the marriage 'tax penalty') factions which made the, unavoidable, possibility of increased tax avoidance worth the risk – 'There will, of course, be nothing to

[12] AWS Minute books, with thanks to Elizabeth Cruickshank for sharing her painstaking research.
[13] HC Deb, 15 March 1988, vol 129 col 997.
[14] ibid.

stop married women from asking their husbands to handle their tax affairs, or vice versa, as before; and many will no doubt do so',[15] acknowledged Lawson.

Under the new provisions, a husband and wife would be taxed independently on income of all kinds. All taxpayers, male or female, married or single, would be entitled to the same personal allowance, which would be available against all income, whether from earnings, pensions or savings. The provisions came into effect in 1990, from which time married couples in the UK (unlike many other countries) have been separately taxed.

To soften the blow, at the same time the government introduced a Married Couple's Allowance which could be claimed by all married couples.[16] This was resisted slightly by Labour MPs, although it eventually passed. The allowance went at first instance to the husband, to maintain his tax threshold; only if he did not have enough income to set it against could the wife claim it. The allowance was intended to recognise the importance of marriage, a concern that it appears later Governments did not share. Since 2000, the Married Couple's Allowance has been withdrawn in stages from all but the oldest couples. In another measure designed to incentivise marriage, the mortgage interest tax relief that at the time could only be claimed once by a married couple, but by each of two unmarried individuals independently, was linked instead to the property – with the result that it made no difference whether or not a couple were married, the allowance was the same.

Significantly, what the Act did not do was to recognise women's unpaid labour in the home. Unpaid labour forms a significant part of the overall wealth of a household, and the reason why women's finances have tended to be considered within the 'household' is that, when their labour is considered in proportion to the income they receive, there is a clear discrepancy.

## III. What Happened Next

While section 32 of the Finance Act 1988 was a welcome lobbying victory, the enthusiasm of the Inland Revenue has waned. Despite the obvious feminist value of not compelling women to combine their income with that of their husbands for the purpose of taxation, the switch to separate taxation apparently led to a significant amount of reallocation of family assets – with men transferring part of their property to women, who tended to be in a lower tax bracket.[17] This (if they were able to use the assets) gave them greater financial independence, and was sometimes useful for women who wished to separate from their husbands, but caused the Revenue much frustration. The *Arctic Systems*[18] test case in 2007 revealed perceived avoidance through separate taxation, perhaps fuelled in part by the growth of the IT industry and the connected proliferation of one-person companies. Settlement legislation was deployed by the Revenue to tackle the 'problem', and failed.

[15] ibid col 998.

[16] ibid.

[17] See Melvin Stephens Jr and Jennifer Ward-Batts, 'The Impact of Separate Taxation on the Intra-Household Allocation of Assets: Evidence from the UK' (2004) 88 *Journal of Public Economics* 1989.

[18] *Jones v Garnett* [2007] UKHL 35.

## IV. Significance

Separate taxation is significant for women because it gives them privacy as to their earnings. It removes a tool by which they might be persuaded – against their will – to give up paid work and stay home to raise a family. And it is symbolically important in recognising the separation of wives and husbands and the financial independence of women. Although it fails to deal with the issue of their unpaid labour in the home, this is perhaps something best solved by other means than tax reform.

While the introduction of independent taxation gave women greater financial independence, however, it did so at the expense of a potential reduction in the amount of tax recoverable by the Revenue. Views on this differ. On the one hand, tax avoiders – for this is how the Revenue construes families who shift a husband's higher earnings into his wife's lower bracket, through asset transfer – have an ongoing impact on the availability of funding for programmes for the poor (who, largely, will comprise women and their children). On the other hand, it is simply unjustifiable for any reason (perhaps other than the tax avoidance as identified by the Revenue) for a wife's income to be lumped with that of her husband, simply because of the fact of her marriage. In the mid-1970s, US law professor, Boris Bittker suggested that there is no perfect 'tax law' answer to the question of taxing the family. He proposed that ultimately the question comes down to a choice by citizens, after experts have retired from the discussion.[19] Perhaps acknowledging this will allow a more informed analysis of gendered economic inequality within the arenas of taxation, the paid and unpaid markets, and the family.

## Further Reading

- Janet C Gornick, 'Gender Equality in the Labour Market: Women's Employment and Earnings' in Diane Sainsbury, *Gender and Welfare State Regimes* (OUP, 1999) 210.
- JA Kay and C Sandler, 'The Taxation of Husband and Wife: A View of the Debate in the Green Paper' (1982) 3 *Fiscal Studies* 173–87.
- Melvin Stephens Jr and Jennifer Ward-Batts, 'The Impact of Separate Taxation on the Intra-Household Allocation of Assets: Evidence from the UK' (2004) 88 *Journal of Public Economics* 1989.

[19] Boris I Bittker, 'Federal Income Taxation and the Family' (1975) 27 *Stanford Law Review* 1389, 1496.

# 59

# First Woman Court of Appeal Judge in England and Wales, Elizabeth Butler-Sloss, 1988

DANA DENIS-SMITH

In 1988, Baroness Butler-Sloss became the first woman to be appointed to the Court of Appeal of England and Wales. Hers was a speedy rise, after less than a decade as a High Court judge. It was also an historic one; she was – at the time – the highest-ranking woman judge in the country, a position she held until **Lady Hale's** appointment to the Appellate Committee of the House of Lords in 2004. Ten years later, in 1998, she became the first woman President of the Family Division, a role she held until her retirement in 2005, and in which she is yet to be followed by another woman. She chaired a number of high-profile government inquiries, including the Cleveland Child Sex Abuse inquiry and the inquiry into the death of Princess Diana, as well as ruling in high-profile children's rights and capacity cases.

## I. Life

Elizabeth Butler-Sloss (nee Havers) was born on 10 August 1933 in Kew, London, the youngest, and only girl, of four children. She was born when both her parents were in their 40s and, by her own admission, she had a restricted childhood, expected to conform within a strict parenting method:

> [L]ittle things like, I went to church on Sundays with my mother and I wore a hat and of course I wore a skirt. I haven't yet got to the point of going to church in trousers because of that sort of early training.[1]

Educated at the prestigious public (private) girls' school Wycombe Abbey, Butler-Sloss decided at the age of 13 that she wanted to become a barrister. Her father, Sir Cecil Havers, had been a High Court judge, and her brothers were also lawyers. Whilst her brothers discouraged her from following in the family's male tradition, her father was very supportive: 'my father was extraordinarily modern and said if my brothers could do it, so indeed

[1] All quotes by Baroness Butler-Sloss are from an interview with the First 100 Years project on 4 April 2016.

could I, if I was clever enough'. Unlike her brothers, she did not go to university and instead was sent to finishing school in Switzerland for one year. This was standard practice for girls in the upper classes at the time, since they were not expected to need to prepare for a career. The first woman High Court judge, **Elizabeth Lane**, was another prominent legal woman who did not have a university education (although her brothers did). Indeed, it was not uncommon at this time for men to be called to the Bar without a university degree.[2] Butler-Sloss was called the Bar in 1955 as a member of the Inner Temple, one of the four Inns of Court in London. She was 21 years old (the minimum age at which one could be called to the Bar) and became one of about 60 women barristers.[3]

At that time, it was expected that pupils would pay for a tenancy, so any new (male) barrister with some private income could build a career relatively quickly. The same was not true for women barristers, however, as many solicitors would not instruct them: '[N]obody wanted women'. Nevertheless, she secured a tenancy, through family connections, in a criminal Chambers:

> [M]y Chambers took me and I had excellent pupillages and so on, which you needed … to succeed at the Bar … I did get in to court a lot because I was in criminal Chambers to begin with and there was a lot of small work and in those days, you could go in to court.

As time passed, she gradually moved into family law, considered more suitable work for women.

She married Joseph Butler-Sloss, another barrister, at the age of 25 and had three children within five years. Her husband, the son of a solicitor, later became a Recorder of the Crown Court (1972–84) and spent the latter part of his career in Africa as Judge of the High Court of Kenya (1984–90).

As well as legal, Butler-Sloss also had political ambitions and, in 1959, soon after her marriage, she stood for Parliament in the general election as the Conservative Party candidate in the Labour stronghold of Vauxhall and Lambeth, South London. She was one of 81 women running for Parliament.[4] She was unsuccessful. With hindsight, she did not regret the defeat:

> I was nine months pregnant on polling day which wasn't entirely sensible because I misjudged the date of the election, as indeed [did] the chairman of the selection committee … But I realised after the election that with a new baby, and a husband, and a slightly improving career, that to be an MP was a step too far. I think at that stage also, having been a family lawyer for three years, I thought it would put an intolerable strain on the marriage and for me the marriage was more important than being an MP.

Interestingly, another woman barrister – Margaret Thatcher – was also a Conservative Party candidate in 1959. Thatcher, who won the seat in Finchley in 1959, went on to become the first British woman prime minister.

[2] A university degree was not required to be called to the Bar until 1975.

[3] The *Birmingham Daily Post* on 5 March 1968 reported that in the decade up to 1968 the number of women barristers had 'more than doubled' to 123 women practising at the Bar compared to just over 2,200 male barristers.

[4] 'Will of the People', *Birmingham Daily Post*, 9 October 1959. Of the 81 women candidates, 28 were Conservative, 36 Labour, 16 Liberal and one Communist.

Butler-Sloss gave up practising at the Bar in 1970, aged 36, to take up an employed position as a divorce registrar at Somerset House. Her husband's work meant he was often away from home and she took an employed position so she could be at home with her family:

> my daughter, when I told her … she was 11 when I became a registrar, and she said, 'does that mean I'll know where you are Mum?' and I suddenly realised that my father was absolutely right to advise that 'you absolutely owe it to your family to take this job'.

In 1979, she became the fourth woman to be appointed a High Court judge, following in the footsteps of **Elizabeth Lane**, **Rose Heibron**, and Margaret Booth. Tellingly, all four women were appointed to the Family Division, but Butler-Sloss's move was unexpected in other ways:

> I tell you what I felt more about, was being the first District Judge Registrar to go from the registry to the High Court and that was the leap that mattered, because it was and remains exceptional and I certainly did not expect to be promoted. My father had told me I would not be promoted, and he died before I was and so to be asked to become a High Court judge from Somerset House, I mean it hit the headlines of the press with a lot of criticism and nepotism because it was a new government, 1979 and my brother had just been appointed Attorney General.

Butler-Sloss' brother, Michael Havers QC – then MP for Wimbledon and Attorney General and later Lord Chancellor – had a high-profile and controversial legal career. But he would not have been involved with appointments to the High Court in 1979, as that decision rested with the Lord Chancellor, Lord Hailsham at the time.

In January 1988, almost 40 years after the first woman barristers were made QC, and 23 years after Elizabeth Lane was appointed to the High Court, Elizabeth Butler-Sloss became the first woman to be appointed a *Lord* Justice of Appeal. Unlike the widespread press coverage of **Brenda Hale**'s appointment as a law lord in 2004, her ground-breaking appointment did not attract much attention – the media was more interested in her family arrangements (she stayed in the UK, while her husband – now a High Court judge – was based in Kenya).[5] It is likely that her appointment was precipitated by her high-profile chairing of the government inquiry into the unprecedented number of suspected child sex abuse cases detected at Middlesbrough General Hospital in Cleveland: 'After I had done the Cleveland Child Abuse Inquiry, and produced the report in 1988, in a sense I didn't expect to get to the Court of Appeal but I wasn't all that surprised'. Between February and July 1987 over 100 children had been removed from their parents – often in the middle of the night – and placed into care. The Cleveland Child Sex Abuse inquiry is one of the most controversial and lasting legacies of her judicial career.[6] The inquiry – which included 74 days of hearings – concluded that there was miscommunication and lack of cooperation between social services, doctors and the police. It also criticised the methods used by the doctors to assess whether the children had been abused.[7] A number of her recommendations, including that children could not be summarily removed from parents to 'places of safety' unless necessary, were subsequently implemented in the Children Act 1989.[8]

[5] *News of the World*, 17 July 1988.

[6] See eg Beatrix Campbell, 'A child abuse inquiry requires a truth-seeker. Grabbing a grandee isn't enough', *The Guardian*, 14 July 2014.

[7] For a comprehensive summary of the Inquiry see 'Summary of the Cleveland inquiry' (1988) 297 *British Medical Journal* 190–91.

[8] Robert Verkaik, 'Woman judge gets to highest legal rank', *The Independent*, 28 June 1999.

In 1999, Butler-Sloss became President of the Family Division of the High Court. She retired in 2005 and in 2006 joined the House of Lords as a life peer. She views herself as politically non-aligned, sitting on the cross-benches in the House of Lords and focusing on areas that she views to be part of her expertise as a family lawyer:

> I concentrate on children. I concentrate on legal issues. And one of the areas that I'm particularly concerned about is human trafficking and modern slavery. I'm very concerned about children anywhere when they're unaccompanied, they are lost some of them … but I'm also worried that some of them will be sexually exploited.

## II. Context

There were so few women barristers when Butler-Sloss entered the profession, and so few women judges when she was appointed, that we must ask why she succeeded, when so many did not. First, she was a member of a well-known and high-profile legal 'dynasty' and had the support of her distinguished father, if not her brothers, at the start of her career. Through them she also had the good fortune of knowing many of the early women legal pioneers. She counted Elizabeth Lane – a friend of her father's – as 'very much a mentor to me'. She also admired Rose Heilbron:

> I went to listen to Rose Heilbron to see how one should do a good job as a woman in court. But I equally went to listen to the men and it was their expertise that I was interested in rather than the gender.

Yet it would be too easy to dismiss her rise as solely because of her family connections. Her promotion was also a sign of the times. By the time she was appointed to the Court of Appeal, Margaret Thatcher was well into her second term as Britain's first woman prime minister, and Lord Hailsham, the Lord Chancellor, was keen to promote women.

## III. What Happened Next

In 1976, just 10 salaried judges were women. By 1989, this had increased to 34. Further down the legal hierarchy, women made up just over three per cent of QCs and around 13 per cent of the self-employed Bar.[9] Little wonder then that Butler-Sloss remained the only woman – representing a mere 2.5 per cent of Court of Appeal judges – for over a decade. Since then, despite a veritable flood of women into the legal profession, the number of women who have followed in Butler-Sloss's footsteps is depressingly small. In the 30 years since her appointment, there have been just 12 women judges on the Court of Appeal.

Butler-Sloss has only relatively recently spoken about how she found forging a career as a woman in law. Like many of her generation, she made a point of – in her words – 'not making a fuss' about being a woman in seeking to advance her career. She grew up, as she put it, in a world 'where people knew where they stood and people did what was expected of them', and

[9] Erika Rackley, *Women, Judging and the Judiciary: From Difference to Diversity* (Routledge, 2013) 38–39.

were conscious of words like 'service' and 'duty'. Certainly, she was not a campaigner. Helena Kennedy QC, for example, remembers Butler-Sloss advising the newly formed **Association of Women Barristers** 'not to rock the professional boat too strenuously'.[10] Her (perceived) lack of enthusiasm for greater gender diversity whilst at the top of the judiciary has given her a mixed reputation among later generations of (women) lawyers and judges:

> I got quite criticised by my female colleagues on the bench who hadn't yet got confirmed that I wasn't making more of a point of being the first woman. I took the opposite view that I was there. It was my presence that mattered and it was important that I didn't rock the boat. So, they just got used to me and every now and again when they really went too far in meetings, I said come off it chaps. They realised that I was there.

However, she was – and is – a believer that change can be effected by working from within a system, perhaps more gradually, but with similarly positive outcomes, to transform a legal sector that was slow to open to women.

> I see myself as a small cog in the wheel I think. A very important wheel that's turned around to bring people like Brenda Hale as the Deputy President of the Supreme Court, a considerable number of women in the Court of Appeal and I think it's important that women recognise that there's no point appointing a woman to the highest position unless she can cope with it, intellectually, academically and emotionally. We need far more women at every level but they're coming.

## IV. Significance

> I brought about an acceptance that women were in the Court of Appeal, and perhaps the most interesting for me was sitting with the then Master of the Roles, Lord Donaldson, who … was obviously very dubious about me. I was the first woman. What was I going to be like? What was it going to do? Was I going to create waves?

Inevitably perhaps during her judicial career spanning 35 years, Elizabeth Butler-Sloss created more than a few waves, mostly as a consequence of the sensitive nature of the issues under her consideration. She ruled on a number of important and difficult issues including family disputes, child custody, gay adoption, abortion, and capacity.[11] Many of her decisions advanced women's and children's rights, and for this reason often made her a target of criticism – most notably from campaign group Fathers for Justice.[12]

Quietly ambitious, Butler-Sloss embraced her position as a legal pioneer but did not see it as part of her role to create a movement for change. She was not a challenger in the legal profession or a rebel against social conventions at home: she followed the course most married women took in her day – leaving the Bar to focus on her family upon marriage, and taking up an employed role to have steadier hours for her children – but always retained a desire to advance in her career. Presented with the opportunities, she swiftly took them and, in doing so, helped to bring down the barriers to women. She was well aware that it was harder and slower for women to progress in the legal profession (it took **Helena Normanton**

[10] Helena Kennedy, *Eve Was Framed: Women and British Justice* (Vintage, 1993) 62.

[11] See eg ***St George's Healthcare NHS Trust v S* (1989).**

[12] Clare Dyer, 'The Guardian profile: Elizabeth Butler-Sloss', *The Guardian*, 12 November 2004.

almost 30 years to take silk; Butler-Sloss's brother did it in half the time) and she chose to use this insider knowledge to her advantage: to turn her status as an outsider – by virtue of her gender – into a strength rather than a weakness. Making something unusual, like being the first woman on the Court of Appeal, look utterly normal is her legacy to future generations of women lawyers, and is something that might resonate more in the future than was appreciated in her day.

## Further Reading


- Elizabeth Butler-Sloss, 'The Legal Glass Ceiling – Broken or Merely Cracked?' Inner Temple Lecture, 9 November 2015, reprinted in *Inner Temple Yearbook 2016–2017* (Inner Temple, 2017) 114–15.
- First 100 Years archive interview with Baroness Butler-Sloss, 4 April 2016.
- *Richard Susskind, The Susskind Interviews: Legal Experts in Changing Times* (Sweet & Maxwell, 2005) chapter 11, 163–80.

# 60

# Section 5 of the Criminal Law (Rape) (Amendment) Act 1990

SUSAN LEAHY

Until 1990 in Ireland, a husband could not be prosecuted for the rape of his wife as a result of what was known as the 'marital rape exemption'. Abolishing a husband's immunity from conviction for rape of his wife was a significant turning point in the reform of sexual offences law. Section 5 of the Criminal Law (Rape) (Amendment) Act 1990 formally erased a husband's immunity from prosecution for marital rape. This reform marked a break with the idea of rape as a property crime (and husband as sexual proprietor of his wife), as well as sending a message that consent may be absent even where individuals have had sex numerous times before. However, whilst the reform constituted a very significant advance symbolically, its practical effects in terms of convictions and appropriate punishment of marital rape have been less pronounced.

## I. Context

The marital rape exemption is traced to the now infamous words of Sir Matthew Hale, who asserted that a husband could not be found guilty of raping his wife because 'by their mutual matrimonial consent and contract the wife hath given up herself in this kind unto her husband, which she cannot retract'.[1] Despite its serious ramifications for women, Hale's proclamation was neither challenged nor affirmed for several decades. Jennifer Temkin notes that '[l]egal history appears to record a silence on the matter until the nineteenth century'.[2] The first case to consider the marital rape exemption was *R v Clarence*[3] in 1888 where a husband was charged with transmission of a 'venereal disease' to his wife. He was convicted of malicious infliction of bodily harm and malicious infliction of grievous bodily harm. The case was referred to the Court for Crown Cases Reserved where Lois

[1] Sir Matthew Hale, *The History of the Pleas of the Crown* (1736) (Vol 1, Chap 58) 629.
[2] Jennifer Temkin, *Rape and the Legal Process* (2nd edn, OUP, 2002) 78.
[3] *R v Clarence* (1889) 22 QBD 23.

Bibbings notes 'a great deal, if not most, of the two-hour long courtroom argument and discussion which ensued concerned the laws relating to sex and marriage'.[4] The majority of the 13 judges[5] appeared to accept that the marital rape exemption was part of English common law and, although there were minority judgments which questioned its validity, *Clarence* 'came to be seen as a confirmation of Hale's exemption'.[6] There were no reported judgments on marital rape in the Irish courts prior to the 1990 Act but, due to the shared common law history with England and the Irish courts' tendency to follow English judgments post-independence, it was accepted that the exemption was part of Irish law.[7]

Many justifications were propounded for the retention of exemption. These justifications were discussed (and ultimately dismissed) by the Law Reform Commission (LRC) who considered the marital rape exemption in their *Consultation Paper on Rape* in 1987. Hale's original justification for the marital rape exemption was that an irrevocable consent to sexual activity was provided by a wife upon entering into a marriage contract. The LRC noted that the civil law on marriage 'did not proceed on the basis that, by marrying, a woman commits herself to have sexual intercourse with her husband at his demand'.[8] However, according to the LRC, this 'does not necessarily mean that such conduct by her husband should constitute … rape'.[9] Another rationale for the exemption was that allowing wives to make rape allegations could escalate marital disputes and prevent the possibility of reconciliation.[10] Reliance on this rationale is evident in a draft speech prepared for Minister of State at the Department of Justice, Seán Doherty, prior to a Dáil debate on the Criminal Law (Rape) Act 1981.[11] The draft included the following statement: 'I feel that the situation between husband and wife could be irretrievably damaged if it were possible for the wife, however unjustifiably, to allege rape which would require investigation by the gardaí.'

Opposition to abolition of the exemption was also justified because women who were raped by their husbands had alternative remedies such as a prosecution or civil proceedings for assault.[12] There were also concerns about false allegations and difficulties of proving that a rape had occurred where the couple were married.[13]

[4] Lois S Bibbings, *Binding Men: Stories about violence and law in late Victorian England* (Routledge, 2014) 117.

[5] The Court for Crown Cases Reserved was an appellate court for criminal cases. It consisted of all the judges on circuit in England of time (#15). Because this case was contentious, it was decided that all judges should be present. However, two judges were absent on the day (Bibbings, n 4 above, 116). The Court was replaced with the Court Criminal of Appeal in 1907.

[6] Bibbings, n 4 above, 139.

[7] Law Reform Commission, *Consultation Paper: Rape and Allied Offences* (Law Reform Commission 1987) 11. However, drawing on English exceptions to the exemption which it was assumed should also apply in Irish law, the Commission suggested that the exemption was 'confined to circumstances where the spouses are cohabiting and there are no separation proceedings being, or even, perhaps, in contemplation': ibid.

[8] ibid 42.

[9] ibid.

[10] ibid.

[11] This information was made available by journalist, Fiona Gartland, in 2011: Fiona Gartland, 'Marital rape law rejected due to family concerns', *Irish Times*, 31 December 2011.

[12] Law Reform Commission, n 7 above, 43.

[13] ibid 45.

## II. The Landmark

Feminist scholars and activists highlighted the marital rape exemption as an especially pernicious form of discrimination. Catharine MacKinnon declared that the marital rape exemption meant that wives were 'unrapable',[14] noting that:

> the law of rape divides women into spheres of consent according to indices of relationship to men. Which category of presumed consent a woman is in depends on who she is relative to a man who wants her, not what she says or does.[15]

Similarly, Susan Brownmiller argued that if women were to be 'equal partners' within a marriage, 'then intercourse must be construed as an act of mutual desire and not as a wifely "duty", enforced by the permissible threat of bodily harm or of economic sanctions'.[16] The feminist message was clear: the marital rape exemption was a denial of women's sexual autonomy placing them in an inferior position to their husbands, who could force sexual activity upon them with impunity. Further, the rule sent a dangerous message about sexual communication, that is, that consent could be presumed on the basis of a pre-existing relationship or previous consensual sexual encounters.

At grassroots level in Ireland, the women within the Dublin Rape Crisis Centre (DRCC) were the chief campaigners for abolishing the exemption. They campaigned steadily for this reform in the debates surrounding both the Criminal Law (Rape) Act 1981 and the Criminal Law (Rape) (Amendment) Act 1990. The Council for the Status of Women (an organisation which represents women's interests to government) also campaigned for rape law reform at this time, producing a Report, *Rape in Ireland*, which was presented to the Minister for Justice, Gerry Collins, in October 1978.[17] This Report included a call for the criminalisation of marital rape. However, the DRCC led the feminist campaign for reform of the Criminal Law (Rape) Act 1981 (which led to the abolition of the marital rape exemption).[18] The work of the grassroots feminists within the DRCC at this time is thoroughly documented by Susan McKay.[19] In February 1979, the DRCC held a press conference to announce its opening and to launch its first report which called for a range of reforms to Irish sexual offences law, including the abolition of the marital rape exemption.[20] In June 1980, Senator Gemma Hussey brought a Bill on rape to the Seanad which included the abolition of the marital rape exemption.[21] This Private Member's Bill was defeated by the Government majority. The Government-sponsored Criminal Law (Rape) Bill 1980 which was introduced in November 1980 (and which became the Criminal Law (Rape) Act 1981) did not criminalise marital rape. At a meeting between the Minister for State at the Department of Justice (Seán Doherty) and the DRCC in September 1980, 'the [DRCC] women were left in no doubt as to

[14] Catharine A MacKinnon, *Toward a Feminist Theory of State* (Harvard University Press, 1989) 175.
[15] ibid.
[16] Susan Brownmiller, *Against Our Will: Men, Women and Rape* (Fawcett Books, 1975) 381.
[17] Yvonne Galligan, *Women and Politics in Contemporary Ireland: From the Margins to the Mainstream* (Pinter, 1998) 114.
[18] ibid 119.
[19] Susan McKay, *Without Fear: 25 Years of the Dublin Rape Crisis Centre* (New Island, 2005).
[20] ibid 24.
[21] Galligan, n 17 above, 116.

the government's position on marital rape: "Absolute rejection of this proposal. No way will this be in the new legislation"'.[22] Speaking in the Dáil during the passage of the Bill, Minister Doherty indicated that marital rape was an issue of great complexity which merited 'further study' and this is why it was not included in the Bill.[23]

The omission of marital rape from the 1981 Act, along with a number of other shortcomings, resulted in the DRCC being very disappointed with the 1981 Act. McKay reports that the DRCC had 'been campaigning for the repeal of the … Act since it was enacted'.[24] Their drive for further reform gathered momentum in 1986. In April, the DRCC won the support of the Council for the Status of Women.[25] This was significant, as the Council 'had been given consultative status as the official representative of women's interests with the government, making government ministries well disposed to listen to the views of this organisation'.[26] In October, an official launch of the campaign for reform of the 1981 Act was supported by the other Rape Crisis Centres (Galway, Limerick, Cork and Waterford) and by a number of politicians.[27] The Joint Oireachtas Committee on Women's Rights recommended reforms which mirrored the DRCC's calls.[28] This committee was 'a parliamentary voice for women's demands'. Significantly, it was chaired by Monica Barnes TD who had been involved in the women's movement before entering politics.[29] Further, in both its 1987 Consultation Paper and 1988 Report,[30] the LRC recommended the abolition of the marital rape exemption.

When the Criminal Law (Rape) (Amendment) Bill was published in December 1988, marital rape was finally to be criminalised in a provision which would become section 5 of the Criminal Law (Rape) (Amendment) Act 1990. Section 5 provides that:

> (1) Any rule of law by virtue of which a husband cannot be guilty of the rape of his wife is hereby abolished.
>
> (2) Criminal proceedings against a man in respect of the rape by him of his wife shall not be instituted except by or with the consent of the Director of Public Prosecutions [DPP].

Although section 5 finally recognised marital rape as a crime, it was not a perfect provision. Requiring the consent of the DPP for proceedings to be brought marks marital rape for special attention. The section was included 'to prevent the institution of spiteful or mischievous proceedings by a spouse or an interfering third party'.[31] At the time, it was possible for a private prosecution to reach a preliminary hearing at the District Court without the intervention of the DPP. Section 5(2) prevents this. However, commenting on the Act, Caroline Fennell suggested that it is difficult not to perceive section 5(2) as representative of: 'the lingering suspicion that a woman, devious as she is with all the traditions and myths of Eve

[22] McKay, n 19 above, 33. An account of this meeting was published in the DRCC's Annual Report in 1981.
[23] *Dáil Debates*, 7 December 1988, vol 328 cols 1455–1457.
[24] McKay, n 19 above, 105–06.
[25] ibid 106.
[26] Galligan, n 17 above, 118.
[27] Monica Barnes (Fine Gael); Mary O'Rourke (Fianna Fáil); Mary Harney (Progressive Democrats); Proinsias De Ross (Workers' Party) and; Eithne Fitzgerald (Labour Party) (McKay, n 19 above, 111).
[28] McKay, n 19 above, 113.
[29] Galligan, n 17 above, 120.
[30] Law Reform Commission, *Report: Rape and Allied Offences* (LRC 24-1988).
[31] Minister for Social Welfare (Dr Woods), presenting the Criminal Law (Rape) (Amendment) Bill 1988 on behalf of the Minister for Justice: *Dáil Debates*, 18 May 1989, vol 390 col 601.

hanging about her, would once again use rape within marriage as some way of getting back at her husband.'[32]

## III. What Happened Next

Although traditionally Ireland tends to lag behind English reform efforts, Ireland abolished the exemption before England and Wales. The abolition of the exemption was confirmed by the House of Lords in *R v R*.[33] The abolition was subsequently enshrined in legislation in section 142 of the Criminal Justice and Public Order Act 1994. The path to reform in England had been quite different to that in Ireland, with the exemption receiving significant judicial attention which had led to a 'gradual whittling away of the exemption'[34] via the creation of a number of exceptions prior to its complete abolition in *R v R*. The exemption was held not to apply where a non-cohabitation or separation order was in place,[35] where a decree nisi of divorce had been granted,[36] where a non-molestation undertaking had been given by a husband,[37] or where a formal deed of separation had been agreed.[38] The greater volume of jurisprudence on marital rape in England possibly explains why the exemption was judicially, as opposed to legislatively, abolished.

In Ireland, the practical impact of section 5 has been minimal. The first conviction for marital rape was not secured until 2002. This conviction was subsequently overturned by the Court of Criminal Appeal because of deficiencies in the evidence and a retrial was ordered.[39] The conviction was reinstated at a retrial in 2006 and the offender was sentenced to six years in jail. Giving evidence after the second conviction, the victim spoke of the 'nightmare' she had endured as a result of the length of the court processes (the rape occurred in 1997) and having to withstand two trials.[40] There have only been four other convictions for marital rape in Ireland. In October 2015, a man found guilty of marital rape was sentenced to six years' imprisonment. Notably, the man told the gardaí that he did not think it was possible for a man to rape his wife.[41] There were two further convictions for marital rape in 2016. In July 2016, a man was sentenced to 12 years' imprisonment with the final two years suspended for marital rape.[42] This case received significant press attention and was a stark reminder of the levels of violence which women within relationships can be subject to. The husband in this case was also found guilty of the separate offence of threatening to kill his

[32] Caroline Fennell, 'Annotation of the Criminal Law (Rape) (Amendment) Act 1990, *Irish Current Law Statutes Annotated*, paras 32-01, 32-12.

[33] *R v R* [1992] 1 AC 599. The exemption had already been abolished by Scottish judiciary in *Johnson Davis Stallard v HM Advocate* 1989 SCCR 248; 1989 SLT 469.

[34] Graham Virgo, 'Marital Rape – The Fast or Slow Track to Law Reform?' (1991) 50 *Cambridge Law Journal* 19, 19.

[35] *R v Clarke* [1949] 2 All ER 448.

[36] *R v O'Brien* [1974] 3 All ER 663.

[37] *R v Steele* (1976) 65 Cr App R 22.

[38] *R v Roberts* [1986] Crim LR 188.

[39] 'Court overturns man's conviction for rape of wife', *Irish Times*, 12 October 2004.

[40] 'First man convicted of marital rape jailed for six years', *Irish Examiner*, 31 January 2006.

[41] 'Six-year sentence for man convicted of raping his wife', *Irish Times*, 30 November 2015.

[42] Conor Gallagher, 'Man jailed for 10 years for threatening, assaulting and raping his wife', *Irish Times*, 25 July 2016.

wife and pleaded guilty to assaulting her with a hammer. Significantly, this case received further significant press attention in 2018 when the man's appeal against sentence was allowed, reducing it to 10 years, with the final 18 months suspended. This decision received sharp criticism in particular from victims' groups such as Dublin Rape Crisis Centre, who called for an urgent review of the law relating to marital and intimate partner rape.[43] In October 2016, another man was convicted for rape of his wife, having punched her in the face several times during the attack. He was sentenced to seven years' imprisonment with the final two years suspended.[44] Most recently, in May 2017, a man was convicted of raping his wife twice in one night. He was sentenced to nine years' imprisonment in July 2018.[45]

Although there are no official statistics available on the number of complaints of marital rape made to the gardaí or of the number of prosecutions which have been brought since the 1990 Act commenced, it is clear that the criminal justice system's response to marital rape is inadequate. Available statistics show that rape within intimate relationships, including marriage, happens more frequently than the conviction rate would suggest. In *The SAVI Report: Sexual Abuse and Victimization in Ireland* (the most extensive study of the prevalence of sexual abuse and violence ever undertaken in Ireland), 23.6 per cent of perpetrators of sexual violence against women as adults were intimate partners, or ex-partners.[46] More recently, in its *Impact Report 2017*, domestic abuse support group Women's Aid revealed that there were 607 disclosures of sexual abuse by women engaging with their services in 2017. This included 232 disclosures of rape within intimate relationships.[47] The 2015 Annual Report of the DRCC revealed that 24.36 per cent of victims who had used their service had been sexually abused by a boyfriend or partner.[48] Section 5(2) has also been criticised by both commentators and victims' groups for unnecessarily distinguishing rape within marriage from other forms of rape, and there have been a number of calls for its repeal.[49]

## IV. Significance

The removal of the marital rape exemption sent an important signal about women's sexual autonomy. Commenting on the abolition of the marital rape exemption in English law, Sue Lees notes, it: 'carries the clear implication that a woman does have a right to

[43] Shane Phelan, 'Calls for review after man who raped and threatened to kill wife has sentence cut', *Irish Independent*, 1 March 2018.

[44] Isabel Hayes, 'Man gets five years in jail for raping and beating his wife', *Irish Independent*, 21 December 2016. The man in this case lost an appeal against his conviction in May 2018: Ruaidhri Giblin, 'Man (46) fails in appeal against conviction for marital rape', *Irish Times*, 10 May 2018.

[45] Fiona Ferguson, 'Man jailed for nine years for raping wife twice in one night', Irish Times, 20 July 2018.

[46] Hannah McGee, Rebecca Garavan, Mairead de Barra, Joanne Byrne and Ronán Conroy, *The SAVI Report: Sexual Abuse and Victimization in Ireland* (The Liffey Press, 2002) 98.

[47] Women's Aid, *Impact Report 2017* (2018) 3.

[48] Dublin Rape Crisis Centre, *Annual Report 2015* (Dublin Rape Crisis Centre, 2016) 15.

[49] Rape Crisis Network of Ireland (RCNI), *RCNI Agenda for Justice: Discussion Document* (RCNI 2009) 14 and *Agenda for Justice: Towards Ending Injustice for Survivors of Sexual Violence: RCNI Legal Position Paper* (RCNI 2005) 4; Susan Leahy, 'Acknowledging the role of the Criminal Justice System in Combatting Domestic Violence: Assessing the Recent Law Reform Commission's Recommendations' (2014) 1 *Irish Journal of Family Law* 9; Joint Oireachtas Committee on Justice, Defence & Equality, *Report on Hearings in Relation to Domestic and Sexual Violence* (Joint Oireachtas Committee on Justice, Defence & Equality, 2014) 5.

self-determination or to take an active rather than a passive sexual role, and that acceptable forms of sexuality require the presence of mutual desire and consent.'[50]

However, while the landmark was important symbolically, there is still a sense that marital rape is a 'crime apart' from other forms of rape. This is particularly evident in Ireland with the retention of section 5(2), which Campbell et al suggest 'may betray a sentiment on the part of the legislature [that rape] perpetrated by a woman's husband is not truly comparable to rape *per se*'.[51] Thus, although this landmark was symbolically significant, in practice there is more work to be done to ensure that it is as momentous in practice as it is in principle.

## Further Reading

- Anna Carline and Patricia Easteal, *Shades of Grey – Domestic and Sexual Violence against Women: Law Reform and Society* (Routledge, 2014) chapter 10.
- Yvonne Galligan, *Women and Politics in Contemporary Ireland: From the Margins to the Mainstream* (Pinter, 1998) chapter 6.
- Susan McKay, *Without Fear: 25 Years of the Dublin Rape Crisis Centre* (New Island, 2005) chapters 3 and 8.

[50] Sue Lees, *Carnal Knowledge: Rape on Trial* (2nd edn, The Women's Press, 2002) xlv.

[51] Liz Campbell, Shane Kilcommins and Catherine O'Sullivan, *Criminal Law in Ireland: Cases and Commentary* (Clarus Press, 2010) 588.

# 61

# First Woman President of Ireland, Mary Robinson, 1990

LEAH TREANOR

In 1990, Mary Robinson became the first woman President of Ireland, making Ireland the first EU country to elect a woman head of state. Her political career had begun 20 years earlier when she was elected to Seanad Éireann, the Upper House of the Oireachtas. A constitutional lawyer, Mary Robinson championed human rights and gender equality both in her work as a lawyer and as a Senator. Despite the limited constitutional remit of the Irish President,[1] Mary Robinson's presidency was an active and meaningful one. Indeed, many would say that Robinson redefined the office of President itself.

## I. Life

Mary Therese Winnifred Robinson (née Bourke) was born in Ballina, County Mayo, in 1944. Educated in Ballina, Dublin and Paris, she went on to study law at Trinity College, Dublin, where she graduated with first class honours in 1967. The same year, she won a postgraduate fellowship to study a Master's degree at Harvard University, again graduating with first class honours.

In 1967 Robinson was called to the Bar of Ireland, where she built a thriving constitutional law practice; this of itself was something of an achievement, given a broader tendency for women to be channelled into less prestigious areas of legal practice such as family law. In 1980 she was called to the male-dominated Inner Bar of Ireland, becoming a Senior Counsel (SC) – only the third woman to do so.[2] Robinson was not just an eminent lawyer, she was a path-breaking academic too. In 1969 – at the age of 25 – she was appointed Reid Professor of Constitutional and Criminal Law at Trinity College, Dublin. At the time of writing, she is Chancellor of Trinity College, Dublin.

In 1969 she successfully contested an election to Seanad Éireann as an independent candidate. She later held office as a Labour Party Senator from 1976 until 1985 when she

[1] Article 13 Bunreacht na h'Éireann.

[2] **Frances Moran** took silk in 1947, but did not practise. She did, however, become the first woman law professor in Ireland, when she was appointed to a Chair in 1934. The second – and first practising – woman to take silk was Mella Carroll, who took silk in 1976 (Ivana Bacik, Cathryn Costello and Eileen Drew *Gender Injustice: Feminising the Legal Professions?* (Trinity College, Dublin Law School, 2003) 72.

resigned from the party over its support for the Anglo-Irish Agreement. Notwithstanding the fact of her public resignation in 1985, it was the Labour Party that nominated and supported Robinson for election to the presidency in 1990. Indeed, despite much pressure to re-join the party at this juncture, Robinson was firm in her conviction to remain independent.[3]

Robinson sat as a Senator for over 20 years, fighting tirelessly – and successfully – to advance women's rights in Irish society. She successfully campaigned for changes to the law which would have significant impact on women's lives, such as abolishing the requirement for women to resign from the civil service upon marriage, the legal right to contraception,[4] and the right of women to sit on juries.[5] As a lawyer, she took the *Airey* case – involving a woman who was unable to secure a judicial separation from her physically abusive husband because she could not afford the costs of a solicitor – to the European Court of Human Rights and succeeded in obtaining a ruling that Ireland was in breach of the European Convention on Human Rights for failing to provide civil legal aid.[6]

On 7 November 1990 Robinson was elected seventh President of Ireland, with an 86,559 vote majority. Described as 'the most historically significant presidential election in the history of the state',[7] this was the first time a woman had ever held the office of President in Ireland.[8]

Robinson remained as President of Ireland until 1997, when she resigned just before the end of her term to become UN High Commissioner for Human Rights. She was the second person appointed to this role and remained in post until 2002. She is still politically active, having assumed a series of UN roles following her departure from presidential office. She is also involved in the work of the 'Elders', a global network of world leaders founded by Nelson Mandela, who are committed to advancing peace and human rights.[9]

## II. Context

Whilst constitutionally defined as an element of the Oireachtas, the office of President remains distinct from the Irish governmental process, with the office-holder acting in a 'figurehead' capacity with no political involvement. Traditionally the presidency was an office with low political impact, a comfortable 'one to which politicians might retire'[10] after a lengthy career in politics. This is reflected in the profile of previous office-holders: 'elderly

[3] Mary Robinson, *Everybody Matters: A Memoir* (Hodder & Stoughton, 2012) 132.

[4] Michael O'Sullivan, *Mary Robinson: The Life and Times of an Irish Liberal* (Blackwater Press, 1993); Olivia O'Leary and Helen Burke, *Mary Robinson: The Authorised Biography* (Hodder & Stoughton, 1998). See further **Health (Family Planning) Act 1979**.

[5] Following the enactment of the Juries Act 1927, only property owners were eligible for jury service. Whilst women could apply to sit on juries, the legislative framework automatically rendered women exempt as they were not legally entitled to hold property until 1976. See further on the position in England & Wales, **Section 25 of the Criminal Justice Act 1972**.

[6] *Airey v Ireland* [1979] ECHR 3, (1979) 2 EHRR 305.

[7] Patsy McGarry, *First Citizen: Mary McAleese and the Irish Presidency* (The O'Brien Press, 2008) 36.

[8] Robinson was officially inaugurated as the seventh President of Ireland on 3 December 1990.

[9] See further <https://www.theelders.org/>.

[10] McGarry, n 7 above, 198.

former ministers who were not interested in developing the potential of the office'.[11] So uncontroversial was the office that the Irish presidential election of 1990 was just the fifth to be contested by more than one candidate. In real terms, this meant that the Irish presidential election of 1990 was the first in 17 years.

The political affiliation of successful candidates had also become predictable. Ireland being a conservative society, the majority of former Presidents were drawn from the conservative Fianna Fáil party.[12] Robinson herself acknowledged the general assumption that Fianna Fáil's Brian Lenihan would be the successful candidate in 1990.[13] Testament to her power as a revolutionary, Mary Robinson – an independent – was not only the first woman to be elected President but, further, the youngest candidate ever and the first successful non-Fianna Fáil candidate since 1945. As such, it was clear that Robinson's election marked a new beginning for Ireland. As she put it in her acceptance speech,

> there was nothing rational or reasonable about the campaign which developed into a barnstorming, no holds barred, battle between my ad hoc assembly of political activists, amateurs, idealists and romantic realists against the might, money and merciless onslaught of the greatest political party on this island. And we beat them.[14]

Key to understanding the significance of Robinson's presidency is an understanding of Ireland in the late 1980s and early 1990s. Ireland in that era was characterised by a close relationship between Church and State, the Catholic Church enjoying a tremendous degree of political influence and staunchly opposing constitutional amendments antithetical to Catholic teachings such as those proposed in the referenda on abortion (1983) and divorce (1986).[15]

In *this* Ireland, an extremely 'traditional' (and narrow) view of the role of women prevailed. Women were relegated to the domestic sphere, with very few women visible in public life. Undoubtedly patriarchal in nature, Ireland's political culture was defined by political scientists writing at the time as authoritarian,[16] conformist[17] and anti intellectual.[18] It was against this current that Robinson – a liberal, an intellectual, *a woman* – successfully sought election as President of Ireland.

From the moment Robinson was nominated as a candidate for the presidency, it was clear that women would play an important role in both her campaign and her election. Managing to mobilise women to a degree never before seen in Ireland, Robinson's team comprised a number of women. At grass-roots level, women inspired by Robinson's work were a driving force behind the campaign. When it came to casting their vote, women turned out in their

[11] David Gwyn Morgan, 'Mary Robinson's Presidency: Relations with the Government' (1999) 34 *Irish Jurist* 256, 257.

[12] Fianna Fáil (in English, 'Soldiers of Destiny') is an Irish political party which was founded by Eamon DeValera in 1926.

[13] Robinson, n 3 above, 131.

[14] Mary Robinson, 'President Robinson's acceptance speech, 9 November 1990: http://www.president.ie/en/sabina-higgins/speeches/president-robinsons-acceptance-speech.

[15] The 1983 referendum upheld the right to life of the unborn with a majority of almost 67%. In 1986 the proposed amendment to allow dissolution of marriage was rejected with almost 64% voting against. See further **Protection of Life During Pregnancy Act 2013** and **Fifteenth Amendment of the Constitution Act 1995** respectively.

[16] David Schmitt, *The Irony of Irish Democracy: The Impact of Political Culture on Administrative and Democratic Political Development in Ireland* (Lexington Books, 1973) 43–54.

[17] Michael Gallagher, *The Irish Labour Party in Transition* (Gill and Macmillan, 1982) 19–20.

[18] Basil Chubb, *The Government and Politics of Ireland* (3rd edn, Longman, 1992) 18–20.

droves, including some who had never voted before. Robinson recounts stories of women who 'traditionally would have asked or been told by their husbands who to vote for, breaking that mould and giving me their vote'.[19] Irish women had, for the first time, been given a political voice, enabling many to find their own. Recognising the symbolic significance of her election, in her inaugural speech Robinson thanked Irish women, 'mná na hÉireann,[20] who, instead of rocking the cradle, rocked the system, and who came out massively to make their mark on the ballot paper and on a new Ireland'.[21]

## III. What Happened Next

A new Ireland was born. Whilst restricted in terms of how overtly 'political' she could be as President, the thread of Robinson's 'politics' could be easily ascertained from her record in Seanad Éireann. Through 'reinterpreting the traditional limits' of the presidency, Robinson relied on the 'moral influence' of her office and her role as the voice of the people to influence public opinion.[22] Robinson's work contributed to a sea change for women in Irish society, who were now afforded property rights, some reproductive rights and the ability to participate in the public sphere. In 1995 during Robinson's tenure, and owing to her influence, a referendum on the dissolution of marriage resulted in the legalisation of divorce in Ireland.[23]

Robinson was not the last woman President of Ireland. Following her departure from office in 1997, Mary McAleese was elected as her successor. This was the first time in the *world* that a woman had followed another woman into office as elected head of state.[24] The fact that the Irish presidency had been consecutively filled by women contributed to a redefinition of the role of women in Irish society; women were no longer relegated to the domestic sphere, but were key players in the political arena.

## IV. Significance

> … above all, the women of Ireland who are still struggling on the long march to equality and equity. To all those who have no voice or whose voice is weak I say: take heart. There is hope. Look what you did in this election. You made history. As President I hope we will make history together.[25]

With Robinson's election as President in 1990, for the first time the 'Guardian of the Constitution' was a woman – and a feminist woman at that.[26] Robinson commanded a

[19] Robinson, n 3 above, 143.
[20] *Mná na h'Éireann* is Gaeilge for 'Women of Ireland'.
[21] Robinson, 'President Robinson's acceptance speech', n 14 above; and Robinson, n 3 above, 145.
[22] ibid 131.
[23] See further **Fifteenth Amendment of the Constitution Act 1995.**
[24] Yvonne Galligan, 'Women in Politics' in John Coakley and Michael Gallagher (eds), *Politics in the Republic of Ireland* (5th edn, Routledge, 2010) 263.
[25] Robinson, n 14 above.
[26] Ailbhe Smyth, '"A Great Day for the Women of Ireland …":The Meaning of Mary Robinson's Presidency for Irish Women' (1992) 8 *Canadian Journal of Irish Studies* 61, 61.

substantial degree of respect from others. Highly capable, she was properly 'assumed to be as intelligent as any of her male counterparts'.[27] This is significant, given the frequency with which gendered assumptions are made about women's competence and ability to 'hold their own' in traditionally male-dominated arenas, and marked an important shift in societal attitudes towards women.

Beyond the personal and professional achievements of Robinson, the election of a woman as head of the Irish state demonstrated that – for women – anything was possible. Women were instrumental to her presidential campaign. Never before had women's voices been regarded as important. In 1990, Irish women made sure they were heard. The role of women in bringing about this monumental change demonstrated the political power women were capable of wielding and set the tone for the future. In the words of one prominent Irish feminist, writing shortly after her election:

> Mary Robinson's very presence is a refutation of stereotypical notions of feminine 'passivity'. She presents an image of ourselves, as women and indeed as Irish, that is positive, modern, sophisticated, independent, and capable of making sense of differences without erasing them. Exploding myths and shibboleths, she allows us to break free of constraints and to set about re-creating ourselves.[28]

It has been almost 30 years since Ireland elected its first woman President, yet the legacy of Mary Robinson, and of the women who supported her, remains vibrant in Ireland today as ever. Irish women continue to claim their rightful place in public office and continue to demand more for themselves, particularly in their quest for further reproductive rights.[29] As Mary Robinson said, 'Feel empowered. And if you start to do it, if you start to feel your voice heard, you will never go back'.[30]

## Further Reading

- Fergus Finlay, *Mary Robinson: A President with a Purpose* (The O'Brien Press, 1990).
- Mary Kenny, *Goodbye to Catholic Ireland: A Social, Personal and Cultural History from the fall of Parnell to the realm of Mary Robinson* (Sinclair Stevenson, 1997).
- Mary Robinson, *Everybody Matters: A Memoir* (Hodder & Stoughton, 2012).

[27] Valerie Bresnihan, 'The Symbolic Power of Ireland's President Robinson' (1999) 29 *Presidential Studies Quarterly* 250, 260.

[28] Ailbhe Smyth, n 26 above, 73.

[29] See further **Protection of Life During Pregnancy Act 2013; Thirty-sixth Amendment to the Irish Constitution, 2018**.

[30] Khadija Patel, 'Getting Our Irish Up: Interview with Mary Robinson', *The Daily Maverick* (South Africa, 10 August 2012).

# 62

# Foundation of the Association of Women Barristers, 1991

FRANCES BURTON*

The Association of Women Barristers (AWB) was founded in 1991 to provide a support network for women barristers, to press for reform to benefit women barristers and to influence gender-related law reform generally.

## I. Context

Unlike the **Association of Women Solicitors**, with its origins in the period immediately before and after 1919, the Association of Women Barristers (AWB) did not play even a minor role in or around the year of the professional enabling Act. The Bar is the more conservative and the more powerful arm of the legal profession in England and Wales. Barristers represent clients in court and are usually briefed by solicitors. Trainee barristers must undergo a period of pupillage or apprenticeship before being accepted into Chambers, groups of barristers administered by a clerk. For many decades after the **Sex Disqualification (Removal) Act 1919**, qualified women faced difficulties in finding pupillage opportunities, Chambers that would admit them, solicitors who would brief them, and clerks who would allocate work to them. Even past the 1970s, because barristers are self-employed and so not covered by the **Sex Discrimination Act 1975**, discrimination against women was widespread. In the 1990s the scale of sexual harassment of young women at the Bar was becoming known.

By the late 1980s, it had become apparent that the Bar Council lagged far behind mainstream recognition of the need to consider the still manifestly unequal position of women in the profession. The leadership of the time was more concerned with more general reform and reorganisation, such as the blueprints for Chambers governance, which was then still run mainly through 'the old boys' network' approach without any kind of constitution; the latter was required only from 1995.[1] These were also the days of the pre-Judicial Appointments

* Former chair (2000–02) and current Vice-President and committee member of the Association of Women Barristers.

[1] See eg *Practice Management at the Bar*, the Bar Council's report of that year on optimum chambers' management, commissioned from Central Law Training and recommending a formal system of governance by committee to replace the then common 'benevolent despotism' of the Head of Chambers.

Commission 'tap on the shoulder' for elevation to the Bench, when the patronage of the Lord Chancellor – for both appointments to the judiciary and as QCs (from which the judiciary was mostly selected) – was the only route to ultimate career advancement.

## II. The Landmark

The foundation of the AWB in 1991 came about as the result of an initiative of a group of Common Law and Chancery women barristers, who called a meeting to discuss the concept of an association which would provide mutual support to women in all sectors of the Bar and to lobby for some of the equality and diversity measures then significantly lacking in the profession generally. The Association's first Chairwoman was Jennifer Horne-Roberts from the Common Law Bar. At the time it was clear that today's standards of equal treatment and opportunity were not available even to many *men*, a lack felt by many of them as much as by women, and particularly by black, Asian and other minority ethnic barristers as well as those who had no strong family or other connections with the Bar or otherwise with the Establishment.

With the benefit of hindsight, the establishment of the AWB in 1991 was as much in its way a watershed as the 1919 Act or the gradual evolution of the AWS. Women barristers looked with envy on the AWS. Indeed, it was the precedent of the AWS, with its Law Society budget and Law Society administrative support, that generated discussion amongst women at the Bar: first, as to why there should not be a similar organisation of women *barristers*, and, secondly, why the establishment of the AWB should not encourage other specialist minority groups whose collective voices – soon including lesbian and gay perspectives as well as the main ethnic groups – would swell the movement for genuinely equal treatment. The AWS was a significant inspiration and support to the AWB: indeed at the very time when the AWS's role has been declining towards its closure by the Law Society in the early years of the twenty-first century, the influence and remit of the AWB have grown. At the same time it has resisted suggestions by the Bar Council that it is irrelevant in modern times. This growth and development would almost certainly not have taken place without the established model of the AWS.

## III. What Happened Next

In the early years the AWB's primary focus was on generating solidarity amongst women at the Bar and in public relations. Its early activities were mainly social and profile-raising through, for example, regular early evening drinks meetings for members in a bar off Chancery Lane and a garden party, following the model of other Bar Associations such as the Bar Association for Commerce, Finance and Industry (BACFI), to which many AWB members who were employed as in-house counsel belonged.

By the mid-1990s, however, the Association had a constitution, a membership of several hundred, a woman High Court judge as President (Mary Arden),[2] and a proactive

[2] **Elizabeth Butler-Sloss** had declined the invitation, advising that the Association might 'antagonise the men', although she attended the Association's launch in Inner Temple.

committee chaired successively by Chancery, Employment and Common Law women barristers. This brought the perspectives of women in all these sectors of the Bar to the Association's work. Additional benefit came from a concurrent equality and diversity movement at the Bar generally when the Bar Council's Equality Committee and Sex Discrimination Sub-Committee (SDC) were set up. This enabled the AWB to achieve representation on the Sub-Committee, to send a delegate to the European Women Lawyers' conference held in Paris on the 1981 UN Convention on the Elimination of All Forms of Discrimination Against Women (CEDAW),[3] and to participate in some, if not all, of the formal work of the Bar Council.

More importantly, membership of the Bar Council's Sex Discrimination Sub-Committee allowed the AWB to play an active part in early efforts to widen the pool of appointable women from which both the judiciary and QCs could be selected. The 1997 Labour Government, which included Lord Irvine as Lord Chancellor, was the catalyst in this respect. At the Association's Dinner that year, Irvine announced the first relaxations in the rigid rules previously surrounding qualification for judicial office, which had made many women's domestic commitments an ill fit for the then standard terms of judicial appointment. Introducing the changes, he exhorted his female audience with the encouraging words 'Don't be shy, apply'.

This was the first of several advances achieved by the Association in the late 1990s. The second, even more far-reaching, was membership for the Chairwoman of the Association on the Lord Chancellor's Working Party on Judicial Appointments and Silk. The initial key report was drafted by the holder of that office at the time, Chancery barrister Josephine Hayes, who had already flexed the Association's growing collective muscle by successfully suing the Attorney-General for indirect discrimination in making an unadvertised appointment through secret consultations, in contravention of the accepted principle that all such appointments would be open to fair competition. When this was followed by the appointment of the Commissioners for Judicial Appointments, led by Sir Colin Campbell, the Association's third achievement was the successful lobby for severance of all judicial and Silk appointments from the remit of the Lord Chancellor. This was generated by the plenary meeting of the full panel of all the Commissioners with leaders of all the interested groups in which the key paper was presented by the AWB, urging that only a completely independent Judicial Appointments Commission could achieve the transparency in equality and diversity which a modern appointments system required.[4]

From this point the Association went from strength to strength, although it did not achieve (and still has not achieved) the seat on the Bar Council which would give them the same voting rights as other Bar Associations such as the Sole Practitioners' and the Employed Bar Associations. This was a disappointment, since at the Law Society the AWS received not only equivalent recognition but also a formal budget, administrative support and a place for its Chair at the annual ceremonies at the Opening of the Legal Year. In contrast, the Chairwoman of the AWB was only given a seat in the congregation at Westminster Abbey and, unlike the AWS Chair, was not included in the procession. This exclusion

[3] On CEDAW see further **UK Ratification of the Optional Protocol to the Convention on the Elimination of all Forms of Discrimination Against Women (CEDAW), 2005**.

[4] The Judicial Appointments Commission established in the Constitutional Reform Act 2005 started work in April 2006.

was justified on the ground that the AWB did not qualify as a 'Bar Association' (defined as one of practitioners in a specialist field) entitled to such Bar Council representation, according to the report of a working party set up by the Bar Council and chaired by Lord Alexander of Weedon QC to consider the composition of the Bar Council. Women barristers, they argued, did not represent a specialist field of practice but only a group defined by gender.[5]

In practical terms, this has mattered little. The first Chair of the Employed Bar Association, Susan Ward, a Vice-President of BACFI, happened also to be a former Chair of the AWB and was happy to represent its interests at Bar Council meetings. Others with seats on the Bar Council, such as the then Leader of the South Eastern Circuit, Stephen Hockman QC (later Chairman of the Bar), then offered to do the same. Hockman did his best to see that the AWB was included in Bar Council events where other Bar entities were represented, while the next Chairmen of the Bar invited the Association's Chairwoman to attend meetings. When Peter Goldsmith QC was Chairman of the Bar in the mid-1990s he went a step further by deciding to become the first of several men at the Bar who indicated that they would like to be associate members.

However in 2002, to the Association's surprise, the Chairwoman of the AWB was formally invited (as a member of the SDC) to the Queen's Golden Jubilee Service in St Paul's and, with a variety of other representatives of the legal profession, to the Buckingham Palace Garden Party. The same year, Carolyn Kirby, the first woman President of the Law Society, invited the AWB Chair to dinner at her official residence and thereafter the Law Society's Chief Executive, Janet Paraskeva, made sure that the AWB was included in every women-related event held by the Society.

Over the years, the Association has been involved in every major consultation and advance in equality and diversity, which has benefited not only women barristers but also men at the Bar, including pressing for an effective Equality Code for the Bar – although, sadly, incidences are still reported of discrimination, since there are clearly still many ways of evading the letter of the Code. In November 2011, for example, the Association joined with the AWS to give oral evidence to the House of Lords' Constitution Committee Inquiry on of Judicial Appointments, where several passages of the AWB's prior written submissions were quoted with approval by the Constitution Committee, and the AWB was able to press home the message that while quotas or any dilution of the merit criterion should not be allowed to impact on appointments of those best suited to the achievement of a quality judiciary, it was clear that there are still some unexplored avenues through which the appointment pool might usefully be widened.[6]

In 2011 the AWB celebrated 20 years of such work with a dinner arranged by one of its former Presidents, **Lady Hale**, at the House of Lords; and in 2016 she hosted another to celebrate the Association's 25th anniversary. Under the recent presidency of Mrs Justice

[5] The Alexander Report (2000) was the report of a working party, chaired by Lord Alexander, set up by the Bar Council to consider the composition of the Bar Council following the decision to give full advocacy rights to barristers employed as in-house counsel. Lord Alexander was an innovative former Chairman of the Bar Council, whose year of office in 1985 had set the Bar on a pathway to reform in various respects, but whose 2000 leadership of this important working party proved to be somewhat conservative.

[6] See Select Committee on the Constitution, Judicial Appointments, Oral and Written Evidence (no date); Select Committee on the Constitution, *Judicial Appointments* (HMSO, March 2012) [102]–[105].

Cox, a former equality and human rights barrister, a strong link was forged between the AWB and the UK Association of Women Judges, set up by Lady Hale in 2003. The current President, Lady Justice Hallett, who took office in 2017, had herself been the first woman Chair of the Bar Council. Current concerns include retention rates for women at the Bar, especially those returning after maternity leave or a career break; the concentration of women in criminal and family law (the least remunerative areas of work, and most likely to be subject to funding cuts); representation of women among 'Silks' or Queen's Counsel, the senior barristers; and women's issues generally such as the legal enforcement of the prohibition of FGM. Mentoring continues to be an important activity, and the Association recently responded to the government's consultation on flexible working hours for court work.

## IV. Significance

As Lady Justice Hallett puts it:

> I was called to the Bar in the 'Dark Ages' of the 1970s. By the time the Association of Women Barristers was founded in 1991, much had changed; but not enough. The same can be said for the last 25 years … I had hoped that, by 2017, there would be no need for an association dedicated to monitoring and representing the interests of women at the English Bar. I was overly optimistic. As I have travelled round the country talking to female practitioners of all ages, I have been left in no doubt that the AWB is as necessary now as it was when it was founded.[7]

In recent years, the Association has become much younger in membership and outlook, and now largely communicates in modern idiom through news posted on its website and through Facebook and Twitter, which have also become indispensable professional marketing tools even at the Bar. Unfortunately, however, this immediacy in contemporary forms of communication – motivated in part by desire to conserve the Association's restricted resources (which still depend entirely on member subscriptions) has also had a downside. The Association's printed Newsletter has been discontinued.[8]

Such economies have also enabled delivery of as many practical services to members, for example, the development of the Association's pupillage and judicial appointment advice evenings, as well as regular modest social events which enable the membership to keep in touch. The Association also plays a key role in providing information and a valuable practical communication channel by their attendance at the annual pupillage fair, its clinics to support the various stages of women barristers' career advancement, its now annual appearance in a workshop at Bar Conference each autumn and its ongoing campaigning.

This holistic advancement of women's interests has added a vibrant new dimension in the AWB's work. It is clearly an extremely positive development in supporting women at the Bar, especially given research by the Bar Council and others which details the ongoing

[7] Heather Hallett, 'Welcome from the President the Right Honourable Lady Justice Hallett' (The Association of Women Barristers' website, 2017: https://www.womenbarristers.com).

[8] Attempts are being made to locate and assemble a collection of past memorabilia, including some of the early editions of the Newsletter which record interesting perspectives on the development of the Association in serving women's interests, for deposit in the Women's Library at LSE before these are lost to future researchers.

difficulties in retention after a few years' practice.[9] As Lady Justice Hallett said, the AWB remains as relevant as ever.

## Further Reading

- *Counsel*, the monthly journal of the Bar: www.counselmagazine.co.uk.
- The Association of Women Barristers' website: www.womenbarristers.com.

[9] See, eg, Bar Council, Gender and diversity at the Bar, (Bar Council, 23 July 2015); Bar Standards Board, *Women at the Bar* (Bar Standards Board, July 2016).

# 63

# *R v Ahluwalia* (1993)

SIOBHAN WEARE

The landmark case of *R v Ahluwalia*[1] liberalised the defence of provocation for women who kill their abusive partners, and acknowledged that Battered Woman Syndrome (BWS)[2] *could be* a relevant characteristic of the defendant's for the purposes of the defence. The case began a process of law reform culminating in the abolition of the defence of provocation and its replacement with a new partial defence to murder – loss of control, found in the Coroners and Justice Act 2009.

## I. Context

Historically, domestic violence was seen as a private matter. The state and police largely steered clear of 'domestics' (usually) between husband and wife, though the issue had been raised by first-wave feminists who campaigned for, and succeeded in getting passed, the Matrimonial Causes Act 1878, allowing women to separate from violent husbands and receive maintenance.[3] However, it was not until the rise of the Women's Liberation Movement in the 1970s that the matter began to be taken seriously. The first women's refuge was opened in Chiswick in 1971, documented in Erin Pizzy's ground-breaking book *Scream Quietly or the Neighbours will Hear* (published in 1974).[4] At the same time a number of feminist organisations – including Women's Aid (established in 1974), Southall Black Sisters (established in London in 1979) and Women Against Violence Against Women (established in 1980), were set up to campaign against domestic and gender-related violence and to provide support services for women. These feminist groups co-ordinated campaigns and lobbied for the introduction of legislation and policies to support women experiencing domestic violence.

[1] *R v Ahluwalia* [1992] 4 All ER 889, [1992] EWCA Crim 1, (1993) 96 Cr App R 133.

[2] Battered Woman Syndrome can be experienced by women who suffer ongoing abuse from violent partners and 'is something akin to a state of fear, trauma and shock, characterised by anxiety and depression, a perception that death is likely, a total inability to escape and a feeling of helplessness' (Susan Edwards, 'Battered Woman Syndrome' (1992) 142 *New Law Journal* 1350).

[3] Frances Power Cobbe, 'Wife Torture in England' (1878) reprinted in Susan Hamilton (ed), *Criminals, Idiots, Women and Minors: Victorian Writing by Women on Women* (Broadview Press, 1995) 132–70.

[4] **First Women's Refuge, 1971.**

By the late 1980s quite significant progress had been made in relation to domestic violence and supporting women victims. The Domestic Violence and Matrimonial Proceedings Act 1976 enabled married women to obtain injunctions against their violent husbands to exclude them from the home.[5] However, women who killed their partners in response to the violence they experienced faced ongoing hurdles and injustices when interacting with a criminal justice system tailored to respond to male violence. In particular, abused women found it difficult to use provocation as a partial defence to murder, whilst men who killed their wives when discovering their infidelity could successfully raise the defence and receive a reduced sentence.

Women killing their male partners are a relatively rare phenomenon, especially when compared with the number of men who kill their female partners.[6] Under the law, murder is defined as the unlawful killing of another human being in the Queen's peace,[7] with the intention to either kill or cause grievous bodily harm.[8] There are multiple defences to murder, only three of which will be considered for the purposes of this landmark:

1. Self-defence, which if successful leads to a complete acquittal.
2. Provocation (now abolished and replaced with loss of control), a partial defence to murder based on loss of self-control, which reduced the offence to manslaughter if successfully used.
3. Diminished responsibility, a partial defence to murder based on the defendant suffering an abnormality of the mind, reducing the offence to manslaughter.

Before *Ahluwalia*, for women who killed their abusive partners, access to only one of these defences – diminished responsibility – was readily available, with abused women struggling to successfully use either self-defence or provocation. The use of diminished responsibility as a defence per se was unproblematic. However it pathologised the actions of women (often unnecessarily and inaccurately), and did not accurately reflect their lived experiences of acting out of fear and in response to a campaign of violence and abuse, rather than as a result of an abnormality of the mind.

Self-defence, whilst appearing prima facie to be the most appropriate defence for women who kill their abusers, was, and continues to be, precluded from use because it requires consideration of the reasonableness of the defendant's resort to force and, in particular, whether an attack was imminent when the self-defensive action was taken. This is a problematic requirement for battered women to satisfy, as many act whilst not facing a threat of imminent violence, whilst their abusers are asleep or otherwise incapacitated, for example, by intoxication, because they are too frightened to fight back whilst being threatened. They are also often perceived as reacting disproportionately in inflicting fatal violence when not facing an imminent threat. The gendered construction of this defence also 'prevents its use by women. Behind it lies an image, a stereotype, of isolated, (man to man) violence. Domestic violence is outwith this paradigm.'[9]

[5] ***Davis v Johnson* (1978).**

[6] Office for National Statistics, 'Homicide – Relationship between victim and principal suspect' (11 February 2016).

[7] Edward Coke, *The Third Part of the Institutes of the Laws of England* (Printed by Miles Flesher, 1633) 47.

[8] *R v Cunningham* [1982] AC 566.

[9] Celia Wells, 'Battered woman syndrome and defences to homicide: where now?' (1994) 14 *Legal Studies* 266, 272.

Before *Ahluwalia*, battered women were also unsuccessful in using the defence of provocation, defined most famously by Devlin J at trial in *R v Duffy* and approved by the Court of Appeal, as

> some act or series of acts, done by the dead man to the accused which would cause in any reasonable person … a sudden and temporary loss of self-control, rendering the accused so subject to passion as to make him or her for the most part not master of his mind.[10]

Section 3 of the Homicide Act 1957 codified this definition, but excluded the requirement that the loss of control be 'sudden and temporary'.

Provocation was developed in recognition of 'human frailty – that under certain circumstances everyone has the potential to suddenly "snap" and kill another person'.[11] The narrative that emerged from the case law was typically one of a jealous man discovering his wife in the act of infidelity, as in the case of *Mawgridge* in 1707: 'for jealousy is the rage of a man, and adultery is the highest invasion of property'.[12] Alongside a woman's adultery, a wife's sustained nagging was also found to be sufficient provocation in a case in 2001.[13] Thus the law on provocation was one created by men, for men, 'with emphasis on masculine metaphors of temperature, speed and pressure'.[14] Consequently the experiences of battered women who acted out of fear, rather than anger, were excluded from recognition within the defence.

Despite the exclusion of the 'suddenness' requirement from the statutory definition of provocation, the *Duffy* definition, as it came to be known, proved to be salient in subsequent case law. This meant that the defence was difficult to satisfy where there had been a lapse of time or 'cooling off period' between the provocative conduct and the defendant's actions. As with self-defence, this was problematic for women who did not kill their abusers immediately following, or during, the provocative conduct, but instead experienced a 'slow-burn reaction' to the provocation, killing their partner hours or days later whilst he was unable to fight back. Thus for women who killed their abusers, provocation, which was based around discourses of anger, did not recognise the cyclical reality of domestic abuse, in particular the woman's fear, victimisation, and paralysis. This issue came to the fore following numerous high-profile cases in the late 1980s. The injustice experienced by these women, combined with outrage at the availability of the defence of provocation for men who killed their adulterous wives, was seized upon by feminist campaigners, including Southall Black Sisters and Justice for Women, established in 1990 as 'a feminist campaigning organisation that supports, and advocates on behalf of, women who have fought back against or killed violent men'.[15]

One of the most high-profile cases was that of Sara Thornton, convicted of murder after she stabbed her husband once with a knife resulting in his death. She had suffered years of physical and emotional abuse from him and on the night she killed him in June 1989 he returned from the pub drunk, called her a 'whore', and told her to leave their home. Thornton

[10] *R v Duffy* [1949] 1 All ER 932 (CA).
[11] Danielle Tyson, *Sex, Culpability, and the Defence of Provocation* (Routledge, 2013) 26.
[12] *R v Mawgridge* (1707) Kel J 119, 84 ER 1107, 1114–15.
[13] *R v Betambeau* (unreported) Winchester Crown Court, 2 February 2001.
[14] Alison Young, 'Conjugal Homicide and Legal Violence: A Comparative Analysis' (1993) 31 *Osgoode Hall Law Journal* 761, 771.
[15] Justice for Women, 'What we do': https://www.justiceforwomen.org.uk/what-we-do/.

appealed her murder conviction in 1991 but was unsuccessful.[16] Thornton's defence counsel had sought to challenge the requirement of a 'sudden' loss of control in provocation as laid down in *Duffy*. They argued that Devlin J's wording was inappropriate in cases involving domestic abuse and provocative conduct over a prolonged period, and that in such cases it was 'misleading to talk of a sudden loss of control'.[17] The Court of Appeal rejected this argument, holding that the requirement of a 'sudden and temporary loss of control' was correct and well understood by juries. Thus the decision in *Thornton* confirmed the 'criminal law's imperviousness to the battered women's perspective'.[18]

A few months later *Ahluwalia* came before the Court of Appeal, resulting in a liberalisation of the provocation defence for women who killed abusive partners.

## II. The Landmark

On 9 May 1989, Kiranjit Ahluwalia killed her husband after experiencing severe violence and abuse from him over the 10 years of their marriage. That evening, Ahluwalia's husband had indicated that their marriage was over, demanded she give him £200, and threatened to beat her and burn her face with an iron. Ahluwalia went to bed but, unable to sleep, went to get petrol that she had previously bought and used it to set fire to her husband's bedding whilst he slept. He died several days later in hospital and she was charged with murder.

During her trial she did not give evidence and no medical evidence was introduced to support her defence, which focused on the argument that she did not intend to kill her husband or cause him serious harm, but only wanted to cause him some pain. Provocation was introduced secondarily, with reliance placed upon the abuse she experienced throughout their marriage, as well as the specific incidents on the night of the homicide. Despite the defence seeking a lesser conviction of manslaughter, Ahluwalia was convicted of murder and sentenced to life imprisonment with a minimum tariff of 12 years.

Southall Black Sisters, a not-for-profit organisation run by, and for, black and minority women, were involved in Ahluwalia's case from the outset and led her appeal. After her conviction they began to prepare her grounds of appeal as well as beginning a major campaign around the experiences of women who kill abusive partners, holding public meetings and demonstrations. They were supported by Justice for Women and the solicitor Rohit Sanghvi.

In September 1991, Ahluwalia was given leave to appeal, and her case was heard by the Court of Appeal in July 1992. Her counsel, Geoffrey Robertson QC and Andrew Nicol, appealed on three grounds:

1. That the direction in *Duffy* regarding a 'sudden and temporary loss of control' in provocation was wrong.
2. That the trial judge ignored that she was suffering from BWS, which was a characteristic relevant to, and affecting the gravity of, the provocation.

[16] *R v Thornton* (1993) 96 Cr App R 112.
[17] ibid 118.
[18] Rohit Sanghvi and Donald Nicolson, 'Battered Women and Provocation: The Implications of *R v Ahluwalia*' [1993] *Criminal Law Review* 728–38, 728.

3. That the defence of diminished responsibility should be available to her as a result of newly submitted psychiatric reports.

Her appeal succeeded on the third ground as a result of new psychiatric evidence documenting her long-standing depression due to her experiences of violence and abuse. A retrial was ordered and in September 1992, the Crown accepted Ahluwalia's plea of manslaughter on the basis of diminished responsibility. She was released immediately due to time served.

Although the first and second grounds of appeal relating to provocation were rejected, the Chief Justice, Lord Taylor, giving judgment for the Court, liberalised the requirements for provocation. In relation to the *Duffy* requirement of a 'sudden and temporary loss of self-control', the Court accepted that a delayed reaction would not in itself prove a bar to using provocation. However, Lord Taylor made it clear that 'the longer the delay … the more likely it will be that the prosecution will negative provocation'.[19] Moreover, the Court held that suffering from BWS *could be* a relevant characteristic of the defendant's for the purposes of provocation.

## III. What Happened Next

These liberalisations resulted in a flurry of appeals. Perhaps the most famous of these involved Sara Thornton, whose initial appeal, as noted above, had been dismissed. In May 1995, with the support of Justice for Women, she was granted a further appeal by the Home Secretary and her case was heard in the Court of Appeal in December 1995. Following *Ahluwalia*, the Court affirmed that BWS could 'constitute a significant characteristic relevant to how the reasonable person would have reacted to the trigger incident'[20] in cases of provocation, and ordered Thornton's conviction quashed and a re-trial held. In May 1996 at her re-trial, counsel raised the defences of both diminished responsibility and provocation, not wanting to risk only relying on provocation. The jury accepted her manslaughter plea (but it was not clear on what ground) and Thornton was released immediately due to time served.

Despite making the provocation defence more accessible to women who killed their abusers, concerns arose about the use of BWS evidence, in particular over the way that it pathologised the actions of these women. As Celia Wells argued, the use of BWS evidence 'undermines the claim that the battering itself is sufficient excuse for the loss of self-control',[21] suggesting that abused women not diagnosed with BWS would not succeed with the defence. Women therefore had to be syndromised through evidence of BWS being introduced in order to be successful with provocation, implying 'that it is their reaction to the violence which is the problem, not the violence itself'.[22]

The high-profile nature of *Ahluwalia* and *Thornton* ensured continuation of debates around the use of BWS evidence. This, combined with successful campaigns run by Justice for Women and Southall Black Sisters, and the Law Commission's review of the defence of

[19] *R v Ahluwalia* (1993) 96 Cr App R 133, 139.

[20] *R v Thornton (No 2)* [1996] 1 WLR 1174, 1175.

[21] Wells, n 9 above, 274.

[22] ibid.

provocation in 2004,[23] contributed substantially to the government announcing a review of the law of homicide in July 2005. Central to the review was the defence of provocation and concerns that the defence continued to exclude women who killed abusive partners specifically out of fear, rather than anger, or because they were suffering from BWS. Feminist campaign groups and women's organisations including Rights of Women, Refuge, and Southall Black Sisters played central roles in the consultation process, submitting contributions and publicly commenting on the issues involved. Justice for Women was particularly involved, submitting two memoranda to the House of Commons Public Bill Committee,[24] and providing oral evidence to the Committee.[25] Harriet Harman QC MP was also instrumental in the reform process as part of her wider campaign to have domestic violence placed firmly on the then Labour Government's agenda. She publicly pressed for the reforms, in particular focusing on the inequality of provocation in providing a defence for men who killed their adulterous or nagging wives.

Following the consultation process and debates in the Houses of Parliament, the Coroners and Justice Act 2009 received Royal Assent on 12 November 2009. The Act abolished provocation, replacing it with a new partial defence to murder of loss of control, found in sections 54–55. The defence requires that the defendant lost self-control as a result of a qualifying trigger, and that a person of the defendant's sex and age, with a normal degree of tolerance and self-restraint, and in the circumstances of the defendant, might have reacted in the same or similar way. Three qualifying triggers are outlined, requiring that the defendant's loss of self-control could be attributable to:

1. A fear of serious violence from the victim.
2. Things said or done (or both) which constituted circumstances of an extremely grave character and caused the defendant to have a justifiable sense of being seriously wronged.
3. A combination of factors one and two.

Rather than focusing on the defendant's characteristics (the approach taken in provocation, allowing for inclusion of BWS evidence), loss of control focuses on their circumstances. This ensures that the focus of the case remains on the violence experienced by the woman. When referring to her circumstances, the jury will need to consider the history of violence in the relationship – that is, cumulative provocation – as well as her previous behaviour in considering whether her fear of serious violence (as a qualifying trigger) is justified. Concerns around the use of BWS evidence have also been alleviated, with such evidence most likely to now be useful in relation to a plea of diminished responsibility.

In an attempt to remedy the inequality of provocation, loss of control excludes sexual infidelity as a qualifying trigger.[26] This limitation represents a major change from provocation and received criticism, particularly from within the judiciary, with concern raised that men who killed in such circumstances under the 'red mist of anger' would be

[23] Law Commission, *Partial Defences to Murder: Final Report* (Law Com No 290, 2004).

[24] Coroners and Justice Bill Committee, 'Memorandum Submitted by Justice for Women (CJ09)' (February 2009); 'Memorandum Submitted by Justice for Women (CJ20)' (February 2009).

[25] House of Commons Public Bill Committee, Coroners and Justice Bill, 4th sitting, 5 February 2009, col 103.

[26] Section 55(6)(a) of the Coroners and Justice Act 2009.

disadvantaged.[27] Consequently, this limitation around sexual infidelity was interpreted by the Court of Appeal in *R v Clinton*.[28] The Lord Chief Justice, Judge LCJ, delivering judgment for the Court, confirmed that in cases where sexual infidelity was the sole trigger for a loss of control the defence must be disregarded. However, where other things were said or done that constituted a qualifying trigger, these should be considered *in the context* of any sexual infidelity that occurred. This decision thus diluted the sexual infidelity exclusion, undermining the reasoning behind its inclusion in the 2009 Act.

## IV. Significance

*Ahluwalia* is an overwhelmingly positive legal landmark for women, beginning a process of reforms which provided increased protection for women who kill their abusive partners, and reigniting discussions around the unequal treatment of men and women within the criminal justice system. It followed decades of significant campaigning by women and feminist organisations. But like many of the landmarks in this collection, it was not the end of the story. The gendered nature of the justice system remains. This is perhaps most clearly seen in the dilution of the sexual infidelity exclusion, as well as in interpretations of the requirement to focus on the circumstances of the defendant's loss of control. This focus includes all of the abused woman's circumstances, and thus also her behaviour. Therefore, in order to be viewed as a 'true' victim of domestic abuse, a woman must conform to cultural and gendered stereotypes around who or what a battered woman is, presenting herself as faithful and devoted in her familial relationships, including with her abuser, and having previously reacted passively to the violence experienced.[29] If she is unable to do so then she may be viewed as not 'truly' fearing serious violence from her partner, and thus as undeserving of successfully using the loss of control defence. It is clear that, despite progress made, the pervasiveness of gendered stereotyping around (battered) women remains. So too do the feminist organisations and campaigns keeping these issues firmly on the public and political agenda.

## Further Reading

- Susan Edwards, 'Anger and Fear as Justifiable Preludes for Loss of Self-Control' (2010) 74 *Journal of Criminal Law* 223–41.
- Kate Fitz-Gibbon, 'Replacing Provocation in England and Wales: Examining the Partial Defence of Loss of Control' (2013) 40(2) *Journal of Law and Society* 280–305.
- Law Commission, *Murder, Manslaughter and Infanticide* (Law Com No 304, 2006).

[27] Gaby Hinsliff, 'Harman and Law Lord clash over wife killers', *The Guardian*, 9 November 2008.
[28] *R v Clinton; R v Parker; R v Evans* [2012] EWCA Crim 2.
[29] Sanghvi and Nicolson, n 18 above, 735.

# 64

## *Feminist Legal Studies* Journal, 1993

ROSEMARY HUNTER

The first issue of *Feminist Legal Studies* was published in March 1993. Its appearance was a significant moment in feminist (legal) publishing and in feminist legal studies more generally in the UK. *Feminist Legal Studies* was the first UK peer-reviewed, scholarly journal to focus specifically on feminist legal scholarship. At a time when it was difficult to get feminist work published in established 'malestream' legal journals, it provided a venue for that work and in doing so, helped to nurture and develop the field of feminist legal studies, both in the UK and internationally. I played a small part in the journal's subsequent history, having been the Academic Editor of *Feminist Legal Studies* from 2006 to 2010 and a member of the journal's editorial board from 2006 to 2012.

### I. Context

The rise of second wave feminism in the 1960s and 1970s precipitated, among other things, the blossoming of academic feminism across a range of humanities and social science disciplines and the development of women's studies as a specifically feminist, interdisciplinary field of study. Academic feminists challenged the partiality of male-defined and male-centred knowledge and knowledge-production, and instead sought to generate and promote knowledge based on the realities of women's lives. Feminist historians focused on new sites of concern – the domestic as much as the public – making women's lives the subject of history and restoring women who had been written out of history. Feminist literary scholars similarly focused on women writers, and particularly writers who had articulated women's experience. Feminist sociologists insisted on gender as an essential category of social analysis, and demonstrated the manifold ways in which social experience was gendered. Feminist philosophers contested the masculine canon of Western thought and the hierarchies and exclusions of masculine reason. The first postgraduate women's studies courses were offered by the Polytechnic of Central London in 1978 (PG Dip) and the University of Kent in 1980 (MA).

Academic legal feminism arrived on the scene relatively late. In the words of Reg Graycar:

> The law is one of the last areas of academic work to have for so long withstood the scrutiny of feminists. Whereas in the last two decades, feminist scholarship has provided important insights and new ways of seeing to the humanities and social sciences, legal scholarship has proceeded in

> apparent ignorance of, and with blissful disregard to, the concerns of women generally, and feminist modes of analysis in particular.[1]

But by the late 1970s and early 1980s in the USA, and the mid-1980s in the UK, feminist legal theory had gained at least a toehold in the academy, evidenced by the fact that in 1988, the *Index to Legal Periodicals* added 'feminist jurisprudence' to its list of subject headings.[2] The first feminist legal text to be published by British academics, Susan Atkins' and Brenda Hoggett's ***Women and the Law***, appeared in 1984.

Across the academic spectrum, however, feminist work was often regarded as marginal, not of general interest, or as intellectually suspect, lacking in rigour or academic credibility. It could be treated by non-feminist (or anti-feminist) book publishers and journal editors with indifference at best, hostility at worst. Feminists responded by setting up their own journals. The first interdisciplinary journal in women's studies, *Feminist Studies*, was published in the USA in 1972. In the UK, *Feminist Review* first appeared in 1979, describing itself as a socialist and feminist journal, 'a vehicle to unite research and theory with political practice, and contribute to the development of both'.[3]

Feminist legal scholars faced the same problems as their sisters in other disciplines. Feminist legal scholarship was considered personal, political and polemical, far from the detached objectivity required of authoritative legal scholarship,[4] or as a form of devalued women's work on a par with 'basket weaving'.[5] Doing feminist research was a career impediment and feminist legal academics were turned down for promotion, as their work was seen to lack intellectual credibility. The pages of established law journals were largely closed to feminists. Sally Sheldon, for example, recalled being told a story by a 'prominent feminist legal scholar' 'about having sent a paper to a mainstream law journal, which rejected it, saying: "No sorry, but we published something on feminism last year so we don't want anything this soon"'.[6] The response from legal feminists, again, was to set up their own journals. The *Harvard Women's Law Journal* (now the *Harvard Journal of Law and Gender*) began publishing in 1978, initially with an issue commemorating the twenty-fifth anniversary of women's admission to Harvard Law School. *The Canadian Journal of Women and the Law/Revue Femmes et Droit*, *Wisconsin Women's Law Journal* (now *Wisconsin Journal of Law, Gender and Society*) and *Berkeley Women's Law Journal* (now *Berkeley Journal of Law, Gender and Justice*) followed in 1985, and the *Yale Journal of Law and Feminism* and *Hastings Women's Law Journal* in 1989. These journals published important early feminist legal texts, including work by Christine Boyle, Ruth Colker, Lucinda Finley, Kathleen Lahey, Diana Majury, Sheila McIntyre, Mary Jane Mossman, Jennifer Nedelsky, Judy Scales-Trent and Robin West.

[1] Reg Graycar, 'Yes Virginia, There Is a Feminist Legal Literature' (1986) 3 *Australian Journal of Law and Society* 105, 106.

[2] Reg Graycar, 'Foreword' (2016) 39 *University of New South Wales Law Journal* 744, 754.

[3] Springer, *Feminist Review*: 'Aims and Scope': http://www.springer.com/social+sciences/journal/41305.

[4] Clare McGlynn, *The Woman Lawyer: Making the Difference* (Butterworths, 1998) 50.

[5] Anecdote related by one of the participants in the Women's Legal Landmarks workshop, Institute of Advanced Legal Studies, London, 17 November 2016.

[6] Sarah Lamble et al, 'Twenty Years of Feminist Legal Studies: Reflections and Future Directions' (2014) 22 *Feminist Legal Studies* 109, 126.

# II. The Landmark

The fact that feminist legal journals existed in the USA and Canada did not mean that UK feminist legal scholars had access to them, either as readers or as authors. Before journal publishing moved online in the 2000s, academics were reliant on their institutional library's hard copy subscriptions, which rarely included feminist legal journals. Academics also tended to publish in their own national journals, unless they happened to give a paper at an overseas conference and were invited to submit it to a local journal. For UK feminist legal scholars, it was therefore necessary to set up a UK feminist law journal to get their own work published.

The idea of *Feminist Legal Studies* (*FLS*) came about in conversations between Anne Bottomley, Maria Drakopoulou, Belinda Meteyard and Joanne Conaghan at the University of Kent in 1991. They set up a collective to run the journal, consisting of all the women of Kent Law School. Although only women could be on the editorial board, the Department as a whole was highly supportive of the venture. The first editorial board of *FLS* consisted of academics Anne Bottomley, Joanne Conaghan, Maria Drakopoulou, Nancy Fulton, Marianne Giles, Belinda Meteyard, Katherine O'Donovan and Joanne Scott, the Law Librarian Sarah Carter, together with PhD students Hazel Biggs, Deborah Cheney, Yves Schelhaus and Denise Twomey. In the following quotation Joanne Conaghan describes both the rationale for the journal and its feminist ethos:

> we were there to provide a support and a global resource for feminists working with law around the world … [W]e did engage in a rigorous review process but very much from the point of view of generosity and care and connectedness. And when we had all those meetings, many, many of them, years and years of them, yes there were old grudges and new ones, personality clashes galore, moans and complaints, but we always joined together. Because we were in one department, we always joined together in our sort of mutual dislike of the isolation of gender issues by our male colleagues in the department, so that always sort of bonded us together.[7]

*FLS* was published by Deborah Charles Publications, a small legal theory press established by former Kent colleague and subsequently Liverpool Law professor Bernard Jackson. As Conaghan recalls:

> The original subscription for individuals was £14 a year and we relied on subscriptions, and every year you'd get your list of subscribers and it was really nice, it was like this international community, 'Oh Look, Reg Graycar, I haven't seen her for 8 years but she's buying our journal'.[8]

The first issue published articles by a senior feminist (Katherine O'Donovan), an early career scholar (Gillian More), a PhD student (Sally Sheldon), and a man (Philip Thomas). All were British, but More's article was based on an LLM thesis written in Canada and Sheldon was studying at the European University Institute in Florence. The topics covered enduring feminist themes: reproduction, marriage, family ideology and equality law. Sheldon has described how positive and kind the review process was for her article, being rigorous but at the same time constructive and helpful – especially compared with her subsequent experience with other journals.[9] These features became hallmarks of *FLS*'s feminist approach to

[7] ibid 118.
[8] ibid 118–19.
[9] ibid 114–15.

the publication process, and particularly of the support and encouragement it offered to early career feminist legal scholars.

## III. What Happened Next

The early 1990s were a peak period for the creation of new feminist law journals. Alongside *FLS* these included *Columbia Journal of Gender and Law* (1991); *UCLA Women's Law Journal* (1991); *Circles: Buffalo Women's Journal of Law and Social Policy* (now *Buffalo Journal of Gender, Law and Social Policy*) (1992); *Southern California Review of Law and Women's Studies* (now *Southern California Review of Law and Social Justice*) (1992); *Texas Journal of Women and the Law* (now *Texas Journal of Women, Gender and the Law*) (1992); *American University Journal of Gender and the Law* (now *American University Journal of Gender, Social Policy and the Law*) (1993); *Cardozo Women's Law Journal* (now *Cardozo Journal of Law and Gender*) (1993); *Michigan Journal of Gender and Law* (1993); *Duke Journal of Gender, Law and Policy* (1994); *William and Mary Journal of Women and the Law* (1994); and the *Australian Feminist Law Journal* (*AFLJ*), which, like *FLS*, published its first issue in 1993. One important difference between these journals, however, was that US law journals are primarily managed and edited by law students, whereas *FLS* and the *AFLJ* were established and edited by academics. Notably, too, *FLS* and the *AFLJ* were the only two of these new journals to include the word 'feminist' in their titles.

*FLS* initially published two issues per year, increasing to three in 1999. As it grew and developed it was inevitably affected by changes in the academic research environment, in feminist scholarship, and in international scholarly publishing.

Changes in the academic research environment included the increasing importance and refinement of research assessment exercises in distributing funding to UK universities. Although the first Research Assessment Exercise (RAE) was held in 1986, the 1996 RAE was the first to be based solely on the qualitative assessment of research outputs submitted by eligible staff. The RAE helped to make feminist legal scholarship respectable, as it was often original and could establish claims to international excellence.[10] In turn, having consolidated a reputation for rigorous peer review, *FLS* itself became respectable as a venue for the publication of RAE outputs and recognised as the leading specialist law journal for the publication of feminist scholarship.[11] Although journal metrics must be treated with caution, *FLS*'s 'impact factor' (a figure which measures the average citation frequency of articles published in the journal in the previous two years) is now higher than that of several other leading specialist and generalist British law journals such as the *Journal of Law and Society*, *Social and Legal Studies* and the *Cambridge Law Journal*.[12]

[10] Rosemary Auchmuty, 'Feminist Stakeholders in the Law School' in Fiona Cownie (ed), *Stakeholders in the Law School* (Hart Publishing, 2010) 35, 57.

[11] See Kevin Campbell, Douglas W Vick, Andrew D Murray and Gavin F Little, 'Journal Publishing, Journal Reputation and the United Kingdom's Research Assessment Exercise' (1999) 26 *Journal of Law and Society* 470, 499; Yvette Russell in Lamble et al, n 6 above, 110.

[12] Impact factors taken from journal websites on 24 February 2017: *FLS* 0.731, *Journal of Law and Society* 0.686, *Social and Legal Studies* 0.620, *Cambridge Law Journal* 0.353.

Over time, too, many more venues opened up in the UK for the publication of feminist legal research.[13] Feminist legal conversations also became much more consistently international, and *FLS* became an important venue for the publication of work by feminist legal scholars across the common law world and beyond. While the second issue of *FLS* had included contributions from Australian and Irish authors, this internationalisation intensified in the 2000s,[14] partly because feminist publishing outlets were not necessarily available in the authors' own countries, and partly because of encouragements in some countries for academics to publish in 'international' journals. In 2009–10 the journal established an International Advisory Board with representation from Africa, Australia and New Zealand, Central and South America, Europe, India and North America.

Changes over time in academic fashions and scholarly preoccupations were inevitably reflected in the pages of *FLS*. Feminist (legal) scholarship responded to the various 'turns' in the wider academy, including the post-structuralist turn, intersectionality and anti-essentialism, the third wave, the new materialism, the affective turn, the spatial turn and more. (These changes of fashion were also reflected in the name changes of the US journals listed above, from being about 'women' to being about 'gender', and sometimes adding wider social justice concerns.) The cover of volume 1 of *FLS* simply stated 'The Editorial Board is happy to receive unsolicited articles irrespective of theme'. By the mid-2000s, *FLS* welcomed 'contributions of original feminist scholarship, both "legal" and interdisciplinary, both theoretical and substantive, aimed at an international readership'.[15] In 2008 the Editorial Board adopted a revised statement of Aims and Scope, specifying that:

> *Feminist Legal Studies* aims to publish critical, interdisciplinary, theoretically engaged feminist scholarship relating to law (broadly conceived). It has a particular interest in work that extends feminist debates and analysis by reference to critical and theoretical approaches and perspectives, including postcolonial, transnational and poststructuralist work.[16]

Rather than embracing the full spectrum of feminist legal work, therefore, it now aimed to provide space for the cutting edge of feminist legal scholarship. At around this time, too, the number and diversity of women academic staff and postgraduate students at Kent Law School were making it more difficult to maintain the earlier solidarity referred to by Conaghan, and, in the face of so many other agendas, activities and commitments, there was less of a shared interest in running a feminist law journal. The decision was ultimately taken to break the link between *FLS* and Kent Law School, and from January 2013, just before the twentieth anniversary of its first issue, *FLS* moved to a new editorial board, now made up of academics from 12 different UK institutions, with a strengthened commitment to critical race feminism and the inclusion of women of colour.

The other major change occurred as *FLS* became part of the global publishing industry. Its original publisher, Deborah Charles Publications, was ultimately sold to Kluwer, which in turn was taken over by the publishing giant Springer in the mid-2000s. This was not a comfortable transition and the editors battled to maintain *FLS*'s standards and ethos against a multinational company based in the Netherlands for whom the journal was merely a tiny part of its vast – and mainly scientific – stable of journals. In 2007, for example, the editors

[13] McGlynn, n 4 above, 51; Rosemary Hunter in Lamble et al, n 6 above, 112.
[14] Hunter in Lamble et al, n 6 above, 112–13.
[15] Rosemary Hunter, 'Editorial' (2007) 15 *Feminist Legal Studies* 1.
[16] Revised website and journal text, author's files.

wrote to the journal's publishing editor detailing six areas of dissatisfaction with the service received from Springer in recent years.[17] At around the same time, the editorial board of *FLS* actively sought a different publisher, but although Sage expressed interest, Springer refused to sell the title.

While some of the matters of concern were addressed, other problems continued and new ones arose, for example, when the publisher introduced standard formatting more appropriate to scientific journals. One of the key strategies of feminist publishing has been to give the full names of authors in footnotes and lists of references, in order to make women's contribution to scholarship visible. Springer's standard formatting, however, provided only for authors' initials, thereby reverting to the assumed masculine of supposed gender neutrality, requiring insistence on the continued use of full names in *FLS*. Similarly, the online submissions system Springer introduced needed extensive customisation to retain the kinds of categories and supportive responses developed for *FLS*'s editorial process. Moreover, unlike some other major journal publishers, the editorial fees paid by Springer were minimal and did not include any share of royalties, making it difficult for the journal to sponsor symposia or even to provide catering for editorial board meetings without university or other external support.

Above all the fact that *FLS* was a subscription journal made it practically unavailable to feminists outside the academy, outside the Anglo-Commonwealth – including to members of its International Advisory Board – and even outside the old university sector in the UK, if institutional libraries did not have or could not afford subscriptions. This limitation ultimately resulted in some members of the *FLS* editorial board breaking away to establish in 2011 the UK's second journal of feminist legal scholarship, *feminists@law*, an online open access journal built on the Open Journal System platform. This format makes the journal accessible to anyone with an internet browser, and gives the editorial board complete control over production.[18] Subsequently, *FLS*'s new editorial board has been successful in increasing the funding provided by Springer and in securing open access to editorials and other journal content.[19]

## IV. Significance

The publication of the first issue of *FLS* began a process which nurtured and provided a home for the work of successive generations of feminist scholars both in the UK and internationally. It occurred at a time when the increasing numbers of feminist legal academics had created both a need for publishing venues for their research, and a movement to meet that need by launching new publishing ventures. In turn, as university law schools began to offer more 'feminist perspectives' courses and to incorporate feminist material into mainstream courses,[20] articles from *FLS* made their way into anthologies and textbooks and onto reading lists, thereby coming to play a role in the education of future lawyers and academics.

[17] Rosemary Hunter and Joanne Conaghan to Neil Olivier, 7 November 2007, author's files.

[18] *feminists@law: an open access journal of feminist legal scholarship*: http://journals.kent.ac.uk/index.php/feministsatlaw/index.

[19] See, for example, Ruth Fletcher et al, 'Wench Tactics? Openings in Conditions of Closure' (2017) 25 *Feminist Legal Studies* 1.

[20] See McGlynn, n 4 above, 14–15.

## Further Reading

- Rosemary Auchmuty, 'Feminist Stakeholders in the Law School' in Fiona Cownie (ed), *Stakeholders in the Law School* (Hart Publishing, 2010) 35.
- *Feminist Legal Studies*: http://link.springer.com/journal/10691 (most journal content accessible only to subscribers, but some open access content available).
- Sarah Lamble et al, 'Twenty Years of Feminist Legal Studies: Reflections and Future Directions' (2014) 22 *Feminist Legal Studies* 109.

# 65

## *Barclays Bank v O'Brien* (1993)

SARAH GREER

In *Barclays Bank v O'Brien*[1] the House of Lords formulated an approach which, although far from perfect, provided some clarity for women and lenders about how the court would approach a situation where undue influence or misrepresentation by the husband had induced the woman to agree to additional borrowing on the family home. The House of Lords held that the bank was fixed with constructive notice of Mr O'Brien's misrepresentation to his wife of the amount and effect of the loan they had provided, secured upon the couple's jointly-owned home, to provide funds for a struggling company in which Mr O'Brien had an interest. In consequence, the bank could not enforce the charge against Mrs O'Brien.

Because family homes were usually held in the joint names of husband and wife after the landmark case of ***Williams & Glyn's Bank v Boland***,[2] situations where wives agreed to act as guarantor (surety) for their husband's debts had become common: in the eight years before *O'Brien*, the same issue had been before the appellate courts no fewer than 11 times. In each case, women had been persuaded, misled or compelled to agree to risk losing their family home – for most families, the major and sometimes only asset – by acquiescing to their husband's request for further borrowing from a lender, secured upon their home. This rare victory for a woman against a lender led eventually to changes in lending practice – although the protection for wives proved to be short-lived.

## I. Context

The increase in the number of cases before the decision in *O'Brien* is unsurprising given the tumultuous events in women's lives in the three decades leading up it. The Thatcher dream of a 'property-owning democracy' embodied in the Right to Buy Act 1980 and tax incentives for borrowers contributed to a rising tide of home ownership in the UK.[3] This was coupled with the deregulation of the mortgage market and the wider deregulation of the financial markets (the Big Bang reforms) in the 1970s and 1980s. Banks entered the mortgage market, which led to increased competition for and availability of mortgage funds.

[1] *Barclays Bank v O'Brien* [1994] 1 AC 180.
[2] *Williams & Glyn's Bank v Boland* [1981] AC 487.
[3] Office for National Statistics, 'A Century of Home Ownership in England and Wales' (April 2013).

They started offering riskier high-loan-to-value mortgage products, with low or no deposit required. House prices had also been rising steadily since the 1970s,[4] and this combination of factors led to the realisation that the family home was a valuable asset, which could be used to borrow money to fund other projects including small business enterprises, another priority of the Government of the time.

Throughout the 1970s and 1980s, there were a number of significant cases involving the potential problems which could arise when a couple lived in a family home owned in the sole name of one of the partners – usually the man. *Williams & Glyn's Bank v Boland* addressed the position of the wife in relation to a mortgagee seeking possession of the family home when the husband had, unknown to her, mortgaged the property and then defaulted on the mortgage. Lenders began to be more aware of the potential legal risks of sole legal ownership, when the home was also occupied by a spouse or cohabitant. As a result, to avoid being inadvertently bound by an equitable owner, they became more insistent about homes being registered in joint names.

In the era of the UK's first woman prime minister, increasing numbers of women worked outside the home,[5] and contributed more directly to the family in a way which the law recognised – economically. Women could now make a direct financial contribution to purchasing the property, by adding their earnings to their partner's, enabling couples to borrow more money from lenders by combining their borrowing power. Thus as the 1980s progressed, more family homes were purchased and owned in the names of both partners.

This trend resolved at least some of the long-standing legal difficulties for women in respect of the family home owned in the husband's sole name, but as *O'Brien* illustrates, it gave rise to other complications. Men could no longer raise funds on the family home unilaterally. Instead, they had to obtain their wife's consent to raise additional borrowing on the property as joint owner. Wives were often reluctant to agree, recognising the potential risks attached. As *O'Brien* and the cases preceding it demonstrate, this sometimes resulted in husbands – typically already in a precarious financial situation and desperate to obtain the additional borrowing – exerting increased pressure on their wives.

When *O'Brien* was heard, there was a growing acceptance – in legal form, if not in social substance – of equality between the sexes, thanks in large part to feminist campaigns in the 1970s and '80s. These decades saw Parliament pass a raft of significant equality legislation to protect women's rights in the workplace. However, in financial matters, women were still fighting for equal treatment.[6] As Lord Browne-Wilkinson recognised in *O'Brien*: in 1994 the practice of equality had not yet necessarily caught up with the ideal – and as Scott LJ observed in the Court of Appeal 'the degree of emancipation of women [was still] uneven'.[7]

## II. The Landmark

Mr and Mrs O'Brien owned their home in joint names, with a mortgage of around £25,000 secured upon it. Mr O'Brien had an interest in a company which was struggling financially.

[4] Nationwide Building Society, 'House Price Index': www.nationwide.co.uk/hpi.
[5] Office for National Statistics, 'Women in the Labour Market' (25 September 2013).
[6] See eg **Section 32 of the Finance Act 1988**.
[7] *Barclays Bank v O'Brien* [1993] QB 109, 139 (CA).

He agreed with the Bank that he would remortgage the family home as security for further lending to the company totalling £135,000: an agreement which his wife was required to sign, as joint legal owner. Mr O'Brien then set to persuading his reluctant wife to agree to the additional borrowing. In the County Court, Mrs O'Brien gave evidence that she was unhappy with the suggestion of additional secured borrowing and that she considered it a great risk. Her husband had been very insistent, and had not accepted her misgivings. She refused to agree to sign the paperwork on a number of occasions, until finally Mr O'Brien appeared in an agitated state at the church where she was arranging flowers for a wedding. She described him as 'going white and in tears' as he tried to persuade her to sign the papers.[8] He said that if she did not sign, their son, who worked in the troubled company, would lose his job, as the company would fail completely. Mr O'Brien had also misrepresented the amount of the liability significantly to his wife, saying that it would only be £60,000, and led her to believe that the loan would be repaid within three weeks. Eventually, she agreed to sign, and visited the Bank with her husband to do so.

In the course of the transaction with the Bank, nobody explained to Mrs O'Brien the possible consequences of her agreeing to remortgage her home in this way and nobody suggested to her that she should obtain independent legal advice.[9] When she went to the Bank with her husband to sign the papers, the clerk presented the documents with the pages folded back, so that Mrs O'Brien saw only where she had to sign them. She did so without reading them, and nobody suggested that she should do so. In due course the company failed and the Bank sought to recover its debt by executing the legal charge over the O'Briens' home. Mrs O'Brien claimed that the charge against her should be set aside on the grounds that she had been induced to enter into the loan agreement by her husband's undue influence and misrepresentation.

At first instance, the Bank was awarded possession. In reaching its decision to reverse the first instance judgment, the Court of Appeal identified a line of authority which assumed a special equity for married women whereby they received special protection from the courts because of their vulnerability in such situations, given the nature of the relationship between the parties. The Court of Appeal did not find that Mr O'Brien exerted undue influence over Mrs O'Brien. Although there were 'heavy family pressures' they were 'not particularly unusual or sufficient … to overset and bear down the will of Mrs O'Brien'.[10] However, Mr O'Brien had misrepresented the extent of the liability and the timescale for repayment. In addition, the Bank should have taken steps to ensure that Mrs O'Brien's consent had been truly obtained and that she had made an informed decision. As it had not done this, the Court of Appeal held that Mrs O'Brien was liable only for the amount that she believed that she had consented to: £60,000.

The Bank appealed to the House of Lords, on the grounds that – amongst other things – the concept of a 'special equity' for married women was wholly incompatible with the status of modern women. In considering the case, the House of Lords recognised that there was a balancing act between the need for Banks to be able to lend with certainty – given that the matrimonial home was a useful asset from which to raise such capital – and the need for the law to protect the vulnerable wife. Lord Browne-Wilkinson accepted that the risk of undue

[8] ibid 118.

[9] The documents included a side-letter suggesting that Mrs O'Brien take independent legal advice, but the letter was not pointed out to her, and she did not read it.

[10] [1993] QB 109, 141 (CA).

influence was greater in cases where 'sexual or emotional ties affect the free exercise of the individual's will'.[11] However, in this case, he did not see any undue influence. Mrs O'Brien was financially aware: she had handled the family's finances when Mr O'Brien had worked overseas, and had for a short time worked as an office manager. Mr O'Brien had, however, misrepresented the additional borrowing to his wife, and because the Bank had not taken reasonable steps to ensure that Mrs O'Brien had really understood the agreement that she had entered into, the Bank was fixed with constructive notice of that misrepresentation. For that reason, the Bank could not enforce its charge against Mrs O'Brien.

In reaching its decision, the House of Lords rejected the theory, derived from Australian case law,[12] of a 'special equity' in favour of married women. Unlike the Court of Appeal, it could find no legal basis for protection for such a limited class of claimants in relation to only one type of transaction. In any event, the House deemed it unnecessary to find a special equity because it laid down some clear guidelines for creditors to follow in all cases. *O'Brien* established that the lender is put upon enquiry where the transaction is not on the face of it to the financial advantage of the wife and there is a substantial risk that the husband has committed a legal or equitable wrong in obtaining the wife's consent to act as surety.

In these circumstances, the lender must take steps to advise the wife of the risk she is running and to advise her to get independent legal advice. Lord Browne-Wilkinson suggested that although these steps may vary from case to case, for future cases it would usually be sufficient for the Bank to insist that the wife 'attend a private meeting (in the absence of the husband) with a representative of the creditor at which she is told of the extent of her liability as surety, warned of the risk she is running and urged to take independent legal advice'.[13] By establishing clear guidelines, the House of Lords intended to balance the interests of the innocent creditor and the interests of the equally innocent surety wife.

*O'Brien* offered surety wives a degree of protection that they had not enjoyed previously. It did not, however, address all the underlying issues in such cases. Feminist academic commentators have observed that the decision evidences a judicial acceptance of the gendered power imbalance and of the influence which husbands routinely exert over their wives since, in order to establish 'undue' influence rather than this seemingly acceptable 'routine' influence, the case would need to be extreme. Despite Mrs O'Brien's description of the pressure put upon her by her husband in the County Court, she did not establish undue influence in the appellate courts: she did not fit the stereotype of a 'down-trodden, uneducated wife'[14] whose will had been overborne.

## III. What Happened Next

As predicted by Lord Browne-Wilkinson, lenders complained that the additional responsibility placed upon them by the House of Lords in respect of surety wives was too onerous. In the years following the case, it was evident that neither the banks nor the courts felt required to follow the *O'Brien* guidelines. In particular, the most robust protection for the surety wife – the requirement for a separate interview with her – was largely

[11] *Barclays Bank v O'Brien* [1994] 1 AC 180, 191 (HL).
[12] *Yerkey v Jones* (1939) 63 CLR 649.
[13] [1994] 1 AC 180, 196.
[14] [1993] QB 109, 117 (CA).

dispensed with: describing it as 'best practice', some judges felt it only important that the 'substance' of the *O'Brien* guidance was to be observed, and that the 'guidance ought not to be mechanically applied'.[15] Most respondents simply required the wife to seek independent legal advice. By the time that the House of Lords considered the eight conjoined appeals in *Royal Bank of Scotland v Etridge (No 2)*,[16] it was apparent that the lending institutions had quietly subverted the *O'Brien* decision.

This may partly explain the nature and focus of the discussion by the House in *Etridge*. Despite many references to the need to balance protection for vulnerable sureties against the need for certainty in business transactions, it reads as an exercise in removing lenders' responsibility to consider carefully the situation of individuals to whom they lend. The House of Lords attached no significance to the fact that each of the appeals before it had been brought by a wife against her husband, in relation to her family home. Nor did it consider the particular significance of that home to the surety wives in the context of their gender and their situation in life.

Early in their decision their Lordships sidestepped the issue of how to address and remedy the wives' complaints by saying that what happened between a husband and wife in reaching a decision to secure additional borrowing upon that home was 'not capable of regulation or investigation'.[17] The clear priority for their Lordships was to lay down guidelines – minimum requirements for lenders – which were 'clear, simple and practically operable'.[18] The *O'Brien* requirement for a private meeting with the wife was officially dispensed with, on the grounds that lenders might expose themselves to further risk by complying. The House of Lords decided that this was a job for the legal adviser, and laid down guidelines about how and what the legal adviser should explain to the wife. The lender would be protected if it proceeded on the basis of a confirmation from a solicitor that the wife had received independent legal advice.

By removing the requirement for a private meeting with the wife, *Etridge* accelerated and approved the covert process of erosion of the protection for women which had been established in *O'Brien*. Nevertheless, for better or for worse, *Etridge* seems to have reduced the number of surety wife undue influence cases before the appellate courts. The subsequent cases that have emerged in favour of the influenced surety, such as the mother/son case of *HSBC v Brown*,[19] only demonstrate the importance to lenders of following the *Etridge* guidelines carefully, and equally importantly, documenting and recording their compliance. The courts seem to have decided that the real and complex position of the surety wife is a problem consigned to history, solved by a simple lenders' checklist.

## IV. Significance

*O'Brien* was an important decision for women, because it provided a degree of protection in a very common situation, where women were persuaded or compelled to agree to risk their

[15] See Mark Pawlowski and Sarah J Greer, 'Constructive notice and independent legal advice: a study in lending institution practice' [2001] Conv 229.

[16] *Royal Bank of Scotland v Etridge (No 2)* [2001] UKHL 44,

[17] See Rosemary Auchmuty's feminist judgment in *Etridge* in Rosemary Hunter, Clare McGlynn and Erika Rackley (eds), *Feminist Judgments: from Theory to Practice* (Hart Publishing, 2010).

[18] [2001] UKHL 44, [2].

[19] *HSBC Bank PLC v Brown* [2015] EWHC 359 (Ch).

home in circumstances that were highly unlikely to benefit them or their children. It also has much wider significance: it sparked huge debate in the years after the decision. For feminists, the decision encapsulates the dilemma of whether it is better that vulnerable women have special legal treatment by virtue of their status as women, even though that marks them out as a different and unequal class, in need of special protection – in which case they are protected – or whether it is better that in order to demonstrate equality, they are not given special legal treatment – in which case they may not have a remedy at all. The case even helped to coin a new and memorable international phrase that still resonates: 'sexually transmitted debt'.[20] Feminist legal academics are broadly divided between both arguments, although all are generally in agreement, on the evidence of the case law, that institutions – whether banks or courts – continue to work to the advantage of men.

Although great injustice remains for women in economic matters,[21] the improvement in women's legal and financial status in the 25 years since *O'Brien* has done a great deal to strengthen their position in respect of home ownership. The matter perhaps remains more complicated than that. In her interviews with surety wives, Fehlberg concluded that many of them would have agreed to risk their home even if the potential consequences had been clearly explained to them. It seems that the underlying power imbalance and complexities of human relationships still remain a challenge for the courts and the women who seek redress through them.

## Further Reading


- Rosemary Auchmuty, 'Men Behaving Badly: an analysis of English Undue Influence Cases' (2002) 11(2) *Social & Legal Studies* 257–82.
- Belinda Fehlberg, *Sexually Transmitted Debt: Surety Experience and the English Law* (Clarendon Press, 1997).
- Lorna Fox, *Conceptualising Home: Theories, Laws and Policies* (Hart Publishing, 2007).


[20] See Belinda Fehlberg, *Sexually Transmitted Debt: Surety Experience and the English Law* (Clarendon Press, 1997).

[21] Not least in the gender pay gap, which the World Economic Forum estimates will take 170 years to close.

# 66

# *Webb v EMO Air Cargo (UK) Ltd (No 2)* (1994)

DEBRA MORRIS

In *Webb v EMO Air Cargo (UK) Ltd (No 2)*,[1] the House of Lords held that dismissing a pregnant woman was contrary to the **Sex Discrimination Act 1975**, even though a man in similar circumstances (that is, unable to work for a time) would also have been dismissed. Significantly, it was finally recognised that no comparison (for example, to a sick man) was necessary to establish discrimination against a pregnant woman.

## I. Context

In 1995, when this landmark judgment was delivered, women's employment levels were rising, with over 62 per cent of women aged 16–64 participating in the labour market.[2] The Women's Liberation Movement had been campaigning to support women working outside the home, learning new skills and receiving a decent wage, and most of the shift towards more working women and fewer working men happened between 1971 and 1991.[3] Many women would experience pregnancy during their working lives, often more than once. Motherhood was to be encouraged, to ensure a strong population, but working mothers also needed to be accommodated and the law began to recognise this, with legislation such as the Sex Discrimination Act 1975 being enacted. Enlightened employers could also see the economic benefits of retaining working mothers, with the alternative being to replace them through costly recruitment and additional training.

In 1987, the total fertility rate (the number of children that would be born to each woman if current fertility patterns persisted throughout her child-bearing life) was predicted to be 1.81.[4] In July of that year, Carole Webb, who had recently joined the work-force, was surprised to discover that she was pregnant, but was even more surprised when told that she would lose her job as a result.[5] She decided not to accept this outcome and

[1] *Webb v EMO Air Cargo (UK) Ltd (No 2)* [1995] 1 WLR 1454.

[2] 10 years earlier, in 1985, the figure was 56%; Office for National Statistics, 'Labour Market Statistics' (February 2015).

[3] Office for National Statistics, 'Full report – Women in the labour market' (September 2013).

[4] Office for National Statistics, 'Birth Summary Tables, England and Wales 2010' Table 1.

[5] Kirsty Walker, 'The five women who turned the tide', *The Express*, 27 May 2000.

consequently her case considered the correct approach under the Sex Discrimination Act 1975 to the unfavourable treatment of a pregnant woman in the workplace. Did her treatment need to be compared with how a man would be treated in comparable circumstances so that an employer would have a defence if such a man would have been treated no more favourably? Or did the fact that pregnancy is gender-specific mean that unfavourable treatment would amount to sex discrimination without the need for a comparison with how a man might be treated? Earlier cases used the male comparison approach[6] despite the fact that logic would dictate that the normality of pregnancy and the rarity of sickness are not comparable, not least because many working women will experience pregnancy more than once whereas many working men will not even suffer one bout of sickness that results in long-term leave.

In both the Employment Appeal Tribunal[7] and the Court of Appeal,[8] Carole Webb unsuccessfully challenged the initial ruling that there was no unlawful discrimination since a man similarly incapable of working for medical or other reasons would have been dismissed. This was despite the (then) recent decision of the Court of Justice of the European Union (CJEU) in Case C-177/88 *Dekker v Stichting Vormingscentrum voor Jonge Volwassen (VJV-Centrum)*,[9] which had determined that it is a breach of the Equal Treatment Directive to refuse to employ a woman because of the possible adverse consequences for the employer of employing a pregnant woman.

Although Carole Webb had been employed indefinitely, she was initially recruited to replace another employee due to go on maternity leave. In the House of Lords, the judges considered that she was not dismissed simply because she was pregnant, but because her pregnancy meant that she would not be available for work during the critical period. In such circumstances, it was held that, as a matter of UK law, it was legitimate to make a comparison between the non-availability of a woman due to pregnancy and the non-availability of a man at the relevant time. The House of Lords accepted that the UK courts were required to construe domestic legislation in any field covered by an EU Directive so as to accord with its interpretation laid down by the CJEU, if that could be done without distorting the meaning of the domestic legislation. In this case, however, the judges were unclear whether the CJEU would regard the fundamental reason for dismissal as being the employee's unavailability for work or her pregnancy. They were uncertain as to how much weight, if any, should be given to the reasons why Carole Webb was recruited. Accordingly, the House of Lords in *Webb v EMO Air Cargo (UK) Ltd (No 1)*[10] referred questions on the construction of Article 2(1) of the Equal Treatment Directive, to the CJEU under what is now Article 267 of the Treaty on the Functioning of the EU.[11] Under Article 2(1), the principle of equal treatment means that there shall be no discrimination whatsoever on grounds of sex, either directly or indirectly. Additionally, Article 5(1) provides that the application of the equal

[6] See eg *Turley v Allders Department Stores* [1980] ICR 66, holding that it was impossible to compare the two cases.

[7] *Webb v EMO Air Cargo (UK) Ltd* [1990] ICR 442 (EAT).

[8] *Webb v EMO Air Cargo (UK) Ltd* [1992] 2 All ER 43 (CA). Applying *Hayes v Malleable Working Men's Club and Institute* [1985] ICR 703.

[9] Case C-177/88 *Dekker v Stichting Vormingscentrum voor Jonge Volwassen (VJV-Centrum)* [1990] ECR I-3941.

[10] *Webb v EMO Air Cargo (UK) Ltd (No 1)* [1993] 1 WLR 49.

[11] Formerly Article 177 of the EEC Treaty.

treatment principle with regard to working conditions, including those governing dismissal, means that men and women shall be guaranteed the same conditions without discrimination on grounds of sex.

The CJEU in Case C-32/93 *Webb v EMO Air Cargo*[12] decided that pregnancy was a condition unique to women, and dismissal on grounds of pregnancy amounted to direct discrimination on grounds of sex. They held that pregnancy is not in any way comparable with a pathological condition, and even less so with unavailability for work on non-medical grounds. The Equal Treatment Directive precluded dismissal of an employee who was recruited for an unlimited term with a view, initially, to replacing another employee during the latter's maternity leave and who could not do so because, shortly after recruitment, she was herself found to be pregnant. It was irrelevant that the employer would have dismissed a male employee engaged for this purpose who required leave of absence at the relevant time for medical or other reasons.

## II. The Landmark

When the case returned to the House of Lords, the judges were able to construe the Sex Discrimination Act 1975 so as to accord with the CJEU decision as to the meaning of the European legislation. The House of Lords therefore allowed Carole Webb's appeal from the decision that she had not been discriminated on the ground of sex, and remitted the case to an industrial tribunal to assess compensation. The decision accords with the CJEU ruling that it is unlawful sex discrimination to dismiss a woman who, having been employed for an indefinite period, was immediately afterwards found to be pregnant. This would apply even if she was initially recruited specifically to replace another employee due to go on maternity leave.

Lord Keith, however, emphasised the fact that both the CJEU and the Advocate General had considered it to be relevant that Carole Webb had been employed for an indefinite period. That suggested the possibility of a distinction between such a case and the case where a woman's absence due to pregnancy would have led to her being unavailable for the *whole* of the period for which she had been engaged. Lord Keith suggested that the outcome may well have been different in that situation, adding that if this were not the correct approach then surprising results could follow. He gave the example of an employer wishing to employ someone for a specific and fixed period, such as Wimbledon fortnight or the Olympic games. If one of the applicants was expecting a baby on the first day of the event, it seemed absurd, to his Lordship, that she should be able to complain of unlawful sex discrimination if she were not selected on the basis of her unavailability, simply because she was pregnant. He was of the view that were the distinction not made – so that an employer would still be unlawfully discriminating in refusing to employ a woman who was employed for a fixed period during the whole of which she would be unable to work due to pregnancy – 'the result would be likely to be perceived as unfair to employers and as tending to bring the law on sex discrimination into disrepute'.[13]

[12] Case C-32/93 *Webb v EMO Air Cargo* [1994] ECR I-3567.
[13] *Webb (No 2)*, n 1 above, [1995] 1 WLR 1454, 1459.

## III. What Happened Next

The CJEU had made it clear that, for the purpose of EU law, pregnancy discrimination is sex discrimination. Eventually, the House of Lords, in a decision predicted at the time to be a 'landmark',[14] had no choice but to apply this interpretation. The CJEU later also held that the protection applied to those with contracts for both fixed and indefinite periods.[15] Counsel for Carole Webb in the House of Lords, Stephen Sedley (later Sedley LJ), commented:

> My junior, Laura Cox (now Cox J) and I had known from the start that we were going to lose at home but would eventually win in Europe. What made the difference was the English courts' focus on conventional wisdom and pragmatism, and the European court's focus on principle and underlying purpose – a form of choice with which courts with constitutional underpinnings are perhaps more familiar than the English courts are, or at least were until the Human Rights Act 1998 came into force.[16]

In some ways, the decision has been overtaken by events. Since this case, statutory rights have been strengthened. Nevertheless, even though pregnancy-connected dismissals are now automatically unfair,[17] it often remains beneficial to claim both sex discrimination[18] and unfair dismissal. Unlike the caps on unfair dismissal awards,[19] compensation for sex discrimination is not subject to a statutory maximum and there is the additional possibility of recovering damages for injury to feelings.

Along with Gabrielle Defrenne (a Belgian flight attendant who successfully challenged her employer's women-only compulsory retirement age)[20] and Helen Marshall (who successfully challenged her dismissal on the basis that she had passed state pension age),[21] Carole Webb has been described as one of 'three woman litigants who have contributed much to the state of EC equality law'.[22] It took the dedicated Carole Webb eight years and a trip to Luxembourg (the location of the CJEU) to win her case. Her tenacity is to be admired, especially when one learns that she was only a teenager when she was told that she would be sacked for being pregnant. Her counsel later noted: 'Carole Webb's child will have been almost eight years old by the time the House of Lords finally gave judgment in her favour; but perhaps the compensation she finally recovered will have paid for a family holiday.'[23] In fact, we know that she has a framed copy of the cheque for £7,500 which she eventually received in compensation.[24]

[14] Elizabeth Buie, 'Pregnancy: illness or unique condition?', *The Herald*, 20 October 1995.
[15] Case C-438/99 *Maria Luisa Jiménez Melgar v Ayuntamiento de Los Barrios* [2001] ECR I-6915.
[16] Stephen Sedley, 'Constitutional Law and the Right to Equality' (2014) 13 *Equal Rights Review* 11, 18.
[17] See now sections 99 and 108 of the Employment Rights Act 1996.
[18] Any unfavourable treatment because of pregnancy, pregnancy-related sickness or maternity leave is unlawful under section 18 of the Equality Act 2010. The Recast Equal Treatment Directive 2006/54/EC also prohibits less favourable treatment of women related to pregnancy or maternity leave.
[19] Section 124 of the Employment Rights Act 1996.
[20] See eg Case 80/70 *Defrenne v Belgium* [1971] ECR 445.
[21] See eg Case 152/84 *Marshall v Southampton & Southwest Hampshire Area Health Authority (Teaching)* [1986] ECR 723.
[22] Holly Cullen and Andrew Charlesworth, 'Portia's Daughters: The Role of the Individual Litigant in Developing European Community Sex Discrimination Law' (1994–95) 97 *West Virginia Law Review* 751, 752. She is later referred to as a 'Euro-heroine' (770).
[23] Sedley, n 16 above.
[24] Walker, n 5 above.

When the CJEU decision was delivered, the chair of the Equal Opportunities Commission said: 'It will have major implications for employers who will need to change their employment culture and practices'.[25] Unfortunately, that is a message that still needs to be brought home. In 2016, the Equality and Human Rights Commission (EHRC) published results of research which investigated the prevalence and nature of pregnancy discrimination and disadvantage in the workplace.[26] While the majority of employers reported that they were firm supporters of female staff during and after pregnancy and found it easy to comply with the law, 77 per cent of mothers – an increase from 45 per cent in a similar survey 10 years earlier[27] – said that they had a negative or possibly discriminatory experience related to pregnancy or maternity leave. In the context of this landmark specifically, 11 per cent of mothers reported being dismissed, made compulsorily redundant where others in their workplace were not, or treated so poorly that they felt that they had to leave their job. There is a clear difference between employers' views on how easy it is to protect women from being treated unfavourably and the extent to which mothers feel that they have been protected. These experiences adversely affect the lives of individuals and their families, but also mean that businesses lose skilled and productive workers, who may well be deterred from bringing employment tribunal claims.[28]

One notable feature of this landmark is that the applicant was represented throughout by her local community law centre. This is in contrast to many key cases which have resorted to EU law to promote gender equality, where support has come from the Equal Opportunities Commission (now the EHRC) or a UK trade union. The many pressures now placed on law centres, including increased demand, lack of available funding and reductions in legal aid, mean that is highly unlikely that such a case would be supported again.[29] There is also a concern as to what the future may hold, once the UK has left the EU, for women whose maternity leave may be perceived by a potentially business-friendly government as a cost that employers would prefer to avoid.[30] Some commentators have begun to talk of the possibility of the 'return of the sick man'.[31]

## IV. Significance

*Webb* is significant because it meant that employers could no longer excuse unfavourable treatment of women who were pregnant or on maternity leave by reference to how sick or

[25] Frances Gibb, 'Landmark victory for woman sacked when pregnant', *The Times*, 15 July 1994.

[26] Equality and Human Rights Commission, 'Pregnancy and Maternity-Related Discrimination and Disadvantage: Summary of key findings' (HM Government, 2016).

[27] Equal Opportunities Commission, 'Greater expectations – final report of the EOC's investigation into discrimination against new and expectant mothers in the workplace' (EOC, 2005).

[28] At least fees for bringing employment tribunal cases (introduced in 2013) have been abolished, following the Supreme Court Decision in *R (UNISON) v Lord Chancellor* (Equality and Human Rights Commission Intervening) [2017] UKSC 51, which held that the fees were unlawful.

[29] The 2016 Annual Report of Hillingdon Law Centre, that supported Carole Webb, described the last year as 'one of the toughest the Law Centre has ever encountered.'

[30] See eg Robert Wintemute, 'Goodbye EU Anti-Discrimination Law? Hello Repeal of the Equality Act 2010?' (2016) 27 *King's Law Journal* 387.

[31] Eg Rachel Crasnow QC, 'Brexit and Mrs Webb: Return of the sick man versus pregnant woman?' (Cloisters Blog, 22 June 2016).

incapacitated men would be treated. The decision finally put paid to the idea that a pregnant woman should be equated with a sick man.

Looking back, we can appreciate how the English courts made heavy weather of this issue. If discrimination is because of pregnancy, it must, by definition, be sex discrimination because only one sex can experience it. Also, even if a man who required time off for any reason would be treated equally unfavourably, the grounds for his treatment would not be his sex. The sex discrimination comes in treating a pregnant woman unfavourably on grounds of her pregnancy. That a man is treated equally badly is irrelevant as a defence. As Anne Morris commented at the time, 'Nowhere was the reluctance to promote equality of opportunity for pregnant workers more apparent than in the long, tortuous saga of Mrs Webb'.[32]

*Webb* is a landmark decision because it emphasises the reality that employers must accept: that pregnancy is a normal part of the lives of many working women. Despite contemporary newspaper reports referring to the employer in this landmark case being 'hit by double baby shock',[33] pregnant workers are a standard feature of the workplace and employers must learn to accept them as such. Any time off due to pregnancy will form only a small proportion of a woman's total working life and must be accommodated by employers. The introduction of shared parental leave rights in 2015,[34] which now allow a mother to transfer periods of leave to the father, has the potential to further normalise pregnancy and work, although take-up rates for fathers are likely to remain low.[35]

In 1994, Carole Webb commented on her own CJEU victory, saying 'I feel relief that somebody's backed me after all this time … All this fighting's got to go somewhere. It's got to help other women who get pregnant'.[36] The 2016 results of the EHRC research remind us that this fight continues.

## Further Reading

- Clare McGlynn, 'Pregnancy dismissals and the *Webb* litigation' (1996) 4(2) *Feminist Legal Studies* 229.
- Anne Morris, 'The death throes of the sick man: *Webb v EMO Air Cargo (UK) Ltd (No 2)*' [1995] 5 *Web Journal of Current Legal Issues.*
- Erika Szyszczak, 'The Status to be Accorded to Motherhood: *Case C-32/93, Webb v EMO Air Cargo (UK) Ltd*' (1995) 58 *Modern Law Review* 860.

[32] Anne Morris, 'The death throes of the sick man: *Webb v EMO Air Cargo (UK) Ltd (No 2)*' [1995] 5 *Web Journal of Current Legal Issues.*

[33] Anthony Doran, 'Euro defeat for firm hit by double baby shock', *Daily Mail* (London, 20 October 1995).

[34] As a result of Children and Families Act 2014, Pt 7.

[35] Women and Equalities Committee, *Report on Gender Pay Gap* (HC 2015–16, 584) [156].

[36] Clare Dyer, 'Bosses Who Sack Mothers-to-be Risk Huge Claims', *The Guardian*, 15 July 1994.

# 67

# First Woman to Lead a Top 10 Law Firm in England and Wales, Lesley MacDonagh, 1995

STEVEN VAUGHAN

In 1995, Lesley MacDonagh was appointed as the managing partner of Lovell White Durrant (now Hogan Lovells).[1] It was the first time a woman had been elected to lead a top 10 law firm in England & Wales. At the time of her appointment, the firm comprised 1400 partners and associate lawyers spread across nine offices in Europe and Asia. By the time MacDonagh stepped down as managing partner, 11 years later, Lovells had doubled in size, due mostly to its merger with German firm Boesebeck Droste, which she led at the beginning of the millennium. MacDonagh was voted 'Legal Business Managing Partner of the Year' for the year 2000 and was the first woman elected as a member of the Justinians, a previously all-male legal dining club.

## I. Life

Born in April 1952, Lesley MacDonagh joined Lovell White & King (as it then was) in 1978. A real estate and environmental law specialist, she was made a partner by the firm in 1981 (the firm's second woman partner),[2] became head of the firm's property, planning and environmental practices in 1987, and joined Lovells' executive committee in 1993. At the time of her appointment as Lovells' managing partner, MacDonagh had three children (the youngest was nine months old) and had her fourth child during her second term as managing partner.[3]

There were no legal connections in her family. Her father was a Dorset businessman, although her mother, as MacDonagh recounted in an interview with Elizabeth Cruickshank

[1] A role she shared initially with fellow managing partner, Michael Maunsell ('Glass ceiling shattered – Lesley MacDonagh, the first woman to become managing partner of a top ten City firm', *Law Society Gazette*, 8 February 1995).

[2] Harriet Maunsell, the first woman partner at the firm, was appointed a year earlier.

[3] Indeed, the visibility of her family responsibilities in the reporting of her appointment and later interviews is striking (cf Clare McGlynn, *The Woman Lawyer: Making the Difference* (Butterworths, 1998) 100–103).

in 2003, 'worked in the RAF for a while, so perhaps she was a bit of a role model'.[4] It was 'a complete outsider' who suggested that she might have some legal talent, a town clerk at a local authority for whom MacDonagh had worked during a six-month internship. Eschewing university, the local authority sponsored MacDonagh's qualification as a solicitor by the apprenticeship route (through five years of 'articles') and paid for her College of Law fees.

Away from her practice, MacDonagh has served on various boards and committees, holding a number of concurrent non-executive directorships of FTSE 100 and FTSE 250 companies. She was a Governor of the London School of Economics, a member of the Property Advisory Group for the UK Government, and a Council Member of the Law Society (there one of eight women out of 75 members). She was also a Supervisory Board Member of the Citizenship Foundation and is currently a trustee of Sadler's Wells. With her husband, another Lovells partner, MacDonagh spends her spare time renovating old houses and talks of her love for shopping, and her 'feminine side', when interviewed about her life away from work.[5]

## II. Context

The number of women solicitors did not begin to grow markedly until the 1970s, but by 1980 the proportion of new solicitors who were women equalled the number of law graduates who were women.[6] Rosalind Bax became the first female partner of an elite law firm in 1971 (at what was then Coward Chance and is now Clifford Chance, a top five law firm). By the time of MacDonagh's appointment in the late 1990s, women made up just under a third of the solicitors' profession, and 15 per cent of partners in private practice.[7] By 2000, they numbered 17 per cent of partners in the 100 biggest firms in England and Wales.

Today, women law students outnumber male law students (10:6), women trainee solicitors hold over 60 per cent of training contracts,[8] and the number of practising women solicitors in 2016 equalled (for the first time) the number of practising male solicitors.[9] The same, however, is not true of women partners in law firms. Episodic research by the trade publication *The Lawyer* has shown that the proportion of partners at the UK's top 100 law firms who are women stayed static at 22 per cent in the five years 2012–17, despite the introduction of aspirational targets by many firms (and some limited regulatory efforts in relation to diversity by the Legal Services Board and the Solicitors Regulation Authority).[10] Little change has thus occurred in the last 20 years.

[4] 'Lesley McDonagh' in Elizabeth Cruickshank, *Women in the Law: Successful Career Management* (Law Society Publishing, 2003) 190.

[5] ibid 195–96.

[6] Richard L Abel, 'England & Wales' in Richard L Abel and Phillip SC Lewis (eds), *Lawyers in Society* (Beard Books, 1988) 36.

[7] Erika Rackley, *Women, Judging and the Judiciary: From Difference to Diversity* (Routledge, 2013) 46.

[8] Normally, a two-year apprenticeship post-university as part of the pathway to becoming a solicitor.

[9] Law Society, *Annual Statistical Report 2016* (April 2017).

[10] 'The UK 200 Diversity Audit', *The Lawyer*, November 2015. On diversity regulation, see: Steven Vaughan, 'Going Public: Diversity Disclosures by Large Law Firms' (2015) 83 *Fordham Law Review* 101.

The rise of the 'mega' law firm has been one of the most interesting and important changes to the legal profession in England and Wales in the last five decades. Until 1967, law firms could, by statute, have no more than 20 partners. Since then, there has been massive expansion in corporate finance law firms. The lawyers who work for these firms bill thousands of hours each year, working late into the night and many weekends. They are paid well for their efforts, with equity partners (those who own the firm) at some 'mega' law firms taking home millions of pounds each year. Numerous commentators have reflected on the 'heterosexual masculinity' which pervades these firms and which is said to be one of the reasons why so few women make it to the top.[11] This is despite 'feminisation' (and the general opening up of the profession to 'outsiders') being one of the other significant trends in the legal profession over the last five decades. At the top end, the largest law firms have been accused of embedding and encouraging 'macho' ways of working (long hours, casual sexism, a drinking culture and so on) to the detriment of women lawyers who are said to face a lifetime of formal and informal processes and initiatives that act as barriers to their advancement in these practices.[12] It is notable, but unsurprising, that the trade publication the *Law Society Gazette*, in an article to mark her ground-breaking appointment, included, without comment, a fellow Law Council member's description of MacDonagh: 'Oh yes, blonde, spikey hair, very tasty' alongside its own description of her as 'a good looking woman and a very snappy dresser, [who] cuts quite a dash amongst the "suits" on the Law Society's Council'.[13]

At the same time, these mega law firms appear relatively impervious to pressure to change. The clients of large law firms have a powerful role in deciding exactly who works for them and what work is done by which of their lawyers.[14] Despite this, the ability for demand-side diversity drivers (that is, clients improving the diversity of their service providers via terms of engagement through, for example, requiring a woman partner to be present on work done for them) to lead to positive change has so far been limited. The exact causes for this intractability are unclear. The results are more so. In 2015, during a panel session on women and senior management inside law firms at the Global Law Summit, celebrating 800 years of Magna Carta and the rule of law, the General Counsel of Yum! Brands, Sarah Nelson-Smith, observed that, 'In our last panel review [where businesses choose the law firms who will work for them on a recurring basis] we met more people named Mark than women'.

## III. What Happened Next

MacDonagh spent 11 years (three terms) as Lovells' managing partner, stepping down in 2006. In the accounts of her time as managing partner, much is made of MacDonagh's oversight of the firm's international expansion (via mergers with other law firms in Germany,

[11] Hilary Sommerlad and Peter Sanderson, *Gender, Choice and Commitment: Women Solicitors in England and Wales and the Struggle for Equal Status* (Dartmouth Publishing, 1998) 199.

[12] Hilary Sommerlad, Lisa Webley, Daniel Muzio, Jennifer Tomlinson and Lizz Duff, *Diversity in the legal profession in England and Wales: a qualitative study of barriers and individual choices* (Legal Services Board, 2013).

[13] *Law Society Gazette*, n 1 above.

[14] See: Joanne P Braithwaite, 'The Strategic Use of Demand-side Diversity Pressure in the Solicitors' Profession' (2010) 37(3) *Journal of Law and Society* 442.

Paris and the Netherlands) and her management of the firm's move to a custom-built, flag-ship office space on Holborn Viaduct. Much is also made of her love of detail, and of her views on the importance of the right culture in the workplace. As MacDonagh said in an interview with *The Lawyer* in 2001,

> I'm very keen on lifestyle issues, trying to make sure that it's a good place to work. Obviously, it's a place you come to work and not a holiday camp. But there are cultures and behaviours that you can reinforce. Courtesy and fun are catching – if someone is fun, you're likely to pass that on.[15]

Not that she was entirely unaware of her novelty as a woman. In a candid 'day in the life' report in 2002, she notes

> 10.45 Walk a few hundred yards from our offices, don hard hat and fetching day-glo jacket to check out progress on the fitting-out of our 300,000sq ft new London headquarters. … I have to check out the proposed computer room (which is a part of the site women don't usually visit …) and try not to let my eyes be drawn to the builders' pin ups of scantily clad ladies. I note that I win more points on this part of the agenda, due to the distraction levels of others (males) in the team. Resolve to hold whole of next meeting in computer room.[16]

While MacDonagh was only the second woman partner made up at Lovells, she refused to accept a glass ceiling (at her firm).[17] Indeed, in various interviews (while acknowledging that gendered discrimination is present elsewhere in the legal profession) MacDonagh has attributed the lack of women peers to a lifestyle choice. She maintained that rather than being blocked by prejudice, many women with family commitments had 'no inclination to get involved with partnership'.[18] Heteronormative and highly-gendered view of family life aside, this view is not uncommon. Nor is it without (some) foundation. Data collected by the Law Society and research on diversity in the profession consistently suggests that the biggest drop-off point for women lawyers is when they are in their late 20s and early 30s, often for family-related reasons. Since the mid-1990s a number of law firms have taken steps to try and encourage women to stay on in practice, through a combination of: mentoring schemes (often under the auspices of a firm's 'women's network'); increasing commitment to flexible and part-time working; the introduction of maternity provisions (often for the first time) into partnership agreements; return to work schemes; and public declarations of aspirational targets.[19]

These have had varying degrees of success. In 2017, 10 law firms in the UK top 200 have partnerships that are at least 50 per cent women, including Kingsley Napley, a top 100 firm, which has women in both senior partner and managing partner roles, and where three-quarters of the firm's lawyers are women. At the top 100 law firms, women make up

[15] 'Lady of little leisure', *The Lawyer*, 1 October 2001.

[16] 'Day in the Life: Lesley MacDonagh, managing partner, international law firm' (efinancialcareers, 22 April 2002): https://news.efinancialcareers.com/uk-en/7405/day-in-the-life-lesley-macdonagh-managing-partner-international-law-firm/.

[17] See eg Sharon Wallach, 'First woman among equals', *Independent*, 8 February 1995; Criukshank, n 4 above, 192.

[18] 'Research shows stagnation in number of female partners working at large firms', *Law Society Gazette*, 31 July 2001.

[19] See further McGlynn, n 3 above, 93–124. At present, Ashurst, Eversheds, Herbert Smith Freehills (HSF), Pinsent Masons and Taylor Wessing are aiming for 25% women partners, while Berwin Leighton Paisner, Clifford Chance, Clyde & Co and Norton Rose Fulbright are aiming for a more ambitious 30%.

25 per cent or more of the equity partnership at 24 firms. As of July 2017, nine women hold senior management roles in UK top 50 law firms.[20] Three of these are women at UK top 20 firms. There has yet to be a woman senior or managing partner at a 'magic circle' law firm (the top five in the UK).

## IV. Significance

In a sector that is known for its macho, long-hours culture, the appointment of a woman as managing partner of a top 10 law firm in 1995 was striking. The successes of Lovells during MacDonagh's time as managing partner (including significant international expansion and significant increases in partnership profits) are proof (if such proof was ever needed) that a woman can lead an elite law firm; and lead it well. MacDonagh's life away from the office (as a mother to four children) is evidence that it is also possible for a woman to combine a family with elite law firm management (such a combination seeming to be a given for men in law firms).

> One of the things I'm happiest about is that I haven't had to abandon my family or my career for the other. I have a rich family life, but I enjoy coming to the office every day. Children are such a great relaxer. As you walk in the door they require you to focus on them immediately. It's a wonderful mind-clearer.[21]

### Further Reading

- Sharon C Bolton and Daniel Muzio, 'Can't Live with 'Em; Can't Live without 'Em – Gendered Segmentation in the Legal Profession' (2007) 41(1) *Sociology* 47.
- 'Lesley MacDonagh' in Elizabeth Cruickshank, *Women in the Law: Successful Career Management* (Law Society Publishing, 2003) 190–96.
- Hilary Sommerlad, Lisa Webley, Daniel Muzio, Jennifer Tomlinson and Liz Duff, *Diversity in the legal profession in England and Wales: a qualitative study of barriers and individual choices* (Legal Services Board, 2013).

[20] HSF CEO Sonya Leydecker; Berwin Leighton Paisner managing partner Lisa Mayhew; Addleshaw Goddard senior partner Monica Burch; CMS Cameron McKenna senior partner Penelope Warne; Hogan Lovells London managing partner Susan Bright; Stephenson Harwood chief executive, Sharon White; Withers managing director, Margaret Robertson; Trowers & Hamlins senior partner Jennie Gubbins; and Shoosmiths' CEO, Claire Rowe.

[21] Lesley MacDonagh in Wallach, n 17 above.

# 68

# Fifteenth Amendment of the Constitution Act 1995

LAURA CAHILLANE

The Fifteenth Amendment of the Constitution Act 1995 removed the ban on divorce from the Irish Constitution. It was the second attempt at removing the ban; the first in 1986, ended with a substantial victory for the no-divorce campaigners. This was perhaps surprising: by the 1980s, Ireland stood apart; most other Western countries had long since introduced divorce laws. When the referendum came, one would have assumed that there would be a strong vote for divorce in Ireland. In fact, the proposal was easily defeated and the majority (including the majority of women) voted against removing the ban in 1986.

By the time of the second referendum in 1995, a number of changes had taken place which had liberalised laws and altered attitudes to women. For example, women had won the right to sit on juries, and to use contraception, marital rape had been criminalised, gender discrimination had been legislated for, **Mary Robinson** had been elected as President of Ireland, and the Irish Supreme Court had allowed a 14-year-old rape victim to travel abroad for an abortion.[1] The 1995 campaign was presented as a women's rights issue and a continuation of the fight for freedom of choice for women and while the proposal passed with only the narrowest of margins, the victory demonstrates, in a microcosmic sense, that the position and status of women in modern Ireland had changed forever.

## I. Context

Before Irish Independence, as Ireland was a part of Great Britain, a person domiciled in Ireland could petition the British Parliament for a divorce by private bill.[2] However this was a very expensive process and divorce was rare. While the new Irish Free State Government did not openly ban divorce (and the 1922 Constitution was silent on the issue), the first petitions were never progressed and no further petitions were received. Thus, while divorce was not prohibited in the Irish Free State, it was not practically possible either.

[1] *Attorney General v X* [1992] 1 IR 1. See further **Thirty-sixth Amendment to the Irish Constitution, 2018**.
[2] The **Divorce and Matrimonial Causes Act of 1857** regulated divorce in England and Wales but this was never extended to Ireland.

In 1937 the new Constitution, Bunreacht na hÉireann, was promulgated and this document placed a new emphasis on the family, pledging to protect it and declaring that it possessed 'inalienable and imprescriptible rights antecedent and superior to all positive law.' This has been interpreted as the family based on marriage, with another provision pledging to 'guard with special care the institution of Marriage, on which the Family is founded, and to protect it against attack'. Moreover, for the first time, there was an explicit ban on divorce. Article 41.3.2 stated 'No law shall be enacted providing for the grant of a dissolution of marriage'.[3] The then Taoiseach, Eamon De Valera's, vision of women as 'comely maidens' abounded; women were expected simply to marry and produce children.[4] The institution of marriage was highly respected, and unhappy or violent marriages were conveniently ignored. Of course, in reality separation existed, though it was usually disguised by the man 'going to England for work.'

The problem was that while couples did in fact separate, there was no legal structure around separation, division of property and assets, child custody, etc. This meant all of these issues had to be sorted out informally, and only if the couple could come to an agreement on such issues. Inevitably, many couples did not. The idea of providing for divorce meant providing the scaffold which would give rights to women in the context of a marital separation, provide a legal basis for dealing with property etc, and allow for the possibility of remarriage. One major downfall of the first divorce campaign, as we will see below, was that this legal scaffold had yet to be erected.

In 1986, the Fine Gael-Labour coalition government proposed a referendum to remove the ban. Opinion polls indicated that the proposal would be successful and so campaigning was limited. The Council for the Status of Women[5] supported the measure, but did not actively campaign. Apart from this organisation, women in favour of the amendment were not generally organised. A few high-profile women such as **Mary Robinson** (later to become the first woman President of Ireland), argued fervently in favour of the amendment, but such examples were few and far between.

As a result, most campaigning was carried out by the 'no'-side, consisting mainly of Catholic organisations. The no-campaign portrayed divorce as something which would devastate Irish society and encourage widespread marital breakdown and sexual promiscuity. Mags O'Brien, member of the Divorce Action Group (founded in 1980 to campaign for divorce), described how the pro-divorce women were targeted and subjected to many taunts; they were described as sluts and harlots.[6] Single career women were portrayed as predators of married men and it was alleged that for men, divorce was simply a way to escape from their obligations and 'get away with it'. The campaign played on married women's fears that they might be divorced against their will and left destitute and subject to the shame of

[3] Despite the ban, termination of marriage was still possible by either a divorce *a mensa et thoro* ('judicial separation' – a limited form of divorce for adultery, cruelty or unnatural practices) or by a decree of nullity. However, neither of these permitted remarriage and while an ecclesiastical annulment (which declares that the marriage was invalid to begin with) did technically allow for remarriage, the State did not recognise this as valid and required a civil termination. The consequences of an annulled marriage, whether by Church or State, meant that any children of that marriage would be regarded as illegitimate.

[4] The 1937 Constitution was his 'brainchild'.

[5] An umbrella organisation for women's groups. Now called the National Women's Council of Ireland.

[6] Interview with Mags O'Brien, 21 December 2016.

society. Conservative Fine Gael TD Alice Glenn famously claimed that a woman voting for divorce was like 'a turkey voting for Christmas'.[7]

It was an effective campaign, so while early opinion polls showed strong support for the amendment, in the end it was rejected by a margin of almost two to one. It was a devastating blow to those who had campaigned for a yes vote. However, the mistakes of the campaign were quickly realised. One of the major problems of the 1986 campaign was that many of the legal details surrounding divorce had not been worked out. So over the next nine years, 18 pieces of legislation were passed in order to provide the detail and foundation which was missing in 1986. The most important pieces of legislation were the Judicial Separation and Family Law Reform Act 1989 and the Family Law Act 1995, which paved the way for the second referendum in 1995. In fact, in extending the grounds for judicial separation and providing for ancillary orders such as maintenance, property adjustment and custody of children in the context of separations, these statutes had gone so far as to almost provide for divorce in everything but name, albeit a 'divorce' which did not allow for remarriage.

## II. The Landmark

The Fifteenth Amendment of the Constitution deleted Article 41.3.2 in its entirety. It provides that a court may grant a dissolution of marriage if the spouses have lived apart for at least four out of the previous five years and there is no reasonable prospect of a reconciliation. The court must also be satisfied that proper provision will be made for the parties and any children involved. Despite the fact that this introduced a limited form of divorce with a long waiting period, the measure passed only by the skin of its teeth by 9114 votes in the national referendum.

While the 1995 campaign was every bit as bitter as nine years previously, the difference this time was that all the political parties supported the measure and that women, particularly women politicians, were much more active in the campaign. Whereas in 1986, the 'no'-side had presented themselves as being pro-women, this time the 'yes' campaign pointed to the benefits of divorce for women. Both sides acknowledged that marital breakdown existed in Ireland and the 'yes'-side pointed to the need to give deserted spouses a second chance. In essence, they based the campaign on the right to remarry. Crucially, divorce was seen as a rights issue, particularly a *women's* rights issue. Marian McGennis, for example, a Fianna Fáil Senator who had voted no in 1986, admitted that she had done so in the mistaken belief that the prohibition strengthened and protected marriages. However, in light of the dramatic rise in marriage breakdowns she realised that this was not the case and now recognised that what divorce offered was a second chance – or, more accurately, a second marriage – to those whose marriages had broken down.

Key figures of the 'no'-campaign such as Professor William Binchy, Nora Bennis and Una Bean Mhic Mhathúna, took the same line as the 1986 campaign: divorce was contrary to Catholic social teaching and Irish traditional values and it would lead to the disintegration of family life in Ireland. The campaign is now famously remembered for its billboard slogan: 'Hello Divorce … Bye Bye Daddy'.[8]

[7] The Alice Glenn Report, May 1986, vol 1, no 3.

[8] This slogan was famously re-worked during the 2015 same-sex marriage referendum, this time emphasising that a child needs a mother: 'Hello same-sex marriage … Bye Bye Mammy'.

On referendum day, the voting came 'down to the wire' and on the morning of the count it was too close to call but by the afternoon it was clear the amendment would pass by a whisker, the strong 'yes'-vote in Dublin swinging it. The reasons for success in 1995 are varied. The fact that the Catholic Church now held less sway following the various scandals which had emerged in the intervening years was a major factor. The fact that all political parties supported the change would also have been influential. Perhaps the biggest change, however, has been referred to as the 'Robinson factor'.[9] Mary Robinson had been a major proponent of divorce during the earlier campaign when she was a Senator. In 1995, as President of Ireland, she was unable to take part in the debate but she was a highly respected figure whose views were well-known. As Christine James has pointed out,

> as a young professional, lawyer, professor, mother, former Seanad member, and President who is Catholic but married to a Protestant, Mary Robinson in lifestyle, belief, and political views embodied the essence of the modern and increasingly Euro-conscious Irish identity.[10]

Irish views on the role and status of women had also changed by 1995. While family and motherhood were still cherished, work outside the home had come to be seen as normal.[11] As Carol Coulter has noted:

> The social base for the ideology of the anti-divorce lobby had, therefore, been eroded. Social, attitudinal, and legislative changes had brought about a situation where lone parents made up a significant, and no longer stigmatized, minority, where many married women with children worked outside the home and favoured a sharing of responsibility in providing for the family and in domestic tasks between partners. The presentation of female dependency as either the ideal or the norm was no longer acceptable.[12]

The 'yes'-campaign also appealed to people's sympathy for friends or family who were separated or in unhappy marriages. One Fine Gael poster displayed a woman with children with the caption: 'If she was your daughter, would you give her a second chance?' Anne Connolly, one of the leaders of the 'yes'-campaign believes that this was a decisive influence in 1995. Speaking about the success of the campaign she noted that on analysing the mistakes from 1986, the pro-divorce side realised they had to be 'a lot warmer, more inclusive and understanding'.[13]

## III. What Happened Next

Once the referendum had passed, the legislation containing the details on divorce could pass through the Oireachtas. In fact, the Family Law (Divorce) Act 1996 was not passed until seven months later due to a separate court action related to equality in funding for

[9] Christine P James, 'Céad Míle Fáilte? Ireland Welcomes Divorce: The 1995 Irish Divorce Referendum and the Family (Divorce) Act of 1996' (1997) 8 *Duke Journal of Comparative and International Law* 175, 215.

[10] ibid.

[11] Carol Coulter, '"Hello Divorce, Goodbye Daddy" Women, Gender and the Divorce Debate' in A Bradley and M Valiulis (eds), *Gender and Sexuality in Modern Ireland* (University of Massachusetts Press, 1997) 193.

[12] ibid.

[13] Jack Gibson, 'How to Win Your Referendum' (*Totally Dublin*, 7 April 2015): www.totallydublin.ie/more/how-to-win-your-referendum/.

referendum campaigns.[14] The Act itself was quite restrictive, since the constitutional provision which had been added by the referendum required a separation period of at least four out of the previous five years with no reasonable prospect of reconciliation. The Act encouraged couples to attend counselling and mediation first and only then to pursue separation and divorce proceedings. It also provided for joint custody, addressing the fear that fathers would be deprived of their rights.

The first divorce case, *RC v CC*,[15] to reach the courts involved a man with a terminal illness who wished to marry the woman he had been living with for many years and with whom he had a daughter. The children from his first marriage were adult and he wished to provide for his new family on his death. The court granted the application, despite being before the official date of enforcement, due to the severity of his illness.

While the no-side had predicted a flood of divorce applications were the measure to pass, in fact, applications for divorce were, and still are quite low. While more than 60,000 people qualified for a divorce when the Act came into force in February 1997, only 1,000 people had made applications and only a further 1,146 applications were made that year.[16] This is probably because the legislation which had been passed in the years between the two votes on this issue had gone a long way in resolving issues surrounding marriage breakdowns. Couples could now separate and deal with issues involving property, finances and children under these Acts. The biggest change brought in by the removal of the ban on divorce was that divorce, as opposed to judicial separation, allowed for remarriage.

In comparison to most other jurisdictions, divorce in Ireland continues to be relatively rare. Applications rose to a peak in 2007 with 3,684 divorces granted but since 1997 there have only been about 50,000 divorces granted in total. Figures from the Courts Service also show that women are more likely to seek divorce than men.[17]

In April 2017, the government accepted Fine Gael TD Josepha Madigan's proposal to reduce the waiting time for a divorce from four years to two. This will require a further referendum to amend the provision inserted in 1995. Ireland has again changed a lot in the 20 years since the last referendum on this issue. 'We have become a more open, welcoming society, less willing to judge the personal lives of others … I do not believe the attitudes towards divorce, expressed in the 1995 referendum, are a reflection of today's Ireland'.[18]

## IV. Significance

The removal of the ban on divorce is one of a long line of reforms which gradually gave women the freedom which had been lacking in many areas of their lives up to that point. Freedom of choice is something which was denied to Irish women for many years as a result

[14] See *McKenna v An Taoiseach (No 2)* [1995] 2 IR 10.

[15] *RC v CC* [1997] 1 ILRM 401.

[16] Jenny Burley and Francis Regan, 'Divorce in Ireland: the fear, the floodgates and the reality' (2002) 16(2) *International Journal of Law, Policy and the Family* 214.

[17] See Irish High Court Divorce Archive.

[18] Madigan, quoted in Michael O'Regan, 'Government accepts Bill to reduce waiting time for divorce', *The Irish Times*, 6 April 2017.

of the prohibitions on divorce, contraception,[19] abortion, and even things like sitting on juries[20] and working in the civil service after marriage. The removal of the ban on divorce meant that Irish women had the freedom to leave an unhappy marriage and remarry. Of course second marriages break down too and women often suffer financially after a divorce but crucially they now have the choice and, as the statistics demonstrate, many women have chosen to exercise that choice.

The success of the referendum in 1995 is often pointed to as one of the major turning points in modern Irish society. It showed that Ireland had begun to shed many of its traditional, conservative societal notions. Divorce was presented as a women's issue. Before this, such issues were often regarded as unimportant and women themselves were slow to support campaigns lest they be seen as immoral or promiscuous.

The 1995 result had both narrow and wider significance for women. In the narrow sense, it was an equality measure since a woman with a foreign divorce (a divorce granted in another jurisdiction) would, once she had met the domicile qualifications, be treated by the Irish legal system as a single woman, whereas an Irish woman who had separated from her husband faced significant difficulties with regard to property distribution, custody battles and registration of children, particularly before the 1989 Act. The advent of legal divorce meant that there was now a legal avenue for such situations. Irish women were given the opportunity of a clean break and a chance to start again, and crucially, Irish society had recognised that women deserved this chance.

In a wider sense, the referendum altered perceptions of women in Irish society. Previously, a woman who did not marry and have children was regarded as a 'failure'. Now it was increasingly accepted that she might choose not to marry or have children, and that she might want – and be entitled to – a career. As divorce became more normal in society, so too did single, separated and divorced women.

The referendum campaign was evidence of the tension between old conservative Ireland and new more liberal Ireland. Paul Ryan explains 'we were coming off the back of Mary Robinson's selection in 1990, the decriminalisation of homosexuality and the birth of the Celtic Tiger. There was this kind of movement towards a more secular, liberal society'.[21] In fact, Ryan credits the campaigns for divorce reform with inspiring campaigners for marriage equality (that is, same-sex marriage):

> People kind of pointed back and said look, the sky didn't fall in, the Irish family is a pretty robust institution, people are very committed to the idea of family. We can do gay marriage – there's not going to be a huge impact.[22]

Without doubt, the success of the marriage equality referendum in 2015, a move which many believed would never happen in Ireland, is testament to the focus of the campaigners 20 years earlier and their commitment to empathy, rights, and equality.

[19] *McGee v Attorney General* [1974] IR 284.

[20] *de Burca v Attorney General* [1976] IR 38.

[21] *Newstalk Breakfast*, 17 January 2017: http://www.newstalk.com/Unwedded-bliss-twenty-years-since-the-divorce-was-granted-in-Ireland-whats-changed.

[22] ibid.

## Further Reading

- Carol Coulter, '"Hello Divorce, Goodbye Daddy" Women, Gender and the Divorce Debate' in A Bradley and M Valiulis (eds), *Gender and Sexuality in Modern Ireland* (University of Massachusetts Press, 1997).
- David Fitzpatrick, 'Divorce and Separation in Modern Irish History' (1987) 114 *Past and Present* 172.
- Christine P James, 'Céad Míle Fáilte? Ireland Welcomes Divorce: The 1995 Irish Divorce Referendum and the Family (Divorce) Act of 1996' (1997) 8 *Duke Journal of Comparative and International Law* 175.

# 69

## *St George's Healthcare NHS Trust v S* (1998)

KAY LALOR, ANNE MORRIS AND ANNAPURNA WAUGHRAY

Although the case of *St George's Healthcare NHS Trust v S*[1] reiterates general principles of patient autonomy and self-determination, it is of special significance for women because of its unequivocal affirmation that a competent pregnant woman can refuse medical treatment even if that refusal may result in harm to her or the foetus.[2] It also establishes that mental health legislation cannot be used to prevent a competent pregnant woman from exercising this right. In confirming that the right of an adult of sound mind to refuse any or all medical treatment 'reflects the autonomy of each individual and the right of self-determination' (ibid), the Court of Appeal held that

> while pregnancy increases the personal responsibilities of a woman it does not diminish her entitlement to decide whether or not to undergo medical treatment … an unborn child is not a separate person from its mother. Its need for medical assistance does not prevail over her rights.[3]

*St George's Healthcare Trust v S* thus addresses three important issues: first, a pregnant woman's right to decline medical treatment even where this may harm her unborn child; second, that this right is not diminished because her decision to exercise it contravenes societal expectations of pregnant women or appears morally repugnant; and third, mental health legislation cannot be deployed to detain and treat an individual against her will merely because her thinking process is unusual or even bizarre, irrational, and contrary to the views of most people. In the case of a pregnant woman, the fact that her thinking may result in harm to her unborn baby does not mean that she must therefore be mentally disordered.

### I. Context

Historically, women have existed in the domain of the 'private', especially in relation to pregnancy and motherhood. Often this meant that the voices and experiences of pregnant women were silenced or minimised. There is a long association of female reproduction with weakness or 'hysteria', which was said to show that women were unfit to participate in

[1] *St George's Healthcare NHS Trust v S* [1999] Fam 26, [1998] 3 All ER 673.
[2] ibid 43.
[3] ibid 50.

the 'public', masculine world.[4] The view that pregnant women should surrender decision-making to doctors and that women's own experiences and preferences were less important than the opinions of the medical profession persisted into the twentieth century, as expressed in particularly extreme form in a 1980s handbook on pregnancy and labour:

> why do women have to recount such stories to one another, especially when the majority of them are so blatantly untrue … Probably more is done by wicked women with their malicious lying tongues to harm the confidence and happiness of pregnant woman than by another other single factor.[5]

Hostility to the notion that women may wish to have some control over their experience of pregnancy and childbirth is reflected in attitudes to the capacity of pregnant women to make decisions about their own bodies. The law presumes that every adult is competent provided she is able to understand and retain information and weigh it as part of the process of arriving at the decision.[6] The presumption is not displaced simply because a decision is not one of which most people would approve, nor is it rebutted simply because a person has a mental illness. Nevertheless, pregnant women often find themselves absorbed into a medical process in which it is assumed that they will defer to the expertise of those treating them. This expectation of deference is bolstered by prevailing expectations of how pregnant women should behave – as captured in Anne Morris's discussion of the Victorian poem 'Angel in the House', which praises the 'sublime altruism of one whose desires are subordinated to the happiness of others'.[7] A pregnant woman is expected to do all she can to promote the welfare of the foetus. Those women who fail to do this have been labelled 'bizarre',[8] 'not very bright',[9] 'difficult',[10] 'angry … and uncooperative'[11] or simply mad or bad mothers.[12] In other words, a woman's refusal to follow medical advice is taken not just as an indication of a lack of proper femininity, but also as a lack of competence.[13] In 1996, in *Rochdale Healthcare NHS Trust v C*, Johnson J held that the 'acute emotional stress and physical strain' of labour rendered C incapable of making a decision even of the most trivial kind.[14] This was despite the fact that C had refused a caesarean based on her previous bad experience of such intervention, and that her obstetrician was of the opinion that she was competent to refuse.

A further challenge to women's control over their bodies and their pregnancies has been the increasing medicalisation of pregnancy and childbirth, which has accompanied

[4] Ann Oakley, *Women Confined: Towards a Sociology of Childbirth* (Martin Robertson, 1980); Jo Murphy-Lawless, 'The Silencing of Women in Childbirth: Or Let's Hear It for Bartholomew and the Boys' (1988) 11(4) *Women's Studies International Forum* 293.

[5] Gordon Bourne, *Pregnancy* (Cassell, 1984) 15.

[6] *Re C (Adult, refusal of treatment)* [**1994**] 1 All ER 819 and see now section 1(2) of the **Mental Capacity Act 2005**.

[7] Anne Morris, 'The Angel in the House: Altruism, Competence and the Pregnant Woman' in Anne Morris and Susan Nott, *Well Women: The Gendered Nature of Health Care Provision* (Ashgate, 2002).

[8] *St George's Healthcare Trust v S* [1999] Fam 26, 51.

[9] *Re MB (An adult: medical treatment)* [1997] 2 FCR 541, 546.

[10] *Whitehouse v Jordan* [1981] 1 WLR 246, 250.

[11] Julia Burrows, 'The Parturient Woman: Can There be Room for More than One Person with Full and Equal Rights inside a Single Human Skin?' (2001) 33(5) *Journal of Advanced Nursing* 689, 693.

[12] See eg Emily Jackson, *Regulating Reproduction: Law, Technology and Autonomy* (Hart Publishing, 2001) 135.

[13] Sheena Meredith, *Policing Pregnancy: The Law and Ethics of Obstetric Conflict* (Ashgate, 2005).

[14] *Rochdale Healthcare NHS Trust v C* [1997] 1 FCR 274, 275.

a shift from childbirth at home to delivery in hospital, and from midwifery to obstetrics.[15] While the increased availability of free ante-natal care and hospital delivery following the creation of the NHS in 1948 was an important factor in reducing maternal mortality rates, Ann Oakley suggests that that the move from midwife-managed home delivery to delivery by obstetricians in hospitals was not simply due to social and medical advances but was part of a power struggle over the language, control and cultural construction of childbirth. Oakley argues that assumption of control of pregnancy and childbirth by doctors in the second half of the twentieth century was accompanied by a side-lining and denigration of midwives who were represented as 'half taught' or 'totally ignorant'.[16] Increased medical control of pregnancy has been accompanied by its 'pathologisation': treating pregnancy as illness with imminent complications.[17] Pregnant women undergo (usually very willingly) tests, scans and screenings which can enhance the experience of pregnancy and be life-saving, but which may also lead to an increased number of interventions. Deliveries by caesarean section in England, for example, have risen from four per cent of births in 1970 to 26.5 per cent in 2014–15.[18]

## II. The Landmark

The socio-historical context sheds light on why the question of pregnant women's autonomy became so highly contested in *St George's Healthcare NHS Trust v S* and why S's refusal to have a caesarean section presented such a strong challenge to the dominant assumptions that regulate pregnancy and labour.

S was 29 years old and 36 weeks pregnant when on 25 April 1996 she sought to register at a doctor's surgery in London, having not received any previous ante-natal care. She was diagnosed with pre-eclampsia, a condition that can endanger the life of the woman and foetus. S declined the recommended treatment, which included an early induced delivery. Her refusal led to her immediate compulsory detention in hospital under section 2 of the Mental Health Act 1983 for assessment because it was feared that her mental state 'may be compromising her ability to make decisions' and that she was 'probably depressed'. In the face of her continuing refusal to consent to treatment, an application was made to the High Court by the hospital for a declaration that it would be lawful to proceed with a caesarean section without her consent.

The Court did not hear from S, even though she had instructed solicitors and had expressed very clearly in writing that she understood the risks of pre-eclampsia, but that she had always held 'very strong views' with respect to medical and surgical treatment and opposed medical intervention in her pregnancy. She emphasised her own strong belief that 'natural events', including death, should not be interfered with. At the hearing, however, the fact that S had instructed solicitors was not made clear, nor were S's solicitors made aware

[15] Oakley, n 4 above, 12; Jackson, n 12 above, 119–36. In 1955, 33% of births were in the home. In 2006, the rate was 2.7%: Home Births in the UK, 1955–2006 (Andrea Nove et al, 'Population Trends No. 133' (Office for National Statistics, 2008). The rate is fairly stable.

[16] Oakley, n 4 above.

[17] Jackson, n 12 above, 120.

[18] NHS Maternity Statistics – England, 2014–2015 (NHS Digital, 25 November 2015).

of the proceedings. The judge was informed that S was suffering from severe pre-eclampsia, that she had been admitted to hospital under section 2 of the Mental Health Act 1983, that an assessment of her mental and psychiatric condition was 'ongoing', that 'moderate depression' had been diagnosed, and that she was refusing any intervention. Beyond that, the question of her capacity to consent was not addressed. It was also – mistakenly – claimed that S had been in labour for 24 hours, when in fact labour had not yet begun.

Permission to perform a caesarean section was granted and S was delivered of a baby girl by emergency caesarean section. While not resisting sedation or anesthetisation, S refused to sign the operation consent form and so it proceeded on the basis of the court order.

Several months after these events, S applied for judicial review of the High Court order, arguing that her admission, detention and treatment were unlawful. She also appealed against the declaration authorising the caesarean section. The Court of Appeal found in her favour in all aspects. In relation to her detention under the Mental Health Act 1983, it was held that

> The [Mental Health] Act cannot be deployed to achieve the detention of an individual against her will merely because her thinking process is unusual, even apparently bizarre and irrational, and contrary to the views of the overwhelming majority of the community at large.[19]

The court noted that the approach taken to S by those around her had been that it was so bizarre for a pregnant woman to refuse treatment for herself and the foetus that she had to be mentally ill. Under the Mental Health Act, however, compulsory detention for assessment is lawful only where certain conditions are met and, in particular, the mental disorder must be serious enough to warrant detention. Here, it was clear that detention had occurred not because of S's supposed mental disorder, but because of her physical condition (pre-eclampsia). If she had not been pregnant and physically unwell, there would have been no question of detaining her under the Act. Her detention was therefore unlawful. As far as the non-consensual treatment was concerned, the Court upheld the right of a competent adult to refuse even life-saving treatment. This extends to pregnant women even though 'pregnancy increased the personal responsibilities of a woman'.[20] The needs of the unborn child do not 'prevail over her right not to be forced to submit to an invasion of her body against her will' and that right 'was not reduced or diminished merely because her decision to exercise it might appear morally repugnant'.[21] In the absence of lawful justification, removal of the baby from within S's body under physical compulsion was an infringement of her autonomy and a trespass to her person.

## III. What Happened Next

Five days after the emergency caesarean, S discharged herself from hospital. Initially, she rejected her baby and considered having her adopted or fostered. However, she later reconsidered, fought for, and won custody of her daughter.[22] In part, it was this battle for

[19] [1999] Fam 26, 51.
[20] ibid 50.
[21] ibid.
[22] Kate Watson-Smyth, 'Appeal on forced birth is refused', *Independent*, 15 March 1997.

custody, which led to the lengthy delay between S's detention and the Appeal Court hearing. The Appeal Court's judgment itself was generally well-received, with a leader in the *Independent* newspaper proclaiming it a 'loud clear blast on the trumpet of liberty from the Court of Appeal'.[23] The paper went on to say that 'women have been bullied and coerced into Caesareans and hysterectomies to an extent which is an affront to the liberal values of a civilised society.'

Of course, one judicial decision is not going to bring about a sudden transformation of attitudes to pregnant women. Indeed, *St George's Healthcare NHS Trust v S* had been foreshadowed by an earlier Court of Appeal decision in *Re MB*,[24] in which the Court had again asserted the right of a pregnant woman to refuse treatment but then went on to find that MB was lacking in capacity because of her phobia of needles. The Courts have continued to authorise caesarean sections on non-consenting women, including those who are compulsorily detained under the Mental Health Act 1983.[25] Moreover, despite policies which aim to put the woman at the heart of maternity care, and national guidance which states that 'women's decisions should be respected, even when this is contrary to the views of the healthcare professional',[26] women are not always listened to. One survey suggested that only 50 per cent of women questioned felt they had experienced the birth they wanted.[27] It is undeniable that pregnancy and childbirth remains a contested sphere.

## IV. Significance

What then is the significance of *St George's Healthcare NHS Trust v S*? First, it should be noted that the case is not primarily about the rights and wrongs of medical intervention in pregnancy. Nobody would suggest that women would be better off without the life-saving technologies and procedures to which women in the developed world have access. Nor would it be fair to overlook the fact that those involved in this case were motivated by what they saw as the interests of the woman and her foetus. Rather, the legacy of *St George's Healthcare NHS Trust v S* is the clear statement that a pregnant woman is not be treated as incapable of making a decision *simply* because she chooses something that many would judge to be misguided, or even immoral. Equally important is the finding that competent pregnant women may not be detained under mental health legislation in order to be compulsorily treated for a physical rather than a mental condition.

The case sets out clear markers against which court-authorised caesareans must be tested and affirms the autonomy of the pregnant women in medical decision-making. It also highlights the importance of listening to women and involving them in the decision-making processes during pregnancy and childbirth. The ongoing influence of the case can

[23] Anon, 'Leading article: Judges strike a blow for freedom', *Independent*, 7 May 1998.

[24] *Re MB* [1997] 2 FCR 541.

[25] See eg *Re AA (Mental Capacity: Enforced Caesarean)* [2012] EWHC 4378 (COP).

[26] National Institute for Health and Care Excellence: Antenatal care for uncomplicated pregnancies, Clinical Guideline [CG62] (2008), 1.1.1.7. See also NICE Clinical Guidelines [CG132] (2011), 1.2.9.5 on choosing a planned C-Section.

[27] Dignity in Childbirth, 'The Dignity Survey 2013: Women's and Midwives' Experiences of UK Maternity Care' (Birthrights, 2013) 7.

be seen in *Montgomery v Lanarkshire Health Board*.[28] Here, an obstetrician took the view that it was not 'in the maternal interests for women to have caesarean sections', and failed to offer a woman with a high-risk pregnancy a caesarean section, despite the risks of vaginal delivery.[29] In her judgment **Lady Hale** commented that the doctor seemed to have judged that vaginal delivery was 'morally preferable' to caesarean section. Referring to *St George's Healthcare NHS Trust v S*, she held:

> A patient is entitled to take into account her own values, her own assessment of the comparative merits of giving birth in the 'natural' and traditional way and of giving birth by caesarean section, whatever medical opinion may say, alongside the medical evaluation of the risks to herself and her baby. She may place great value on giving birth in the natural way and be prepared to take the risks to herself and her baby which this entails. The medical profession must respect her choice, unless she lacks the legal capacity to decide … There is no good reason why the same should not apply in reverse, if she is prepared to forgo the joys of natural childbirth in order to avoid some not insignificant risks to herself or her baby. She cannot force her doctor to offer treatment which he or she considers futile or inappropriate. But she is at least entitled to the information which will enable her to take a proper part in that decision.[30]

This shows the positive impact of the landmark decision, but it should not be overlooked that the Court of Appeal in *St George's Healthcare NHS Trust v S* did not suggest that S's refusal of treatment was to be condoned or approved. This is important because the historical context of pregnancy, maternity and motherhood continues to influence views and attitudes going far beyond the issue of non-consensual caesarean sections. Campaigns concerned with foetal rights, abortion, new technologies, IVF and surrogacy have all raised issues of decision-making, autonomy and capacity. Lady Hale noted in *Montgomery*: 'Gone are the days when it was thought that, on becoming pregnant, a woman lost, not only her capacity, but also her right to act as a genuinely autonomous human being.'[31] The decision in *St George's Healthcare NHS Trust v S* remains a landmark because it insists that we are vigilant in ensuring that women are not silenced or side-lined within their own experiences of pregnancy and childbirth.

## Further Reading

- Emily Jackson, *Regulating Reproduction: Law, Technology and Autonomy* (Hart Publishing, 2001).
- Anne Morris, 'The Angel in the House: Altruism, Competence and the Pregnant Woman' in Anne Morris and Susan Nott (eds), *Well Women: The Gendered Nature of Health Care Provision* (Ashgate, 2002).
- Ann Oakley, *Essays on Women, Medicine and Health* (Edinburgh University Press, 1993).

[28] *Montgomery v Lanarkshire Health Board* [2015] UKSC 11.
[29] Discussed [2015] UKSC 11, [13].
[30] ibid [114]–[116].
[31] ibid [116].

# 70

# Section 41 of the Youth Justice and Criminal Evidence Act 1999

SONIA KALSI

Sexual offences are unlike other crimes. The majority of victims are women, many offences go unreported, and conviction rates are low. Myths and stereotypes linger about who is a 'real' victim and that sexually promiscuous women are more likely to consent to intercourse and less likely to tell the truth. The use of a woman's sexual history at trial plays into – and perpetuates – these myths. It is used to discredit the complainant by humiliating and degrading them to such an extent that they feel violated all over again. It deters many women from reporting sexual offences and when they do, can lead to the withdrawal of complaints. And it contributes to the woefully poor conviction rate.

Women's activism played a key role in keeping sexual history evidence on the public and political agenda when the first legislative attempt to limit admissibility proved unsuccessful. This paved the way for section 41 of the Youth Justice and Criminal Evidence Act 1999 (YJCEA), which excludes evidence and questions on a complainant's sexual history unless specific requirements are met. However, while section 41 stands as a symbolic challenge to the myths and stereotypes around the relevance of a woman's sexual history, its success has been limited in practice. In a recent court observer scheme, the results suggested that previous sexual conduct was used to discredit complainants 'in precisely the way that section 41 was intended to prevent'.[1]

## I. Context

During the late 1960s and early 1970s, the prevalence and impact of rape and sexual violence were key motivators for the emerging Women's Liberation Movement. Organisations such as Women's Aid, Women Against Rape (WAR), and Rape Crisis[2] – galvanised by the House of Lords' decision in *DPP v Morgan*[3] that the defendant's honest belief that the complainant was consenting (even if unreasonable) was sufficient to secure an acquittal on rape – campaigned

[1] Ruth Durham, Rachel Lawson, Anita Lord and Vera Baird, *Seeing is believing: the Northumbria Court Observers Panel Report on 30 Rape trials 2015–2016* (Newcastle, Northumbria Police and Crime Commissioner, 2017) 39.

[2] **First Rape Crisis Centre, 1976.**

[3] *DPP v Morgan* [1976] AC 182.

widely for changes to the law,[4] as well as for better treatment of complainants by the police and within the criminal justice system. One aspect of this was the introduction of so-called 'rape shield' legislation, restricting the use of a complainant's sexual history (either with the accused or with a third party) as evidence.

As early as 1975, the Advisory Group on the Law of Rape, led by **Rose Heilbron**, set up by the Government in the wake of *Morgan*, expressed concern that the complainant's sexual activity, then admissible under the common law, was frequently being used to prejudice the jury against the victim and was 'inimical to the fair trial of the essential issues'.[5] However, its recommendation that sexual history evidence be strictly regulated by statute, so that 'in general' *third-party* sexual history evidence 'ought not to be introduced', was ignored.[6] Section 2 of the Sexual Offences (Amendment) Act 1976 allowed judges to give leave for evidence of a complainant's previous sexual experience with a third party to be adduced provided they were satisfied that it would be unfair to refuse it. This meant admissibility was essentially left to the discretion of the same judges who had freely permitted the introduction of sexual history evidence under common law.[7] Moreover, it reinforced the distinction drawn by the common law between evidence relating to sexual activity with the accused and that with a third party. Section 2 only applied in relation to the latter, leaving the assumption that the former is always relevant unchallenged. Unsurprisingly, this did little to restrict its use.[8] In 1987 Zsuzssana Adler's study found 75 per cent of applications made to allow sexual history into evidence were successful.[9]

In the meantime, feminist activism on rape issues became more organised. WAR advocated that a woman's sexual history should not be raised in court in *any* circumstances.[10] It sought to increase awareness of the widespread nature of rape by publishing pamphlets, holding meetings, picketing courts, and 'invading' places such as private members' clubs, the Ministry of Defence and the offices of *The Guardian* newspaper. They even held a 'women's court' in Trafalgar Square where judges and ministers were called to account for their failure to satisfactorily address rape issues.[11]

By the 1990s, the (mis)use of sexual history evidence in rape trials had been well documented by feminist academics such as Jennifer Temkin, who highlighted that the few cases in which sexual history evidence *was* restricted were being successfully appealed,[12] and Sue Lees, who found that almost three-quarters of the rape complainants she interviewed believed they had been treated unsympathetically and/or were asked irrelevant and unfair questions.[13] At the same time there were a number of important related legal developments, including the removal of the marital rape exclusion in *R v R*,[14] and the

[4] **Section 1 of the Sexual Offences Act 2003.**

[5] Heilbron Committee, *Report of the Advisory Group on the Law of Rape* (Cmnd 6352, 1975) [92].

[6] ibid [134].

[7] See Jennifer Temkin, 'Sexual history evidence – the ravishment of section 2' [1993] *Criminal Law Review* 3–20.

[8] Eg *R v Lawrence* [1977] *Criminal Law Review* 492 and *R v Viola* [1982] 3 All ER 73.

[9] Zsuzssana Adler, *Rape on Trial* (Routledge & Kegan, 1987) 73.

[10] Women Against Rape, *Introduction & Statement of Aims* (WAR, 1977).

[11] Ruth Hall, 'Up from Under' in Women Against Rape, *Women at W A R* (Falling Wall Press, 1978).

[12] For a detailed discussion see Jennifer Temkin, 'Sexual History Evidence – Beware the Backlash' [2003] *Criminal Law Review* 217.

[13] Sue Lees, *Carnal Knowledge: Rape on Trial* (Hamish Hamilton, 1996) 31.

[14] *R v R* [1992] 1 AC 599 and see section 5 of the Criminal Law (Rape) (Amendment) Act 1990.

abolition of the compulsory corroboration warning in sexual cases.[15] In 1995, two prostitutes, supported by WAR, successfully brought the first private prosecution for rape in the English courts following the CPS's decision not to prosecute.[16] Attitudes towards rape and rape victim-survivors were also gradually changing. 'Date rape' had entered the public consciousness – challenging the myth of the stranger rapist. There was widespread public condemnation when, in 1996, Julia Mason endured the horror of being questioned in court about her sex life by her attacker for six days.[17] And in October 1997, the ITV programme *Thursday Night Live* debated 'Is sexual history evidence ever relevant?'.

## II. The Landmark

It was against this backdrop that the Labour party came to power in May 1997, with 101 newly-elected Labour women MPs (unhelpfully dubbed 'Blair's babes' by the *Daily Mail*).[18] With hopes of a new focus on women-related issues, women's organisations seized this opportunity to lobby for change. Rights of Women worked closely with other organisations and MPs,[19] including Debra Shipley MP who drafted an Early Day Motion calling for a total overhaul of rape law in June 1997 (though there was no mention of restricting sexual history evidence directly).[20] An independent review of arrangements to assist and protect vulnerable and intimidated witnesses soon followed. The *Speaking Up for Justice* report, published by the Home Office in 1998, took into account information provided by the Rape Crisis Federation, Rape Crisis Centres, WAR, and Victim Support, as well as research by feminist academics, and concluded that there was overwhelming evidence that the practice in the courts on sexual history evidence was unsatisfactory.[21] Its recommendations included the creation of a stricter regime of admissibility and preventing defendants from personally being able to cross-examine complainants.

The Government responded by introducing the Youth Justice and Criminal Evidence Bill which had its second reading in April 1998. It outlined a new scheme to restrict sexual history evidence far more rigorously. However, while feminist and women's organisations welcomed the removal of judicial discretion, for some the proposed changes did not go far enough. In July 1998, WAR wrote an open letter to then Home Secretary, Jack Straw, signed

[15] Sections 32 and 33 of the Criminal Justice & Public Order Act 1994.

[16] Sally Weale, 'Private Case Brings Rapist to Justice', *The Guardian*, 18 May 1995.

[17] Helen Nowicka, 'Rape Victim's Foul Court Ordeal', *Independent*, 22 August 1996.

[18] Suzanne Moore, 'Welcome to "Blair's Babes" but the struggle goes on', *Independent*, 8 February 1997.

[19] Margaret Greenfields, 'Rape and the legal process: the implications of recent developments' in *Rights of Women Bulletin* (Rights of Women, Summer 1998).

[20] It was supported by 126 MPs and read: 'That this House believes that there should be a change towards the law concerning rape and a better understanding of the needs of rape victims; urges the removal of the defendant's right to cross-examine the victim; requests the restriction of multiple cross-examination of the victim in cases where there is more than one defendant; requests that ID parades be conducted behind mirror glass; urges more consistent sentencing and help for rape victims to re-enter society; urges charges to be brought against people who falsely claim to have been raped; requests that victims be represented in court by their own barrister; and urges that British people who have been raped by British people while overseas should be able to turn to the British legal system for justice' ('Rape Law Review', Early Day Motion 101, tabled by Debra Shipley (10 June 1997)).

[21] Home Office, *Speaking Up for Justice: Report of the Interdepartmental Working Group on the treatment of vulnerable or intimidated witnesses in the criminal justice system* (June 1998).

by over 200 women's, BME, and other community organisations, calling for the law to be amended so that sexual history evidence was not admissible in *any* circumstances.

> We are very concerned about the ordeal victims of rape experience in court ... Women describe court as a 'second rape' because they, not the accused, are effectively put 'on trial'. In most cases the accused claims the woman consented, and defence barristers trawl through her sexual or medical history in order to discredit her evidence that she didn't consent. Women are routinely cross-examined about sexual abuse in childhood, whether they were sexually active before 16, when they last had sex, how they dress, abortions, contraception, menstrual cycle, the number and race of previous boyfriends, whether they drink, take tranquilisers or other drugs ... Even children are not protected from such deeply prejudiced questions. The evidence presented in this way invites the jury to decide not whether a person was raped but whether she is entitled to the law's protection.[22]

In March 1999, the Campaign to End Rape, a national campaign that included the Rape Crisis Federation, Justice for Women, Action Against Child Sexual Abuse, and the YWCA of Great Britain, presented a petition to the Government as further evidence of renewed public concern about rape and sexual assault.[23] They were concerned that Parliament's intention to change the law on sexual history evidence would be watered down by the courts as had happened before. Unfortunately the Government's Women's Unit did not share these concerns, insisting in a letter to WAR that there were times when a woman's sexual history may be relevant in rape cases in relation to belief in consent.[24] It was left to the newly elected women MPs – sometimes criticised for not having transformed gender politics[25] – to take the issue forward. A number had an impact on changes to rape policy and legislation, including Caroline Flint MP, Julia Drown MP, Margaret Moran MP, Angela Smith MP and Beverly Hughes MP, all of whom were on the Standing Committee that considered the proposed changes on sexual history evidence.[26]

The response from the House of Lords – particularly those members with a legal background – was mixed. While some, such as Baroness Mallalieu, Lord Thomas and Lord Bingham, considered section 2 of the 1976 Act to be operating satisfactorily, others, including Lord Lester, were more supportive of the new proposals and reassured that judicial discretion would not be removed, but rather the new provisions sought 'to structure, guide and narrow' it.[27]

The result was section 41 of the YJCEA, which provides a more structured approach to the exercise of judicial discretion when deciding whether to allow sexual history evidence. Such evidence is to be excluded *unless* it falls into one of four exceptions. The first is that the sexual history evidence relates to a relevant issue in a case other than whether the complainant consented, including the defendant's *belief* in consent (section 41(3)(a)). If consent *is* an issue, sexual history evidence can be admitted in two further situations: either when the

[22] Against Rape, 'Open letter to Jack Straw', July 1998: www.womenagainstrape.net/content/open-letter-jack-straw.

[23] 'Justice for a Change, Rape and the Criminal Justice System', Campaign Pack (Campaign to End Rape, March 1999).

[24] Frances Gibb, 'Jay faces row on change in rape evidence', *The Times*, 1 March 1999.

[25] Lucy Ward, 'Learning from the "Babe" experience: how the finest hour became a fiasco' in Anna Coote (ed), *New Gender Agenda: Why Women Still Want More* (IPRR, 2000) 29.

[26] Fiona Mactaggart, *Women in Parliament: Their Contribution to Labour's First 1000 Days* (Fabian Society, 2000) 7; Youth Justice and Criminal Evidence Bill, Standing Committee E, Thursday 24 June 1999.

[27] HL Deb, 8 Feb 1999, vol 597 col 47.

evidence relates to sexual behaviour which is alleged to have taken place 'at or about the same time' as the event which is the subject matter of the charge' (section 41(3)(b)) (which the Act's Explanatory Notes say is expected to be not more than 24 hours before or after the offence) or if the defendant can show that the past sexual behaviour is so similar to the complainant's behaviour on the occasion in question 'that the similarity cannot be explained by coincidence' (section 41(3)(c)). Finally, sexual history evidence can be raised to rebut or explain evidence adduced by the prosecution, so long as it goes no further than to directly contradict or explain claims made by or on behalf of the complainant (section 41(5)). In addition to one of these requirements being met, the court must also be satisfied that the purpose or main purpose of the evidence is not to impugn the credibility of the complainant as a witness (section 41(4)), that the evidence relates to a specific instance(s) of sexual behaviour (section 41(6)) and that refusal of leave might render a conclusion of the jury or court on any relevant issue unsafe (section 41(2)).

## III. What Happened Next

Section 41 was immediately challenged in the courts on the basis that it contravened the defendant's right to a fair trial under article 6 of the newly enacted Human Rights Act 1998 (HRA). The defendant in question wanted to raise evidence and cross-examine the complainant on their having had consensual sex on several occasions in the month before the offence – something which did not fit within any of the four 'gateways'. The case – *R v A (No 2)*[28] – became something of a feminist cause célèbre.[29]

A joint written intervention from the Rape Crisis Federation, the Campaign to End Rape, the Child and Woman Abuse Studies Unit and Justice for Women presented the House of Lords with evidence that rape when parties are known to each other is the most frequent type of rape, the least likely to be reported and the least likely to result in conviction.[30] While the Fawcett Society branded the all-male composition of the House of Lords 'internationally embarrassing and unacceptable in a modern, democratic society',[31] it went on to suggest that without the benefit of a woman's perspective, the Court 'might unconsciously prefer the interests of the male defendant over the female complainant when deciding how to strike a balance between their rights'.[32] Their argument was refused by an all-male panel of three, without an oral hearing or explanation.[33]

The House of Lords agreed that on a straightforward reading of section 41 the evidence was inadmissible and that this would endanger the defendant's right to a fair trial. Lord Steyn, while acknowledging the desirability of protecting a complainant from unwarranted intrusions into their private life, believed that section 41 amounted to 'legislative overkill'.[34]

[28] *R v A (No 2)* [2001] UKHL 25.

[29] See further Clare McGlynn, '*R v A (No 2)*' in Rosemary Hunter, Clare McGlynn and Erika Rackley (eds), *Feminist Judgments: From Theory to Practice* (Hart Publishing, 2010) 211–27.

[30] [2001] UKHL 25, [52].

[31] Mary Ann Stephenson, 'Bad Judgment', *The Guardian*, 27 March 2001.

[32] ibid.

[33] See further Erika Rackley, 'Why Feminist Legal Scholars Should Write Judgments: Reflections on the Feminists Judgment Project in England & Wales' (2012) 24(2) *Canadian Journal of Women and Law* 389–413, 408–09.

[34] [2001] UKHL 25, [43].

However, rather than issuing a declaration of incompatibility under section 4 of the HRA, the law lords opted to interpret section 41 in line with the 1998 Act by reading gateway section 41(3)(c) as permitting evidence where it was so relevant to the issue of consent that to exclude it would endanger the fairness of the trial.[35] The case was returned to the lower courts for a decision on its facts.

So where does this leave the use of sexual history evidence in rape trials? Certainly, there was disappointment from those who had campaigned for and supported the legislative changes. In the words of Vera Baird QC at the time, the upshot of *R v A (No 2)* is that when it comes to deciding when to admit such evidence 'we're back to the discretion of a lot of male judges'.[36] Clare McGlynn, in her feminist re-writing of the case, described the approach of the law lords as 'veer[ing] towards judicial vandalism'.[37]

Unsurprisingly, there continue to be calls for further legislative and procedural reform. The most recent example followed the conviction and subsequent acquittal for rape of Premier League footballer Ched Evans. Although Evans's appeal was initially refused, after his defence team and private investigators dug up evidence of sexual activity involving the complainant and two men around the time of the alleged rape, the Criminal Cases Review Commission referred the case to the Court of Appeal in October 2016, which determined that the evidence of sexual activity with third parties 'would have been relevant and admissible'.[38] His conviction was quashed. Women's groups such as the End of Violence Against Women Coalition and WAR expressed dismay at how the complainant's sex life had been put on trial – initially in the press and on social media, and subsequently in the courtroom – and the impact this would have on women reporting rape.[39]

In February 2017, Liz Saville-Roberts MP introduced a Sexual Offences (Amendment) Bill 2017 which sought to further limit cross-examination of complainants.[40] The following month, former Solicitor General, Harriet Harman MP tabled an amendment of the Prison and Courts Bill 2017 to prohibit sexual history evidence completely.[41] In December 2017, the Ministry of Justice rejected such a ban, arguing on the basis of evidence collected in a review of 309 sample cases that section 41 was working effectively. Sexual history evidence had only been adduced in 25 of those cases.[42] In January 2018, Harman and former Solicitor General Vera Baird QC, supported by a number of MPs and women's charities, including the End Violence Against Women Coalition, Rape Crisis and Victim Support, called again for section 41 to be strengthened. Speaking ahead of the launch of the campaign, Harman argued the current situation is

> not what women should have to put up with; it's not what Parliament intended … It's not a fair trial if prejudicial, irrelevant evidence is allowed in. The Government cannot go on ignoring the

[35] ibid, [46].

[36] Clare Dyer, 'Lords rule rape shield law unfair', *The Guardian*, 18 May 2001.

[37] McGlynn, n 29 above, [71].

[38] *R v Ched Evans* [2016] EWCA 452, [72].

[39] John Bingham and Nicola Harley, 'Victims' groups cry foul as footballer Ched Evans is cleared of raping teenager after complainant's sexual history is put before the court', *The Telegraph*, 15 October 2016.

[40] Sexual Offences (Amendment) Bill (HC Bill 137), 8 February 2017.

[41] Notice of Amendment: Public Bill Committee, Prisons & Courts Bill, 23 March 2017.

[42] Ministry of Justice and Attorney General's Office, *Limiting the use of complainants' sexual history in sex cases* (Cm 9547, December 2017). See also Clare McGlynn, 'Why Laws On Sexual History Evidence Still Need Reform', *Huffington Post*, 17 December 2017.

> evidence of the scale and nature of the problem. We need a change in the law to ensure that trials are fair and that complainants do not face the ordeal of their sexual history being dragged through the courts.[43]

While the possibility of legislative change is uncertain, there have been procedural changes aimed at addressing the balance between complainants and the accused. In August 2017, it was reported that the Director of Public Prosecutions, Alison Saunders, directed prosecuting counsel to tell jurors more about the *accused's* sexual history, including 'situations where an alleged rapist exercised controlling or coercive behaviour towards other women, including previous girlfriends'.[44]

## IV. Significance

> Myths are powerful tent pegs which secure the status quo. In the law, mythology operates almost as powerfully as legal precedent in inhibiting change, and the law is full of mythology. Women are particularly at its mercy … mythology is a triumph of belief over reality, depending for its survival not on evidence but on constant reiteration.[45]

Section 41 of the YJCEA was an important attempt to tackle the myth that sexually experienced women are more likely to consent to sexual acts. Battered, and perhaps a little bruised, it regulates the use of complainant sexual history evidence both in relation to the defendant/s as well as third parties, and applies to sexual offences other than rape.

However, two decades later the myths and stereotypes that it was hoped would be challenged stubbornly remain. According to Rape Crisis figures '85,000 women and 12,000 men are raped in England and Wales alone every year; that's roughly 11 rapes (of adults alone) every hour'.[46] In 2015–16 there were 2,689 rape convictions, around 7.5 per cent of recorded allegations.[47] This represents, on Rape Crisis figures, just 2.8 per cent of all rapes. There is clearly much to be done to challenge and eradicate the myths and cultural practices that dissuade complainants from reporting rape and sexual violence and that make it harder for those who do. And even more needs to be done to defeat the societal assumptions that make a woman's sexual history prejudicial in the first place. The struggle to fully eradicate rape myths and further change the law is far from over. And if the past is any predictor of the future, feminist lawyers, MPs, academics and activists – who not only paved the way for the enactment of section 41, but have since monitored and exposed its flaws – will be a key part of this process.

[43] Lizzie Dearden, 'MPs launch campaign to stop sexual history being used unfairly against rape complainants in court', *Independent*, 29 January 2018.

[44] Martin Evans, 'Rape juries hear about men's sexual history to increase chance of conviction', *The Telegraph*, 8 August 2017.

[45] Helena Kennedy, *Eve was Framed* (revd edn, Vintage, 2005) 32.

[46] Rape Crisis, 'Statistics': https://rapecrisis.org.uk/statistics.php.

[47] Vikram Dodd and Helena Bengtsson, 'Reported rapes in England and Wales double in four years' *The Guardian*, 13 October 2016.

## Further Reading


- Ruth Durham, Rachel Lawson, Anita Lord and Vera Baird, *Seeing is believing: the Northumbria Court Observers Panel Report on 30 Rape trials 2015–2016* (Newcastle, Northumbria Police and Crime Commissioner, 2017).
- Clare McGlynn, Rape Trials and Sexual History Evidence: Reforming the Law on Third-Party Evidence (2017) 81(5) *Journal of Criminal Law* 367–92.
- Clare McGlynn, '*R v A (No 2)*' in Rosemary Hunter, Clare McGlynn and Erika Rackley (eds), *Feminist Judgments: From Theory to Practice* (Hart Publishing, 2010) 211–27.

# 71

# *Islam v Secretary of State for the Home Department, R v Immigration Appeal Tribunal and Another, ex parte Shah* (1999)

NORA HONKALA

*Islam v Secretary of State for the Home Department, R v Immigration Appeal Tribunal and Another, ex parte Shah (Conjoined Appeals)*[1] (*Islam* and *Shah*) concerned two women – Syeda Shah and Shahanna Islam – from Pakistan who were subjected to serious physical abuse by their husbands and were forced to leave their homes. They applied for asylum in the UK claiming that they feared that if returned to Pakistan they would be subjected to domestic violence from which there was no state protection, as well as severe sanctions arising from false allegations of adultery made against them. The House of Lords decision was the first time the highest court in the UK recognised gender as a protected characteristic and women as a particular social group within the meaning of the United Nations Convention Relating to the Status of Refugees (1951) ('the Convention').[2]

## I. Context

In 2016, women represented half of the world's 19.6 million refugees.[3] Women and children are often part of large-scale movements of people who flee persecution and human rights abuses, poverty and lack of economic opportunities, as well as escaping conflicts and devastation in their home countries. The significant increase in the number of armed conflicts around the world since the early 1990s has forced millions of women and girls to flee and many remain, often for years, in overcrowded refugee camps or as displaced persons within their home countries. Women and children also form the overwhelming majority of internally displaced persons (IDPs) who are especially at risk of violent attacks, sexual violence and abduction and who are frequently deprived of adequate shelter, food and health services.

[1] *Islam v Secretary of State for the Home Department, R v Immigration Appeal Tribunal and Another, ex parte Shah* [1999] UKHL 20.

[2] 1951 Convention Relating to the Status of Refugees.

[3] UN General Assembly, 'In Safety and Dignity: Addressing Large Movements of Refugees and Migrants, Report of the Secretary-General' (2016), UN Doc A/70/59.

The position of women in society, their frequent lack of means to travel and/or knowledge of their rights, as well as the particular risks they face during flight, mean that it is generally more difficult for women than men to reach a country where they can safely seek asylum. More generally women and girls continue to be subjected to serious human rights violations, including rape and other forms of sexual violence, resulting from discrimination and/or violence against them because of their gender, age and other factors.

Those women who are able to flee their home state, which is either unwilling or unable to protect them, can seek protection under the UN Refugee Convention. The Convention and its 1967 Protocol form the foundations of international refugee protection. Today, 145 states are signatories to the Convention and it is the sole legally binding international instrument that provides protection for refugees. The Convention sets out the definition of a refugee, outlines their rights, and the obligations of states to protect them. Article 1A(2) defines a refugee as a person who has a well-founded fear of persecution for reasons of race, religion, nationality, membership of a particular social group (PSG) or political opinion.[4] The absence of sex or gender from this list can in large part be explained by the historical context in which the Convention was drafted and adopted. The Convention was adopted in the aftermath of the Second World War. This, together with the backdrop of the Cold War, informed its understanding of who might become a refugee – namely a single, male, political activist fleeing persecution by the state. As a result, neither sex nor gender was included in the definition, indeed it was doubted whether there would ever be refugee cases on these bases.[5]

Subsequent feminist critique has demonstrated not only the historical contingency of this view, but its adverse impact on women claiming asylum. This critique built on the international women's rights movement – which advocated for women's rights to be taken seriously and showed the androcentric nature of international law[6] – and the challenge by second-wave feminists of the public/private distinction. In these ways, feminist lawyers and others have challenged the apparent downplaying of gender-related persecution within the Convention,[7] and have argued for the recognition of serious harm committed against women by private individuals as a matter of public concern in international law.[8]

As there was no realistic option of expanding the wording of the Convention itself, strategic advances have come through ensuring gender-sensitive interpretations of the Convention. The late 1980s and early 1990s saw sustained pressure from women's rights activists, immigration advocates and scholars across a number of jurisdictions.[9] The leadership and staff at the Office of the United Nations High Commissioner for Refugees (UNHCR) responded to calls for a more inclusive and proactive approach to refugee women

[4] The 1967 Protocol removed the temporal limitations of the 1951 Convention so that refugee status could be sought by all. Refugees are protected by the customary international law principle of non-refoulement (non-expulsion or return), which prohibits the return of a refugee to a territory where she faces serious threats to her life or freedom. See also Article 33 of the Refugee Convention.

[5] Thomas Spijkerboer, *Gender and Refugee Status* (Ashgate, 2000) 1.

[6] Article 7 of the Covenant of the League of Nations, 1919.

[7] Jane Freedman, *Gendering the International Asylum and Refugee Debate* (Palgrave Macmillan, 2015) 75.

[8] Deborah Eve Anker, 'Legal Change from the Bottom Up: The Development of Gender Asylum Jurisprudence in the United States' in Efrat Arbel, Catherine Dauvergne and Jenni Millbank (eds), *Gender in Refugee law: From the Margins to the Centre* (Routledge, 2014) 54.

[9] Deborah Eve Anker, ibid 53.

sympathetically.[10] In 1991, the UNHCR published its Guidelines on Refugee Women and the UNHCR Executive Committee issued several recommendations for states to adopt national guidelines in order for women's experiences to be recognised under the Convention, including the provision that 'women … fearing persecution or severe discrimination on the basis of their gender should be considered a member of a social group.[11] At the same time at state level, feminist collaboration and lobbying were starting to have an impact. Pressure from these groups, as well as the UNHCR,[12] led to the adoption of national Gender Guidelines recognising the particular protection needs of refugee women. They also supported and advocated for women refugees in a number of high-profile immigration and asylum cases including *In Re Kasinga* in the United States.[13] It is against this backdrop that *Islam* and *Shah* came before the House of Lords in 1999.

## II. The Landmark

Syeda Shah was 43 and pregnant when she was turned out of her marital home. Shahanna Islam was a teacher in Pakistan where she lived with her husband and two children. Just prior to her leaving she had intervened in a fight at her school between two rival political factions. One of the factions subsequently made allegations of adultery against her to her husband. Both women had suffered severe violence at the hands of their husbands in Pakistan (Islam was twice admitted to hospital). They sought asylum in the UK on the basis that if they returned to Pakistan they were at risk of false allegations of adultery and would be unprotected by the state. The punishment upon a court's finding of sexual immorality includes flogging or stoning to death. The Court of Appeal had rejected the women's claim – their fear of persecution, while well-founded, was not (as required under the Convention) for reasons of their membership of a PSG. (It was not open for the women to argue that they feared persecution *as women* as this was excluded from the categories in Article 1A(2)).

Prior to *Shah and Islam*, no case on whether women amounted to a PSG had reached the House of Lords. The Home Office had consistently attempted to stymie such cases by offering to some women exceptional leave to remain – as it had done in this case. However, both Islam and Shah wanted to obtain refugee status, which provides a stronger form of protection as a result of international law obligations toward refugees placed on receiving states. Emboldened by progress overseas, feminist and refugee advocates in the UK had been working hard to get a test case heard. The Refugee Women's Legal Group (RWLG), set up by feminist scholars, refugee women, lawyers and activists in 1996, was instrumental in raising awareness on the particular difficulties women asylum-seekers faced when their claims were decided. Its founding members were Hildegard Dumper (Refugee Action), Minoo Jalali (Avon and Bristol Law Centre), Monireh Moftizadeh (Asylum Aid), Heaven Crawley (academic), Jane Coker and Alison Stanley (ILPA) and Victoria Tennant

[10] Arbel, Dauvergne and Millback, n 8 above, 3.

[11] UNHCR: *Guidelines on the Protection of Refugee Women* (July 1991), UN Doc ES/SCP/67.

[12] UNHCR Executive Committee, 'Refugee Protection and Sexual Violence', Conclusion No 73 (XLIV) (1993).

[13] *In Re Kasinga* 21 I & N 357 (BIA 1996). See also *In Re Acosta* 19 I & N Dec 211 (BIA, 1985); *Canada (Attorney General) v Ward* [1993] 2 SCR 689; New Zealand Refugee Status Appeals Authority (RSAA), *Refugee Appeal No 1312/93 Re GJ* (30 August 1995).

(Refugee Legal Centre), and others soon joined. The group's aim was to bring a gendered perspective to refugee law and policy. In June 1997, written by Heaven Crawley and together with ILPA and Refugee Action, the RWLG produced *Women as Asylum Seekers: A Legal Handbook*. The Handbook sought to provide information for legal practitioners and others working with asylum-seeker women about the ways in which the asylum procedure could be made more accessible and sensitive to asylum-seeker women's experiences.

Following the publication of the Handbook and responding to international developments of provision of national gender guidelines in other countries, RWLG established a drafting committee in order to produce Gender Guidelines for determination of women's claims for refuge in the UK. The drafting committee drew from a wide range of experiences including members of the legal profession, academics and representatives from NGOs and other organisations (Amnesty International, Asylum Aid, ILPA, the Joint Council for the Welfare of Immigrants (JCWI), the Immigration Advisory Service (IAS), Refugee Action, the Refugee Council, the Refugee Legal Centre (RLC), Southall Black Sisters and the UNHCR). The draft document was then circulated for consultation and discussion to refugee community organisations, women's groups, human rights groups and NGOs working with refugees and asylum-seekers in the UK, as well as crucially to asylum-seeking women themselves. The *Gender Guidelines for the Determination of Asylum Claims in the UK* were published in July 1998.[14] These defined gender-specific persecution as comprising serious harm and a failure of state protection. In *Shah and Islam*, Lord Hoffmann referred to the Guidelines and accepted their formulation

> What is the reason for the persecution which the appellants fear? Here it is important to notice that it is made up of two elements. First, there is the threat of violence to Mrs Islam by her husband and his political friends and to Mrs Shah by her husband. This is a personal affair, directed against them as individuals. Secondly, there is the inability or unwillingness of the State to do anything to protect them. There is nothing personal about this. The evidence was that the State would not assist them because they were women. It denied them a protection against violence which it would have given to men. These two elements have to be combined to constitute persecution within the meaning of the Convention. As the *Gender Guidelines for the Determination of Asylum Claims in the UK* (published by the Refugee Women's Legal Group in July 1988 [*sic*]) succinctly puts it (at p 5): 'Persecution = Serious Harm + The Failure of State Protection'.

The Lords, by a majority, held that the women had a well-founded fear of persecution because they would not be protected by their state, which partly tolerated and partly sanctioned their discrimination. Vitally, the Lords also accepted that their fear of persecution was for reasons of their membership of a PSG. The Lords held that while members of a PSG shared a common, immutable characteristic that was either beyond the power of an individual to change or was so fundamental to the individual's identity that it ought not to be required to be changed, it was not required under Article 1A(2) of the Convention that a PSG should be cohesive, although cohesiveness could prove the existence of a particular social group. On this basis, gender was considered to be an immutable characteristic allowing the women to be members of a necessary PSG, defined variously as 'women of Pakistan'

[14] Refugee Women's Legal Group, *Gender Guidelines for the Determination of Asylum Claims in the UK* (RWLG, 1998). See further discussion in Sue Kirvan, 'Women and Asylum: A particular Social Group' (1999) 7(3) *Feminist Legal Studies* 333, 337–40.

and 'Pakistani women … accused of transgressing social mores (in the instant case, adultery, disobedience to husbands) … who were unprotected by their husbands or other male relatives'.

## III. What Happened Next

Since *Shah and Islam*, courts have accepted arguments that persecutory actions toward a PSG may be a relevant factor in determining the visibility of that group in a particular society. Women fleeing domestic violence from China, Ethiopia, Iran, Kenya, Moldova, Sierra Leone, Somalia, Albania, Afghanistan and Ukraine have been recognised as refugees on the basis of entrenched discrimination and lack of state protection.[15] *Shah and Islam* has been followed and further developed in other jurisdictions, including New Zealand[16] and Australia, where Gleeson CJ commented:

> It is power, not number, that creates the conditions in which persecution may occur. … Women in any society are a distinct and recognisable group, and their distinctive attributes and characteristics exist independently of the manner in which they are treated, either by males or by governments.[17]

In 2002, the UNHCR published its guidelines specifically addressing gender-related persecution in which it stated that: 'Gender-related claims have typically encompassed, although are by no means limited to, acts of sexual violence, family/domestic violence, coerced family planning, female genital mutilation, punishment for transgression of social mores, and discrimination against homosexuals.'[18]

In the UK, the Asylum Directorate's instructions to decision-makers on the definition of particular social groups within the meaning of the Convention have been revised.[19] Gender Guidelines specifically aimed at the judiciary, which drew from the RWLG Guidelines, were adopted in 2000.[20] The RWLG continued to lobby members of Parliament to ensure the official adoption of their guidelines by the Home Office.[21] With the help of RWLG, Asylum Aid set up its Refugee Women's Resources Project to deal with questions of gender and asylum and to work with RWLG in lobbying the government. Finally, the Home Office agreed to work together with RWLG and with the UNHCR's representative in the UK to draw up its own guidelines, which were adopted in 2004.

*Shah and Islam* was not the last time the House of Lords considered the scope of a PSG. In *Secretary of State for the Home Department v K; Fornah v Secretary of State for the Home*

[15] Frances Webber, '"As a woman I have no country": The Denial of Asylum to Women Fleeing Gender-based Persecution' (Women for Refugee Women, 2012) 5.

[16] New Zealand Refugee Status Appeals Authority (RSAA), *Refugee Appeal No 71427/99* (16 August 2000).

[17] *Minister for Immigration & Multicultural Affairs v Khawar* [2002] HCA 14 [33], [35].

[18] UNHCR, *Guidelines on International Protection: Gender-Related Persecution within the Context of Article 1A(2) of the 1951 Convention and/or its 1967 Protocol relating to the Status of Refugees* (Geneva, May 2002), UN Doc HCR/GIP/02/01 [3].

[19] Heaven Crawley, *Refugees and Gender: Law and Process* (Jordans, 2001) 77.

[20] *Immigration Appellate Authority (UK): Asylum Gender Guidelines*, 1 November 2000.

[21] Freedman, n 7 above, 102.

*Department*[22] they considered whether it extended to women fleeing the threat of Female Genital Mutilation (FGM). Overturning the Court of Appeal, and following *Shah and Islam*, the Lords held that it did. It is perhaps unsurprising that the most strongly-worded response came from **Lady Hale** – the first woman and openly feminist – member of the Appellate Committee. For her the answer as to whether FGM amounted to gender-related and gender-specific persecution was

> so blindingly obvious that it must be a mystery to some why [the cases] had to reach this house … the world has woken up to the fact that women as a sex may be persecuted in ways which are different from the ways in which men are persecuted and that they may be persecuted because of their inferior status accorded to their gender in their home society.[23]

## IV. Significance

The decision in *Shah and Islam* was groundbreaking in its acceptance of gender as a protected characteristic under the Convention. In so doing, the House of Lords demonstrated not only a willingness to take women's rights seriously but, more broadly, the non-discriminatory objective and purpose of the Refugee Convention. The case consolidated emerging consensus on the need for a gender-sensitive interpretation of PSG and took a holistic approach in its recognition of the women, who were persecuted because they were women, as refugees.

Of course, challenges remain for refugee women and the advocates supporting them. There is still much work to do to achieve gender-sensitive interpretation of the Convention. Research suggests that first-instance decision-makers in the UK systematically fail to consider PSG in relation to gender-persecution claims and that the Gender Guidelines are regularly not adhered to.[24] Moreover, a political climate which has seen increasing support for restrictive immigration and asylum policies has contributed to fears of less generous interpretations of PSG in the future, where the category of 'women' is at risk of being seen as too wide and an implicit 'floodgates' risk.

In the meantime, however, Sue Kirvan suggests, 'for feminists the cases of *Islam* and *Shah* address debates as to the most empowering arguments and useful strategies to employ in order to further the protection of refugee women'.[25] Without doubt, the claimants in *Islam* and *Shah* were beneficiaries of the feminist strategies of the 1970s, the legacy of Women's Aid and others in moving understandings of, and responses to, 'domestic' violence out of the 'private' and into the 'public' sphere. However, it is important that the debate continues to move on. More recently, the focus of feminists working in this area has shifted to challenging the tendency to deploy the PSG in all women refugees' claims. In fact, many asylum

[22] *Secretary of State for the Home Department v K; Fornah v Secretary of State for the Home Department* [2006] UKHL 46.

[23] ibid, [83], [86].

[24] See, Helen Muggeridge and Chen Maman, 'Unsustainable: The Quality of Initial Decision-making in Women's Asylum Claims' (Asylum Aid, 2011) and Sophia Ceneda and Clare Palmer, '"Lip Service" or Implementation?; The Home Office Gender Guidance and Women's Asylum Claims in the UK' (Asylum Aid, Women's Refugee Project, 2006).

[25] Kirvan, n 15 above, 340.

cases involving women might also (or instead) involve a well-founded fear of persecution for reasons of a 'political opinion'. The women have been involved in active resistance, transgression of social norms and/or institutional discrimination. The inherently political nature of these – and other – asylum claims means that feminist activism in this area is as important as ever.

## Further Reading


- Efrat Arbel, Caterine Dauvergne and Jenni Millbank (eds), *Gender in Refugee Law: From the Margins to the Centre* (Routledge, 2014).
- Heaven Crawley, *Refugees and Gender: Law and Process* (Jordans, 2001).
- Alice Edwards, 'Transitioning Gender: Feminist Engagement with International Refugee Law and Policy 1950–2010' (2010) 29(2) *Refugee Survey Quarterly* 21.

# 72

## *White v White* (2000)

JONATHAN HERRING

The decision of *White v White*[1] is one of the most striking acknowledgements of the value of carework in the law and provides a powerful statement of equality between husbands and wives. That said, the fact that at the turn of the twenty-first century it could regarded as revolutionary to declare that the courts should ensure there should be no discrimination between husbands and wives in financial orders on divorce might also be seen as evidence of the tenacious hold of patriarchy.

## I. Context

Prior to the Married Women's Property Acts of 1870 and 1882,[2] on marriage a woman's property passed in common law to her husband. Since then married women have been able to own their own property, but English law has never adopted a system of community of property, as is normal in many American States and continental jurisdictions, according to which property is equally shared between the spouses. As a result, in English law during marriage each spouse owns the property they brought into the marriage and the property they earned during it. Historically, this worked to the disadvantage of women, given the limited access that women had to the labour market, the strong social norms that the husband was the breadwinner and the wife has primary responsibility for home-making and childcare; and the lack of public child care and poor family friendly policies. On divorce, before 1970, courts had power only to order maintenance payments to an ex spouse, not to re-distribute capital property. This meant that a divorcing husband could, and usually did, walk away with all or a large proportion of the marital assets.

Under the Matrimonial Causes Act 1973, which incorporated the ancillary relief provisions of the Matrimonial Proceedings and Property Act 1970, courts have a broad discretion to distribute the assets of a couple on divorce, taking into account the factors listed in section 25. These include the income, property, obligations and needs of the parties; the length of the marriage; and the contributions of the parties to the relationship, including to the welfare of the family. However, initially the courts restricted the application of these to

[1] *White v White* [2000] UKHL 54, [2001] 1 AC 596.
[2] **Married Women's Property Act 1882.**

the wife claiming for her needs or 'reasonable requirements'. In the case of wealthy couples needs were 'generously interpreted', so that the needs of the wife of a millionaire were seen as very different from the needs of the wife of a man of limited means. But she could not claim more than she needed.

This was well illustrated by the case of *Dart v Dart*,[3] where the wife's needs were found to be met by a lump sum of £9 million. His precise wealth was unclear: was it £400 million or £700 million? For the Court of Appeal it simply did not matter; he could clearly afford to pay the £22 million assessed as necessary to meet her needs and there was nothing more to ask. Whether the husband needed the millions left was not considered a question that needed to be considered. It was simply accepted that the husband had earned the fortune and so in the absence of an especially good reason he should keep it. The wife's contribution to the marriage was ignored. Indeed, there is no mention of what specifically her contribution was, although they had two children together. She was presented simply as a dependant who needed to plead for her needs to be met. As Alison Diduck suggests, the approach of the courts can be seen as an attempt to ensure that husbands with property rights were protected from potential plunder if wives' claims were not kept under control.[4] From this perspective, the 'very generous' interpretation of 'reasonable requirements'[5] was seen as the courts being at their most beneficent towards wives.

The law prior to *White v White*, as set out in *Dart v Dart*, was generally seen as providing a degree of certainty, at least in big money cases. The question at least was clear: 'how much money was needed to meet the reasonable requirements of the wife?'. The difficulty was in interpreting what 'reasonable requirements' meant in this context. The cases that are reported in the law reports nearly all involve millionaires and so give little guidance on the meaning of 'needs'.

The truth is that only in the wealthiest cases is the court likely to be able to meet the needs of both spouses. For many couples, indeed most, there are no assets to divide on divorce, or very few. The court reports focused on wealthy cases and so the law was criticised, predominantly in terms of the courts stretching the concept of needs beyond any sensible interpretation.[6] There was also considerable unhappiness with the resulting paradox that, the longer the marriage, the older the wife and hence the less that was needed for future needs. 'Tycoons' ex-wife to lose her jet' was the headline in the *Irish Times*[7] in response to *Dart v Dart*, indicating that the perception that, if anything, the law was being too generous to wives.

## II. The Landmark

Mr and Mrs White had operated two dairy farms in partnership. They ran the business together, although Mr White had used capital from his father to buy the first farm and

[3] *Dart v Dart* [1996] 2 FLR 286.

[4] Alison Diduck, 'Fairness and Justice for All? The House of Lords in *White v White*' (2001) 9 *Feminist Legal Studies* 173.

[5] *Miller v Miller; McFarlane v McFarlane* [2006] UKHL 24 [144] (Lady Hale).

[6] Peter Singer, 'Sexual Discrimination in Ancillary Relief' (2001) 31 *Family Law* 115.

[7] 3 July 1996, *The Irish Times*.

obtained the second farm from the father on advantageous terms. The marriage lasted 33 years and there were two adult children. The net assets were £4.6 million.

Holman J, who heard the case at first instance, relied on the *Dart* approach and assessed the wife's reasonable requirements. There were seen to be met by awarding the husband to pay her £800,000, in addition to the £200,000 she had in her own name. The Court of Appeal emphasised the fact that the farm in this case had been a partnership and increased her award to £1.5 million. The very fact that Holman J applied *Dart* in a case where the money was generated by a spousal partnership is striking. It demonstrates the assumption that women make no financial contributions or, even if they make some, they do not count. Indeed, taking on board the Court of Appeal's approach – **Butler-Sloss LJ** notably pointed out that Mrs White was entitled not only to her share of the partnership but also a recognition of her contribution of child care – that could have led to a claim of more than 50 per cent of the assets.

The House of Lords dismissed both the husband's appeal, which sought a restoration of Holman J's order, and that of the wife seeking to increase the Court of Appeal's order.

While the judgment in the House of Lords contains statements of grand principle, its central argument was that the approach characterised in *Dart v Dart* over-emphasised the 'needs' factor in section 25(2) and ignored the other factors listed, particularly a consideration of the contributions of the parties to the marriage. It is in that regard that the House of Lords made its most notable remarks. Lord Nicholls, in a much-quoted passage, said:

> In seeking to achieve a fair outcome, there is no place for discrimination between husband and wife and their respective roles. Typically, a husband and wife share the activities of earning money, running their home and caring for their children. Traditionally, the husband earned the money, and the wife looked after the home and the children … But whatever the division of labour chosen by the husband and wife, or forced upon them by circumstances, fairness requires that this should not prejudice or advantage either party … If, in their different spheres, each contributed equally to the family, then in principle it matters not which of them earned the money and built up the assets. There should be no bias in favour of the money-earner and against the home-maker and the child-carer.[8]

The claim in *White v White* that the contributions of a child-carer and a money-maker were equal was not novel. Lord Denning MR observed in *Wachtel v Wachtel* that 'the wife who looks after the home and family contributes as much to the family assets as the wife who goes out to work'.[9] However, Denning's view was largely ignored, and it was the use of his approach to explain why the starting-point of the law should be an equal division of the couple's assets which was novel.

The House of Lords were clear that they were not creating a presumption of equal sharing. Lord Nicholls preferred the language of a yardstick which should be used after all the factors had been taken into account and a provision award assessed to see if there was discrimination. He explained that 'equality should only be departed from only if, and to the extent that, there are good reasons for doing so'.[10] He also noted that in more cases than not, there would be a good reason for departing from an equal division.

[8] [2001] 1 AC 596, 605.
[9] *Wachtel v Wachtel* [1973] Fam 72, 93–94.
[10] [2001] 1 AC 596, 605.

## III. What Happened Next

One might have been forgiven for thinking that *White v White* heralded a new era of greater fairness for women as well as certainty for the law, and that future cases could be easily resolved by relying on the yardstick of equality. This seemed especially likely following the House of Lords' decision in *Miller v Miller; McFarlane v McFarlane*,[11] which built upon the reasoning in *White* to emphasise the importance of fairness in financial orders on divorce, claiming that equality would produce fairness. However, since these decisions there has been a gradual withdrawal from the statements of equality in *White*. The lower courts have found numerous ways of ensuring, even in cases of a wealthy couple, that an equal division does not occur. This has been done through a range of devices.

First, the sharing principle has been said to apply only to 'marital property'; that is, property generated during the marriage which could be attributable to the matrimonial relationship.[12] Inheritance, lottery winnings, and solo business projects could be designated as not marital and so not subject to sharing. Although *White* had indicated that in the case of a lengthy marriage all property could be shared and no distinction would be drawn between marital and non-marital property, this has largely been ignored in recent cases.[13]

Second, the courts have been willing to use the notion of 'extraordinary contribution' to suggest that an extensive money-earner has made an extraordinary contribution and so is entitled to more than a half share.[14] Note that this potential argument has not been applied to a home-maker and, indeed, the courts have indicated that it could not, indicating that there are still differences in attitudes towards money-making and child care – they cannot conceive of an 'extraordinary contribution' to home-making.

Third, the courts have become increasingly reluctant to make awards based on compensation for lost earnings or enhancement of earning potential.[15] As had been emphasised in *Miller; McFarlane*, an award which shared the current assets equally, but paid no attention to the impact of the marriage on the earning potential of the parties, risked failing to compensate the carer for the negative impact of the marriage and permitting the money-maker to take all the benefit for the positive impact. Yet the courts have in recent years found claims for both compensation for lost earning capacity and enhancement of the money-maker's too speculative to form the basis of an award.[16] This means that, although there may be some degree of equality at the date of divorce, the wildly different earning capabilities caused by child care mean that very quickly dramatic inequalities in their wealth will arise. As Hayler Fisher and Hamish Lowe in their survey of the research conclude:

> The stark conclusion is that men's household income increases by about 23 per cent on divorce once we control for household size, whereas women's household income falls by about 31 per cent. There is partial recovery for women, but this recovery is driven by repartnering: the average effect of repartnering is to restore income to pre-divorce levels after nine years. [For] those who do not repartner … the long term economic consequences of divorce are serious.[17]

[11] *Miller v Miller; McFarlane v McFarlane* [2006] UKHL 24, [2006] 1 FLR 1186.
[12] *B v PS* [2015] EWHC 2797.
[13] *JL v SL (No 2) (Financial Remedies: Rehearing: Non-Matrimonial Property)* [2015] EWHC 360.
[14] *Cowan v Cowan* [2001] EWCA Civ 671.
[15] *SA v PA (Pre-Marital Agreement: Compensation)* [2014] EWHC 392.
[16] *SS v NS (Spousal Maintenance)* [2014] EWHC 413.
[17] Hayler Fisher and Hamish Low, 'Who Wins, Who Loses and Who Recovers from Divorce?' in Jo Miles and Rebecca Probert (eds), *Sharing Lives, Dividing Assets: An Interdisciplinary Study* (Hart Publishing, 2009) 254.

Fourth, and significantly, ***Radmacher v Granatino***[18] permitted the courts to give effect to pre-nuptial agreements. These appear to have grown in popularity among the wealthiest couples, upon whom the *White* equal-division principle was most likely to have impact. Significantly, *Radmacher* makes it clear that a departure from equality will not be regarded as a reason for not giving effect to a pre-nuptial agreement. Indeed, unless the agreement is leaving a party in a 'real predicament of need', it is likely to be given effect. *Radmacher*, as **Lady Hale** recognised in her dissenting judgment in that case, opens the door to many spouses receiving even less than they would have under the old 'reasonable requirements approach' prior to *White*.

These developments have meant that the promise of an equal division of assets being a norm, at least for wealthy couples, and a determination that there would be no discrimination between husbands and wives, seems a distant call. As Mostyn J recently noted, cases of equal sharing of assets are as rare as the sighting of a snow leopard.[19]

## IV. Significance

The significance of this case is that it is one of the few areas of law in which care work is valued and recognised, and even said to be valued as equal to money-making. In much law, care work is invisible and offered no recognition or respect. This is despite the fact that care work is about meeting the most essential and basic needs that humans have. It deserves to be valued as at least as important as financially productive work, indeed more so. To date, care work has been largely invisible to the legal and political discourses. There have been strong expectations that mothers and daughters will care for family dependants, and women are often willing to do this out of love or the weight of expectation, even if it does not receive financial or social acknowledgment. Part of the difficulty is that care work cannot be readily reduced to a figure on a balance sheet. It is literally and metaphorically beyond value.

Although *White* is a rare example of acknowledging the value of care work, there are real dangers in getting carried away with the welcome rhetoric of the decision. First, it is notable that even in the case itself, despite the particularly compelling case for at least an equal division, reasons were found not to grant equality. Indeed, as outlined above, the judgment laid the seeds for later case law to develop a wide number of ways to get around equal division, always to the disadvantage of the caregiver.

Second, only for the very wealthy married couples is *White v White* equal division an option. For the vast majority of cases, couples have no or very few assets and it is a pretence to assume then that caregiving is valued by the law. Even for middle-class couples it is earning capacity and pensions which are the most valuable assets available, yet the courts appear particularly reluctant to deal with them.

Third, the recognition of caregiving in *White* is limited only to married or civilly partnered couples. For those who care outside this privileged sphere care continues to go unrecognised and unrewarded by the law and the state. Cohabitants and those informally caring for adults gain nothing from *White*.

[18] ***Radmacher v Granatino*** [2010] UKSC 42.
[19] *JL v SL (No 2) (Financial Remedies: Rehearing: Non-Matrimonial Property)* [2015] EWHC 360.

Fourth, equality was interpreted to mean formal equality. As noted above, even among fairly wealthy couples, an equal division of assets would leave the parties in a very unequal position in the years following the marriage, given the likely impact of the marriage on their earning potential and the ongoing responsibilities of care. Indeed, for many less-well-off couples, the limited assets there are given to the wife and children, giving them significantly more than half the assets. If formal equality were to become the norm for all divorcing couples, wives in non-millionaire households would significantly lose out in many cases.

Fifth, *White* seems to be based on an image of relationships from a bygone era. Even Mrs White was combining her child care with money-making. Gay and lesbian relations rarely fall into a straight forward division of money-maker and child-carer. The dangers are that the realities of low-paid, part-time work being undertaken by those raising children falls out of the picture. The 'double' or 'triple' shift of combing employment, child care, and care of dependent relatives can be masked with the talk of the equal contributions of the money-maker and home-maker.

If the law is serious about the claim in *White v White* that we should value equally caregiving and money-making we need vast changes in the law and societal structures.[20] The achievement in *White v White* hardly deserves being called a scratch on the surface of that aim. Perhaps for those seeking greater valuing of care the rhetoric of *White* is welcome. But the rhetoric of autonomy and self-sufficiency are more commonly found in the more recent case law on financial orders. As Alison Diduck has argued, we have shifted from a language of paternalism, which portrayed women as supplicants, to one which emphasises the ideas of equality and sharing in *White* itself.[21] However, now 'individualism, autonomy and choice' dominate. The 'White revolution' nowadays looks more the speech of a politician: strong on rhetoric, but slow in action.

## Further Reading

- Alison Diduck, 'Fairness and Justice for All? The House of Lords in *White v White*' (2001) 9 *Feminist Legal Studies* 173.
- Lisa Glennon, 'The Limitations of Equality Discourses on the Contours of Intimate Obligations' in Julie Wallbank, Shazia Choudhry and Jonathan Herring (eds), *Rights, Gender and Family Law* (Routledge, 2010).
- Brenda Hale, 'Equality and Autonomy in Family Law' (2011) 33 *Journal of Social Welfare and Family Law* 3.

[20] Jonathan Herring, *Caring and the Law* (Hart Publishing, 2013).
[21] Diduck, n 4 above.

# 73

# Sex Discrimination (Election Candidates) Act 2002

SUSAN ATKINS

The Sex Discrimination (Election Candidates) Act 2002 allowed political parties in the UK to use positive discrimination to tackle persistent under-representation of women in Parliament and other elected bodies. It did so by excluding from the **Sex Discrimination Act 1975** (SDA) and Sex Discrimination Order 1976 (which applied to Northern Ireland) any arrangements made by political parties for the purposes of reducing inequality in the numbers of men and women elected by them as candidates.

Proposals for a Bill were announced in the first Queen's speech after the 2001 election, which saw a fall in the numbers of women MPs. This was in marked contrast to the doubling of the number of women MPs (to 18 per cent) following the 1997 election in which all-women shortlists had been used by the Labour Party for half its 'winnable' seats, until stopped by a legal challenge. Passed with all-party support in 2002, the Act put positive action to increase female representation in Parliament firmly on the map. Representation of women as MPs (which had remained at under five per cent until 1987) increased at every subsequent election to 32 per cent by the General Election in June 2017.

## I. Context

The Labour Party started to consider the issue of whether and how to increase the number of women MPs after losing the 1987 General Election, when their research showed that voters found its masculine images old-fashioned and unattractive.[1] This was especially so amongst women, who had been found to be more likely to vote Conservative in every election since 1945. The 1990 Labour Party Conference adopted a policy of a 40 per cent quota for women's representation throughout the party, but the selection of candidates was excluded when Party rules were changed in 1991 to implement that policy. The fall-back position, that if a woman was nominated at the first stage of the selection process at least one woman should be on the final shortlist, resulted in a small increase in the number of

[1] Maria Eagle and Joni Lovenduski, *High time or high tide for Labour women* (The Fabian Society, 1998).

women elected in the 1992 General Election, which Labour again lost. As a result senior party officials were persuaded to make a greater representation of women an integral part of the modernisation agenda and strategy for electoral success.[2]

The Labour Party's National Women's Conference had for many years advocated the use of all-women shortlists. With the backing of its popular leader, John Smith MP, in 1993 the Labour Party adopted the use of all-women shortlists for half its 'winnable' seats (that is, those where the previous Labour MP was stepping down, or 'target' seats which could be gained for Labour with a relatively small swing of voters). The choice of which seats should have all-women shortlists was decided by regional committees on which women were well represented, because of the quota policy previously adopted. Despite some resistance, by January 1996 most candidates had been chosen and half of the key target seats (33) and two empty seats had women candidates.[3]

In 1996, however, an Industrial Tribunal held the use of all-women shortlists to be unlawful under the SDA.[4] Until that point it had been assumed that the SDA did not apply – the job of an MP not being 'employment' and section 33 of the SDA exempting political parties from the provisions outlawing discrimination in the provision of goods facilities and services, thus allowing women's associations to continue. The Tribunal held that all-women shortlists contravened section 13(1) of the SDA prohibiting discrimination by bodies which can confer an authorisation or qualification needed for engagement in a particular profession or trade. In order to complete the selection process in good time and not jeopardise the position of candidates already selected under the process, the Labour Party decided not to appeal. The remaining selections were made from open lists and some women were selected, although not as many as would have been on the all-women shortlists policy.[5]

Of the 158 Labour women candidates in the 1997 election, 101 were elected to be MPs. Women accounted for half the MPs elected in key target seats; just over a third of seats previously held by Labour, and nearly 17 per cent of unexpected gains.[6] Women made up almost a quarter of Labour MPs after the 1997 election and the number of female MPs from all parties doubled to 120. That number dropped to 118 in the 2001 election,[7] the number of women Labour MPs falling by six to 95.

The Labour Party's experience focused attention across political parties on how to increase women's representation. The Scottish National Party (SNP), Plaid Cymru and the Liberal Democrats had voted in favour of an amendment to the 1998 Bills setting up the new Devolved legislatures, which would have allowed positive action measures in elections to those bodies. Although the amendments failed, women made up a much higher proportion of Members of the Scottish Parliament (MSP) and Members of the Welsh Assembly (MWA) – 36.4 per cent and 38.3 per cent respectively – in part due to the different electoral systems used[8] and because these were totally new legislatures, with no existing members.

[2] ibid 4.

[3] ibid 5–6.

[4] *Jepson and Dyas-Elliott v The Labour Party and others* [1996] IRLR 166.

[5] Eagle and Lovenduski, n 1 above, 6–7.

[6] ibid 8.

[7] After the *Jepson* case the Labour Party adopted a policy that *half* of every shortlist should be women. This did not translate into women being 50% of candidates.

[8] Elections to the Scottish Parliament and Welsh Assembly use an Additional Member system by which every elector has two votes, one for the constituency chosen on a first-past-the-post basis and a second for the region

In both elections the Labour Party used a twinning process, combining two constituencies for the selection process and selecting one man and one woman, a process which is easier where there are no incumbents. In the 1999 European Parliamentary election, the Liberal Democrats adopted a policy of zipping; that is, placing men and women alternately on the list of Parliamentary candidates, which achieved a 50 per cent representation of women MEPs. Despite resistance to positive action within the Conservative Party, the announcement by the Labour Government of its intention to prepare legislation allowing positive action in the selection of candidates was welcomed by Caroline Spelman MP, Conservative spokesperson on Women's Issues and by Michael Portillo MP, a candidate in the Conservative leadership election.[9]

## II. The Landmark

After the 1997 General Election, the Labour Government established a Women's Unit in the Cabinet Office to support two new Ministers for Women and I became its second Director in 2000. The 2000 Labour Party Conference resolved to review the law on positive action. In 2001 the then Minister for Women, Baroness Jay, and the then Home Secretary, Jack Straw MP (who had the departmental lead for electoral policy), agreed to undertake this review with a view to introducing legislation enabling all-women shortlists to be re-introduced. Officials in the two departments worked together on the review. We were greatly helped by the work of Meg Russell, then Senior Research Fellow at the Constitution Unit, University College London (UCL), who had undertaken a short project to investigate the legal obstacles and whether these could be overcome. Her report, *Women's representation in UK politics: What can be done within the law?*, published in June 2000, reviewed domestic and EU law and concluded that a change in the law was possible and necessary to allow positive action to be used with confidence.

The Labour Party Manifesto in 2001 included a commitment to legal change. After Labour were returned to government, they announced a commitment to prepare legislation to allow political parties to make positive moves to increase the representation of women in public life. After the election, responsibility for electoral law transferred to the Department for Transport, Local Government and the Regions (DTLR) but the Women's Unit (renamed the Women and Equality Unit (WEU) to reflect its extended scope to co-ordinate equality policy across government) hosted the Bill team and remained the driving force.

Meg Russell's second report in 2001, *The Women's Representation Bill: Making it Happen*, looked at the legal and political issues, legal options, different types of positive action measures and experience from across Europe. WEU worked closely with her, helping to ensure a wide range of representation from political parties and government departments at a UCL seminar on the subject, at which speakers from other EU Member States explained their laws. The WEU talked to a group of expert lawyers and asked the Equal Opportunities

from a party list. Elections to the Northern Ireland Assembly are by the single transferable vote form of proportional representation.

[9] Meg Russell, *The Women's Representation Bill: Making it Happen* (The Constitution Unit, University College London, 2001).

Commission (EOC) and Fawcett Society to share their research in helping to develop policy. The EOC and Fawcett took the findings of their research[10] to all the party-political conferences. The WEU Gender Research Forum meeting had presentations from Paul Chaney (Wales), Fiona Mackay (Scotland) and Margaret Ward (Northern Ireland) on the difference having a higher percentage of women in the Devolved Assemblies had made. The Women's National Commission also undertook research on this difference from the perspective of women's organisations.[11] This activity and briefing sessions for spokespersons on women's issues across political parties generated a groundswell of support for the Bill.

Support was also given within the machinery of government. Potential obstacles, such as a heavy legislative programme and resulting pressure on Parliamentary time and lack of capacity in the Parliamentary Counsel's office, were overcome with the support of the leaders of both Houses (Robin Cook MP[12] and Lord Williams) and from a former Parliamentary Counsel who volunteered his services for the Bill. The inclusion of a sunset clause, providing that the provisions of the legislation would expire at the end of 2015 (unless previously extended by affirmative resolution regulations), also overcame some potential opposition to the Bill. It was passed with the support of all parties in both Houses and received Royal Assent on 26 February 2002.[13]

## III. What Happened Next

The legislation prompted renewed interest in positive action. In 2001 the Liberal Democrats agreed that 40 per cent of their 'winnable' seats should be fought by female candidates, to monitor progress towards that target and to review selection processes. After the Act was passed, the Labour Party reinstated the all-women shortlist policy, increasing the number of women returned as Labour MPs in the 2005 election.

Having failed to win the 2005 election, the Conservative Party focused on increasing and supporting more women candidates (including some women-only training) and on changing the selection process rules. Baroness Jenkin and Theresa May MP set up a Women2Win campaign and David Cameron MP, then new Party Leader, championed diversity and change. In 2006 the party established a priority list of candidates (to be 50 per cent women) from which local associations in vacant Conservative-held seats would be expected to select.[14]

In 2010 five organisations came together to form the 'Counting Women In' coalition to raise awareness about the absence of women from the highest levels of politics in

[10] Judith Squires and Mark Wickham-Jones, *Women in Parliament: a comparative analysis* (EOC, 2001) and Jessica Elgood, Louise Vinter and Rachel Williams, *Man Enough for the job? A Study of Parliamentary Candidates* (EOC, 2002).

[11] The Women's National Commission was abolished in 2010 as part of the reductions in Non Departmental Public Bodies.

[12] Robin Cook also introduced a number of family-friendly reforms to the workings of the House of Commons as part of a modernisation programme.

[13] For background to the Bill, see Pat Strickland, Oonagh Gay, Julia Lourie and Richard Cracknell, *The Sex Discrimination (Election Candidates) Bill* (House of Commons Research Paper 01/75, 2001).

[14] These rules were subsequently amended to extend the requirement of 50% representation of women at every stage of the selection process and increase oversight by the party central machinery.

the UK.[15] Developments within Parliament included, in 2008, a Speaker's Conference to consider and make recommendations for rectifying disproportionate under-representation of women and ethnic minorities in the House of Commons,[16] and the establishment of an All-Party Parliamentary Group for Women in Parliament in 2010[17] and a Women and Equalities Committee of the House of Commons (WEC) in 2015. The Equality Act 2010, which consolidated and updated the then extant equalities statutes, extended the sunset clause provisions of the 2002 Act to 2030, allowed parties to use all-disabled shortlists and to reserve some (but not all) places on shortlists for candidates on grounds of ethnicity or sexual orientation,[18] and provided for regulations to require political parties to publish data relating to diversity of candidates.[19] In 2016 the Speaker of the House of Commons set up a new group, 'The Commons Reference Group on Representation and Inclusion', made up of men and women MPs, to consider 43 proposals made in 'The Good Parliament Report' by Sarah Childs, to improve representation, and the working practices and culture of the UK Parliament.[20] In January 2017 the WEC's report *Women in the House of Commons after the 2020 election* made five recommendations including extending the provisions of the 2002 Act to elections for Mayors and Police and Crime Commissioners and beyond 2030.[21]

## IV. Significance

The political landscape has changed dramatically, and symbolically women are better represented in the legislature and executive. In 2003, the Welsh Assembly became the first Parliament in the world to be made up of equal numbers of men and women.[22] By early 2017 women made up 30 per cent of MPs,[23] Britain had its second female Prime Minister, Theresa May, and eight of the 22 Cabinet Ministers were women, including the third female Home Secretary. While the proportion of MPs increased by two per cent following the 2017

[15] The Centre for Women and Democracy, the Electoral Reform Society, the Fawcett Society, the Hansard Society and Unlock Democracy.

[16] A rarely used procedure, a Speaker's Conference on Electoral Reform was also used in 1916 to consider extending the vote to women.

[17] In 2014, this Group published a report *Improving Parliament: creating a better and more representative House*, with a number of recommendations to encourage more women and under-represented groups to consider a role in public life, to improve professional behaviour in the House and to establish a Women and Equalities Committee.

[18] Political parties gave evidence to the WEC on the use of positive action measures. All have programmes for training, mentoring and support for women and other minority groups. The Liberal Democrats and Scottish National Party have recently adopted a policy of all-women shortlists, still used by Labour. The Liberal Democrats have used an all-disabled shortlist for one of its most winnable seats.

[19] Section 106 Equalities Act 2010 which has not yet been brought into force. The WEC's report on Women in the House of Commons after the 2020 election recommended that it should be.

[20] Sarah Childs, *The Good Parliament* (University of Bristol, 2016). Professor Childs was seconded to the House of Commons in 2015, at the Speaker's request, to work on the report. In Northern Ireland a Speaker's Reference group on a Gender Sensitive Assembly was set up in February 2016 and a Women's Caucus set up in March 2016 to develop a three-year action plan.

[21] House of Commons Women and Equalities Committee, *Women in the House of Commons after the 2020 election* (HMSO, HC 630, 2017).

[22] See **National Assembly for Wales Election, 2003.**

[23] After 5 by-elections which increased the number of women MPs by 4.

General Election, the number of women in Cabinet fell from eight to five.[24] Women's representation in two of the Devolved legislatures and the European Parliament was even higher.[25] The First Ministers in both Scotland and Northern Ireland were women, six political parties were led by women,[26] and Nicola Sturgeon, Scottish First Minister, had a gender-balanced cabinet.

Political parties now seem to have embraced the importance of gender in their selection processes as an integral part of modernisation and election strategies, recognising it as a matter of democratic legitimacy as well as individual justice. Achieving women's full and equal participation in elected bodies is one of the Sustainable Development Goals agreed by 193 United Nations member states (including the UK) in 2015.

The 2002 Act has also resulted in more attention being given by Parliament and political parties to other types of diversity. This is equally an issue for women, who may face multiple barriers due to their gender, ethnicity, religion, sexual orientation or disability. After the 2015 election the number of ethnic minority women MPs nearly doubled from 11 to 21 out of 650 MPs and constitute over half of the 41 of ethnic minority MPs.[27] In 2017, the number of ethnic minority MPs increased to 52 including 26 women.[28]

The 2002 Act was an enabling measure which allowed political parties to change their internal processes to improve women's representation in elected bodies. The experience of the Devolved Assemblies shows that other factors are equally important, and attention within the UK Parliament is now focusing on working practices, culture and measures that can be taken to attract women as potential candidates and retain women as MPs once elected. The Inter-Parliamentary Union reported in 2016 on the global prevalence of sexism, harassment and violence against women MPs, which affects women's political engagement.[29] Concern about this phenomenon in the UK was raised by the House of Commons Administration Committee in 2015 and again by the Women and Equalities Committee a year later in the aftermath of the murder of a woman MP, Jo Cox, outside her constituency office in June 2016.[30] In late 2017 the issue of sexual harassment within public life, following the #me too campaign, led to the resignation of a senior Cabinet Minister and an all-party agreement to introduce a new independent complaints procedure for members and staff within the UK Parliament.

There is debate as to whether the increased number of women in the various Parliaments of the UK has led to substantive changes: do more women MPs lead to more attention and

[24] Though two more attend Cabinet (November 2017 figures).

[25] In July 2017, 42% of the National Assembly for Wales, 35% of the Scottish Parliament, 30% of the Northern Ireland Assembly and 41% of the UK's MEPs are women (See Vyara Apostolova and Richard Cracknell, *Women in Parliament and Government* (HC Library Briefing Paper SN01250, July 2017)).

[26] The Conservatives (for the UK and in Scotland), SNP, Plaid Cymru, the Democratic Unionist Party and Green Party. The Liberal Democrats in Wales were led by a woman from 2008–16. UKIP had a female leader briefly in 2016 before being replaced by a man.

[27] Lukas Audickas, *Ethnic Minorities in Politics and Public Life* (HC Library Briefing Paper SN01156, March 2016): http://www.obv.org.uk/sites/default/files/images/downloads/SN01156-Ethnic-Minorities-in-Politics-and-Public-Life.pdf.

[28] Lukas Audickas and Vyara Apostolva, *Ethnic Minorities in Politics and Public Life* (HC Library Briefing Paper SN01156, June 2017): http://researchbriefings.files.parliament.uk/documents/SN01156/SN01156.pdf.

[29] House of Commons Women and Equalities Committee, n 21 above.

[30] Report of a survey of women MPs and staff by the House of Commons Administration Committee in 2015: https://www.parliament.uk/documents/commons-committees/admin-committee/Memoranda.pdf, and House of Commons Women and Equalities Committee, n 21 above.

action on matters of particular concerns to women?[31] The Speaker's Conference Report in 2010 concluded that there was evidence that, with increased representation, both the content and style of politics changes, and that the development of policy and legislation on social issues was higher on the agenda.

There is also a question as to whether the UK has reached a critical mass at which women's representation as MPs has become normalised. The WEC feared not, calling the 30 per cent figure 'a serious democratic deficit' and noting the vulnerability of having the majority of women MPs in one party. The Committee's recommendations included a 45 per cent target to be set by the Government for women in Parliament and local government by 2030 and legislation setting a statutory minimum of 45 per cent for women's representation on party shortlists, to be brought into force if the numbers and proportion of women failed to increase significantly after the 2020 election.[32] Since the WEC Report there has been a very slight increase in the representation of women. Should this fall back in future, the 2002 Act and subsequent institutional developments should maintain attention on the issue of democratic equality.

## Further Reading

- House of Commons Women and Equalities Committee, *Women in the House of Commons after the 2020 election* (HMSO, HC 630, 2017).
- Richard Kelly and Isobel White, *All Women Shortlists* (House of Commons Library Briefing Paper SN05057, March 2016).
- Meg Russell, *The Women's Representation Bill: Making it Happen* (The Constitution Unit University College London, 2001).

[31] See Sarah Childs, Joni Lovenduski and Rosie Campbell, *Women at the Top 2005: Changing Numbers, Changing Politics* (Hansard Society, 2005); Sarah Childs and Mona Lena Krook, 'The substantive representation of women' in Sarah Childs (ed), *Women and British Party Politics* (Routledge, 2008).

[32] House of Commons Women and Equalities Committee, n 21 above.

# 74

# Section 1 of the Sexual Offences Act 2003

NIKKI GODDEN-RASUL

The Sexual Offences Act 2003 radically altered the archaic sexual offences laws in England and Wales. Section 1 defines rape as the intentional penile penetration of the vagina, anus or mouth of another person without that person's consent and without a reasonable belief that s/he consents. The most significant change was the move from 'honest' to 'reasonable' in relation to the defendant's belief in consent – the former having been widely decried by feminists as a 'rapist's charter'.[1] Section 1 must be read alongside section 74 which not only includes, for the first time, a definition of consent, but one which emphasises women's autonomy over men's desires.

The new legislation was the culmination of a detailed review process informed by contributions of feminist scholars, organisations and campaigns, drawing on decades of feminist anti-rape work. Through rape law reform the then Labour Government aimed to improve the reporting and conviction rates, but the inclusion of feminist perspectives in the legislative process meant that the law now also better recognises and protects women's sexual autonomy.

## I. Context

By the turn of the twenty-first century, a wealth of feminist work on sexual violence had accumulated. By the 1970s, women had begun sharing their experiences of men's violence in consciousness-raising groups which revealed the prevalence of rape. Rape Crisis Centres were opened to provide victim-survivors with support which was sorely lacking from public institutions.[2] There was an increasing recognition that, contrary to the public and legal image of rape as a crime perpetrated by a stranger who uses physical force or threats, most women are raped by their (ex)partner, friend, or acquaintance. At the same time, it was becoming clear that the criminal law did not reflect women's lived experiences. Little wonder that rape victim-survivors seldom turned to it. When they did they were commonly treated with suspicion and there was little chance of the perpetrator being convicted.

Within the academy, feminist scholars such as Catharine MacKinnon and Liz Kelly were asking why rape is prevalent, and why the criminal justice system fails to address it.

[1] Jennifer Temkin, *Rape and the Legal Process* (2nd edn, OUP, 2002) 119.
[2] **First Rape Crisis Centre, 1976.**

They linked rape to social norms which imbue men with a sense of entitlement to use women's bodies for their own pleasure.[3] It is these gendered norms, they suggested, that underpin the many and varied 'myths' about rape, such as that consent can be assumed if a woman has not communicated 'no' clearly enough, or that a woman's sexual behaviour and dress are indicative of consent. And it was these myths that led criminal justice personnel, and victim-survivors' friends and family, to blame them for precipitating rape, and which the law on rape did little to dispel.

Prior to the 2003 Act, rape law was based on statutes from the 1950s and 1970s, with roots dating back to the nineteenth century. Section 1 of the Sexual Offences Act 1956, as amended by section 1 of the Sexual Offences (Amendment) Act 1976, defined rape as a man having sexual intercourse with a woman without her consent.[4] Under this definition, a man must have either known the woman was not consenting, or be reckless as to whether she was consenting. This endorsed – and put on a statutory footing – an earlier House of Lords' decision, *DPP v Morgan*,[5] that a defendant's honest belief in the victim-survivor's consent would absolve him of liability. The defendant was one of three Royal Air Force colleagues taken by a fourth man to the latter's house where they had sex with his wife. They were told that this was part of a game she liked, and that her apparent resistance was pretence. Its focus on the *defendant's* perception of events, at the expense of the complainant's experience and sexual autonomy, meant that the '*Morgan* defence' was detested by feminists.[6]

Crucially, the concept of consent itself was undefined and left to the jury to interpret. Rape cases were susceptible to being judged against antiquated notions – previously legally accepted – that only force, fear or fraud proved lack of consent. Sexual relations, rather than being understood as a mutual agreement, were typically presented as an act pursued by men to which women consensually submit. Indeed, it was not until 1998 in *R v Malone*[7] that the Court of Appeal highlighted that the complainant did not need to communicate or demonstrate lack of consent.

The 1990s saw piecemeal reform of substantive and procedural laws, some of which were in response to feminist concerns about the poor treatment of complainants and the continuing influence of rape myths. In 1991 the House of Lords allowed, for the first time, the possibility of rape within marriage.[8] As well as protecting married women's rights, this reflected the reality that most victim-survivors intimately know their rapists. Shortly after, in section 142 of the Criminal Justice and Public Order Act 1994, the act of rape was broadened to include non-consensual penile penetration of a person's anus in response to public concerns about the rape of men. At the end of the decade, the Youth Justice and Criminal Evidence Act 1999 was enacted, providing for special measures to protect vulnerable witnesses and assist in obtaining best evidence, such as, in section 41, restricting when a complainant's sexual history can be used as evidence of consent in a sexual offence trial.[9]

[3] Catharine MacKinnon, *Toward a Feminist Theory of the State* (Harvard University Press, 1989); Liz Kelly, *Surviving Sexual Violence* (Polity, 1988).

[4] See also **Section 4 of the Sexual Offences (Amendment) Act 1976**.

[5] *DPP v Morgan* [1976] AC 182,

[6] Temkin, n 1 above, 122–28.

[7] *R v Malone* [1998] 2 Cr App R 447.

[8] *R v R* [1992] 1 AC 599. See further, **Section 5 of the Criminal Law (Rape) (Amendment) Act 1990**.

[9] **Section 41 of the Youth Justice and Criminal Evidence Act 1999**.

In practice, however, these rape law and procedural amendments made little difference to complainants. Marital rape cases were not usually investigated or prosecuted in the criminal justice system, and suspicion of rape complaints in the absence of physical violence and resistance remained.[10] Public and legal understandings of rape continued to be informed by problematic gendered expectations as to when, where, and with whom women have consensual sex.

By the end of the twentieth century, a number of factors coalesced to instigate significant legal change. The 2000 British Crime Survey estimated that in the course of a year 61,000 women between ages 16 and 59 were raped in England and Wales.[11] Police records, therefore, reflected just 20 per cent of rapes, and of those, only eight per cent resulted in a conviction.[12] Political parties faced pressure to reform rape laws, as had been done in other Commonwealth jurisdictions, including New Zealand and Australia. The Labour Party manifesto prior to the 1997 General Election promised to improve the criminal law and justice response to sexual offences. In addition, under section 4 of the Human Rights Act 1998, judges were able to declare legislation incompatible with the European Convention on Human Rights. This also ensured that the Government would have to act, particularly as the European Court of Human Rights had already held that a state could be in violation of human rights where appropriate rape legislation was lacking.[13] In 1999 a lengthy review process was initiated, which culminated in the Sexual Offences Act 2003.

## II. The Landmark

The Labour Government had three aims in reforming the law of rape, set out in the policy paper *Protecting the Public*: to modernise the law on rape; to improve conviction rates; and to encourage victim-survivors to report rape.[14] The policies set out in the paper were based on the recommendations in a Law Commission Report (*Consent in Sex Offences*)[15] and a Home Office review of sex offences (*Setting the Boundaries: Reforming the Law on Sex Offences*).[16] The review process, explained in *Setting the Boundaries*, was 'open, inclusive and evidence based'. It included an advisory External Reference Group and consultation conferences involving feminist organisations, such as Rape Crisis and the Campaign to End Rape, as well as leading feminist academics, most notably Jennifer Temkin, whose evaluation of the law was described as 'of particular importance'.[17]

The policy paper adopted the modernising recommendation in *Setting the Boundaries* to extend the definition of rape to include non-consensual penile penetration of the mouth, accepting the view that it is as 'horrible, as demeaning and as traumatising as other forms

[10] Temkin, n 1 above, chapter 1.
[11] ibid 17, citing the survey alongside other studies from 1947–2000 (11–30).
[12] ibid 27.
[13] *X and Y v Netherlands* [1985] ECHR 4.
[14] Home Office, *Protecting the Public* (Cm 5668, 2002) [8]–[10].
[15] Law Commission, *Consent in Sex Offences* (HMSO, 2000).
[16] Home Office, *Setting the Boundaries: Reforming the Law on Sex Offences, Vol 1* (HOCD, 2000).
[17] ibid [2.5.1]. For Temkin's evidence, see Home Office, *Setting the Boundaries: Reforming the Law on Sex Offence, Vol 2* (HOCD, 2000) 77–124.

of forced penile penetration'.[18] This view was repeated by Cathy Halloran, representing the Rape Crisis Federation and Campaign to End Rape, in her evidence to the Home Affairs Committee.[19] Despite concerns that juries would refuse to convict for rape in cases of non-consensual oral penetration,[20] neither the Government nor Parliament were persuaded to change this aspect of the Sexual Offences Bill.

Another key aim of the policy paper was to communicate more clearly what constitutes acceptable and unacceptable behaviour in the context of sexual relations.[21] To this end, section 74 of the Sexual Offences Act 2003 defines consent as where a person 'agrees by choice, and has the freedom and capacity to make that choice'. Consent is a shared agreement between active subjects, rather than women's acquiescence to men's desires. In addition, the Act introduces circumstantial facts which raise either an evidential (rebuttable) presumption or a conclusive presumption that consent and a reasonable belief in consent were lacking (sections 75 and 76). Disappointingly, the presumptions do not mark out the clearest cases of non-consent – for example, incapacity to consent by way of intoxication is only presumed where it was defendant-induced. This provides limited protection to self-intoxicated complainants and reinforces the moral 'victim hierarchy' of which feminists have been critical. However, in broad terms, the consent provisions convey important messages about the value of sexual autonomy.

The most significant change in the law is, however, the 'reasonable belief in consent' requirement. This allows for a rape to be committed where a defendant lacks a *reasonable* belief in the complainant's consent. Interestingly, this requirement was not recommended in either the Law Commission or Home Office reports. Both suggested a subjective test with added qualifications, for example, that the defence of honest belief in consent is not available when the defendant was voluntarily intoxicated.[22] Crucially, the Government refused to entertain a subjective standard, maintaining that it did not provide enough protection for victim-survivors and hampered the conviction rate.[23] In fact, the original Sexual Offences Bill set the bar even higher at 'what the reasonable person would have believed'.[24] However, following extensive debate in Parliament, in which the measure was criticised for unfairly punishing a person who makes an honest mistake and does not have the same capacity for reason as the reasonable person,[25] the Bill was revised to ask what is reasonable for the *defendant* to believe 'in all the circumstances'.[26] And so, while the shift to a reasonable belief standard was hailed at the time as a feminist victory, there were immediate concerns that the concessions made would invite the jury to consider circumstances which are only loosely related – if at all – to consent.[27]

The Bill received Royal Assent on 20 November 2003 and came into effect in May 2004.

[18] Home Office, n 14 above [0.6] and [2.8.5].
[19] Home Affairs Committee, *Sexual Offences Bill – Fifth Report of Session 2002–03* (HC 639, 2003) 7.
[20] For example, see Peter Rook QC, Chair of the Criminal Bar Association, ibid.
[21] Home Office, n 14 above, [9–11].
[22] *Setting the Boundaries*, n 16 above, [2.13.14].
[23] Home Office, n 14 above, [32].
[24] Sexual Offences HL Bill (2002–03) 26.
[25] HL Deb, 2 June 2003, vol 648 cols 1061–1077.
[26] Sexual Offences HL Bill (2002–03) 128.
[27] Andrew Ashworth and Jennifer Temkin, 'The Sexual Offences Act 2003: (1) Rape, Sexual Assaults and the Problems of Consent' [2004] *Criminal Law Review* 328, 342.

## III. What Happened Next

The high hopes for the Sexual Offences Act 2003 were dampened relatively quickly. A 'stocktake' by the Home Office in 2006 concluded that the 2003 Act had 'modernised rape law as the Government intended, but had not encouraged victim-survivors to report rape and had no discernible impact on the conviction rate.[28] While feminists were pleased that the 2003 Act took some important *symbolic* steps in the protection of sexual autonomy, they were sceptical as to whether the substantive legal changes would translate into *practice*. As Andrew Ashworth and Jennifer Temkin summarise, assumptions and stereotypes as to when, where and with whom women have consensual sex are left unchallenged in the law.[29]

As a result, the concept of consent has been interpreted and applied in light of social norms and rape myths. Mock jury studies reveal that continuing gendered assumptions about sexual behaviour, for example that a woman has consented to sex unless there is evidence of force or resistance, still influence jury decision-making.[30] Similarly, (mock) jurors' consideration of 'all the circumstances' which may have induced a defendant's 'reasonable' belief in consent include largely – if not entirely – irrelevant factors such as the complainant's behaviour or sexual history.[31] While this may be inevitable for some – MacKinnon, for example, argues that any consent standard is doomed to fail to protect women from sexual violations in a context of gender inequality where men's perspectives are privileged – it is no less disappointing.[32]

The defendant-perspective-focus has been slightly weakened by judicial interpretations of section 1(1)(c) of the Act. In *R v B*[33] the Court of Appeal would not allow a jury to take into account a defendant's mental disorder to render an irrational belief in consent a reasonable one for the defendant to have held. However, the Court of Appeal made clear that in some cases the defendant's particular characteristics will be relevant to determine whether a belief in consent was reasonable. In addition, presumptions raised about lack of consent and belief in consent in the 2003 Act have been of limited guidance in improving understandings of consent and reasonable belief in consent. Some have been interpreted narrowly by judges, and others need little evidence to be rebutted and are complicated for jurors to understand.[34] The definition of consent, presumptions about consent, and the requirement of a reasonable belief in consent are symbolically significant in recognising violations of sexual autonomy, but they have had little practical effect in punishing such violations.

Knowing that the Sexual Offences Act 2003 would not address problematic attitudes held within the criminal justice system, feminist scholars, activists and commentators have continued to focus on procedures and policies which offer victim-survivors better

[28] Home Office, *Sexual Offences Act 2003: A Stocktake of the Effectiveness of the Act Since its Implementation* (Home Office, 2006).

[29] Ashworth and Temkin, n 27 above, 342.

[30] Emily Finch and Vanessa E Munro, 'Breaking the Boundaries: Sexual Consent in the Jury Room' (2006) 26 *Legal Studies* 303.

[31] ibid.

[32] MacKinnon, n 3 above.

[33] *R v B* [2013] EWCA Crim 3.

[34] Catarina Sjölin, 'Ten Years On: Consent Under the Sexual Offences Act 2003' (2015) 79 *Journal of Criminal Law* 20, 27–30.

treatment within the criminal justice system and the possibility of justice in more cases. These include police investigation improvements, such as having women police officers and forensic examiners available,[35] or providing rape complainants with independent legal representation,[36] as well as the use of restorative justice processes.[37] While not all feminist proposals have been taken up, recent reports do highlight many good processes and policies that have been adopted by the Government or local police forces.[38]

However, the problem remains with implementing such policies.[39] Other continuing challenges are to secure resources for victim-survivor-centred initiatives, such as the funding of Rape Crisis Centres, and to achieve social changes through addressing gender inequalities and stereotypes. Gendered expectations and rape myths still hold strong, masking the realities of rape and protecting men's access to women's bodies.[40] Fourteen years on, victim-survivors continue to be treated with scepticism and hostility in the criminal justice system, and few receive justice. Of the estimated 60,000–95,000 rapes a year, in 2012, for example, 15,670 were recorded by the police and just 1,070 resulted in a conviction.[41]

## IV. Significance

Section 1 of the Sexual Offences Act 2003 is of considerable symbolic significance for women.

While the Government's motivations for rape law reform focused on increasing the conviction rate, the process provided feminist scholars and activists with the opportunity to influence the legislation to reflect women's lived experiences of rape and to encourage belief in complainants throughout the criminal justice process.[42] Decades of feminist research and the views of feminist academics and organisations were incorporated into the legislative process and final law. This was no mean feat. Throughout history laws have been made by men for men, including – or perhaps especially – those which primarily concern women. The result of this feminist input was a revised definition of rape which – while not perfect – better reflects the fundamental violation of rape and the realities of women's experiences of men's sexual violence. It is a law which conveys important messages about the regard which should be given to a woman's sexual autonomy, and provides a platform from

[35] Liz Kelly, Jo Lovett and Linda Regan, *A Gap or a Chasm? Attrition in Reported Rape Cases* (Home Office, 2005).

[36] Fiona Raitt, 'Independent Legal Representation for Complainants in Rape Trials' in Clare McGlynn and Vanessa E Munro (eds), *Rethinking Rape Law: International and Comparative Perspectives* (Routledge, 2010) 267.

[37] Clare McGlynn, Nicole Westmarland and Nikki Godden, '"I Just Wanted Him to Hear Me": Sexual Violence and the Possibilities of Restorative Justice' (2012) 39 *Journal of Law and Society* 213–40.

[38] Jennifer Brown and others, *Connections and Disconnections: Assessing Evidence, Knowledge and Practice in Response to Rape* (Government Equalities Office, 2010) 6; Baroness Vivien Stern, *The Stern Review – An Independent Review into how Rape Complaints are Handled by Public Authorities in England and Wales* (Home Office, 2010).

[39] ibid.

[40] Jennifer Temkin and Barbara Krahé, *Sexual Assault and the Justice Gap: A Question of Attitude* (Hart Publishing, 2008).

[41] Ministry of Justice, Home Office and ONS, *Statistics Bulletin: An Overview of Sexual Offending in England and Wales* (January 2013).

[42] Wendy Larcombe, 'Falling Rape Conviction Rates: (Some) Feminist Aims for Rape Law Reform' (2011) 19 *Feminist Legal Studies* 27.

which to articulate feminist conceptions of consent and to continue to challenge pernicious and damaging rape culture and myths.

## Further Reading


- Andrew Ashworth and Jennifer Temkin, 'The Sexual Offences Act 2003: (1) Rape, Sexual Assaults and the Problems of Consent' [2004] *Criminal Law Review* 328.
- Wendy Larcombe, 'Falling Rape Conviction Rates: (Some) Feminist Aims for Rape Law Reform' (2011) 19 *Feminist Legal Studies* 27.
- Catarina Sjölin, 'Ten Years On: Consent Under the Sexual Offences Act 2003' (2015) 79 *Journal of Criminal Law* 20.

# 75

# National Assembly for Wales Election, 2003

CATRIN FFLÛR HUWS

On 2 May 2003 the National Assembly for Wales (Cynulliad Cenedlaethol Cymru) became the first legislative body in the world to have an equal number of men and women returned as Members. Coming 75 years after the Representation of the People (Equal Franchise) Act 1928 had ensured that all women had the vote on the same footing as men,[1] it was a significant achievement for women's political representation internationally, nationally and locally. For the first time women and men were able to participate on an equal footing in a political process, transforming not only its external output and priorities but also its workplace culture.

## I. Context

The National Assembly for Wales was created in 1999 following the 1997 devolution referendum. It is a democratically elected devolved legislature that is entitled to enact primary legislation on the matters detailed in the Government of Wales Act 2006 and the Wales Act 2017 as they affect Wales. There are 60 Assembly Members (AMs), 40 of whom are elected at constituency level using a first-past-the-post system.[2] The remaining 20 members are selected from regional party lists, and four members are selected from each Welsh region according to the proportion of votes cast for each party.[3]

From the outset, the Assembly returned a high number of women members. Following the first election in 1999, women made up 40 per cent of AMs. To put this in context, prior to 1997, Wales had only returned four women MPs to *any* Parliament – Megan Lloyd George (1929–51 and 1957–66), Eirene White (1950–70), Dorothy Rees (1950–51) and Ann Clwyd (1984–present). The UK General Election of 1997 had returned 120 (18.2 per cent) woman MPs to Westminster – although this was double the number of women MPs returned in 1992. In Northern Ireland, 14 women became MLAs (Members of the Legislative Assembly) (7.7 per cent) following the first election in June 1998.[4] In the Scottish Parliament, 48 women

[1] As noted at the time by Laura Turquet for the Fawcett Society in Nicolas Watt, 'Women win half Welsh seats', *The Guardian*, 3 May 2003.

[2] Parliamentary Constituencies and Assembly Electoral Regions (Wales) Order 2006 (SI 2006/1041), Schedule 1.

[3] ibid, Schedule 2.

[4] Michael Potter (2016) Female Members of the Northern Ireland Assembly 1998–2016 (Northern Ireland Assembly Research and Information Service Briefing Paper, 30/16, NIAR 035-16, February 2016).

became MSPs (Members of the Scottish Parliament) following the Parliament's first elections, just over 37 per cent of the total number of MSPs.

## II. The Landmark

In May 2003, the National Assembly for Wales became the first legislative body in the world with equal numbers of men and women, when 30 women were returned as Assembly Members, representing exactly half of the legislature. The importance of the 2003 election result arises from the fact that there was a strong commitment in the early years of the National Assembly for Wales to create a working environment that would not deter women from becoming AMs. Flexible working schemes and family-friendly working hours[5] were introduced in order to take account of the fact that women were more likely to be the primary carer in a family, and in 2012, the National Assembly for Wales was listed as one of the top 10 family-friendly workplaces in the UK.[6] A commitment was made to ensuring that maternity leave did not disadvantage women in terms of securing promotion and ensuring that pay did not become unequalised over time.[7]

Several factors may be identified as having contributed to the achievement of this landmark. First, the National Assembly for Wales was created at a time when increasing the proportion of women in Parliament was high on the UK Government's agenda and the political climate was encouraging for women.[8] Second, as a new institution the Assembly and its actors were able to be more progressive in the policies and strategies adopted because they were not fighting centuries of entrenched attitudes. Third, it had size on its side. Fifty per cent of 60 is a more achievable target than 50 per cent of the 650 MPs returned to Westminster. Fourth, the AMs were elected by virtue of an electoral system which includes an element of proportional representation – 40 AMs are elected to a constituency on the basis of a first past the post system, while a further 20 are selected from regional lists to represent the proportion of votes for each party. This enables regional lists to be used to create a gender-balance, with the result that if a party selects a male candidate at the constituency level, the regional lists can be composed of women – or vice versa. Prior to 2003, attempts had been made to create women only lists for elections in order to combat the historical inequality and the possibility that voters would be prejudiced against a woman candidate. However, the case of *Jepson and Dyas-Elliott v The Labour Party*[9] caused some unease with this approach. The *Jepson* case concerned a male prospective election candidate for the Labour party who failed to be selected because the Labour Party at the time favoured women-only shortlists. Jepson and his co-applicant successfully argued that they had been the victims of discrimination as a result of this policy. However, the **Sex Discrimination**

[5] Paul Chaney, 'Women and Political Change in Wales' (2004) 14(2) *Regional and Federal Studies* 281.

[6] National Assembly for Wales Press Release, 'National Assembly joins leading FTSE 100 companies in top 10 family-friendly places to work' (National Assembly for Wales, 27 September 2012).

[7] National Assembly for Wales Committee on Equality of Opportunity, *National Assembly for Wales Equal Pay Audit 2001* (13 June 2001).

[8] Fiona Mackay and Laura McAllister, 'Feminising British Politics: Six Lessons from Devolution in Scotland and Wales' (2012) 83(4) *Political Quarterly* 730.

[9] *Jepson and Dyas-Elliott v The Labour Party* [1996] IRLR 116.

**(Election Candidates) Act 2002**, meant that women-only shortlists are now permitted, and both the Labour Party and Plaid Cymru utilised this, along with other measures in order to increase the proportion of women standing for election.

## III. What Happened Next

Since 2003, Wales has seen other notable landmarks in the importance of women in the law-making process. The results of this election represent a significant change in attitudes. Although affirmative action was used to ensure that more women were listed as candidates, the First Minister, Rhodri Morgan AM,[10] stated that the change was a genuine one, and that to have 30 women AMs elected to one Assembly represented an enormous change that had taken place within a six-year period. In June 2006, following a by-election, Trish Law AM took the seat of Blaenau Gwent. This resulted in women holding 31 seats out of 60, outnumbering men in the Assembly for the first time.[11] Since 2003, the proportion of women AMs has remained consistently high – 47 per cent in 2007, 43 per cent in 2011 and 42 per cent in 2016. It is also significant that in all three of these elections, near-equality of representation was achieved, not through the use of the regional list process, but rather, with women standing as constituency candidates in their own right. In the 2007 election, therefore, more women than men were elected using the first-past-the-post system. Even though the proportion of women elected in 2011 and 2016 was slightly lower than in 2007, the ratios of 17 women to 23 men and 19 women to 21 men still fall within a 40:60 target (whereby there are no fewer than 40 per cent and no more than 60 per cent of men and women).

Indeed, the importance of the 2003 election result as a landmark for women is not simply about numbers. It created an environment where women could challenge established strongholds and win – not because of affirmative action, but by gaining the respect of the electorate and proving themselves to be deserving of their vote. Take, for example, Leanne Wood AM's election to the Rhondda constituency seat in 2016. Despite having initially been elected to the National Assembly for Wales in 2003 as a regional candidate, Wood won the seat for Plaid Cymru with 51 per cent of the votes, defeating the incumbent Labour AM. The significance of this becomes manifest when one considers that, at the UK parliamentary level, Rhondda was a Liberal-Labour seat from 1886 to 1910 and has returned a Labour MP to Westminster in every election since 1910. Put simply, no political party other than Labour has ever won a parliamentary seat in the Rhondda constituency. Rhondda, a former mining district, was also a Labour constituency at the National Assembly elections from 2003 to 2016, yet Wood – a woman – won it for Plaid Cymru.

The 2003 election result not only reflected and nurtured a culture in which women AMs could contribute to political decision-making, but it also created a climate in which they could lead it. Since 2011, the office of the Presiding Officer of the National Assembly for Wales has been filled by a woman (Rosemary Butler AM, 2011–16, followed by Elin Jones

[10] Watt, n 1 above.

[11] Vyara Apostolova, Carl Baker and Richard Cracknell, *Women in Public Life, the Professions and the Boardroom* (HC Library Paper SN5170, 27 July 2017).

AM, 2016–present). Moreover, since 2012 the leaders of two of four parties represented in the National Assembly for Wales have been women – Leanne Wood AM for Plaid Cymru and Kirsty Williams AM for the Liberal Democrats. Following the 2016 election, Leanne Wood AM and Carwyn Jones AM received an equal number of votes from the Assembly Members in the election for the post of First Minister. The deadlock was broken by an acceptance that the Labour Party would govern as a minority Government as opposed to Plaid Cymru (led by Wood) leading a coalition-Government. However, Wood has stated that she would not rule out a coalition with the Labour Party in the future, which could see her in an Assembly leadership position within the fifth term of the National Assembly for Wales.

Since 2003, the other devolved legislatures in the United Kingdom have established their own landmarks for women. In Scotland, three of the five party leaders in the Scottish Parliament are women and in both Northern Ireland and Scotland, the First Minister is a woman – Nicola Sturgeon MSP in Scotland, and until 2017, Arlene Foster MLA in Northern Ireland. In Scotland and Northern Ireland, women also lead the second largest parties in those territories. In Scotland, the Conservative Party is the second biggest party, and is also led by a woman – Ruth Davidson MSP – while in Northern Ireland, the second largest party is Sinn Féin, whose Assembly Leader is Michelle O'Neill MLA.

Change is also taking place in the UK Parliament. The 2015 General Election was the first time the number of women who stood as parliamentary candidates exceeded 1000.[12] In 2016, Theresa May MP became the UK's second woman Prime Minister. The 2017 General Election saw a significant increase in the number of women elected as MPs (208 compared with 143 at the 2010 election).[13]

The equal representation of women in the National Assembly for Wales also created more scope for issues that would otherwise have been overlooked, such as domestic violence and equal pay, to be debated in a consensual way with a 'complete absence of chest thumping and table thumping'.[14] For example, the National Assembly for Wales has passed the **Violence Against Women, Domestic Abuse and Sexual Violence (Wales) Act 2015** – an Act which endeavours to ensure that the public sector response to gender-based violence is more effective in supporting victims and making people more aware of the problems caused by violence in order to prevent its occurrence and tackle it more effectively when it does occur. Despite not having the power to legislate directly in relation to criminal law, Wales is using the powers it does have to effect change on gender-based issues, and the presence of women in the legislative process has been a key driver in enacting legislation of this nature. Paul Chaney argues that the presence of women in the National Assembly for Wales has had a positive impact in terms of ensuring that the equality impact of proposed policies is considered.[15] It is hoped that, as with innovations like the creation of a Children's

[12] Richard Keen and Richard Cracknell, *Women in Parliament and Government* (HC Library Commons Briefing papers SN01250, 6 February 2018).

[13] On the position in Ireland see **Electoral (Amendment) (Political Funding) Act 2012**.

[14] Stephanie Jones, Nickie Charles, and Charlotte Aull Davies, 'Transforming masculinist political cultures? Doing politics in new political institutions' (2009) 14(2) *Sociological Research Online*.

[15] Paul Chaney, 'Devolved Governance and the Substantive Representation of Women: The Second Term of the National Assembly for Wales, 2003–2007' (2008) 61(2) *Parliamentary Affairs* 272.

Commissioner and of an Older People's Commissioner, other legislatures will follow where Wales has led.

Despite these advances though, a number of potential weaknesses still exist. When she was Presiding Officer, Rosemary Butler AM considered that one issue is that women are still not putting themselves forward for public office as often as men.[16] A report by the Scottish Parliament and the National Assembly for Wales from 2011[17] argues that the alpha-maleness of the political arena has crept back into Welsh and Scottish politics, despite an initial commitment to consensus politics. For the moment, however, the National Assembly for Wales continues to be experienced as less 'masculinised'[18] than other political environments, and women feel far more able to participate effectively.

The depiction of women candidates by the press, by voters and by political parties continues to be a significant factor affecting women's participation in politics. A young woman candidate is perceived as lacking experience or is described in sexualised terms (the so-called 'Blair Babe' which was the epithet popularly used in the media and in other contexts to describe the 101 women elected to the UK Parliament in 1997, when Tony Blair became Prime Minister), while older women are criticised for being ugly, with little regard being had to what they say and do. According to Assembly Member Bethan Jenkins,[19] there continues to be a focus on a woman's inexperience or her looks, while her contribution to politics is underplayed. Jenkins comments:

> So, is there really more equality within politics? Do more women want to be involved in politics in Wales, or does sexism still exist here? Do women still get treated differently to men despite the progress made? These are questions that I can only answer on a personal level … People have a tendency to judge what I look like before they judge what I say. Being included in degrading polls such as the *Western Mail*'s 'Wales' Sexiest Women' poll merely intensifies the situation. In many newspaper articles, the tag line will refer to me being 'one of Wales's sexiest women,' as opposed to noting the serious political issue that I am campaigning on. Or on other occasions there are huge pictures of me, or more than one picture of me printed alongside an article, which I believe takes people's initial focus away from the seriousness of my words. Do men in politics have to struggle with this?

Jenkins also notes that she had to combat very traditional views from voters regarding a woman's role, with viewpoints expressed either regarding the suitability of women in politics at all, or assumptions being made that a woman could not devote herself to politics if she was, or was likely to become a mother.

The latter aspect is something that is both challenged and undermined by the family-friendly working practices of the National Assembly for Wales. It is challenged by the fact that it is easier for women who do have the reality of juggling family commitments with political office to participate in the political process, but it is undermined by the fact that it reinforces gender stereotypes because it reiterates the idea that women are also mothers who

[16] 'Rosemary Butler launches training for women seeking public office', *BBC News online*, 30 January 2014.

[17] Scottish Parliament and Welsh Assembly, *Women's Representation in Scotland and Wales: Report and analysis* (Electoral Reform Society and Centre for Women and Democracy, 2011).

[18] Nickie Charles, 'Doing Gender, Practising Politics: Workplace Cultures in Local and Devolved Government' (2014) 21(4) *Gender, Work and Organization* 368.

[19] Bethan Jenkins AM, 'Gender equality and the Welsh Assembly', *Wales Arts Review*, 28 November 2013. Now known as Bethan Sayed, having married in 2018.

need different (ie less onerous) working patterns because they have commitments outside their working life. It also reinforces the perception that women will focus on 'women's' issues, and that they therefore have little to offer the population in general, even though issues such as inequality, violence and family structures ought to be public issues and should not be perceived as matters that only affect women.

## IV. Significance

2 May 2003 can be regarded as an important landmark in that the last 15 years have seen women becoming mainstream and important in Welsh politics in ways that have not been encountered before. But breaking through a wall is not the end of the story. Ron Davies MP, The Secretary of State for Wales at the time of the devolution referendum in 1997, remarked that devolution is a process not an event.[20] So too is the representation of women in politics. Accordingly, what is required is to continue building on the success of 2003 in order to effect change in other areas of life. A report published in 2012[21] indicates for example that the lead set by the National Assembly for Wales has not been followed in other territories, or indeed in other areas of Welsh politics. Only 17 women MPs have ever been returned to Westminster from Wales, and the proportion of women in local government is a very modest 25 per cent, with Ynys Môn (Anglesey) having the lowest proportion of women councillors – a mere five per cent. A landmark may mean different things. It may be something unique in an otherwise uninspiring landscape. Or it may be an indicator that from here on in the terrain changes. Let's hope that 2 May 2003 is an example of the latter.

## Further Reading


- Stephen Brooks and Owain Ap Gareth, *Women in Public Life* (Electoral Reform Society Cymru, 2013).
- Fiona Mackay and Laura McAllister, 'Feminising British Politics: Six Lessons from Devolution in Scotland and Wales' (2012) 83(4) *Political Quarterly* 730.
- Scottish Parliament and Welsh Assembly, *Women's Representation in Scotland and Wales: Report and analysis* (Electoral Reform Society and Centre for Women and Democracy, 2011).


[20] Ron Davies, *Devolution: A Process Not an Event* (The Gregynog Papers, Vol 2 No 2, Institute of Welsh Affairs, 1999). Over the following years, the phrase 'devolution is a process not an event' became a popular meme for describing the evolution of devolution in Wales.

[21] Equality and Human Rights Commission, *International Women's Day 2012 Update. Who Runs Wales? The Journey toward gender Equality* (National Assembly for Wales, 2012).

# 76

# Mental Capacity Act 2005

ROSIE HARDING

The Mental Capacity Act 2005 (MCA), which applies in England and Wales, makes legal provision for a wide range of people (family members, health and social care professionals, courts) to make decisions in the best interests of people who lack the capacity to make a decision for themselves (section 3). It applies to anyone who has impaired decision-making capacity as a result of 'an impairment of the mind or brain' (section 2). Two of the guiding principles of the MCA hold the key to considering this piece of legislation to be a women's legal landmark.

The first, and most important, is the statutory presumption that: 'a person must be assumed to have capacity unless it is established that he lacks capacity' (section 1(2)). This creation of a statutory presumption of capacity is powerful, and of great importance for vulnerable women. Prior to the MCA, there was a common law presumption of capacity, but this was not clearly extended to those with impaired capacity 'due to mental illness or retarded development'.[1] The common law presumption was also narrower than the statutory presumption in the MCA, applying primarily in the context of medical decision-making. The consequence of this statutory presumption is that it is for the person alleging a lack of capacity to prove that the person is unable to make their own decision, rather than the person having to provide evidence that they have capacity.

The second significant aspect of the MCA is that where a 'best interests' decision is made or action taken because a person is unable to make their own decision, the least restrictive option is to be preferred (section 1(6)). This approach prioritises the autonomy rights of disabled people, ensuring that any action taken in the best interests of the person is proportionate, and that their freedoms are appropriately protected. In the case of women with intellectual disabilities, the pre-MCA approach often resulted in court-approved sterilisation procedures, and this issue will serve as the primary exemplar of the importance of this legal landmark for women.

## I. Context

Difficulty making decisions, or being considered to lack the capacity to make one's own decisions, can affect a remarkably large proportion of the population over the life course.

[1] *In re T (Adult: Refusal of Treatment)* [1993] Fam 95, 112 (Lord Donaldson MR).

Over 3 million people in the UK live with conditions that can cause difficulties with capacity, including learning disabilities, acquired brain injuries and dementia.[2] According to Mind, the mental health charity, one in four people in the UK will experience a mental health problem each year.[3] Whilst not all mental health problems result in diminished mental capacity, some mental health problems (like, for example, depression and anxiety) can make it very difficult for people to make decisions about their lives. More importantly, in the context of a legal landmark for women, gender has always played a considerable role in questions of (in)capacity in law and society. Women have higher rates of diagnosis with common mental disorders than men;[4] women are at higher risk of developing Alzheimer's Disease than men;[5] and women were historically more likely than men to be diagnosed with 'madness', admitted to asylums, or given psychiatric 'treatment'.[6] The MCA's legislative enactment of a presumption of capacity, and the requirement for the least restrictive option, have acted as an important legal corrective against the marginalisation of women through findings of incapacity or 'madness'.

The legal regulation of incapacity was historically a matter for the Royal Prerogative, the history of which can be traced back as far as 1339.[7] The Royal Prerogative gave the King entitlements to land belonging to 'idiots' or 'lunatics', a duty to make provision for the 'idiot', and a requirement to return the land to the right heir of the 'idiot' on his death.[8] The specific regulatory dimensions of the Royal Prerogative changed in scope over the centuries, eventually vesting in the Lord Chancellor and the court, to allow a wide inherent jurisdiction to do 'whatever is necessary for the benefit of Lunatics'.[9] The Royal Prerogative relating to property and affairs was formally abolished by the Mental Health Act 1959, and the power to administer the affairs of those who lacked capacity passed to the (old) Court of Protection. Under that legislation, whose powers were re-enacted under the Mental Health Act 1983, capacity was an 'all or nothing' determination: either a person had the capacity to deal with all of their property or they were considered to have no capacity at all. The Court of Protection jurisdiction under the 1959 Act only extended to property and affairs, usually exercised through the appointment of a 'receiver'.[10] Personal decision-making about health and welfare matters were addressed through a combination of compulsory treatment powers regarding hospital admissions,[11] and guardianship.[12] Under the

[2] Rosie Harding, 'Statutory Wills and the Limits of Best Interests Decision-Making' (2015) 78(6) *Modern Law Review* 945–70.

[3] Mind (2017) *Mental Health Facts and Statistics*: http://www.mind.org.uk/information-support/types-of-mental-health-problems/statistics-and-facts-about-mental-health/how-common-are-mental-health-problems/#.

[4] One in five women, compared to one in eight men: Sally McManus, Paul Bebbington, Rachel Jenkins and Tralach Brugha (eds), *Mental health and wellbeing in England: Adult Psychiatric Morbidity Survey 2014* (NHS Digital, 2016).

[5] Women are approximately 1.5 times more likely to develop Alzheimer's Disease (the most common form of dementia) than men (Rosie Erol, Dawn Brooker and Elizabeth Peel, *Women and Dementia: A Global Research Review* (Alzheimer's Disease International, 2015)).

[6] Jane M Ussher, *The Madness of Women: Myth and Experience* (Routledge, 2011).

[7] TCS Keely, 'One Hundred Years of Lunacy Administration' (1943) 8(2) *Cambridge Law Journal* 195–200.

[8] Margaret McGlynn, 'Idiots, Lunatics and the royal prerogative in early Tudor England' (2005) 26(1) *The Journal of Legal History* 1–24.

[9] Keely, n 7 above, 195.

[10] Sections 100–121 of the Mental Health Act 1959.

[11] Sections 25–29 of the Mental Health Act 1959.

[12] Sections 33–34 of the Mental Health Act 1959.

1959 Act, guardianship was a wide-ranging personal power, akin to that of a father over his under-age children. Guardianship powers were narrowed significantly under the Mental Health Act 1983, but this left a legal lacuna relating to health and welfare decision-making. Enduring Powers of Attorney were introduced in 1986 for property and financial affairs decisions,[13] but no equivalent power was available in respect of health and welfare decisions until the MCA.

## II. The Landmark

The Law Commission, under Commissioner Brenda Hoggett (now **Lady Hale**), began a review of the law relating to mental incapacity in 1989. The first consultation paper[14] set out the problems with the law at that time, particularly highlighting the lack of legal framework relating to consent to serious medical treatment.[15] Around that period there had been a series of cases relating to sterilisation of mentally disabled young women,[16] the most influential of which was the decision in *Re F (Mental Patient: Sterilisation)*.[17] As well as authorising the sterilisation of an intellectually disabled woman, *Re F* has been credited with the foundation (or re-discovery)[18] of what has become known as the 'inherent jurisdiction' of the High Court to make decisions on behalf of vulnerable and incapacitated adults. In that case, the House of Lords held that serious medical treatment could be given without consent to adults who lacked the capacity to give consent, where such treatment was justified by the doctrine of necessity. The Law Commission's consultation paper highlighted three problems with this approach to medical decision-making concerning adults with impaired capacity: the limitations of the doctrine of necessity; the suitability of a 'best interests', rather than substituted judgment approach; and the use of the clinical negligence standard[19] as the standard to be applied in determining best interests.[20] Importantly, similar questions about the scope and appropriateness of best interests remain salient to this day.[21]

Following a series of consultations on different aspects of the law,[22] the final report on Mental Capacity, including a draft Mental Incapacity Bill, was published in 1995.[23] A further decade passed, however, before the recommendations from the Law Commission were enacted through the Mental Capacity Act 2005. In that time, use of the inherent jurisdiction

[13] Enduring Powers of Attorney Act 1985.
[14] Law Commission, *Mentally Incapacitated Adults and Decision-Making: An Overview* (Law Comm Consultation No 119, 1991).
[15] ***St George's Healthcare NHS Trust v S* (1998)**.
[16] See Law Commission, n 14 above, [1.9].
[17] *Re F (Mental Patient: Sterilisation)* [1990] 2 AC 1.
[18] Ruth Hughes, 'The Inherent Jurisdiction over Vulnerable Adults' [2013] *Private Client Business* 132.
[19] *Bolam v Friern Hospital Management Committee* [1957] 1 WLR 582.
[20] See Law Commission, n 14 above, 29–34.
[21] Harding, n 2 above.
[22] Law Commission *Mentally Incapacitated Adults and Decision-Making: A New Jurisdiction* (Law Comm Consultation No 128, 1993); Law Commission *Mentally Incapacitated Adults and Decision-Making: Medical Treatment and Research* (Law Comm Consultation No 129, 1993); Law Commission *Mentally Incapacitated Adults and Decision-Making: Public Law Protection* (Law Comm Consultation No 130, 1993).
[23] Law Commission *Mental Incapacity* (Law Comm No 231, 1995).

had grown to fill the void left by the removal of most forms of guardianship. A group of 28 organisations and groups representing the interests of people with a range of intellectual and psychosocial disabilities came together to form the Making Decisions Alliance, and to lobby for the legislation. The Mental Capacity Act 2005 came fully into force on 1 October 2007. The process of enacting the MCA therefore, took nearly two decades. At time of writing, the MCA approaches its tenth anniversary, and the legal landscape for people with impaired capacity has changed a great deal as a result of this statute.

## III. What Happened Next

The MCA changed the shape of capacity law in England and Wales, catalysing a shift in understandings of 'capacity' in law from global, or person-specific, towards being granular and decision-specific. The central principles of the Act regarding decision-making by people with impaired capacity are: the presumption of capacity; the requirement to provide support and assistance in making decisions; and the requirement to respect unwise, but capacitous, decisions. These three principles all foreground decision-making by people with intellectual and psychosocial disabilities, supporting their rights to enjoy legal capacity on an equal basis with others.[24] Where a person with an 'impairment of the mind or brain' is shown (on the balance of probabilities) to lack the capacity to make a decision for themselves, any decision made must be in their 'best interests' (section 1(5)).

The inclusion of 'best interests' as an alternative when a person lacks decision-making capacity, however, creates a point of tension between English law in this area and international human rights law.[25] Under the MCA, where a person lacks the capacity to make a decision, then decisions can (and must) be made in their 'best interests'. In contrast, the UN Committee on the Rights of Persons with Disabilities have called for the abolition of objective best interests decision-making in favour of a much more subjective approach focusing on the 'best interpretation of the will and preferences' of the individual.[26]

The changes sparked by the MCA took some time to filter through to judicial decisions. Early cases decided under the MCA continued to use phrases like 'P lacks capacity',[27] which have little meaning in the context of a law that presumes capacity and requires decision-specific capacity determination.[28] Initially, jurisprudence from the Court of Protection considered 'best interests' as an objective test, rather than a reflection of the person's wishes and feelings. The reasons for this include the guidance given in the explanatory notes to the MCA,[29] alongside the continued use of the 'best interests balance sheet' approach developed prior to the MCA in *Re A (Male Sterilisation)*.[30] A turning point in consideration of the best interests approach under the MCA came when the first case under the MCA,

[24] UN Convention on the Rights of Persons with Disabilities, Article 12.

[25] See further, Harding, n 2 above.

[26] Committee on the Rights of People with Disabilities (2014) General Comment No 1 on Article 12: Equal recognition before the law CRPD/C/GC/1.

[27] Under the MCA, the person at the centre of proceedings is referred to as 'P'.

[28] Rosie Harding, 'Legal Constructions of Dementia: Discourses of autonomy at the margins of capacity' (2012) 34(4) *Journal of Social Welfare and Family Law* 425–42.

[29] MCA Explanatory Notes [28].

[30] *Re A (Male Sterilisation)* [2000] 1 FLR 549.

*Aintree University Hospitals NHS Foundation Trust v James*,[31] was heard before the Supreme Court. In that case, Lady Hale took the opportunity to clarify that, 'the purpose of the best interests test is to consider matters from the patient's point of view'.[32] This shift in the understanding of best interests has since been instrumental in two important cases deciding on matters relating to the withdrawal of artificial hydration and nutrition.[33] Lady Hale was, of course, both the architect of the MCA whilst at the Law Commission, and the arbiter on its meaning whilst a Justice of the Supreme Court. It is likely that Lady Hale's feminist principles have shaped the form and interpretation of the MCA.

## IV. Significance

Returning to the example of sterilisation of intellectually disabled women, which initially acted as a catalyst for law reform back in the late 1980s, helps to draw out the significance of the MCA as a women's legal landmark. Comparing cases from that period with similar cases under the regulatory regime introduced by the MCA, we can excavate a shift in understandings of capacity and towards the least restrictive option for women. In the late 1980s a series of cases had authorised the sterilisation of disabled women, under the inherent jurisdiction, as necessary medical procedures. In *Re F*, for example, sterilisation was considered by the court to be in F's best interests because she was in a sexual relationship, there was a 'serious objection to each of the ordinary methods of contraception', and becoming pregnant would 'from a psychiatric point of view, be disastrous'.[34] Importantly, and perhaps surprisingly, no consideration was given to F's capacity to consent to sex, despite the (infantilising) way the court described her mental capacity: 'she has the verbal capacity of a child of two and the general mental capacity of a child of four to five'.[35] Nor was any substantive consideration given to F's views about either the sterilisation operation or her sexual relationship. Rather, it was stated by the Court that 'she is unable to express her views in words but can indicate what she likes or dislikes … there is, however, no prospect of any development in her mental capacity'.

By way of contrast, in *A Local Authority v K*,[36] decided under the MCA, the court declined to make an order that sterilisation was in the best interests of K, a young woman with Down's Syndrome. This was because she was not sexually active, and less restrictive forms of contraception were considered to be a more appropriate first-line response if the situation arose where it was required. There have continued to be cases under the MCA where sterilisation has been thought to be in the best interests of the person at the centre of MCA proceedings. In *Re DD (No 4) (Sterilisation)*,[37] for example, sterilisation through the

[31] *Aintree University Hospitals NHS Foundation Trust v James* [2013] UKSC 67.

[32] ibid, [45].

[33] *M v Mrs N* [2015] EWCOP 76; *Briggs v Briggs* [2016] EWCOP 53.

[34] *Re F*, n 17 above, [1990] 2 AC 1, 53–54.

[35] ibid 53.The first civil case to consider capacity to consent to sex was *X City Council v MB, NB and MAB* [2006] EWHC 168 (Fam); [2006] 2 FLR 968. See Ralph Sandland, 'Sex and Capacity: The management of monsters?' (2013) 76(6) *Modern Law Review* 981–1009.

[36] *A Local Authority v K* [2013] EWHC 242 (COP).

[37] *Re DD (No 4) (Sterilisation)* [2015] EWCOP 4 (Fam).

occlusion of the fallopian tubes was considered to be in the best interests of an intellectually disabled woman who had previously had six pregnancies, and the medical evidence suggested that a further pregnancy would seriously endanger her life. Importantly, in *Re DD (No 4)*, it was noted that 'considerable efforts … have been made to enable her to make the relevant decisions'.[38] The difference the MCA has made in this area is that rather than sterilisation being considered as a first step in preventing pregnancy, for the convenience of those who care for women with intellectual disabilities, it is now appropriately considered a 'last resort', when other methods of contraception and sex education have failed.

The MCA has made a great deal of difference to the lives of women with intellectual and psychosocial disabilities. The statutory presumption of capacity means that those who seek to override the wishes of disabled people must first prove that they lack capacity to make their own decisions. The focus in the MCA on the least restrictive option has ensured that fewer disabled women are subjected to sterilisation procedures. The MCA has also reflected, and perhaps catalysed, a shift in the discursive construction of capacity and intellectual disability. Yet the MCA model of using a functional test of capacity, alongside status provisions, and backed up by best interests substituted decision-making, has come under increasing levels of criticism in recent years.[39] The tension between objective best interests and prioritising the will and preferences of the individual, as suggested by the Committee on the Rights of Persons with Disabilities,[40] is now posing significant challenges. Finding a way to achieve the right balance between supporting disabled people's autonomy and continuing to provide an appropriate level of protection for vulnerable people is the next big challenge in mental capacity law. The MCA has put England and Wales in a strong position to rise to that challenge, but we may well need to build another landmark to get us there.

## Further Reading

- Rosie Harding 'Statutory Wills and the Limits of Best Interests Decision-Making' (2015) 78(6) *Modern Law Review* 945–70.
- Genevra Richardson, 'Mental Disabilities and the Law: From substituted to supported decision-making?' (2012) 65 *Current Legal Problems* 333–54.
- Alison Stansfield, AJ Holland and ICH Clare, 'The sterilisation of people with intellectual disabilities in England and Wales during the period 1988 to 1999' (2007) 51(8) *Journal of Intellectual Disability* 569–79.

[38] ibid, [7].

[39] Eilionoir Flynn and Anna Arstein-Kerslake, 'Legislating personhood: realising the right to support in exercising legal capacity' (2014) 10 *International Journal of Law in Context* 81; Harding, n 2 above.

[40] CRPD/C/GC/1, n 26 above.

# 77

# UK Ratification of the Optional Protocol to the Convention on the Elimination of all Forms of Discrimination Against Women (OP-CEDAW), 2005

MEGHAN CAMPBELL

The Optional Protocol to the Convention on the Elimination of all Forms of Discrimination Against Women (OP-CEDAW) opens up exciting new forums to enforce women's civil, political and socio-economic rights. The OP-CEDAW allows individual women in the UK to hold the government accountable on the international stage for its commitment under The Convention on the Elimination of All Forms of Discrimination Against Women (CEDAW) to eliminate discrimination against women and achieve gender equality.

## I. Context

CEDAW is the pre-eminent instrument on women's human rights. It was drafted in the 1960s and 1970s in response to the failure of the mainstream international human rights system to take seriously women's rights. The Convention was open for signature in 1981. The UK signed the treaty that year but did not ratify it till 1986. CEDAW is a sophisticated instrument in that it protects women's civil and political rights and socio-economic rights in one treaty. Its unique perspective is that it investigates from an asymmetrical standpoint how gender discrimination and inequality have a negative impact on women's human rights. Under CEDAW the state is required to ensure women's equality in public life, education, employment, health care, family life and socio-economic life (Articles 7–13, 16, CEDAW). There are specific provisions ensuring women's equality before the law and equality for rural women (Articles 14–15, CEDAW). Unlike other UN human rights treaties, CEDAW also has provisions on negative cultural attitudes and stereotypes on the roles of men and women (Article 5, CEDAW).

The implementation of the treaty is monitored by the CEDAW Committee, a body of 23 independent experts on gender equality drawn from around the globe. The CEDAW Committee's initial methods for holding states accountable were the General Recommendations and Concluding Observations. First, the General Recommendations are a legal analysis of specific aspects of CEDAW such as harmful cultural practices and women's rights in conflict scenarios. Second, every four years the UK submits a report to the CEDAW Committee detailing the measures it has taken to implement CEDAW. After a written and oral dialogue session between the CEDAW Committee and the representatives of the UK government, the CEDAW Committee releases Concluding Observations, which highlight the positive developments and express concerns in areas where the UK has fallen short of its treaty commitments, and provide recommendations to ensure greater gender equality within the UK.[1] In the latest Concluding Observations for the UK, the CEDAW Committee expressed concern on the gendered impact of austerity measures and budgetary cuts, the Universal Credit system of welfare benefits, the lack of representation of minority women in Parliament, female genital mutilation and the objectification of women in the media.[2] Neither the General Recommendations nor the Concluding Observations are legally binding. However, the output of the CEDAW Committee can be extremely useful and has been relied upon by apex courts and law reform commissions. The General Recommendations and Concluding Observations provide a holistic understanding of gender equality in each state, but this comes at the expense of an in-depth understanding of crucial aspects of gender inequality.

There was a sustained campaign from women's organisations within the UN, academics and civil society organisations (CSOs) to develop an individual communications procedure for CEDAW. Advocates for the individual communications procedure argued that it 'will promote the more effective implementation of [CEDAW] and thereby enhance the enjoyment by women of the rights it guarantees'.[3] More specifically, the individual decisions can bring tangible relief to individuals; allow for in-depth examination of specific legislation, policies and programmes on gender equality; encourage governments to ensure more effective and available domestic remedies; contribute to changes in domestic law and practices which discriminate against women; and 'give [women's] rights a salience in terms of political concerns … that those rights lack.'[4]

## II. The Landmark

The lack of individual accountability under CEDAW was routinely identified as a weakness in the treaty's implementation mechanisms, especially when compared with other UN treaty bodies. An individual petition was proposed during the drafting of CEDAW but this never came to fruition. During the 1980s and early 1990s, individual Committee members, the UN Secretary-General and UN-appointed expert groups, raised the possibility of an individual communications procedure. At the Vienna World Conference on Human Rights in 1993 the advocacy of the women's movement resulted in the Vienna Declaration and Programme of Action calling on the CEDAW Committee 'to examine the possibility of including the

[1] See eg **Concluding Observations of the UN Committee against Torture, Recommendation to Ireland Regarding the Magdalene Laundries (2011)**.

[2] CEDAW Committee, 'Seventh Concluding Observations: UK' (2013) CEDAW/C/GBR/CO/7.

[3] Andrew Byrnes and Jane Connors, 'Enforcing the Human Rights of Women: A Complaints Procedure for the Women's Convention?' (1995–96) 21 *Brooklyn Journal of International Law* 679.

[4] ibid.

right to petition'.[5] In 1994 an independent group of experts drafted an optional protocol which was adopted by the CEDAW Committee. Between 1996 and 1999 the CEDAW Committee and the UN Commission on the Status of Women drafted the OP-CEDAW. In 1999 the OP-CEDAW, which allows the CEDAW Committee to consider individual communications and conduct inquiries into grave and systemic abuses, was adopted by the UN General Assembly and open for signature. Six years afterwards, the OP-CEDAW came into force in the UK.

The OP-CEDAW provides two new avenues for women in the UK to access justice and hold the state accountable for its commitment to eliminate discrimination against women under CEDAW. First, it empowers individuals or groups of individuals to submit communications to the CEDAW Committee arguing that the UK has failed to fulfil its CEDAW obligations (Article 2, OP-CEDAW). Second, on the receipt of reliable information the Committee can initiate an inquiry procedure to investigate grave or systemic violations of CEDAW (Article 8, OP-CEDAW). Similarly to the General Recommendations and Concluding Observations, the individual communications and inquiry procedures are not legally binding on the UK but in practice can have authoritative and significant legal weight. The jurisprudence developed under the OP-CEDAW can support and invigorate women's movements within the UK.[6]

The UK expressed serious reservations on signing the OP-CEDAW. Its initial concerns were that the individual communications procedure would undermine the implementation of the Human Rights Act 1998 (HRA).[7] Even after the HRA came into force the UK Government argued that it needed time to 'bed down' and that the OP-CEDAW would interfere with this process. When challenged in the House of Lords, the Government took a different argument. It stated '[we] believe that the UK already complies with the CEDAW convention ... we already have extensive legislation that deals with virtually all the issues that are covered by CEDAW'.[8] The implication was that OP-CEDAW was redundant because the UK had provided sufficient domestic accountability and remedies. The veracity of this statement is highly questionable as the periodic review of the UK by the CEDAW Committee in 1999 highlighted numerous areas where the UK fell short of achieving gender equality.[9] Moreover, at this time gender equality legislation in the UK was fragmented and arguably only narrowly focused 'on discrimination against women in the employment'.[10] In contrast, under the OP-CEDAW women can hold the state accountable to its obligations under CEDAW such as eliminating all forms of gender discrimination and achieving substantive gender equality, remedying negative gender stereotypes and cultural attitudes and ensuring women's equal rights in broad areas of life such as political participation, education, health and economic and social life. The Government's thin arguments against acceding to the

[5] Vienna Declaration and Programme of Action (1993) UN Doc A/CONF.157/23 (Part II), ch 111, sec II, [40].

[6] International Network for Economic, Social and Cultural Rightsand International Women's Rights Action Watch, 'Claiming Women's Economic, Social and Cultural Rights' (ESCR-Net and IWRAW, 2013).

[7] Christine Chinkin and Jane Gordon, 'The UK CEDAW Story' [2011] *European Human Rights Law Review* 274, 286.

[8] HL Deb, 31 January 2020, vol 631 cols 346–349 (**Baroness Scotland**, Parliamentary Secretary, Lord Chancellor's Department) as cited in Chinkin and Gordon.

[9] CEDAW Committee, 'Fourth Concluding Observations: UK' (1999) A/54/38 Rev 1 (SUPP).

[10] Chinkin and Gordon, n 7 above.

OP-CEDAW suggest a deep reluctance to acknowledge the embedded structural gender inequalities that exist and of the important role of international accountability forums.

In March 2002 an Interdepartmental Review of International Human Rights Instruments was undertaken to consider allowing individual complaints to the UN treaty bodies. After a two-year review, the Government announced in 2004 that

> we have decided to accept the Optional Protocol to CEDAW, which will help us to assess the effects of individual petitions to the UN generally. By accepting the Protocol we are also confirming the [UK's] commitment to women and equality issues.

Christine Chinkin and Jane Gordon noted that 'the Government appears to have … acceded to the [OP-CEDAW] more as a test case than a demonstration of its commitment … to women's rights in the UK'.[11] In fact the Government stated that the 'practical value to individual citizens to individual petition to the UN is unclear'.[12] In December 2004 the UK acceded to the OP-CEDAW and it came into force in March 2005.

## III. What Happened Next

At the beginning there was promising enthusiasm for the OP-CEDAW in the UK, but it has only been used twice in the 13 years it has been in force. This in part might be due to the fact that both communications were found to be inadmissible.

In *Constance Ragan Salgado v UK*,[13] the individual argued that the UK was in violation of Article 9 of CEDAW (equality in nationality) because the law did not permit her to transmit her citizenship to her son. Her son was born in 1954 and at that time British nationality came through the paternal line. The discriminatory provisions on nationality were amended in 1981 and made retroactive but only to children born between 1961 and 1983, so she was still unable to pass her citizenship on to her child. Her communication was deemed inadmissible because the events that formed the basis of the claim occurred before the coming into force of CEDAW and she had not exhausted domestic remedies.

In *NSF v UK*,[14] the individual claimed that her proposed deportation to Pakistan put her life and safety at risk from her abusive and violent ex-husband. The UK argued that she had not exhausted domestic remedies as she could still seek permission to apply for judicial review of the refusal to grant her leave to remain in the UK on humanitarian grounds. It further argued that NSF had never raised any issue of sex discrimination before the domestic authorities. The CEDAW Committee accepted the arguments of the UK and the communication was inadmissible. Although it is unfortunate that both claims did not proceed to investigate the merits of the communication, it is noteworthy that the UK provided 'full and careful legal arguments against the admissibility of these communications', suggesting that despite earlier resistance it takes the OP-CEDAW seriously.[15]

[11] ibid.
[12] ibid.
[13] *Constance Ragan Salgado v United Kingdom* (2007) CEDAW/C/37/D/11/2007.
[14] *NSF v United Kingdom* (2007) CEDAW/C/38/D/10/2007.
[15] Chinkin and Gordon, n 7 above, 288.

In October 2008, Jim Murdoch conducted a review for the Ministry of Justice on the OP-CEDAW to ascertain its value added and to assess whether the UK should recognise the competence of other UN treaties bodies to hear individual petitions. The report concludes that beyond a symbolic effect 'it is otherwise difficult to identify any real practical benefits'.[16] The OP-CEDAW, he observes, has not had any wider impact upon policy-making and has not been used to 'highlight systemic problems of discrimination against women' and there remains some doubt as to whether the OP-CEDAW is 'in any event an appropriate mechanism to achieve more authoritative determinations on tackling systemic issues in societies preventing the realisation of equality between the sexes'.[17] The conclusions from the study are dispiriting, but this is partly because the study was conducted very early in the history of the OP-CEDAW when the CEDAW Committee had not yet had a chance to build up a body of jurisprudence.

## IV. Significance

In the 13 years the OP-CEDAW has been in force in the UK, it has made significant contributions to the development of women's rights and brought into focus grave, systemic and entrenched gender inequalities. The most important contributions are in relation to gender-based violence. The individual communications under the OP-CEDAW have further developed the due diligence requirement of the state to protect women against violence. It has repeatedly held in the context of other signatory states that the 'perpetrator's rights cannot supersede women's human rights to life and to physical and mental integrity'.[18] It has conducted four inquiries, two of which (those on Mexico and Canada) focus on systemic and grave cases of violence against women. The inquiry into missing and murdered Indigenous women in Canada emphasised the importance of ensuring that frameworks to address violence must be de facto effective and available. It also held that the state needs to address poverty and socio-economic rights as part of a holistic strategy to eliminate violence. In relation to health, the individual decisions of the OP-CEDAW have emphasised the importance of informed consent to medical treatments, held that access to therapeutic abortion is important to ensure women's physical *and* mental health, and analysed how maternal health care policies did not address the needs of poor, Afro-Brazilian women. An inquiry procedure in the Philippines established the need for access to multiple types of contraception as a matter of women's right to health, and the inquiry in Northern Ireland concluded the severe restrictions on accessing abortion violated women's rights to health, education and family life. The OP-CEDAW has also protected women's right to public housing and right to inherit under customary law. The decisions are influential and in numerous instances have resulted in changes to domestic legislation and policies.

While the OP-CEDAW is under-used, it remains a significant legal landmark that furthers women's access to justice, particularly in the context of the substantive cuts to legal aid services in the UK. Individual women are empowered by the OP-CEDAW to claim

[16] Jim Murdoch, 'The OP-CEDAW: The Experience of the United Kingdom' (UK Ministry of Justice, 2008).
[17] ibid 25–27.
[18] *Sahide Goeke v Austria* (2007) CEDAW/C/39/D/5/2005 [12.1.5].

their rights to gender equality. The primary challenge is that CEDAW and the OP-CEDAW are in the shadows in the UK. They are 'virtually unknown among the general public and possibly across the branches of government too … the result is that they are not utilised by women to any great extent or operationalised by the government'.[19] In 2010 the Equality and Human Rights Commission (EHRC) published guidance on how to use the OP-CEDAW, but this has not resulted in an increase use of the individual communications procedure.[20] This neglected position is undeserved, as the OP-CEDAW has limitless promise to ensure greater gender equality within the UK.

There are many compelling reasons why women and women's organisations in the UK should engage further with the OP-CEDAW. It is an affordable mechanism. UK women can submit their individual petition in a simple email. There is no requirement to use a lawyer; there are no complex evidentiary procedures or rules or costly oral hearings. In deciding claims under the OP-CEDAW, the CEDAW Committee is not a judicial body and there is no requirement of particular professional qualifications. This means that CSOs within the UK can support individual women or groups of individual women throughout the entire individual petition process. Furthermore, CSOs in the UK can provide reliable information of systemic abuses and begin the process of initiating an inquiry procedure. This was the case for the inquiry procedures in Northern Ireland and Canada. Information from CSOs resulted in a country visit from the CEDAW Committee, and numerous interviews with police, justice officials, advocacy groups and individual women. In the case of Canada, the CEDAW Committee made 38 recommendations to address this grave violation of CEDAW, 34 of which the Canadian government accepted. The OP-CEDAW can act as a bridge between local and grassroots organisations and the state. Additionally, the jurisprudence from the individual communications can serve an important symbolic function and act as an authoritative legal tool in both political and legal forums to lobby for change in the UK.

Most importantly, the OP-CEDAW allows women in the UK to bring to international attention overlooked aspects of gender equality and makes them active participants on the international legal stage. Although the UK has sophisticated laws, policies and programmes on gender equality, there are still many severe and pressing gaps in its approach to eliminating discrimination against women. For example, the HRA does not explicitly ensure the protection of women's socio-economic rights. Rights that are not protected in the domestic context, for example women's rights to education and health care, are protected under CEDAW and reviewable under the OP-CEDAW. Contrary to the original position of the UK Government, the OP-CEDAW fills an important accountability gap. For example, the lack of legal regulation on the provision of sex education in schools can be the subject of an individual claim under the OP-CEDAW. Woman can claim before a body of international experts that by not ensuring sufficient access to domestic violence shelters the UK has not fulfilled its obligations under CEDAW. The individual decisions provide specific recommendations to address the individual wrong and general recommendations to address the systemic issues raised by the communication. Women in the UK can seek both individual

[19] Sandra Fredman, 'CEDAW in the UK' in Anne Hellum and Henriette Sinding Aasen (eds), *Women's Human Rights: CEDAW in International, Regional and National Law* (Cambridge University Press, 2013) 516.
[20] Ceri Hayes and EHRC CEDAW Project team, 'A Lever for Change: Using the OP-CEDAW' (EHRC 2010).

redress and broader transformative change. As the example of other countries demonstrates, the individual decisions and inquiry procedure can be a powerful catalyst to effect domestic change.

Domestic legislation or even regional instruments that protect women's right can be amended, changed or withdrawn, but there is no precedent for a country withdrawing from an international human rights treaty. What the future holds for human rights in the UK remains uncertain. Regardless of any domestic shifts, the OP-CEDAW remains. It is time for individual women in the UK to take advantage of the potential of the OP-CEDAW and hold the Government accountable for its commitment to realise substantive and transformative gender equality.

## Further Reading


- Andrew Byrnes, 'CEDAW and the Committee: Reflections on Their Role in the Development of International Human Rights Law and as a Catalyst for National and Legislative Policy Reform' *University of New South Wales Law Research Paper* (No 2010-17, 2010).
- Meghan Campbell, 'Women's Rights and the Convention on the Elimination of Discrimination Against Women: Unlocking the Potential of the Optional Protocol' (2016) 34(4) *Nordic Journal of Human Rights* 242.
- Jane Connors, 'Optional Protocol' in Marsha Freeman, Christine Chinkin and Beate Rudolf (eds), *The UN Convention on the Elimination of All Forms of Discrimination Against Women: A Commentary* (OUP, 2012).
- Loveday Hodson, 'Women's Rights and the Periphery: CEDAW's Optional Protocol' (2014) 25 *European Journal of International Law* 561.

# 78

# Forced Marriage (Civil Protection) Act 2007

PRAGNA PATEL

The Forced Marriage (Civil Protection) Act 2007 introduces a civil remedy – a Forced Marriage Protection Order (FMPO) – to stop a person being married against their will and to help remove them from a situation where such a marriage has already taken place (section 1). The introduction of the Act marked a ground-breaking moment in the history of black and minority ethnic (BME) women's struggles in the UK, against violence against women and for equality. It represented the culmination of BME women's struggles against the powerful multicultural precept that legal and other state responses to the needs of BME women should be guided by cultural relativism rather than by secular, universal human rights norms and standards on gender equality. The Act signalled a human rights-based approach to all forms of gender-based violence against BME women, who otherwise remained invisible in the social contract that had been forged between the British state and its minorities.

## I. Context

BME populations have had a presence for centuries in the UK but post-war experiences of discrimination and racism – in the streets, and in workplaces and institutions – produced local and national anti-racist struggles. By the mid-1980s, anti-racist, feminist organisations like Southall Black Sisters (SBS) had set their face against what had become the orthodoxy within the anti-racist movement – the myth of black 'communities of resistance'.[1] This construction lent itself to the portrayal of such 'communities' as monolithic entities involved only in a singular perpetual struggle against racial injustice.[2] This ignored internal fault-lines of power based on class, gender, sexuality and caste divisions; processes that often

[1] Southall Black Sisters is a not-for-profit, secular organisation established in 1979 to address the needs of black and minority ethnic women experiencing gender-based violence and related issues. It operates a specialist advocacy and campaigning centre aimed at empowering minority women to assert their rights. Although based in West London, it has a national reach.

[2] See the Campaign Against Racism and Fascism and Southall Rights, *Southall: the birth of a black community* (Institute of Race Relations, 1981).

intersected, reproducing other forms of inequality and resistance.[3] The silencing of women and other powerless sub-groups within minorities compelled SBS to call for engagement in simultaneous struggles against racial, gender and other forms of oppression, even if this created complexities and brought with it other challenges.[4]

This crucial feminist struggle was made more difficult by the state's own shift in its race relations approach from assimilation to the relatively more progressive policy of multiculturalism. First introduced in education, the multicultural model was the dominant approach to race relations from the mid-1980s to the late 1990s, and was quickly accepted as a tool of national policy across a range of issues at the local and national levels.[5] Although a more enlightened framework – multiculturalism recognised difference and promoted tolerance and co-existence based on mutual respect – it was not without its flaws. It drew on previous models of British colonial rule whereby indigenous populations were homogenised and divided according to their perceived cultural and religious identity. The strategy relied on the creation of male gatekeepers drawn from powerful religious and caste elites, with whom the British could engage.[6] In this way, internal gender, caste and class divisions and contestations were flattened and the anti-democratic and patriarchal power of the selected 'community leaders' legitimated and strengthened. Moreover, under this model, minorities were primarily viewed as targets of social policy, rather than as actors with citizenship rights within the democratic system.[7]

SBS was one of the first BME women's organisations to mount a strident feminist critique of multiculturalism, maintaining that, whilst it had a place in challenging racism, it had very negative consequences for minority women. Against a backdrop of changing perceptions of women's socio-political role in the wider society, the lives of minority women continued to be determined only by reference to cultural and religious values which took precedence over fundamental rights and freedoms. Whilst increasingly visible feminist campaigns on violence against women in the wider society were finally receiving state recognition, multicultural approaches to BME women had the effect of masking oppressive practices within minority communities and constraining BME women's bid for autonomy and rights.

The consequences of adopting a 'hands off' approach to the family affairs of minority communities was the lack of state recognition for BME women's experiences of gender-based violence such as domestic violence, forced marriage, honour-based violence, marital captivity, ritual and child abuse and sexual and domestic slavery. Instead, institutional policy and practices dictated that they be tolerated to avoid causing offence to cultural and religious sensibilities.[8]

[3] See Gita Sahgal, 'Fundamentalism and the Multi-Culturalist Fallacy' in Southall Black Sisters (eds), *Against the Grain: A celebration of survival and struggle – Southall Black Sisters 1979–1989* (SBS, 1990).

[4] ibid.

[5] Floya Anthias and Nira Yuval-Davis, *Racialised Boundaries: Race, Nation, Gender, Colour and Class and the Anti-racist Struggle* (Routledge, 1992).

[6] Gita Sahgal, 'Secular Spaces: The Experience of Asian Women Organising' in Nira Yuval Davis and Gita Sahgal (eds), *Refusing Holy Orders: Women and Fundamentalism in Britain* (Virago Press, 1992).

[7] Yasmin Ali, 'Muslim Women and the Politics of Ethnicity and Culture in Northern England' in Yuval-Davis and Sahgal, *Refusing Holy Orders*, ibid.

[8] Pragna Patel, 'Faith in the State? Asian Women's Struggles For Human Rights in the UK' (2008) 16(1) *Feminist Legal Studies* 9–36.

The close connection between SBS' struggles against violence against women and the politics of multiculturalism is perhaps nowhere better encapsulated than in the 1989 case of 'Afia'. Afia was a 13-year-old Bangladeshi girl of Muslim background from East London who contacted SBS because she was afraid she would be taken to Bangladesh during the school holidays and forced into a marriage. Her eldest sister had run away from just such a fate and her father wanted to prevent Afia and her sisters from following suit. Afia approached social services for protection but was met with indifference and inflexibility. Operating within the multicultural framework, they rejected her fears, stating that she was a 'typical' young Asian adolescent experiencing nothing more than 'a touch of the culture clash'. With the help of SBS and her lawyers, Afia was temporarily made a ward of court. However, at a final court hearing, social services argued for the discontinuation of the wardship proceedings, stating that 'insensitive intervention' in her family would 'diminish her father's confidence and authority' and 'distort the balance of power within the family'. In effect, social services argued that any state intervention would exacerbate the reality of racism in which the family lived and from which the father was trying to shield his daughters. The presiding judge agreed and decided to de-ward Afia, adding that there were bound to be 'stresses and strains in any family but that did not mean that the state should intervene'.[9] Following Afia's return home, SBS was denied all contact with her by her father and have since been unable to locate her.

## II. The Landmark

Despite such legal setbacks and political acquiescence, SBS continued to challenge the politics of multiculturalism and to press for the recognition of forced marriage as a specific form of violence against women and a violation of their human rights to freely enter into marriage, and to bodily and sexual integrity. Links were also made between forced marriage, honour-based violence and serious sexual and psychological harm and suicide, significantly affecting women of South Asian origin.

By 1999, a series of high-profile cases of 'honour killing' and forced marriage like that of Rukshana Naz[10] and 'Jack and Zena',[11] together with mounting criticism from groups like SBS, led to a break-through in the state's response to gender-based violence in BME communities. In 1999, the then Junior Home Office Minister, Mike O'Brien MP, set up a working group on forced marriage which included SBS as a member, along with a range of community and religious 'leaders'. SBS mobilised a large number of predominantly Asian and minority women's groups and women's refuges in support of its recommendations to the group. Though problematic in parts (especially its simplistic distinction between forced and arranged marriage), the working group produced a report, published in 2000, that

[9] See Pragna Patel and Hannana Siddiqui, 'Shrinking Secular Spaces: Asian Women at the intersect of race, religion and gender' in Ravi K Thiara and Aisha K Gill (eds), *Violence Against Women in South Asian Communities* (Jessica Kingsley Publishers, 2010) ch 4, 107.

[10] Rukshana Naz was 19 years old when her brother strangled her while her mother held her down by her feet. Her mother said, 'it was written in her kismet [fate]' (Kate Watson-Smyth, 'Mother murdered pregnant daughter', *The Independent*, 25 May 1999).

[11] Patel and Siddiqui, n 9 above, 108.

explicitly recognised forced marriage as an abuse of women and children's rights and made specific recommendations for better protection, including effective monitoring, training and support for statutory agencies and women's organisations at the front line of supporting vulnerable women, including victims and potential victims of forced marriage.[12] An unprecedented announcement followed when O'Brien broke with the multicultural consensus by stating in Parliament that 'multicultural sensitivity is no excuse for official silence or moral blindness'.[13] He advocated a 'mature' multicultural approach that allowed for forced marriage and other forms of gender-based violence against BME women to be framed within a human rights discourse. This was a historical and potentially liberating moment for BME women.[14]

It created momentum. **Patricia Scotland**, the then Home Office Minister, spearheaded the government's campaign against forced marriage. January 2005 saw the establishment of the Forced Marriage Unit (FMU) with the aim of conducting policy, outreach and casework on forced marriage in the UK and abroad. In 2006, Lord Lester approached SBS with the aim of introducing a civil law by way of a Private Member's Bill on forced marriage. The move followed SBS' public opposition to the Labour Government's intention of making forced marriage a specific criminal offence.[15] SBS argued that civil remedies were more viable and that a new criminal law, whilst symbolic, would be unworkable and potentially counter-productive.[16] Drawing on their experiences, SBS maintained that whilst victims do not want to be coerced or deceived into marriage, few – if any – are willing to see their parents prosecuted. Most want better protection and adequate resources to escape forced marriage. It was a position supported by the majority of women's organisations across the UK, including the Newham Asian Women's Project, Ashiana Network and Women's Aid.

Lord Lester's proposal was better tailored to provide protection from forced marriage, in addition to serving an important educative function within and outside of BME communities. The Forced Marriage Bill garnered considerable support from a range of organisations, including Liberty and the NSPCC, during its passage in Parliament. In a key debate on 26 January 2007, 34 speakers lined up mainly in its support,[17] causing the then Prime Minister, Tony Blair, to 'U-turn' and provide Government backing for the Bill.[18]

The Forced Marriage (Civil) Protection Act came into force in November 2008, creating a new part 4A of the Family Law Act 1996.[19] It defines forced marriage as based on the

[12] Home Office Working Group on Forced Marriage, *A Choice by Right: The report of the working group on forced marriage* (Home Office, June 2000).

[13] HC Deb, 10 February 1999, vol 325 col 277.

[14] At the same time, however, SBS had resigned from the working group on account of the Home Office seeking to appease 'community leaders' who wanted mediation to remain a legitimate option when addressing forced marriage and related issues. SBS went on to produce its own report, *Forced marriage: an abuse of human rights* (SBS, 2001) a year later. See further Hannana Siddiqui, 'It was written in her kismet: forced marriage' in Rahila Gupta (ed), *From Homebreakers to Jailbreakers* (Zed Books, 2003).

[15] Home Office, *Forced Marriage: A Wrong not a Right.* A consultation paper on the criminalisation of forced marriage (December 2005).

[16] Rahila Gupta, 'Pressure and Appeasement', *The Guardian*, 20 June 2006.

[17] HL Deb, 26 January, vol 688 cols 1319–1367.

[18] Significantly, it was Labour Peer, Catherine Ashton, then Constitutional Affairs Minister, who had campaigned privately for Lester's Bill. **Patricia Scotland** was reported as being against it (Mary Riddell, Gaby Hinsliff and Jamie Doward, 'Blair U-turn over forced marriages', *The Guardian*, 4 March 2007.

[19] The Act applies to England & Wales and Northern Ireland. Scotland adopted similar provisions in 2011 in the Forced Marriage etc. (Protection and Jurisdiction) (Scotland) Act 2011.

absence of free and full consent, though this remains a contested concept within feminist debates.[20] It gives family courts at local and High Court levels wide powers to make Forced Marriage Protection Orders (FMPOs) to secure the health, safety and well-being of the person to be protected; it permits applications from survivors as well as third-party applicants; and crucially, it has extra-territorial effect. An order can prohibit conduct occurring abroad in connection with a forced marriage. FMPOs can prohibit and restrict the conduct, not only of those parties who are directly subjecting the victim to duress, but also other parties who may become involved in such conduct, including those involved in aiding, abetting, counselling, procuring, encouraging, conspiring or assisting another person to force, or to attempt to force a person to enter into a marriage. The duration of a FMPO may be for a specified period or may last until varied or discharged, thus providing important judicial oversight in respect of continuing or future risks.

## III. What Happened Next

Following the 2007 Act's introduction, other significant measures were introduced such as the first statutory guidance on forced marriage,[21] followed by guidance in other areas such as female genital mutilation (FGM), all of which have vastly improved state responses to BME women. These are all now recognised as specific forms of gender-based harms. The FMU has also taken measures to provide more effective action to help British and dual nationals overseas, and further and improved statutory guidelines have been created, including the publication of new multi-agency guidelines on forced marriage (March 2013) and FGM (April 2016).[22] These measures have greatly improved policy and practice within key front-line agencies, such as the police, health care and social services.

There are no solid data on the incidence of forced marriage or other forms of gender-based violence against BME women in the UK, though it is recognised that there is serious under-reporting.[23] Figures from the FMU show that there has been a steady increase in applications involving predominately young women seeking FMPOs, although the numbers tend to fluctuate. The most recent figures, for April–June 2017, indicate that there were 78 applications and 72 orders made. Of the applications 77 per cent involved applicants under the age of 17.[24]

While the implementation of the Act has revealed ongoing weaknesses,[25] overall it has improved protection for the most vulnerable in ways that could not have been imagined by SBS and other feminist campaigners when they first challenged multicultural policies for their effect in reinforcing patriarchal power relations within BME communities.

[20] Sundari Anitha and Aisha Gill, 'Coercion, Consent and the Forced Marriage Debate in the UK' (2009) 17 *Feminist Legal Studies* 165–84.

[21] HM Government, 'The Right to Choose: Multi-agency statutory guidance for dealing with forced marriage' (November 2008).

[22] See Guidance 'Forced marriage' (Gov.UK, 20 March 2013, updated 9 March 2017); Statutory Guidance, 'Multi agency statutory guidance on female genital mutilation' (Gov.UK, 1 April 2016).

[23] Oonagh Gay, 'Forced marriage' (HC Library Briefing Paper SN01003, 21 January 2015).

[24] Ministry of Justice and Office for National Statistics, 'Family Court Statistics Quarterly, England and Wales, April to June 2017', 28 September 2017.

[25] *Bedfordshire Police Constabulary v RU and Another* [2013] EWHC 2350 (Fam).

The Act has also led to important developments in case law involving the overlap between forced marriage and children's rights, including the recognition that forced marriage can amount to 'significant harm' within the meaning of the Children Act 1989.[26] Significantly, the Act has also brought feminist debates on consent and coercion into the legal arena. Marriage may be forced by a range of coercive measures, including duress and emotional blackmail (such as appeals to duty and for the maintenance of social norms and values), that can blur the distinction between a forced and arranged marriage – although the law has yet to catch up with the nuanced and layered social realities in which women give consent.

Further afield, developments in the UK have mirrored events on the world stage where forced marriage has fast gained recognition as a violation of women's human rights. At the same time that the 2007 Act was introduced in the UK, forced marriage was being recognised as a pervasive feature of armed conflicts around the world. This led to important debates concerning whether the issue of forced marriage should be subsumed within the category of other inhumane acts, such as sexual slavery, or distinguished as a specific crime against humanity.[27] More recently, governments across Europe have looked to Britain when enacting measures to address forced marriage. The Istanbul Convention, though not yet ratified by the UK, stipulates that all Contracting States are required to take effective steps to address forced marriage and honour-based violence and the serious consequences including sexual violence and physical and psychological health risks associated with it.[28]

Despite these developments, parallel moves in recent years give cause for concern. The growing political consensus across Europe is to shift the focus away from implementation and from the need for more resources, to criminalisation and the adoption of stringent immigration policies as a means of combating the problem. In 2012, following a short consultation,[29] the then Prime Minister, David Cameron, announced his intention to introduce a new criminal law on forced marriage: 'Forced marriage is abhorrent and is little more than slavery. To force anyone into marriage against their will is simply wrong and that is why we have taken decisive action to make it illegal.'[30]

The same day the Government published a response to its consultation. Of the 297 responses, just over half were in favour of a criminal offence, with 37 per cent against. The consultation process was, however, challenged by a number of women's NGOs who had in 2011 responded to an independent and more detailed survey conducted by Roehampton University, which showed that 74 per cent of the respondents opposed the criminalisation of forced marriage.[31] Nevertheless, the Government's report did show that 80 per cent of respondents – including SBS – believed that current remedies were not being used effectively.[32] Despite these concerns, in June 2014, section 121 of the Anti-Social

[26] *London Borough of Camden v RZ* [2015] EWHC 3751 (Fam).

[27] Jennifer Gong-Gershowitz, 'Forced Marriage: A "New" Crime Against Humanity?' (2009) 8 *Northwestern Journal of International Human Rights* 53.

[28] The UK government is a signatory to the Istanbul Convention. In June 2017 it announced new measures as part of the Domesic Abuse Bill to allow ratification.

[29] Home Office, *Forced Marriage: A Consultation* (December 2011).

[30] Number 10 Downing Street press release, *Forced Marriage to become a criminal offence*, 8 June 2012.

[31] Aisha Gill, *Exploring The Viability of Creating A Specific Offence For Forced Marriage In England and Wales: Report of Findings* (University of Roehampton, July 2011).

[32] Home Office, *Forced Marriage – A Consultation: Summary of Responses* (June 2012) 9.

Behaviour, Crime and Policing Act 2014 made it an offence to force someone to marry, with a maximum penalty of seven years' imprisonment.[33] Additionally, populist discourses on immigration and integration have become 'vortex' issues sucking in questions of forced marriage, honour killings and other forms of 'harmful cultural practices' that apparently signify the lack of integration by minorities into the 'British way of life'.[34] With the result that forced marriage has consistently been primed for moral panic by the media and politicians seeking to impose immigration controls, and the fluidity of the boundaries between the concepts of coercion and consent has been deliberately misused to reinforce the view that all migrant family arrangements are suspect.[35]

## IV. Significance

During the passage of the Forced Marriage Bill, Lord Lester said of its purpose:

> The serious social evil which the Bill seeks to combat and remedy is the forcing of children and young adults to marry against their will. It gives rise to gross abuses of human rights especially affecting children and young people … It involves inhuman and degrading treatment and punishment of those who resist coercion, even their murder. It is a form of domestic violence and there is a direct link between forced marriages and honour killings … Forced marriage is, of course, an oxymoron … It is a form of sexual enslavement, sometimes amounting to domestic slavery … As we mark the bicentenary of the abolition of the slave trade, we should surely take effective measures to tackle this gross abuse.[36]

These sentiments have been echoed by many in the judiciary, who just two decades earlier were reluctant to intervene in forced marriage cases like that of Afia. As Munby LJ noted in *Re K, A Local Authority v N*: 'Forced marriage is intolerable. It is a gross abuse of human rights. It is a form of domestic violence that dehumanises people by denying them their right to choose how to live their lives.'[37]

While, as Lord Lester noted, forced marriage is not limited to Asian communities – it 'affects children, teenagers and adults from all races and religions, including Christians, Hindus, Jews, Muslims and Sikhs'[38] – the contextualisation of forced marriage within a continuum of gender-based violence and within a human rights framework represents a high point in black feminist struggles. It signified a shift in the basis of ethical judgement and reconfigured the law's approach to BME women.

More recently, feminist campaigns against forced marriage and violence against BME women appear to have reached a crossroads. Struggles against the politics of multiculturalism by organisations like SBS led to significant shifts in legal and state responses to

[33] To date there has been just one conviction under the new law (Josh Halliday, 'Boy aged eight among known potential victims of forced marriage in UK', *The Guardian*, 20 April 2016).

[34] Shamit Saggar and Will Somerville, *Building a British Model of Integration In An Era of Immigration: Policy Lessons for Government* (Migration Policy Institute, May 2012).

[35] Pragna Patel, 'Moral panics and social evils: forced marriage and gender-related violence in immigration law and policy in the UK' in Floya Anthias and Mojca Pajnik (eds) *Contesting integration, engendering migration: theory and practice* (Palgrave Macmillan, 2014).

[36] HL Deb, 26 January 2007, col 1319.

[37] *Re K, A Local Authority v N* [2005] EWHC 2956 (Fam), [85].

[38] HL Deb, 26 January 2007, col 1319, referring to speech by Baroness Scotland.

gender-based violence in minority communities. They have been heralded most clearly by the introduction of the Forced Marriage (Civil) Protection Act. Yet these same organisations now find themselves in the paradoxical situation of building on the landmark achievement whilst simultaneously resisting the instrumentalisation of forced marriage by those seeking to mount a wholesale assault on the more positive aspects of multiculturalism.

## Further Reading


- Home Office Working Group on Forced Marriage, *A Choice by Right: The Report of the Working Group on Forced Marriage* (Home Office, 2000).
- Hannana Siddiqui, 'There is no "honour" in domestic violence, only shame! Women's struggles against "honour" crimes in the UK' in Lynn Welchman and Sara Hossain (eds), *'Honour' Crimes, Paradigms, And Violence Against Women* (Zed Books, 2005).
- Nira Yuval Davis and Gita Sahgal (eds), *Refusing Holy Orders: Women and Fundamentalism in Britain* (Virago Press, 1992).

# 79

# First Woman Attorney General for England, Wales and Northern Ireland, Patricia Scotland, 2007

LINDA MULCAHY

In June 2007 Patricia Scotland became the first woman to take up the position of Attorney General for England, Wales and Northern Ireland since its foundation in 1315.[1] She was also the first black woman, and indeed the first black person, to be elevated to the post. On her appointment, members of the press described her as the most prominent black woman in government and as a leading voice on racial, feminist and equality issues.[2] She held the post for three years until the fall of the Labour Government but went on to serve as Shadow Attorney General from 2010 to 2011.

## I. Life

Patricia Scotland was born in 1955 in the small village of St Joseph in Dominica, to Antiguan and Dominican parents. She was the tenth of 12 children and was raised in the Roman Catholic faith. Her family moved to live in North East London when she was two years old. After completing her schooling she went on to study and practise law despite one of her lecturers warning that being black and female might be too big a hurdle to overcome in a legal career.[3] Patricia Scotland was called to the Bar at Middle Temple in England in 1977, where she specialised in family, constitutional, public, anti-corruption law and human rights.[4] She was a founding member, and head of chambers, at 1 Gray's Inn Square before moving to 4 Paper Buildings.

In 1991, at 35 she was the youngest woman and first black woman to ever become Queen's Counsel. The appointment was made under a system which had been criticised

[1] Since 2010 this post has been re-named 'Advocate General for Northern Ireland' in respect of Northern Ireland.

[2] See for instance Chukka Umunna, 'The Duty to Inspire', *New Statesman*, 3 September 2007 and Dan Newling, 'The Future QC born into a family of 14', *Daily Mail*, 17 September 2009.

[3] Mark Tran, 'Profile: Lady Scotland', *The Guardian*, 28 June 2007.

[4] ibid. See further Baroness Scotland QC's 4 Paper Buildings profile: http://www.4pb.com/barrister-profile/baroness-scotland/.

for its over-reliance on secret soundings about applicants drawn from a narrow selection pool in which women, ethnic minorities and those with a lack of judicial connections were under-represented.[5] At the time of her appointment those most likely to succeed in the appointments process were white male Oxbridge graduates, and those least likely were women non-Oxbridge graduates. Patricia Scotland had neither been to public school nor studied at Oxford or Cambridge.[6] She attended Walthamstow School for girls and obtained a law degree from the University of London External Programme.

Patricia Scotland was also the first black woman to be appointed Deputy High Court Judge, Recorder and Master of Middle Temple. During his term as Lord Chancellor, Lord MacKay is understood to have wanted Patricia Scotland to become the first black High Court judge, but the Conservative party's 1997 election defeat meant that he left office before this could be achieved.[7] Instead she was appointed as a peer in the House of Lords by the new Labour government, where she chose to be designated Baroness Scotland of Asthal in recognition of the Oxfordshire town where she lived with her husband and two sons. She was made a Privy Councillor in 2001 and became the first black woman ever to become a minister in a UK Government when she was appointed Parliamentary Secretary for the Lord Chancellor's Department in the same year. She also served as Minister of State for Criminal Justice Reform from 2003 to 2007.

Patricia Scotland's career has been characterised by ongoing links with, and an engaged interest in, the Caribbean. She maintained her connections with the region when she was called to the Bar in Antigua and Barbuda, and then Dominica in 1978. She has been a patron of Lifeline, a suicide hotline based in Trinidad and Tobago, and chaired HM Government's Caribbean Advisory Group from 1997 to 1999. During the period 1999–2001 she served as Parliamentary Under-Secretary of State for the Foreign and Commonwealth Office. Patricia Scotland went on to become the first woman Secretary-General of the Commonwealth in 2016 and in her inaugural address she described herself as a classic child of the Commonwealth, born in the Caribbean and brought up in London.[8]

Her many achievements have been recognised in a host of awards including Channel 4 Peer of the year (2004); the Political Studies Association Parliamentarian of the Year (2004); *The Spectator* Parliamentarian of the Year (2005); the London Black Leaders Award (2007); the Caribbean World Award (2008); *The Guardian's* Most Powerful Black Female Briton (2009) and The Black Solicitors Network Lifetime Achievement Award (2009).

## II. Context

As a first officer of the Crown, the Attorney General has considerable influence on affairs of state. In their modern form they are the co-ordinator of legal advice to ministers, responsible

[5] See Michael Blackwell, 'Taking Silk: An Empirical Study of the Award of Queen's Counsel Status 1981–2015' (2015) 78 *Modern Law Review* 971 and Kate Malleson and Fareda Banda, *Factors Affecting the Decision to Apply for Silk and Judicial Office* (Lord Chancellor's Department Research Series No 2/00, 2000).

[6] Blackwell, ibid.

[7] The first black judge to be appointed to the High Court bench was Linda Dobbs, QC who was appointed in 2004.

[8] 'Baroness Scotland becomes first woman Secretary General of the Commonwealth', *MercoPress South Atlantic News Agency*, 6 April 2016.

for overseeing the conduct of criminal prosecutions[9] and responsible to Parliament for the effectiveness of prosecuting authorities such as the Crown Prosecution Service, Serious Fraud Office and the Treasury Solicitor's Department.[10] Having simultaneously to weigh the balance of conflicting considerations derived from the law, the general interest and the realm of politics means that the role is a complex one which has often attracted criticism.[11] The dual responsibility of the Attorney General as government minister and legal adviser renders the post-holder both an important law practitioner and a law-maker.

Patricia Scotland was neither the first nor the last woman to have been made an Attorney General in the common law world. Anne Halpern was elected to the role of US State Attorney General for Pennsylvania in 1959, Janet Reno was appointed the first female US Attorney General in 1995 and Margaret Wilson became the first Attorney General in New Zealand in 1999. However, a woman was not appointed to the post in Australia until 2011 and in the US, the first African American Attorney General did not take up office until Loretta Lynch in 2015. The ongoing scarcity of women Attorney Generals has been criticised by scholars because of the high-profile nature of the job and the stereotypically masculine assumptions about the qualities needed of the person responsible for overseeing the prosecution of suspected criminals.

It has been argued that the presence of a favourable political culture which supports female incumbents is essential to the appointment process and success of the post-holder.[12] In the UK, it is important to see the appointment of Patricia Scotland as Attorney General in the context of a concerted effort by the Labour party to promote female candidates in public office. In response to the small numbers of women MPs in Parliament, the Labour party adopted a policy of all-women shortlists in half of the vacant seats the party was likely to win in the 1997 election. The policy is thought to have contributed to 120 women MPs entering Parliament in 1997; exactly double the number that had been elected in 1992. The advent of the new Labour administration also saw a substantial increase in the proportion of women appointed to other offices in public life, including the Cabinet, local government, the House of Lords, the Scottish Parliament and the Welsh Assembly.[13] Patricia Scotland was a worthy and direct beneficiary of this policy when she was appointed to the House of Lords as a Labour peer in 1997.

## III. What Happened Next

Since Patricia Scotland was appointed Queens Counsel there has been radical change to the appointments system. An independent Queen's Counsel Selection Panel which is independent of the Bar Council, the Law Society and of Government was established in 2004 and

[9] This is especially the case where there the public interest is involved.

[10] The Attorney may attend, but is not a member of, Cabinet. The dual role of independent legal adviser and politician is not without its critics: see House of Commons Constitutional Affairs Committee, (2006–7) Constitutional Role of the Attorney General, London: House of Commons.

[11] John Edwards, *The Attorney General, Politics and the Public Interest* (Sweet & Maxwell, 1984).

[12] Elizabeth Ellen Gordon, 'Female Candidates, Sociopolitical Subculture, and State Attorney General Elections' (2016) 37 *Justice System Journal* 63.

[13] Pippa Norris and Joni Lovenduski, 'Blair's Babes: Critical Mass Theory, Gender, and Legislative Life' (2001) Social Science Research Network Electronic Paper Collection; and Sarah Childs and Mona Lena Krook, 'Critical Mass theory and Women's Political Representation' (2008) 56 *Political Studies* 725. See also National Assembly for Wales Election, 2003.

modified in 2006. In the aftermath of the 2016–17 appointments the Panel reported that the number of women applying and being successful continues to rise. Whilst recognising that there was still scope for improvement, the proportion of women amongst those appointed is at its highest level ever. Of the 113 appointments made, 31 were women.[14]

The use of gender quotas by the Labour party provoked a considerable amount of discussion in the UK, though the approach is far from unusual when viewed from an international perspective. Gender quotas have been extensively used across the globe to improve the representation of women in politics and by 2014 more than 130 countries had witnessed the adoption of some kind of electoral quota.[15] Researchers have found the impact of these policies to be uneven, but dramatic. One obvious impact has been that the world average of women in national parliaments has nearly doubled since 1997.[16]

The adoption of affirmative action policies across the globe has raised hopes about the likelihood that this development will alter the policy agenda, tone of debate and the representation of women's interests in parliament and legislation.[17] Research has thrown some doubt on the expectation that the presence of more women in legislatures is capable of facilitating the emergence of feminist policies in the short term. Against this backdrop, Patricia Scotland stands out as someone who has remained committed to, and vocal about, initiatives that protect the interests of women. This is particularly true of her involvement in projects that aim to eliminate domestic violence. As the chair of the Inter-Ministerial Group on Domestic Violence she helped introduce major changes to address the identification and management of domestic violence, including the introduction of multi-agency risk assessment conferences, Independent Domestic Abuse Advisers and specialist domestic violence courts. According to the British Crime Survey, this led to a 64 per cent reduction in the number of reported domestic violence incidents between 2004 and 2009. From 2011 to the present day she has also acted as co-founder and patron of the Global Foundation for the Elimination of Domestic Violence. More recently, she has identified tackling domestic violence as a key priority during her time as Secretary General of the Commonwealth and has launched an appeal to bring together charities, voluntary and statutory agencies to raise awareness of the issue in the UK.[18]

## IV. Significance

The office of the Attorney General is an ancient one which can be traced back to the thirteenth century, when Attorneys General and their medieval precursors were charged with the responsibility of maintaining the Sovereign's interests before the royal courts.[19] The bar

[14] See further: http://www.qcappointments.org/about-us/introduction/.

[15] See further, Sex Discrimination (Election Candidates) Act 2002; Electoral (Amendment) (Political Funding) Act 2012.

[16] Mary K Nugent and Mona Lena Krook, 'All Women Shortlists: Myths and Realities' (2016) 69 *Parliamentary Affairs* 115.

[17] Norris and Lovenduski, n 13 above.

[18] 'Commonwealth Secretary-General says "No More: to Domestic Violence"', *The Commonwealth*, 17 May 2016.

[19] There has been extensive scholarly debate about the exact origins of the post and who it was that first held the position of Attorney General. For an extensive discussion of the role see further John Edwards, *The Law Officers of the Crown* (Sweet & Maxwell, 1964); Edwards, n 11 above; Rosamund M Thomas, 'The Attorney-General for

on women qualifying as lawyers in England and Wales until the twentieth century[20] and the fact that the vast majority of monarchs have been male mean that for many hundreds of years this powerful role was performed by men for men. Patricia Scotland was succeeded in the post of Attorney General by Dominic Grieve (2010–14), Jeremy Wright (2014–2018) and Geoffrey Cox (2018–) and as a result she continues to be the only woman, as well as the only black person, to have held the post.

## Further Reading

- Michael Blackwell, 'Taking Silk: An Empirical Study of the Award of Queen's Counsel Status 1981–2015' (2015) 78 *Modern Law Review* 971.
- Kate Malleson and Fareda Banda, *Factors Affecting the Decision to Apply for Silk and Judicial Office* (Lord Chancellor's Department Research Series No 2/00, 2000).
- Pippa Norris and Joni Lovenduski, 'Blair's Babes: Critical Mass Theory, Gender, and Legislative Life' (2001) Social Science Research Network Electronic Paper Collection.

England and Wales, and Northern Ireland: His Role in Civil and Criminal Proceedings' (1991) 57 *International Review of Administrative Sciences* 209.

[20] Sex Disqualification (Removal) Act 1919.

# 80

# Section 14 of the Policing and Crime Act 2009

F VERA-GRAY

Coming into force on 1 April 2010 through the addition of a new section (section 53A) to the Sexual Offences Act 2003, section 14 of the Policing and Crime Act 2009 made it a strict liability offence in England and Wales to pay for, or promise to pay for, the sexual services of a person who has been coerced, deceived, forced or threatened by a third party into prostitution. Section 14 is a landmark in women's legal history because not only was it the result of concerted and coordinated campaigning from feminist activists both within and outside of government, it also marked an important shift in policy focus for England and Wales, moving legislative attention away from women and onto the choices of men.

## I. Context

In January 1999 the then Home Secretary, Jack Straw, announced a review of sexual offences.[1] The review was in recognition of the patchwork nature of the criminal provisions up until that point: a mixture of amendments, such as the extension of the definition of rape in 1994 to include male rape, and legislation dating as far back as the nineteenth century. Feminists had long highlighted the problems with the sexual offences provisions as they stood,[2] including the use of sexual history evidence in court and the ruling in *DPP v Morgan*.[3] The review itself was guided by a strong feminist influence, including the establishment of an external reference group featuring prominent feminist academics including Professors Liz Kelly and Jennifer Temkin, as well as the national umbrella organisation for Rape Crisis Centres. Significantly, this group was the first time feminists were formally involved in the process of law reform in England and Wales from the outset.[4]

[1] Gavin Berman and Grahame Danby, The *Sexual Offences Bill* [HL]: Policy Background Bill 128 2002–03 (House of Commons Research Paper 03/61, 10 July 2003).

[2] For a useful overview of the criticisms feminists have made about rape law in England and Wales, see Nicole Westmarland, *Rape Reform Law in England and Wales*, School for Policy Studies Working Paper Series Paper Number 7, 2004.

[3] *DPP v Morgan* [1976] AC 182.

[4] Personal communication with member of the group.

The consultation process also marked an official acknowledgment by the Labour Government of the need to review issues surrounding prostitution specifically, particularly, though not solely, the role of exploitation and coercion in experiences of, and routes through, the prostitution system. Prostitution is a long-standing fault line in feminism. Though there is broadly agreement that the prostitution system can act as what Liz Kelly has called a 'conducive context' for men's violence,[5] whether prostitution itself is a form of violence against women is fiercely contested, with the impact of these divergent perspectives on policy illustrated in a recent article by Maddy Coy.[6] The lack of political will to take a distinct position on prostitution has meant that, as shall be seen below, it has been subject to multiple reviews, from the sexual offences review through to the Labour-led *Paying the Price* consultations in 2004 and 2006,[7] the Conservative and Liberal Democrats' *Review of Effective Practice in Responding to Prostitution* in 2011,[8] and the All-Party Parliamentary Group (APPG) report *Shifting the Burden* in 2014[9] – all of which have generated substantial discussion but as yet no definitive statement from government.

The recommendations on prostitution arising out of the review of sexual offences in 2000[10] formed the basis of *Protecting the Public* and what became the prostitution-related offences in the Sexual Offences Act 2003. However, the government signalled their intention to examine the scope for a review of the broader issues surrounding prostitution. This intention was formalised in the 2004 consultation document, *Paying the Price*, which marked the next stage of reform seeking to address the wider issues associated with prostitution.[11]

The timing of both the review of sexual offences, and then of prostitution itself, was connected to an international drive around trafficking that called upon states to take action to discourage the demand for exploitation.[12] However, the action during this period must be attributed not only to the government's international obligations but also to the clear role of feminist activism and campaigning. In the Labour Government of 1997–2010, there was a cohort of women who were also long-standing feminist activists. Vera Baird, Harriet Harman, Fiona MacTaggart, Clare Short, and Jacqui Smith had all participated in a range of forms of feminist activism before coming to the House of Commons. These women were supported by feminist activists in frontline support services, as well as in the academy, where women such as Liz Kelly, Linda Regan, Marianne Hester, and Nicole Westmarland were producing comprehensive research on the experiences of women within

[5] Liz Kelly, '"A Conducive Context": Trafficking of Persons in Central Asia' in Maggy Lee (ed), *Human Trafficking* (Willan Publishing, 2007) 73–91. Liz Kelly 'The conducive context of violence against women and girls', *Discover Society*, 1 March 2016: https://discoversociety.org/2016/03/01/theorising-violence-against-women-and-girls/.

[6] Maddy Coy, 'Prostitution in (and out of) policy on violence against women and girls in the UK' (2017) 1(1) *Journal of Gender-Based Violence* 117–26.

[7] Home Office, *Paying the Price: a consulation paper on prositution* (Home Office, July 2004) and Home Office, *A Coordinated Prostitution Strategy and a summary of responses to Paying the Price* (Home Office, January 2006).

[8] Home Office, *A Review of Effective Practice in Responding to Prostitution* (13 October 2011).

[9] All-Party Parliamentary Group on Prostitution and the Global Sex Trade (APPG), *Shifting the Burden: Inquiry to Assess the Operation of the Current Legal Settlement on Prostitution in England and Wales* (March 2014).

[10] Home Office, *Setting the Boundaries: Reforming the Law on Sex Offences, Vol 1* (HOCD, 2000) and Home Office, *Setting the Boundaries: Reforming the Law on Sex Offence, Vol 2* (HOCD, 2000).

[11] Home Office 2004, n 7 above.

[12] For example, the UN Palermo Protocol in 2000 (formally known as the Protocol to Prevent, Suppress and Punish Trafficking in Persons Especially Women and Children, supplementing the United Nations Convention against Transnational Organized Crime), and the 2005 Council of Europe Convention against trafficking in human beings.

the prostitution system, including street-based prostitution and trafficking. Denise Marshall, who ran the feminist organisation Eaves Housing, set up the Poppy Project as a result of women using Eaves services disclosing experiences of trafficking for sexual exploitation. At the time of its creation in 2003, the Poppy Project was the only dedicated specialist service for this group of women.[13] The establishment of this service meant that for the first time in England and Wales, women's accounts of trafficking and coercion in the prostitution system were being recorded by a frontline feminist organisation, which was to play a key role in the evidence submissions to support what was to be section 14.

The 2004 consultation document, *Paying the Price*, aimed at prompting an informed debate of the issues to help in the development of a coordinated strategy on prostitution for England and Wales. The document was explicit in its understanding of demand and economic necessity as driving factors, as well as recognising the gendered nature of the prostitution system; however, the need to protect neighbourhoods and communities from prostitution also played a key role in the consultation's framing. This approach, though broadly well-received, was criticised by feminists across different positions in the debates, as when communities are seen as *victims* of prostitution, the most visible *perpetrators*, and thus the targets for criminal sanctions, are the (typically) women selling, not the male clients. It is important to recognise that whilst feminists diverge on the issue of criminalising demand – broadly supported by those within the 'violence against women' movement, and opposed by many within sex-worker rights organisations – both perspectives advocate for the removal of criminal sanctions from those who directly sell or are sold for sex. Though full decriminalisation includes decriminalising those organising or profiting from the sale of someone else's sexual services (a 'pimp' or 'manager'), the Equality model is not just about criminalising demand, but also about decriminalising the sellers in the immediate exchange, as well as embedding responses outside of criminal justice (such as support for exiting, help with housing, benefits, or advocacy around immigration rights) within the policy frame.[14] Given these competing frames, the coordinated prostitution strategy published in 2006 as a result of the consultation has been called 'opaque and contradictory' by those supporting a full decriminalisation model.[15] It was also denounced by the 2014 APPG report (which recommends an approach informed by the Nordic model), which called the law on prostitution in England and Wales: 'incoherent at best and detrimental at worst'.[16]

## II. The Landmark

Given this dissatisfaction across feminist positions, combined with the UK's international obligations to reduce the demand for sexual exploitation, the then Home Secretary, Jacqui

[13] See further, Eaves: putting women first: http://www.eavesforwomen.org.uk/about-eaves/our-projects/the-poppy-project/.

[14] This approach was typically referred to as the 'Nordic' model, but as more countries outside of the Nordic region have taken it on, including France, Northern Ireland and the Republic of Ireland, and a version in Canada, it is increasingly known as the 'Equality' model.

[15] Jane Scoular and Maggie O'Neill, 'Regulating Prostitution Social Inclusion, Responsibilization and the Politics of Prostitution Reform' (2007) 47(5) *British Journal of Criminology* 764–78.

[16] APPG, n 9 above, 4.

Smith, commissioned a six-month review in 2008 to assess the need for further measures. Published as *Tackling the demand for prostitution*, the review concluded that there was evidence to support the development of a new offence to criminalise those who are found to be paying for sex with a person who is being controlled against their wishes for someone else's gain.[17] The recommendation was that the new offence should be 'a strict liability offence meaning that it will be irrelevant whether the sex buyer knew that the prostitute was controlled or not'.[18]

The recommendation became section 14. It provoked lengthy and sometimes heated discussion during the parliamentary process,[19] and Eaves came together with the feminist grassroots lobbying organisation Object during the House of Lords stage to launch a more formal campaign supporting the amendment. Called 'Demand Change!', the campaign focused on encouraging women to send template letters of support for section 14 to local MPs and members of the House of Lords. It was assisted by feminist lawyers Gunilla Ekberg, who was able to give campaigners in the UK support around how the Equality model worked through her familiarity of the model in Sweden, and Cate Briddick, who later drafted the joint statement of support for section 14 from the feminist legal charity Rights of Women. **Baroness Scotland** also helped drive support from within the Lords. This coordinated campaign resulted in success, with the amendment passing in November 2009. A joint statement issued by Rights of Women, together with 67 prominent signatories from across the women and human rights sectors, expressed its support with key caveats around implementation. Signatories clearly stated that

> in order to be effective in reducing demand for commercial sexual exploitation, there needs to be: a concerted publicity campaign to raise awareness of the new offence and the harm cause by prostitution to those involved, and to the status of women in society as a whole; and a commitment from agencies in the criminal justice system, particularly the police and Crown Prosecution Service to the effective investigation and prosecution of this offence.

On 1 April, 2010, the new section 53A of the Sexual Offences Act 2003 came into effect in England and Wales: a strict liability offence which made it an offence to pay or attempt to pay for sexual services from someone who has been subject to force or exploitation. An offence is committed if a person (A) 'makes or promises payment for the sexual services of a prostitute (B)' and 'a third person (C) has engaged in exploitative conduct of a kind likely to induce or encourage B to provide the sexual services for which A has made or promised payment' and; 'C engaged in that conduct for or in the expectation of gain for C or another person (apart from A or B).' It is irrelevant where in the world the sexual services are to be provided, and whether the buyer (A) is aware of the exploitative conduct of C. 'Gain' here refers to both any financial advantage, including the discharge of an obligation to pay or the provision of goods or services gratuitously or at a discount; or the goodwill of any person which is or appears likely, in time, to bring financial advantage. Person C engages in exploitative conduct if they use force, threats (whether or not relating to violence) or any other form of coercion; or they practise any form of deception.

[17] Home Office, *Tackling the Demand for Prostitution: A Review* (Home Office, November 2008).

[18] ibid 3.

[19] Natahsa Mulvihill, 'Gender, power and the translation of English prostitution policy' in Nadia Aghtaie and Geetanjali Gangoli (eds), *Understanding Gender Based Violence: National and international contexts* (Routledge, 2014) 110–29.

An identical amendment, section 15, came into effect at the same time in Northern Ireland – though this has since been superseded by new legislation across both Northern Ireland and the Republic that makes it completely illegal to pay for sex and decriminalises the sellers.

## III. What Happened Next

Despite the need for investment in implementation, identified both in the statement of support from the Rights of Women in 2010 and in 2006 by the responses to the *Paying the Price* consultation, a long-term public-facing government campaign of this nature has yet to be implemented. Seven years on from its introduction, section 14 is largely seen to have been weakly enforced. This is due in no small part to a lack of political will, and the over-reliance on victim testimony rather than other evidentiary techniques such as those now in use around domestic violence offences. A 2014 study found that only 29 per cent of police forces used the legislation at all, with only 43 convictions between its implementation and November 2012.[20] However, these figures have been disputed.

Records for the period 2010–12 provided by the Ministry of Justice after a Freedom of Information (FOI) request show 61 convictions for the offence of 'paying or promising to pay a person to provide sexual services, where that person is subject to exploitative conduct to induce or encourage them to provide those services' under the Sexual Offences Act 2003 53A.[21] Though this number is higher than that in the 2014 study, it is also given with references to the limitations of relying on police and court data systems, as well as explaining that when a defendant has been found guilty of two or more offences it is the offence for which the heaviest penalty is imposed that is recorded. As such, this higher number may still not represent all of the convictions under section 53A. Subsequent research using FOI requests has found significant shortcomings and inaccuracies in police data on section 14 of the Policing and Crime Act 2009. For example, Andrea Matolcsi's work on section 14 shows that the 2014 study was based on police statistics received after requesting information on section 14 rather than section 53A of the Sexual Offences Act (where section 14 was incorporated into law) which may mean some forces reported a 'nil' usage as the request did not relate to what offenders would have been questioned on or arrested under.[22] Thus, while there may indeed be a lack of use of section 14 (also seen in the relatively low number of convictions – approximately 60 by 2014), Matolcsi's in-depth work in this area suggests it is highly likely that relying solely on police or Crown Prosecution Service figures cannot give an accurate picture of implementation.

[20] Sarah Kingston and Terry Thomas, 'The police, sex work, and Section 14 of the Policing and Crime Act 2009' (2014) 53(3) *Howard Journal of Criminal Justice* 255–69.

[21] How many people convicted under s53A Sexual Offences Act 2003: https://www.gov.uk/government/uploads/system/uploads/attachment_data/file/306063/how-many-people-convicted-under-s53A-sexual-offences-act-2003.xls.

[22] Andrea Matolcsi, *Section 53A of the Sexual Offences Act 2003 (inserted by section 14 of the Policing and Crime Act 2009) on 'paying for the sexual services of a prostitute subject to coercion etc': Implementation and the views of practitioners* (Unpublished PhD thesis, University of Bristol, 2017).

Alongside these considerations, the debates on prostitution, and government reviews, continue without a clear or definitive position from government. In 2011, the Coalition Government delivered their *Review of Effective Practice into Prostitution*,[23] informed by a localism agenda that claimed to take 'no position', although initial working groups contained only academics and representatives who supported full decriminalisation and, at the time, did not even support the provision of exiting services.[24] In January 2016, an inquiry was called by the Home Affairs Select Committee to assess the evidence about the impact of the different regulatory approaches – legalisation, full decriminalisation, and the Nordic or Equality model – and to consider whether there might be benefits to changing the existing legal framework in England and Wales. However, in September 2016 the chair of the inquiry, Keith Vaz – who had publicly stated his resistance to legislative approaches that focused on sex buyers – had to stand down after it was revealed that he was in fact a sex buyer himself. Given this, though the published report from the committee in July 2016 was intended to be (and was responded to by government as) an interim report,[25] currently the inquiry is listed as concluded.[26]

## IV. Significance

The limitations of section 14 sit within what is seen by many as a weak legislative response to prostitution in England and Wales. As the importance of supporting women in the prostitution system is a shared priority for feminists advocating legal reform across the debates, the perceived ineffectiveness of section 14 in this area needs to be one of the important measures for its significance as a landmark for women. However, it is important to remember the warnings given by those who campaigned for the amendment about the potential for its failure, without government will and resources, to ensure effective implementation. This suggests that the problem is not the legislation itself but rather its dependence on wrap-around measures such as police training and public awareness campaigns, to ensure its success.[27]

Additional factors include a lack of resourcing to police to deal with prostitution and sex-trafficking generally, including the elimination or broadening of mandates of specialist units; priorities, including whether buyers are targeted at all; and inadequate training and awareness-raising of the offence among police. Matolcsi's recent study, for example, uncovered a relatively low level of understanding of the offence (some of the 10 police interviewed in different locations in England mistakenly thought it had to be proved that the buyer was aware of the exploitation, which is not the case), or even awareness, with several police participants seemingly not aware of the offence. Evaluating the significance of section 14

[23] Home Office, n 7 above.

[24] I am indebted to Heather Harvey for her discussion of this.

[25] House of Commons Home Affairs Committee, *Prostitution* (HC 26, July 2016); Home Office, 'The Government Response to the Report from the Home Affairs Select Committee Session 2016–2017 HC 26: Prostitution' (Cm 9361, December 2016).

[26] See Home Affairs Committee, 'Prostitution inquiry': https://www.parliament.uk/business/committees/committees-a-z/commons-select/home-affairs-committee/inquiries/parliament-2015/prostitution/.

[27] My thanks to Ruth Breslin for her insights here.

requires not only attention to how the legislation has been utilised, and its substantive effects, but also consideration of the law's symbolic role and the lessons learnt around implementation. These lessons form part of its significance, offering a warning to feminist activists that political will is integral in translating legislative change into real change in women's lives.

Together with this, the value of legislation should not only be measured by criminal justice statistics. Prostitution is undeniably gendered, and the significance of section 14 lies in the ways in which it sought to take account of gender inequality in situating agency. The amendment marked a shift in attention for prostitution legislation in England and Wales, away from the public nuisance discourse towards a more informed understanding of the role of material inequalities and the operations of coercion. As such, whilst the shift it signalled fell short of providing the breadth of supportive measures for those in prostitution that are embedded in the Equality model, it demonstrated a more complex understanding of the prostitution system than had previously been evidenced in law.

## Further Reading


- Maddy Coy, 'Prostitution in (and out of) policy on violence against women and girls in the UK' (2017) 1 *Journal of Gender-Based Violence* 117–26.
- Andrea Matolcsi, *Section 53A of the Sexual Offences Act 2003 (inserted by section 14 of the Policing and Crime Act 2009) on 'paying for the sexual services of a prostitute subject to coercion etc': Implementation and the views of practitioners* (Unpublished PhD thesis, University of Bristol, 2017).
- Natasha Mulvihill, 'Policy Briefing: Prostitution Law and Policy in England – The Limits of Liberalism' (*Discover Society*, 1 March 2016).

# 81

# *Radmacher v Granatino* (2010)

MARIE PARKER

In *Radmacher v Granatino*[1] the UK Supreme Court ruled for the first time that a pre-nuptial agreement could be binding on divorcing parties but that the courts would still have the discretion to waive any such agreement if it had been obtained unfairly or was unfair to any children of the marriage.

## I. Context

Traditionally, pre-nuptial and post-nuptial agreements have been held to be void as a matter of public policy, for three reasons. First, a couple about to enter into a marriage should not be able to contemplate a future divorce. This was rejected by the majority of the Supreme Court in *Radmacher* on the basis that it was 'obsolete and should be swept away'.[2] Second, a person should not be able to contract out of their responsibilities towards their children. There have been no changes to cast any doubt on this rule.[3] Third, an agreement should not be able to oust the jurisdiction of the court, because people should always able to access the protection of legislative provisions. The Law Commission consulted on this in 2014 and proposed in its subsequent report a draft Bill indicating how a qualifying nuptial agreement could be created.[4] This is yet to be taken forward.

The desire to protect the financial security of women exercising contractual capacity can be found at the source of the rule which prevents such agreements from ousting the jurisdiction of the court. The passing of the **Married Women's Property Act 1882** meant that everything a woman owned upon marriage, and anything she acquired during the marriage, became her separate property. The Act also conferred on women full contractual capacity, although husbands also remained responsible for their wives' contractual debts until 1935.[5] The most commonly cited case concerns a separation agreement from the

[1] *Radmacher v Granatino* [2010] UKSC 42.

[2] [2010] UKSC 42, [52]. For further commentary see Marie Parker, 'The draft Nuptial Agreements Bill and the abolition of the common law rule: 'swept away' or swept under the carpet?' (2015) 27(1) *Child and Family Law Quarterly* 63.

[3] Law Commission, *Marital Property Agreements – A Consultation Paper* (Consultation Paper No 208, 2012).

[4] Law Commission, *Matrimonial Property, Needs and Agreements* (Law Com No 343, 2014).

[5] Law Reform (Married Women and Tortfeasors) Act 1935.

late 1920s, *Hyman v Hyman*.[6] Mr Hyman and Mrs Hyman were married in 1912, and in 1919 – after Mr Hyman left Mrs Hyman for another woman – a deed of separation was executed (adultery by the husband was not at the time a ground for divorce unless aggravated by an additional factor such as incest).[7] The couple remained legally obliged to live together. This could be enforced by self-help or by obtaining a decree of restitution of conjugal rights. Their private agreement set the amount of maintenance to be paid by the husband and also prevented the wife from taking any action which would force her husband to cohabit with her. After the **Matrimonial Causes Act 1923** gave equality to wives with regard to grounds for divorce, Mrs Hyman's options altered and she started divorce proceedings in 1927. She obtained a decree nisi and applied for maintenance. Her husband tried to rely upon the separation deed. The case went to the House of Lords where it was decided that the deed of separation did not prevent a petition to the court for maintenance upon divorce. Lord Atkin stated:

> In the absence of any statutory enactment the former wife would be left without any provision for her maintenance other than recourse to the poor law authorities. In my opinion the statutory powers of the Court to which I have referred were granted partly in the public interest to provide a substitute for this husband's duty of maintenance and to prevent the wife from being thrown upon the public for support.[8]

Since 1973, financial settlements on divorce have been governed by the factors in section 25 of the Matrimonial Causes Act 1973, as refined by case law including ***White v White*** and *Miller v Miller; McFarlane v McFarlane*.[9]

## II. The Landmark

Katrin Radmacher and Nicolas Grantino were both living in London when they met in a Mayfair nightclub in November 1997. Both were from wealthy families, but Radmacher, coming from a very rich German business family, was significantly wealthier than Granatino. Granatino, a French national, was working as an Investment Banker when the couple met, earning a very high wage. The couple become engaged in June 1998 and married in November 1998.

In August 1998, prior to their marriage, they signed a pre-nuptial agreement written by a Notary in Germany. It had been made at the instigation of Radmacher, who had already received some of her family wealth and expected to receive further transfers in the future. Her father insisted that these future transfers would only occur with the protection of a pre-nuptial agreement in place. The agreement set out that Granatino would receive none of Radmacher's fortune should they divorce. Granatino explained that he had understood that, without a pre-nuptial agreement in place, his wife would have been disinherited. He wished to marry her and did not want to cause any problems within the family, but was unaware of

[6] *Hyman v Hyman* [1929] AC 601.

[7] **Matrimonial Causes Act 1857**.

[8] [1929] AC 601, 603.

[9] ***White v White*** [2001] 1 AC 596 and *Miller v Miller; McFarlane v McFarlane* [2006] UKHL 24.

how important the contract was to his wife. Radmacher stated that she was anxious that any man should want to marry her for love, and not for her money.

The couple lived in a rented flat in Knightsbridge, London, during their marriage. Their first daughter was born in September 1999. They moved to New York for the husband's work in April 2000, but Radmacher returned to London in May 2001, her husband following later that year. Their second daughter was born in May 2002. In July 2003, Granatino left his employment to undertake research for a doctorate in biotechnology at Oxford. This meant that his earning capacity was significantly reduced and he spent many nights away from home. As promised, Radmacher's father had transferred further capital to her during the marriage. In August 2006, with their marriage in difficulties, Radmacher moved to another rented flat in Knightsbridge with the children. The couple divorced in 2007. Granatino claimed for ancillary relief, as it was then termed – a financial settlement including maintenance and a share of the property.

The case came to the High Court in 2008. Baron J found the pre-nuptial agreement to be defective on the basis that Granatino had received no independent legal advice; the agreement sought to deprive him of all claims, which she considered to be manifestly unfair; there had been no disclosure by Radmacher and there had been no negotiations; and two children had been born during the marriage.[10] A more limited award was granted than Granatino would have ordinarily been awarded on divorce, on the basis that he had agreed to take nothing in the event of a divorce.

Radmacher appealed successfully to the Court of Appeal. Thorpe LJ's view was that there had been 'a sufficiently erroneous exercise of the judicial discretion'[11] in the lower court. The Court reasoned that the husband's claim should be dismissed because: he was of great ability (so had high potential earning power); such contracts were standard practice in France and Germany; he had been provided with the opportunity to seek independent legal advice; he had known his wife was from a very wealthy family, and it was to be assumed that a young couple anticipated having children after marrying.[12] The Court of Appeal therefore restricted the award to his role as a father and he took nothing as a result of being a former husband. Notably, his home would be held on trust for Radmacher, his debts would be cleared and he was provided with money to buy a car.

On appeal, the majority of the Supreme Court agreed with the award granted by the Court of Appeal. They put forward the following test:

> The court should give effect to a nuptial agreement that is freely entered into by each party with full appreciation of its implications unless in the circumstances prevailing it would not be fair to hold the parties to their agreement.[13]

When considering the fairness of the agreement the Court considered needs, compensation and sharing: the same factors as are considered in all financial settlements on divorce. The majority decided that the needs of the husband did not render the agreement unfair on the basis that he was very capable; the relief granted would enable him to look after his

[10] *NG v KR (Pre-nuptial contract)* [2008] EWHC 153 [137]. This list of reasons is based on factors recommended in Home Office, *Supporting Families: A Consultation Document* (Home Office, 1998).

[11] *Radmacher v Granatino* [2009] EWCA Civ 649 [44].

[12] ibid [33].

[13] *Radmacher v Granatino* [2010] UKSC 42, [75].

two daughters; it would meet his needs for the time being, and his debts had been cleared. They considered there was no compensation element to the case, since his change of career had been driven by his own preference, not the demands of his family. They also considered that he should not be entitled to share a proportion of the wife's wealth when he had agreed he would have no such entitlement.[14]

**Lady Hale**, at the time the only woman Justice in the court, dissented. She did not think that the agreement should be the starting point; rather, the starting point should be the general rules governing financial relief on divorce. She set out her own test:

> Did each party freely enter into an agreement, intending it to have legal effect and with a full appreciation of its implications? If so, in the circumstances as they now are, would it be fair to hold them to their agreement?[15]

When considering needs, Lady Hale pointed to the wider context in which the claimant was more likely to be a woman:

> Each party has a responsibility to try to adjust to living without such support. But they may still be entitled to support for requirements which arose as a result of or during the marriage. Usually, of course, this is because of the demands of child-rearing and the (often lifelong) financial disadvantage which results.[16]

She noted that 'choices are often made for the sake of the overall happiness of the family'.[17] She emphasised that marriage makes a difference, and it was therefore wrong to see the parties as freely contracting individuals. She considered that the Court of Appeal was incorrect to equate married and unmarried parenthood, since 'Marriage still counts for something in the law of this country and long may it continue to do so'.[18]

Lady Hale begins her judgment by drawing attention to 'a gender dimension to the issue which' (she added with some point) 'some may think ill-suited to decision by a court consisting of eight men and one woman'.[19] In a lecture delivered in 2014 she noted that there were cases where her 'experience and perceptions of life' made a difference to her view of the law and the realities of owning a family home jointly.[20] *Radmacher* was surely one such case. Although she was advocating further provisions to be made for the husband in this case, and while conceding that 'We have now arrived at a position where the differing roles which either may adopt within the relationship are entitled to equal esteem',[21] she clearly had an eye to the more typical case in this situation where it would be the wife trying to establish provision for her needs. This is evident from her reference to the fact that needs are usually generated by child-rearing and her observation that 'the object of an ante-nuptial agreement is to deny the economically weaker spouse the provision to which she – it is usually although by no means invariably she – would otherwise be entitled'.[22]

[14] ibid [119]–[122].
[15] ibid [169].
[16] ibid [187].
[17] ibid [188].
[18] ibid [195].
[19] ibid [137].
[20] Lady Hale, 'Women in the Judiciary, Fiona Woolf Lecture for the Women Lawyers' Division of the Law Society, 27 June 2014.
[21] [2010] UKSC 42, [132].
[22] ibid [137].

# III. What Happened Next

The test expounded by the majority in *Radmacher* has elevated pre-nuptial and post-nuptial agreements above the factors to be considered under section 25 Matrimonial Causes Act 1973. There are now many subsequent reported decisions which have upheld the *Radmacher* decision. For example, in *Z v Z (No 2) (Financial Remedies: Marriage Contract)*, Moor J refers the 'seismic shift' in this area since the Supreme Court's decision.[23] In *V v V (Prenuptial Agreement)* Charles J acknowledged, 'the need to recognise the weight that should now be given to autonomy'.[24] The Law Commission's consultation paper on marital property arrangements, which was delayed until the Supreme Court's decision in *Radmacher*, refers to it as the 'culmination of this story of the evolution of judicial views'.[25] In their final report, published in 2014, they recommend that the Government should introduce qualifying nuptial agreements, though not so as to contract out of financial needs (thus providing the scope for the type of protection Lady Hale argued for in *Radmacher*).[26] In January 2017, the Government stated that it would consider the Law Commission's recommendations on qualifying nuptial agreements as part of a wider consideration of private family law reforms.[27] Draft legislation is yet to be introduced.

# IV. Significance

The Supreme Court decision in *Radmacher v Granatino* marks a point in history where such agreements became as close to binding as judge-made law can provide. It is a landmark for women for two reasons. First, this case stands out against the vast majority of marital property cases where it is the ex-husband or future husband trying to reduce the maintenance to be awarded to his wife. In largely upholding the agreement, created at the insistence of a woman (albeit one whose wishes were in line with those of her father), the majority of the Supreme Court demonstrated a willingness to acknowledge and enforce the contractual capacity of women in relation to their property and money following marriage (something for which women have fought for centuries), and not to regard them as 'weak-minded women in love'[28] – a view that has shaped and informed the decision-making of judges in the lower courts.

Secondly, the case brings the law a step closer to recognising pre-nuptial agreements as binding. Views differ as to whether this is a positive or negative development for women. While some view such agreements as a step backwards,[29] others argue that many women

[23] *Z v Z (No 2) (Financial Remedies: Marriage Contract)* [2011] EWHC 2878 (Fam), [33].
[24] *V v V (Prenuptial Agreement)* [2011] EWHC 3230 (Fam), [36].
[25] Law Commission, n 3 above, [3.37].
[26] Law Commission, *Matrimonial Property, Needs and Agreements* (Law Com No 343, 2014) [5.84].
[27] Ministry of Justice, *Report on the implementation of Law Commission proposals* (January 2017) [48]–[50].
[28] Lenore J Weitzman, *The Marriage Contract: A Guide to Living with Lovers and Spouses* (Free Press, 1981) 246.
[29] See eg Gail F Brod, 'Premarital Agreements and Gender Justice' (1994) 6 *Yale Journal of Law and Feminism* 229, 279: 'By focusing on women's idealized de jure equality, lawmakers have ignored women's actual, continuing social and economic inequality. By ignoring women's de facto inequality, lawmakers reforming the law of premarital agreements have overlooked the adverse economic impact that premarital agreements have on women as a class.

would be in a better – stronger – financial position if they knew that they would or may not be financially supported were the marriage to end, prior to entering the marriage, rather than have an unwelcome surprise later down the line, when often little can be done. An open discussion about the proposed agreement may result in the woman deciding not to get married at all.[30] Alternatively, it may prompt further negotiations in order to ensure a better outcome for the wife.[31]

In her groundbreaking study of pre-nuptial agreements, Sharon Thompson pointed out that the move to recognise the rights of spouses to make autonomous decisions can, and often does, obscure other key issues, such as the imbalance of power.[32] There is therefore a fine balance to be found between ensuring that the presumed equality between the parties reflects reality[33] and recognising that a person may choose to sign such contracts blinded by romance or love. If this balance can be achieved, then many benefits for women can begin to emerge. Knowing where you stand at the beginning of any relationship is important. Knowing where you stand, as a result of creating a pre-nuptial agreement before you enter into marriage, prevents (or at least limits) false hope of ongoing financial support. And insofar as it presents the opportunity for women to negotiate a better deal, and/or make more fully informed lifestyle choices – which may in turn shape and apprise attitudes toward women's decision-making and competency more generally – this is no bad thing.

## Further Reading

- Brigitte Clark, 'Should Greater Prominence Be Given To Pre-Nuptial Contracts in the Law of Ancillary Relief?' (2004) 16 *Child and Family Law Quarterly* 399.
- Sharon Thompson, *Prenuptial Agreements and the Presumption of Free Choice: Issues of Power in Theory and Practice* (Hart Publishing, 2015).
- Lenore J Weitzman, *The Marriage Contract: A Guide to Living with Lovers and Spouses* (Free Press, 1981).

Lawmakers should recognize premarital agreements for what they are: contracts that violate social norms against gender discrimination'.

30 See eg Twila Perry, 'Dissolution Planning in Family Law: A Critique of Current Analyses and a Look toward the Future' (1990–91) 24 *Family Law Quarterly* 77, 84–85: 'Dissolution planning at the beginning of a relationship could also have a positive effect on the marriage itself. Frank discussions about what the parties expect in the event of termination of the relationship would likely lead to wide-ranging discussions about what they expect during the relationship, and serious differences might be worked out before the marriage takes place. To the extent that any such discussions ultimately reveal differences that turn out to be irreconcilable, they arguably would serve a positive function even if the result is the couples who otherwise would have married do not do so'.

31 Lenore J Weitzman *The Marriage Contract: A Guide to Living with Lovers and Spouses* (Free Press, 1981) 248: 'the explicit agreement would be visible to third parties – her family and friends – and they would be likely to try to exert the pressure necessary both to make her insist on, and to make him grant, more favourable terms'.

32 Sharon Thompson, *Prenuptial Agreements and the Presumption of Free Choice: Issues of Power in Theory and Practice* (Hart Publishing, 2015).

33 Brod, n 29 above, 279.

# 82

# Concluding Observations of the UN Committee against Torture, Recommendation to Ireland Regarding the Magdalene Laundries, 2011

MAEVE O'ROURKE

In June 2011, the United Nations Committee against Torture (CAT) examined Ireland's human rights record for the first time. The CAT's Concluding Observations addressed an issue which had long been ignored by the Irish government and had not yet been considered by any international human rights treaty body or national or international court: the (so-called 'historic') abuse of girls and women in Ireland's Catholic Church-run Magdalene Laundries.

The CAT noted that it was 'gravely concerned' by both 'the failure by the State party to protect girls and women who were involuntarily confined between 1922 and 1996 in the Magdalene Laundries' and the state's failure to investigate allegations of ill-treatment in the institutions. The CAT therefore recommended that the Irish government (a) 'institute prompt, independent and thorough investigations into all complaints of torture and other cruel, inhuman or degrading treatment or punishment that were allegedly committed in the Magdalene Laundries'; (b) 'in appropriate cases, prosecute and punish the perpetrators with penalties commensurate with the gravity of the offences committed'; and (c) 'ensure that all victims obtain redress and have an enforceable right to compensation, including the means for as full rehabilitation as possible'.[1] These recommendations were included in the CAT's urgent follow-up mechanism, requiring the government to respond within one year.

## I. Context

While not uniquely Irish or Catholic in origin, 10 Catholic Church-run Magdalene Laundries remained in operation in Ireland from independence, in 1922, until the last institution closed in Dublin in 1996. The institutions were convents with commercial laundries

[1] United Nations Committee against Torture, *Concluding Observations on the initial report of Ireland*, UN Doc CAT/C/IRL/CO/1 (17 June 2011), [21].

attached, where thousands of women and girls as young as nine were detained and forced into unpaid labour for indeterminate periods of time. The girls and women confined in Magdalene Laundries included those taken into state care as children, those who had given birth outside of marriage (and had been forced to relinquish their infants on that basis) and those who had been sexually abused. Magdalene Laundries also confined girls and women in the criminal justice system, girls and women with disabilities, girls and women whose families or communities considered them to be a burden or 'promiscuous', and girls and women who were in need of shelter. Records indicate that state officials directly placed at least 26 per cent of girls and women in Magdalene Laundries, frequently in contravention of or in the absence of authorising legislation. Nuns, priests, doctors and family members were also among those who referred girls and women to the institutions.

Ireland's Magdalene Laundries were understood by both the general public and the girls and women confined in them to be places of punishment and shame. A contribution by the Minister for Industry and Commerce in the Seanad in 1955 illustrates the official attitude towards Magdalene girls and women at that time: 'the persons concerned here are not ordinary factory workers. They are miscreants of one kind or another. They are people who are in there, in these institutions, for the public good'.[2] In 1960, Senator Nora Connolly O'Brien criticised the Criminal Justice Bill, 1960, which provided for girls to be detained in a Magdalene Laundry on remand, on the basis that:

> I do not think there is any member of this House who is ignorant of what the stigma would mean to a girl if she had mended her ways, if she had been corrected and was leading a normal and upright life, and had to spend the rest of her life in the fear and terror of being charged with having in her youth been an inmate of St. Mary Magdalen's Asylum … If I were asked to advise girl delinquents … whether to go to prison on remand, or to go to St Mary Magdalen's Asylum on remand, I would advise them wholeheartedly to choose prison, because I think having a record of having been in prison as a juvenile delinquent would not be so detrimental to the afterlife of the girl as to have it legally recorded that she was an inmate of St. Mary Magdalen's Asylum.[3]

Survivor testimony reveals that, once inside the institutions, girls and women were frequently denied information about the reason for their detention or when they would be released (if at all). The girls and women were routinely stripped of their identities through the imposition of numbers, 'house' names, uniforms and/or haircuts and through constant surveillance, prohibitions on speaking, and denial of contact with the outside world. They were forced to work for no pay, six days per week from morning until evening, at heavy commercial laundry work, other manual labour and sometimes needlework and other crafts. Many survivors have recounted being subjected to repeated verbal denigration and to punishments for failure to work or for otherwise stepping out of line, including humiliation rituals and physical abuse. *An Garda Síochána* (the Irish police force) is known to have returned escapees to the Magdalene Laundries, and women have spoken of being punished for their escape attempts, including by transfer to a different Magdalene institution and solitary confinement.[4]

[2] Seanad Éireann Debate, Vol 44 No 15, 11 May 1955 (Factories Bill – Committee).

[3] Seanad Éireann Debate, Vol 52 No 19, 13 July 1960 (Criminal Justice Bill, 1960 – Second Stage).

[4] See Justice for Magdalenes Research, NGO Submission to the UN Committee Against Torture in respect of Ireland (for the session), July 2017, citing numerous sources of evidence, including the *Report of the Inter-departmental Committee to establish the facts of State involvement with the Magdalen laundries* (February 2013).

James Smith contends that the Magdalene Laundries formed part of Ireland's 'architecture of containment' – an architecture of physical, legal and other more abstract structures which the Irish Free State (1922–37) erected in cooperation with the powerful Catholic Church hierarchy in order to discipline and mould the image of the citizens of the newly independent nation.[5] The new state's identity was bound up with the proclaimed moral virtue of its society and women in particular.[6] The nation's 'architecture of containment', according to Smith, encompassed not only a network of institutions (including industrial and reformatory schools, Magdalene Laundries, mother and baby homes, County Homes and prisons), but also 'official and public discourses that concealed the existence and function of these facilities' and 'legislation that proscribed contraception, cultivated ignorance regarding human sexuality, and fostered intolerance for illegitimacy'.[7] As Smith notes, 'the availability of this containment infrastructure empowered the decolonising nation-state to confine aberrant citizens, rendering invisible women and children who fell foul of society's moral prescriptions.'[8]

## II. The Landmark

In 2003, three adoption rights activists (Mari Steed, Claire McGettrick and Angela Murphy), two of whom are the daughters of women detained in Magdalene Laundries for a combined total of approximately 60 years, established the *Justice for Magdalenes* (JFM) advocacy group. JFM's predecessor organisation, the *Magdalen Memorial Committee*, had successfully lobbied the Irish government for a memorial to the women whose bodies were exhumed in 1993 from a grave at the site of the High Park Magdalene Laundry in Dublin and cremated by the Sisters of Our Lady of Charity of the Refuge so that the nuns could sell their land.[9] The driving force behind JFM's establishment was the revelation in 2003 by the late journalist Mary Raftery, that the Sisters of Our Lady of Charity of Refuge had received exhumation licences from the Department of the Environment in 1993 for 155 women's bodies, without producing death certificates for 80 women or the full names of 46 women.[10]

JFM's aims were to

> promote and represent the interests of the Magdalene women, to respectfully promote equality and seek justice for the women formerly incarcerated in Magdalene Laundries, and to seek the establishment and improvements of support as well as advisory and re-integration services for survivors.[11]

[5] James M Smith, *Ireland's Magdalen Laundries and the Nation's Architecture of Containment*, (University of Notre Dame Press, 2007) Introduction and Chapter 2.

[6] See, for example, Lindsey Earner-Byrne, 'Illegitimate motherhood, 1922–60' in Earner-Byrne, *Mother and Child: Maternity and child welfare in Dublin, 1922–60* (Manchester University Press, 2007); Una Crowley and Rob Kitchin, 'Producing "decent girls": governmentality and the moral geographies of sexual conduct in Ireland (1922–1937)' (2008) 15(4) *Gender, Place and Culture* 355.

[7] Smith, above n 5, 46.

[8] ibid.

[9] 'Magdalene women plaque unveiled', *The Irish Times*, 22 April 1996; Mary Raftery, 'Restoring dignity to Magdalenes', *The Irish Times*, 21 August 2003.

[10] Raftery, ibid.

[11] Justice for Magdalenes, 'About Justice for Magdalenes': www.magdalenelaundries.com/what.htm.

Specifically, JFM sought an apology from the state to former Magdalene women and their family members and a comprehensive redress scheme.

In July 2009, upon the publication of the Ryan Report – the product of a nine-year investigation into the abuse of children in state-funded, Church-run residential schools, which was accompanied by a state apology to survivors of the schools and a redress scheme – JFM renewed its campaign for an apology and redress for survivors of the Magdalene Laundries. The government's response was to deny state liability for the institutions. The Minister for Education insisted that the Magdalene Laundries 'were privately owned and operated institutions which did not come within the responsibility of the State.'[12] He stated that the institutions 'were not subject to State regulation or supervision' and that '[t]he State did not refer individuals to Magdalen Laundries nor was it complicit in referring individuals to them.'[13]

By this point, JFM had gathered archival evidence of significant state involvement with the Magdalene Laundries. Between 2009 and 2010, JFM continued its campaign for an apology and redress by meeting officials from numerous government departments, obtaining formal support from Labour Women and the National Women's Council of Ireland for a redress scheme, and achieving the formation of a cross-party, ad hoc parliamentary committee dedicated to addressing the issue of redress for Magdalene survivors. Government TDs submitted an online petition to the Taoiseach, and TDs from all parties submitted approximately 30 parliamentary questions to government Ministers. JFM also wrote to each of the relevant religious congregations several times to request a meeting, to no avail. The group did, however, meet with the Primate of All Ireland, Cardinal Sean Brady, and Archbishop of Dublin, Diarmuid Martin.

In 2010, JFM decided to take a human rights approach to its campaign for reparation. The group's first step was to request that the Irish Human Rights Commission (IHRC) conduct an inquiry into 'the State's failure to protect the constitutional and human rights of women and young girls in the nation's Magdalene Laundries' and the state's obligation to provide redress to survivors.[14] The IHRC's response was swift: in November 2010 it published a 27-page 'Assessment of the Human Rights Issues Arising in relation to the "Magdalen Laundries"' which concluded with a formal recommendation to government 'that a statutory mechanism be established to investigate the matters advanced by JFM and in appropriate cases to grant redress where warranted.'[15]

In the absence of a response to the IHRC's Assessment, in April 2011 JFM this author submitted an NGO report on behalf of JFM to the UN Committee against Torture (CAT) for its first periodic review of Ireland.[16] Appended to this shadow report were the detailed, anonymised testimonies of four women incarcerated in different Magdalene Laundries between the late 1950s and late 1960s, and further shorter testimonies transcribed from radio and television programmes in which Magdalene survivors had recounted their experiences.

[12] Letter from Batt O'Keeffe, Minister for Education and Science to Tom Kitt, TD (4 September 2009), reproduced in JFM, *Information Booklet*: http://www.magdalenelaundries.com/jfm_booklet.pdf 6.

[13] ibid.

[14] See Justice for Magdalenes, Submission to the Irish Human Rights Commission (10 June 2010).

[15] Irish Human Rights Commission, *Assessment of the Human Rights Issues Arising in relation to the 'Magdalen Laundries'*, November 2010, 28–29.

[16] Justice for Magdalenes, Submission to the United Nations Committee against Torture (May 2011).

The governmental delegation which attended the CAT's examination of Ireland in Geneva in May 2011 held fast to the line that the state held no responsibility for abuse in Magdalene Laundries. The Secretary General of the Department of Justice argued that 'these alleged events happened in most cases a considerable time ago, in privately run institutions' and that 'the vast majority of women who went to these institutions went there voluntarily or, if they were children, with the consent of their parents or guardians'.[17] In response, the acting Chairperson of the CAT, Felice Gaer, noted that Magdalene survivors 'are alive' and questioned the assertions that the Magdalene Laundries were 'private' and 'voluntary':

> Do you have anything to suggest that the vast majority of women who went there were aware of the conditions … if they made a choice, if they were given information?
>
> We had testimony about locked doors and people being captured by police and returned …
>
> An act of torture may also arise from an act of omission and not just a positive act. So this appears to include failure to inspect or regulate the place where acts of torture occurred … wouldn't this apply to the Magdalene Laundries?[18]

Following the session in Geneva, the CAT issued its formal Concluding Observations in which it recommended the immediate investigation of allegations of abuse in Magdalene Laundries, the prosecution and punishment of perpetrators, and the provision of full redress.

## III. What Happened Next

The CAT's recommendations to Ireland regarding the Magdalene Laundries gained national and international press attention (including in the *New York Times*, *Time* Magazine, *The Guardian* and the BBC), and over the following days JFM organised an email campaign directed at Cabinet members, and numerous Senators and TDs called for parliamentary debates on the IHRC and CAT recommendations.[19]

Then, just over a week after the CAT issued its recommendations, on 14 June 2011, the Irish Minister for Justice announced that the government had 'considered the circumstances of the women and girls who resided in the Magdalene Laundries' and would establish an 'Inter-departmental Committee [IDC] to clarify any State interaction with the Magdalene Laundries and to produce a narrative detailing such interaction'.[20]

The IDC published its findings 18 months later, on 5 February 2013.[21] The report demonstrated numerous forms of state involvement with the Magdalene Laundries, including placements of girls and women, the provision of financial support, and widespread

[17] 'Sean Aylward from the Dept of Justice at UNCAT 1', 24 May 2011, <https://www.youtube.com/watch?v=tSrDbeO5wYs>; See also UN Committee against Torture, Summary record of the 1005th meeting held at the Palais Wilson, Geneva, on Tuesday, 24 May 2011, 3pm, UN Doc CAT/C/SR 1005, http://www.bayefsky.com/summary/ireland_cat_c_sr1005_2011.pdf.

[18] Felice Gaer, 24 May 2011, https://www.youtube.com/watch?v=YsUMPiFjUuk; See also UN Committee against Torture, Summary record of the 1005th meeting, n 17 above.

[19] Justice for Magdalenes, 'Letter to Cabinet Ministers', 13 June 2011: http://www.magdalenelaundries.com/dear_minister.htm.

[20] Department of Justice and Equality, Statement on the Magdalene Laundries, 14 June 2011.

[21] Ireland, *Report of the Inter-departmental Committee to establish the facts of State involvement with the Magdalene Laundries* (February 2013).

commercial dealings with the institutions through contracts for laundry services. The report further revealed the state's concomitant failure to regulate or monitor the institutions beyond treating them as factory premises (and even at that, its failure to properly supervise the institutions as factories) and its passing of legislation in 1936 to permit the non-payment of wages to the girls and women.

The Government had not given the IDC the mandate to make any legal findings or findings of wrongdoing in its report, nor had it given the IDC the mandate to investigate allegations of abuse. However, even without such findings the report's release only added to the momentum of the public pressure campaign for reparation. While the IDC had been conducting its research, JFM had gathered almost 5,000 pages of archival and testamentary evidence concerning human rights abuses in Magdalene Laundries, which the group summarised in a public report.[22] JFM and other NGOs had publicised the CAT's one-year deadline for Ireland to respond to its recommendations, and Ireland had come before the UN Human Rights Council's Universal Periodic Review process, where the Magdalene Laundries were again highlighted. In July 2012, Ireland's Special Rapporteur on Child Protection called for 'concrete provision' for Magdalene survivors and investigations capable of leading to criminal prosecutions where appropriate, on the basis that 'slavery' and 'forced labour' appeared to have occurred in the institutions.[23] In addition, the state broadcaster, RTE, for the first time aired a television investigative news feature on the Magdalene Laundries (which featured Felice Gaer, Acting Chairperson of the CAT).[24]

Finally, on 19 February 2013, the Taoiseach issued a state apology to all survivors of the Magdalene Laundries.[25] During his speech, the Taoiseach also promised the establishment of a fund to provide for 'payments and other supports, including medical cards, psychological and counselling services and other welfare needs'.[26]

## IV. Significance

In the space available, it is possible only to highlight – rather than fully discuss – the significance of the CAT's intervention in 2011. Four aspects, in particular, deserve brief mention.

First, the CAT's engagement with the Magdalene Laundries issue gave the women's complaints legal weight. Throughout the JFM campaign Magdalene survivors had alleged what, in principle, amounted to grave breaches of constitutional and human rights obligations (and, indeed, crimes and tortious causes of action). However, the passage of time and

[22] Justice for Magdalenes, *State involvement in the Magdalene Laundries: Principal Submissions to the Inter-departmental Committee to establish the facts of State involvement with the Magdalene Laundries* (18 September 2012).

[23] Geoffrey Shannon, Fifth Report of the Special Rapporteur on Child Protection (2012), 81: https://www.dcya.gov.ie/documents/publications/5RapporteurRepChildProtection.pdf.

[24] *RTE Prime Time*, 'The experiences of some of the Magdalene Laundry women' (25 September 2012).

[25] Dáil Éireann, *Magdalen Laundries Report: Statements* (19 February 2013). See also https://www.youtube.com/watch?v=hOQyl7ZpoH8.

[26] Continuing shortcomings in the implementation of the Magdalene 'restorative justice' scheme and in the state's provision of redress more generally are discussed in Justice for Magdalenes Research, NGO Submission to the UN Committee Against Torture in respect of Ireland (for the session) (July 2017); Maeve O'Rourke and James M Smith, 'Ireland's Magdalene Laundries: Confronting a history not yet in the past' in Alan Hayes and Maire Meagher (eds) A Century of Progress? Irish Women Reflect (Arlen House, 2016).

the civil Statute of Limitations in Ireland barred the women from pursuing these claims in court. The government used the absence of court judgments to support its claim that the state was not liable for any unlawful conduct – notwithstanding that Magdalene survivors were rendered unable to complain or seek justice, in large part, due to the state's involvement in the women's exploitation, its prolonged failure to investigate and its failure to afford any redress or rehabilitation. The CAT's intervention shifted the balance of power, restoring importance to the women's claims of rights violations and forcing the state to engage with questions of legality.

Second, the CAT's involvement kept the issue of redress for Magdalene survivors high up on the domestic political agenda. In its debate with government officials and its extraction of policy responses from those officials, the CAT process provided material which elected representatives in Ireland, and JFM, could harness in continuing to demand reparation. The CAT process also garnered the attention of the national and international press, and consequently the attention of the general public.

Third, the CAT's periodic review process and the periodic review processes of other UN human rights treaty bodies have provided mechanisms by which the state's response to the Magdalene Laundries abuse can be kept under continual review. Although JFM retired its political campaign following the establishment of an 'ex gratia' scheme for Magdalene survivors in 2013, the subsequently formed *Justice for Magdalenes Research* organisation continues to make submissions to the CAT and other human rights treaty bodies regarding the ongoing need for a thorough, independent investigation into human rights violations in Magdalene Laundries and numerous other forms of redress, including access to records, access to court, and legal reforms to guarantee non-repetition.

Fourth, the CAT's recommendations regarding the Magdalene Laundries are significant on an international jurisprudential level. They contribute to the body of jurisprudence which recognises violence against women and the so-called 'private' realm in which it commonly occurs as engaging the rule against torture and ill-treatment and states' positive obligations under the norm. In addition, they are a significant addition to the CAT's fledgling jurisprudence recognising the rights to an investigation, access to justice and comprehensive redress regarding torture or ill-treatment which occurred prior to the state's ratification of the Convention Against Torture and which has produced 'continuing violations'.

## Further Reading

- Justice for Magdalenes Research: www.jfmresearch.com.
- Maeve O'Rourke and James M Smith, 'Ireland's Magdalene Laundries: confronting a history not yet in the past' in Alan Hayes and Maire Meagher (eds), *A Century of Progress? Irish Women Reflect* (Arlen House, 2016).
- James M Smith, *Ireland's Magdalen Laundries and the Nation's Architecture of Containment* (University of Notre Dame Press, 2007).

# 83

## *Birmingham City Council v Abdulla* (2012)

HARINI IYENGAR

Just over 40 years after the Equal Pay Act 1970, 11,000 low-paid women local authority employees brought equal pay claims against Birmingham City Council. Mrs Abdulla was the lead claimant in a test case involving 170 women and four men. The claimants (the '*Abdulla* Group') were ostensibly too late to bring their claims in the Employment Tribunal, where the limitation period for such claims is fixed at just six months. So they boldly challenged the received wisdom that equal pay claims belonged in the specialist tribunal, and instead lodged their claims at the High Court. When Birmingham City Council challenged this, they took their case all the way to the United Kingdom Supreme Court and won.

*Birmingham City Council v Abdulla*[1] is superficially a procedural case about the interpretation of the defence of limitation. It typifies the abstruse, technical skirmishes which characterise the law on equal pay, where choices made in an exercise of legal interpretation create or deny transfers of wealth worth billions of pounds from large organisations dominated by men leaders to individual women workers. Nevertheless, in establishing that equal pay claimants can elect to bring their claims either in the Employment Tribunal (with a six-month time limit) or the High Court (with a six-year time limit), the case enhances the opportunities of thousands of women to enforce their equal pay rights.

## I. Context

The campaign for women's right to 'equal pay for equal work' was long-argued and hard won.[2] Despite the apparent success of the campaigns of the 1960s, culminating in the enactment of the Equal Pay Act 1970, the promise of equal pay for equal work remains difficult, expensive and time-consuming for women to enforce. Pay inequality because of sex is subject to a unique and eccentric system of legal regulation, which has been ineffective as a tool for eliminating either unequal pay for equal work (which is unlawful) or the gender pay gap (which is not unlawful unless sex discrimination puts men into the higher-value jobs).

[1] *Birmingham City Council v Abdulla* [2012] UKSC 47.
[2] **Dagenham Car Plant Strike, 1968.**

The British labour market remains highly segregated by gender. Women are typically concentrated in the lower-paid occupations and at the most junior levels of workplace hierarchies. Segregation routinely corresponds to traditional gender-based stereotypes about what work is suitable for each gender, which in turn impacts on whether that work is perceived as 'low' or 'high' value and how it is remunerated. When increasing numbers of women enter a field of work or profession – say, teaching – a gradual decline in wages and status usually follows. In comparison, where a large number of men enter a previously 'feminised' profession the opposite effect occurs – as happened, for example, in the move from 'librarianship' to 'data control'.

The Equal Pay Act 1970 created an unwieldy and technically complex regime in which enforcement of the right to equal pay requires the individual woman employee to sue her employer, or former employer, for breach of contract. In contrast to the statutory torts which protect women against sex discrimination at work, which define and proscribe unlawful treatment and provide for enforcement mechanisms in the Employment Tribunal,[3] the equal pay regime, now found in the Equality Act 2010, perpetuates the legal fiction created by the Equal Pay Act 1970 which implies into every contract of employment an equality clause. The legislation which Parliament, heavily dominated by men, has chosen to enact and preserve provides that by operation of law any terms of a woman's contract shall be modified so that they are no less favourable than the terms of her male colleague's contract, if they are doing equal work. If a woman believes she is being paid less than a male colleague doing equal work, she must sue her employer for breach of that implied equality term in her contract of employment.[4]

A consequence of the inherent difficulties in bringing equal pay claims is that the gender pay gap has narrowed at a glacial speed. All women – whether low-paid and high-paid – are affected. There are wide variations in the gender pay gap between the public and private sector, different industries, ages of employees, and regions.[5] It tends to be wider in the private sector, in more skilled occupations, and in more senior roles, and is widest in financial services.[6] Generally speaking, the gender pay gap is lower in the public sector, but it is here that unequal pay has the greatest practical impact. Women in the public sector, and women of colour,[7] tend to be concentrated in the lowest-paid jobs, such as cooks, cleaners and care workers; and it is these women who are most deeply affected by the gender pay gap, because of their relatively low earnings.

[3] See further, the Equality Act 2010, Parts 2, 5 and 9, generally updating provisions originally contained in the Sex Discrimination Act 1975.

[4] One consequence of this is that it is extremely rare in practice to see an express sex equality clause in any contract of employment. Interestingly, claims of pay inequality on the grounds of other 'protected characteristics' (race, disability, sexual orientation, religion or belief, age, pregnancy, gender reassignment, or marital status) are all brought as claims of discrimination, with no fiction involving the implication of an equality clause into the contract of employment. Such claims, however, are subject to a three-month time limit and may be brought only in the Employment Tribunal.

[5] Tom Evans, 'Understanding the Gender Pay Gap in the United Kingdom' (Office for National Statistics, 17 January 2018).

[6] 55% gender pay gap in 2009. See further Haroon Siddique, 'City's "shocking" gender pay gap revealed in equality report', *The Guardian*, 9 April 2009 reporting on Equality and Human Rights Commission report: https://www.equalityhumanrights.com/en/publication-download/research-report-14-pay-gaps-across-equality-strands (1 April 2009).

[7] Antony Breach and Yaojun Li, *Gender Pay Gap by Ethnicity in Britain – Briefing* (Fawcett Society, March 2017).

## II. The Landmark

The claimants in *Abdulla* were mainly women, some of whom had worked for Birmingham City Council for many years, who worked in traditionally female roles, such as cooks, cleaners and carers. As one carer said, 'We did everything [in our jobs] – we washed, dressed, cooked, cleaned, got pensions, everything … We were dedicated to looking after those people'.[8] They argued that Birmingham City Council was in breach of the 'equality clause' inserted into their contracts of employment by section 1(1) of the Equal Pay Act 1970, as substituted by section 8(1) of the Sex Discrimination Act 1975, by failing to provide certain benefits and other payments which were payable to workers of the opposite sex employed on work rated as equivalent. They sought sums equivalent to bonus payments and other additional payments which their male colleagues working in traditionally male-dominated jobs (such as refuse collection, street cleaning, road works and grave digging) were receiving and they were not, despite their jobs having been rated as equivalent in formal job evaluation schemes.[9] According to a BBC news report, the court heard that 'the annual salary of a female Manual Grade 2 [Birmingham City Council] worker was £11,127, while the equivalent male salary was £30,599'.[10]

Until *Abdulla*, it was routinely accepted that, despite its characterisation as a breach of contract claim, an equal pay claim was subject to a six-month limitation period and to be resolved by an Employment Tribunal, rather than the six-year limitation period which applies to other kinds of breach of contract claims, which are dealt with by the High Court. It is very unusual to bring an equal pay claim in the County Courts or the High Court, perhaps because in the civil courts the losing party generally has to pay the winning party's legal costs. By contrast, the Employment Tribunal is still supposed to be an informal forum in which the employer and employee can represent themselves, and so costs are awarded only in exceptional cases. This makes the Employment Tribunal a more attractive and less risky forum for most employees. However, over the years, the Employment Tribunal has acquired great experience and skill in determining complex equal pay claims. As a result, it is very unusual to find a woman representing herself in an equal pay claim, let alone an employer, despite the court system's insistence of informality. Facilitated by a no-win-no-fee agreement with their solicitors, the *Abdulla* Group deliberately brought their equal pay claims in the High Court, because they knew that they were out of time to bring claims in the Employment Tribunal.

In bringing mass equal pay claims, the claimants created a huge unforeseen financial problem for Birmingham City Council. Nevertheless, even by the time the case had reached the Supreme Court, the City Council had still not submitted a substantive defence. Rather they relied on every available technical defence in costly litigation on preliminary legal issues – the most important of which was that the claims 'could more conveniently be

[8] Joan Clulow, 71, who worked for the city council for 25 years as a home help, quoted in 'Birmingham City Council loses equal pay appeal bid', *BBC News online*, 24 October 2012.

[9] Although many formal job evaluation exercises were conducted in the public sector, mass equal pay litigation against local authorities from the 1990s onwards established that there was structural unfairness and even sex discrimination in trade union negotiation systems (eg *Allen v GMB* [2008] EWCA Civ 810), leading to a situation in which male-dominated jobs were often assessed as being more demanding. Regularly, male pay also crept up through 'bonuses' introduced after the conclusion of job evaluation studies.

[10] *BBC News online*, n 8 above.

disposed of' by an Employment Tribunal, in accordance with section 2(3) of the Equal Pay Act 1970. This provided:

> Where it appears to the court in which any proceedings are pending that a claim or counterclaim in respect of the operation of an equality clause could more conveniently be disposed of separately by an employment tribunal, the court may direct that the claim or counterclaim shall be struck out; and (without prejudice to the foregoing) where in proceedings before any court a question arises as to the operation of an equality clause, the court may on the application of any party to the proceedings or otherwise refer that question, or direct it to be referred by a party to the proceedings, to an employment tribunal for determination by the tribunal, and may stay or sist the proceedings in the meantime.

The reasons why the women failed to present their case to the Employment Tribunal were – Birmingham City Council argued – 'irrelevant'.

The High Court rejected this argument. Given their presentation outside the six-month Employment Tribunal limitation period, the Employment Tribunal would not have had jurisdiction to determine the claims and, accordingly, the disposition would not be 'more convenient'. By the time the case reached the Court of Appeal, the City Council had conceded that the reasons why each claimant had failed to present her claim in time in the Employment Tribunal were relevant, and argued instead that each claim should be struck out unless the claimant could provide a reasonable explanation for the failure. This argument also failed.

In the Supreme Court, Birmingham City Council's focus changed. They asked the Court to consider what Parliament's purpose had been in providing a strict time limit in the Employment Tribunal, if women could simply fail to comply and then have their claims heard in the civil courts.

The majority in the Supreme Court[11] concluded that Parliament had not ousted the jurisdiction of the ordinary courts over equal pay claims, despite the fact that, in practice, over four decades, equal pay claims were always brought in the Employment Tribunal, to the extent that even the employment specialist, Court of Appeal judge Mummery LJ, 'whose experience in this area of the law is unrivalled, … had never previously encountered a claim under the [Equal Pay] Act which had been presented to a court rather than a tribunal'.[12] Moreover, the Supreme Court disagreed with the approach of Slade J (a rare female High Court judge), who had concluded in *Ashby v Birmingham City Council* (a separate case on the identical issue to *Abdulla*)[13] that the reason why the women had not presented their claims in time to the Employment Tribunal should be determinative of whether the claims should be struck out. They decided the case on the 'natural reading' of what Parliament had provided:[14] it could never be 'more convenient' to dispose of a claim in the Employment Tribunal if it would be time-barred.[15] The claimants were again successful.

[11] Lord Wilson gave the leading judgment, with which Lady Hale and Lord Reed agreed. Lord Sumption gave a dissenting judgment with which Lord Carnwath agreed.

[12] [2012] UKSC 47, [6].

[13] *Ashby v Birmingham City Council* [2012] EWHC 424 (QB), [2012] ICR 1.

[14] [2012] UKSC 47, [27].

[15] ibid, [29].

## III. What Happened Next

Birmingham City Council never filed a substantive defence. The litigation illustrates the way in which the equal pay statutes have encouraged technical defences rather than promoted practical pay equality. As very often happens in equal pay litigation, the parties settled after the preliminary skirmishes. It was reported in 2014 that Birmingham owed £1.1 billion in settlement of 11,000-odd claims, including the *Abdulla* Group of test cases,[16] towards which central government gave Birmingham City Council a £530,000,000 loan. It was widely stated that Birmingham also sold the National Exhibition Centre to fund the equal pay settlements. Nevertheless, years after the claims were presented, it was reported that final figures of settlement had still not been agreed in thousands of cases and so the women still had not received their back-pay.[17] This pattern is a familiar one: enormous sums are bandied about but it takes years, if not decades, for the cash to reach the women's own pockets.

In July 2013, the Government introduced Employment Tribunal fees of up to £1,200, triggering an immediate 85 per cent drop in equal pay claims.[18] Over the next four years, fees depressed the number of equal pay claims to around half of previous levels. In 2015, the trade union UNISON brought proceedings for judicial review on the basis that the introduction of fees was unlawful on a number of grounds, including as a matter of access of justice, but also because it discriminated unlawfully against women and other protected groups. In July 2017, the Supreme Court held that Employment Tribunal fees were unlawful.[19] The Government abolished fees and began trying to reimburse claimants.[20] There are early indications that the number of equal pay claims is now increasing.

The gender pay gap continues to dominate public and political debate. In 2017, Equal Pay Day – the date from which women in the UK (compared to the average earnings of their male counterparts) 'start working for free' – fell on 21 November.[21] Journalists continue to develop stories on the gender pay gap, ranging from sensational revelations involving glamorous stars of the screen to serious business analysis of gender disparities in the labour market. The first reports under the Equality Act 2010 (Gender Pay Gap Information) Regulations 2017[22] were published in April 2018. Around 9,000 employers with 250 or more employees will now have to calculate their gender pay gaps and publish the data on a government website. No sanctions are imposed for non-compliance – although non-compliance or wide gender pay gaps may attract negative media reports, or encourage women employees to make equal pay claims.

[16] Neil Elkes, 'Council is "stalling" on equal pay settlements', *Birmingham Post*, 3 May 2014.

[17] '"Thousands of" Birmingham City Council equal pay claims "not settled"', *BBC News online*, 27 August 2015.

[18] Her Majesty's Courts and Tribunals Service: Tribunals Quarterly and Annual Reconciled Returns.

[19] *R (on the application of UNISON) v Lord Chancellor* [2017] UKSC 51.

[20] '"Employment tribunal fees unlawful", Supreme Court rules', *BBC News online*, 26 July 2017.

[21] Claire Cohen, 'Women of Britain work for free from today – so here's how to leave work on time', *The Telegraph*, 10 November 2017.

[22] Equality Act 2010 (Gender Pay Gap Information) Regulations 2017 (SI 2017/172).

## IV. Significance

> The council could have saved an awful lot of money if they had listened to us in the first place. I worked hard – I worked on Christmas Day, whenever they wanted me to. I don't feel guilty at all. I did a good job and I enjoyed my job – I deserved that pay.[23]

*Abdulla* established an important legal principle, namely that women had a right to bring equal pay claims in the civil courts, even when out of time in the Employment Tribunal, and even though it had been unheard of for women to exercise that right during four decades of operation of the equal pay legislation.

Despite their victory, equal pay litigation remains cumbersome and complex. The statutory provisions continue to be grounded in legal fictions and increasingly unjustifiable distinctions between sex-based and other kinds of pay inequality. Although *Abdulla* has established a clear path open to equal pay claimants which leads to the High Court, that court lacks expertise and experience in equal pay litigation.

For now, the campaign for equal pay for equal work goes on. Feminist lawyers and political activists continue to press for reform of both equal pay law and socio-economic policy, including British working women's access to affordable childcare, effective maternity rights, flexible working, equal job opportunities, and equal pensions.[24] Equal pay litigation tells only part of the story.

## Further Reading


- Antony Breach and Yaojun Li, *Gender Pay Gap by Ethnicity in Britain – Briefing* (Fawcett Society, March 2017).
- Tom Evans and Anna Ardanaz-Badia, 'Understanding the Gender Pay Gap in the United Kingdom' (Office for National Statistics, 17 January 2018).
- Fawcett Society, *Sex Discrimination Law Review* (January 2018).
- Harini Iyengar, *A Practical Guide to the Law of Gender Pay Gap Reporting* (Law Brief Publishing, September 2018).
- Women's Equality Party General Election Manifesto 2017: Equal Pay Policies: http://www.womensequality.org.uk/equal_pay_and_opportunity.


[23] Joan Clulow (see n 8 above) in 'Birmingham City Council liable for £757m equal pay claims', *BBC News online*, 12 November 2012.

[24] Women's Equality Party, 'Objectives': http://www.womensequality.org.uk/objectives.

# 84

# Electoral (Amendment) (Political Funding) Act 2012

IVANA BACIK

The Electoral (Amendment) (Political Funding) Act 2012 introduced a political gender quota in Ireland. Section 42 provides that political parties will have their state funding cut by half, unless at least 30 per cent of their General Election candidates are of each gender. This quota will rise to 40 per cent in 2023.

The Act has already begun to have a transformative effect on Irish politics. It was applied for the first time in the 2016 General Election, in which a record 35 women were elected to the Dáil Éireann out of 158 TDs (Teachtaí Dála or members). Women now make up 22 per cent of TDs for the first time; 16 per cent was the highest percentage previously achieved.

## I. Context

The story of this ground-breaking legislation dates back to the time of the Irish women's suffrage movement, the work of early-twentieth-century feminist activists, and more recent campaigning work of feminist groups and women in the Oireachtas.

A century ago, the campaign seeking votes for women internationally was divided between moderate suffragists and more radical 'suffragettes'. In Ireland, the moderate wing of the suffrage campaign was represented by activists like Anna and Thomas Haslam, described as 'genteel revolutionaries'.[1] However, a more radical approach was adopted by many women also prominent in the struggle for Irish independence, like Constance Markievicz, who was active in both the suffrage and nationalist campaigns.[2] Hanna Sheehy-Skeffington was a well-known feminist contemporary of Markievicz. Along with her husband Francis, she set up the Irish Women's Franchise League, the equivalent of Emmeline Pankhurst's WSPU (Women's Social and Political Union) in England.[3] The Sheehy-Skeffingtons were nationalists but, unlike Markievicz, took a pacifist position in the Easter Rising 1916.

[1] Carmel Quinlan, *Genteel Revolutionaries: Anna and Thomas Haslam and the Irish Women's Movement* (Cork University Press, 2005).

[2] Anne Haverty, *Constance Markievicz: Irish Revolutionary* (New York University Press, 1993).

[3] Margaret Ward, *Hanna Sheehy-Skeffington: A Life* (Cork University Press, 1997).

For activists like Markievicz and the Sheehy-Skeffingtons, even where they disagreed on the adoption of particular tactics in the nationalist campaign, the causes of Irish independence and women's suffrage were closely linked by the same motivating force.[4] Indeed, some years later Markievicz, then a TD, described in a Dáil speech how the women's suffrage movement had led to her embracing of other campaigns:

> My first realisation of tyranny came from some chance words spoken in favour of woman's suffrage and it raised a question of the tyranny it was intended to prevent – women voicing their opinions publicly in the ordinary and simple manner of registering their votes at the polling booth. That was my first bite ... at the apple of freedom and soon I got on to the other freedom, freedom to the nation, freedom to the workers.[5]

As it happened, the campaign for women's suffrage achieved partial success even before Irish independence, when the right to vote was extended to some women across the then United Kingdom in February 1918 through the **Representation of the People Act**. This Act applied more restrictive conditions to women than to men, extending the franchise to almost all men over 21, but only to women over 30, subject to property qualifications.

This was followed by the Parliament (Qualification of Women) Act, passed in November of the same year, which allowed women to become MPs. In the December 1918 UK election that followed, Constance Markievicz was the only woman elected. She became the first woman MP and TD, choosing to sit in the first Dáil Éireann but not to take up her seat at Westminster. She also became one of the first women government ministers in the world, as Minister for Labour in the 1919–22 Sinn Féin Government formed following that election. In the months following independence in 1922, women in Ireland obtained the right to vote on an equal basis to men through the Electoral Act 1923, an important assertion of equal rights for the nascent Irish Free State. This Act extended the vote to all women over 21 and abolished any remaining property qualifications – some years before women in Britain obtained equal voting rights.

However, after the creation of the Irish Free State in 1922 and ensuing Civil War, Irish women like Markievicz, and many other 'unmanageable revolutionaries', became much less visible publicly, their voices suppressed by the deeply conservative Catholic nationalism that dominated in the new state.[6] Few women were involved at a policy-making level, and women's groups were generally organised around women's domestic roles as wives and mothers. It would be several decades before a second-wave feminist movement began to seek more substantive change for women's rights.

The achievement of women's equal right to vote in 1923 may be seen as the last feminist law for a generation. Over the following decades, only a tiny number of women stood for election. Those few women who became TDs were later described as the 'silent sisters' for their lack of opposition to the insertion of a clause recognising mothers specifically as having 'duties in the home' in the 1937 Irish Constitution.[7]

[4] Sinéad McCoole, *No Ordinary Women: Irish Female Activists in the Revolutionary Years 1900–1923* (first published 2003, O'Brien Press, 2015).

[5] Speech to Dáil Éireann, 2 March 1922, vol S2 No 3 (Irishwomen and the Franchise).

[6] Margaret Ward, *Unmanageable Revolutionaries: Women and Irish Nationalism* (Pluto Press, 1996).

[7] See Yvonne Scannell, 'The Constitution and the Role of Women' in Brian Farrell (ed), *De Valera's Constitution and Ours* (Gill & Macmillan, 1988).

Even the resurgence of women's activism and the emergence of a fledgling women's movement during the 1970s did not bring about any notable increase in the numbers of women elected to the Oireachtas.[8] While progress was made on issues like equal pay, many setbacks for feminist campaigners occurred during the last two decades of the twentieth century; notably the passage in 1983 of the 'Eighth Amendment' to the Constitution, which declared the foetus to have a right to life equal to that of the 'mother'.[9] This provision generated many tragic cases over 35 years, until its deletion from the Constitution by way of referendum in May 2018.[10]

Despite the lack of progress over many decades, at one time it did appear that the number of women in politics might rise organically, without positive action measures. In 1990, in a surprise result, feminist lawyer **Mary Robinson** was elected as the first Irish woman President. In the General Election of 1992, 20 women were elected as TDs (12 per cent of the total), a new high. Ireland was then ranked internationally in 37th place in the Inter-Parliamentary Union (IPU) rankings of women's representation in the lower or single chamber of national parliaments; it was predicted that numbers would keep increasing.

However, that did not prove to be the case. The numbers of women TDs failed to rise during subsequent decades, and Ireland's international ranking fell over successive elections. Until the 2012 Act was passed, the Dáil had never been less than 84 per cent male. The proportion of women in the Oireachtas had not actually fallen between 1990 and 2012, but any rise was minimal, in contrast with other countries which had adopted positive action measures.

In particular, those European countries which had introduced political gender quotas had seen significant change over intervening years. Belgium, for example, was ranked alongside Ireland in 1990; it is now ranked 20th in the world with 38 per cent women in parliament, having adopted positive action legislation. Similar measures were adopted in Spain, also ranked alongside Ireland in the 1990s, but now at 14th place with 39 per cent women.[11]

Thus, until the Irish law reform was introduced in 2012, there was a striking contrast between the lack of action to address low levels of women's representation in Ireland and the positive measures taken elsewhere. This was highlighted in the early years of the twenty-first century by a number of women's groups, led by the National Women's Council of Ireland (NWCI).

## II. The Landmark

In December 2008, to focus public attention on this ongoing problem, and to celebrate the 90th anniversary of the 1918 election, an 'Oireachtas Women' day was organised by this

[8] Yvonne Galligan, *Women and Politics in Contemporary Ireland: From the Margins to the Mainstream* (Pinter, 1998).

[9] Article 40.3.3 of the Constitution.

[10] See also **Protection of Life During Pregnancy Act 2013; Thirty-sixth Amendment to the Irish Constitution, 2018.**

[11] Inter-Parliamentary Union website: www.ipu.org. Ireland is now ranked at 81st place (as of 3 July 2018).

author in the Dáil Chamber, with invitations issued to all women still living who had ever been elected TDs or Senators. About 80 women were present, and the photograph taken of the event became a significant visual image of parity democracy – for the first time ever, a Dáil chamber half full of women.

As a follow-up, the Joint Oireachtas Committee on Justice commenced research on women's participation in politics, holding hearings with relevant experts, and a number of women who had achieved high political office. During the hearings, one former Minister remarked memorably that democracy in Ireland would remain 'unfinished' until the numbers of women TDs increased. The Committee's report was published in October 2009.[12] It emphasised the need to take positive steps to address the low levels of women entering politics, noting that the scarcity of women candidates constitutes a serious restriction on voter choice. In at least 60 per cent of constituencies in Ireland in the 2007 election, no women candidates had stood from either of the two largest parties, Fine Gael and Fianna Fáil. In five constituencies, there had been no women candidates from any party.

The report found that women face serious obstacles in entering politics. From the accounts given of women's experiences, and the international literature, these obstacles were identified as the 'five Cs': childcare, cash, confidence, culture and candidate selection procedures. In short, women tend to bear the bulk of child caring responsibilities; they earn less than men, lack sufficient confidence to put themselves forward as candidates, and have to endure a male-dominated culture in political parties. The parties operate as 'gatekeepers' to the 'secret garden' of candidate selection,[13] often a highly-complex process which operates to obscure the existence of 'secret quotas' based on a candidate's name, sporting achievements or geographical base.

These obstacles are difficult to tackle, but the report made a number of recommendations to address them, drawing on experience of successful initiatives in other jurisdictions. These included the introduction of family-friendly parliamentary procedures, public advertising campaigns to challenge gender stereotypes, and leadership training programmes within political parties.

However, the most controversial recommendation related to candidate selection procedures. The report recommended that statutory political gender quotas be imposed on political parties, based on the 1994 Belgian law providing that no more than two-thirds of candidates from any political party in a general election could be of the same gender.[14] This effectively put a cap on the number of men a party could select, and had a significant effect on the numbers of women elected subsequently in Belgium. This law amounts to an 'opportunity quota' rather than an 'outcome quota'. It simply requires political parties to put forward a minimum number of candidates of each gender, but no parliamentary seats are reserved for women, leaving voters free to make the ultimate choice.

Despite the moderate nature of the quota recommended in Ireland, this was seen as a highly controversial recommendation. It was strongly supported by the NWCI, but was opposed vocally by many individuals, including several high-profile women TDs. The outgoing Government did not act on the report's recommendation. There was little improvement

[12] Joint Oireachtas Committee on Justice, Equality, Defence and Women's Rights, *Report on Women's Participation in Politics* (Oireachtas, 2009). This author was the Rapporteur for the Report.

[13] ibid 17.

[14] Smet-Tobback Act 1994.

in women's representation rates in the ensuing General Election, held in February 2011. Only 25 women TDs were elected, constituting 15 per cent of the total. This represented only a marginal increase from the outgoing Dáil, and provided strong evidence of the need for change.

Two new feminist groups emerged around this time, working to support the campaign for quota legislation, and to encourage more women to put themselves forward as candidates. Both groups, *Women for Election* and *50/50 by 2020*, played a key role in making an evidence-based case for quotas, and in changing public opinion through their campaigning and advocacy work.[15] Members of these groups, along with supportive academics and politicians, argued strongly that the numbers of women politicians would not increase without positive intervention. They showed that of the total 4,744 Dáil seats that had been filled from 1918–2011, just 260 had been taken by women (five per cent); only 91 women TDs had ever been elected since the foundation of the Irish State.[16] Perhaps most effective was the statistic used by the NWCI, asserting that, without any intervention, it would take 370 years for Ireland to reach a 50/50 gender balance in politics.

The new Government elected in February 2011 included the Labour Party as a minority coalition partner with Fine Gael. Labour members had been actively engaged in the quota campaign, and the party had called for the introduction of a quota in its election manifesto. As a result, gender quotas were included in the negotiations around Government formation, and a commitment to introduce this reform was given in the Programme for Government agreed between the coalition partners. Campaigning by the pro-quota feminist groups intensified to ensure that this became a reality, and proved successful with the introduction in December 2011 of the Electoral (Amendment) (Political Funding) Bill.

The Bill was first debated in the Seanad in February 2012. As the report had recommended, section 42 of the Bill creates an 'opportunity quota' for political parties, and imposes a significant sanction for those which do not comply. It provides that parties must select at least 30 per cent of candidates of each gender nationally for the next General Election; this will rise to 40 per cent seven years after that election. State funding for political parties which do not comply will be reduced by half – a really meaningful sanction, as Irish political parties are heavily reliant upon state funding.

During the debates on the new law, some opposition was expressed to the concept of a quota. Conversely, many of those who supported the concept argued that it did not go far enough, and should apply not only to Dáil elections, but also to Seanad, local and European elections. The Minister for the Environment responded that it was more practical to link the quota to Dáil elections, given that state funding for parties is largely calculated based on General Election results. He also suggested that political parties would be keen to nurture prospective women Dáil candidates through selecting them as candidates in preceding local elections.

The Act finally passed on 20 July 2012, and Ireland became the seventh country in the EU to introduce a gender quota mechanism.

[15] See National Women's Council of Ireland: www.nwci.ie; Women for Election: www.womenforelection.ie; the 50/50 Group: www.5050-group.com.

[16] Fiona Buckley and Claire McGing, 'Women and the Election' in Michael Gallagher and Michael Marsh (eds), *How Ireland Voted 2011: The Full Story of Ireland's Earthquake Election* (Palgrave Macmillan, 2011).

## III. What Happened Next

The next elections were local elections held in 2014. Despite the absence of any statutory quota at that level, the proportion of women elected as councillors increased significantly, from 16 per cent in 2009 to a new high of 20 per cent – proving that political parties were indeed preparing women as Dáil candidates. The General Election took place in February 2016, and again saw a notable increase in the number of women entering the Dáil. As previously outlined, a record number of 35 women were elected, amounting to 22 per cent of TDs – the first time women had broken through the 20 per cent barrier.

The 2012 Act is not formally opposed by any political party, but continues to attract criticism from certain public figures, and is currently the subject of a constitutional challenge. In February 2016, the High Court dismissed a case taken by Fianna Fáil Party member Brian Mohan, seeking to strike down section 42 on the grounds that it had discriminated against him as a potential male candidate for his party.[17] During the court hearing, the state argued that its right to enact legislation regulating the conduct of elections included an entitlement to legislate to promote the constitutional guarantee of equality. Fiona Buckley from University College Cork, a leading academic expert, gave evidence for the state that financial sanctions were necessary to ensure political parties would run more women candidates. Mr Justice David Keane rejected Mohan's challenge on the basis that he lacked *locus standi* (legal standing to bring the case). The judge ruled that a political party would have been better placed to bring the case, since Mohan could not prove that his interests were adversely affected by the Act, or that he would have been chosen as a party candidate had section 42 not been passed. Mohan's appeal against this decision was heard by the Court of Appeal in July 2017,[18] where the decision of the High Court was upheld on the basis that, as the High Court had held, Mohan lacked standing to take the case since the quota measure is 'directed to political parties' and not to individual members.

Feminist campaigners were hopeful that the appeal would not succeed. There is a sense that most people now accept the need for positive action measures to address Ireland's historically low levels of women's political representation, and the 2016 General Election results have bolstered the case for quotas, with several new women TDs elected who are very publicly supportive of quotas. Section 42 has had a positive effect already for greater gender diversity in politics, and undoubtedly represents a true legal landmark for Irish women.

## IV. Significance

Experience elsewhere, and now in Ireland, clearly shows that, without enforceable legal targets or quotas, the numbers of women in politics will not rise. Without this landmark law, the work of the suffrage campaigners would not have been fully vindicated, and Irish democracy would have remained unfinished and incomplete.

[17] *Mohan v Ireland & Another* [2016] IEHC 35.
[18] *Mohan v Ireland & Another* [2018] IECA 13.

## Further Reading

- Alan Hayes and Máire Meagher (eds), *A Century of Progress: Irish Women Reflect* (Arlen House, 2016).
- Joint Oireachtas Committee on Justice, Equality, Defence and Women's Rights, *Report on Women's Participation in Politics* (Oireachtas, 2009).
- Maedhbh McNamara and Paschal Mooney, *Women in Parliament: Ireland 1918–2000* (Wolfhound Press, 2000).

# 85

# Protection of Life During Pregnancy Act 2013

FIONA DE LONDRAS

The Protection of Life During Pregnancy Act 2013 (PLDPA) is the first piece of legislation to outline the mechanisms by which women can access abortion in Ireland.

As a general matter, abortion is unlawful and constitutionally prohibited except where there is a 'real and substantial risk' to the life of a pregnant women, the risk can only be averted by termination of the pregnancy, and the foetus is not yet viable. This is the combined legacy of the Offences Against the Person Act 1861 (criminalising abortion), the 8th Amendment to the Constitution of 1983 (providing a constitutional right to life to the foetus in Article 40.3.3 of the Constitution), a highly conservative jurisprudence on the meaning of the 8th Amendment in subsequent years, and a political establishment seemingly unwilling to acknowledge or tackle the harms done by a lack of access to abortion care. All of this means that pregnant people who do not wish to continue with their pregnancies in Ireland have very few options. Although feminist activists, courts, medics, and international organisations had long called for a legislative scheme to be introduced that would allow women (and medics) to determine whether they fell within the very limited allowance for lawful abortion, it was not until the death of Savita Halappanavar and the European Court of Human Rights decision in *A, B & C v Ireland*[1] that an Irish parliament took on this task.

## I. Context

For thousands of women in Ireland who do not wish to continue with pregnancy, travelling to England to access abortion has been the least bad option, although it carries significant financial and practical costs. Feminist activism has made it easier than it might have been for Irish women to access abortion care in England. Even in the 1980s there was a valuable diaspora movement in the UK, well documented by one of its leading figures Ann Rossiter,[2] supporting women in Ireland in finding information, sourcing finance, and

[1] *A, B & C v Ireland* (2011) 53 EHRR 13.

[2] Ann Rossiter, *Ireland's Hidden Diaspora: The 'Abortion Trail' and the Making of a London-Irish Underground 1980–2000* (LASC Publishing, 2009).

making arrangements to access abortion care. While this started out as a relatively covert set of feminist practices, there is now a well-established NGO, the Abortion Support Network, which provides structured support to women seeking support to access abortion care in those parts of the UK where it is available.

Until 1992 practically no information was available about abortion in Ireland; family planning and women's services were not permitted to tell women about where they could access abortion, or what an abortion even was in practical terms, and Irish and European Courts upheld this.[3] In response, phone helplines were established to help women find out how, where and when to access abortion. However, many pregnant people could not access these services; in the 1980s telephones were sparse, especially in rural Ireland, and where available they were often run through an operator or accessed only in public telephone boxes or by using the phone of a friend or neighbour. Privacy was in short supply.

Presumably linked to the lack of reproductive autonomy imposed by the legal and social context, self-harm and infanticide were not uncommon, and unknown numbers of women persisted with pregnancies that they did not want. Until 1992 it was not clear that pregnant people had a right to travel to another jurisdiction in order to access abortion; the view of the superior courts was that anything that facilitated the 'destruction of unborn life' was prohibited by the state's commitment to 'vindicate the right to life of the unborn'.[4] The Attorney General considered it his constitutional obligation to attempt to prevent travel to access abortion where it came to his attention,[5] as it did in the case of *Attorney General v X*.[6]

*X* involved a 14-year-old girl who was pregnant as a result of rape and in respect of whom the High Court had issued an injunction to prevent her travelling to access abortion. Although the Supreme Court held that 'X' was entitled to access abortion in Ireland because there was a real and substantial risk to her life (a risk from suicide), the case highlighted the extremity of a ban on travel for pregnant women. Following this, in 1992, a referendum was held to confirm that the protection of unborn life in Article 40.3.3 did not undermine the rights to travel or to access information.

While travel to access abortion was then legally possible, it was utterly inaccessible for many, due to the cost of taking time off work, taking a plane or ship to the UK, paying for the abortion, and getting home. Even though many abortion care providers in the UK provide discounted abortion care to women from Ireland, the costs remain too high for many. The right to information is very limited; only non-directive information about abortion can be provided, and it is a criminal offence for a medical practitioner to refer a patient abroad for abortion care.[7]

It was in this context that three women – known as 'A', 'B' and 'C' – took a case to the European Court of Human Rights. Although the Court found that deciding on the extent to

[3] *Attorney General (ex rel The Society for the Protection of Unborn Children) v Open Door Counselling Limited and the Dublin Wellwoman Centre Ltd* [1988] 1 IR 593; Case C-159/90, *Society for the Protection of Unborn Children Ireland Ltd v Grogan* [1991] ECR I-4685.

[4] *Attorney General (ex rel The Society for the Protection of Unborn Children) v Open Door Counselling Limited and the Dublin Wellwoman Centre Ltd* [1988] 1 IR 593.

[5] Interview with the then Attorney General, Harry Whelehan, broadcast on *Scannal* (RTÉ), 22 February 2010; 'Scannal Web Notes': http://www.rte.ie/tv/scannal/xcase.html.

[6] *Attorney General v X* [1992] 1 IR 1.

[7] Regulation of Information (Services Outside the State for Termination of Pregnancies) Act 1995.

which abortion was available was within a state's discretion (so it could be as narrow as in Ireland), where there was a right to access abortion, there had to be a way to exercise it.[8] The fact that there was no legal structure through which the limited right to abortion in cases of real and substantial risk to life could be accessed, in itself constituted a violation of the European Convention on Human Rights.

This judgment echoed a clear demand from pro-choice, feminist groups such as 'Action on X' that the Oireachtas should 'legislate for *X*',[9] and led to an expert committee being established that would consider how the state might respond to the judgment. Around the time that group reported, it was reported that a woman in the West of Ireland, Savita Halappanavar, had died during a protracted miscarriage in a Galway hospital.[10] It was reported that she had requested an abortion once it became clear that a miscarriage was underway, but was denied one because there was still a foetal heartbeat and, as far as the hospital was concerned, there was no sufficient risk to her life to justify intervention. By the time there was, the risk was too acute. Savita Halappanavar died of sepsis.

Halappanavar's death led to huge national protests. Vigils were held outside Leinster House (the Irish Houses of Parliament), and prominent politicians and feminist activists such as Senator Ivana Bacik led the way in demanding a legislative response. The exact parameters of that response were, of course, limited by the Constitution: to legalise abortion in a wide range of scenarios required a constitutional amendment, but to 'legislate for *X*' did not. Feminist activists were clear on that too; legislation was required, but was not enough. Constitutional change was ultimately needed.[11]

## II. The Landmark

The PLDPA provides for abortion where medical practitioners certify 'in good faith' that there is a real and substantial risk to the pregnant woman's life, and that it is their reasonable opinion that this can only be averted by terminating the pregnancy. 'Reasonable opinion' is defined as 'an opinion formed in good faith which has regard to the need to preserve unborn human life as far as practicable'.[12] If the risk to the pregnant woman's life emanates from a physical illness two medical practitioners must certify to this; if it emanates from a risk of suicide three practitioners must so certify. In an emergency a single medical practitioner must certify that it is her reasonable opinion that an abortion is 'immediately necessary in order to save the life of the woman'.[13] Should a woman wish to challenge a refusal to provide her with abortion care she can apply for the decision to be reviewed either by two doctors (where she claims there is a risk to life from physical illness) or by three (where the risk is

[8] *A, B & C v Ireland* (2011) 53 EHRR 13.

[9] Action on X was a feminist organisation advocating for legislation to give effect to the *X Case*, led by Ailbhe Smyth.

[10] Kitty Holland, 'Woman "denied a termination" dies in hospital', *The Irish Times*, 14 November 2012.

[11] See the comments reported from eg Ailbhe Smyth (then Action on X; now Coalition to Repeal the 8th), Orla O'Connor (National Women's Council of Ireland), and Abigail Rooney (Choice Ireland) in Maire O'Halloran, 'X Case Legislation "Most Restrictive"', *The Irish Times*, 10 January 2013.

[12] PLDPA 2013 ss 7(1)(a)(ii), 8(1)(b), 9(1)(a)(ii).

[13] PLDPA 2013 ss 8(1)(b).

said to be one of suicide), and that panel should decide within 10 days of the review request having been made.

All arguments that the risk of death by suicide should be treated the same as other risks of death were rejected. There is no legal basis for treating suicide differently from physical illness in respect of abortion law: in both cases the pregnant woman has a *constitutionally protected* right to access abortion. However, for anti-abortion advocates, allowing abortion in cases of a risk of suicide fundamentally undermines the constitutional protection of the right to life of the foetus, the implication of course being that women might claim to be suicidal 'simply' to access abortion. The words of one TD, Brian Walsh, are representative of the objections of many. He claimed that the suicide provision would 'defile the Statute Book with the absurd premise that the suicidality of one human being can be abated by the destruction and killing of another'.[14] Others argued that it would 'open the floodgates to widespread abortion'[15] (Eamon O'Cuiv TD), and 'normalise suicidal ideation'[16] (Lucinda Creighton TD). Creighton, who was a Cabinet minister, ultimately voted against the Bill, losing her Cabinet role as a result. But the truth is that the suicide provision is highly restrictive.

Having been referred for assessment under the PLDPA, a woman must be assessed by three psychiatrists, one of whom 'provides, or who has provided, mental health services to women in respect of pregnancy, childbirth or post-partum care' (section 8(3)). This is a significant restriction in itself. Perinatal psychiatry is such a small field of specialised practice in Ireland that it is not even listed as a specialism on the Irish College of Psychiatry website. In 2004 perinatal psychiatry represented only six per cent of psychiatric services in Ireland,[17] and in 2003 there were only three perinatal psychiatrists in the country.[18] Thus, while the Act made abortion available for suicidal women as a matter of law, the combination of hyper-restrictive legal provisions and chronic under-resourcing means that, realistically speaking, the 'right' can hardly ever be exercised.

The Act allows for medical practitioners to refuse to provide or assist in providing abortion care on the basis of *conscientious objection* (section 17), except in cases of emergency. However, the PLDPA says nothing about whether institutions have a right to assert conscientious objection. This is significant, as a large proportion of Irish hospitals are under the patronage of the Roman Catholic Church, including many of the 25 listed 'appropriate institutions' in the PLDPA. The extent to which these hospitals can restrict treatments to those that comply with a Catholic ethos remains unsettled in Ireland, although in 2017 public outrage at the prospect of the new National Maternity Hospital being owned by and under the patronage of a religious order, and resultant doubts about the availability there of abortion and other reproductive health treatments, led to the order in question (the Sisters of Mercy) divesting themselves of the project.

Apart from the circumstances already described, the intentional destruction of unborn human life is a criminal offence (section 22(1)), punishable by up to 14 years imprisonment.

[14] Dáil Debates, 10 July 2013.

[15] Dáil Debates, 1 July 2013.

[16] Dáil Debates, 1 July 2013.

[17] V O'Keane, A Jeffers, E Moloney and S Barry, 'Irish Psychiatric Association Survey of Psychiatric Services in Ireland' (2004) 28 *Psychiatry Bulletin* 364.

[18] Judith Crosbie, 'Abortion proposals are a "sick joke" and "abusive" – psychiatrist', *The Irish Times*, 22 April 2013.

Both those who provide and those who procure abortions (ie providers and pregnant women) are committing an offence. This is significant, as many women in Ireland order online and then self-administer abortion pills. In doing so, they are committing an offence. All attempts to remove the criminalisation provision from the Bill, or to ensure that pregnant women would not be criminalised even if medical practitioners or others who provided abortions outside of the Act would be, fell on deaf ears and continue to do so: in 2017 Brid Smith TD proposed amending the Act to reduce the penalty to €1. The Government refused, arguing that protecting the constitutional right to life of the unborn requires criminalisation and a serious penalty. Anything less would be a neglect of the state's constitutional duty.

## III. What Happened Next

The PLDPA 2013 did not fundamentally change life for women in Ireland; rather, it is utterly inadequate to meet women's needs. Its terms are simply too restrictive, even to give real effect to the existing constitutional right to access abortion where there is a real and significant risk to life.

In one well-publicised case ('*Y*'), medical processes moved so slowly that by the time the pregnant woman was certified as being at real and substantial risk of suicide the pregnancy was so advanced that the foetus was viable and an abortion was not permitted.[19] When the pregnant woman refused food or water in protest a High Court order for forced hydration was sought. A C-section was performed and a baby boy was born.[20] The woman is now pursuing legal action for the harm done to her through the application of the Act.[21]

In another case, a suicidal, pregnant girl believed she was being brought to a hospital to be given an abortion but was actually involuntarily detained under the Mental Health Act 2001. Deemed not to be suicidal, she was simultaneously determined to require involuntary detention to 'care' for her. The detention order was discharged by the District Court,[22] but we do not know whether that child was then able to access abortion care. Her story illustrates starkly the power that the PLDPA places in the hands of doctors who hold the legal power, simultaneously, to deny an abortion and detain the woman seeking it.

Furthermore, the state has not provided sufficient resources to support the administration of the abortion law regime in the PLDPA. There are still only three perinatal psychiatrists in Ireland, all working part-time, and all located in Dublin.[23] How suicidal women are realistically supposed to access their legal rights in such a situation is difficult to imagine. Indeed, very few women access abortion under the 2013 Act; in 2015, for example, only 26 abortions were carried out under the Act.[24] We do not know how many women were denied abortions they asked for, how many might have been placed in mental health deten-

[19] Mark Tighe, 'State "denied abortion" to rape victim', *Sunday Times*, 17 August 2014.
[20] Dearbhail McDonald and Fioannan Sheahan, 'Baby delivered as woman refused abortion under law', *Irish Independent*, 16 August 2014.
[21] Kitty Holland, '"Ms Y" to sue 11 respondents over abortion refusal', *The Irish Times*, 19 September 2015.
[22] Child Care Law Reporting Project, *Order detaining pregnant girl seeking abortion discharged*: https://www.childlawproject.ie/publications/order-detaining-pregnant-girl-seeking-abortion-discharged/.
[23] Confirmed by the Irish College of Psychiatry (correspondence with author).
[24] Paul Cullen, 'Terminations carried out on 26 women last year', *The Irish Times*, 29 June 2016.

tion afterwards, how many went directly to England for an abortion rather than navigate the Irish law, and how many women continue to be pregnant against their will.

## IV. Significance

The PLDPA is unsatisfactory, insufficient, and ineffective. But it is still a landmark for women. It was the first time that the Irish parliament gave effect to the (very limited) constitutional right to access abortion. The fact that this right had lain effectively unusable for more than 30 years had not only made it more or less illusory but had also hidden in plain sight the true scale of its restrictiveness. While people were aware that abortion was not available in Ireland, the combination of Savita Halappanavar's death, the passage of the Act, and the spectacle of Irish politicians arguing in the Parliament that women would fake suicidal ideation to access abortion awoke something in the population.

The movement to 'legislate for *X*' quickly morphed into movement to 'Repeal the 8th', and the Coalition to Repeal the 8th, led by Ailbhe Smyth, a longtime feminist activist in Ireland, held its first conference in Dublin in September 2014. The Abortion Rights Campaign started a March for Choice in 2011, and in 2016 there were an estimated 20,000 participants in solidarity marches all over the world. 'Repeal' merchandise and public art is widespread, and increasing numbers of (public and private) figures are speaking out about their experience of acquiring abortion to tackle the stigma associated with it in Ireland. In 2017 a 'Citizens Assembly' recommended repeal of the 8th Amendment, its replacement with an obligation on the Oireachtas to legislate, and a legislative framework that permitted abortion without the need to specify reasons, up to 14 weeks gestation and for a wide range of reasons, thereafter.

These developments are the product of decades of activism, and come too late for the thousands of women who have been x-iled[25] for abortion care elsewhere, continued with pregnancies without their consent, and died or suffered severe health difficulties because of a lack of access to abortion. But they are also partly the legacy of the PLDPA. The passage, terms, and documented violence of the PLDPA have written large the continuing and abject failure of the Irish state to meet the needs of pregnant women. The Act has made abundantly clear that the 8th Amendment must be repealed if women in Ireland are to have real access to effective abortion care, and thus helped to create a momentum for change that, at the time of writing, seems close to unstoppable. A referendum to repeal the 8th Amendment was held in May 2018; 66.4 per cent voted 'yes'.[26]

## Further Reading

- Fiona de Londras, 'Constitutionalizing Fetal Rights: A Salutary Tale from Ireland' (2015) 22(2) *Michigan Journal of Gender and the Law* 243–89.

[25] The X-ile project is an ongoing online gallery of women who have accessed abortion services outside of Ireland and Northern Ireland: http://www.x-ileproject.com.

[26] **Thirty-sixth Amendment to the Irish Constitution, 2018**.

- Fiona de Londras and Mairead Enright, *Repealing the 8th: Reforming Abortion Law in Ireland* (Policy Press, 2018).
- Ann Rossiter, *Ireland's Hidden Diaspora: The 'Abortion Trail' and the Making of a London-Irish Underground 1980–2000* (LASC Publishing, 2009).
- Ailbhe Smyth, *The Abortion Papers: Ireland* (Attic Press, 1992).

# 86

## *R v Nimmo and Sorley* (2014)

KIM BARKER

*R v Nimmo and Sorley*[1] changed the perception of social media offences in England and Wales. The decision followed a short – but significant – period whereby social media abuses such as trolling and harassment, although increasing in number, often remained outside of the focus of the criminal law. This decision saw the first custodial sentences issued to the defendants for their sustained abusive messages made via social media platform Twitter to two women – Caroline Criado Perez and Stella Creasy – for campaigning to have women on banknotes.[2] It was the first decision handed down under the revised guidance on social media prosecutions from the Director of Public Prosecutions[3] issued in light of *Chambers v DPP*.[4] Without doubt, *R v Nimmo and Sorley* is a legal landmark in the prosecution of social media offences. However, it is also a legal landmark *for women* because this decision represents an important step forward in the recognition and tackling of online harassment, abuse and other forms of threatening behaviour, from which women continue to suffer disproportionately.

## I. Context

March 2006. Twitter is founded. Within a decade, the global micro-blogging site claims user numbers of over 300 million,[5] with 500 million tweets a day.[6] Along with other social media sites such as Facebook and Snapchat, Twitter has changed the way we interact with one another. However, it has not – it seems – changed *what* we say. Reports of social media harassment highlight that, alongside perfectly pleasantly online interactions, there are a growing number of nasty and abusive comments.[7] This is not Twitter's 'fault'. Online bullying

[1] *R v Nimmo and Sorley*, Westminster Magistrates Court, judgment of 24 January 2014 (unreported)

[2] Alice Phillipson, 'Woman who campaigned for Jane Austen bank note receives Twitter death threats', *The Telegraph*, 28 July 2013.

[3] CPS (2013), *Social Media: Guidelines on prosecuting cases involving communications sent via social media*. The current (revised) guidelines are available at: http://www.cps.gov.uk/legal/a_to_c/communications_sent_via_social_media/.

[4] *Chambers v DPP* [2012] EWHC 2157 (Admin).

[5] Rose McGrory, 'UK Social Media Statistics for 2016' (*Rose McGrory Social Media Ltd*, 1 April 2016).

[6] Susanna Kim, 'Twitter's IPO Filing Shows 215 Million Monthly Active Users' *ABC News*, 3 October 2013.

[7] 'Five internet trolls a day convicted in UK as figures show ten-fold increase', *The Telegraph*, 24 May 2015.

takes a number of different forms and is particularly hard to define, but there are some common threads to such activity, including repetition, power imbalances, aggression and intention[8] – factors relevant to the significance and impact of online abuses on victims. The rise of social media has been mirrored by an increase in social media offences. However, in some cases, these have simply added to the problems faced by those seeking to regulate the online arena.[9] These challenges were recognised by the House of Lords Communications Select Committee, which noted in 2015 that there a number of terms – including cyber bullying, revenge porn, trolling, virtual mobbing – which are used to describe online abuse, many of which refer to one and the same thing.[10]

Of course, the trend in social media use – and abuse – was not something witnessed for the first time in *R v Nimmo and Sorley*. Other cases dealing with aspects of social media had already made their way before the courts – for example, the successful claim brought by Lord McAlpine in respect of a defamatory Tweet sent by Sally Bercow.[11] However, the most significant in the context of *R v Nimmo and Sorley* was the decision in *Chambers v DPP*, where the courts faced an appeal against a criminal conviction for sending a message of 'menacing character' in contravention of section 127(1)(a) of the Communications Act 2003. The message in question concerned a jokey threat to blow up Doncaster Sheffield airport: 'Crap! Robin Hood Airport is closed. You've got a week and a bit to get your shit together otherwise I'm blowing the airport sky high!' The relevance of the humorous nature of the communication was rejected at first instance: the message had been sent via a public electronic communications network (Twitter) and no specific intention is required for an offence under section 127(1)(a). The decision was overruled by the Court of Appeal, which highlighted – in a similar vein to earlier judgments of the European Court of Human Rights – the need to balance free and robust speech, and messages which pose a threat, or are of a menacing character.[12] In the words of Judge LCJ:

> Satirical, or iconoclastic, or rude comment, the expression of unpopular or unfashionable opinion about serious or trivial matters, banter or humour, even if distasteful to some or painful to those subjected to it should and no doubt will continue at their customary level, quite undiminished by this legislation.[13]

In response, after a prolonged period of consultation, the Director of Public Prosecutions released updated guidance on social media prosecutions. This identified four categories into which potential prosecutions may generally fall:

- Communications which may constitute credible threats of violence to the person or damage to property;
- Communications which specifically target an individual or individuals and which may constitute harassment or stalking within the meaning of the Protection from Harassment Act 1997 or which may constitute other offences such as blackmail;

[8] Colette Langos, 'Cyberbullying: The Challenge to Define' (2012) 15(6) *Cyberpscyhology, Behaviour and Social Networking* 285.
[9] ibid.
[10] Communications Select Committee, *Social Media and Criminal Offences* (HL Paper 37, 2014–2015).
[11] *McAlpine v Bercow* [2013] EWHC 1342 (QB).
[12] *Jersild v Denmark* (1994) 19 EHRR 1; Damian Carney, 'Football banning orders and Twitter – bomb joke on Twitter' (2012) *Police Journal* 255, 262.
[13] [2012] EWHC 2157 (Admin), [28].

- Communications which may amount to breach of a court order;
- Communications which do not fall into the categories above and which fall to be considered separately, ie those which may be considered grossly offensive, indecent, obscene or false.[14]

A key context surrounding the imposition of custodial sentences in *R v Nimmo and Sorley* lies in the gender-focused abuse perpetrated by Nimmo and Sorley: the abusive messages were sent to two prominent women in the context of a campaign to increase the number of women appearing on banknotes in the UK.

## II. The Landmark

In 2013, the Bank of England announced a change in the ten-pound bank note.[15] From 2017, the image of Charles Darwin would be replaced by one of Jane Austen. The announcement came after a short but intense period of campaigning, gaining over 35,000 supporters,[16] led by Caroline Criado Perez in response to the upcoming absence of women on banknotes following an earlier announcement that social and prisoner reformer, Elizabeth Fry, would be replaced by Winston Churchill on the five-pound note.[17]

However despite their success, Criado Perez and Stella Creasy MP, who supported the campaign, found themselves victims of multiple abusive messages sent through social media, including death and rape threats. At its height Criado Perez received around 50 abusive Tweets an hour for a 12-hour period.[18] This was partially a backlash against the notion of 'swapping' a man for a woman on a banknote to introduce a notion of equality, but is symptomatic of the wider prevalence and visibility of online abuse. The most severe threats to Criado Perez and Creasy were sent by John Nimmo and Isabella Sorley, who posted abusive messages on Twitter, publicly abusing Criado Perez, and in turn, Creasy. This led to a sustained level of personal abuse against the women. The abusive messages, reported in the judge's sentencing comments, are partially reproduced here to challenge the 'tyranny of silence'. It is recognised that such reproduction is not unproblematic. The abusive messages from Isabella Sorley included the following:

> Fuck off and die … you should have jumped in front of horses, go die; I will find you and you don't want to know what I will do when I do … kill yourself before I do; rape is the last of your worries; I've just got out of prison and would happily do more time to see you buried [s; seriously go kill yourself! I will get less time for that; rape?! I'd do a lot worse things than rape you.[19]

[14] CPS Guidance, n 3 above.

[15] 'Jane Austen to be face of the Bank of England £10 note', *BBC News Online*, 24 July 2013.

[16] Caroline Criado Perez, 'We need women on British banknotes': https://www.change.org/p/we-need-women-on-british-banknotes.

[17] Caroline Criado Perez, 'Women on bank notes: is the Bank of England finally listening?', *The Guardian*, 4 July 2013.

[18] Philipson, n 2 above.

[19] Judge Howard Riddle, Senior District Judge (Chief Magistrate) in the Westminster Magistrates Court, *R v John Ramond Nimmo and Isabella Kate Sorley*, Sentencing Comments, 24 January 2014, 2. https://www.judiciary.uk/wp-content/uploads/JCO/Documents/Judgments/r-v-nimmo-and-sorley.pdf.

John Nimmo's Tweets were in a similar vein:

> Ya not that gd looking to rape u be fine; I will find you; come to geordieland (Newcastle) bitch; just think it could be somebody that knows you personally; the police will do nothing; rape her nice ass; could I help with that lol; the things I cud do to u; dumb blond bitch.[20]

Both Creasy and Criado Perez reported the Tweets to the police – first via Twitter and later in person. However, despite the police's arguable *over*-reaction in *Chambers v DPP* their response was one of *in*-action and indifference. Creasy was told in response to that message that reporting abusive Twitter messages through Twitter to the police was insufficient to launch an investigation. Moreover, in deciding to charge Nimmo and Sorley under the Communications Act 2003 for improper use of a public communications network, the CPS focused on the medium of the messages, rather than the threats they contained. The messages could – and should – have been prosecuted under the Criminal Justice Act 1988 or the Offences Against the Person Act 1861. Threats made via Twitter are still threats. A prosecution under either of those pieces of legislation could have resulted in a custodial sentence of years rather than weeks.[21]

Fortunately, the courts – on this occasion – were more responsive. Nimmo and Sorley pleaded guilty to sending 'menacing' tweets and both received custodial sentences of eight and 12 weeks respectively. Commenting on their actions in his sentencing comments, Judge Howard Riddle, noted that 'the serious harm caused by the offending behaviour makes it inappropriate to impose anything other than an immediate custodial sentence … The harm caused is very high'.[22] Victim statements from Creasy and Criado Perez underline the impact of Nimmo and Sorley's actions. Creasy had installed panic buttons in her home. For Criado Perez the effects of the harassment were 'life-changing'. She spent time and money making herself untraceable, and describes the messages as 'imprinted' on her mind such that she doesn't think she 'will ever be free of them'.

## III. What Happened Next

Before *Chambers* in 2012, there were just 25 prosecutions for social media offences. Since then the number of prosecutions has more than doubled. 55 cases were brought in 2013 alone. Indeed, the explosion in prosecutions for social media abuses is so great that the 'Working to Halt Abuse Online' group has stopped recording online harassment cases.[23] (That said, Crown Prosecution Service figures suggest, the number of offences reaching a court hearing was in decline by 2014.)[24] There are three reasons for this increase in prosecutions. First, the prominence of the (largely negative) coverage in the mainstream media that

[20] ibid.

[21] The fact that the threats were conveyed via Twitter not only distracted the CPS and Police from the essence of the case, but also opened up the decision to prosecute to 'free speech' objections. See for example: Joseph H Rowbotham, 'To Rant, Vent and Converse: Protecting Low Level Digital Speech' (2012) 71(2) *Cambridge Law Journal* 355.

[22] Judge Riddle, n 19 above.

[23] WHO@, 'Online Harassment / Cyberstalking statistics': http://www.haltabuse.org/resources/stats/.

[24] House of Lords Select Committee on Communications, *Social Media and Criminal Offences* (HMSO, HL Paper 37, July 2014) 35.

trolls and social media abuses now receive. It is also attributable, secondly, to the revised and clearer DPP guidance on prosecuting social media offences. And finally, in light of both of these, social media platform providers like Twitter are beginning to take steps to protect their users and become involved in the policing of their own platforms,[25] although it has taken a significant amount of time to reach this point.

There have been a number of other high-profile cases dealing with similar issues. In just over six months in 2012, community orders or custodial sentences were impose in relation to racial abuse of retired footballer Stan Collymore,[26] and the (then) seriously ill footballer Fabrice Muamba[27] as well as abusive messages on Facebook concerning Madeline McCann and April Jones.[28] However, while all of these cases involve abuse via social media, and in many the abuse is directed against various protected characteristics – typically race or sexuality – none have considered in the same way the gender-based, misogynist abuse seen in *Nimmo and Sorley*. And so, while the sentencing in these latter cases recognises the harm caused by abusive messages, there is less indication, despite *Nimmo and Sorley*, that online gender harassment is recognised and taken seriously. The application of existing law is spasmodic.

Moreover, in all these cases, the law applied is not specific to abuse via social media. In 2014, the House of Lords Communications Select Committee noted that, whilst there may be a basis for legislative changes, they saw no reason to alter existing legislation. In the opinion of the Committee, the legal provisions appear to be working well enough to remain unchanged: 'Although we understand that "trolling" causes offence, we do not see a need to create a specific and more severely punished offence for this behaviour'.[29] This position has been criticised by prominent figures state such as the Children's Commissioner for Wales, Keith Towler, who has called for legal changes to be made to address the distinction between offline and online activity.[30] Feminist politicians – including Yvette Cooper MP and Natalie McGarry MP – have also called for change.[31] The 'Recl@im the Internet' campaign was launched by Cooper in 2016, supported by a number of women's organisations including the Fawcett Society, EVAW and Women's Aid, with the aim of 'taking a stand against online abuse'.[32]

## IV. Significance

*Nimmo and Sorley* is significant because it is the first case imposing custodial sentences for misogynistic Twitter abuse. It shone a light onto the murky world of online misogynist abuse and the harm it inflicts on its victims. It is significant because it brought the issue of

[25] 'Twitter announces more tools for dealing with abuse', *BBC News Online*, 15 November 2016.

[26] Claire Duffin, 'Police criticise Twitter over Stan Collymore racial abuse case', *The Telegraph*, 29 July 2014.

[27] Steven Morris, 'Student jailed for racist Fabrice Muamba tweets', *The Guardian*, 27 March 2012.

[28] 'April Jones: Matthew Woods jailed for Facebook posts', *BBC News Online*, 8 October 2012.

[29] Communications Select Committee, n 24 above, 32.

[30] 'Cyberbullying law needed, says children's commissioner for Wales', *BBC News Online*, 15 October 2013; Maggie Brown, 'Labour calls for better laws to stop cyberbullying', *The Guardian*, 30 January 2014.

[31] Katie Forster, 'Jo Cox Death: Calls for violent threats against female MPs to be taken more seriously', *Independent*, 17 June 2016.

[32] Yvette Cooper, 'Why I'm campaigning to reclaim the internet from sexist trolls', *The Telegraph*, 26 May 2016.

gender-based online abuse into the mainstream. It made women, and the abuse of women who campaign for women, visible. And it made clear that it was wrong.

Its most significant legacy then is, perhaps, the ongoing debate that has arisen at all levels – from the House of Lords to the social media users and platform providers, in the mainstream media, academic journals and classrooms – about how to challenge and end all forms of misogynistic abuse – whether online or offline.

## Further Reading


- Kim Barker, 'Virtual spaces and virtual layers – governing the ungovernable?' (2016) 25(1) *Information and Communications Technology Law* 62–70.
- Andy Phippen, and Jennifer Agate, 'New Social Media Offences Under the Criminal Justice and Courts Act and Serious Crime Act: The Cultural Context' (2015) 26(3) *Entertainment Law Review* 82.
- Laura Scaife, 'The DPP and Social Media: A New Approach Coming Out of the Woods?' (2013) 18(1) *Communications Law* 5.

# 87

# Bishops and Priests (Consecration and Ordination of Women) Measure 2014 and Canon C2 'Of the Consecration of Bishops', 2014

MIRANDA THRELFALL-HOLMES

On 17 November 2014 the Church of England's General Synod formally changed the Church's Canon Law when it passed legislation enabling women to be consecrated as bishops, and formally amended Canon C2 of the Canons of the Church of England to state that 'a man or a woman may be consecrated to the office of bishop' (C2.1). For the avoidance of doubt, the Canon also made explicit that 'In the forms of service contained in The Book of Common Prayer or in the Ordinal words importing the masculine gender in relation to bishops are construed as including the feminine' (C2.6).

For the Church of England, this was the culmination of theological debates over women's ordination which had spanned the twentieth century. From a legal perspective it was even more significant. Because the Church of England is an established Church, the Canon Law which governs its operation forms part of the law of the land. The position of Church of England bishops is enshrined in the British parliamentary system. The House of Lords comprises both Lords Temporal (those holding hereditary or life peerages) and Lords Spiritual (the most senior Church of England bishops). The Lords Spiritual had until this point been the last element of the Houses of Parliament that was legally barred to women, and so this Canon removed the final constitutional barrier to women's full participation in parliament (although this was consistently resisted as an argument in the debates as being a purely secular consideration).

## I. Context

Women's ordination had been debated for over a century.[1] There is considerable evidence that women were ordained as deaconesses in the early Church, and some contested and

[1] Trevor Beeson, *The Church's Other Half: Women's Ministry* (SCM Press, 2011); Gary Macy, *The Hidden History of Women's Ordination: Female Clergy in the Medieval West* (OUP, 2007).

inconclusive evidence to suggest that they may, on occasion, have been ordained as priests or even bishops. Women were certainly ordained as abbesses in the medieval period. Women's ordination had been occasionally discussed by theologians throughout the history of the Church, and new religious movements were often marked by a willingness to ordain or be led by women, but there was little serious attempt to ordain women in the established Churches until the nineteenth century.

The Church of England, as established in the late sixteenth century, maintained the historic three-fold ordering of deacons, priests and bishops as those ordained to lead the Church. It was widely believed that this ecclesiastical hierarchy was essential to guarantee the integrity and security of the aristocratic hierarchy – 'no Bishop, no King', as King James I of England and V of Scotland declared.[2] It survived the turmoil of seventeenth-century England and the period of parliamentary Puritan rule following the English Civil War, and was enshrined in the structures of parliamentary monarchy that emerged in the early eighteenth century. Church of England Bishops, the Lords Spiritual, sat in the House of Lords as of right. Even after the unification of the crowns, the Church of Scotland remained an entirely separate entity, with no representation at Westminster, whilst the Church in Wales was part of the established Church of England until 1914 when it was split off and disestablished.

By the mid-nineteenth century, women were becoming vocal about their exclusion from the ministry of the Church. Elizabeth Ferard successfully campaigned to be ordained as the first Church of England deaconess in 1862. She was followed by Isabella Gilmore, whose work firmly established the order of deaconess in the Church of England.

The office of deaconess, however, was not part of the three-fold order of deacons, priests and bishops but an adjunct to it. Campaigners for women's ordination to the three-fold orders of the Church fought throughout the twentieth century. Most prominent was Maude Royden, the first chair of the Church League for Women's Suffrage in 1909. Women's ordination was added to their mandate in 1915, a move which drew the comment from the *Church Times* 'that women be ordained is for any sane person so absolutely gross that he must refuse to discuss it'.[3]

Women's ordination was put on the agenda of the Lambeth Conference, the worldwide gathering of Anglican bishops that happens every 10 years, in 1920. That conference affirmed that deaconess was the only office of the Church open to women, but did clarify that women could be lay members of synods, which are Church councils and legislative bodies comprising lay and ordained members.[4] The 1930 conference reaffirmed this decision and made it clear that deaconesses were not equal to (male) deacons.[5] However, events overtook the synods in 1941. Florence Li Tim-Oi was a theologically trained minister in Hong Kong, and was ordained deaconess in 1940. When the Japanese occupied Hong Kong in 1944, Bishop Hall ordained her a priest there. The Lambeth Conference of 1948 refused to accept this,[6] and Tim-Oi voluntarily refrained from exercising her priestly ministry until women were ordained elsewhere in the Anglican communion.

[2] William Barlowe, *The Sum and Substance of the Conference at Hampton Court* (1604).

[3] Beeson, n 1 above, 133.

[4] Lambeth Conference 1920, **Resolutions 46–54: The Position of Women in the Councils and Ministrations of the Church (1920). Official papers of the General Synod are available online via the Church of England website.**

[5] Lambeth Conference 1930, **Resolutions 66–72 The Ministry of the Church – The Ministry of Women.**

[6] Lambeth Conference 1948, Resolutions 114–115 Proposed Chinese Canon.

Campaigning for women's ordination continued in the Church of England, and in 1979 the Movement for the Ordination of Women (MOW) was founded.[7] Key women in its life included Una Kroll and Monica Furlong, and its first moderator was the Bishop of Manchester, Stanley Booth-Clibborn. In 1978, the MOW succeeded in having the removal of the legal obstacles to women's ordination debated in General Synod, but the vote was lost in the House of Clergy. (Important votes in Synod have to be passed by a two-thirds majority in each of the three houses – laity, clergy and bishops). Eventually, after continued campaigning by members of MOW – including silent demonstrations at ordination services, and a succession of books by Furlong – the first women deacons in the Church of England were ordained in 1987,[8] and the first priests in 1994.[9] Women were still, however, barred from becoming bishops.

## II. The Landmark

After women were ordained as priests in 1994, many in the Church believed that the matter had been settled. Those who pointed out that the legislation was flawed, and that women as bishops was 'unfinished business', were widely criticised for disturbing the fragile status quo. MOW disbanded in 1994. However, it quickly became apparent that the need for feminist campaigning was far from over. The vote to allow women to be priests had created a new piece of companion legislation, the 'Episcopal Ministry Act of Synod', which legitimated continued discrimination against ordained and lay women in the Church. This Act had been rushed through Synod with none of the usual scrutiny and consultation because the bishops feared that the legislation to allow women's ordination would not be passed without greater 'protection' for those who objected. Furlong founded a campaigning group, the Group for Rescinding the Act of Synod (GRAS), and a new successor to MOW was formed, Women and the Church (WATCH), with a wider remit to encourage feminist theology and, among other things, to campaign for the consecration of women as bishops.[10]

These campaigns were met with widespread resistance and resentment by opponents, who were vehemently opposed to the consecration of women as bishops. Women priests could be largely avoided by simply going to another church, but a woman bishop would be the bishop of the whole diocese and would be ordaining clergy. Some opponents argued that this meant that the integrity of the transmission of orders from one generation to the next would be put in jeopardy. Societies such as 'Forward in Faith' (from an Anglo-Catholic perspective) and 'Reform' (from the Evangelical wing) were formed specifically to campaign

[7] The archieve of the MOW has been catalogued and is available to view at the LSE library (Fabiana Barticioti, 'Archive of the Movement for the Ordination of Women' (*LSE History Blog*, no date)).

[8] Yvonne Clarke was the first black woman Deacon in the UK. She was ordained on 15 March 1987 ('Yvonne Clarke, Ordained Female Deacon, 15th March 1987. A celebration of 30 Years', *Women and the Church*, 18 March 2017).

[9] The first 32 women to be ordained priests were ordained in Bristol Cathedral on 12 March 1994, in alphabetical order, so the first woman ordained priest was Angela Berners-Wilson. Some of their stories are told in Helen Thorne, *Journey to Priesthood: An In-Depth Study of the First Women Priests in the Church of England* (Centre for Comparative Studies in Religion & Gender Monograph, 2000), and Beeson, n 1 above, chapter 22; Huma Qureshi, 'Angela Berners-Wilson: "I was first female priest in England"', *The Guardian*, 7 November 2012.

[10] Women and the Church, 'About WATCH': https://womenandthechurch.org/about-watch/.

against women bishops and to promote the theologies that rejected women's ordination. They argued that their position was theological not misogynistic, and pointed to the fact that they rejected not just the ministry of women but that of male bishops who had ordained women. Some arguments were based on ecumenism – that this was an unhelpful or invalid innovation that the Church of England should not do without the Roman Catholic and Orthodox Churches. Others argued that the Bible taught that women were simply not designed by God for leadership, but should be subordinated to male authority.

Opponents were keen to ensure that the debates were almost entirely theological in nature and internally focused. Little attention was paid to the legal point that the Lords Spiritual were part of the Houses of Parliament. Indeed, any arguments on the grounds of employment law, discrimination, equality or fairness were routinely dismissed with scorn as being secular and untheological and therefore irrelevant to the Church debates – or indeed, as demonstrating just how unfit women were for ordination since their arguments were so untheological.

GRAS and WATCH continued the pressure for further change, however, and in 2003 Southwark Diocesan Synod passed a motion requesting the Church of England's General Synod to rescind the Episcopal Ministry Act of Synod. Normally, motions that come to General Synod from dioceses are taken in the order in which they are received, but this one was then 'parked' for over a decade. The bishops decided that they would instead commission reports on the issue, and a series of alternative proposals began to be considered.

The debates over the following decade were distinguished by not being primarily about the substantive issue of whether women could become bishops or not, but rather about what kind of provisions should be put in place for those who disagreed with women's ordination as a matter of theological principle.

In 2005, a Legislative Drafting Group was established to begin the process of shaping legislation. When this group reported to Synod in 2008, it recommended that arrangements be made within the existing structures of the Church of England for those who 'as a matter of theological conviction will not be able to receive the ministry of women as bishops or priests'. This meant rejecting the proposal of Forward in Faith and other campaigners for a new 'Third Province' to enable those who objected to women's ministry to opt out of any contact with women or those who supported women's ministry. In a long session Synod debated and voted down a series of amendments. I myself had originally proposed an amendment to introduce a 'sunset clause' limiting any arrangements for objectors to a 40-year period, but withdrew it before it was debated. Synod therefore agreed to draw up legislation to allow women to be consecrated as bishops, with a statutory code of practice for the care of objectors.

In July 2010 the first draft of the Bishops and Priests (Consecration and Ordination of Women) Measure and draft Amending Canon 30 were debated at revision stage. For legislation which touches on the doctrine and belief of the Church a reference stage to the synods of each of the Church of England's dioceses must also be included. Accordingly this legislation was remitted to the 43 diocesan synods for their consideration, a process which took 18 months. Each synod voted on it, and a majority of synods were needed to vote in favour for the legislation to be taken further. The motion was carried in every single diocese and returned to General Synod in February 2012. The only further stage to happen was a reference to the House of Bishops, who were to meet in May, and it was expected that they would formally agree to present the legislation to the July meeting of Synod for Final Approval.

In that February meeting, however, concerns began to emerge that the House of Bishops might amend the legislation that had been so widely agreed. Worried that the legislation might not command the necessary two-thirds majority in each House, the bishops were suggesting that they might make changes to give further reassurances. Worried in turn that the last-minute panic that had led to the ill-considered Act of Synod was in danger of happening again, Synod took the unusual step of passing a motion asking for the House of Bishops not to amend the legislation substantially. Despite this, when the House met in May they did indeed change the legislation, adding a small clause – 'Clause 5.1.c' – which would have enshrined sex discrimination on the face of the measure, and thus in the law of the land. In the event, there was so little consensus at the Final Approval debate in the July Synod that the bishops were persuaded to withdraw the amended legislation and try again.

Hasty revision took place over the summer months, and revised legislation was brought before the Synod at a special session in November. After a tense debate, it was lost: a majority of the Synod approved it, but the required two-thirds majority was missed by a mere five votes in the House of Laity. The atmosphere in Synod was sombre, but the whole Church was taken aback by the outpouring of public rage and disappointment. The Archbishop of Canterbury elect was summoned to the Commons to explain what had happened, and it was made clear to the Church that if Synod could not deliver the result that was expected by the country, Parliament might step in and do it over the heads of the Church.[11]

This pressure from Parliament was at least partly the fruit of sustained campaigning and educative work by WATCH with Members of Parliament. The appointment at just this time of a new Archbishop of Canterbury, Justin Welby, was also key, as up until this point the leadership from the top had been ambivalent. Welby and his team were keen that his new tenure as Archbishop should not be overshadowed by this issue, and were keen to clear the ground so that they were free to address the building tensions within the Anglican Communion over same-sex relationships.

New legislation was drafted very quickly, and the whole legislative process was accelerated. In July 2014, this second attempt secured the necessary two-thirds majorities in Synod, and parliamentary time was found over the summer for the necessary parliamentary approval stage.[12] Hansard records an overwhelmingly positive debate in Parliament that day.[13] The legislation received Royal Assent and was finally enacted in a special session of General Synod on 17 November 2014.

## III. What Happened Next

National rejoicing was followed by an impatience for the appointment of the first woman bishop. On 17 December 2014, Reverend Libby Lane, a parish priest, was announced as the

[11] HC Deb, 22 November 2012, vol 553 col 717.

[12] House of Lords and House of Commons Ecclesiastical Committee 'Bishops and Priests (Consecration and Ordination of Women) Measure' (HL Paper 45; HC 622, September 2014).

[13] HL Deb, 14 October 2014, vol 756 cols 166–188 (Bishops and Priests (Consecration and Ordination of Women) Measure).

next Bishop of Stockport and the first woman bishop in the Church of England. She was consecrated in York Minster in January 2015 with great celebration.

Meanwhile, consideration was being given to the question of how to get women bishops into the House of Lords as soon as possible. Bishop Lane was not eligible for the Lords, as she was a suffragan (assistant) bishop, rather than a diocesan bishop, and in any case the Lords Spiritual are appointed on a seniority basis. Until the middle of the nineteenth century there were 26 bishops in the Church of England. When new dioceses began to be created, it was agreed that the number of bishops in the Lords would remain fixed at 26. Five bishops have a seat in the Lords by right (Canterbury, York, Durham, London and Winchester), with the remaining 21 seats being filled based on length of service.

It was realised that, if this order of seniority were maintained, there would not be a woman bishop in the House of Lords for about 10 years, and it was clear that this would be politically unacceptable. In consultation with WATCH and senior women clergy the Archbishop of Canterbury introduced into the House of Lords legislation to 'fast-track' the first women bishops into the Lords. For the first 10 years, any woman appointed as a diocesan bishop would go to the front of the queue for the next available seat in the Lords.

In June 2015 Rachel Treweek became the Bishop of Gloucester, and the first diocesan bishop in the Church of England. When Parliament met after the summer recess in autumn 2015 she became eligible to take her seat, but she sent back the first writ of summons that she received because she objected to being referred to as 'right reverend father in God'. It was agreed that she be addressed simply as 'right reverend bishop', and she became the first female member of the Lords Spiritual when she was introduced to the House by the Archbishop of Canterbury and the Bishop of London on 26 October 2015.

## IV. Significance

Around a third of the Church of England's 12,000 clergy are women, and women are about a half of those being currently ordained each year. For us, women bishops have been symbolic of the full acceptance of our orders in the Church of England. It remains a point of sadness and some tension, however, that there are still formal and legislatively binding arrangements to cater for those who oppose women's ministry. The Code of Practice that accompanied the legislation contains five guiding principles, four of which concern the special provisions for those who do not accept the validity of the women's ordination, and currently all new candidates for ordination or senior office are required to sign these. There is currently little political will for this to change.

The focus for tensions and dissent within the Church of England and the wider Anglican Communion has moved on from women's ordination to same-sex relationships, and particularly to the question of same-sex marriage and the ordination of those in same-sex relationships. Some conservatives are keen to stress that this is a very different debate from that about women, and it is primarily being framed as a moral and ethical issue. However, there are clear links with this debate, in terms both of the validity of differing interpretations of and approaches to the Bible, and of how essentialist a view is taken of gender and sexuality. This debate may well run for the next century.

## Further Reading

- Trevor Beeson, *The Church's Other Half: Women's Ministry* (SCM Press, 2011).
- Monica Furlong (ed), *Act of Synod, Act of Folly: Episcopal Ministry Act of Synod 1993* (SCM Press, 1998).
- Julia Ogilvy, *Women in Waiting: Prejudice at the heart of the Church* (Bloomsbury, 2014).

# 88

# *In the Matter of an Application for Judicial Review by the Northern Ireland Human Rights Commission* (2015)

MARIE FOX AND SHEELAGH McGUINNESS

In 2015, the Northern Ireland Human Rights Commission (NIHRC) brought a ground-breaking judicial review seeking a declaration that the law in Northern Ireland breached the human rights of women seeking abortion care. Sitting in the High Court in Belfast, Horner J ruled that the law was not human rights compliant (under Article 8 of the European Convention on Human Rights (ECHR)) in denying terminations to women who were carrying a foetus with a fatal abnormality or who had become pregnant as a result of rape or incest.[1] He held that abortion should be permitted on these grounds, noting that to force women to travel in such circumstances would cause enormous stress. While the exceptions carved out in Horner J's ruling were very limited, his ruling nevertheless represented a significant legal advance. Northern Ireland has one of the most restrictive abortion regimes in Europe, which has been facilitated by women travelling to access abortion care or accessing abortion pills online. The action taken by the NIHRC and Horner J's ruling acknowledges the importance of abortion as a human rights issue and carries the potential to contest the criminalisation of the actions of significant numbers of Northern Irish women.

## I. Context

In 2015 (indeed to date), abortion law in Northern Ireland lagged behind that elsewhere in the UK and Europe, aside from the Republic of Ireland[2] and Malta. The **Abortion Act 1967** has never applied to the jurisdiction.[3] Instead, abortion was governed primarily by the Offences Against the Person Act 1861 (which prohibits the procuring of a miscarriage) and

[1] *In the Matter of an Application for Judicial Review by the Northern Ireland Human Rights Commission* [2015] NIQB 96.

[2] See further **Protection of Life During Pregnancy Act 2013**.

[3] The criminal law relating to abortion in Northern Ireland falls within the legislative competence of the Northern Ireland Assembly by virtue of section 4(1) of the Northern Ireland Act 1998.

the Criminal Justice Act (Northern Ireland) 1945 which prohibits child destruction, subject to a defence where it was performed to preserve the life of the pregnant woman. Moreover, it was unclear until a series of cases in the mid-1990s[4] whether *R v Bourne*[5] (which as a jury direction in a Crown Court trial was technically not binding in Northern Ireland) applied. In *Bourne*, McNaghten J had ruled that if the doctor took the view that continuing the pregnancy would render the woman 'a physical or mental wreck' a termination was permissible. While ultimately the vagueness of this test prompted the medical profession in Great Britain to push for more liberal abortion provision, culminating in the enactment of the Abortion Act 1967, in Northern Ireland the so-called *Bourne* exception – while lawful – has been interpreted restrictively. Most significantly, in *Re AMNH*[6] it was held that continuation of the pregnancy must pose a 'real and serious risk' to the woman's health, while *Western Health and Social Services Board v CMB*[7] emphasised that the risk must be 'permanent or long term'. In summary then, in twenty-first-century Northern Ireland abortion was only available if termination was necessary to preserve the life of the woman, or if continuing the pregnancy posed the risk of a real and serious adverse effect on her physical or mental health, which would be long term or permanent.[8]

By 2015, the restrictive abortion regime was having a huge impact on women. Those with much wanted pregnancies who sought termination because the foetus had been diagnosed with a fatal condition had to convince health professionals that the impact on their mental health was such that they came within the restrictive interpretation of *Bourne*, as did women who had become pregnant following a sexual offence. More generally, all women of child-bearing age risked criminalisation if they sought to end an unwanted pregnancy. In the previous year, 802 abortions had been carried out in Great Britain on women resident in Northern Ireland,[9] a figure which is likely to be a significant underestimate of overall abortions, since many women will not disclose their actual address or will have procured abortion pills online.[10] As noted in an influential Amnesty International Report in 2015:

> For many women, demonstrating a long-term risk to health, particularly mental health, and overcoming barriers to access to abortion in Northern Ireland is often an unsurmountable challenge. Women's access to and experience with health services also varies depending on the attitude of and availability of services within each of Northern Ireland's NHS health trusts … which leads to further inequity.[11]

Perhaps surprisingly, throughout the late twentieth century this regime generated little feminist opposition. Eileen Fegan and Rachel Rebouche attribute this to the 'Troubles',

[4] Starting with *Northern Health and Social Services Board v F and G* [1993] NILR 268.

[5] *R v Bourne* [1938] 3 All ER 615.

[6] *Re AMNH, sub nom Northern Health and Social Services Board v A and Others* [1994] NIJB 1.

[7] *Western Health and Social Services Board v CMB*, High Court (Family Division), 29 September 1995 (unreported).

[8] Department of Health, Social Services & Public Safety *Guidance for Health and Social Care Professionals on Termination of Pregnancy in Northern Ireland*, March 2016: https://www.health-ni.gov.uk/publications/guidance-hsc-professionals-termination-pregnancy-northern-ireland.

[9] Department of Health, *Abortion Statistics, England & Wales: 2013* (June 2014).

[10] See further Tamara Hervey and Sally Sheldon, 'Abortion by telemedicine in Northern Ireland: patient and professional rights across borders' (2017) 68 *Northern Ireland Legal Quarterly* 1–33.

[11] Amnesty International, *Barriers to Accessing Abortion services* (February 2015).

which prompted the women's movement to suppress potentially divisive issues which could threaten consensus-building and cross-community political organising. They point to the high-profile Northern Ireland Women's Coalition – a cross-community political party which existed from 1996–2006 – which, though it campaigned on social issues such as inclusion of women in public life, found it challenging to frame a reproductive health strategy that encompassed choice about pregnancy.[12] In consequence, feminist campaigning was limited to somewhat sporadic single-issue organisations. The Northern Ireland Abortion Law Reform Association (NIALRA), established in the 1960s, was modelled on the British Abortion Law Reform Association (ALRA) which had successfully lobbied David Steele MP to introduce his private member's bill on abortion in 1967. NIALRA's demise was followed by the creation of the avowedly feminist Northern Ireland Abortion Campaign (NIAC) in the 1970s, which explicitly advocated women's right to choose. Its campaign for safe legal abortion was galvanised by the death from septicaemia of a young Belfast woman following an unlawful termination in 1980. In 1984 some members of NIAC formed the NIALRA (Mark 2) with the single aim of influencing Westminster MPs to extend the 1967 Act to the jurisdiction.[13] More recently this has been a key demand of 'Alliance for Choice', which was formed in 1996 to pressurise the incoming Labour Government to reform the law. Their demands chimed with those of the medical profession, which has long expressed concern about the uncertain legal climate in which health professionals work.

Since the 1980s, the British Medical Association (BMA) has advocated the extension of the 1967 Act to Northern Ireland. However, although it reaffirmed this policy in 2014, stating 'BMA policy supports the extension of the Abortion Act to Northern Ireland', it went on to caution that 'The Westminster Government has made it clear that any changes in abortion legislation in Northern Ireland would have to be instigated by the Northern Irish public'.[14] Meanwhile inside Parliament, a series of amendments to the Human Fertilisation and Embryology Bill in 2007 which would have extended the Abortion Act to Northern Ireland were dropped by the Labour Government, allegedly to secure the support of the Democratic Unionist Party on other issues.

Perhaps the most striking feature of abortion law reform campaigns in Northern Ireland, however, has been the extent to which they have been segregated from broader human rights policy and feminist activism. Tellingly, until the publication of the 2015 Amnesty Report, mainstream human rights organisations (including statutory bodies such as the NIHRC) had eschewed the issue, as had prominent NGOs, notably the Committee on the Administration of Justice, which was otherwise at the forefront of human rights campaigns. The 2015 judicial review case is therefore significant not only for the court ruling, but because of the shift it represents in NIHRC strategy.[15]

[12] Eileen Fegan and Rachel Rebouche, 'Northern Ireland's Abortion Law: The Morality of Silence and the Censure of Agency' (2003) 11 *Feminist Legal Studies* 221–54, 247–49.

[13] NIALRA, *Abortion in Northern Ireland: The Report of an International Tribunal* (Beyond the Pale Publications, 1989).

[14] BMA Views, *The law and ethics of abortion* (November 2014; updated June 2017).

[15] See further Marie Fox and Sheelagh McGuinness, 'The highs and lows of one hectic day in Northern Ireland's abortion struggle', *The Conversation*, 2 July 2017; Ruth Fletcher, Marie Fox, and Sheelagh McGuinness, 'Trial and Error in Northern Irish Abortion Law' (*London Irish Abortion Rights Campaign*, 7 July 2017).

## II. The Landmark

Although the Northern Ireland Human Rights Commission, established in 1998 as part of the Good Friday Agreement, initially refrained from engaging with abortion,[16] this position shifted in 2013 when, the NIHRC expressed concern that abortion law was not ECHR compliant. The Department of Justice responded by announcing a consultation on whether the law should be reformed to permit abortion in limited circumstances, namely 'if there has been a diagnosis that the foetus is a result of rape or where the foetus was diagnosed with a fatal foetal abnormality (FFA)'.[17] A joint consultation with the Health Department had been vetoed by then Northern Ireland Health Minister, Jim Wells. However, by the time the Department of Justice, in April 2015, recommended legislation to allow terminations in cases of fatal foetal abnormality but not rape, the NIHRC, under a newly-appointed Chief Commissioner Les Allamby, had instituted judicial review proceedings. It contended that the failure to provide for termination of pregnancy in cases where the pregnant woman was carrying a foetus with a serious malformation or a fatal foetal abnormality, or where her pregnancy was a result of rape/incest breached Articles 3 (protection against inhuman and degrading treatment), 8 (protection of private and family life) and 14 (protection from discrimination) of the ECHR.

Horner J was a relatively new appointment to the High Court of Northern Ireland when he heard the case, which remains his most high-profile ruling to date. The issue was whether he should issue a declaration of incompatibility pursuant to sections 6 and 4 of the Human Rights Act 1998 on the grounds that the law, as outlined above, breached the ECHR. Having outlined Northern Irish law as well as that in other European jurisdictions,[18] Horner J concluded that the position in both Irish jurisdictions was out of line with a 'European consensus' that suggested 'that the right to abortion on both sides of the border in Ireland should be extended'.[19] Situating the case in the context of the UK's obligations under international human rights law, he detected:

> a groundswell of support for the view that the UK's international obligations, even though they are not incorporated into Northern Ireland law, require exceptions so as to permit abortion for pregnancies which are a consequence of rape and/or incest and where there is a FFA.[20]

A notable feature of the ruling was the High Court's willingness to contextualise the issues. A range of oral and written submissions were received from organisations representing a wide spectrum of views, including Alliance for Choice, the Abortion Support Network (ASN), Amnesty International, and the Society for the Protection of the Unborn Child (SPUC). Most importantly, the Court heard from individual women denied abortions in Northern Ireland. Waiving anonymity, Sarah Ewart, whose story had attracted sympathetic media coverage, testified about the negative impact of having to travel to England for a

[16] Fegan and Rebouche, n 12 above.

[17] Department of Justice, *The Criminal Law on Abortion: Lethal Foetal Abnormality and Sexual Crime. Response to the Consultation and Policy Proposals* (April 2015).

[18] See generally on ECHR jurisprudence and abortion, 'Reproductive Rights' (European Court of Human Rights Press Unit Factsheet April 2018).

[19] [2015] NIQB 96, [58].

[20] ibid [68].

termination following a diagnosis of anencephaly.[21] Ewart described her experience in an interview on the Stephen Nolan show: 'This is destroying me … I don't want to go out and face people. It is just emotionally wrecking. This is not the way I should be. This is not who I am. This needs to change'.[22] These narratives were critical to the outcome of the case. Also crucial was Horner J's willingness to recognise the broader political context and likely consequences of judicial inaction, given his view that the prospects for legislative action were 'gloomy'.[23]

Turning to the Convention rights at stake, Horner J stated '[t]he position in Northern Ireland law can reasonably be summed up by concluding that the unborn child does not enjoy a full "right to life" under Article 2'.[24] However, the NIHRC's claims under Articles 3 and 14 failed. As regards the claim under Article 3, he held that no breach had occurred, as the state's obligations were primarily negative and it was not responsible for the circumstances in which these women found themselves. Since the women were not entirely prevented from having abortion, this claim rested purely on the 'additional stress of having to travel' which did not, in his view, satisfy the high severity threshold for finding breach of Article 3.[25] Although ruling that it was not necessary to make a finding on the alleged breach of Article 14[26] Horner J held that the Commission had also failed to prove that the law was discriminatory.[27]

At the heart of the case, however, was his ruling that the state had breached its obligations under Article 8. Having analysed relevant ECHR jurisprudence which offered 'limited' guidance, since each state was accorded a wide margin of appreciation in determining the legality of abortion,[28] Horner J concluded that it was up to the domestic court to determine whether Article 8 was breached. He held that it was not legitimate, proportionate or necessary in a democratic society to prohibit a termination following a diagnosis of FFA since:

> the mother's inability to access an abortion in those circumstances constitutes a gross interference with her personal autonomy. As discussed, a normal foetus does not have an article 2 right to life … in the case of a FFA, there is no life to protect … There is nothing to weigh in the balance.[29]

In the case of pregnancy resulting from a sexual crime he observed:

> Sexual crime is the grossest intrusion on a woman's autonomy … Weighed in the balance is the foetus, incapable of an independent existence for many weeks into the pregnancy. [I]mposing a blanket ban on abortion … effectively prevents any consideration of the interests of any woman whose personal autonomy has been so vilely and heinously invaded. A law so framed can never be said to be proportionate.[30]

[21] Amelia Gentleman, 'I needed an abortion but my consultant told me: "I'm not going to prison"', *The Guardian*, 7 January 2016; 'Sarah Ewart: her story of having an abortion in England', *Channel 4 News*, 29 June 2017: https://www.channel4.com/news/sarah-ewart-her-story-of-having-an-abortion-in-england.

[22] 'Sarah Ewart's Abortion Journey from Northern Ireland', Stephen Nolan *BBC Radio 5 Live*, 11 October 2013: http://www.bbc.co.uk/programmes/p01jmx4x.

[23] [2015] NIQB 96, [34].

[24] ibid [109],

[25] ibid [121].

[26] ibid [168].

[27] ibid [170].

[28] ibid [144].

[29] ibid [160].

[30] ibid [162].

Horner J made a subsequent additional judgment in December 2015 to clarify some aspects of the November decision.[31] Most importantly he issued a declaration of incompatibility, stating:

> There is near unanimity among the parties in this judicial review, and that includes the Commission, that for this court to try and read the impugned provisions in a Convention-compliant way would be a step too far. Having given due consideration to all the submissions and the arguments raised therein, I conclude that such a view is correct. Accordingly, as indicated in my judgment, and for the reasons set out in that judgment and as a matter of last resort, I make a declaration of incompatibility.[32]

## III. What Happened Next

The latest Department of Health statistics show that in 2016–17 only 13 women met the threshold for abortions in Northern Ireland in the year to March 2016.[33] In the same period 919 women travelled from Northern Ireland to Great Britain to access abortion, which is an increase of over a quarter from 2016 and the highest level since 2011, likely owing to the funding announcement noted below. The actual number of women – including those risking prosecution by purchasing pills online – will be much higher.[34]

The period since the 2015 ruling has witnessed an unprecedented degree of political and legal activity on the issue of abortion in Northern Ireland. A controversial appeal by the Attorney-General and Minister of Justice against Horner J's December 2015 incompatibility ruling was allowed by the Northern Ireland Court of Appeal (NICA) in June 2017, primarily on the grounds that abortion was a matter for the legislature.[35] Notwithstanding a disappointing outcome, the judgment also contained positive judicial reasoning. Weatherup LJ, for example, concurred with the High Court that current restrictions on access to abortion were in breach of Article 8, while Morgan LCJ and Gillen LJ stated that women pregnant as a result of rape or having had a diagnosis of foetal anomaly *should* be entitled to treatment in Northern Ireland under the existing legal framework.

Leave was granted to NIHRC to appeal to the UK Supreme Court, but before the case was heard in June 2017 another important legal challenge to the restrictiveness of abortion provision in Northern Ireland failed in the Supreme Court. In this case, the claimants challenged the refusal of the Secretary of State for Health to fund terminations for women travelling from Northern Ireland to England on the NHS unless it was an emergency. The need to travel means that women in Northern Ireland often spend upwards of £900 in order to access an abortion. The majority of the UK Supreme Court[36] held that the

[31] *In the Matter of an Application for Judicial Review by the Northern Ireland Human Rights Commission* [2015] NIQB 102.

[32] [2015] NIQB 102, [5].

[33] Department of Health, *Abortion Statistics, England & Wales: 2017* (June 2018).

[34] Tamara Hervey and Sally Sheldon, 'Abortion by telemedicine in Northern Ireland: patient and professional rights across borders' (2017) 68 *Northern Ireland Legal Quarterly* 1–33.

[35] *In the matter of an Application by the Northern Ireland Human Rights Commission for Judicial Review* [2017] NICA 42.

[36] Lord Wilson gave the lead majority judgment, with which Lord Reed and Lord Hughes agreed. Lord Reed gave a concurring judgment, with which Lord Hughes agreed. Significantly, Lady Hale and Lord Kerr gave dissenting judgments.

Secretary of State was not obliged to fund abortion services for Northern Irish women who had abortions in England and Wales, even though they were UK taxpayers.[37] As Lady Hale noted in her dissenting judgment:

> The right of pregnant women to exercise autonomy in relation to treatment and care has been hard won but it has been won[38] … This is to deny pregnant women from Northern Ireland the same right to choose what is done with their bodies as is enjoyed by all other pregnant citizens of the United Kingdom. It is inconsistent with the principle of equal treatment which underlies so much of our law. This is not to say that the law in Northern Ireland has to be the same as the law in the rest of the United Kingdom. That is not what this case is about. But it is to say that a woman from Northern Ireland who is in Great Britain ought not to be denied, as a matter of policy, the same rights as other women here enjoy.[39]

The decision prompted Stella Creasy MP to table an amendment to the Queen's Speech which would have committed the Westminster Government to funding abortion services for Northern Irish women who travelled to England for abortion care. Ultimately this forced the Conservative Government to commit to funding these procedures in order to avert a potentially divisive vote when it was dependent on the political support of the Democratic Unionist Party, and Creasy withdrew the amendment. Notably, however, this funding was made available through the Government Equalities Office, not the Department for Health. Moreover, as a recent highly critical CEDAW report concluded, travel to Great Britain can never be an optimal solution given the emotional burden and lack of follow up care.[40] In March 2018, over 130 MPs and peers from all parties called on then Home Secretary, Amber Rudd, to allow women in Northern Ireland to be able to access abortion locally.[41] As their letter noted, '50 years after the Abortion Act 1967 women and girls in Northern Ireland still face up to life in prison for accessing a service which is provided on the NHS in England and Wales'.[42]

In June 2018, just weeks after citizens in the Republic of Ireland voted to Repeal the 8th Amendment,[43] the Supreme Court finally handed down its judgment in this case. In an unusually split decision a (4–3) majority of the Supreme Court disagreed with the unanimous view of the Northern Irish courts, ruling that the NIHRC lacked standing to bring the case, and hence that there was no jurisdiction for the Court to make a declaration of incompatibility on the basis of the substantive conclusions reached by the Court.[44] On the

[37] *R (on the application of A and B) v Secretary of State for Health* [2017] UKSC 41.

[38] See ***St George's Healthcare NHS Trust v S* (1998)**.

[39] [2017] UKSC 41, [93], [95].

[40] CEDAW, *Report of the Inquiry concerning the United Kingdom of Great Britain and Northern Ireland under Article 8 of the* ***Optional Protocol to the Convention on the Elimination of all Forms of Discrimination against Women*** (23 February 2018). See also *Who Decides? We Trust Women. Abortion in the Developing World and the UK. A Report by the UK All-Party Parliamentary Group (APPG) on Population, Development and Reproductive Health* (March 2018) which highlighted the need for clear guidance on funding, and provision of a care pathway for women travelling from Northern Ireland (p 38).

[41] Jane Martinson, 'MPs from all sides call for abortion law in N Ireland to be relaxed', *The Guardian*, 7 March 2018.

[42] Letter to Amber Rudd MP (8 March 2018): https://static1.squarespace.com/static/581f830fbebafba66ba1a131/t/5aa043f14192027fb3d4e6b1/1520452597370/Letter+to+Amber+Rudd+MP.pdf.

[43] See **Thirty-sixth Amendment to the Irish Constitution, 2018.**

[44] *In the matter of an Application by the Northern Ireland Human Rights Commission for Judicial Review* [2018] UKSC 27. For an incisive critique of the majority's reasoning on the standing issue see Jane Rooney, 'Standing

substantive issues, by a majority the Supreme Court ruled that the law in Northern Ireland was incompatible with Article 8 in respect of women whose foetus was diagnosed with a FFA (on this issue the split was 5–2), and in respect of women whose pregnancy resulted from rape or incest (4–3 Split). Two judges also held that the current law breached Article 3. All were agreed that there was no breach of Articles 8 or 3 in respect of serious foetal abnormality cases and that there was no need to address the Article 14 claim.

## IV. Significance

In 2005, in the wake of the Northern Ireland Family Planning Association (NIFPA) litigation,[45] Ruth Fletcher called for the adoption of a human rights-based strategy to 'positively and generally assert women's reproductive rights at the same time that it seeks to accommodate the needs of the most vulnerable'.[46] The NIHRC litigation can be situated within such a strategy, and when the NICA upheld the High Court's ruling that the NIHRC had legal standing to bring the case it averted the need for women to undertake individual human rights challenges. This makes it desperately disappointing that the Supreme Court overturned this by ruling that under the Northern Ireland Act 1998 the Commission lacked competence to bring 'abstract' proceedings 'where the only complaint is that primary legislation, such as the 1861 [Offences Against the Person] Act, is incompatible with Convention rights'.[47]

Yet, notwithstanding the finding on standing and the reversal of Horner J's declaration of incompatibility by the superior courts, his judgment, and indeed the fact that the case was ever litigated, have marked an important shift in the legal and political culture within which abortion is debated in Northern Ireland. The symbolic significance of Horner J's declaration that denial of a woman's ability to make choices about her pregnancy can in certain circumstances breach her human rights was huge, and was accepted by the Supreme Court judges, all of whom agreed that legislative reform was necessary. The key question now is whether this action will be taken by the Northern Ireland Assembly if it is restored in the near future or whether intervention by the Westminster Parliament will be necessary.

of the Northern Ireland Human Rights Commission in the UK Supreme Court Abortion Decision': https://legalresearch.blogs.bris.ac.uk/2018/06/standing-of-the-northern-ireland-human-rights-commission-in-the-uk-supreme-court-abortion-decision/.

[45] In 2001, in the first judicial review of the provision of abortion services and medical practices relating to abortion in Northern Ireland, Kerr J held that while the Department of Health, Social Services and Public Safety was not failing in its statutory duty not to produce guidelines on these issues, it would be prudent to do so. The NIFPA appealed his decision and the NICA ruled that the Department was obligated to provide the guidance. Following a series of drafts and a further legal challenge by SPUC, guidance was finally produced in March 2016: Department of Health, Northern Ireland Executive (2016) *Guidance for Health and Social Care Professionals on Termination of Pregnancy in Northern Ireland.* Belfast: Department of Health, Social Services and Public Safety. For details see Catherine O'Rourke, 'Advocating Abortion Rights in Northern Ireland: Local and Global Tensions' (2016) 25 *Social and Legal Studies* 716–40, 719–21.

[46] Ruth Fletcher, 'Abortion needs or abortion rights? Claiming state accountability for women's reproductive welfare' (2005) 13 *Feminist Legal Studies* 123–34, 123.

[47] [2018] UKSC 27, Lord Mance at [58].

## Further Reading


- Eileen Fegan and Rachel Rebouche, 'Northern Ireland's Abortion Law: The Morality of Silence and the Censure of Agency' (2003) 11 *Feminist Legal Studies* 221–54.
- Marie Fox, 'The Consequences of Criminalisation: Abortion in Northern Ireland' in Amel Alghrani, Rebecca Bennett and Suzanne Ost (eds), *The Criminal Law and Bioethical Conflict* (Cambridge University Press, 2012) 203–20.
- Catherine O'Rourke, 'Advocating Abortion Rights in Northern Ireland: Local and Global Tensions' (2016) 25 *Social and Legal Studies* 716–40.

# 89

# Violence Against Women, Domestic Abuse and Sexual Violence (Wales) Act 2015

OLGA JURASZ

The Violence Against Women, Domestic Abuse and Sexual Violence (Wales) Act 2015 (VAW Act) is the first piece of legislation in the United Kingdom to explicitly and specifically address violence against women as opposed to 'domestic violence' generally. Following a unanimous vote of the National Assembly for Wales, it became law in Wales on 29 April 2015. Its key purpose is to improve the public sector response in relation to the prevention of acts of gender-based violence, domestic abuse, and sexual violence, the protection of victims, and support of those affected (section 1).

The VAW Act represents a devolved[1] response to a key social and legal problem: violence against women and girls. It is significant for women as it sets out practical steps which national and local government and public sector bodies ought to implement in order to work together to prevent violence against women. In so doing, it places Wales at the forefront of the UK's continuing efforts to combat all forms of violence against women. Despite a plethora of legislation in England and Wales seeking to address and reduce violence against women in its many and varied forms, to date it has typically focused on specific forms of violence and/or remedies for victims, rather than on preventative measures per se. The VAW Act marks an important shift in this respect: it focuses on establishing strategic and coherent public sector mechanisms aimed at prevention of and protection from gender-based violence, domestic abuse, and sexual violence in Wales. The Act also aims to strengthen the support available to the victims of gender-based violence, domestic abuse, and sexual violence.

[1] Devolution is a process of delegation of legislative or executive functions (or both) relating to the issues within the region by the central government to a regional authority. In Wales, the Government of Wales Act 1998 established the National Assembly for Wales, a body with powers of making laws on devolved issues for Wales. Since May 2007 the National Assembly has had powers to legislate for Wales in specific areas without the need for approval from the UK Parliament. These areas include education, culture, health and social welfare (for a complete list of areas in which the National Assembly can legislate, see National Assembly for Wales website: http://www.assembly.wales/en/abthome/role-of-assembly-how-it-works/Pages/Powers.aspx.).

# I. Context

The prevalence and perniciousness of violence against women and girls is a global problem.[2] It transcends international borders. A 2014 survey *Violence Against Women: an EU-wide survey* carried out by the EU Agency for Fundamental Rights found that around 13 million women in the European Union experienced physical violence in the previous year.[3] However, of course, violence against women and girls is not limited to physical violence. It also includes psychological violence, sexual violence, honour-based violence, and economic harms. And, following the developments at an international level, it is now generally accepted that violence against women is a form of discrimination against women and a violation of human rights. Nor – despite the title of the Act and as recognised in its gender-neutral language – is gender-based and sexual violence and domestic abuse limited to women and girls, though they are disproportionately affected by it.

Violence against women continues to be a significant problem in England and Wales. In the time leading up to the VAW Act coming into force, an increase in reporting of crimes committed against women and girls was observed in England and Wales. In June 2015, the Crown Prosecution Service (CPS) reported the highest number ever of cases involving crimes of violence against women and girls in England and Wales. In 2014–15, the CPS prosecuted 6878 cases involving violence against women and girls in Wales, securing a conviction in 74.5 per cent of these cases.[4] The cases in Wales constituted 6.42 per cent of the total number of cases involving violence against women and girls across England and Wales in 2014–15. Whilst women also are perpetrators of domestic abuse and VAW, the CPS data confirms that 93 per cent of defendants in cases involving violence against women and girls were men.[5]

Prior to the enactment of the VAW Act, a number of domestic laws in England and Wales provided protection for women from certain types of gender-related, domestic and sexual violence as well as remedies against such acts. Specific acts of violence against women (as well as remedies) have been covered under various pieces of legislation such as the Matrimonial Causes Act 1878 (allowing women to separate from violent husbands), the **Housing (Homeless Persons) Act 1977** (giving increased legislative protections to women who were homeless or at risk of becoming homeless as a result of domestic violence), the Domestic Violence and Matrimonial Proceedings Act 1976 (allowing courts to exclude legal owners from their own property if violent to their wife or cohabitant),[6] the **Sexual Offences Act 2003** (covering rape and sexual violence), the Female Genital Mutilation Act 2003,[7] **Forced Marriage (Civil Protection) Act 2007**, and section 121 of the Anti-Social Behaviour Act 2014 (forced marriage). These were all the result of strenuous lobbying by feminist groups such as WAVAW (Women Against Violence Against Women). In cases

[2] The term 'violence against women' (VAW) is understood as inclusive of acts of violence affecting both women and girls.

[3] EU Agency for Fundamental Rights (FRA), *Violence Against Women: an EU-wide survey* (Publications Office of the European Union, 2015).

[4] Crown Prosecution Service, *Violence Against Women and Girls: Crime Report* 2014–2015 (CPS, 2015) 98.

[5] ibid 21.

[6] ***Davis v Johnson* (1978)**.

[7] See further **Prohibition of Female Circumcision Act 1985**.

concerning domestic violence, civil and criminal remedies such as occupation and non-molestation orders as well as restraining and non-harassment orders were legislated for in the Family Law Act 1996 (as amended by the Domestic Violence, Crime and Victims Act 2004) and by the Protection from Harassment Act 1997. Indeed, in the year leading up to the VAW Act's enactment, several domestic laws relating to domestic violence and some forms of violence against women were adopted which applied in both England and Wales. These included Domestic Violence Protection Orders and the Domestic Violence Disclosure Scheme (also known as Clare's Law), which gives persons in new relationships a right to make a request to the police to disclose whether their new partner has a history of committing domestic abuse. Other significant developments include provisions addressing harms that disproportionately affect women in the Criminal Justice and Courts Act 2015, relating to pornographic images of rape (section 37) and some forms of image-based sexual abuse (sections 33–35).

However, despite – and maybe even because of – this legislative output, victims of violence and abuse continued to be under-protected and/or unsure about the support and remedies available.

## II. The Landmark

Efforts to enact specific legislation aimed at combatting violence against women in Wales go back to 2009 when the Wales Violence Against Women Action Group (a coalition of organisations working to end violence against women in Wales) campaigned for the Welsh Government to introduce the first Welsh strategy and appropriate legislation to tackle all forms of violence against women, not solely domestic abuse. In the same year, the Group published a report, *Violence Against Women: Why an Integrated Strategy in Wales?*, which made a case for such a strategy.[8]

In 2012, the Welsh Government proposed the Domestic Abuse (Wales) Bill. In introducing the Bill, the Government recognised violence against women and girls in Wales as an enduring social problem and a barrier to 'Wales becoming a fair and prosperous society'.[9] It considered 'better education and awareness of gender-based violence from the "cradle to the grave", which includes the public, frontline staff and professionals' as one of the three priorities of the legislation.[10]

By the time the Bill was formally introduced to the National Assembly by Lesley Griffiths AM, Minister for Local Government and Government Business, in June 2014, it had already garnered support from a number of influential Assembly Members. Set against the backdrop of growing awareness of violence against women issues, the Bill was given much political support, particularly from the two Welsh Labour politicians, Carl Sargeant AM and Joyce Watson AM, who openly supported the introduction of the Bill. Outside the Assembly, other initiatives aimed at combatting and raising awareness of

[8] Wales Violence Against Women Action Group, *Violence Against Women: Why an Integrated Strategy in Wales?* (Wales Violence Against Women Action Group, 2009).

[9] Welsh Government, *White Paper: Consultation on legislation to end violence against women, domestic abuse and sexual violence (Wales)* (WG17102, 26 November 2012) [2].

[10] ibid [12].

violence against women – such as the One Billion Rising Campaign and Not in My Name Campaign – were also taking place.[11] Capitalising on this, and coinciding with the launch of the Bill the Welsh Government launched an advertising campaign calling for people 'to take a stand' against VAW and domestic abuse. Its purpose, Griffiths noted, was 'to empower people with information to act in the right way if they suspect abuse may be taking place'.[12]

Despite the eventual unanimous vote, the passage of the VAW Bill through the National Assembly was not straightforward. Although the proposals for new legislation on tackling violence against women were generally welcomed by women's groups and campaigners, earlier versions of the Bill met with a strong response from women's groups, including Welsh Women's Aid, who called for improvements in the proposed legislation, especially in relation to its gender-neutral provisions.[13] Shortly after the Bill was introduced, the Wales Violence Against Women Action Group launched a petition and an accompanying online campaign #WhereAreTheWomen.[14] The aim of the campaign was to increase the focus on *women* victims of violence in recognition of the disproportionate levels of violence and abuse suffered by them. While the campaign secured a significant symbolic victory – a change in the Bill's title, replacing 'Gender-based violence' with 'Violence Against Women' – and had some success in relation to the education provisions, it was less successful in securing substantive change to the majority of provisions in the VAW Act.

The VAW Act does not introduce any new statutory offences. Rather, it imposes various obligations on local authorities as well as on the Welsh Government in order to support the delivery of the primary purposes of the Act. Under section 3, Welsh Ministers have a duty – established using the strong phraseology of 'must' – to prepare, publish, implement, and review a National Strategy for tackling violence against women and girls, domestic abuse, and sexual violence. This should take the form of an 'action plan' containing an outline of concrete goals contributing to the realisation of the objectives of the Act, specific actions taken towards fulfilment of these goals, and the time-scale in which these objectives are to be achieved. The Act places an equivalent duty on Welsh local authorities and health boards to prepare joint local strategies for the particular area in Wales that they govern (section 5). As with the National Strategy, the aim of the local strategies is to contribute to the fulfilment and realisation of the purposes of the Act. In addition, under section 15 of the Act, Welsh Ministers may issue guidance to a relevant authority (that is, local authorities, Local Health Boards, fire and rescue services, and the NHS) on how it should exercise its functions to contribute to the purposes of the Act.

The Act also recognises that education plays a major role in the prevention of gender-based violence and domestic abuse. Accordingly, sections 9 and 10 of the Act allow Welsh Ministers to require local authorities to publish information about how their education functions are being exercised (including in schools, further education, and higher education institutions) to promote the purposes of the Act.

[11] Carl Sargeant, 'Wales Leads the Way in Tackling Violence against Women' (14 February 2013); The Women's Institute, 'No More Violence Against Women': https://www.thewi.org.uk/wi-in-wales/current-campaigns/no-more-violence-against-women.

[12] Daniel Davies, 'Domestic violence bill 'disappointment' from campaigners', *BBC News online*, 30 June 2014.

[13] ibid.

[14] 'Campaigners launch #WhereAreTheWomen petition demanding Welsh Government tackle violence against women', *Wales Online*, 25 September 2014).

Finally, the Act includes measures for systematic monitoring of progress in relation to its implementation. Welsh Ministers as well as local authorities and Local Health Boards are under an obligation to submit annual reports on their progress in the implementation of measures which were identified in their respective strategies and subsequently undertaken in pursuit of the purposes of the Act (sections 12 and 13). In addition, the Act establishes an office of a National Adviser on Violence Against Women and other forms of Gender-based Violence, Domestic Abuse and Sexual Violence (section 21), whose primary role is to advise Welsh Ministers on matters concerning VAW, domestic abuse and sexual violence in Wales. The role also involves carrying out research into these matters, publishing reports on specific issues within the scope of the Act, and reporting annually on activities undertaken within the scope of the role.

## III. What Happened Next

The final provisions of the VAW Act came into force in January 2016. In the same month, the National Training Framework on Violence Against Women, Domestic Abuse and Sexual Violence was issued by Public Services Minister, Leighton Andrews AM.[15] This contains statutory guidance (in accordance with section 15) setting minimum standards of training and professional requirements for all those working with the victims of gender-based violence, sexual violence, and domestic abuse across Wales. The Framework is designed to bring a consistent, gender-sensitive, and specialist response to gender-based violence and domestic abuse through professional training of relevant authorities. The Framework refers to the principle of 'Ask and Act' – a system of early identification of victims of gender-based violence and domestic abuse – which had arisen in recognition of the importance of the role played by public services in identifying and addressing violence against women, domestic abuse and sexual violence.[16] In November 2016, the Government adopted the National Strategy on Violence Against Women, Domestic Abuse and Sexual Violence 2016–2020.

However, while the full impact of the VAW Act on prevention of and response to gender-based violence and domestic abuse in Wales is still unknown, its implementation has not been entirely smooth. In July 2016, Welsh Women's Aid published a report – *Are you listening and am I being heard?* – which drew on consultations with 66 survivors of violence and abuse, aimed at informing the National Strategy.[17] It made 10 key recommendations, including the introduction of dedicated specialist services, better responses by professionals involved in the family justice system, compulsory prevention education in all schools

[15] Welsh Government, *The National Training Framework on Violence Against Women, Domestic Abuse and Sexual Violence: Statutory guidance under section 15 of the Violence against Women, Domestic Abuse and Sexual Violence (Wales) Act 2015 and section 6 of the Government of Wales Act 2006* (Welsh Government, January 2016).

[16] The Welsh Government completed a consultation on draft statutory guidance on 'Ask and Act' in January 2016 (Welsh Government, *A consultation on draft statutory guidance on 'Ask and Act' under section 15 of the Violence against Women, Domestic Abuse and Sexual Violence (Wales) Act 2015 and section 60 of the Government of Wales Act 2006* (WG26746, November 2015). As of 19 March 2018, there has been no response from the Government.

[17] Welsh Women's Aid, *Are you listening and am I being heard? Survivor Consultation: A report of the recommendations made by survivors of violence against women, domestic abuse and sexual violence, to inform the National Strategy in Wales* (Welsh Women's Aid, March 2016).

and colleges, accessible refuge support, and increased women's support groups, with one survivor commenting

> Government should hear from women, women who've been through it, on an ongoing basis; otherwise they'll come up with these ideas that won't work. Any of us could … there's enough of us who've gone through it so we can help.[18]

Similarly, further post-legislative scrutiny of the VAW Act delivered in December 2016 found that whilst the Act remains recognised as a ground-breaking piece of legislation, further practical improvements are necessary in order to improve the public sector response and effective implementation of the Act.[19] Welsh Women's Aid, again, called for a more integrated approach to delivery of the Act nationally and locally, and highlighted the resource implications of implementing the Act and the National Strategy in light of increasing demand for specialist services for survivors.

## IV. Significance

The VAW Act is a significant piece of legislation and the first in the UK to explicitly refer to violence against women in its title. However, it is not only the name of the Act that sets it as a landmark – its significance goes much further than that.

The Act introduced specific mechanisms which place duties on the Welsh Ministers as well as relevant authorities in Wales with regard to prevention of and response to gender-based violence, domestic abuse and sexual violence. As such, it places these bodies under a positive obligation to take practical and transparent steps to fulfil the purposes of the Act. An obligation to publish national and local strategies, as well as regular reporting mechanisms established under the Act, ensure a much needed level of transparency and accountability of the public sector with regard to preventing and responding to gender-based violence and domestic abuse. In addition, the role of National Adviser contributes towards an effective implementation of the Act and ensures regular monitoring of the situation in Wales regarding gender-based violence, domestic abuse and sexual violence. Placing positive duties on the Welsh Government and public sector authorities ensures a proactive and practical approach to combatting violence against women and domestic abuse and represents a new line of attack.

Furthermore, the context and history of drafting of the VAW Act highlight the significant role of Welsh women's organisations in raising public awareness about violence against women in Wales and taking practical steps to combat it. The activism of women's organisations, in particular the Wales Violence Against Women Action Group, was instrumental in influencing the National Assembly to prioritise combatting violence against women and girls and gave the necessary impetus for the legislative change in this area. Since the VAW Act came into force, Welsh women's organisations continue to play an essential role in scrutinising the progress of implementation of the Act, making suggestions for the necessary

[18] ibid 2.

[19] National Assembly for Wales Equality, Local Government and Communities Committee, *Is the Violence Against Women, domestic Abuse and Sexual Violence (Wales) Act 2015 working? Post-legislative scrutiny* (December 2016).

improvements, and monitoring the Welsh Government's compliance with its obligations set out in the VAW Act.

At the very least, the VAW Act reshaped the way in which the public sector in Wales is responding to violence against women, domestic abuse, and sexual violence. The new legislation made those issues a priority, both for the local government and public sector in Wales. It is certainly hoped that, in the long-term, the measures introduced by the Act will also have a transformative effect on public attitudes towards violence against women – a crucial element in prevention of these acts.

## Further Reading

- Christine Chinkin, 'Addressing violence against women in the Commonwealth within states' obligations under international law' (2014) 40(3) *Commonwealth Law Bulletin* 471–501.
- Sylvia Walby, 'Official statistics mask the extent of domestic violence in the UK', *The Conversation*, 15 July 2015.
- Welsh Women's Aid: http://www.welshwomensaid.org.uk/ (for up-to-date information regarding VAW in Wales).

# 90

# Section 2 of the Abusive Behaviour and Sexual Harm (Scotland) Act 2016

ERIKA RACKLEY

Section 2 of the Abusive Behaviour and Sexual Harm (Scotland) Act 2016 makes it a criminal office to disclose, or threaten to disclose, a photograph or film which shows, or appears to show, another person in an intimate situation. Introduced in response to the growing phenomenon of 'revenge porn', whereby vengeful ex-partners distribute private sexual images without the consent of their former partners, the offence also extends to the non-consensual distribution of other forms of image-based sexual abuse, notably so-called 'upskirt' images, those that are (often but not always) surreptitiously taken up a woman's skirt, and pornographic photoshopping, where, for example, an individual's Facebook profile picture is superimposed onto an explicit image. As such it was the first – and to date only – legislation in the UK and Ireland addressing varied forms of image-based sexual abuse.

## I. Context

Abuse and harassment of women are not new. Nor is the taking/distribution of private sexual images, with or without the party's consent, whether for sexual or non-sexual purposes. Without doubt, however, the prevalence of such behaviours has increased exponentially with the ubiquity of the smartphone and 'cloud' technology. Images quickly go viral, travelling around the world by text, email, or on dedicated 'revenge porn', regular pornography and/or social media websites. They are big business. Hunter Moore's notorious 'Is Anyone Up?' website, which regularly featured 'revenge porn', was said to receive over 300,000 unique visitors a day before it was closed down in 2012.[1] In 2016, it was estimated that there were around 3,000 dedicated 'revenge porn' websites worldwide[2] and more than 30 sites operating in the UK.[3] Although these sites host images of men as well as women,

[1] Dave Lee, 'Is Anyone Up's Hunter Moore: "The net's most hated man"?', *BBC News Online*, 20 April 2012.

[2] Walter DeKeseredy and Martin D Schwartz, 'Thinking Sociologically about Image-Based Sexual Abuse: The Contribution of Male Peer Support Theory' (2016) 2(4) *Sexualisation, Media, & Society* 1–8.

[3] Louise Ridley, 'Revenge Porn is Finally Illegal: Who are the Victims and Perpetrators of this Growing Phenomenon?', *Huffington Post*, 12 February 2015.

it is the images of women that are more frequently viewed and commented on.[4] The impact on the victim-survivor can be devastating: unemployment, loss of job opportunities, family and relationship breakdown, death and rape threats, physical and mental health difficulties, even suicide.

While revenge porn is perhaps the most familiar example of such behaviour, it is just one form of a range of gendered, sexualised forms of abuse which sit on a 'continuum of image-based sexual abuse'.[5] Other examples include the non-consensual creation and/or distribution of upskirt images, images that have been subject to pornographic photoshopping, recordings of sexual assaults and rape, and 'sextortion', whereby perpetrators typically coerce victims into creating and sharing images or performing sexual acts and threaten them with exposure unless they continue the activities. At other times, the images themselves may have been consensually taken but are non-consensually distributed after they have been hacked or stolen by a third party. Nor, often, does this form of abuse occur in isolation: research has demonstrated that threats to ensure the production of and then to reveal intimate photos are common within abusive relationships.[6]

Whatever the moniker, all forms of image-based sexual abuse share the same characteristics. They are all pernicious and gendered forms of sexual abuse. Not only are victim-survivors mostly women and girls, but the abuse and harassment they are subjected to are sexualised and misogynistic. The persistence of sexual double standards enables perpetrators to shame and humiliate victims. They all constitute a fundamental breach of the victim-survivor's privacy, dignity and sexual autonomy. They are all a form of cultural harm, contributing to the normalisation of non-consensual sexual activity and creating a climate in which women's sexual expression is not respected.[7]

In June 2013, Scottish Woman's Aid launched the 'Stop Revenge Porn Scotland' campaign.[8] Drawing inspiration from Holly Jacobs' 'End Revenge Porn' campaign launched in the US the previous year,[9] this was the first campaign in the UK to address the issue.[10] Its purpose was to 'start a public conversation about revenge porn: why it happens, how we can respond, and importantly, how we can prevent it'.[11] And they did. Women began to 'speak out' about their experiences of revenge porn.[12]

> I had never done anything like this before, but I trusted him and thought it might be fun. We made the video, and then watched a film and went to bed. I never thought much about what

[4] Abby Whitmarsh, 'Analysis of 28 Days of Data Scraped From a Revenge Pornography Website'. (*Everlasting Student*, 13 April 2015); Abby Whitmarsh, 'I wanna get statistical, Let me hear your numbers talk' (*Everlasting Student*, 14 April 2015).

[5] Clare McGlynn, Erika Rackley and Ruth Houghton, '"Beyond 'Revenge Porn': The Continuum of Image-Based Sexual Abuse' (2017) 25(1) *Feminist Legal Studies* 25–46; Clare McGlynn and Erika Rackley, 'Image-Based Sexual Abuse' (2017) 37(3) *Oxford Journal of Legal Studies* 534–61. On the problems associated with the term 'revenge porn', see Clare McGlynn and Erika Rackley, 'Not "revenge porn", but abuse: let's call it image-based sexual abuse' (*Everyday Victim Blaming*, 6 March 2016).

[6] Anastasia Powell, Asher Flynn and Nicola Henry, 'The picture of who is affected by "revenge porn" is more complex than we first thought', *The Conversation*, 8 May 2017.

[7] McGlynn and Rackley (2017), n 5 above.

[8] Women's Aid, 'Stop Revenge Porn Scotland': www.stoprevengepornscotland.wordpress.com/.

[9] Cyber Civil Rights Initiative, 'About': www.cybercivilrights.org/welcome/.

[10] Ellie Hutchinson, 'We need to talk about revenge porn', *New Statesman*, 5 October 2013.

[11] Ellie Hutchinson, 'Stop revenge porn' (*the f word blog*, 5 August 2013).

[12] See eg the Women's Aid, 'Women Speak Out': www.stoprevengepornscotland.wordpress.com/women-speak-out/.

> would happen to it if we split up. I suppose most normal people would delete it! As time went on he started criticizing me, but I was still pretty smitten. He used to come to my house and make remarks about how I did things. He was a little bit obsessive … I carried on with my life, started university. I had almost forgotten about the video. 11 months later I received a message asking 'is this you?' and a link to a video, the video had my name in it and where I lived … [Though the video has been taken down] I check the sites …, maybe 3 times a week, but in the beginning it was becoming an obsession 3 or 4 times a day. I felt worried if I couldn't access a computer. I still feel depressed, dirty and have self harmed a few times. I do feel I am doing much better and now I just want to be there for other victims, and raise awareness in the UK.[13]

A number of roundtables involving Rape Crisis Scotland, White Ribbon Scotland, Victim Support, and Police Scotland followed. In July 2013, a motion commending Scottish Women's Aid on its campaign received cross-party support[14] and was later debated in the Scottish Parliament.[15] Opening the debate, Nationalist Party MSP Christina McKelvie commented:

> Decades ago, domestic abuse was not talked about or recognised – women walked into doors or fell downstairs. Things have moved on, although sadly there are still people in abusive relationships who are too frightened to come forward. Their confidence has been eaten away by their partners so effectively that many end up convinced that somehow the abuse is all their own fault. It is therefore vital that the new stop revenge porn Scotland site gains the maximum profile. That is why I am having this debate in the chamber.[16]

Less than a year after the start of their campaign, the Lord Advocate (the chief public prosecutor for Scotland), Frank Mulholland QC, called for specific legislation to deal with growing problem of individuals posting so-called revenge porn on the internet.[17]

Meanwhile in England and Wales a campaign to introduce similar legislation, led by Maria Miller MP, was gaining ground.[18] In July 2014 Justice Secretary Chris Grayling MP told the House of Commons that there would be a 'serious discussion' in Government about the practice,[19] and by the following autumn a series of amendments were added to the Criminal Justice and Courts Bill then making its way through parliament. In February 2015, section 33 of the Criminal Justice and Courts Act 2015 made it a criminal offence to disclose private, sexual[20] photographs and films with intent to cause distress.[21] The Revenge Porn

[13] 'Emma's story', ibid.

[14] Motion S4M-07333: Christina McKelvie, Hamilton, Larkhall and Stonehouse, Scottish National Party, 24 July 2013.

[15] 'End Revenge Porn', Official Report: Meeting of the Parliament, Session 4, 11 September 2013: http://www.parliament.scot/parliamentarybusiness/report.aspx?r=9019&i=81427&c=0&s=revenge%2520porn.

[16] ibid 17:36.

[17] Jonathan Whitelaw, 'Call for internet revenge porn legislation', *The Scotsman*, 10 April 2014.

[18] See eg 'Revenge Pornography' HC Deb, 19 June 2014, vol 582 cols 1368–1376; Maria Miller, 'We must treat revenge porn as the crime it is', *The Telegraph*, 6 October 2014.

[19] Owen Bowcott, '"Revenge pornography" could soon be outlawed, says Chris Grayling', *The Guardian*, 2 July 2014.

[20] According to section 35(2) and (3) of the Act, a 'photograph or film is "private" if it shows something that is not of a kind ordinarily seen in public' and 'is "sexual" if (a) it shows all or part of an individual's exposed genitals or pubic area, (b) it shows something that a reasonable person would consider to be sexual because of its nature, or (c) its content, taken as a whole, is such that a reasonable person would consider it to be sexual'. A photo is not private and sexual if it is only such because it has been altered – thereby excluding so-called 'fake porn' or AI-assisted revenge porn (section 35(4) and (5)).

[21] The intent to distress requirement has been criticised. It means that a perpetrator who distributes private, sexual images without the consent of the individual/s depicted for, say, a joke or financial reward has not committed an offence.

Helpline, founded by Laura Higgins and later funded by the UK Government Equalities Office, opened in the same month.[22]

## II. The Landmark

As the House of Lords voted unanimously to support the new 'revenge porn' laws in England and Wales,[23] pressure was growing on the Scottish Government to introduce similar legislation. The Scottish Woman's Aid campaign was continuing and, in October 2014, Scottish Liberal Democrats wrote to the Scottish Justice Secretary, Kenny MacAskill, urging him to consider introducing a bespoke law.[24] In March 2015 the Scottish Government launched its *Equally Safe – Reforming the criminal law to address domestic abuse and sexual offences* consultation, which sought views on a number of criminal offences targeted at preventing violence against, and maximising the wellbeing and safety of, women and girls.[25] In particular, views were sought on a proposal to create a specific criminal offence aimed at addressing revenge porn.[26] Ninety-nine per cent of respondents agreed that a specific offence should be created.[27]

In October 2015, the Cabinet Secretary for Justice, Michael Matheson MSP, introduced the Abusive Behaviour and Sexual Harm Bill to the Scottish Parliament, which included a new specific offence for the non-consensual sharing of private, intimate images, intended to cover instances of 'revenge porn'.[28] This proposed to make it a criminal office to share or to threaten to share, without the consent of the person depicted, 'intimate' photographs or films; that is, showing people engaged in a sexual activity which would not usually be done in public, or with their genitals, buttocks or breasts exposed or covered only with underwear. Crucially, unlike the law in England and Wales, the offence would extend to threats to share a relevant image, to digitally enhanced or manipulated photographs or films (that is, so-called 'fake porn'), and would include situations where the perpetrator had recklessly caused fear, alarm or distress to the person shown in the image – such as forwarding the image for a joke or financial gain.

However, as in England and Wales, it did not extend to the distribution of 'upskirt' images as it was proposed that perpetrator would have a defence if the intimate image was taken in a public place and other members of the public were present.[29] Thus, though the *taking* of such images was prohibited under section 9 of the Sexual Offences (Scotland) Act 2009,

[22] Gareth May, 'What It's Like to Run a Phone Line for Victims of Revenge Porn' (*Broadly*, 10 May 2016). Since its launch in January 2015, the Helpline has received over 11,000 calls, three-quarters of which were from women. Numbers have increased by around 40% each year (Rebecca Sharp, Helpline Practitioner, Revenge Porn Helpline speaking at *Combating Revenge Pornography: Tackling Perpetrators, Supporting Victims and Raising Awareness*, Public Policy Exchange, 19 April 2018).

[23] The provisions were later extended to Northern Ireland by virtue of sections 50–53 of the Justice Act (Northern Ireland) 2016.

[24] 'New law to tackle "revenge porn" in Scotland', *BBC News Online*, 22 October 2014.

[25] Scottish Government, *Equally Safe – Reforming the criminal law to address domestic abuse and sexual offences*, Scottish Government Consultation Paper, March 2015.

[26] ibid [2.12]–[2.33].

[27] Graham Ross, 'SPICe Briefing: Abusive Behaviour and Sexual Harm (Scotland) Bill', 12 November 2015, 9.

[28] ibid 3.

[29] ibid 11.

their subsequent distribution – whether by the person taking the image or another – was not. This omission did not go unnoticed.[30] Giving oral evidence to the Justice Committee, Clare McGlynn commented:

> *Clare McGlynn*: ... we need to be discussing the examples where real harm is caused to many victims – upskirting is an example of that ... I think that we should be ... worried about the prevalence of images being taken surreptitiously up women's skirts and then being distributed without their consent. At the moment, such activity would not be covered by the bill's provisions.
>
> *Elaine Murray*: Upskirting is not a term that I have ever heard before – I rather wish I never had.
>
> *Clare McGlynn*: There are whole websites dedicated to upskirting ...
>
> *Elaine Murray*: Goodness![31]

By the time the Bill had reached its second stage, Murray was convinced. Introducing an amendment to the Bill to cover the distribution of upskirt images, she continued

> Such images often end up on websites that are dedicated to the sharing of non-consensually taken private sexual photographs and/or pornographic websites. I understand that those sites are big business. In May 2015, one such site was exposed by the *Mail on Sunday*, and it was said to be receiving 70,000 views a day and was valued at £130 million.[32]

At the third stage, others agreed. An additional sentence was added to the 'public place' defence, limiting it to situations where the person in the image 'was not in the intimate situation as a result of a deliberate act of another person to which [they] did not agree' (section 2(5)(b)), making the distribution of upskirt images a criminal offence.

The Bill was passed unanimously on 22 March 2016 and received Royal Assent on 28 April 2016.

## III. What Happened Next

In March 2017, the Scottish government ran a large public awareness campaign, supported by Scottish Women's Aid, Rape Crisis Scotland, and others and featuring nude images covered in crime tape, ahead of the law coming into force in July 2017.[33] Reports of the first conviction followed in September.[34] However, concerns have since been raised about the number of cases reaching court. Reports in March 2018, indicated that just 39 per cent of reported cases between July and December 2017 were classed as 'detected' or ready to be referred to the courts.[35] The same reports revealed that 92 per cent of victims were women, with just under 50 per cent in their 20s.[36]

[30] See Written Submission to the Justice Committee from Clare McGlynn and Erika Rackley, 5 November 2015 (ABSH3); Justice Committee, Stage 1 Report of the Abusive Behaviour and Sexual Harm (Scotland) Bill (SP Paper 885, 21 January 2016) [81].

[31] Evidence given to Justice Committee, 'Abusive Behaviour and Sexual Harm (Scotland) Bill: Stage 1', 17 November 2015, col 62.

[32] Official Report: Justice Committee, 1 March 2016, col 42.

[33] 'Hard-hitting posters highlight new "revenge porn" law', *BBC News Online*, 26 March 2017.

[34] 'First conviction under new "revenge porn" law in Scotland', *BBC News Online*, 4 September 2017.

[35] Chris Green, 'Less than half "revenge porn" cases in Scotland reach courts', *The Scotsman*, 7 March 2018.

[36] The figures for England and Wales were, at least initially, slightly better. In 2016–17, the CPS prosecuted 465 cases in relation to the offence of disclosing private sexual photographs and films with an intent to cause

In England and Wales high-profile campaigns – involving victim-survivors of upskirting,[37] academics,[38] and women's organisations, including Rape Crisis, Women's Aid, the Women's Institute, Mumsnet, Girlguiding and Everyday Sexism[39] – arguing for further legal changes to criminalise upskirting images, have finally been heeded. In June 2018, after Liberal Democrat MP, Wera Hobhouse's Private Member's Bill on the topic was controversially objected to by Christopher Chope MP, the Government introduced the Voyeurism (Offences) (No 2) Bill 2017–2019.[40] Given the strength of feeling on the issue, and level of high-profile support, at the time of writing (June 2018) its progression to the statute book seems assured.

However, while this new law would criminalise the creation of such images, it would not criminalise their *distribution*. It is a further example of an ad hoc and piecemeal approach to legal regulation in this area. As noted by the Fawcett Society in their *Sex Discrimination Law Review*, published in 2018, victim-survivors of other forms of image-based sexual abuse – such as pornographic photoshopping or so-called 'fake porn' – or whose perpetrators are motivated by something other than 'an intention to cause distress' – financial gain or amusement, for example – remain unprotected.[41] Nor are victim-survivors of image-based sexual abuse – with the exception of those who have been upskirted – guaranteed the anonymity provided to victim-survivors of other sexual offences.[42]

In the meantime, other victim-survivors of revenge porn have turned to the civil law. The beginning of 2018 saw the success of two such claims. In the first, Facebook accepted liability under misuse of private information, negligence and a breach of data protection laws after a naked photo of a teenager from Northern Ireland was posted on a so-called 'shame page'. In the second, Chrissy Chambers (a singer and video blogger) sued her former boyfriend for harassment, breach of confidence and misuse of private information after he secretly recorded them having sex and posted the recording on a pornographic website. Both cases were settled out of court, and so offer little by way of clarity as to the potential success of the various actions. However, what they do is put both website and social media

distress, an increase from 205 the previous year (Crown Prosecution Service, *Violence against Women and Girls Report 2016–2017* (10th edn, November 2017) A43). However, while the number of reported cases continues to increase, figures obtained by the BBC in June 2018 suggested that of the 7,806 incidents of revenge porn reported since the new law in 2015, 2,813 were dropped by the victim ('Revenge porn: one in three allegations dropped', *BBC News Online*, 14 June 2018).

[37] 'I had upskirt photos taken of me – sign to make this a sexual offence in England & Wales': https://www.thepetitionsite.com/takeaction/887/239/401/. Currently the law on voyeurism, introduced in 2003 to capture 'peeping toms', requires that the perpetrator spy on people in private – such as in changing rooms or toilets – for sexual gratitification. As upskirting mostly takes place in public – in supermarkets, on public transport, at music festivals – voyeurism does not apply. See further Clare McGlynn and Erika Rackley, 'Why "upskirting" needs to be made a sex crime', *The Conversation*, 15 August 2017.

[38] See eg Clare McGlynn's evidence to the House of Commons Women and Equalities Committee (Oral evidence: Women's everyday experience of sexism and sexual harassment, HC 592, 6 December 2017); Erika Rackley and Clare McGlynn, '"Upskirting" and "revenge porn": the need for a comprehensive law', *The Conversation*, 16 June 2018.

[39] End Violence Against Women, 'Women's groups urge Government to "go further" with proposed Domestic Violence Bill': www.endviolenceagainstwomen.org.uk/womens-groups-urge-government-to-go-further-with-proposed-domestic-violence-bill/.

[40] 'Upskirting law to be passed soon, says Theresa May', 16 June 2018.

[41] Fawcett Society, *Sex Discrimination Law Review: Final Report* (January 2018) 8.

[42] See further, Clare McGlynn, 'The Law Must Protect All Victims Of Image-Based Sexual Abuse – Not Just Upskirting', *Huffington Post*, *BBC News Online*, 9 March 2018.

operators and perpetrators of image-based sexual abuse on notice: the civil law has teeth in this context and – if it bites – you will be liable for substantial damages.[43]

## IV. Significance

Section 2 of the Abusive Behaviour and Sexual Harm (Scotland) Act 2016 is unusual in delivering more than it promised. Sold as a new law to address the problem of revenge porn, from the outset its provisions have gone beyond this. By the time it was passed, the so-called 'revenge porn law' provides a bespoke response to multiple forms of image-based sexual abuse. As such it is a key milestone in ongoing efforts to protect and respect women's privacy and sexual autonomy both on and off line.

Of course there is more to do. A new law is not – and can never be – a silver bullet. The fight to ensure the safety and wellbeing of women and girls continues. But law can be, and often is, a key lever for cultural change. The Act is also a clear example of the power of sustained and collective feminist campaigning. The legacy of Scottish Women's Aid and the women to whom they gave a voice in June 2013 can be seen not only in legislative change in Scotland in 2016, but in the ongoing visibility of and societal responses to image-based sexual abuse across the UK and beyond. The tide of abuse, harassment and violence against women and girls will – we have to believe – one day stop. And when it does, the extent to which feminist activists, academics and parliamentarians have stood on the shoulders of each other and those who have gone before will be apparent.

## Further Reading

- Clare McGlynn and Erika Rackley, 'Image-Based Sexual Abuse' (2017) 37(3) *Oxford Journal of Legal Studies* 534–61.
- Clare McGlynn, Erika Rackley and Ruth Houghton, '"Beyond Revenge Porn": The Continuum of Image-Based Sexual Abuse' (2017) 25(1) *Feminist Legal Studies* 25–46.
- Clare McGlynn and Erika Rackley, 'Not "revenge porn", but abuse: let's call it image-based sexual abuse' (*Everyday Victim Blaming*, 6 March 2016).

[43] See Alan Reid, 'Landmark revenge porn cases are a stark warning for perpetrators and social networks', *The Conversation*, 17 January 2018; Kirsty Horsey and Erika Rackley, 'Tort Law' in Rosemary Auchmuty (ed), *Great Debates in Gender and Law* (Palgrave, 2018).

# 91

# First Woman President of the UK Supreme Court, Brenda Hale, 2017

ERIKA RACKLEY

In September 2017, Brenda Hale became the first woman President of the UK Supreme Court. Her appointment follows her other ground-breaking appointments as the first woman Deputy President, as the first woman appointed to the newly-established Supreme Court and as the first – and only – woman law lord, following her elevation to the Appellate Committee of the House of Lords. Without doubt, Hale is – both currently and historically – the UK's most senior woman judge. Feminist academic, law reformer, judge; she has played a key role in improving the position of many women, children and men.

## I. Life

Born in Leeds in 1945, Hale has spent much of her life in male-dominated institutions. As a young girl she lived in the boarding house of Scorton Boys Grammar School where her father was headmaster and her mother (who had had to give up teaching when she married)[1] ran the boarding house. Excelling at school – she was the only pupil in her primary school class to pass the eleven-plus examination, enabling her to attend a selective grammar school – and encouraged by her headmistress,[2] Hale won an open exhibition to Girton College, Cambridge, joining the handful of women at the University reading law. On graduating, top of her class and with a starred first, she joined the law school at Manchester University in 1966, combining an academic post initially with study for, and later practice at, the Manchester Bar.[3] At Manchester, she specialised in social welfare and family law, authoring a number of groundbreaking texts including *Mental Health Law* (1975), *Parents and Children: The Law of Parental Responsibility* (1977), *Family, Law and Society: Cases and Materials* (1983) and ***Women and the Law*** (with Susan Atkins) (1984), and founding and

[1] **Education Act 1944**.

[2] Paula Thompson interview with Brenda Hale for the National Life Story Collection (Hale, Brenda Marjorie, *National Life Story Collection: Legal Lives, British Library Sounds*, recorded 25 November 2008, 16, 22, 23 March 2010).

[3] It is worth noting here that Hale chose to go the Law School at Manchester because of its policy of encouraging its academics also to practise. Had she not, she would not have met the statutory qualifying criteria to be a judge (Thompson, ibid).

editing the *Journal of Social Welfare Law*. Following stints as a legal member of the Mental Health Review Tribunal for the North West and as a member of the Council on Tribunals (a watchdog body for Tribunal System), she was the first woman from an academic non-practising background to be appointed as an assistant recorder in 1982, a part-time position which involved sitting as a judge for 20 days a year in the County and Crown Courts. Two years later, she became the first woman (and youngest ever) Commissioner at the Law Commission, leading the family law team. Over the next 10 years, she was at the forefront of a number of law reform projects on children, divorce and mental capacity, the benefits of which can still be seen today, most notably in the Children Act 1989 and the **Mental Capacity Act 2005**.

Hale continued to sit as a part-time judge while at the Law Commission, both as a recorder (after her promotion in 1989) and as a Deputy High Court judge in the Family Division. In 1994, she was 'tapped on the shoulder' to become a full-time judge sitting in the Family Division of the High Court. She joined the Court of Appeal five years later, when **Elizabeth Butler-Sloss** became President of the Family Division, and remained there until her elevation to the House of Lords in 2004 – an achievement which, like so many senior women in the legal profession, she has suggested was (at least in part) the result of being the 'right woman at the right time'.[4]

## II. Context

Though formal barriers preventing women from becoming lawyers were removed by virtue of the **Sex Disqualification (Removal) Act 1919**, as recently as the mid-1970s men solicitors continued to outnumber their women counterparts by 20 to one, while nearly half of all sets of chambers were still to have their first woman member.[5] In 1976, just over two per cent of full-time, salaried judges were women, and only two women – **Elizabeth Lane** and **Rose Heilbron** – sat in the High Court.[6] However, by 1987 women not only accounted for just under half of law graduates in England and Wales, but were also outperforming their male counterparts.[7] At the same time women accounted for 37 per cent of those called to the Bar, an increase from just 8.2 per cent in 1970.[8] By 1992–93 half of those entering the solicitor's profession[9] and 42.7 per cent of those called to the Bar were women.[10]

Despite this apparent 'flood' of women entering the judicial pipeline, far fewer have made it into the upper echelons of the judiciary. When Hale joined the High Court

[4] ibid.

[5] Albie Sachs and Joan Hoff Wilson, *Sexism and the Law: A Study of Male Beliefs and Judicial Bias* (Martin Robertson, 1978) 174.

[6] Helena Kennedy, 'Women at the Bar' in Robert Hazell (ed), *The Bar on Trial* (Quartet Books Ltd, 1978) 148, 149. Kennedy strongly refutes the assumption that there were not sufficient women in the pool of potential judges to allow for the appointment of more women judges, even in 1976. She suggests that there were 80 women eligible for judicial appointment, of whom just 17 (21%) were appointed, compared to 53% of the 150 men in the same pool.

[7] Peter Marks, *Annual Statistical Report 1988* (Law Society, 1988) figures 6.2 and 6.4.

[8] Bar Council figures (on file with author).

[9] John Jenkins and Danielle Walker, *Annual Statistical Report 1993* (Law Society, 1993) tables 11.8 and 12.7.

[10] Bar Council figures (on file with author).

bench in 1994 she was only the tenth woman ever to do so. Indeed, so few women had been appointed to the High Court that she inherited the judicial robes of Margaret Booth (the third woman appointee to the Court (1979)) who had in turn acquired them from Elizabeth Lane (1965).[11] Further up the judicial hierarchy, it took 32 years following Lane's groundbreaking appointment to the High Court bench for a woman to be promoted to the Court of Appeal (Butler-Sloss in 1988) and a further 11 years until she was joined by another woman (Hale in 1999). By the turn of the millennium, just 14 women had made it into the senior judiciary; that is, the High Court and above, in England and Wales.[12] And, crucially, no woman had ever been appointed to the UK's most senior court.

Hale's appointment to the Appellate Committee of the House of Lords in 2004 was thus made against a background of increasing disquiet at the absence of women in the senior judiciary. The failure to appoint a woman following the retirement of Lord Slynn in 2002 had been met with widespread dismay. On any measure the appointment of a woman to the House of Lords was long overdue, not least because the United States had appointed its first woman Supreme Court Justice some 23 years earlier (Sandra Day O'Connor in 1981), followed quickly by Canada, Australia and New Zealand. Hale's appointment also came at a time of significant constitutional change resulting in, among other things, the creation of the UK Supreme Court and the Judicial Appointments Commission (which started work in 2006). The then Lord Chancellor, Lord Falconer, had promised to go not only go 'boldly' but also 'further and faster' than any of the previous incumbents of his role in order to deliver 'real change' to the judiciary.[13] By the mid-2000s, buoyed by reports that the number of women and BME judges was 'rocketing',[14] expectations were high – a more diverse judiciary seemed – at last – to be a real possibility. After all, now that the final judicial glass ceiling had been broken there was no reason why Hale's appointment would not be the first of many. And, if that was the case, then not only would this ensure the legitimacy of the judiciary itself but there was also a possibility that the influx of women judges would, to use Hale's words, 'make a difference to how judging is done'.[15]

## III. What Happened Next

Unlike the appointment of Lord Walker 15 months earlier, Hale's appointment was widely reported in the British press. With the exception of the *Daily Mail* (which inevitably saw it as 'the worst thing that had happened since the last bad thing that happened involving a

[11] Thompson, n 2 above. The robes were later passed on to Jill Black, now Lady Black, the second woman appointed to the UK Supreme Court.

[12] Lady Hazel Cosgrove was appointed to the Court of Session (Scotland's highest civil court) having sat on a temporary basis since 1992, and was promoted to the Inner House in 2003. Denise McBride and Siobhan Keegan, the first women appointed to the Northern Irish High Court, were appointed in 2015.

[13] Lord Falconer, 'Increasing Judicial Diversity: The Next Steps', Commission for Judicial Appointments, Institute of Mechanical Engineers, London, 2 November 2005.

[14] Frances Gibb, 'More women join the judiciary', *The Times*, 1 February 2006.

[15] Brenda Hale, 'Equality and the judiciary: why should we want more women judges?' [2001] *Public Law* 489, 496.

woman and an important job'),[16] it was widely welcomed, with Vera Baird MP suggesting that Hale would 'outshine' her male colleagues.[17]

And so she has. In 2009, she moved with a number of her colleagues out of the Parliament buildings over the road to the refurbished Middlesex Guildhall, the site of the new Supreme Court, to become one of the first cohort of, and first woman, Supreme Court Justices. In 2013, she became the Court's second Deputy President, and in 2017 its third President. Not only is she the longest serving Supreme Court Justice, she is also one of the hardest working. To date, Hale has contributed to more Supreme Court decisions than any other serving or retired Justice.[18] Over the years she has brought her sharp intellect and distinctive perspective to many of the key issues of the day, including Female Genital Mutilation, family home ownership, mental health and capacity, religious freedom, equality and children's rights, pre-nuptial agreements, pensions, domestic abuse and sexual violence and social welfare provision. Unlike many other women judges, who dismiss their gender as 'irrelevant', Hale has been highly conscious of her position as, the (then) only woman on the Supreme Court, alluding to it in her judgments – see for example, her comment in ***Radmacher v Granatino***[19] that there was 'a gender dimension to the issue' under consideration by the Court (the enforcement of a pre-nuptial agreement) 'which some may think ill-suited to decision by a court consisting of eight men and one woman'[20] – and referring to it more starkly in extra-judicial speeches and interviews:

> It would be good to think that you had invited me here because I am the wisest, most learned, but yet most approachable and entertaining judge you can think of. But I know that that is not true. You have invited me here because of my scarcity value: I am the only woman judge in the highest court of the United Kingdom and indeed the only woman judge there has ever been at that level in this country. This is a truly lamentable state of affairs.[21]

In fact, it took 17 years and 18 appointments for another woman to be appointed to the Supreme Court. Hale's first duty as President in October 2017 was to swear in her first woman judicial colleague since her time in the Court of Appeal: Lady Black. The slow progress toward diversity is not for want of effort on Hale's part. Over the years, she has given countless speeches and interviews, as well as evidence to Parliamentary committees and reports, on the importance of a diverse judiciary. She has mentored and supported

[16] Hale referring to Melanie Phillips when introducing Helena Kennedy's 'Human Rights for Women: Liberation or Mere Rhetoric?' (Lecture at the London School of Economics, 8 March 2004).

[17] Robert Verkaik, 'Hale appointed first ever law lady', *The Independent*, 23 October 2003.

[18] Lords Mance, Kerr and Clarke were also part of the first cohort of Supreme Court Justices. However Lords Mance and Kerr were elevated to the House of Lords after Hale, and Lord Clarke was appointed directly to the Supreme Court (Rosemary Hunter and Erika Rackley, 'Judicial Leadership on the UKSC' (2018) 38 *Legal Studies* 191–220).

[19] *Radmacher v Granatino* [2010] UKSC 42.

[20] [2010] UKSC 42, [137]. Not that Hale's self-reflection is limited to her gender. In *Edwards v Chesterfield Royal Hospital NHS Foundation Trust* [2011] UKSC 58 – a case concerning the availability of damages for employees dismissed for good reasons, but in breach of the procedures specified in their contracts of employment – she dissented from the majority's decision in favour of the employers, beginning her judgment with the recognition that 'I should perhaps declare an interest, as the only member of this court to have spent a substantial proportion of her working life as an employee rather than as a self-employed barrister or tenured office holder': [104].

[21] Hale, 'It's a man's world: redressing the balance', Norfolk Law Lecture, University of East Anglia, 16 February 2012.

women law students, lawyers and judges – through her work, among other things, with the UK Association of Women Judges and International Association of Women Judges. She has even, on occasion, given suitably qualified women a gentle poke to put themselves forward:

> I may well have been appointed because the powers that be realised the need for a woman. I am completely unembarrassed about that, because they were right, and I hope that I have justified their confidence in me. I don't think that all the talk about the best women being deterred is a plot to put [suitably qualified women] off, but I am sure that they should not be deterred by talk such as this. We owe it to our sex, but also to the future of the law and the legal system, to step up to the plate.[22]

With the appointment of Lady Arden, who joins the Court in October 2018, Hale's efforts appear to be bearing fruit.

## IV. Significance

Of course, the appointment of the first woman President of the UK Supreme Court was always going to attract attention,[23] as was the appointment of the first woman to the UK's most senior court – ending over 600 years of male exclusivity – and rightly so. Both are key strategic milestones in the glacial progress toward a diverse judiciary.[24] For over a decade, Hale's solitary presence acted as a beacon exposing the continued isolation of woman within the judiciary and public life more generally.

However, Hale's contribution to the history of women in law and significance for women more generally is not limited to her landmark appointments. It lies also in what she has done in this and previous roles to reform, interpret and develop the law and in her willingness to 'take a different line' to her male colleagues.[25] As journalist Anne Perkins wrote,

> Let in someone from outside, and it becomes clear what's been missing. Lady Hale has politely jolted the thinking of some of her peers on to a different track; she has shown how the law can be approached from more than one perspective without undermining the law itself. She has done it against that chorus of disbelief so familiar to women in authority, a muttering of criticism that has not always been discreet, and she has survived to change the law.[26]

## Further Reading

- Rosemary Hunter, 'A Conversation with Brenda Hale' (2008) 16 *Feminist Legal Studies* 237.

[22] Hale, 'Appointments to the Supreme Court' in Graham Gee and Erika Rackley (eds), *Debating Judicial Appointments in an Age of Diversity* (Routledge, 2017) 302, 312.

[23] Erika Rackley, 'Celebrate Lady Hale – then make senior judiciary more diverse', *The Guardian*, 23 July 2017.

[24] Colm O'Cinneide and Kate Malleson, 'Are quotas for judicial appointments lawful under EU law?' (*UK Constitutional Law Blog*, 12 November 2014).

[25] Alan Paterson, *Final Judgment: The Last Law Lords and the Supreme Court* (Hart Publishing, 2013) 134–35.

[26] Anne Perkins, 'Thank you, Lady Hale, for shifting the supreme court's view on marriage', *The Guardian*, 8 February 2017.

- Rosemary Hunter and Erika Rackley, 'Judicial Leadership on the UKSC' (2018) 38 *Legal Studies* 191.
- Erika Rackley, *Women, Judging and the Judiciary: From Difference to Diversity* (Routledge, 2013) chapters 5 and 6.
- First 100 Years Interview with Lady Hale: https://www.youtube.com/watch?v=ZokbQ4e312M.

# 92

# Thirty-sixth Amendment to the Irish Constitution, 2018

FIONA DE LONDRAS

On 25 May 2018 Article 40.3.3 of the Irish Constitution was repealed by majority vote in a referendum.

The provision, introduced in 1983 and known as 'the 8th Amendment', imposed a near-absolute ban on abortion in Ireland as a result of its recognition of the 'right to life of the unborn … with due regard to the equal right to life of the mother'. Subsequent amendments introduced in 1992 ameliorated some of the worst effects of the provision by allowing for a right to travel to access medical services that were legal abroad, and a right to information on such services, albeit on a very tightly regulated basis. On 29 January 2018 the Irish Government announced that a referendum would be held to repeal Article 40.3.3 and replace it with the 36th Amendment to the Constitution ('Provision may be made by law for the regulation of termination of pregnancies'). In March 2018 the Oireachtas passed the Thirty-sixth Amendment to the Constitution Bill 2018, and the referendum took place on 25 May 2018.

Once certified by the President (when all legal challenges to the referendum have been concluded), this will be followed by the introduction of new legislation allowing for lawful abortion in Ireland. The proposed new law would allow abortion without restriction as to reason up to 12 weeks, where there is a risk to the pregnant person's life or a risk of serious harm to her health after 12 weeks and until foetal viability, and in cases of fatal foetal anomaly without gestational time limit. This will replace the **Protection of Life During Pregnancy Act 2013**, which only allows abortion where there is a real and substantial risk to the life of the pregnant person. It will also repeal legislation that censors, prohibits, and regulates abortion information.[1]

## I. Context

Abortion has been a crime throughout the entire existence of the Irish state. Until 2013 this was by means of the Offences against the Person Act 1861. Criminalisation was reaffirmed in section 22 of the Protection of Life During Pregnancy Act 2013.

[1] Regulation of Information (Services Outside the State for Termination of Pregnancies) Act 1995, s 16; Censorship Act 1929, s 7; Censorship Act 1946.

In 1983 the 8th Amendment was put to the People following a concerted effort by the Pro-Life Amendment Campaign, which leveraged the dominance of the Catholic Church, the intense conservatism of politics, medicine and law, and a period of extreme political instability to extract a promise from the Government that a referendum would be held. So strong was their influence that the referendum went ahead even though the proposed wording was opposed by the then Attorney General, Peter Sutherland, who expressed concerns about its lack of clarity and its potential to place Ireland in breach of its international human rights obligations in the future.[2] A majority voted in favour of its installation in the Constitution.

This provision had significant political and legal impacts that greatly restricted the reproductive agency of women in Ireland.

Contraception only became legal in 1979,[3] and then only for bona fide family planning purposes (in practice, only for married women whose husbands consented). Women who became pregnant when unmarried were still routinely confined to carceral institutions such as Magdalene Laundries and Mother and Baby Homes.[4] In that socially repressive context, the 8th Amendment was both a backlash against the limited gains of women's liberation movements and a pre-emptive strike against any further such gains. It meant, in political terms, that even if the Oireachtas wanted to make abortion legal in anything other than the most limited circumstances of near-certain death for the pregnant woman it could not; any such legislation would be challenged and struck down as unconstitutional. It also meant that successive Governments could (and did) abrogate responsibility for this essential part of reproductive healthcare, not even providing bereavement counselling for people who travelled to end a pregnancy following a diagnosis of a fatal foetal anomaly until 2016 when the UN Human Rights Committee found that Irish law violated the right to be free from torture, inhuman and degrading treatment or punishment under the International Covenant on Civil and Political Rights.[5]

The legal impacts were also significant. In spite of claims to the contrary during the 1983 referendum campaign, court cases were brought to ensure that the 8th Amendment would isolate women in crisis pregnancy to the greatest extent possible. The Society for the Protection of Unborn Children successfully litigated to ensure that foetal rights could be vindicated at the suit of someone not directly involved in a case because of the public interest involved in protecting unborn life, and also succeeded in securing injunctions against the provision of any kind of information or assistance to women about abortion services elsewhere.[6] Women's health initiatives such as Open Door Counselling and the Well Woman Centre were prevented from supporting women in making appointments for abortion in the UK.[7] Student activists – including Ivana Bacik, who contributes to this volume – were

[2] Peter Sutherland's 1983 advice on the 8th Amendment, published in the *Irish Times*, 13 January 2018.

[3] **Health (Family Planning) Act 1979**.

[4] **Concluding Observations of the UN Committee against Torture, Recommendation to Ireland Regarding the Magdalene Laundries (2011)**.

[5] UN Human Rights Committee, *Mellet v Ireland*, Comm No 2324/2013, UN Doc CCPR/C/116/D/2324/2013 (17 November 2016).

[6] *Attorney General (ex rel The Society for the Protection of Unborn Children Ireland Ltd) v Open Door Counselling Limited and the Dublin Wellwoman Centre Ltd* [1988] 1 IR 593; Case C-159/90, *The Society for the Protection of Unborn Children Ireland Ltd v Grogan* [1991] ECR I-4685.

[7] ibid.

threatened with imprisonment for printing the contact details of abortion clinics in student union publications. Women and girls were stopped at ports if they were considered to be travelling for abortion. Legally, pregnancy was a trap from which a woman could not escape, or at least not without undertaking significant illegal activity.

Activist groups such as the Women's Information Network and the Irish Women's Abortion Support Group did what they could subversively to distribute information, providing material and moral support to women who travelled to England for abortion. However, basic amenities such as telephones were not yet available in every home (sometimes not even every village), and many women were simply forced to continue with their pregnancies.

The harrowing reality of the impact of the 8th Amendment was made clear to all in 1992 when the High Court enjoined a teenage girl, who had been the victim of rape and was suicidal, from travelling for an abortion. In the High Court's estimation, the certain death of the foetus in abortion outweighed the possible death of the girl by suicide, which could be averted by the provision of appropriate care. The *X Case*, as it is known, led to mass public demonstrations and outrage. Famously, the Martyn Turner cartoon in the *Irish Times* – a cultural staple of Irish political and newspaper life – depicted a young girl holding a teddy bear, in an Ireland surrounded by a fortress, with the caption '17th February 1992 – the introduction of internment in Ireland … for 14 year old girls'. The Supreme Court then found that abortion was legal under the 8th Amendment where there was a 'real and substantial risk to the life as distinct from the health' of the pregnant person, and that risk to life could include a risk of suicide.[8]

Since then, anti-abortion campaigners have focused on efforts to reverse this: to say that suicide is not a risk to life that would allow for legal abortion. The People rejected such a reversal twice – in 1992 and 2002 – but even in the debates on the Protection of Life During Pregnancy Act 2013, the implicit assumption that women would pretend to be suicidal – and that doctors would believe them – in order to access abortion was propagated.[9] The 2013 Act made it considerably harder to access abortion in cases of suicidal ideation than in cases of risk to life from physical illness.

Although information and travel were constitutionally protected by referenda that directly followed the *X Case* described above, these rights were not positively constructed. The state would not stop someone from travelling for abortion, but it would not help either, no matter how poor, sick or isolated a pregnant person was.

Women who did travel often did so alone, in secrecy. During abortion travel they were vulnerable to abusive partners, and to predators who knew that Irish women who came for abortion often did so in secret, and that if they assaulted them the women would never tell because nobody knew they had travelled for abortion. Many women who told of their abortion experiences reported realising that if something went wrong nobody would know because they had not told anyone where they were. Activism helps: the Abortion Support Network provides funds, support, beds and assistance to women who seek it. Networks of activists across the island of Ireland also help. The online availability of the abortion pill means that thousands of Irish women self-medicate, either getting pills from Women on

[8] *Attorney General v X* [1992] 1 IR 1.

[9] See eg Brian Walsh TD, Dáil Debates, 10 July 2013 and further discussion of the Protection of Life During Pregnancy Act 2013 in this collection.

Web or Women Help Women, sometimes delivered to Northern Ireland and then brought to the Republic through an activist trail, or from activist networks acting illegally in Ireland. In practice, abortion is available, but a crime.

The 8th Amendment impacted all pregnancies. The state's duty under the 8th Amendment to defend and vindicate the right to life of the unborn, deployed in the patriarchal and sometimes violent context of obstetric medicine, meant that women were often directly or indirectly threatened with court action if they tried to make decisions about pregnancy considered to endanger foetal life or health. Women who sought natural labour against the advice of their doctors were sometimes brought to court to seek orders compelling C-sections.[10] Pregnant women are still the only category of adults with capacity who do not have the right to refuse consent to medical treatment in Ireland.[11]

The 8th Amendment made pregnancy a profoundly diminishing experience for women; for the duration of a pregnancy the state's only duty to a woman was to ensure that she was still alive at the end of the pregnancy. Her bodily integrity, privacy, right to information, sense of self, autonomy and agency were all subordinated to the constitutional right to life of the foetus.[12]

## II. The Landmark

In 1983, the Anti-Amendment Campaign, led by barrister Catherine Forde, forecast that the 8th Amendment would harm women. The Campaign, and activists in the women's movement who supported it, agitated constantly for the whole 35 years of the 8th's existence for its repeal. Then, in the early 2010s, this activism began to become a social movement.

The death of Savita Halappanavar, who died from sepsis during a miscarriage in 2011, mobilised new activists to demand change articulated in a simple but profoundly powerful word: REPEAL. The Abortion Rights Campaign (ARC) swelled in numbers. The March for Choice became a yearly show of strength with tens of thousands of people taking to the streets. The Coalition to Repeal the 8th was founded, bringing together dozens of interest groups, from trades unions to pro-choice groups across professions (doctors, lawyers, pharmacists etc). There were significant artistic interventions, and first-person narrative projects aiming to de-stigmatise abortion.[13] People began to buy and wear merchandise (most notably the black sweaters with white 'REPEAL' decal designed by Anna Cosgrave), and Irish diaspora organised to mobilise significant international solidarity (for example, the London-Irish Abortion Rights Campaign).[14]

Pro-choice politicians began to speak out, sometimes from unexpected places such as local politics and the back benches of conservative Fine Gael, as well as from well-established socialist and feminist pockets of Irish politics: Independent TDs and Senators,

[10] *Health Service Executive v B* [2016] IEHC 605.

[11] HSE, *National Consent Policy* (2014, revised May 2016).

[12] Fiona de Londras and Mairead Enright, *Repealing the 8th: Reforming Irish Abortion Law* (Policy Press, 2018), chapter 1.

[13] See, eg, Jesse Jones, *Tremble Tremble* (57th International Art Exhibition of La Biennale di Venezia); Sarah Maria Griffin, 'We Face this Land' (2016); x-ile (http://www.x-ileproject.com); Everyday Stories (http://everydaystories.org).

[14] London-Irish Abortion Rights Campaign: https://londonirisharc.com.

the Labour Party, Solidarity, People Before Profit, the Anti Austerity Alliance.[15] In the General Election campaign of 2016, all political parties apart from Fianna Fáil addressed the 8th Amendment in their manifestos, promising everything from repeal and the introduction of lawful abortion in some or all circumstances (Labour, Sinn Féin, Anti-Austerity Alliance, People Before Profit, Green Party), to the establishment of some form of deliberative assembly to discuss potential constitutional and/or legislative change (Fine Gael, Social Democrats; such a proposal was also endorsed by Fianna Fáil leader, Micheál Martin, in a radio interview during the campaign).

Following an indecisive election a Fine Gael-led Government was formed, with a small number of Independent deputies joining Cabinet in ministerial roles, including long-time social justice advocate Katherine Zappone, who had made repeal part of her election manifesto. As a result, the *Programme for Partnership Government* included a commitment to establish a 'Citizens' Assembly' to discuss, *inter alia*, the future of the 8th Amendment.[16]

The Citizens' Assembly comprised 99 people selected from the electoral register and was chaired by Supreme Court judge, Ms Justice Mary Laffoy. Following months of deliberations and evidence, and the receipt of over 13,000 submissions from the public, the Assembly recommended constitutional change to enable the Oireachtas to legislate for access to abortion, which it considered should be available without restriction in early pregnancy and on liberal grounds thereafter.[17] The *ad hoc* Joint Oireachtas Committee, established specifically to consider the report, went on to endorse almost all of the Assembly's recommendations (albeit recommending a slightly different form of constitutional change), although it proposed more restrictive grounds for abortion in later pregnancy.[18]

By early 2018, the Cabinet had announced that it would propose a referendum to replace the 8th with the 36th Amendment. The referendum date was set for 25 May 2018. The Department of Health published an outline of the proposed legislation, should the referendum be successful.[19] This proposed legislation became a focal point of the anti-repeal campaign, even though the referendum was strictly on the proposed constitutional change alone.

The 'yes' campaign was led by Together for Yes (TFY), a bespoke civil society group that brought together three key organisations: the Coalition to Repeal the Eighth Amendment (and all its members), the ARC, and the National Women's Council of Ireland (NWCI). It had three co-directors: Ailbhe Smyth, Orla O'Connor and Grainne Griffin. Deirdre Duffy managed the campaign. All had long experience of social justice leadership: Smyth had campaigned against the 8th for decades and also been a leader of the Marriage Equality campaign in 2015, O'Connor was (and still is) director of the NWCI, and Griffin led the ARC. Duffy had spent a number of years as head of policy with the Irish Council for Civil Liberties.

TFY focused on three core arguments: (i) that abortion was already happening in Ireland, but illegally and unsafely; (ii) that the 8th Amendment impacted negatively on

[15] See in particular the comments and positions of (Labour) Senator Ivana Bacik, (Independent) then-Senator Katherine Zappone, and TDs Clare Daly, Ruth Coppinger and Bríd Smith.

[16] *A Programme for Partnership Government* (May 2016), 153: https://merrionstreet.ie/MerrionStreet/en/ImageLibrary/Programme_for_Partnership_Government.pdf.

[17] First Report and Recommendations of the Citizens' Assembly, 29 June 2017.

[18] Report of the Joint Committee on the Eighth Amendment to the Constitution, 20 December 2017.

[19] Department of Health, General Scheme of a Bill to Regulate Termination of Pregnancy, 27 March 2018.

medical practice in Ireland, and (iii) that repeal was the only way to make provision for abortion in so-called 'hard cases' of rape, incest, and fatal foetal anomaly. In doing so TFY garnered the support, in particular, of medical professionals, with prominent obstetricians (especially Professors Mary Higgins, Louise Kenny and Peter Boylan), GPs (especially Dr Mary Favier and Dr Mark Murphy), and specialists in sexual violence (especially Dr Maeve Eogan) playing important roles in the public debates, and the Masters of two of the three Dublin maternity hospitals (Professors Rhona Mahony and Fergal Malone) also intervening in support of repeal.

Questions of law were not prominent in the Yes campaign, although more than 1,000 lawyers signed a petition in favour of repeal.[20] The pre-existing pro-choice lawyers' group, 'Lawyers for Choice', together with some individual academics (including this author and Máiréad Enright), led the provision of public legal education on the 36th Amendment and proposed legislation through street stalls, at town hall meetings around the country, and through online and hard copy resources.[21]

Although the pre-referendum polling suggested that the electorate was tightly divided, the 'yes' side consistently held the lead, and incidents such as the raising of €1 million in a few days through a crowd-funding appeal intended to raise around €50,000 indicated significant and widespread support for the campaign. The interventions of Terminations for Medical Reasons – an advocacy and support group established to ensure that the experiences and voices of people who had received fatal diagnoses for their foetuses – were especially important, as were some key political interventions such as the performance of Sinn Féin leader, Mary Lou McDonald, in the first television debate, the strong performance of Minister for Health, Simon Harris, on the main 'Prime Time' debate, and the intervention of Fianna Fáil leader, Micheál Martin, supporting repeal.

On the local and individual level, pro-choice activism was in evidence across the country. There was at least one 'for Choice/TFY' group in every county, and thousands of volunteers – many of whom had never been engaged in politics before – canvassed, held public meetings, had street stalls in towns and villages, wrote letters to editors, and appeared on local radio in order to discuss and advocate for a yes vote. Parents for Choice – another pre-existing group with thousands of members – mobilised volunteers in every corner of the country. Local teams were coordinated by TFY head office in Dublin, which provided them with official merchandise. Badges and buttons were a key mechanism of ensuring visibility: the official TFY badges said 'yes' or 'tá' (the Irish for 'yes' in a referendum context), but there were also dozens of different variations of badges created by local and thematic groups. From '[county] together for yes' to 'culchies together for yes', 'gays together for yes', and even 'witches', 'dogs' and 'cats' together for yes. Collecting and displaying badges, wearing TFY t-shirts, and placing decal stickers on cars, front doors and windows was widespread. Reports began to circulate of people walking out of Mass if priests preached against repeal. Facebook was a critical location for online canvassing, not only through campaign Facebook ads and videos, but also through grassroots activism. 'In Her Shoes – Women of

[20] Together for Yes, Lawyers: https://www.togetherforyes.ie/lawyers/.

[21] See, especially About the 8th: www.aboutthe8th.com.

the Eighth', a Facebook page that welcomed anonymous submissions of first-person experiences of the 8th Amendment, was inundated with submissions and published at least one every day. These were shared thousands of times, and the power of these anonymised narratives was such that a booklet was made, highlighting some of them, to be distributed to people who were not online. Street and door-to-door canvassers tended to reserve it for the truly undecided: it was both powerful and expensive to produce, but for many it and the *In Her Shoes* page were indispensible in changing hearts and minds. At the time of writing – in early July 2018 – it continues to publish the backlog of the hundreds of stories received, and still has more than 110,000 followers.

The centrist nature of the official TFY campaign – perceived to be required in order to win majority support – arguably resulted in the presentation of a 'tragic' narrative in respect of abortion that marginalised people who had had 'ordinary' abortions (including comedian Tara Flynn and *Irish Times* columnist Roisín Ingle who were among the first to speak about their abortions), and presented self-medication using the abortion pill as dangerous in spite of the very low complication rate associated with these medications. Even though Savita Halappanavar was a totemic figure in the campaign, the voices and experiences of brown and migrant women were largely marginalised in the official campaign. Similarly, trans* narratives of abortion were barely heard, notwithstanding the long-standing trans* inclusivity of the Irish reproductive rights movements. Politicians and advocates who had long presented a pro-choice agenda from a socialist perspective, such as TDs Ruth Coppinger and Clare Daly, Solidarity, People Before Profit, and socialist feminist group ROSA, were sidelined in favour of more 'mainstream', albeit passionate, advocate voices such as Fine Gael politicians Kate O'Connell TD and Senator Catherine Noone. As Máiréad Enright put it,

> In Ireland in May we re-learned the painful old feminist lesson that official campaigns for law reform come to stand for more hope than they can ever possibly bear; that they are shaped by patriarchy even in the very moment of its overcoming. We learned again – as smaller groups departed selectively from official campaign lines, or stuck with them for one more day – that each cluster of us could make its own bargain with the status quo, or none at all. And we learned that official campaigns and the compromises they solder can be temporary, while the movements and friendships that enable them need not disappear.[22]

In this, the successful campaign for a yes vote found itself struggling against and sometimes conceding to the well-known dangers of translating feminist demands into a movement for liberal law reform; a maneuver arguably required by the nature of constitutional change in Ireland, which can only take place through a majority vote in a referendum. However, the referendum succeeded with an overwhelming and unanticipated majority, and the exit poll shows that for most 'yes' voters a woman's right to choose – rather than the 'hard cases' – was the key influencing factor.[23]

[22] Máiréad Enright, 'The Labour of Legal Change: On the Final Days of the Irish Pro-Choice Referendum', Critical Legal Thinking, 20 June 2018: http://criticallegalthinking.com/2018/06/20/the-labour-of-legal-change-on-the-final-days-ofthe-irish-pro-choice-referendum/.

[23] RTE Exit Poll, Thirty-sixth Amendment to the Constitution, 25 May 2018: https://static.rasset.ie/documents/news/2018/05/rte-exit-poll-final-11pm.pdf.

# III. What Happened Next

At the time of writing a number of challenges to the referendum result are on-going in the Irish courts; the referendum result cannot be certified by the President until these are concluded. As a result, the 8th Amendment remains part of the Constitution but the likelihood of success in these challenges is negligible. It is anticipated that legislation will be passed by the end of 2018 and abortion services introduced in January 2019. Given the restrictive nature of lawful abortion after 12 weeks of pregnancy, abortion travel will almost certainly continue. It is also anticipated that for as long as women in Northern Ireland do not have access to lawful abortion a new abortion trail between the North and the Republic will emerge, with the Taoiseach confirming that he anticipates abortion services in Ireland will be available to women from Northern Ireland.[24]

# IV. Significance

The significance of the repeal referendum in May 2018 can hardly be overstated. If the 8th Amendment was a pre-emptive strike against women's liberation, its repeal was a decisive rejection of the principle that the Church, the state, and the mores of an imagined, post-colonial Ireland – with a morally particular protectionist approach to foetal life – should determine women's reproductive lives. As Clare Daly TD put it in the Dáil, the yes vote was a weight being lifted, and society 'atoning for everything it's done' to stigmatise women's sexuality and reproductive agency.[25] Through this vote, 1.4 million Irish people affirmed the principle that it is pregnant people who should decide what happens to their bodies, and that those pregnant bodies are no longer constitutional property.

## Further Reading

- Máiréad Enright, 'The Labour of Legal Change: On the Final Days of the Irish Pro-Choice Referendum', *Critical Legal Thinking*, 20 June 2018: http://criticallegalthinking.com/2018/06/20/the-labour-of-legal-change-on-the-final-days-of-the-irish-pro-choice-referendum/.
- Fiona de Londras and Máiréad Enright, *Repealing the 8th: Reforming Irish Abortion Law* (Policy Press, 2018).
- Department of Health, General Scheme of a Bill to Regulate Termination of Pregnancy, 27 March 2018.

[24] 'Leo Varadkar: "North's women may be able to have abortions here"', *Irish Times*, 29 May 2018.
[25] Dáil Debates, 29 May 2018.

# INDEX

www.ingramcontent.com/pod-product-compliance
Ingram Content Group UK Ltd.
Pitfield, Milton Keynes, MK11 3LW, UK
UKHW051416150926
475561UK00005B/201

9 781509 935666